Oracle Press

PeopleSoft PeopleTools Tips & Techniques

About the Author

Jim Marion is an AICPA Certified Information Technology Professional who currently works as a Principal Applications Technology Consultant at Oracle. He runs a popular blog for the PeopleSoft community at http://jjmpsj.blogspot.com. Jim is also an international presenter of PeopleTools development topics at conferences such as Oracle OpenWorld; UKOUG events; HEUG's Alliance; and Quest's, IOUG's, and OAUG's Collaborate.

About the Technical Editors

Tim Burns is a PeopleSoft Certified Developer and has been teaching PeopleSoft technical courses since 1997. He was a technical instructor at PeopleSoft for more than seven years, where he was often recognized for the quality of his teaching. He is a Master Instructor, the highest level recognized by PeopleSoft. Tim now writes his own training manuals and teaches PeopleSoft technical courses on site at corporations, government agencies, and universities throughout the United States and abroad. Tim is well known in the PeopleSoft community and is a regular speaker at PeopleSoft conferences and user group meetings.

Graham Smith is a software engineer, PeopleSoft developer, and infrastructure analyst currently working for Oxfam GB. Still in awe of the PeopleTools development framework, Graham is proud to have been asked to be part of this book project. Graham is a believer in community-built software and currently chairs the PeopleSoft Technology SIG at the UKOUG. He is a husband and father of six, enjoys fishing and trains, and fights with The Salvation Army. His PeopleSoft blog can be found at http://i-like-trains.blogspot.com.

Oracle Press™

PeopleSoft PeopleTools Tips & Techniques

Jim J. Marion

New York Chicago San Francisco
Lisbon London Madrid Mexico City Milan
New Delhi San Juan Seoul Singapore Sydney Toronto

The McGraw-Hill Companies

Cataloging-in-Publication Data is on file with the Library of Congress

McGraw-Hill books are available at special quantity discounts to use as premiums and sales promotions, or for use in corporate training programs. To contact a representative, please e-mail us at bulksales@mcgraw-hill.com.

PeopleSoft PeopleTools Tips & Techniques

3 4 5 6 7 8 9 0 DOH 1 6 1 5 1 4 1 3 1 2

ISBN 978-0-07-166493-6
MHID 0-07-166493-9

Sponsoring Editor
Lisa McClain

Editorial Supervisor
Patty Mon

Project Manager
Vipra Fauzdar, Glyph International

Acquisitions Coordinator
Meghan Riley

Technical Editors
Tim Burns
Graham Smith

Copy Editor
Marilyn Smith

Proofreader
Bev Weiler

Indexer
Karin Arrigoni

Production Supervisor
Jean Bodeaux

Composition
Glyph International

Illustration
Glyph International

Art Director, Cover
Jeff Weeks

Cover Designer
Pattie Lee

This book is dedicated to my three lovely children. To the Corrick clan and Black tribe for your tremendous encouragement in my life. To our faithful chocolate lab for keeping us company during the past six months of very late nights.

Contents at a Glance

PART I
Core PeopleTools Concepts

1 Application Classes 3
2 The File Attachment API 41
3 Approval Workflow Engine 91
4 Pagelet Wizard 141

PART II
Extend the User Interface

5 Understanding and Creating iScripts 187
6 JavaScript for the PeopleSoft Developer 229
7 AJAX and PeopleSoft 263
8 Creating Custom Tools 303

PART III
Java

9 Extending PeopleCode with Java 337
10 A Logging Framework for PeopleCode 387
11 Writing Your Own Java 415
12 Creating Real-Time Integrations 463
13 Java on the Web Server 505
14 Creating Mobile Applications for PeopleSoft 519

PART IV
Best Practices

15 Test-Driven Development 561
16 PeopleCode Language Arts 579
Index 595

Contents

Acknowledgments xvii
Introduction xix

PART I
Core PeopleTools Concepts

1 Application Classes 3
Our First Application Class 4
Creating an Application Package and Class 4
Coding the Application Class 5
Testing the Application Class Code 6
Expanding the Application Class 11
Inheritance 13
Features of Application Classes 17
Dynamic Execution 17
Construction 17
Stateful Objects 17
Access Control 19
Putting It All Together: The Logging Framework Example 21
Log Levels 22
The Logger Interface 25
The Logger Classes 25
Testing the Framework 31
Dynamic Logger Configuration 32
Factory Test Program 36
Misuses of Application Classes 38
Runtime Context-Sensitive Variables 38
Indiscriminate Usage 38
Conclusion 39
Notes 39

2 The File Attachment API ... 41
Adding Attachments to Transactions ... 42
Investigating the Target Transaction ... 42
Creating the Attachment Storage Record ... 49
Adding the FILE_ATTACH_SBR Subrecord ... 53
Adding Attachment Fields and Buttons to the Transaction Page ... 53
Writing PeopleCode for the Attachment Buttons ... 59
Customizing File Attachment Behavior ... 65
Moving to Level 1 ... 77
Modifying the Page ... 77
Adding the PeopleCode ... 81
Adding Multiple Attachments per Transaction ... 85
Processing Attachments ... 85
Accessing Attachments ... 86
Storing Attachments ... 87
Implementing File Attachment Validation ... 87
Filename Validation ... 87
File Contents Validation ... 89
Conclusion ... 89

3 Approval Workflow Engine ... 91
Workflow-Enabling Transactions ... 92
Creating Supporting Definitions ... 93
Configuring the AWE Metadata ... 102
Modifying the Transaction ... 108
Testing the Approval ... 126
Providing Custom Descriptions for the Approval Status Monitor ... 129
Allowing Ad Hoc Access ... 132
Creating an Event Handler Iterator ... 136
Web Service-Enabling Approvals ... 138
Conclusion ... 140

4 Pagelet Wizard ... 141
Pagelets Defined ... 142
Creating a Pagelet ... 143
Components of a Pagelet Wizard Pagelet ... 148
Pagelet Data Types ... 148
Setup for the Custom Data Type Example ... 148
Coding the Custom Data Type ... 149
Registering the Data Type ... 168
Creating a Test Pagelet ... 168
Pagelet Transformers ... 177
XSL Templates ... 180
Display Formats ... 180
Conclusion ... 183
Notes ... 183

PART II
Extend the User Interface

5 Understanding and Creating iScripts 187
iScripts Defined 188
Our First iScript 189
Coding the iScript 189
Testing the iScript 190
Modifying the iScript 191
A Bookmarklet to Call an iScript 192
Writing the SetTraceSQL iScript 193
Creating a Bookmarklet 194
Desktop Integration 197
Creating an iScript to Serve Calendar Content 198
Building a Parameter Cache 200
Modifying the Transaction 203
Serving File Attachments 209
iScripts as Data Sources 210
Flex Requirements 211
Say Hello to Flex 211
Direct Reports DisplayShelf 220
Conclusion 227
Notes 227

6 JavaScript for the PeopleSoft Developer 229
A Static JavaScript Example 230
A Dynamic JavaScript Example 233
Creating the Derived/Work Record for Dynamic HTML 234
Adding PeopleCode for the HTML Area 234
Creating an HTML Definition 235
Inspecting PeopleSoft's User Interface with Firebug 236
Using Firebug's Console 236
Using Firebug to Enhance the Trace Bookmarklet 237
Styling an Element 239
JavaScript Libraries 240
Serving JavaScript Libraries 241
Using jQuery 243
Making Global User Interface Changes 245
Identifying Common Definitions 245
Minimizing the Impact 247
Coding the Solution 247
Using jQuery Plug-ins 254
Thickbox 254
WEBLIB_APT_JSL iScript Code 260
Performance Issues 261
Conclusion 261
Notes 261

7 AJAX and PeopleSoft 263
Hello AJAX 264
Creating the AJAX Request Handler 264
Ajaxifying a Page 264
Adding Animation 266
Ajaxifying the Direct Reports DisplayShelf 268
Modifying the Flex Source 269
Modifying the Direct Reports Service 270
Creating a New HTML AJAX Service 271
Modifying the Container Page 273
A Configurable User Interface 275
Using a Metadata Repository 275
Modifying the Bootstrap Code 285
Testing the Custom Scripts Component 291
Highlight Active Field Revisited 291
Changing Search Operators 293
Fiddler 298
Conclusion 301
Notes 302

8 Creating Custom Tools 303
The Toolbar Button Metadata Repository 304
Setting Up the Repository Tables 304
Creating the Toolbar Maintenance Page 308
Defining the Toolbar's HTML 311
Attaching the Toolbar to Pages 312
Defining a Custom Script for the Toolbar 312
Adding the Trace Toolbar Button 314
Modifying the Bootstrap Code 316
Separating Common Code from Bootstrap Code 316
Adding New URL-Generation Functions 317
Writing the New Common Code 318
Launching Another Component 324
Creating an iScript to Get CREF Information 324
Adding the Edit CREF Toolbar Button 325
Viewing Query Results 328
Creating a Query to Get a Page's Permission Lists 328
Adding the Query Toolbar Button 329
Leaving the Portal 333
Conclusion 334

PART III
Java

9 Extending PeopleCode with Java . . . 337
Java Overview . . . 338
Why Java? . . . 338
Why Not C++ or .NET or ...? . . . 339
Java and PeopleCode 101 . . . 339
Java Strings . . . 339
Java Arrays . . . 347
Java Collections . . . 349
Writing a Meta-HTML Processor . . . 350
Implementing %Image . . . 350
Implementing %JavaScript . . . 353
Implementing %GenerateQueryContentURL . . . 356
Complete Code for the Meta-HTML Processor . . . 361
Using Third-Party Libraries . . . 364
Apache Commons . . . 365
Apache Velocity . . . 368
Using JSON . . . 373
Conclusion . . . 385
Notes . . . 385

10 A Logging Framework for PeopleCode . . . 387
Investigating Problems . . . 388
Delivered Logging Tools . . . 388
The log4j Java Logging Framework . . . 389
Hello log4j . . . 389
Tracing log4j . . . 392
Configuring log4j . . . 393
Improving Logging Performance . . . 397
Avoiding Logger Reconfiguration . . . 397
Using log4j in the Process Scheduler . . . 398
An Integrated Logging Framework . . . 398
Creating the Level Class . . . 399
Creating the Logger Class . . . 400
The LogManager Class . . . 403
log4j Metadata . . . 410
Testing APT_LOG4J . . . 411
Conclusion . . . 413
Notes . . . 413

11 Writing Your Own Java 415

Your Java Build Environment 416

Your First Java Class 416

- Creating the Source Files 416
- Deploying Java 420
- Creating the Test Program 426

Using PeopleCode Objects in Java 426

- Configuring Your Development Environment 426
- Using PeopleCode System Variables 427
- Accessing Data 429

PeopleSoft Database log4j Appender 436

- Creating the PL/SQL Autonomous Transaction 437
- Writing the Java 441
- Testing the Appender 448
- Static Configuration 449

PeopleSoft Database Velocity Template Data Source 450

- Creating the Template Metadata Repository 450
- Creating the Velocity Repository Java Class 453
- Testing the PSDBResourceLoader 460

Multithreading 461

Conclusion 461

- Notes 462

12 Creating Real-Time Integrations 463

Integration Technologies 464

Setting Up for Database Integration 464

Creating a Custom JDBC Target Connector 466

- Creating the JDBCTargetConnector Class 466
- Predeployment Testing 482
- Deploying the Connector 492

Configuring Integrations 492

- Configuring the Gateway 493
- Creating a Node 494
- Transforming Messages 495
- Creating a Routing 499

Testing the Integrated Connector 501

Troubleshooting Custom Connectors 502

Conclusion 504

- Notes 504

13 Java on the Web Server 505
Extending the PeopleSoft Web Server with JSP 506
Using Servlet Filters 507
Investigating iScript Caching Behavior 508
Creating an HTTP Header Servlet Filter 509
Testing the Servlet Filter 513
Deploying the Servlet Filter 515
Conclusion 516
Notes 517

14 Creating Mobile Applications for PeopleSoft 519
Providing Web Services 520
Enabling a Component Interface as a Web Service 520
Testing the WSDL URL 528
Going Mobile with JDeveloper 528
Creating a Fusion Web Application 529
Creating the Data Control 532
Creating the View 536
Designing the Search Page 540
Testing the Search Page 553
Shortening the Application's URL 555
Requiring Authentication 556
Conclusion 557
Notes 558

PART IV
Best Practices

15 Test-Driven Development 561
Introduction to Test-Driven Development 562
The TDD Approach 562
Some TDD Lingo 563
A TDD Framework 564
Test Driving the Meta-HTML Processor 564
Writing a Test 564
Running the Test 566
Making the Test Pass 569
Running the Test Again 569
Refactoring 570
Repeating the Cycle 573
Conclusion 578
Notes 578

16 PeopleCode Language Arts 579
Composition over Inheritance 580
Façades 581
Factories 582
Inversion of Control 583
Enumerated Types 591
Language Diversity 593
Notes 594

Index 595

Acknowledgments

While I claim full responsibility for the content of this book, including errors and omissions, I cannot take credit for its comprehensibility. For that, I give special thanks to my wife Sarah, who spent countless hours rephrasing and organizing my thoughts to make this book communicate effectively. She is my unsung coauthor. Likewise, Tim Burns and Graham Smith devoted six months of their lives to reading, testing, fixing, and debugging the code samples included with this book. These three people gave six months of their lives to ensure the legibility, accuracy, and integrity of this book. Rebecca and Jo, thank you so much for your extra effort at home that allowed your husbands to help me write this book.

I also want to thank David Kurtz, Tom Kyte, Sheila Cepero, and Lisa McClain for helping me get this project started. Ed Abbo and John Gawkowski, thank you for approving this project. To my managers, Irina Granat and Roger Donaldson, thank you for encouraging me to write this book. Shawn Abernathy, thank you for your valuable insight into the Approval Workflow Engine. Meghan, I appreciate your accountability and dedication to this project. Vipra, Marilyn, and Patty, your style and content editing recommendations were invaluable.

To the PeopleTools giants, Rich Manalang and Chris Heller, I am a dwarf standing on your shoulders. Rich, you opened my eyes to the world of AJAX and PeopleTools. Chris, you taught me the idiosyncrasies of working with PeopleTools and Java. To my PeopleTools instructors, Toby Yoches, Tim Burns, Tom Spol, and Scott Sarris. I wouldn't know an app class from a component interface if it weren't for your thorough instructions. To my fellow PeopleTools presenters, Dave Bain, Jeff Robbins, Greg Kelly, Robert Taylor, Peter Bergmann, and the rest of the demo grounds staff, thank you for giving me your time and energy and helping me further understand how to use and extend PeopleTools. Robert, I specifically credit you with the ideas behind the custom target connector chapter. To the Tipster (Duncan), Digital Eagle, Chili Joe, and the rest of the PeopleSoft bloggers, each of you contributed to the ideas presented in this book. To my friends at the University of Utah, your tough questions and insight move me to new heights. To the PeopleSoft team at Chelan County PUD, thank you for introducing me to PeopleSoft.

Thanks to all the PeopleSoft customers, consultants, and technical presales consultants who visit my blog, ask me questions at user groups, and communicate with me on a daily basis. You inspire me. Learning how you use and customize the product leads me to the solutions I create.

Most important, thank you to my personal Lord and Savior Jesus Christ. Writing a computer programming manual is a monumental effort. To do it in six months, as a second job, requires divine intervention. He is the chief author of all good ideas, the creative force leading all great innovation.

Introduction

As a regular speaker on the PeopleSoft user group circuit, I have the opportunity to present PeopleTools-related tips and techniques to a variety of customers. Audiences are eager to implement the solutions demonstrated, but many people don't know where to start. These one-hour presentations generate excitement by showing what is possible, but they are not detailed enough to teach how to properly implement the solutions. The PeopleTools community needs documentation to bridge the gap between these presentations and the actual implementation.

This book's examples will assist you in your pursuit of knowledge, whether you are looking for more information on application classes and workflow, or are trying to extend your applications with Java and AJAX. The complexity of the examples presented in this book ranges from beginner to expert. The ideas and examples were designed to teach the inexperienced, as well as inspire the seasoned veteran. Each chapter in this book describes tips and techniques for minimizing your modification footprint.

By reading this book, you will learn how to combine PeopleTools with modern, well-known languages, technologies, and methodologies. In the hands of a developer trying to solve a problem, this book is a solution generator. I packed this book with working examples that produce tools and enhancements I hope you will want to incorporate into your PeopleSoft applications.

What's Inside

The content of this book is divided into four parts:

- Core PeopleTools Concepts
- Extend the User Interface
- Java
- Best Practices

I organized the chapters in each part by level of complexity. Except for the chapters in Part II, each chapter is self-contained. For continuity, some examples refer to others presented in earlier chapters. The source code for each chapter is available at www.OraclePressBooks.com.

Each custom object described in this book is prefixed with the letters `APT` to help you distinguish your organization's custom objects from the custom objects in this book (unless, of course, your organization also uses the prefix `APT`). This prefix is an abbreviation for **A** **P**eople**T**ools book.

Core PeopleTools Concepts

Part I contains working examples of core PeopleTools technologies. In Chapter 1, you will learn application class design patterns while you build your own transparent, configurable logging framework. Application classes are relatively new to the PeopleTools toolbox, and represent a significant step forward. The concepts in this chapter form the foundation for many other chapters in this book.

File attachments, workflow, and approvals are key usability features of a good transaction system. Chapters 2 and 3 describe these core PeopleTools features. Chapter 2 covers the File Attachment API by working through examples of adding attachments to transactions. Chapter 3 shows you the inner workings of the Approval Workflow Engine (AWE), which PeopleSoft introduced with PeopleTools 8.48. This chapter walks through the process of writing, configuring, and implementing a new workflow process.

The Pagelet Wizard is PeopleSoft's configurable portlet generator. This tool allows functional superusers to surface actionable business intelligence. In Chapter 4, you will learn how to extend this tool by creating new data types, display formats, and transformers.

Extend the User Interface

Part II of this book dives deep into user interface development. Chapter 5 shows you how to use iScripts to extend your browser through bookmarklets, integrate with desktop calendar systems, and build rich user interfaces using Adobe Flex.

In Chapter 6, you will learn how to use JavaScript and CSS to change the behavior and appearance of PeopleSoft pages. Chapter 7 introduces AJAX and demonstrates how to construct a configurable JavaScript customization framework that allows you to modify the behavior and appearance of delivered pages with zero upgrade impact. Chapter 8 builds on the previous chapters by showing you how to create a custom PeopleTools toolbar that provides access to common online tools, such as tracing and security.

Java

Part III is a six-chapter journey into PeopleSoft's tight integration with the Java language. In Chapters 9, 10, and 11, you will learn how to call Java classes from PeopleCode and how to use PeopleCode functions from Java. These chapters include everything from how to pass data between PeopleCode and Java, to how to write, compile, and deploy your own custom Java classes.

In Chapter 9, you will learn how to call the Apache Velocity Engine from PeopleCode and how to produce and consume JSON-based services using the JSON.simple Java library. Chapter 10 shows you how to use the PeopleSoft-delivered log4j logging framework. Chapter 11 builds on Chapters 9 and 10 by showing you how to create PeopleSoft repositories for Apache Velocity Engine templates and log4j logging statements.

PeopleSoft's Java roots go deeper than PeopleCode integration. Chapter 12 leaves PeopleCode and shifts into PeopleSoft's pure Java realm. In this chapter, you will learn how to create custom Integration Broker target connectors by building a database target connector. By using custom connectors, you can replace many batch-style integrations with real-time integrations.

The PeopleSoft web server is a pure Java 2 Platform, Enterprise Edition (J2EE) application server. Chapter 13 shows you how to leverage the power of J2EE through JavaServer Pages (JSP), servlets, and servlet filters, which offer the opportunity to modify application behavior without changing delivered code.

Chapter 14 closes the Java section by providing a step-by-step tutorial for using Oracle's JDeveloper and Application Development Framework (ADF) framework to create mobile solutions. While the implementation described in this chapter is specific to JDeveloper and Java, you can use the ideas and concepts with any language or technology to create PeopleSoft mobile solutions.

Best Practices

Even though the entire book is devoted to best practices, Part IV wraps up this book with a specific focus on development best practices. Chapter 15 uses a code walk-through to show you how to apply test-driven development (TDD) techniques. Chapter 16 rounds out the best practices discussion by offering implementations of many object-oriented patterns, including composition over inheritance, façades, factories, and inversion of control.

PeopleTools Versions and Approach to HRMS

When I started writing this book, HRMS 9.0 was the newest available HRMS version, and PeopleTools 8.49.14 was the latest PeopleTools version. The images in this book were taken from those versions. Just as I was completing this text, Oracle released HRMS 9.1 and PeopleTools 8.50. To reconcile the differences between this book's images and the latest versions of PeopleSoft, I included notes describing various differences between PeopleTools 8.49 and 8.50.

Even though HRMS is Oracle's most popular PeopleSoft application, as much as possible, I avoided HRMS-specific transactions and references. Some features, however, such as workflow, make sense only in the context of an application-specific transaction. For those examples, I supplied two solutions: one for a custom component that you can create in your application and one that was HRMS-specific.

PART I

Core PeopleTools Concepts

CHAPTER 1

Application Classes

If you are an application class expert, feel free to skim this chapter and quickly move on to the next chapter. On the other hand, if you are new to application classes and object-oriented programming (OOP) in general, then consider this chapter to be an OOP primer. Through the examples in this book, you will learn enough about OOP concepts to create usable, productive application classes. Many of the examples in this book will build upon the application class fundamentals presented in this chapter. So, if this material is new to you, take some time to make sure you fully understand the concepts presented.

Application classes provide PeopleSoft developers with a desperately needed object-oriented complement. The OOP versus procedural debate can be very personal and intense. I don't advocate one over the other. Rather, I believe that both work together to create excellent solutions. Used correctly, application classes can dramatically improve the legibility of your code, provide extensibility, and reduce defects.

In this chapter, you will have the opportunity to create and use several application classes. Through these examples, and the accompanying explanations, you will learn how and when to use application classes.

Our First Application Class

Our first application class is a derivative of the classic Hello World example. Rather than just say "Hello," we will create a `Greeter` application class for use in later chapters. Here are the basic steps to create an application class:

1. Create an application package.
2. Create an application class.
3. Code your class.
4. Test your code.

The following sections provide details about each of these steps.

Creating an Application Package and Class

We define application classes as child objects of application packages. These packages provide structure and qualify application class names in the same way that Java packages organize and qualify Java classes. Therefore, before we create a new application class, we need to create an application package.

If you haven't already done so, launch Application Designer (more commonly known as App Designer). To create a new application package, select File | New from the App Designer menu bar. App Designer will respond by displaying the New Definition dialog box, which contains a list of possible object types. From this dialog, choose Application Package.

We must save and name our new application package before continuing. Click the Save button and name this package `APT_GREETERS`. With our package structure defined, we can add a new class named `Greeter`. To add a new class, select the `APT_GREETERS` package in the Application Package editor and click the Insert Application Class button. App Designer will respond by prompting you for a class name. Enter **Greeter** and click OK. App Designer will add

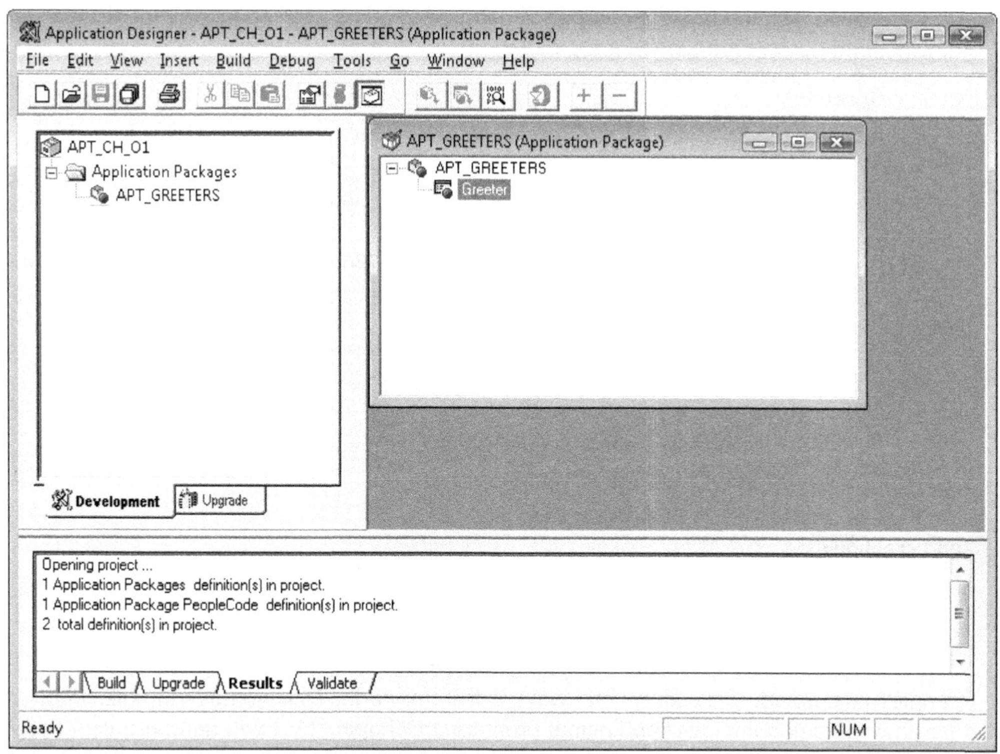

FIGURE 1-1. *Greeter package definition*

the new child item `Greeter` to the `APT_GREETERS` package in the Application Package editor. At this point, your application package should look like Figure 1-1.

Coding the Application Class

Double-click the new `Greeter` element to open the PeopleCode editor. With our package structure in place, we can now write some code for our first application class. Type the following code into the PeopleCode editor window:

```
class Greeter
end-class;
```

Unlike event-based PeopleCode, application class PeopleCode must strictly conform to a contract. The preceding code defines our application class using the reserved word `class` followed by the name of the class: `Greeter`. We conclude our definition with the key phrase `end-class`, followed by the PeopleCode line-terminating semicolon. All class definitions follow this same pattern.

Besides naming a class, the declaration defines a class's characteristics and behaviors. Let's add a behavior to our class definition by creating a new method. The following listing shows a new method declaration named sayHello.

```
class Greeter
   method sayHello() Returns string;
end-class;
```

Notice this method declaration looks similar to a function declaration. Just like functions, methods can accept parameters and return values.

The next listing builds on the previous listings by adding a minimal implementation for our sayHello method. App Designer requires us to provide a minimal implementation for each declared method prior to saving the class.

```
class Greeter
   method sayHello() Returns string;
end-class;

method sayHello
   Return "Hello " | %OperatorId;
end-method;
```

We now have a fully functional application class we can test.

Testing the Application Class Code

PeopleTools provides us with several ways to test this code. To keep this example simple, we will use an Application Engine (App Engine) program. In Chapter 15, I will demonstrate a PeopleCode testing framework designed specifically for unit testing PeopleCode.

Begin by creating a new App Designer definition, just as we did when we created our application package. From the list of definition types, select App Engine. When the App Engine program editor window appears, rename step Step01 to Test1. Then right-click Test1 and choose Insert Action. App Designer will respond by inserting a new SQL action. From the drop-down list, change the action type to PeopleCode. Save this new App Engine as APT_GREETER. Your new App Engine program should look like the one shown in Figure 1-2.

With a basic structure in place, we can add some PeopleCode to test our Greeter application class. Open the PeopleCode editor by double-clicking the gray area under the PeopleCode action, and then enter the following PeopleCode:

```
import APT_GREETERS:Greeter;

Local APT_GREETERS:Greeter &greeter = create APT_GREETERS:Greeter();
Local string &message = &greeter.sayHello();

MessageBox(0, "", 0, 0, &message);
```

The first line of this listing imports the Greeter application class into the current PeopleCode module in a manner similar to a PeopleCode Declare directive. For this example, we used the application class's fully qualified name. When importing several classes from the same package, however, we can use the shorthand wildcard character *, which tells the PeopleCode compiler to

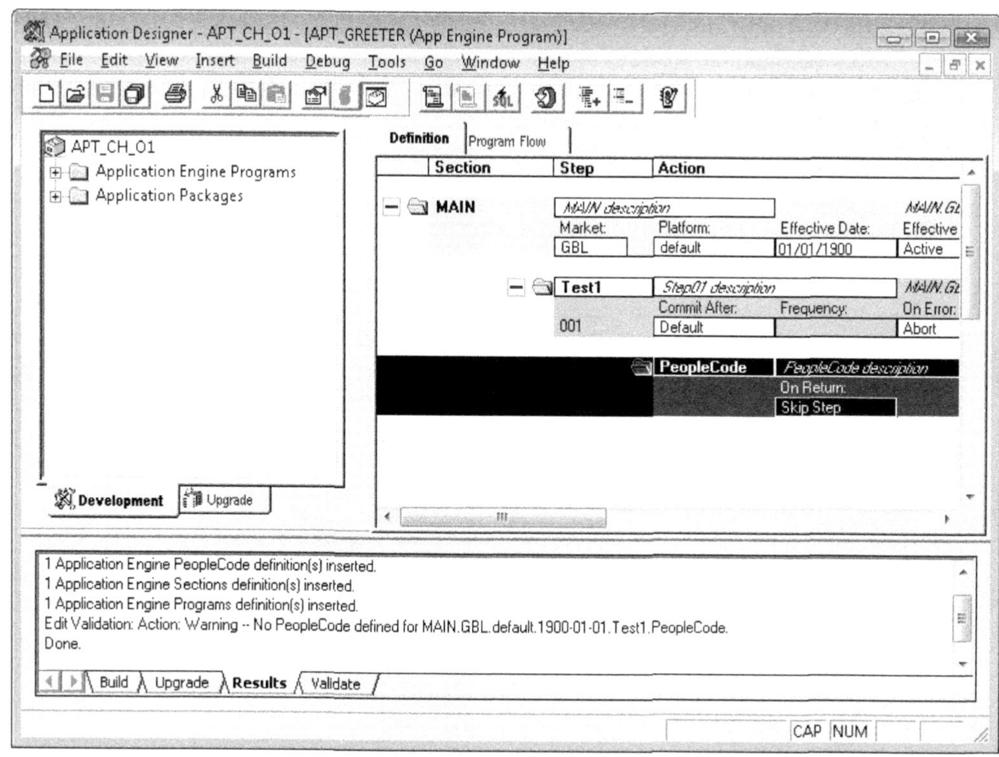

FIGURE 1-2. *New App Engine program*

import all the classes in the given package. For example, we could have written our `import` statement this way:

```
import APT_GREETERS:*;
```

The second line starts by declaring a variable of type `APT_GREETERS:Greeter`. Just as PeopleCode provides us with the loosely typed primitive `Any`, it also provides us with the loosely typed OOP complement `Object`. While it is syntactically correct to loosely declare this variable as type `Object`, the PeopleCode compiler will provide only compile-time feedback if we use strict typing.

The second line also creates a new instance of the `Greeter` class using the `create` keyword. An *instance* is an in-memory object created from the `Greeter`'s application class PeopleCode definition. Besides the `create` keyword, PeopleCode provides two additional object-creation functions: `CreateObject` and `CreateObjectArray`. I will explain these functions later in this chapter, when we build the logging framework example.

The third line executes the new `sayHello` method and assigns the result to a variable named `&message`.

Spartan Programming

Spartan programming[1] seeks to reduce code complexity through minimalistic coding practices. Applying this approach to our test code, we could rewrite it in two lines—one declarative and one executable—as follows:

```
import APT_GREETERS:Greeter;

MessageBox(0, "", 0, 0, (create APT_GREETERS:Greeter()).sayHello());
```

Spartan programming favors inlining over variable usage.[2] Notice our new code example does not use any variables. By reducing our code to one executable line, we have only a single line to read, comprehend, maintain, and test. After removing all the "fluff" from our code logic, flaws are easier to spot. Unfortunately, terse code like this can be difficult to read. Now, with our code reduced to the absolute minimum and any potential logic flaws exposed, let's expand it just a little to make it easier to read,[3] as follows:

```
import APT_GREETERS:Greeter;

Local APT_GREETERS:Greeter &g = create APT_GREETERS:Greeter();
MessageBox(0, "", 0, 0, &g.sayHello());
```

As Albert Einstein said, "Any fool can make things bigger, more complex, and more violent. It takes a touch of genius—and a lot of courage—to move in the opposite direction."[4]

The last line writes the results to the App Engine log using the PeopleCode `MessageBox` function.

We are finished coding this test. Save your work and close the PeopleCode editor. Before running this code, we should disable the App Engine's Restart property. App Engine programs are restartable by default. When an App Engine program fails, PeopleSoft will save the run state of the App Engine so it can be restarted at a later time. Since our program is not restartable, checking this box will save us from needing to manually restart a failed instance of the program.

To disable restart, with the `APT_GREETER` App Engine program open, press ALT-ENTER. App Designer will display the App Engine Program Properties dialog. Switch to the Advanced tab of this dialog and check the Disable Restart check box, as shown in Figure 1-3.

With our test program defined, we can save it and then run it from App Designer. To run the program, click the Run Program button on the App Engine toolbar (see Figure 1-4). App Designer will launch the Run Request dialog. Enable the Output Log to File check box. Before clicking the OK button, copy the name of the log file to your clipboard so you can easily open it in the next step. Figure 1-5 shows the Run Request dialog with all of the appropriate settings.

After clicking the OK button, a new, minimized DOS window should briefly appear in your taskbar and then disappear. To see this program's results, open the log file referenced in the Run

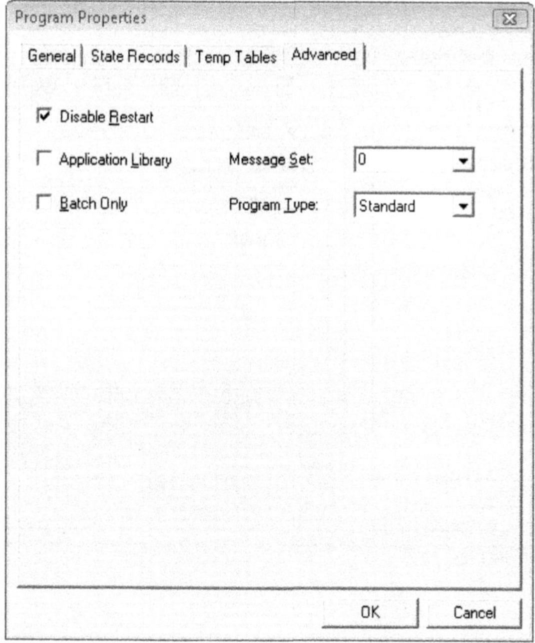

FIGURE 1-3. *Disabling the Restart property*

Request dialog (Figure 1-5), whose name you copied to your clipboard. The contents of the file should look something like this:

```
... PeopleTools version and App Engine details ...

11.54.36 .(APT_GREETER.MAIN.Test1) (PeopleCode)

Hello PS (0,0)
 Message Set Number: 0
 Message Number: 0
 Message Reason: Hello PS (0,0) (0,0)
Application Engine program APT_GREETER ended normally
11.54.36 Application Engine ended normally
```

Because I was logged into App Designer as PS, the program printed `Hello PS`.

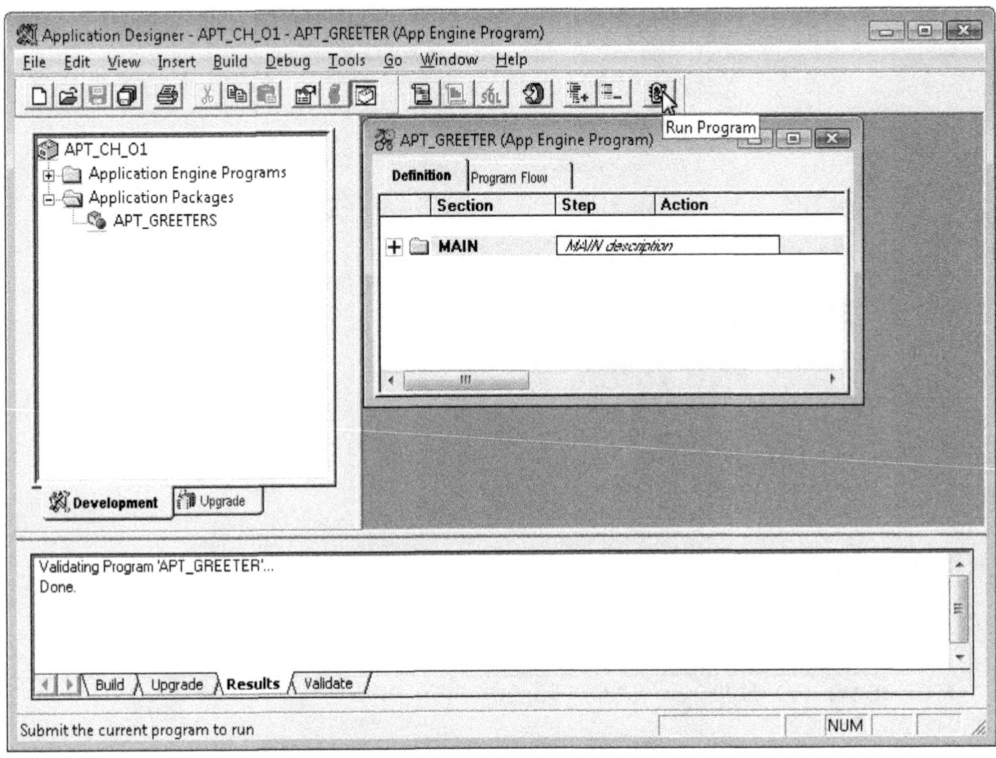

FIGURE 1-4. *Click the Run Program button to open the Run Request dialog.*

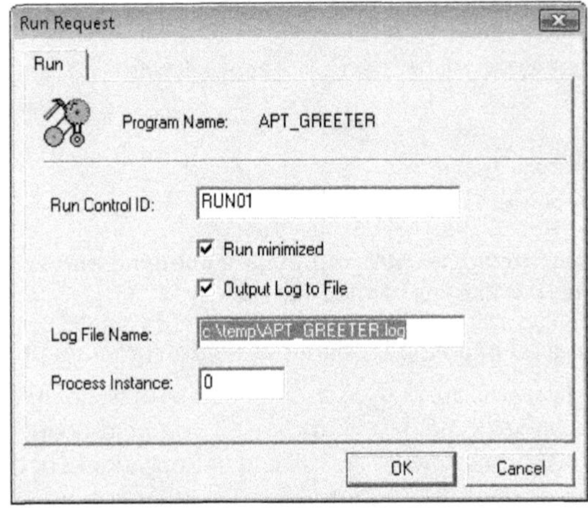

FIGURE 1-5. *Run Request dialog settings for the test program*

Expanding the Application Class

Let's add a method to our `Greeter` class that can greet anyone, not just the logged-in user.

NOTE
The changes to our `Greeter` class are shown in bold text.

```
class Greeter
   method sayHello() Returns string;
   method sayHelloTo(&name As string) Returns string;
end-class;

method sayHello
   /+ Returns String +/
   Return "Hello " | %OperatorId;
end-method;

method sayHelloTo
   /+ &name as String +/
   /+ Returns String +/
   Return "Hello " | &name;
end-method;
```

Embedded Strings

Our `Greeter` class contains a string literal. If my PeopleSoft implementation serves a multilingual audience, I should store the string literal, "Hello," in the message catalog. The message catalog allows developers to store strings by language and maintain those strings online. This allows you to avoid modifying code to update strings. Furthermore, using the message catalog's parameter syntax eliminates messy string/variable concatenations. Here is an example that uses the message catalog:

```
MsgGetText(21000, 2, "Hello %1 [default message]", %OperatorId);
```

In this example, message set 21,000 entry 2 contains the following:

```
Hello %1
```

PeopleCode provides three functions for accessing text stored in a message catalog entry: `MsgGet`, `MsgGetText`, and `MsgGetExplainText`. `MsgGet` and `MsgGetText` both return the main text of a message catalog entry, with the difference being that `MsgGet` appends the message set and entry numbers to the end of the string. `MsgGetExplainText` returns the longer explain text associated with the message catalog entry.

All three of these functions accept a default message as a parameter. Often, you will see the text `Message not found` used as the default message. Avoid this practice. This generic default message offers no help to your users. If you hard-code the message set and entry number, then you should have a reasonable understanding of the message's intent—enough understanding to create a more informative default message.

When creating your own message sets, use the range 20,000 through 32,767. PeopleSoft reserves the right to use message sets numbered from 1 to 19,999.

Naming Classes and Methods

When naming classes and methods, I use a mixture of uppercase and lowercase letters. I begin class names with uppercase letters and method names with lowercase letters. If a name contains multiple words, I capitalize the first letter of each successive word. For example, I will name an application class for processing workflow transactions `WorkflowTransactionProcessor`. If that class contains a method for processing transactions, I will name that method `processTransactions`. I use a similar naming convention for properties and methods with one key difference: I begin method names with verbs that demonstrate the method's action. I adapted this coding convention from those recommended by Sun.[5]

App Designer does not enforce naming conventions. Feel free to use whatever conventions suit your organization.

By now, I am sure you noticed the new `/+ +/` comment style. PeopleCode reserves this comment style for application classes. App Designer regenerates these comments each time it validates an application class and will overwrite any modifications you make to them.

The only difference between our `sayHello` and `sayHelloTo` methods is the name variable. We could centralize our string concatenation logic by calling `sayHelloTo` from `sayHello`. Let's refactor `sayHello` to see how this looks.

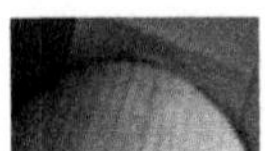

NOTE
Changes are shown in bold text.

```
method sayHello
   /+ Returns String +/
   Return %This.sayHelloTo(%OperatorId);
end-method;
```

NOTE
Code *refactoring is a technique used by software developers to improve on the internal structure of a program without modifying the program's external behavior. Refactoring involves iterative, incremental changes that make the internal code easier to comprehend.*

Our refactored `sayHello` method introduces the system variable `%This`. `%This` is a reference to the current, in-memory instance of the `Greeter` class and qualifies the `sayHelloTo` method as belonging to this class. It is akin to the Visual Basic `Me` or the Java `this`.

Inheritance

Rather than greeting a user by operator ID, it would be more appropriate for the `Greeter` class to address users by name. Since PeopleSoft offers several ways to derive a user's name, rather than modify the `Greeter` class, let's use PeopleCode's inheritance feature to implement this modified behavior. Inheritance allows us to create a new class that inherits the behaviors we want to keep and to override the behaviors we want to change.

We have two options for implementing this modified behavior within our new class:

- Write a new `sayHello` method that returns `sayHelloTo("User's Full Name")`.
- Create a new `sayHelloTo` method that expects an operator ID rather than a name.

Let's choose the latter option to ensure our new class always greets users by name. Because our new class will use the PeopleTools user profile information to look up names, let's call it `UserGreeter`. To begin, open the `APT_GREETERS` application package and add the new application class `UserGreeter`. Your application package should now resemble Figure 1-6.

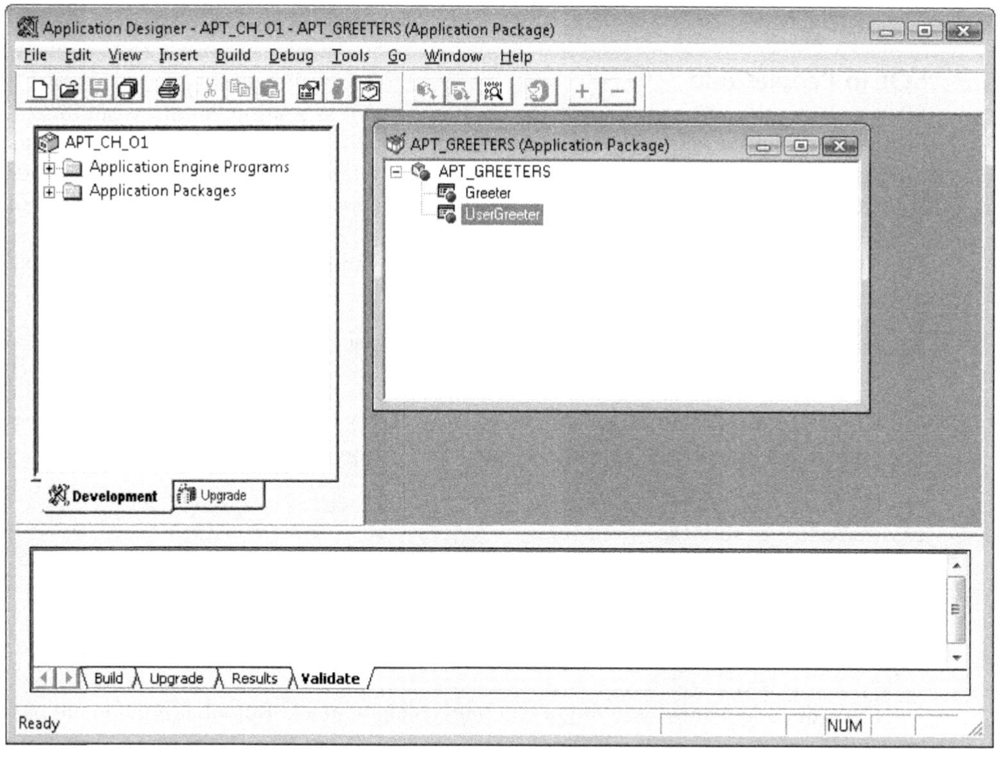

FIGURE 1-6. *Application package with the new UserGreeter class*

Next, open the `UserGreeter` PeopleCode editor and add the following code:

```
import APT_GREETERS:Greeter;

class UserGreeter extends APT_GREETERS:Greeter
   method sayHelloTo(&oprid As string) Returns string;
end-class;

method sayHelloTo
   /+ &oprid as String +/
   /+ Returns String +/
   /+ Extends/implements APT_GREETERS:Greeter.sayHelloTo +/
   Local string &name;

   SQLExec("SELECT OPRDEFNDESC FROM PSOPRDEFN WHERE OPRID = :1",
      &oprid, &name);

   Return %Super.sayHelloTo(&name);
end-method;
```

SQL in PeopleCode

For simplicity, `UserGreeter` embeds a SQL statement as a string literal. Avoid this technique by substituting SQL definitions for string literals. SQL definitions are managed objects that developers can maintain and search independent of the code that uses them. Unlike strings in PeopleCode, you can identify fields and records used in SQL definitions using the Find Definition References feature.

The SQL statement in `UserGreeter` uses SQL bind variables. Alternatively, I could rewrite this embedded SQL using concatenation:

```
SQLExec("SELECT OPRDEFNDESC FROM PSOPRDEFN WHERE OPRID = '" |
      &oprid | "'", &name);
```

Avoid this technique! When you concatenate a SQL statement, you create a potential SQL injection vulnerability. Consider what could happen:

```
REM ** Runs on Oracle and returns the first matching row;
sayHelloTo("Y' OR 'X' = 'X");
```

or

```
REM ** Fails on Oracle, but other DB's?;
sayHelloTo("PS'; DELETE FROM SECRET_AUDIT_TBL WHERE 'X' = 'X");
```

Through code review, you might catch this blatant attack. But what if the value passed to `sayHelloTo` comes from data entered by a user?

Besides providing security, bind variables may offer better performance. Before executing a SQL statement, the database will create an optimal execution plan for that statement and store the compiled execution plan for later reuse.

This new application class, `UserGreeter`, extends the base class `Greeter`. This means that `UserGreeter` inherits all the methods and properties of `Greeter`. Using the `extends` keyword, we can extend a base class by adding new methods or properties, and we can redefine the behavior of a base class by redeclaring methods defined in the base class.

Notice `UserGreeter.sayHelloTo(&name)` uses the `%Super` system variable. Whereas `%This` represents the host object, the instance of the object executing some code, `%Super` represents that host's parent class, more properly known as the object's *superclass*. `%Super` always points to the class the current class extends.

Our new `sayHelloTo` method does not really override the original `sayHelloTo` implementation. Rather, it changes the behavior of the method by executing a few lines of code prior to executing the original implementation. In this scenario, we could describe our extension as a wrapper around the original implementation.

To test this new application class, we will add some code to the `APT_GREETER` App Engine program. Open `APT_GREETER` and add a new step and action. App Designer should automatically name the step `Test2`. Change the step's action type to PeopleCode and save the program. Your App Engine program should now resemble Figure 1-7.

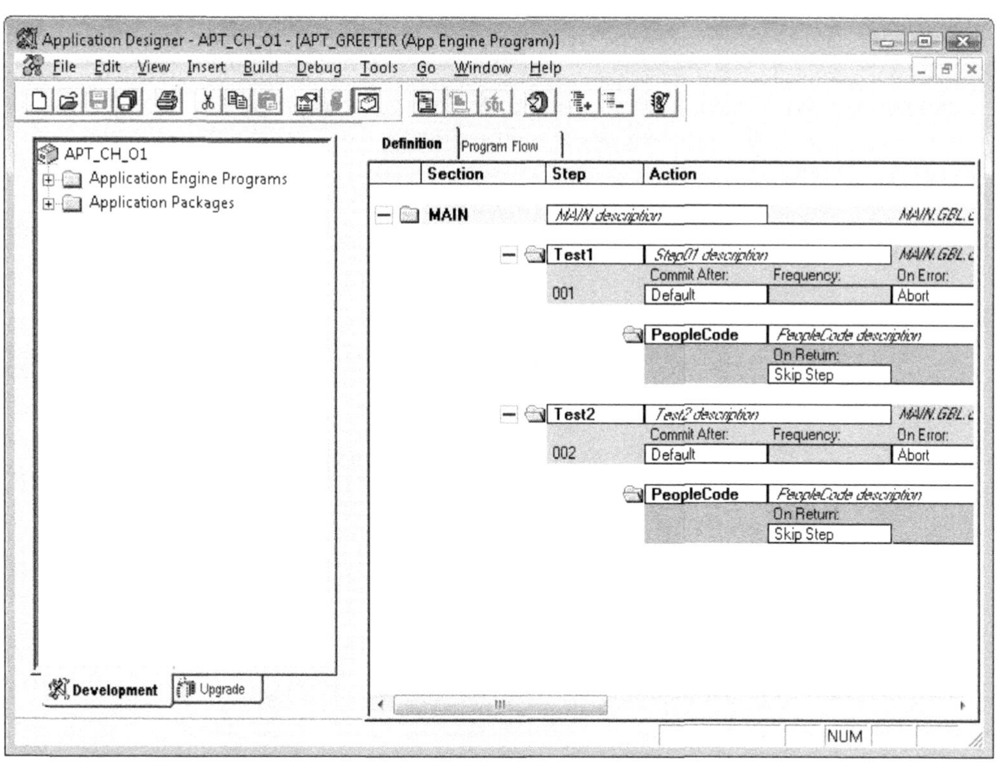

FIGURE 1-7. *App Engine with new step*

Double-click this new PeopleCode action to open the PeopleCode editor and add the following code.

```
import APT_GREETERS:UserGreeter;

Local APT_GREETERS:UserGreeter &greeter = create
      APT_GREETERS:UserGreeter();

REM ** Test the inherited sayHello() method;
MessageBox(0, "", 0, 0, &greeter.sayHello());

REM ** Test sayHelloTo();
Local SQL &cursor = CreateSQL("SELECT OPRID FROM PSOPRDEFN");
Local string &oprid;
Local number &row = 0;

While (&cursor.Fetch(&oprid) And &row < 10)
   &row = &row + 1;
   MessageBox(0, "", 0, 0, &greeter.sayHelloTo(&oprid));
End-While;

&cursor.Close();
```

Let's run this test and see what happens. Specifically, I am curious what will happen when we call `sayHello` on an application class that doesn't define `sayHello`.

When you run this program, you should see output that resembles the following:

```
... PeopleTools version and App Engine details ...

21.53.43 .(APT_GREETER.MAIN.Test1) (PeopleCode)

...

21.53.43 .(APT_GREETER.MAIN.Test2) (PeopleCode)

Hello PS (0,0)
 Message Set Number: 0
 Message Number: 0
 Message Reason: Hello PS (0,0) (0,0)

Hello [PS] Peoplesoft Superuser (0,0)
 Message Set Number: 0
 Message Number: 0
 Message Reason: Hello [PS] Peoplesoft Superuser (0,0) (0,0)...

Application Engine program APT_GREETER ended normally
21.53.44 Application Engine ended normally
```

Calling `sayHello` worked! We can call `sayHello` because `UserGreeter` inherits `sayHello` from its superclass. Notice that `Greeter.sayHello` calls `%This.sayHelloTo`. From the results, we see that, when subclassed, `%This` in `Greeter` refers to an instance of `UserGreeter`. The ability to inherit and/or override a class's behavior is a powerful feature of OOP.

Features of Application Classes

Now that you have created some application classes, let's dive deeper into the features and constructs that differentiate application classes from traditional event-based PeopleCode.

Dynamic Execution

The discussion thus far demonstrates functionality that we could just as easily write using procedural code rather than object-oriented code. But with procedural code, you cannot modify runtime behavior without modifying design-time code. Using interfaces, subclasses, and PeopleCode object-creation functions, you can dynamically execute PeopleCode without knowing the implementation at design time.

Through the creative use of PeopleCode and metadata, this flexibility allows us to wire together business rules through configuration. The Pagelet Wizard offers an excellent example of this. Oracle delivers the Pagelet Wizard with several data sources and display types implemented as application classes. At design time, the Pagelet Wizard knows about interfaces, but not implementations. The actual runtime behavior of the Pagelet Wizard is wired together at runtime using metadata configured by online users. It is this same feature of application classes that allows for online configuration of Integration Broker message handlers, AWE workflow handlers, and Enterprise Portal branding elements.

Construction

Our `UserGreeter` PeopleCode serves as a blueprint that defines the characteristics and behavior of a PeopleCode object. There may be several instances of a `UserGreeter` in memory at a given time, but there is only one class definition. The process for creating an in-memory object from a PeopleCode application class is called *instantiation*. Instantiation occurs when PeopleCode uses the `create` keyword or one of the `CreateObject` or `CreateObjectArray` PeopleCode functions.

The first phase of instantiation is the construction phase. At construction, the PeopleCode processor executes a special application class method called the *constructor*. The constructor is a method that has the same name as the application class and does not return a value. Like other methods, constructors can accept parameters. The constructor is responsible for initializing an object, and therefore should contain the parameters necessary to create a valid, usable object.

Stateful Objects

Just like physical objects, application classes have state. An object's state represents the characteristics of that object. For example, an eight-year-old male chocolate Labrador Retriever could be described as a dog having the following state:

Breed: Labrador Retriever

Color: chocolate

Age: 8 years

Sex: male

The state of an application class is maintained in properties and instance variables. Properties represent the externally visible characteristics of an application class, whereas instance variables represent the object's internal state. Properties comprise a portion of an application class's external interface. Instance variables do not. Consider the following application class declaration:

```
REM ** code for class APT_LOG4PC:Loggers:Logger;
class Logger
   method info(&msg As string);
   method debug(&msg As string);
   property number level;
end-class;
```

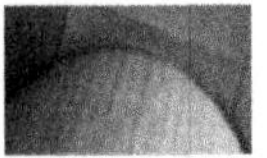

NOTE
The code listings in this section are intended for explanatory purposes only. Unlike prior examples, you are not expected to execute this code directly. After this section, which describes various features of application classes, we will work through a hands-on example of using application classes to build a logging framework.

The preceding `Logger` class declaration contains one read/write property called `level`. The following code adds a read-only property to this class:

```
class Logger
   method info(&msg As string);
   method debug(&msg As string);
   property number level;
   property string lastMessage readonly;
end-class;
```

The keyword `readonly` following the `lastMessage` property marks the property as read-only. This means that the application class declaring this property can modify the property's value, but PeopleCode acting on an instance of this class may only read its value.

Changing a property's value often triggers a change in the internal state of an application class. For example, if the filename of a `FileLogger` instance changes, then the application class may need to close the current file to open a new file. You can use the `set` modifier to execute a block of PeopleCode when a property value changes.

```
import APT_LOG4PC:Loggers:Logger;

class FileLogger extends APT_LOG4PC:Loggers:Logger
   method info(&msg As string);
   method debug(&msg As string);
   property File logFile;
   property number level;
   property string fileName get set;

   ...

end-class;
```

```
set fileName
   /+ &NewValue as String +/
end-set;

get filename
   ...
end-get;
```

Some properties don't have an in-memory representation. The following code block derives a value for the read-only property `isDebugEnabled`:

```
Property boolean isDebugEnabled get;

...

get isDebugEnabled
   return (%This.level > = 100);
end-get;
```

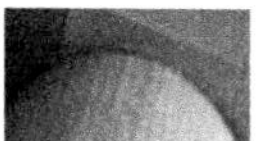

NOTE
The preceding code listing uses an inline expression to return a true or a false value. As with any operation, the parentheses surrounding the comparison, `%This.level > = 100`, tell the PeopleCode runtime to evaluate the statement prior to returning a value. The sample statement returns true if the value in `%This.level` is greater than or equal to 100.

You can define properties as any PeopleCode type. The `get`, `set`, and `readonly` modifiers define a property's mutability (the ability of code acting on a class to change the value of the property). Without any modifiers, a property is defined as read/write. A property defined with the modifier combination `get set` is also a read/write property, with the subtle difference that the PeopleCode runtime executes a block of PeopleCode. This difference provides the application class with the opportunity to validate a value prior to mutation or derive a value prior to access.

The `readonly` and `get/set` modifiers are mutually exclusive. If you specify `get`, then you cannot use `readonly`. You can combine the `get` and `set` modifiers or use the `get` modifier exclusively. The `set` modifier must be accompanied by the `get` modifier.

Access Control

Application classes typically contain stateful information that should be accessed solely by the application class definition. For example, our `FileLogger` class has a `File` object. We should not allow access to this object outside this application class. What if someone executed the `Close` method on our open `File`? These sorts of mutations may introduce undetectable side effects.

PeopleCode allows for three levels of access control:

- **Public** Public instance variables, called properties, are defined as `property number level;`. You have already seen many examples of public method definitions. Combined, public methods and properties form the external interface of an application class.
- **Protected** Protected properties and methods are methods that can be accessed by the defining class and subclasses, but not by PeopleCode outside the class's inheritance structure.

- **Private** Private access control is the most restrictive. Because properties define externally accessible characteristics of an object, we cannot define private properties. Rather, we maintain the private state of an application class using instance variables. Private methods are just like public and protected methods, except that private methods can be accessed only by the declaring class.

These access control modifiers apply to methods, properties, and instance variables, collectively referred to as *members*.

The accessibility of a method or property is determined by its placement in an application class declaration. The following listing provides the syntax for a class declaration in Extended Backus–Naur Form (EBNF), which is an ISO standard syntax for describing computer programming languages.

```
Class
class class_name [[extends | implements] base_class_name]
   [{method_declarations}]
   [{property_declarations}]

[protected
   [{method_declarations}]
   [{instance_declarations}]
   [{constant_declarations}]]

[private
   [{method_declarations}]
   [{instance_declarations}]
   [{constant_declarations}]]
end-Class;


Methods
method_name([Parm1 [{, Parm2. . .}]]) [Returns Datatype] [abstract];


Properties
property DataType property_name [get [set] | readonly] | [abstract];
```

To summarize, you define public methods and properties directly under the class name, protected properties and methods under the `protected` label, and private methods and instance variables under the `private` label.

Some object-oriented languages do not use formal property declarations. These languages expose an object's internal state using an accessor/mutator[6] design pattern. For example, if we wrote `FileLogger` in Java, rather than creating a `fileName` property, we would create an accessor method named `getFileName()` and a mutator method named `setFileName(String parm)`. By convention, methods named `get`*`Xxx`* return the value of a property (accessor), and methods named `set`*`Xxx`* modify a property (mutator). These conventions are very similar to the PeopleCode `get` and `set` modifiers used to declare application class properties.

If you come to PeopleCode from another object-oriented language, you may prefer the accessor/mutator design pattern. PeopleBooks discourages the use of accessor/mutator methods in favor of property declarations, claiming a slight performance gain from avoiding a method call for each property change.[7] Nevertheless, I prefer the `getXxx` and `setXxx` convention used by other object-oriented languages, because these methods communicate the intent of the application class author. Using PeopleBooks' recommendation, the only way to differentiate a property from a method is context:

- Parentheses will never follow a property.
- A property may be used on the left side of an equal sign.

Similarly, without peeking at an application class's declaration, it is impossible to determine the mutability of a property.

On the other hand, by composing the entire external interface of methods, I do not need to consider the differences between properties and methods, and can treat them all as methods. Furthermore, property definitions do not lend themselves to the design of fluent interfaces, which we will discuss later in this chapter.

Putting It All Together: The Logging Framework Example

A common PeopleCode debugging practice involves inserting `MessageBox` statements at strategic locations within a PeopleCode segment. Unlike trace files, this technique allows you to choose what and how statements are logged. This is a very effective technique for peeking into the state of an application at runtime. But what happens to those print statements when you finally discover the code's purpose and resolve any related errors? You delete them, right? Imagine the support calls you would receive if you left those cryptic debug messages in your code! However, although it is effective, this approach suffers from two problems:

- When you're finished debugging, you need to find and remove all those `MessageBox` statements. What if you miss one?
- If the original problem was data-related, then your functional team may call on you to perform this same investigation again.

Finding the right combination of debug statements requires thought and effort. It is a shame to waste that effort by deleting those statements. It would be great if we could place those `MessageBox` statements in our code and leave them there, turning them on and off as needed.

A logging framework provides a solution to this type of problem. Let's take the `Logger` class introduced earlier and convert it into a foundation for an extensible logging framework.

Files are common targets for logging because writing to a file does not interfere with the user interface. From a user's perspective, file logging is transparent. This discussion, however, focuses on a very obtrusive user interface logging technique. Sometimes this obtrusive behavior is preferred. Based on this information, we know we want two logging targets:

- A file target called `FileLogger`
- A message box target called `MessageBoxLogger`

Log Levels

We will want multiple logging levels, as well as corresponding print methods. When setting the level to debug, we want the logging framework to print debug and fatal messages. When the level is set to fatal, however, we want the framework to print only fatal messages.

The following code listing contains the code for a `Level` class. This class has a string representation for printing descriptions and a numeric representation for inclusive comparisons. Following OOP best practices, the `Level` class encapsulates all the logic related to logging levels. The `Level` class is the most complex of all our framework classes because it is responsible for determining what to log.

Create a new application package named `APT_LOG4PC` and add a new class named `Level`. Save the package and add the following code to the `Level` class.

```
class Level
   method enableForFatal() Returns APT_LOG4PC:Level;
   method enableForDebug() Returns APT_LOG4PC:Level;
   method enableFor(&descr As string, &level As number)
      Returns APT_LOG4PC:Level;
   method enableFromNumber(&level As number)
      Returns APT_LOG4PC:Level;

   method toNumber() Returns number;
   method toString() Returns string;

   method isFatalEnabled() Returns boolean;
   method isDebugEnabled() Returns boolean;
   method isEnabledFor(&level As APT_LOG4PC:Level) Returns boolean;



private
   Constant &LEVEL_FATAL = 500;
   Constant &LEVEL_DEBUG = 100;
   Constant &LEVEL_FATAL_DESCR = "FATAL";
   Constant &LEVEL_DEBUG_DESCR = "DEBUG";

   instance number &levelNumber_;
   instance string &levelDescr_;

   method setLevel(&descr As string, &nbr As number)
      Returns APT_LOG4PC:Level;

end-class;

method enableForFatal
   /+ Returns APT_LOG4PC:Level +/
   Return %This.setLevel(&LEVEL_FATAL_DESCR, &LEVEL_FATAL);
end-method;
```

```
method enableForDebug
   /+ Returns APT_LOG4PC:Level +/
   Return %This.setLevel(&LEVEL_DEBUG_DESCR, &LEVEL_DEBUG);
end-method;

method enableFor
   /+ &descr as String, +/
   /+ &level as Number +/
   /+ Returns APT_LOG4PC:Level +/
   Return %This.setLevel(&descr, &level);
end-method;

method enableFromNumber
   /+ &level as Number +/
   /+ Returns APT_LOG4PC:Level +/
   Local APT_LOG4PC:Level &this;

   Evaluate &level
   When = &LEVEL_FATAL
      &this = %This.enableForFatal();
   When = &LEVEL_DEBUG
      &this = %This.enableForDebug();
   When-Other
      &this = %This.enableFor("UNKNOWN", &level);
   End-Evaluate;

   Return %This;
end-method;

method isFatalEnabled
   /+ Returns Boolean +/
   Return (&LEVEL_FATAL >= %This.toNumber());
end-method;

method isDebugEnabled
   /+ Returns Boolean +/
   Return (&LEVEL_DEBUG >= %This.toNumber());
end-method;

method isEnabledFor
   /+ &level as APT_LOG4PC:Level +/
   /+ Returns Boolean +/
   Return (&level.toNumber() >= %This.toNumber());
end-method;

method toString
   /+ Returns String +/
   Return &levelDescr_;
end-method;
```

```
method toNumber
   /+ Returns Number +/
   Return &levelNumber_;
end-method;

method setLevel
   /+ &descr as String, +/
   /+ &nbr as Number +/
   /+ Returns APT_LOG4PC:Level +/
   &levelDescr_ = &descr;
   &levelNumber_ = &nbr;
   Return %This;
end-method;
```

Notice that many of the methods in the `Level` class return a `Level` object. These methods don't actually create a new `Level`. Rather, they return the object itself. This technique facilitates method chaining, a pattern that allows us to chain multiple method calls in a single statement. We will leverage this technique when we implement a `Logger`.

Fluent Interface Design

Eric Evans and Martin Fowler coined the term *fluent interfaces*[8] to describe a design pattern that strives to make code easier to read. By *interface*, I'm referring to the external facing design of an application class (public and protected members), not the interface class type.

A fluent method returns a reference to the object that is most likely to be used next, allowing a programmer to chain the next method call to the previous call. This method-chaining[9] technique is a key component of fluent interface design. For example, our `Logger` will have a `setLevel` method that takes a `Level` object as a parameter. Typical object-oriented code to set the log level would look something like this:

```
Local APT_LOG4PC:Level &debugLevel = create APT_LOG4PC:Level();

&debugLevel.enableForDebug();
&logger.setLevel(&debugLevel);
```

This code requires a temporary variable to hold the `Level` object just so we can set its value. If we could create and configure the `Level` object in one statement, we could eliminate the temporary variable assignment. Here is the same code rewritten using method chaining:

```
&logger.setLevel((create APT_LOG4PC:Level()).enableForDebug());
```

Now, arguably, some might suggest that all of the parentheses required for a PeopleCode constructor make this example a little less *fluent* than other examples. In this book, you will see several examples of method chaining to create fluent interfaces. In fact, when we discuss JavaScript and user interface coding, you will see extensive use of method chaining with the jQuery library.

When using method chaining with PeopleCode, it is very important that you think about fluent interface design. Unlike other languages, PeopleCode doesn't allow you to ignore return values. Rather, you may find that method chaining requires you to create temporary variables where you wouldn't otherwise need them. For example, calling the `enableForDebug` method on a `Level` object already assigned to a local variable would require you to assign the return value to another temporary variable as follows:

```
Local APT_LOG4PC:Level &debugLevel = create APT_LOG4PC:Level();
Local Object &temp = &debugLevel.enableForDebug();
```

When used correctly, method chaining should improve the legibility of your code without requiring unnecessary temporary variables. It is this improved readability that lead Martin Fowler and Eric Evans to name this technique *fluent interfaces*.

The Logger Interface

The following listing defines an interface that both `FileLogger` and `MessageBoxLogger` will implement:

```
import APT_LOG4PC:Level;

interface Logger
   /* Statement logging methods, one for each level */
   method fatal(&msg As string);
   method debug(&msg As string);

   /* Convenience methods for determining the current log level */
   method isFatalEnabled() Returns boolean;
   method isDebugEnabled() Returns boolean;
   method isEnabledFor(&level As APT_LOG4PC:Level) Returns boolean;

   method setLevel(&level As APT_LOG4PC:Level);
end-interface;
```

The Logger Classes

I foresee more similarities than differences between `Logger` implementations. To ensure we hold to the DRY (don't repeat yourself) principle, we'll create a base abstract class that consolidates common logic. This consolidation allows `Logger` implementations to focus on the one feature that makes each `Logger` unique. The intent of this inheritance is to make our final implementation classes easier to write, maintain, and comprehend.

The LoggerBase Class

The following listing contains code for the `LoggerBase` class, which both `FileLogger` and `MessageBoxLogger` will extend.

```
import APT_LOG4PC:Loggers:Logger;
import APT_LOG4PC:Level;

class LoggerBase implements APT_LOG4PC:Loggers:Logger
   method LoggerBase();

   REM ** Statement logging methods, one for each level;
   method fatal(&msg As string);
   method debug(&msg As string);

   REM ** Convenience methods to determine the current log level;
   method isFatalEnabled() Returns boolean;
   method isDebugEnabled() Returns boolean;
   method isEnabledFor(&level As APT_LOG4PC:Level) Returns boolean;


   method setLevel(&level As APT_LOG4PC:Level);

protected
   method writeToLog(&level As APT_LOG4PC:Level, &msg As string) abstract;

private
   instance APT_LOG4PC:Level &level_;

end-class;

method LoggerBase
   &level_ = (create APT_LOG4PC:Level()).enableForFatal();
end-method;

method fatal
   /+ &msg as String +/
   /+ Extends/implements APT_LOG4PC:Loggers:Logger.fatal +/
   If (%This.isFatalEnabled()) Then
      %This.writeToLog(
         (create APT_LOG4PC:Level()).enableForFatal(), &msg);
   End-If;
end-method;

method debug
   /+ &msg as String +/
   /+ Extends/implements APT_LOG4PC:Loggers:Logger.debug +/
   If (%This.isDebugEnabled()) Then
      %This.writeToLog(
         (create APT_LOG4PC:Level()).enableForDebug(), &msg);
   End-If;
end-method;
```

```
REM ** Convenience methods to determine the current log level;
method isFatalEnabled
   /+ Returns Boolean +/
   /+ Extends/implements APT_LOG4PC:Loggers:Logger.isFatalEnabled +/
   Return &level_.isFatalEnabled();
end-method;

method isDebugEnabled
   /+ Returns Boolean +/
   /+ Extends/implements APT_LOG4PC:Loggers:Logger.isDebugEnabled +/
   Return &level_.isDebugEnabled();
end-method;

method isEnabledFor
   /+ &level as APT_LOG4PC:Level +/
   /+ Returns Boolean +/
   /+ Extends/implements APT_LOG4PC:Loggers:Logger.isEnabledFor +/
   Return &level_.isEnabledFor(&level);
end-method;

method setLevel
   /+ &level as APT_LOG4PC:Level +/
   /+ Extends/implements APT_LOG4PC:Loggers:Logger.setLevel +/
   &level_ = &level;
end-method;
```

The previous listing declares `LoggerBase` as an application class that implements the `Logger` interface. This relationship identifies `LoggerBase` as a `Logger`, meaning instances of `LoggerBase` can be assigned to variables declared as type `Logger`. Notice that `LoggerBase` declares and implements every method defined by the `Logger` interface. A class that implements an interface must implement (or declare as abstract) every method defined by the interface.

Look closely at the `writeToLog` method declaration. Notice that it is declared in the *protected* section. By placing this method in the protected members section, we tell the PeopleCode compiler to hide this method from PeopleCode running outside this class's inheritance hierarchy. Only this class and its subclasses can access this method.

We also use the keyword `abstract` to qualify the `writeToLog` method. This keyword tells the PeopleCode compiler that `LoggerBase` does not implement this method. A class with an abstract method is called an *abstract* class. Subclasses of abstract classes must either provide an implementation for abstract methods or redeclare those methods as abstract. We cannot create instances of abstract classes directly. Rather, we create instances of abstract classes through their subclasses.

`LoggerBase` is our first application class with a constructor. As mentioned earlier in the chapter, constructors are methods with the same name as the host class—`LoggerBase` in this case. You need to define a constructor in these cases:

- You need to initialize the application class prior to use.
- Your application class requires parameters.
- You are subclassing another class whose constructor requires parameters.

In our case, we declared a constructor to initialize the `Level` instance variable `&level_`. The `LoggerBase` constructor uses method chaining:

```
&level_ = (create APT_LOG4PC:Level()).enableForFatal();
```

Without method chaining, we would write this statement as follows:

```
&level_ = create APT_LOG4PC:Level();
&level_.enableForFatal();
```

Sometimes method chaining makes code easier to read, and sometimes it doesn't. The way you use method chaining is part of fluent interface design.

Notice that the `LoggerBase` `debug` and `fatal` methods execute the abstract `writeToLog` method. To implement logging functionality, subclasses of `LoggerBase` just need to implement the `writeToLog` method. This frees our `Logger` implementations to focus on their differentiating factor, which is logging.

One of our requirements is to be able to turn logging on and off through configuration. By delegating the on/off decision to the `Level` class, the `LoggerBase` class does not need to know the relationship between logging levels, because that is an implementation detail of the `Level` class. This design decision follows the practice of encapsulation, which suggests that other objects should not know the implementation details of an object.[10] You can see this delegation in the `isFatalEnabled`, `isDebugEnabled`, and `isEnabledFor` methods.

The MessageBoxLogger Class

The following code listing contains the implementation for a logger that writes messages to the PeopleCode `MessageBox` function, creatively named `MessageBoxLogger`.

```
import APT_LOG4PC:Loggers:LoggerBase;
import APT_LOG4PC:Level;

class MessageBoxLogger extends APT_LOG4PC:Loggers:LoggerBase

protected
   method writeToLog(&level As APT_LOG4PC:Level, &msg As string);
end-class;

method writeToLog
   /+ &level as APT_LOG4PC:Level, +/
   /+ &msg as String +/
   /+ Extends/implements APT_LOG4PC:Loggers:LoggerBase.writeToLog +/
   MessageBox(0, "", 0, 0, &level.toString() | ": " | &msg);
end-method;
```

With the boilerplate code handled by the `LoggerBase` superclass, this code is free to focus on the one feature that makes this `Logger` implementation unique. Through inheritance, the `MessageBoxLogger` class contains all the methods of the `LoggerBase` superclass, as well as the one `writeToLog` method that is declared here.

Composition Versus Inheritance

We built loggers using OOP inheritance: A `FileLogger` inherits from `LoggerBase`, which implements `Logger`. Inheritance suffers several design and implementation problems. For example, if you want to format strings prior to logging them, what class would you change? Would you implement this behavior in the `LoggerBase` class? If so, how would you propagate this change to all subclasses? What if one subclass can't interpret the strings formatted by this new string formatting routine?

Composition provides an alternative to inheritance. Using composition, we flatten the `LoggerBase` and `Logger` interface into a single `Logger` class and delegate printing to implementations of a `Target` interface. This one `Logger` class could then print to any destination using a runtime configured `Target`. If we wanted to create a formatter class for formatting strings, we could create a class that implements the `Target` interface and then delegates printing to another `Target` instance.

This book provides several more examples of both inheritance and composition. Chapter 15 covers a design technique called test-driven development, which provides many opportunities to replace inheritance with composition.

Notice the `MessagBoxLogger` class does not have a constructor. If you extend a class whose constructor does not require parameters, and your only purpose for a constructor is to set the value of `%Super`, you do not need a constructor.[11]

The FileLogger Class

Another useful logging target is a file logging target. Rather than obnoxiously displaying messages, a `FileLogger` transparently writes messages to a file. The following code listing contains the implementation for this logger.

```
import APT_LOG4PC:Loggers:LoggerBase;
import APT_LOG4PC:Level;

class FileLogger extends APT_LOG4PC:Loggers:LoggerBase
   method FileLogger(&fileName As string);

protected
   method writeToLog(&level As APT_LOG4PC:Level, &msg As string);

private
   instance File &logFile;
end-class;

method FileLogger
   /+ &fileName as String +/
   %Super = create APT_LOG4PC:Loggers:LoggerBase();
   &logFile = GetFile(&fileName, "A", "A", %FilePath_Absolute);
end-method;
```

```
method writeToLog
   /+ &level as APT_LOG4PC:Level, +/
   /+ &msg as String +/
   /+ Extends/implements APT_LOG4PC:Loggers:LoggerBase.writeToLog +/
   &logFile.WriteLine(&level.toString() | ": " | &msg);
end-method;
```

The `FileLogger` constructor declaration requires a string parameter. Since the purpose of this application class is to write messages to a file, this object would not be valid without this target filename. Put another way, each of the write methods of this logger would fail in the absence of a target filename. We use our constructor to initialize our object, placing it in a usable state.

The constructor creates an instance of the superclass and assigns it to the system variable `%Super`. When implementing a constructor for a class that extends another class, that constructor must assign a value to `%Super`. If you don't define a constructor for a subclass, then the PeopleCode runtime will create an instance of the superclass and assign it to `%Super`.

Figure 1-8 shows the package structure of the `APT_LOG4PC` application package.

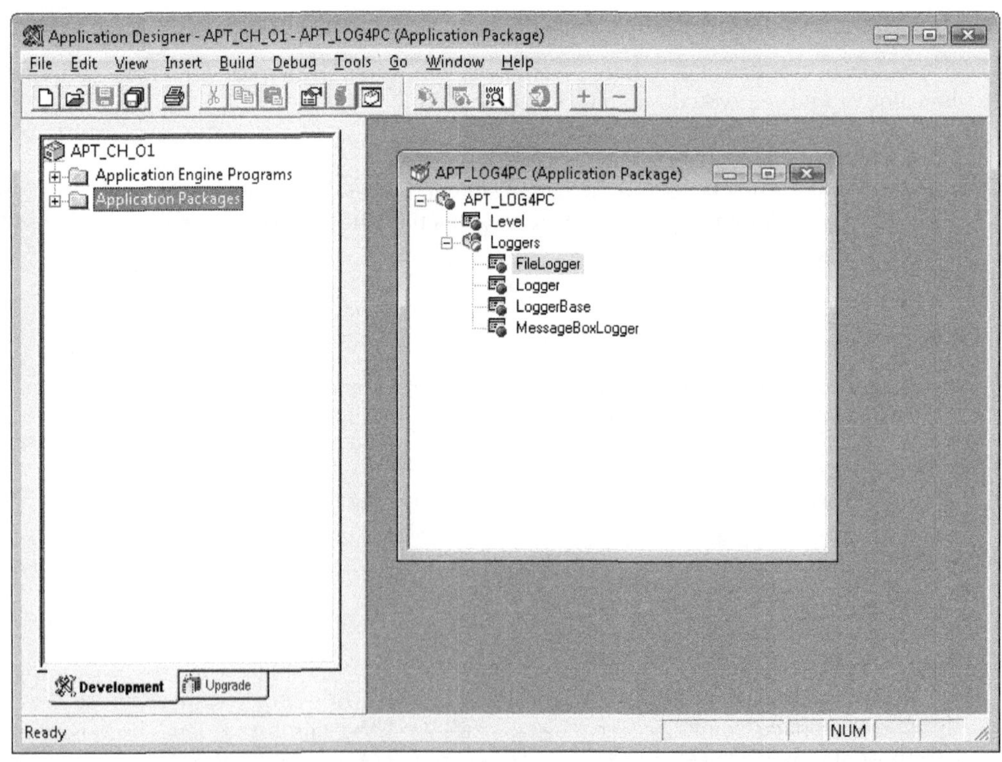

FIGURE 1-8. *APT_LOG4PC package structure*

Testing the Framework

With the code written, we can test this mini logging framework. Now create an App Engine program with a PeopleCode action and enter the following code into the PeopleCode editor:

```
import APT_LOG4PC:Loggers:Logger;
import APT_LOG4PC:Loggers:MessageBoxLogger;
import APT_LOG4PC:Level;

Local APT_LOG4PC:Level &level = create APT_LOG4PC:Level();
Local APT_LOG4PC:Loggers:MessageBoxLogger &logger =
     create APT_LOG4PC:Loggers:MessageBoxLogger();

&logger.setLevel(&level.enableForDebug());
&logger.fatal("This is for DEBUG level");
&logger.debug("This is for DEBUG level");

&logger.setLevel(&level.enableForFatal());
&logger.fatal("This is for FATAL level");
&logger.debug("This is for FATAL level");
```

When you run this program, you should see output that resembles this:

```
... PeopleTools version and App Engine details ...
FATAL: This is for DEBUG level (0,0)
 Message Set Number: 0
 Message Number: 0
 Message Reason: FATAL: This is for DEBUG level (0,0) (0,0)

DEBUG: This is for DEBUG level (0,0)
 Message Set Number: 0
 Message Number: 0
 Message Reason: DEBUG: This is for DEBUG level (0,0) (0,0)

FATAL: This is for FATAL level (0,0)
 Message Set Number: 0
 Message Number: 0
 Message Reason: FATAL: This is for FATAL level (0,0) (0,0)
Application Engine program APT_LOG_TST ended normally
17.15.34 Application Engine ended normally
```

The first five lines of our test code create instances of the logging framework application classes.

The next block of test code sets the log level to debug and then prints two lines of text. The first line of this block makes use of our fluent interface design decision, making it very clear that we are setting the log level to debug. Unlike the constructor example with its parentheses noise, this fluent interface example is very easy to read. We know this test succeeds because we see two corresponding `MessageBox` sections in the program's output.

The final block of code tests our `isEnabledFor`*`Xxx`* methods to see if debug statements print when the log level is set to fatal, which is higher in value than the debug level. Looking at

The Cost of Logging Strings

String construction is expensive. When logging, we don't usually log static strings. Rather, we concatenate static strings with variables that represent the application's state. Even though the `debug` and `fatal` methods test the log level prior to printing, we can further improve performance by using the `Logger` interface's `isDebugEnabled` and `isFatalEnabled` methods to test the log level prior to concatenating strings. Here is an example:

```
If (&logger.isDebugEnabled()) Then
   &logger.debug("This is for " | &level.toString() | " level");
End-If;
```

Executing this code block with the level set to fatal will eliminate the string construction overhead and CPU cycles wasted working through the framework's method hierarchy.

the output, we see the second `DEBUG` message is missing, validating our `isEnabledForXxx` decision logic.

Let's take a closer look at that fluent interface design decision to return a `Level` from the `enableForXxx` methods. This is because we use the `enableForXxx` methods in the context of the `setLevel` method. If `enableForXxx` didn't return a `Level` object, then this statement:

```
&logger.setLevel(&level.enableForFatal());
```

would require two lines:

```
&level.enableForFatal();
&logger.setLevel(&level);
```

More important than line count, the one-line example pairs the purpose of the enable method with the target. It is clear that our intent is to set the logger's level to fatal. This intent is less clear with the separate statements in the two-line example. The intent is hard enough to discern with the two lines paired. Imagine if `&level.enableForFatal()` were several lines removed from `&logger.setLevel(&level)`.

Dynamic Logger Configuration

The code demonstrated thus far builds the foundation for an extensible logging framework. You can use this foundation as is or extend it by creating additional logging targets and levels. For example, you could create a logger that saves messages in a database table (be sure to use autonomous transactions to keep your log from rolling back with failed transactions). We just have one feature left to develop: the ability to configure loggers at runtime.

The Logger Factory

To enable runtime configuration, any code that uses a `Logger` must be ignorant of the actual `Logger` implementation. This ignorance represents a level of abstraction[12] —the use of a `Logger` is not associated with any specific instance of a `Logger`. This abstraction creates a problem:

How do we create instances of an object when we don't know what object to create? In other words, how do we create a `Logger` when we don't know which class provides the `Logger` implementation?

The factory design pattern[13] offers a solution to this problem. With the factory design pattern, we will not create `Logger` instances directly. Rather, we will delegate creation to a *factory* object.

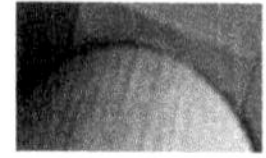

NOTE
This example uses a factory object to encapsulate `Logger` creation logic. Considering the simplicity of `Logger` creation, it is possible to use a PeopleCode function library factory function in place of an application class.

The requirement "runtime configuration" implies some type of runtime accessible storage implemented through a means as simple as transient global variables or as complex as a persistent, configurable database repository. For this example, we will use a configurable repository. We could implement this repository using one of the various structured file formats, or we could use the PeopleSoft database. Because we have various options for implementing a repository, let's keep this framework extensible by defining an interface for factories. Implementations of this interface will create and configure loggers from metadata repositories. The following code contains our interface definition:

```
import APT_LOG4PC:Loggers:Logger;

interface LoggerFactory
   method getLogger(&id As string) Returns APT_LOG4PC:Loggers:Logger
end-interface;
```

Developers can usually create tables in the database, but they may not have access to the application server's file system. Therefore, this example will use a database metadata repository. The record definitions required by this repository are shown in Figure 1-9. Notice the custom field `APT_LOGGER_ID`. It is defined as a character field with a length of 254 and a format of mixed case. `APT_LOGGER_ID` is a key field in both records.

NOTE
I assume you already know how to build fields and records. If not, then I suggest reading Judi Doolittle's book PeopleSoft Developer's Guide for PeopleTools and PeopleCode *(McGraw-Hill/Professional, 2008).*

A logger's constructor can have an unknown number of parameters. To provide the greatest flexibility in the number and type of constructor parameters, we will use the `RECNAME` field of `APT_LOGGER_CFG` to identify the record that holds a logger's constructor argument values. The record `APT_LOGGER_CFG` is the main metadata repository table. The `APT_FILELOG_CFG` record is specific to the `FileLogger` and contains fields corresponding to the parameters required by the `FileLogger` constructor.

The following listing contains SQL `INSERT` statements to populate the metadata repository with test data. The test data identifies two loggers for two tests. The first test will log a fatal and a debug message to the `MessageBoxLogger`, and the second test will log a fatal message to

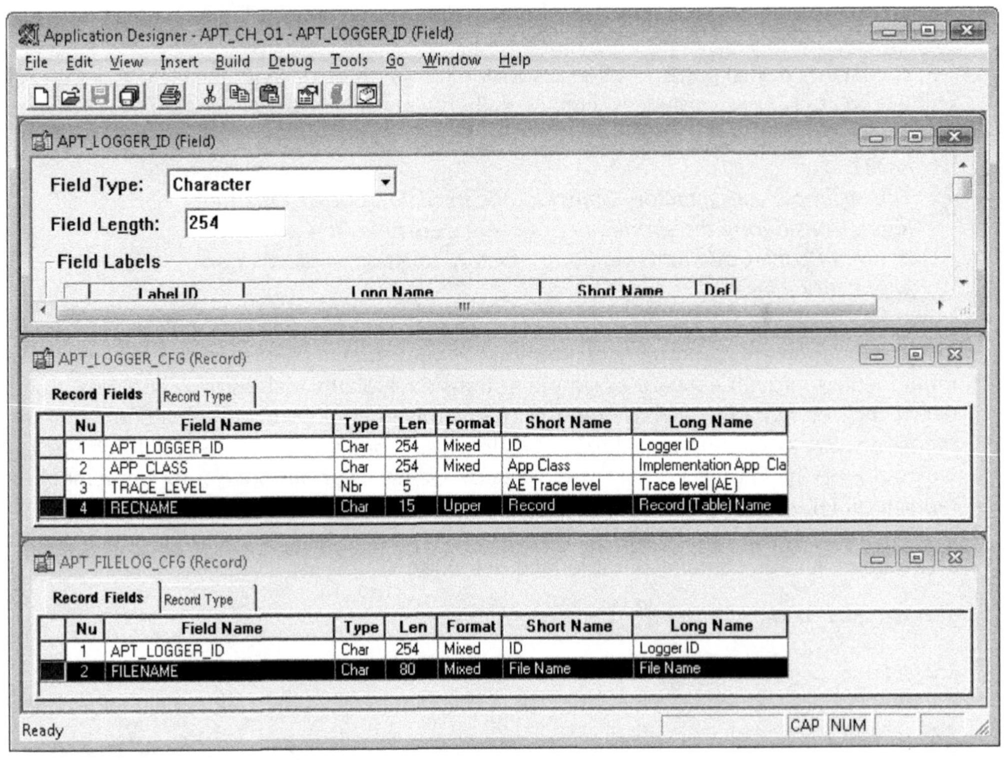

FIGURE 1-9. *Metadata repository*

the `FileLogger`. We will specify the log level for each logger by setting the `TRACE_LEVEL` field to 100 for debug as well as fatal, and 500 for fatal exclusively.

```
-- Logger 1
INSERT INTO PS_APT_LOGGER_CFG VALUES(
   'AE.APT_FACT_TST.MAIN.Step01',
   'APT_LOG4PC:Loggers:MessageBoxLogger',
   100,
   ' ')
/
-- Logger 2
INSERT INTO PS_APT_LOGGER_CFG VALUES
   ('AE.APT_FACT_TST.MAIN.Step02',
   'APT_LOG4PC:Loggers:FileLogger',
   500,
   'APT_FILELOG_CFG')
/
-- Constructor parameters for Logger 2
```

```
INSERT INTO PS_APT_FILELOG_CFG VALUES
   ('AE.APT_FACT_TST.MAIN.Step02', 'c:\temp\factory.log')
/
COMMIT
/
```

The following code listing describes the factory responsible for creating loggers from our database metadata repository:

```
import APT_LOG4PC:Level;
import APT_LOG4PC:Loggers:Logger;
import APT_LOG4PC:Factories:LoggerFactory;

class DBLoggerFactory implements APT_LOG4PC:Factories:LoggerFactory
   method getLogger(&id As string) Returns APT_LOG4PC:Loggers:Logger
end-class;

method getLogger
   /+ &id as String +/
   /+ Returns APT_LOG4PC:Loggers:Logger +/
   /+ Extends/implements APT_LOG4PC:Factories:LoggerFactory.getLogger +/
   Local array of any &parms = CreateArrayAny();
   Local string &loggerClass;
   Local string &parmRecordName;
   Local Record &parmRecord;
   Local number &level;
   Local number &fieldIdx;

   SQLExec("SELECT APP_CLASS, TRACE_LEVEL, RECNAME FROM " |
      "PS_APT_LOGGER_CFG WHERE APT_LOGGER_ID = :1", &id,
      &loggerClass, &level, &parmRecordName);

   If (All(&parmRecordName)) Then
      &parmRecord = CreateRecord(@("RECORD." | &parmRecordName));
      &parmRecord.GetField(Field.APT_LOGGER_ID).Value = &id;
      &parmRecord.SelectByKey();

      REM ** Skip first field, logger name;
      For &fieldIdx = 2 To &parmRecord.FieldCount
         &parms [&fieldIdx - 1] =
            &parmRecord.GetField(&fieldIdx).Value;
      End-For;
   End-If;

   Local APT_LOG4PC:Loggers:Logger &logger =
      CreateObjectArray(&loggerClass, &parms);
   &logger.setLevel(
      (create APT_LOG4PC:Level()).enableFromNumber(&level));

   Return &logger;
end-method;
```

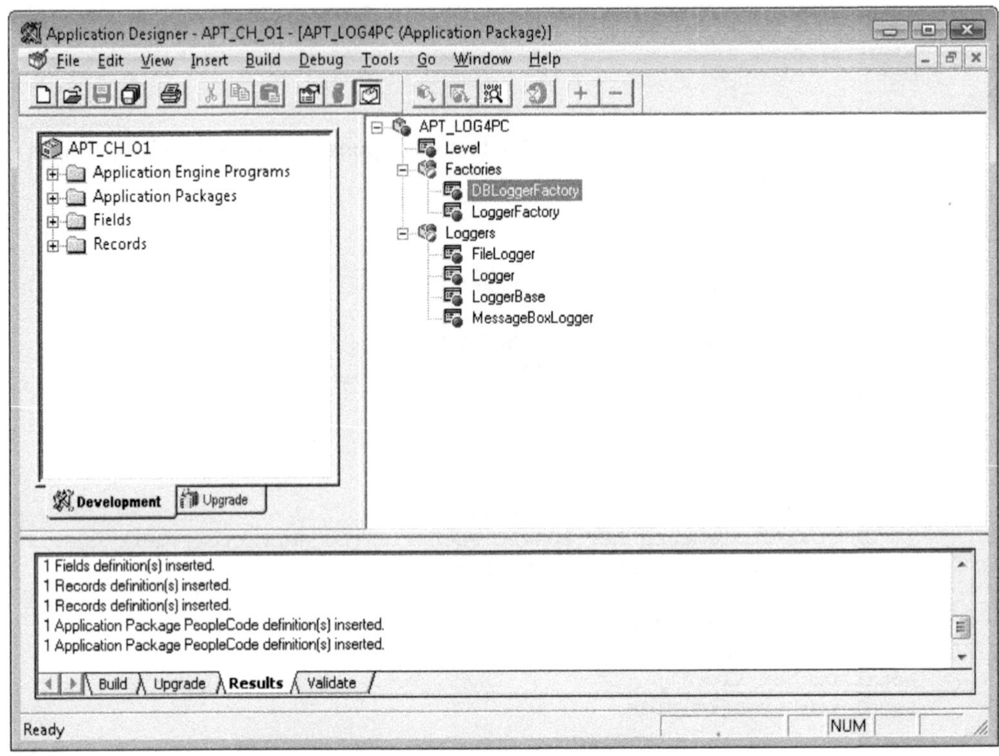

FIGURE 1-10. *APT_LOG4PC application package with factories*

Besides the `create` function, PeopleCode has two additional object-creation functions: `CreateObject` and `CreateObjectArray`. The `getLogger` method uses the `CreateObjectArray` function to create an instance of the correct logger. At design time, if you know the type of object you are creating, then use the strongly typed `create` function. If you don't know the class name, but you do know the number of parameters, then use `CreateObject`. If you don't know the class name or the number of parameters, then use the `CreateObjectArray` function. In this example, we do not know the class name or the number of parameters, so we use the most flexible object-creation method: `CreateObjectArray`.

After adding this code to the `APT_LOG4PC` application package, your final package should resemble Figure 1-10.

Factory Test Program

Keeping with our App Engine test theme, create a new App Engine program called `APT_FACT_TST`. Add two steps to your App Engine, each with its own PeopleCode action. These steps and actions correspond to the `APT_LOGGER_ID` values specified in the prior SQL `INSERT` statement. The next two listings contain the test code for `Step01` and `Step02`, respectively. These listings differ only by the value assigned to the variable `&loggerName`. (Don't forget to disable the Restart property.)

Here is the PeopleCode for `Step01`, which uses logger `AE.APT_FACT_TST.MAIN.Step01`:

```
import APT_LOG4PC:Loggers:Logger;
import APT_LOG4PC:Factories:DBLoggerFactory;

Local string &loggerName = "AE.APT_FACT_TST.MAIN.Step01";
Local APT_LOG4PC:Loggers:Logger &logger =
   (create APT_LOG4PC:Factories:DBLoggerFactory())
      .getLogger(&loggerName);

&logger.debug("This message printed from " | &loggerName);
&logger.fatal("This message printed from " | &loggerName);
```

And here is the PeopleCode for `Step02`, which uses logger `AE.APT_FACT_TST.MAIN.Step02`:

```
import APT_LOG4PC:Loggers:Logger;
import APT_LOG4PC:Loggers:Logger;
import APT_LOG4PC:Factories:DBLoggerFactory;

Local string &loggerName = "AE.APT_FACT_TST.MAIN.Step02";
Local APT_LOG4PC:Loggers:Logger &logger =
   (create APT_LOG4PC:Factories:DBLoggerFactory())
      .getLogger(&loggerName);

&logger.debug("This message printed from " | &loggerName);
&logger.fatal("This message printed from " | &loggerName);
```

When you run this program, you should see output that resembles the following:

```
... PeopleTools version and App Engine details ...
21.22.51 .(APT_FACT_TST.MAIN.Step01) (PeopleCode)

DEBUG: This message printed from AE.APT_FACT_TST.MAIN.Step01 (0,0)
 Message Set Number: 0
 Message Number: 0
 Message Reason: DEBUG: This message printed from
    AE.APT_FACT_TST.MAIN.Step01 (0,0) (0,0)

FATAL: This message printed from AE.APT_FACT_TST.MAIN.Step01 (0,0)
 Message Set Number: 0
 Message Number: 0
 Message Reason: FATAL: This message printed from
    AE.APT_FACT_TST.MAIN.Step01 (0,0) (0,0)
21.22.51 .(APT_FACT_TST.MAIN.Step02) (PeopleCode)
Application Engine program APT_FACT_TST ended normally
21.22.51 Application Engine ended normally
```

Notice that our App Engine log contains debug and fatal statements from `Step01`, but no statements from `Step02`, even though step 1 and 2 use the same code. The logging framework metadata for step 1 described a `MessageBoxLogger` that prints both debug and fatal messages. The metadata for step 2 described a `FileLogger` that logs only fatal messages. If you open the file c:\temp\factory.log, you will see only fatal messages:

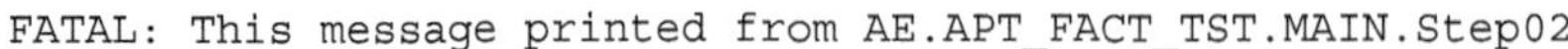

```
FATAL: This message printed from AE.APT_FACT_TST.MAIN.Step02
```

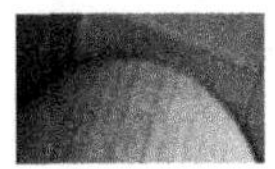

NOTE
When run locally through App Designer, this App Engine program will produce the file c:\temp\factory.log in your local C drive. If you run this same code online, the PeopleCode runtime will place the file in your app server's c:\temp directory.

In Chapter 10, you will learn how to use the log4j Java logging framework, which is a robust, extensible logging solution delivered with PeopleSoft applications.

Misuses of Application Classes

As with any technology, developers can—and frequently do—misuse application classes. This section contains examples and scenarios of application class coding errors and inappropriate use cases.

Runtime Context-Sensitive Variables

Some system variables exist only when code is running in a specific context. For example, if your code is running inside a component, you can use the `%Component` system variable. Similarly, if your code is running from a browser request, you can use `%Portal`, `%Request`, and `%Response`. Avoid using these system variables when writing application class PeopleCode.

Using context-sensitive system variables violates the reusable principle of application classes. The use of these system variables tightly couples application class code to the runtime execution context. For event-based PeopleCode, this is acceptable, because event-based PeopleCode can run only in the context of the event to which it is attached. Application classes, on the other hand, can run in any execution context. Code that uses `%Component` online, for example, cannot be called from Integration Broker subscription handlers, App Engine programs, or iScripts. Furthermore, if you tightly couple application classes to their execution context, you cannot effectively apply test-driven development (discussed in Chapter 15).

Indiscriminate Usage

Application classes provide a mechanism for creating reusable PeopleCode components. Event-based PeopleCode, such as component `SavePostChange` PeopleCode, is not reusable. It is rarely appropriate to delegate event-based processing to application classes. For example, I see programmers try to make application classes into Model-View-Controller (MVC) controllers. MVC is a design pattern used to separate data (the model) from the presentation layer (the view). If you code a component, then you already have a PeopleSoft-managed controller—the component processor.

If you have business logic that you share between online and batch processes, then encapsulating that logic in an application class may make sense. Event-based PeopleCode, however, is usually very component-specific and is not reusable in part, but may be reusable in whole as a component interface.

If you share business logic among events within the same component, then the reusable aspect of an application class is compelling. Application classes and function libraries are the only options for sharing this business logic. Whichever form you choose, do your best to make this shared business logic contextually independent of its runtime environment. While your shared business logic may be tightly coupled to your component's buffer, don't assume that the code is running in the component processor. Rather, pass a `Rowset` buffer structure to your shared code as a parameter. Separating your code from its execution context allows you to test your shared business logic offline. You can replicate a buffer structure using nested `Rowset` structures, but you cannot replicate the component processor's ability to resolve contextual `record.field` references.

Conclusion

If you have a strong OOP background, you may be tempted to write all your code in application classes. On the other hand, if you are new to OOP, you might be tempted to avoid application classes altogether. I suggest a middle road approach. Application classes are not a silver bullet. They were not designed to fit every PeopleCode programming scenario. But they are very good at what they do. The remaining chapters will make extensive use of application classes, providing you with several more excellent examples of their use.

You will also find several excellent examples of applications classes among the PeopleSoft-delivered application PeopleCode. As you will see in Chapter 3, the Approval Workflow Engine is an outstanding framework built using application classes. Likewise, the application package `EOIU:Common` contains several reusable classes for working with collections. I encourage you to investigate the delivered PeopleCode application classes. You will find valuable, reusable application classes and code snippets you can use to improve your own business logic.

Notes

1. Ssdlpedia, "Spartan programming" [online]; available from http://ssdl-wiki.cs.technion.ac.il/wiki/index.php/Spartan_programming; Internet; accessed 18 February 2009.
2. Jeff Atwood, *Coding Horror*, "Spartan Programming" [online]; available from http://www.codinghorror.com/blog/archives/001148.html; Internet; accessed 18 February 2009.
3. Paul E. Davis, "Code Reduction or Spartan Programming" [online]; available from http://willcode4beer.com/design.jsp?set=codeReduction; Internet; accessed 18 February 2009.
4. BrainyQuote, Albert Einstein Quotes [online]; available from http://www.brainyquote.com/quotes/quotes/a/alberteins109011.html; Internet; accessed 18 February 2009.
5. Oracle Corporation, Sun Developer Network, *Code Conventions for the Java Programming Language* [online]; available from http://java.sun.com/docs/codeconv/; Internet; accessed 17 February 2009.
6. Wikipedia, "Mutator method" [online]; available from http://en.wikipedia.org/wiki/Mutator_method; Internet; accessed 18 October 2009.

7. Oracle Corporation, *Enterprise PeopleTools 8.49 PeopleBook: PeopleCode API Reference*, Application Classes, "Differentiating Between Properties and Methods" [online]; available from http://download.oracle.com/docs/cd/E13292_01/pt849pbr0/eng/psbooks/tpcr/book.htm?File=tpcr/htm/tpcr07.htm#d0e17547; Internet; accessed 22 February 2009.

8. Martin Fowler, "FluentInterface" [online]; available from http://www.martinfowler.com/bliki/FluentInterface.html; Internet; accessed 22 February 2009.

9. Martin Fowler, "Method Chaining" [online]; available from http://martinfowler.com/dslwip/MethodChaining.html; Internet; accessed 22 February 2009.

10. Kioskia.net, "OOP–Data encapsulation" [online]; available from http://en.kioskea.net/contents/poo/encapsul.php3; Internet; accessed 22 February 2009.

11. Oracle Corporation, *Enterprise PeopleTools 8.49 PeopleBook: PeopleCode API Reference*, Application Classes, "Constructors" [online]; available from http://download.oracle.com/docs/cd/E13292_01/pt849pbr0/eng/psbooks/tpcr/book.htm?File=tpcr/htm/tpcr07.htm#d0e17124; Internet; accessed 22 February 2009.

12. *TheFreeDictionary*, "abstraction" [online]; available from http://www.thefreedictionary.com/abstraction; Internet; accessed 21 May 2009.

13. Wikipedia, "Factory method pattern" [online]; available from: http://en.wikipedia.org/wiki/Factory_method_pattern; Internet; accessed 19 October 2009.

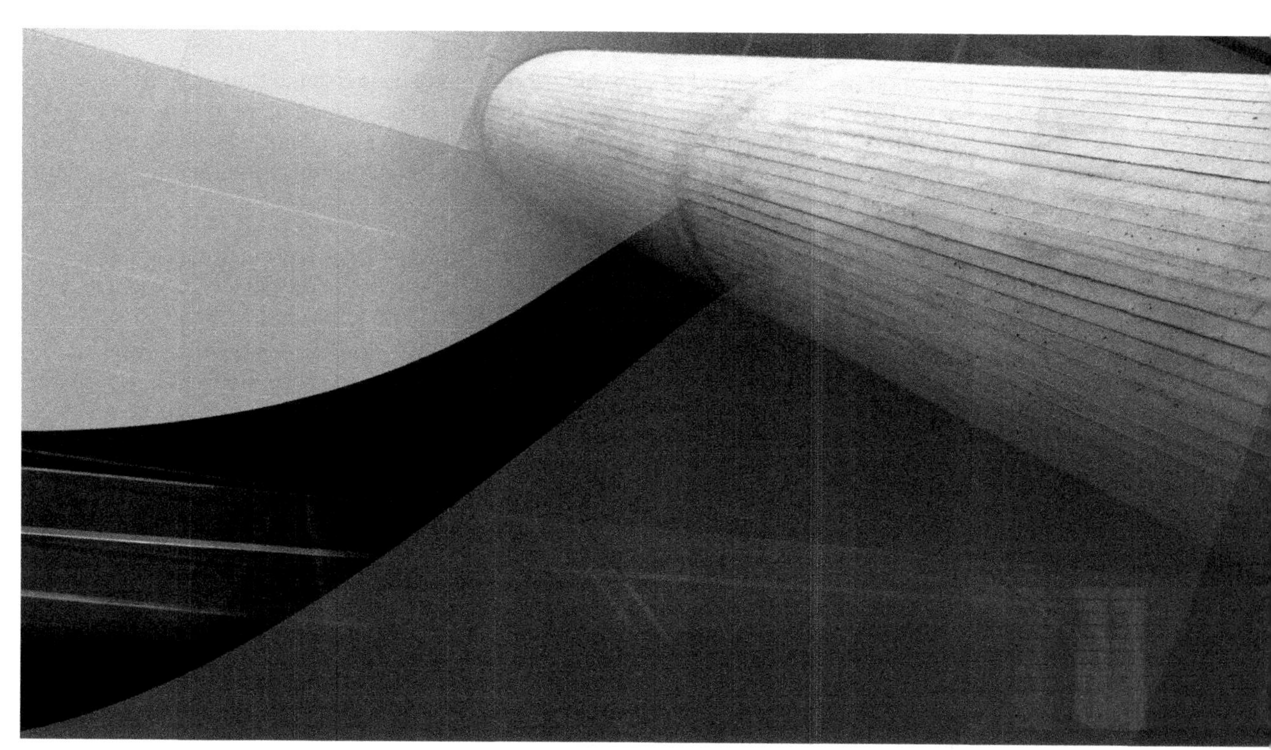

CHAPTER 2

The File Attachment API

pplication users often need to view and store documents related to transactions. For example, an internal auditor needs access to receipts and invoices to validate expense reports and vouchers. The ability to route and view receipts electronically, within the context of the related transaction, improves efficiency in transaction processing.

In addition to attachments, the File Attachment API offers a mechanism for users to transfer files from their desktops to the app server for processing. Consider file-based integrations, which often originate with a user. For example, a training coordinator may use a spreadsheet program to generate a training plan and class schedule for the next quarter. The method used to copy data from that spreadsheet into PeopleSoft's Enterprise Learning Management module can have a significant impact on the training coordinator's PeopleSoft experience.

For users, the File Attachment API provides an experience similar to attaching files to an e-mail message. The difference is the target is a transaction, not an e-mail message.

In this chapter, you will create a new transaction, add file attachment functionality to that transaction, and modify an existing transaction. Along the way, you will learn tips for minimizing the impact of user interface modifications.

Adding Attachments to Transactions

Adding a file attachment requires the following steps:

1. Investigate the target transaction. Identify pages and components.
2. Create a storage record for storing attachments.
3. Add the `FILE_ATTACH_SBR` subrecord to either a transaction record or a custom, related record.
4. Add attachment buttons to a page (Add, Delete, and View).
5. Write PeopleCode for the attachment buttons.

In Part II of this book, we will enhance the user experience through rich Internet technologies. Some of those technologies, such as Flash and JavaFX, require binary files. We need a way to get files from our desktop to the server, where they can enhance the user experience. We will call these binary files *web assets*. In this chapter, we will build a page and a component for developers to upload and describe web assets. The metadata describing these web assets will compose our transaction. We will use the File Attachment API to upload files from our desktop and save them with the transaction.

Investigating the Target Transaction

Since we will be building a new transaction, our investigation will focus on identifying the transaction's requirements. We will then build data and user interface elements to support that transaction.

Each web asset will need an ID field. We will also want a description field that communicates the purpose for the web asset. In Part II, when we write code to serve these web assets to the user's browser, we will need to tell the browser the content type for the binary file. Let's also add a comment field so we can add notes about the asset, annotating the change history or background information of the web asset.

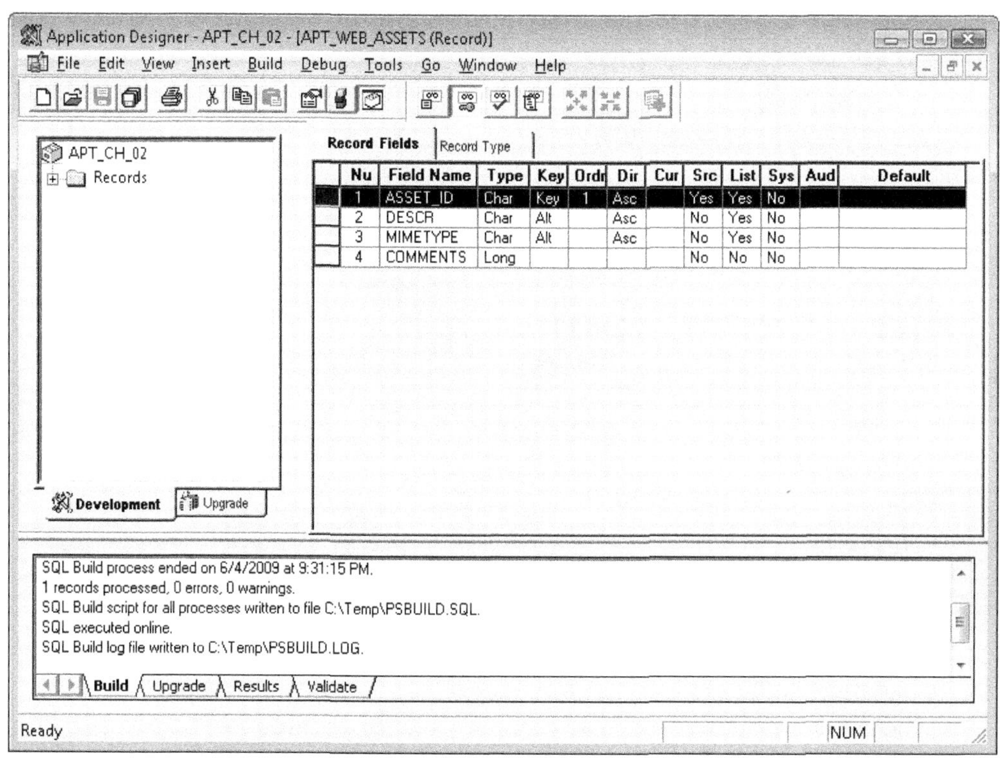

FIGURE 2-1. *The APT_WEB_ASSETS record definition*

With the data elements identified, we can now create the transaction's record definition. Figure 2-1 shows the record that will contain web asset metadata. Notice that `ASSET_ID` is a primary key field. The `DESCR` and `MIMETYPE` fields are alternate search keys. Each of these three fields is selected as a list box item. Save and build the record. When prompted for a record name, enter `APT_WEB_ASSETS`.

Our next step is to create a data-entry page. Figure 2-2 shows this page, named `APT_WEB_ASSETS`. Because the `MIMETYPE` field is 100 characters long, the `MIMETYPE` field text box that App Designer creates is significantly longer than the space available on the page. To change the size of this field, double-click the text box and select Custom from the Size group box. Also notice that `ASSET_ID` is set to display only. Since `ASSET_ID` is our primary key, users cannot edit this field's value. The value for `ASSET_ID` is set when a user adds a new value from the component search page.

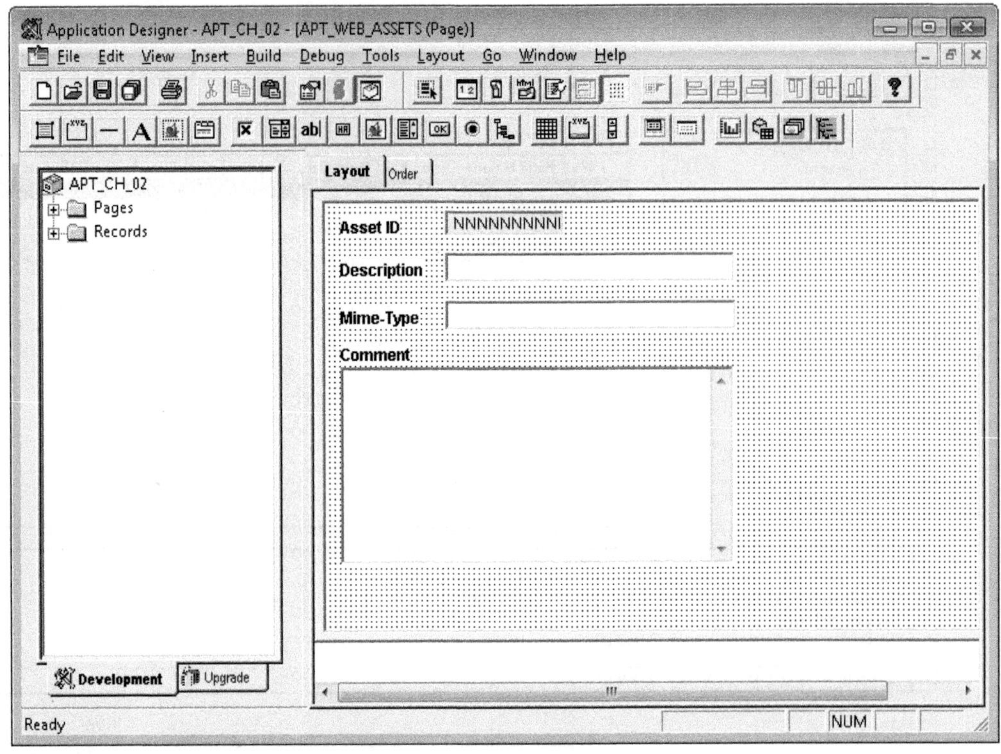

FIGURE 2-2. *The APT_WEB_ASSETS transaction page*

Let's build the APT_WEB_ASSETS component next, as shown in Figure 2-3. After dropping the APT_WEB_ASSETS page on a new component, set the component's search record to APT_WEB_ASSETS and change the page's item label to **Web Assets**.

We are almost ready to register this component. The Registration Wizard requires the following information:

- Menu
- Folder
- Permission list

We need to identify these items before continuing. We will identify the menu and permission list by creating a new menu and a new permission list. The answer to the folder question resides in the portal registry.

Since we don't need to create any objects to answer the folder question, let's answer it now. Log in to PeopleSoft using your web browser and navigate to PeopleTools | Portal | Structure and Content.

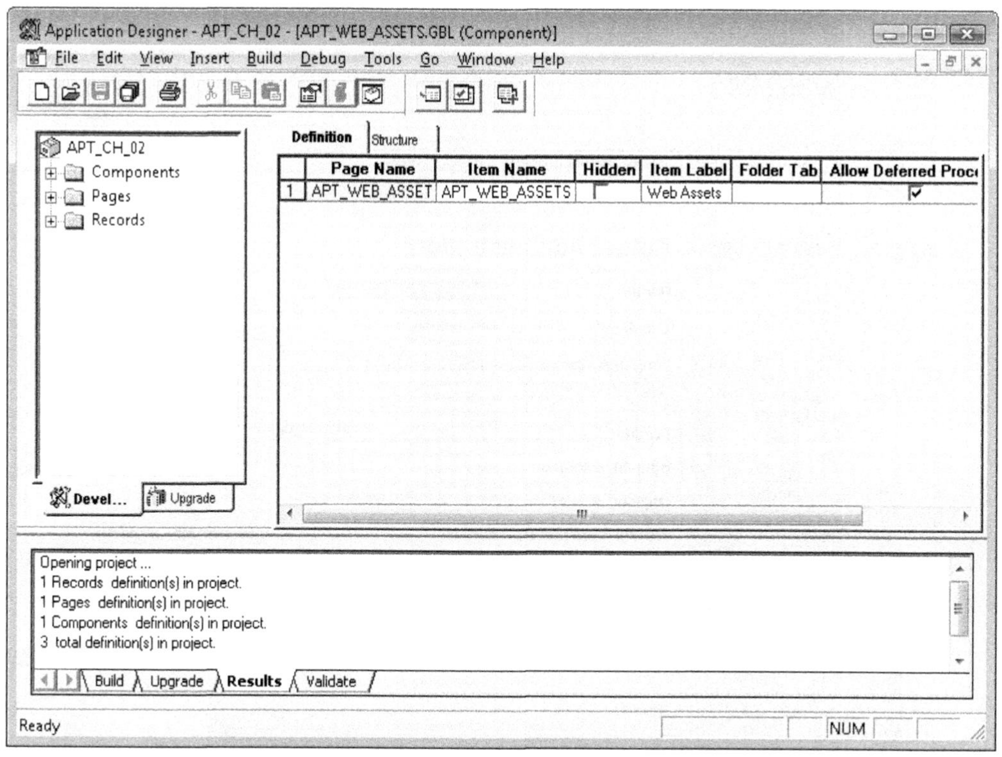

FIGURE 2-3. *The APT_WEB_ASSETS component*

Within the portal registry, navigate to PeopleTools | Utilities. Select the Edit link next to the Administration folder reference. This will allow you to view the name of this folder, as shown in Figure 2-4.

Now we need to create the menu. Figure 2-5 is a screenshot of the empty menu, which is named `CUSTOM`. Unless otherwise noted, the examples in this book will use this menu when registering custom components.

NOTE

Before you can save a new menu definition, App Designer requires you to add one item to the menu. You can delete the item later, or even ignore it indefinitely. Figure 2-5 shows the `CUSTOM` menu with a separator item.

As with all PeopleSoft pages, if you want to view this page online, you need to add it to a permission list. Many examples in this book will require security. Let's create a custom permission

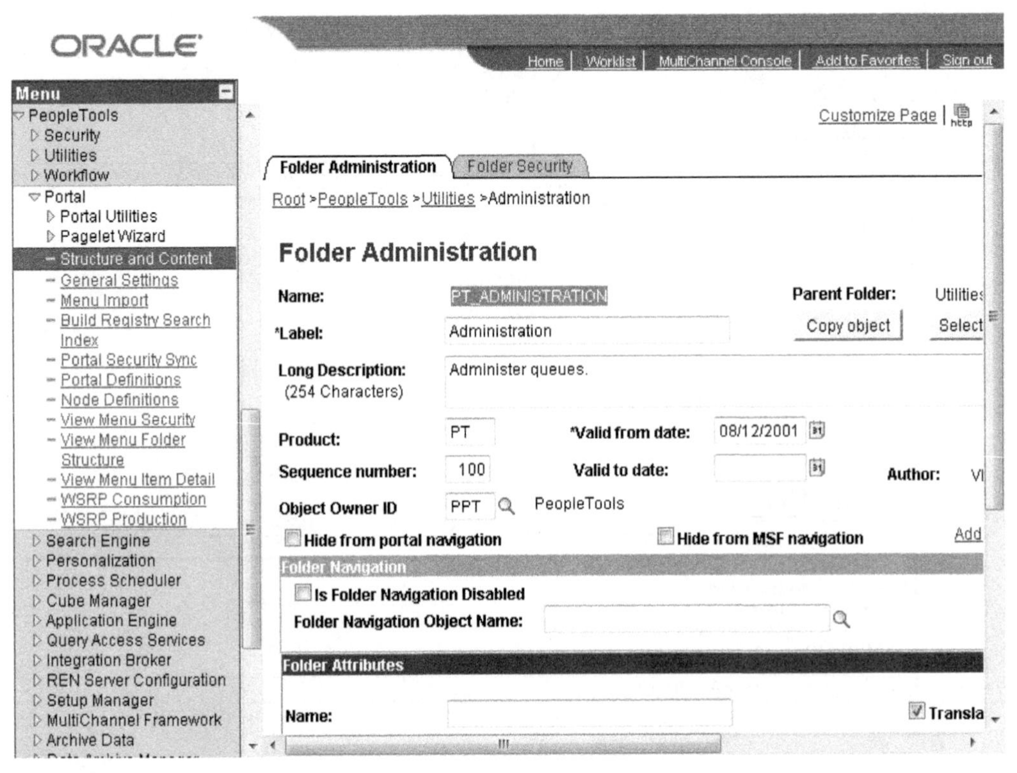

FIGURE 2-4. *Administration folder details*

list and role for use with the rest of the examples in this book. Figure 2-6 shows the custom permission list `APT_CUSTOM`, and Figure 2-7 shows the corresponding role `APT_CUSTOM`.

Now that all registration prerequisites are complete, we can register the component. With the `APT_WEB_ASSETS` component open in App Designer, choose Tools | Register Component. Step through the Registration Wizard as you would when registering any component.

1. On the Start page, choose the following:
   - Add this component to a menu.
   - Add this component to a portal registry.
   - Add this component to a permission list.
2. On the Add to a Menu and Bar page, select the menu `APT_CUSTOM` and the bar `CUSTOM`.

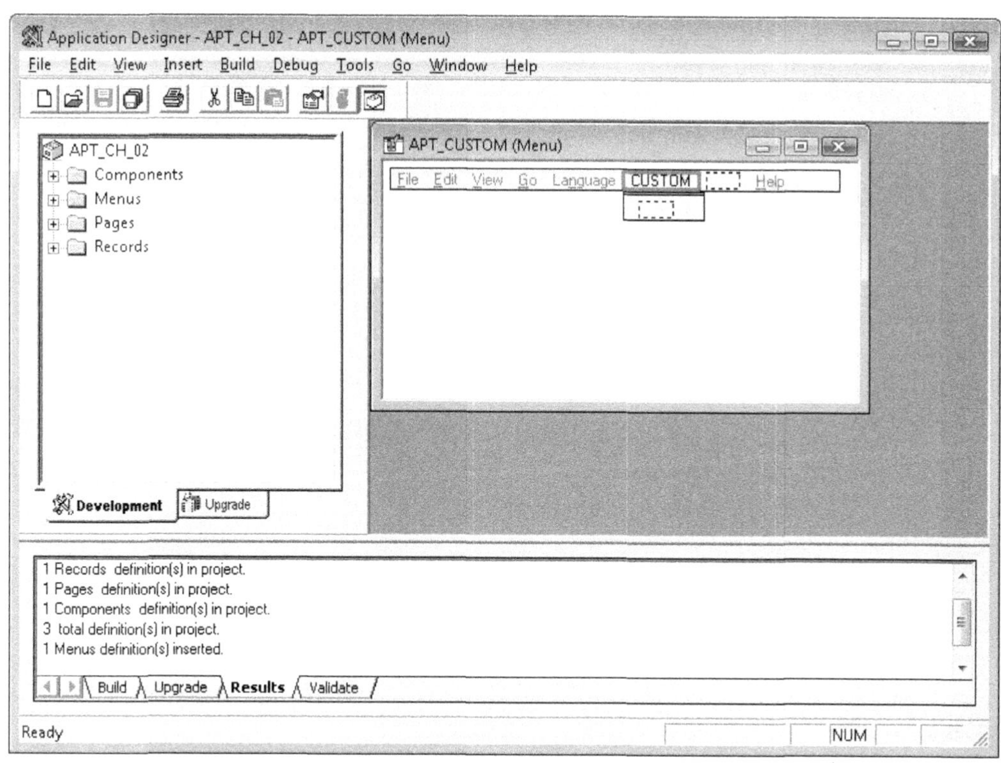

FIGURE 2-5. *APT_CUSTOM menu*

3. On the Create Content Reference page, make these selections:
   - Ensure the Target Content radio button is selected.
   - Select the PT_ADMINISTRATION folder.
   - Change the content reference label to **Web Assets**.
   - Change the long description to **Component for maintaining web user interface assets**.
   - Select the template name of `DEFAULT_TEMPLATE`.
   - Select the appropriate node for your application. (Since I am using an HRMS application, I selected the node named `HRMS`, but your node name may differ.)
4. On the Add to Permission List page, select the `APT_CUSTOM` permission list.
5. On the Finish page, select Menu, Registry Entry, and Permission List to add these items to your project.

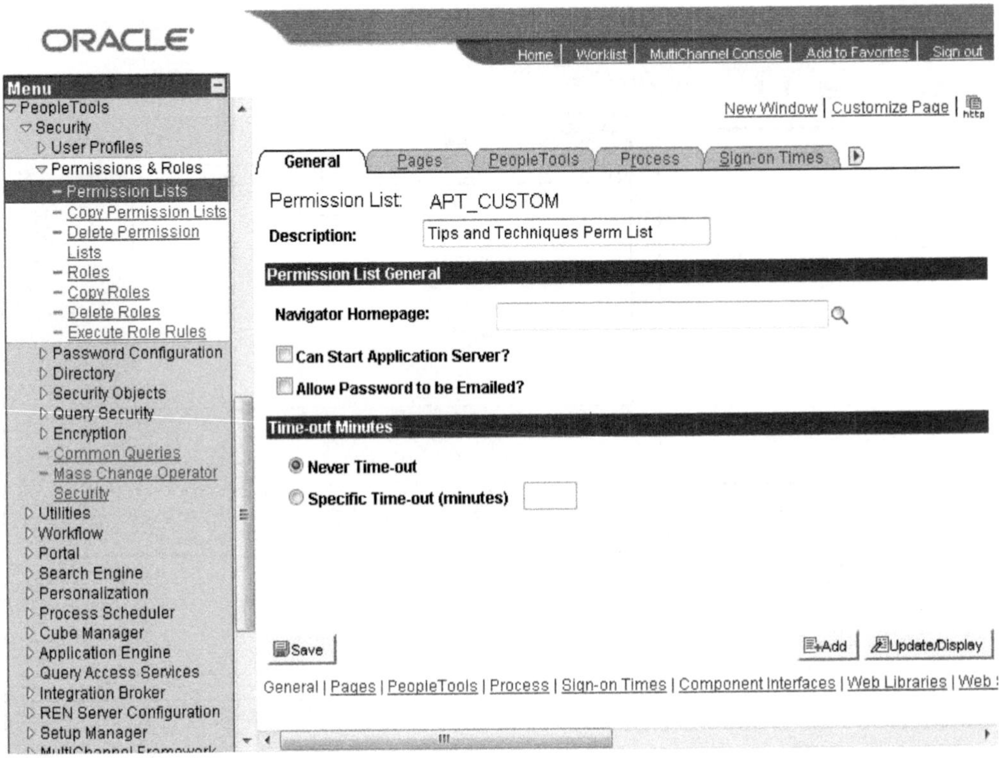

FIGURE 2-6. *APT_CUSTOM permission list*

The Registration Wizard sets the label on the content reference, but not the label on the menu. To set the menu label, open the menu `APT_CUSTOM` and expand the `CUSTOM` menu item. Double-click `APT_WEB_ASSETS` to display the properties for this menu item, and then set the label to **Web Assets**, as shown in Figure 2-8. Save the menu.

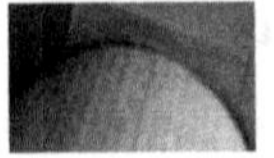

TIP

When migrating projects that contain content references, add the parent folder for the content reference to the project. For example, if you migrate this project, add the PT_ADMINISTRATION folder to your project. Prior to migrating your project, set the upgrade action to Copy and enable the Upgrade check box, even if the parent folder is unchanged. This will cause PeopleTools to recache the contents of the parent folder, making your new content reference available immediately.

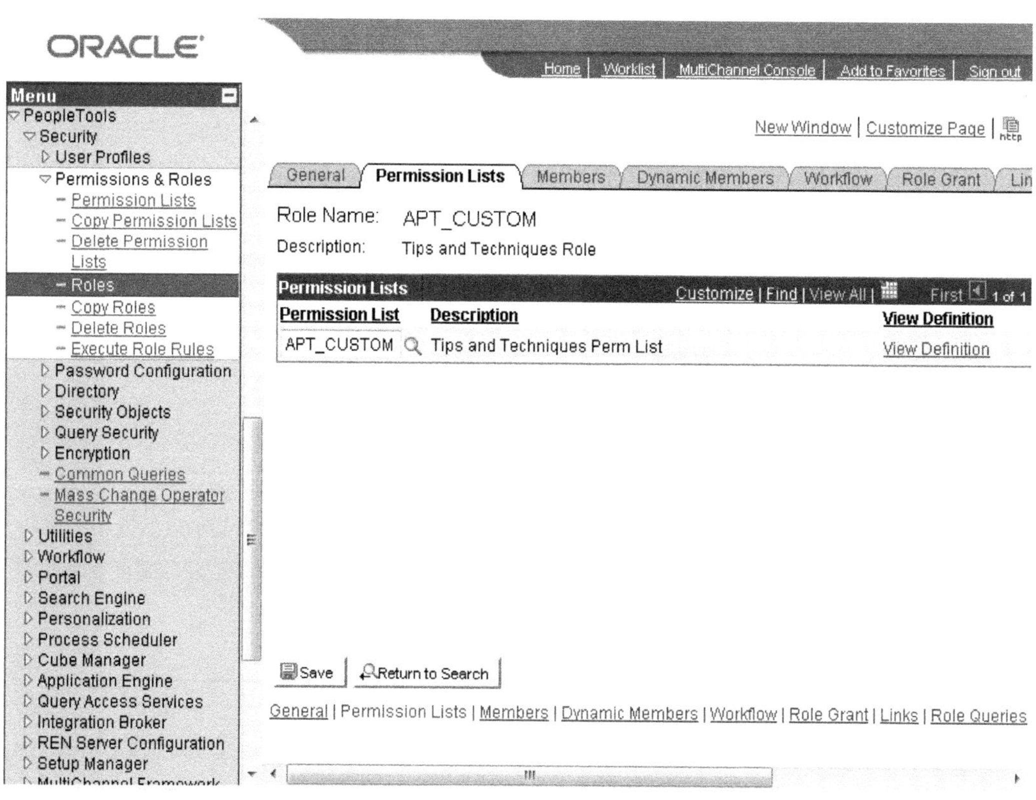

FIGURE 2-7. *APT_CUSTOM role*

Let's test the transaction. First, log in to your PeopleSoft application using your web browser and add the `APT_CUSTOM` role to your user profile. After the role is in your user profile, navigate to PeopleTools | Utilities | Administration. You should see a new item labeled Web Assets. Select this menu item and add the new value **TEST**, as shown in Figure 2-9.

Creating the Attachment Storage Record

Now that we have a working transaction, it is time to add attachment functionality. PeopleSoft offers two attachment storage methods: FTP and record. Both storage methods use HTTP to transfer the file from the client browser to the web server. After the PeopleSoft application receives the file from the user's web browser, it will either forward the attachment to an FTP server or write the attachment to a database record. The choice between FTP and database record is a storage choice, not a transfer choice. Normally, we think of FTP as a method for transferring files, and therefore, may think that an FTP attachment is transferred from the client to the server using FTP, but it isn't.

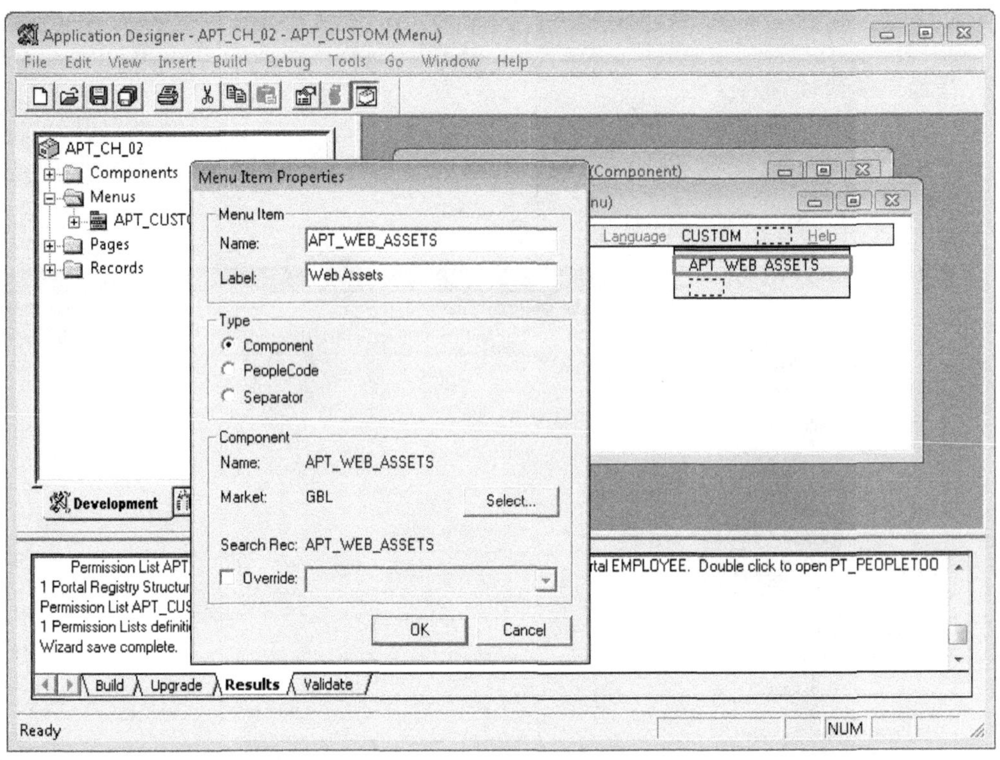

FIGURE 2-8. *Web Assets menu item*

The storage type you choose will differ depending on your attachment purpose, system configuration, and business needs. The File Attachment API functions provide access to attached files for both storage types. One difference between the record and FTP storage options is that the record option actually allows you to read and process a binary file directly from PeopleCode. A record field can contain binary data, and that binary data can be assigned to a PeopleCode variable. However, a binary file cannot be read into a PeopleCode variable, because PeopleCode does not offer functions for reading binary data from binary files.

For this transaction, we will store attachments in a database record. Once you know how to use record storage, then FTP storage is trivial. The page-design considerations for both methods are the same. There are many differences between FTP and record storage from a user and administration perspective. The only difference between the two methods from a developer's perspective is that database record storage requires you to build a new record definition.

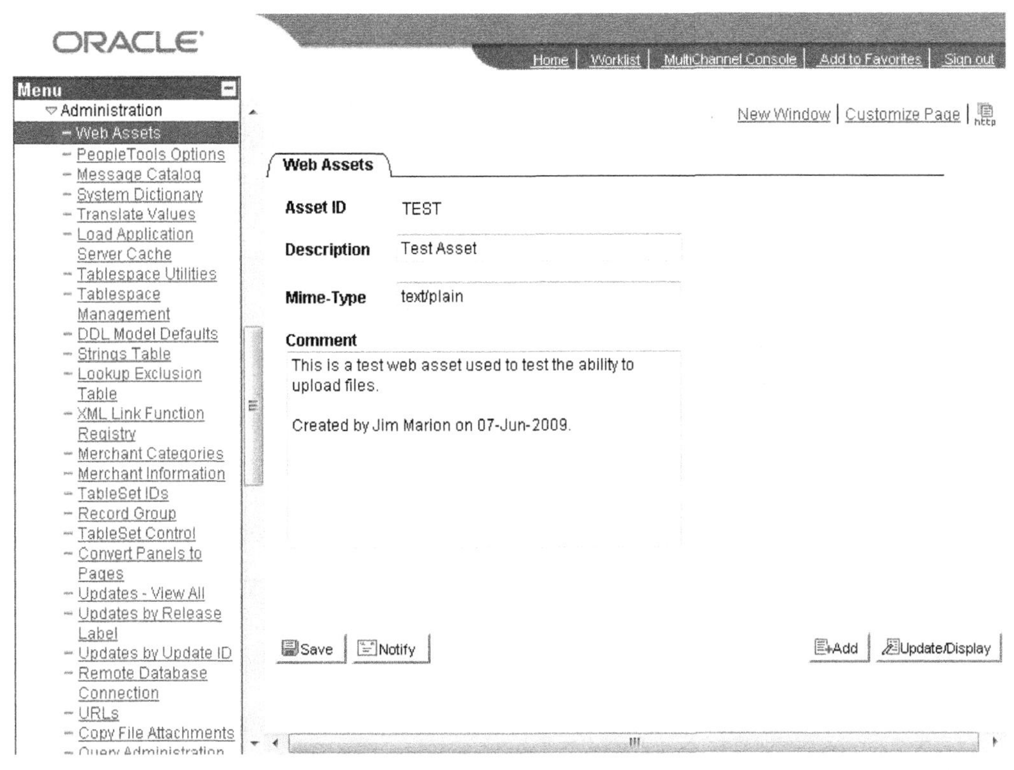

FIGURE 2-9. *Adding the TEST web asset*

FTP or Record Storage—Which Is Better?

PeopleSoft offers FTP or record-based storage solutions for file attachments. While I prefer record-based storage, each has its place. The following are some considerations when choosing between the two methods:

- **Cloning and backup** Since attached files exist within a database record, cloning is a simple matter of copying the database. There are no additional transaction-referenced file system files to copy as there are with FTP storage. Similarly, a standard database backup routine will maintain backup copies of critical transaction-related documents. When storing files in an FTP storage location, you must consider external file backup strategies.
- **Point-in-time recovery** When storing files within the database, your relational database management system (RDBMS) transaction logs maintain rollback and recovery information that identifies file attachments as members of the same database transaction as the online component's transaction. FTP storage does not offer this same capability.

- **Canceled transactions** Another issue with FTP storage that is resolved by standard RDBMS transaction management is dealing with canceled transactions (the user canceled a transaction or, even worse, a transaction was canceled because of an error). When storing attachments in database records, the standard RDBMS rollback will eliminate orphaned attachment data. With FTP storage, if a user cancels a transaction after uploading a file, the attachment file will persist.
- **Accessibility** One of the key benefits of FTP storage over database record storage is accessibility. Users can readily access files residing on an FTP server using standard file browsing, viewing, and administration tools. Through network shares, it is possible for users to view FTP stored files without logging in to PeopleSoft.

To store attachments in the database, we need to create a record definition. Create a new record as you did for the transaction record, but don't add any fields. From the Insert menu, choose Subrecord and insert the `FILE_ATTDET_SBR` subrecord into this new record, as shown in Figure 2-10. Save the record as `APT_WA_ATTDET` and build it.

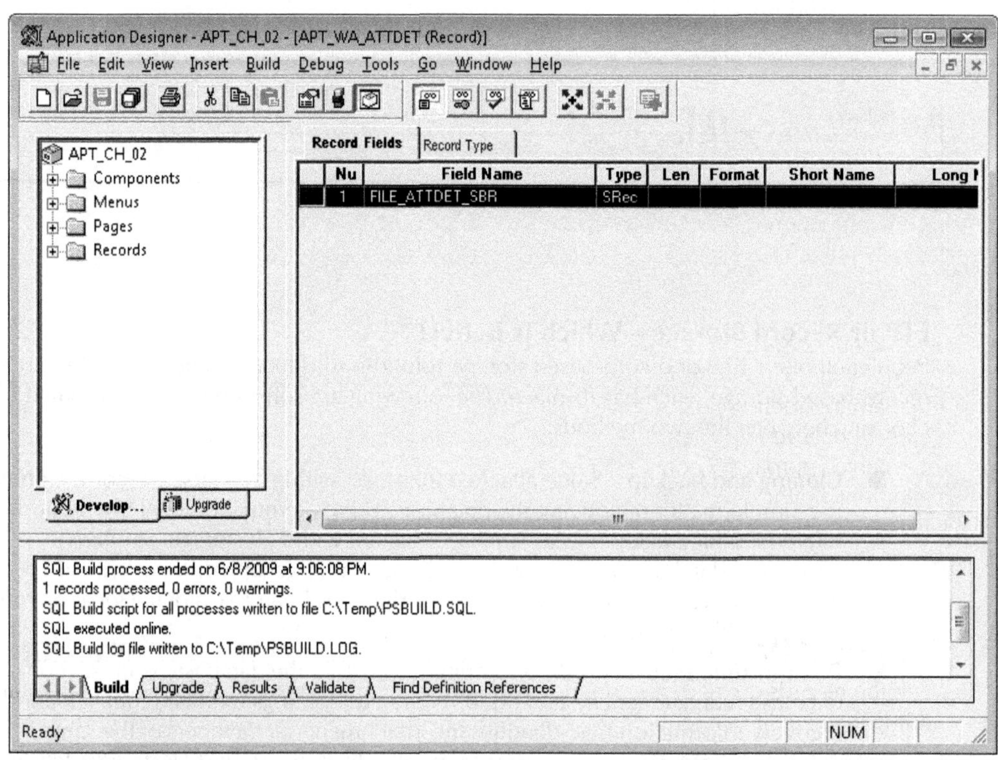

FIGURE 2-10. *APT_WA_ATTDET record definition*

Because PeopleTools limits the length of record names to 15 characters, record names can be quite cryptic. Allow me to decrypt this new record's name. All custom objects in this book's examples are prefixed with APT. Therefore, the APT in this record's name represents our custom object prefix. The WA in the middle of the name is an abbreviation for Web Assets, and the ATTDET is an abbreviation for ATTachment DETails.

This new record, APT_WA_ATTDET, will contain our attachment file data. Let's explore the fields in this record:

- ATTACHSYSFILENAME represents the unique identifier for an attachment. The unique identifier is the original filename with certain characters, such as spaces, replaced with underscores. If we choose, we can prefix the unique identifier with the transaction's keys.
- If the presence of the FILE_SEQ field makes you think of chunked data, you are correct. Attachments stored in database records are chunked according to chunking rules in the PeopleTools Options page. The Max Chunk File Size field on the PeopleTools Options page determines the size of each chunk. If a file is larger than the Max Chunk File Size value, then the File Attachment API will insert multiple rows into APT_WA_ATTDET—one row for each chunk.
- The FILE_SIZE field contains the attachment file's length. If a file is larger than the Max Chunk File Size value specified in the PeopleTools Options page, this field will contain the size of the chunk stored in a given row. The total size of the attached file is the sum of all the FILE_SIZE values for a given ATTACHSYSFILENAME.
- The file's actual data is stored in the FILE_DATA field.

Adding the FILE_ATTACH_SBR Subrecord

Notice that this record definition does not contain any fields to associate the attachment with a transaction. Rather than add the transaction record's keys to the attachment record, we must add the attachment record's keys to the transaction record. This allows the File Attachment API to keep the attachment functions generic enough for use with any transaction. The way we relate a transaction record to an attachment record is through a subrecord called FILE_ATTACH_SBR. The FILE_ATTACH_SBR subrecord contains the ATTACHSYSFILENAME key field you saw in the attachment record.

Since the transaction record is a custom record we created, we could add this subrecord to the main transaction record, APT_WEB_ASSET. However, since I'm sure you are reading this chapter because you want to learn how to add attachments to delivered transactions, let's take an alternative approach. Following best practices, we don't want to modify delivered record definitions. Rather, we can create a secondary record that has the same keys as the transaction, plus the FILE_ATTACH_SBR. This allows us to associate transactions with attachments without modifying delivered records. Figure 2-11 shows this new transaction/attachment record named APT_WA_ATTACH. Note that ASSET_ID is a key field.

Adding Attachment Fields and Buttons to the Transaction Page

With the records defined, we can modify the transaction to include attachment fields. Start by adding a new edit box to the APT_WEB_ASSETS page. Set the field's source record to APT_WA_ATTACH and source field to ATTACHUSERFILE. This is the attachment file display name—the name chosen by the user. Displaying the attachment name is a nice gesture if the transaction contains an attachment.

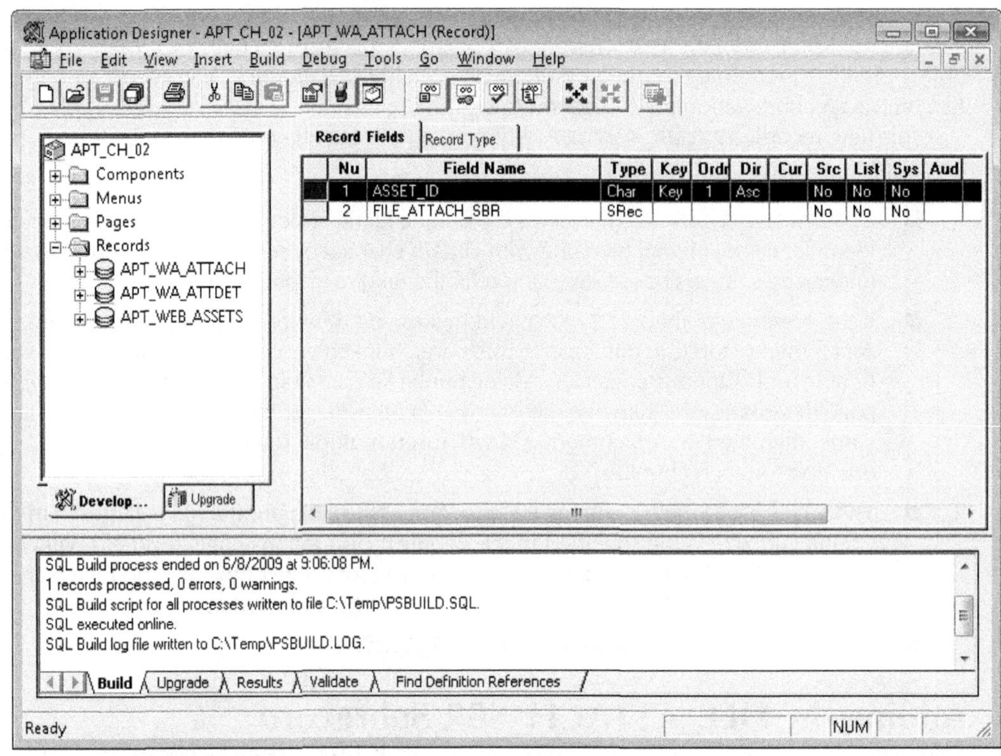

FIGURE 2-11. *APT_WA_ATTACH transaction/attachment record*

We need to modify a few settings for this field. It is too large for our page, and we don't want users typing values into this field. Rather, we want the user to use the designated attachment buttons to add or remove attachments. To change these settings, open the page field's Properties dialog and set the Size to custom. On the Use tab, enable the Display Only check box. After closing the Properties dialog by clicking OK, resize the field to fit on the page.

In a like manner, add the `ATTACHSYSFILENAME` field to the page. We are adding this field to the page just to make it available to PeopleCode. We do not want to display this field to users. Therefore, on the Use tab, mark this field as Invisible. Figure 2-12 shows this modified page within App Designer. Notice that the Sys Filename field appears far off to the right. The display location of this field is irrelevant since it is a hidden field.

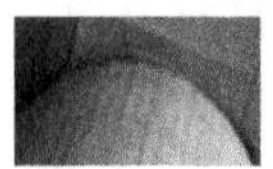

TIP

Placing hidden fields in odd or irregular locations is a good practice. When you open a page with fields in odd places, your eye is drawn to those fields. If hidden fields are placed in standard locations, they blend in with regular fields and are harder to identify.

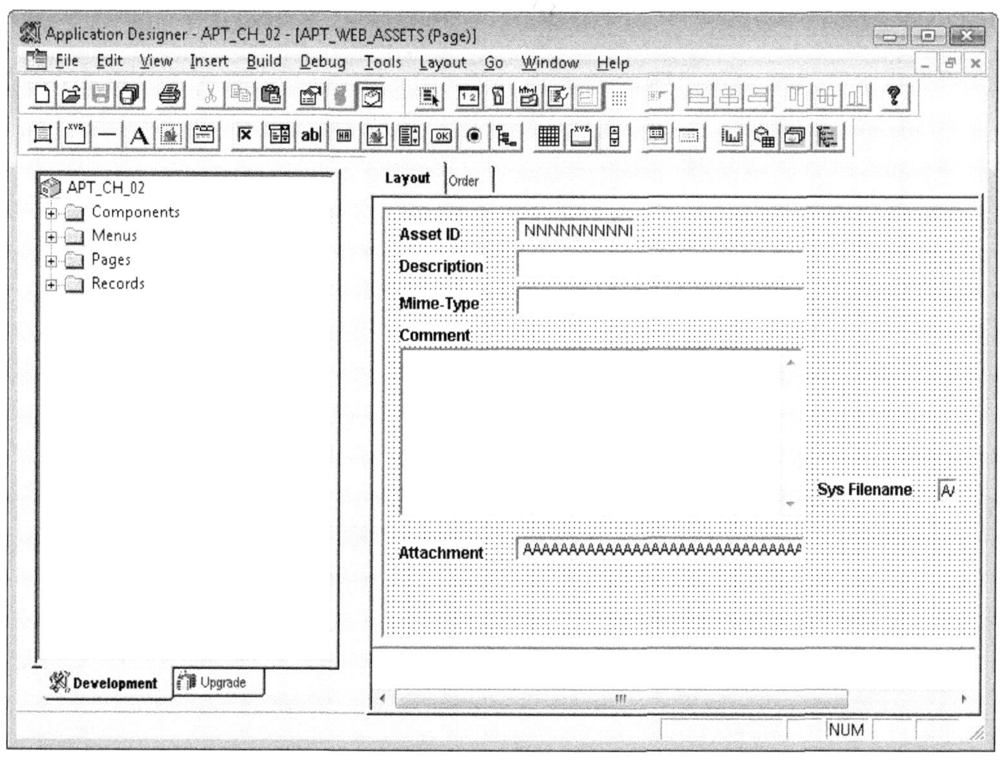

FIGURE 2-12. *APT_WEB_ASSETS page with attachment fields*

Test the page in your browser to make sure it works as expected. When you navigate to the page, PeopleTools | Utilities | Administration | Web Assets, you should see the test transaction we previously created. The new attachment field should be visible, but it will not have a value.

We now have a page and record for adding and storing attachments, but we are missing the PeopleCode and buttons to make it functional. Let's add some buttons to this page to allow users to add, view, and remove, attachments. Adding buttons to a page typically requires creating a derived/work record with fields designated as push buttons. To simplify page development, PeopleTools provides the `FILE_ATTACH_WRK` record with add, view, delete, and detach button fields. Add the `ATTACHADD`, `ATTACHVIEW`, and `ATTACHDELETE` buttons to the `APT_WEB_ASSETS` page. Figure 2-13 shows this transaction page in App Designer with the buttons added. Notice that I added a group box to the bottom of the page and placed the buttons and `ATTACHUSERFILE` field inside this group box.

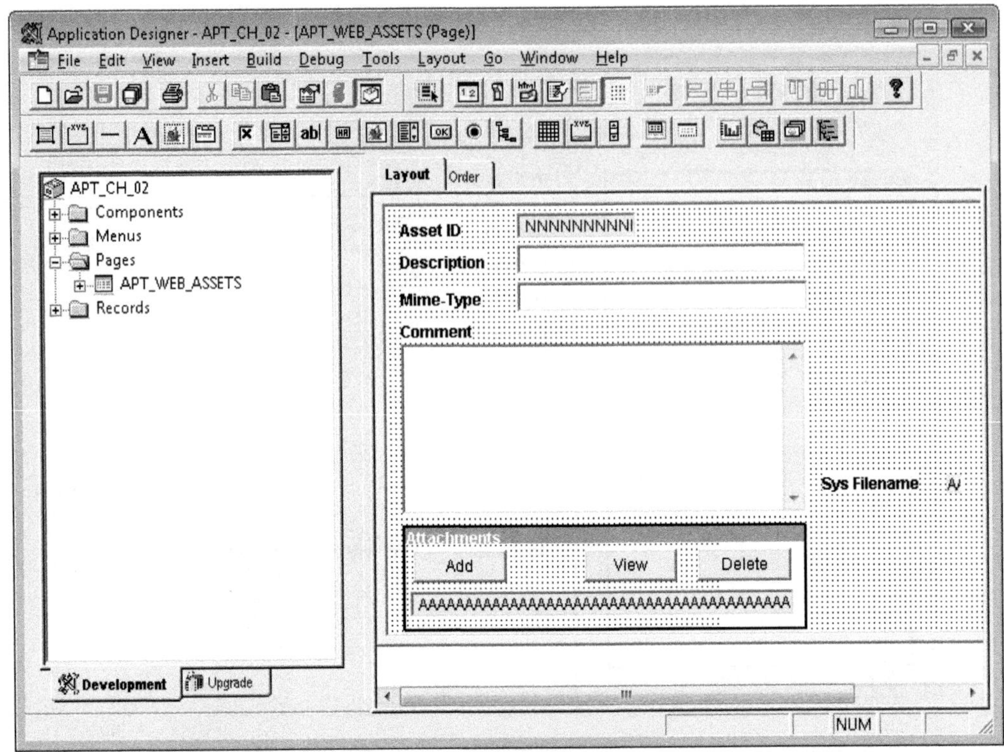

FIGURE 2-13. *APT_WEB_ASSETS page with attachment buttons*

Figures 2-14 and 2-15 show the properties for the Add button. The properties for the View and Delete buttons are the same, except for the field names. For the View button, choose the field name `ATTACHVIEW`. For the Delete button, choose the field name `ATTACHDELETE`.

Reload the page in your browser just to make sure the buttons display properly, as shown in Figure 2-16. We haven't attached any code to the buttons so, at this point, they are still not functional.

When storing attachments using the File Attachment API, you specify the storage location using a URL. For FTP storage, a URL contains all of the information required to log in to an FTP server and save a file. Here is an example of an FTP URL that includes a username and password:

ftp://user:password@servername/folder/for/uploaded/files

For record-based storage, PeopleSoft uses a custom URL specification that looks like this:

record://recordname

where `recordname` represents the name of a database record definition.

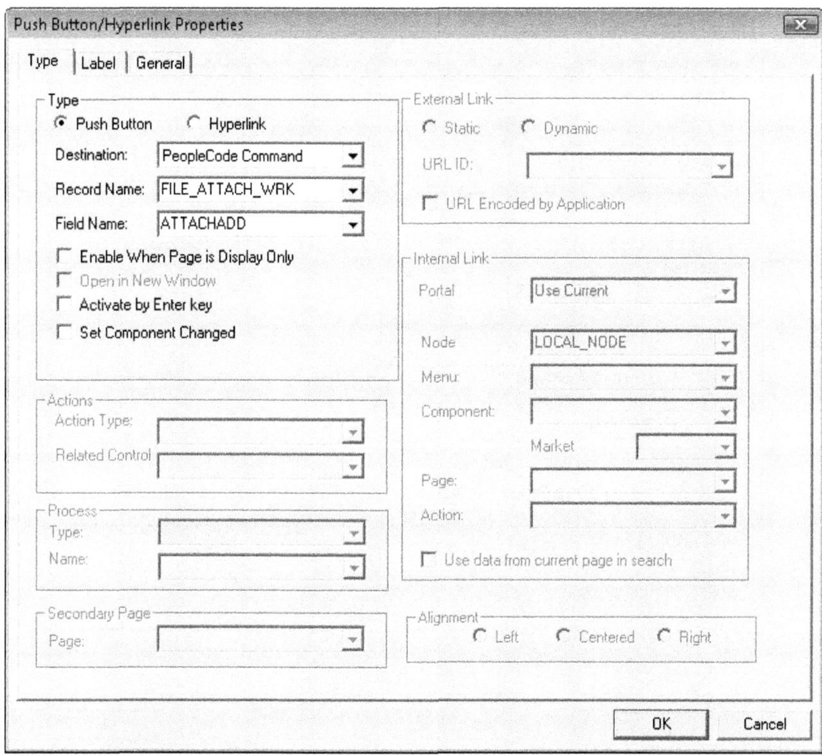

FIGURE 2-14. *ATTACHADD button type properties*

A URL is composed of a protocol and a resource. The PeopleSoft record URL protocol is record, and the resource is recordname. In our case, the URL will be record://APT_WA_ATTDET.

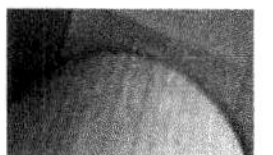

NOTE
Be sure to update your FTP file attachment URLs when migrating code or cloning databases. I recommend storing FTP URLs as URL definitions and adding SQL to your clone scripts to update URL definition values. As a precaution, I also recommend eliminating network routes between your production system and your development, test, quality assurance, and other PeopleSoft systems. In the event that a URL in one of these other systems continues to point to production, eliminating network routes (DNS, proxy, firewall, and so on) will keep your nonproduction systems from affecting your production systems.

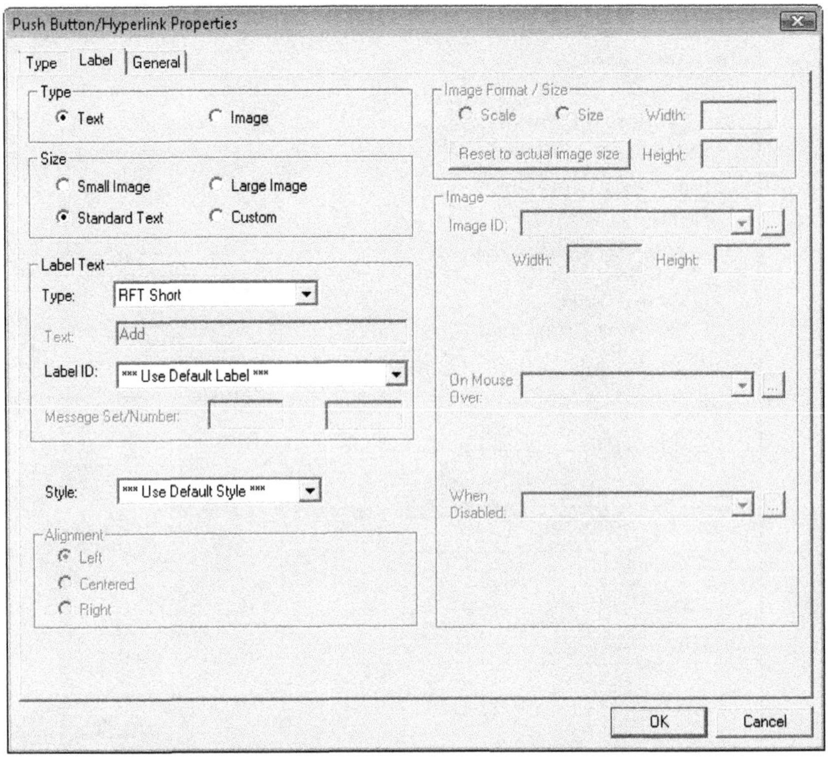

FIGURE 2-15. *ATTACHADD button label properties*

When we attach code to the Add, View, and Delete buttons, we will need to specify the attachment repository's URL. In that code, we can either hard-code the URL as a string literal or store the URL in one of PeopleSoft's configurable string repositories. In Chapter 1, you saw how we could use the message catalog to store strings and retrieve them with `MsgGetText`. PeopleSoft provides another string repository specifically designed for URLs and a corresponding function named `GetURL`. One of the benefits of using the URL catalog is that it allows administrators to maintain URL values without modifying code. We will use this URL catalog to store the URL record://APT_WA_ATTDET.

To add a new URL, log in to your PeopleSoft web application and navigate to PeopleTools | Utilities | Administration | URLs. Add a new value named **APT_WEB_ASSET_ATTACHMENTS**, as shown in Figure 2-17. After creating the URL definition, you can add it to your project and migrate it between environments, just like other PeopleTools-managed definition.

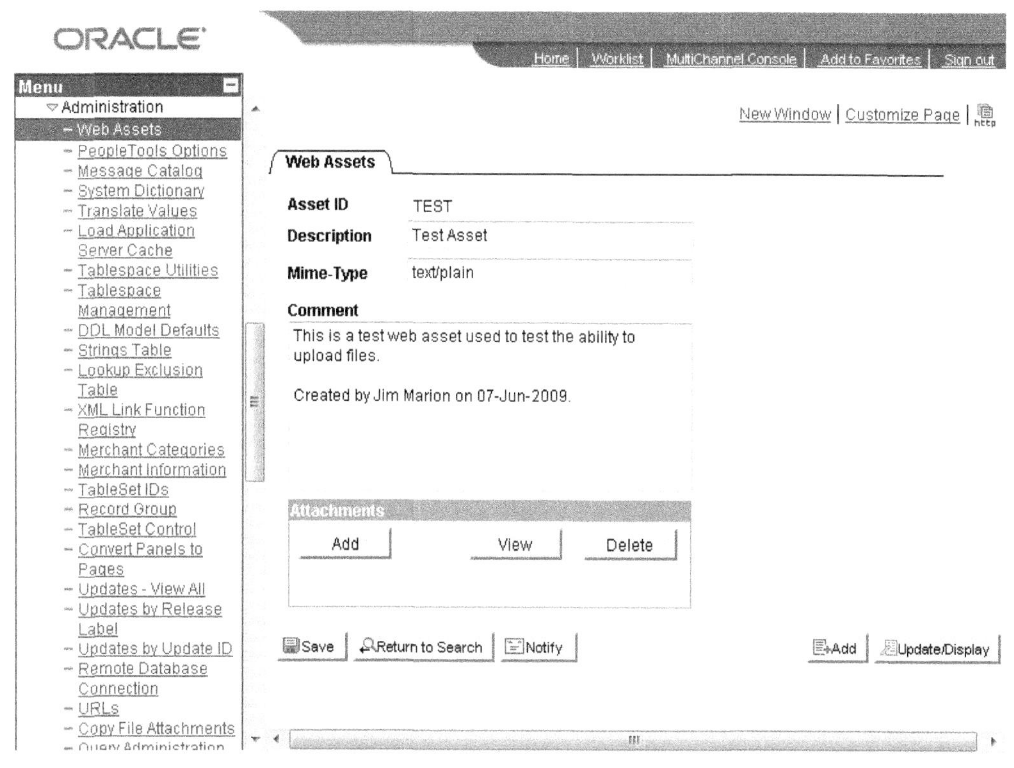

FIGURE 2-16. *Web Assets page online view with attachment buttons*

Writing PeopleCode for the Attachment Buttons

With the user interface elements complete, it is time to make the buttons functional. When adding PeopleCode to buttons, we have a couple of options:

- Add PeopleCode to record events.
- Add PeopleCode to component record events.

Generally speaking, where you place your code (record or component) depends on whether that code should execute every time a button is placed on a page or only for certain components. In this case, our code is specific to the `APT_WEB_ASSETS` component, and therefore, it should be placed at the component level rather than the record level. Furthermore, our buttons are bound to a delivered record, and we don't want to modify delivered definitions if we can avoid doing so.

We will start with the Add button.

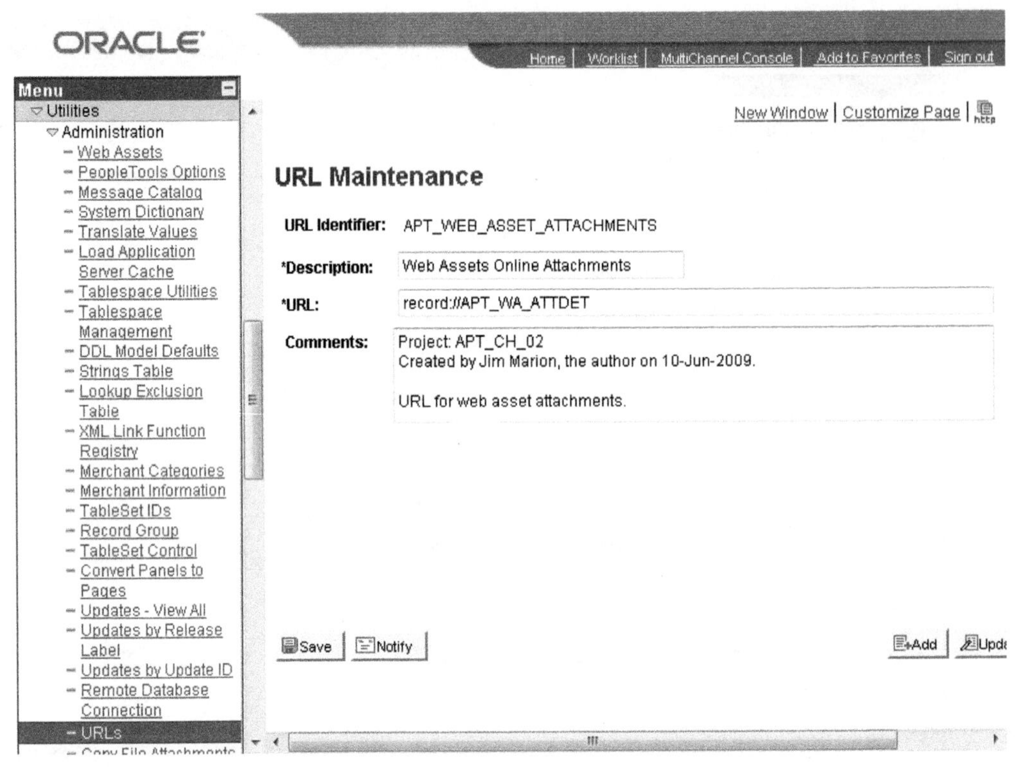

FIGURE 2-17. *APT_WEB_ASSET_ATTACHMENTS URL definition*

The Add Button

Open the component `APT_WEB_ASSETS`. From the View menu, select View PeopleCode. In the first drop-down list, select the `ATTACHADD` field. In the second drop-down list, select `FieldChange`. Figure 2-18 shows the `APT_WEB_ASSETS.GBL.FILE_ATTACH_WRK.ATTACHADD.FieldChange` code editor prior to adding code.

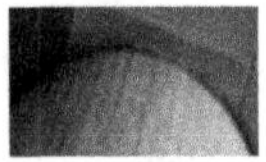

CAUTION

Each of the following PeopleCode events refers to the `APT_WEB_ASSETS` component PeopleCode, not record PeopleCode. Even though the event-based PeopleCode is attached to the `FILE_ATTACH_WRK` record and fields, be sure to add the following PeopleCode to the component, not the record definition. Adding this PeopleCode directly to `FILE_ATTACH_WRK` may cause other attachments to fail, because the `FILE_ATTACH_WRK` record is shared by various transactions.

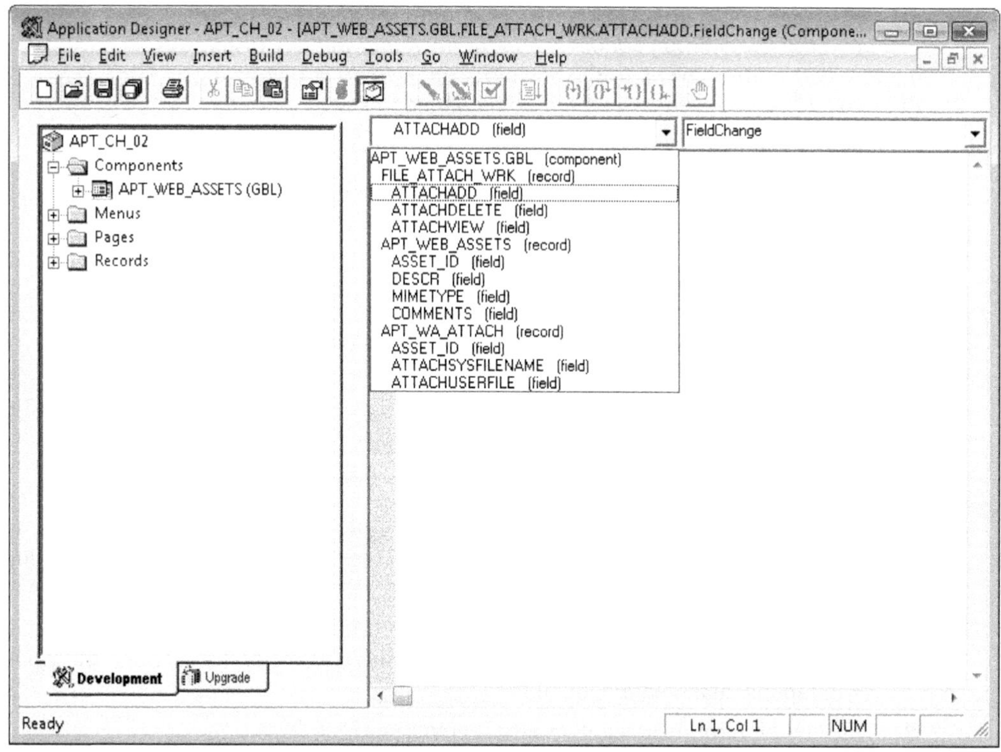

FIGURE 2-18. *ATTACHADD FieldChange event PeopleCode editor*

Add the following code to this editor:

```
Declare Function add_attachment PeopleCode
      FILE_ATTACH_WRK.ATTACHADD FieldChange;
Declare Function display_attachment_buttons PeopleCode
      FILE_ATTACH_WRK.ATTACHADD RowInit;

Local string &recname = "Record." | Record.APT_WEB_ASSETS;
Local number &retcode;

add_attachment(URL.APT_WEB_ASSET_ATTACHMENTS, "", "", 0, True,
      &recname, APT_WA_ATTACH.ATTACHSYSFILENAME,
      APT_WA_ATTACH.ATTACHUSERFILE, 2, &retcode);

If (&retcode = %Attachment_Success) Then
   display_attachment_buttons(APT_WA_ATTACH.ATTACHUSERFILE);
End-If;
```

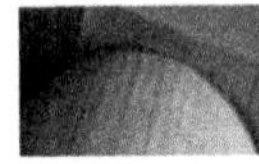

NOTE

Be sure to choose the correct event when adding PeopleCode. When you open the PeopleCode editor for a field, the editor initially displays the `FieldDefault` event. In this scenario, we want to add code to the `FieldChange` event. Make sure you change the event prior to adding your code.

Let's walk through this code line by line. The first two lines declare attachment helper functions:

```
Declare Function add_attachment PeopleCode
      FILE_ATTACH_WRK.ATTACHADD FieldChange;
Declare Function display_attachment_buttons PeopleCode
      FILE_ATTACH_WRK.ATTACHADD RowInit;
```

The `add_attachment` function is a PeopleCode FUNCLIB wrapper around the native `AddAttachment` PeopleCode function. Besides calling `AddAttachment`, the `add_attachment` wrapper function performs the following operations:

- Adds the transaction record's primary key values to `ATTACHSYSFILENAME`, the value that represents the attachment data's primary key. This ensures the primary key for the attachment data is unique.
- Sets the values of the transaction record's `ATTACHUSERFILE` and `ATTACHSYSFILENAME` field values to the values chosen by the user and the values stored in the attachment data table.
- Displays an error message if an error occurs.

The third line declares a variable with the value `Record.APT_WEB_ASSETS`.

```
Local string &recname = "Record." | Record.APT_WEB_ASSETS;
```

Notice that we use concatenation and a PeopleCode definition reference to build this string. If we quoted the name of the record rather than using a definition reference, then the Find Definition References feature would fail to find this usage of the record definition. Even though the syntax looks more cluttered than the string representation, the maintenance impact of this decision makes the extra syntax worth the effort. We will pass this string into the `add_attachment` function to tell the function where to find the transaction's key fields.

Line 4 declares a variable to receive the `AddAttachment` return code:

```
Local number &retcode;
```

The `add_attachment` wrapper function will set this variable to the return value produced by the native `AddAttachment` function.

Line 5 calls the `add_attachment` function, passing in the URL definition, the transaction record, the filename fields, and the return code variable:

```
add_attachment(URL.APT_WEB_ASSET_ATTACHMENTS, "", "", 0, True,
      &recname, APT_WA_ATTACH.ATTACHSYSFILENAME,
      APT_WA_ATTACH.ATTACHUSERFILE, 2, &retcode);
```

The add_attachment declaration follows:

```
add_attachment(&URL_ID, &FILEEXTENSION, &SUBDIRECTORY, &FILESIZE,
      &PREPEND, &RECNAME, &ATTACHSYSFILENAME, &ATTACHUSERFILE,
      &MESSAGE_LVL, &RETCODE);
```

The add_attachment PeopleCode in FILE_ATTACH_WRK.ATTACHADD.FieldChange contains comments describing each of the function's parameters, many of which come from the AddAttachment native PeopleCode function. You can find additional information about the AddAttachment function parameters in the PeopleBooks *PeopleCode Language Reference*.

The first parameter, URL_ID, can be either a string URL or the ID of a URL definition. As you can see, we use the ID of a URL definition. String URLs can be FTP or RECORD URLs of this form:

ftp://user:password@server/directory or RECORD://recordname

We pass empty strings for the file extension and subdirectory parameters. The file extension parameter is not used by modern web browsers. The subdirectory parameter is used only for FTP storage repositories.

The next parameter, identified by the number 0 (zero), represents the maximum file size for an attachment in kilobytes. By specifying 0, we are telling the AddAttachment function to allow files of any size. If you prefer to restrict the maximum allowable file size, then set this to a different value. Because the HTML standard file input button does not provide a mechanism for limiting files by size, the size of the file is not validated until after the file reaches the web server.

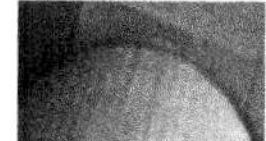

NOTE
If your purpose for limiting a file's size is to reduce bandwidth usage between your client browsers and the web server, then the delivered maximum file size parameter will not satisfy your needs. Nevertheless, it is possible to perform client-side file size validation. A friend of mine uses the Microsoft Scripting.FileSystemObject *script runtime object to restrict uploads by file size prior to submission. Unfortunately, this solution works only with Internet Explorer.*

By passing the Boolean value True and the variable &recname, we are telling the add_attachment function to prefix the ATTACHSYSFILENAME value with the keys from the record &recname. In this example, &recname represents APT_WEB_ASSETS. This ensures the uniqueness of filenames added to APT_WA_ATTDET, our file attachment storage record.

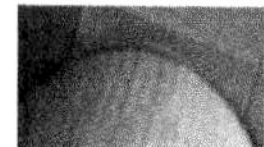

NOTE
Depending on the key structure of your component and the length of the uploaded filename, it is possible that a concatenated filename will exceed the maximum length of 128 characters. The add_attachment *PeopleCode function contains code to limit the concatenated keys to a length of 64 characters, leaving 64 characters for the original uploaded filename.*

The next two parameters, APT_WA_ATTACH.ATTACHSYSFILENAME and APT_WA_ATTACH.ATTACHUSERFILE, represent the relationship between the transaction and the attachment storage location. APT_WA_ATTACH.ATTACHSYSFILENAME is the key value used to map between the storage location and the transaction. APT_WA_ATTACH.ATTACHUSERFILE is the original filename and will be used to display the filename to the user.

&MESSAGE_LVL is an interesting parameter. This parameter tells add_attachment how to handle error notifications. When add_attachment calls AddAttachment, if the return code is an error code, should add_attachment display the error message? A value of 0 suppresses error messages. A value of 1 means display all messages including a success message. We specified a value of 2, which means to display error messages only. If you prefer, you can specify a value of 0, for no messages, and then evaluate the &RETCODE parameter to determine if the function was successful.

The last three lines of code in this FieldChange event enable and disable buttons based on the state of the attachment:

```
If (&retcode = %Attachment_Success) Then
   display_attachment_buttons(APT_WA_ATTACH.ATTACHUSERFILE);
End-If;
```

If the add_attachment function succeeded, then call the display_attachment_buttons FUNCLIB function. The display_attachment_buttons function hides the Add button and shows the View and Delete buttons if the attachment field APT_WA_ATTACH.ATTACHUSERFILE has a value. Otherwise, it hides the View and Delete buttons and shows the Add button.

The Delete Button

Next, add the following code to the ATTACHDELETE FieldChange event. This code is very similar to the ATTACHADD PeopleCode. The delete function needs to know the attachment storage location, the attachment storage key values, and how to handle error messages.

```
Declare Function delete_attachment PeopleCode
      FILE_ATTACH_WRK.ATTACHDELETE FieldChange;
Declare Function display_attachment_buttons PeopleCode
      FILE_ATTACH_WRK.ATTACHADD RowInit;

Local number &retcode;

delete_attachment(URL.APT_WEB_ASSET_ATTACHMENTS,
      APT_WA_ATTACH.ATTACHSYSFILENAME, APT_WA_ATTACH.ATTACHUSERFILE,
      2, &retcode);

If (&retcode = %Attachment_Success) Then
   display_attachment_buttons(APT_WA_ATTACH.ATTACHUSERFILE);
End-If;
```

The View Button

Add the following code to the ATTACHVIEW FieldChange event. This will allow users to download (view) attachments by clicking the View button.

```
Declare Function view_attachment PeopleCode
      FILE_ATTACH_WRK.ATTACHVIEW FieldChange;
```

```
Local number &retcode;

view_attachment(URL.APT_WEB_ASSET_ATTACHMENTS,
      APT_WA_ATTACH.ATTACHSYSFILENAME, APT_WA_ATTACH.ATTACHUSERFILE,
      2, &retcode);
```

Noticing a pattern? The `view_attachment` FUNCLIB function also needs to know the storage location, the attachment key value, and how to handle messages.

Initializing Buttons

The PeopleCode for the Add and Delete buttons hides and shows buttons based on the current state of the transaction's attachment. What about when the page is initially displayed? To hide the Delete and View buttons on new transactions or to show them on existing transactions, add the following PeopleCode to the component's `FILE_ATTACH_WRK RowInit` event. This is the same code we used previously to set the state of our buttons from the Add and Delete `FieldChange` events.

```
Declare Function display_attachment_buttons PeopleCode
      FILE_ATTACH_WRK.ATTACHADD RowInit;

display_attachment_buttons(APT_WA_ATTACH.ATTACHUSERFILE);
```

Testing the Buttons

Using your web browser, navigate to the Web Assets page. Do you see an Add button, but no View or Delete buttons? If so, then your `RowInit` event is working correctly. Use the Add button to add an attachment. Pick any small file from your computer. If you can't find a small file, open Notepad and create text file that contains only the text "Hello World." After uploading a file, you should see the Add button disappear and the View and Delete buttons appear. If you click the View button, your browser should respond by opening that small file in a new browser window. If the file you chose was a type that the browser can interpret, its contents will be shown in the browser window. If the file was a binary file that the browser cannot interpret, such as an .exe file, the browser will prompt you to open or download the file.

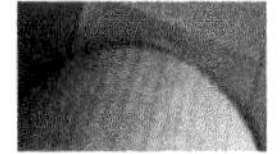

TIP

The `ViewAttachment` function uses JavaScript to open a new window. Modern browsers and browser plug-ins block this behavior, assuming any page that uses JavaScript to display a new window is malicious at worst and annoying at best. If you have a pop-up blocker, or just a modern browser, then you may need to enable pop-ups for your PeopleSoft URL so the `ViewAttachment` function will work properly.

Customizing File Attachment Behavior

The delivered file attachment function library simplifies development by hiding some of the File Attachment API's less common features. In this section we will write our own function library that maintains most of the simplicity of the delivered library while exposing these additional features.

Through writing this custom library, you will learn how to interact directly with the low level File Attachment API.

Button State

Using the delivered `display_attachment_buttons` function, when the transaction has an attachment, the Add button is invisible, and the View and Delete buttons are visible. Conversely, when the transaction has no attachment, the Add button is visible and the View and Delete buttons are hidden. While I certainly advocate disabling features based on the state of a transaction, I am not fond of hiding features users are accustom to seeing. As an alternative, it would be better to enable and disable these buttons based on the state of the transaction. The delivered `display_attachment_buttons` FUNCLIB function also assumes the attachment buttons are bound to the `FILE_ATTACH_WRK` derived/work record. It would be nice to have a more generic version that allows us to bind these buttons to any record. To make these changes, we will create our own function named `APT_set_buttons_state` in a new FUNCLIB.

Before creating the function, we need a new FUNCLIB. A FUNCLIB is a reusable function stored in a derived/work record field event. So, first create a new record and set the record type to Derived/Work. FUNCLIB records do not hold data, so they do not need to exist at the database level. Add the field `ATTACHADD` to this record and save the record as `APT_ATTACH_FUNC`. (The name of the record is not important.) Your record should look something like Figure 2-19.

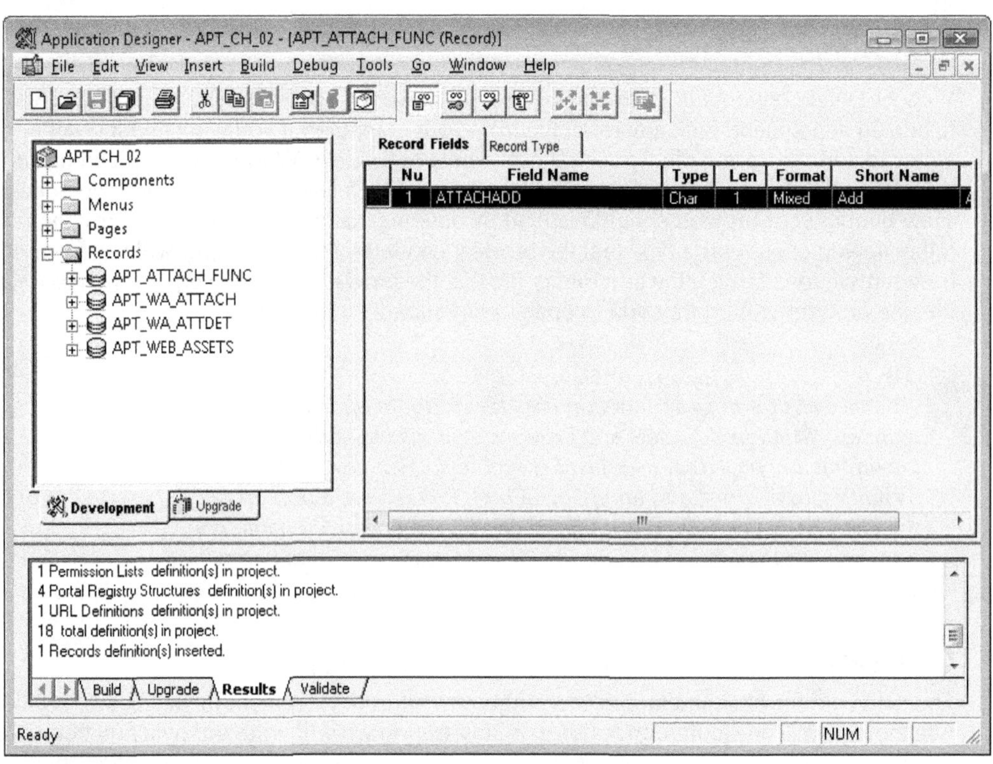

FIGURE 2-19. *APT_ATTACH_FUNC record definition*

NOTE
PeopleSoft recommends that customers suffix FUNCLIB record names with `_FUNCLIB`. This helps differentiate FUNCLIB records from work records and database records. Because record names are limited to 15 characters, and the first 4 are consumed by our prefix, it is a shame to waste the final 8 on the suffix `_FUNCLIB`. That would leave us with only 3 characters to uniquely identify our FUNCLIB. Rather than creating an unintelligible acronym, I chose to shorten the recommended suffix to just `_FUNC`.

PeopleSoft recommends placing FUNCLIB PeopleCode in the `FieldFormula` event, so add the following code to the `FieldFormula` event of the `ATTACHADD` field:

```
/*
 * Function: APT_set_buttons_state
 *
 *   &filename  string  Generally ATTACHUSERFILENAME field
 *   &btn_rec   record  The record bound to the attachment buttons
 *                      This is generally FILE_ATTACH_WRK and has
 *                      the fields ATTACHADD, ATTACHVIEW,
 *                      ATTACHDELETE, and ATTACHDET.
 */
Function APT_set_buttons_state(&attachuserfilename As string,
      &btn_rec As Record)
   Local boolean &add = None(&attachuserfilename);

   REM ** array of possible button names;
   Local array of string &fields =
         Split("ATTACHVIEW ATTACHDELETE ATTACHDET");
   local string &field_ref;
   Local number &field_idx = 0;

   REM ** Assume ATTACHADD is the name of the ADD button;
   &btn_rec.ATTACHADD.Enabled = &add;

   While &fields.Next(&field_idx)
      REM ** try block just in case field doesn't exist;
      try
         &field_ref = "Field." | &fields [&field_idx];
         &btn_rec.GetField(@(&field_ref)).Enabled = ( Not &add);

      catch Exception &e1
         REM ** Field is not in record -- ignore;
      end-try;
   End-While
End-Function;
```

This function introduces some tricks for creating generic routines. The first trick is that we initialize and populate an array of field names in one line by using the PeopleCode `Split` function. We then iterate over that array, checking to see if the field exists in the record. Since all buttons get the opposite state of the Add button, we set the button's state to `Not &add`. The `try` / `catch` / `end-try` construct ignores fields that don't exist in `&btn_rec`. This allows developers to create custom button records without the Delete, View, or Detach buttons. For example, I wrote a batch program once that processed a file. That file came from a file upload on the run control page. I found that users would reuse the same run control, replacing the file with each run. If the process failed, I would not have the file as an audit trail to help me understand why the process failed. To resolve this, I removed the Delete button, requiring users to create new run controls for new files.

We can now replace the `display_attachment_buttons` function in each of the three events (Add `FieldChange`, Delete `FieldChange`, and `RowInit`) with the following declaration and function call:

```
REM ** replace declaration with;
Declare Function APT_set_buttons_state PeopleCode
      APT_ATTACH_FUNC.ATTACHADD FieldFormula;

REM ** replace function call with;
APT_set_buttons_state(APT_WA_ATTACH.ATTACHUSERFILE,
      GetRecord(Record.FILE_ATTACH_WRK));
```

Custom Add Attachment Function

Figure 2-20 shows the delivered File Attachment API file upload page. While the Browse and Upload buttons, in the context of a transaction, may be enough to tell the user what to do, it would be nice to add a little more to this page to provide users with instructions. The native `AddAttachment` PeopleCode function actually allows you to add HTML to this page. Let's create our own version of the `add_attachment` function that takes an HTML parameter.

The current implementation also assumes that the primary key record is available from the current context using `GetRecord()`. This will not work when inserting attachments into a scroll area at a level lower than the row containing the button. Also, if the component contains the same record at multiple levels, then `GetRecord()` will return the instance that is closest to the button's execution context, which may not be the appropriate instance. Furthermore, while it could be argued that the `AddAttachment` function is relevant only within a component context, I prefer to write FUNCLIB functions to be independent of their runtime context.

With this in mind, let's write our own version of the `add_attachment` function. Add the following PeopleCode to the `FieldFormula` event of the `APT_ATTACH_FUNC.ATTACHADD` record field.

```
/*
 * Function: APT_add_attachment
 *
 * Parameters:
 *   &url            string   Either a URL ID or a string in the
 *                            format:
 *                               ftp://user:password@server/
 *                            or
 *                               record://recname
 *   &max_filesize   number   Maximum size of attachment
 *   &prefix_keys    boolean  Add transaction keys to &sys_filename
 *   &key_rec        record   Record containing keys
```

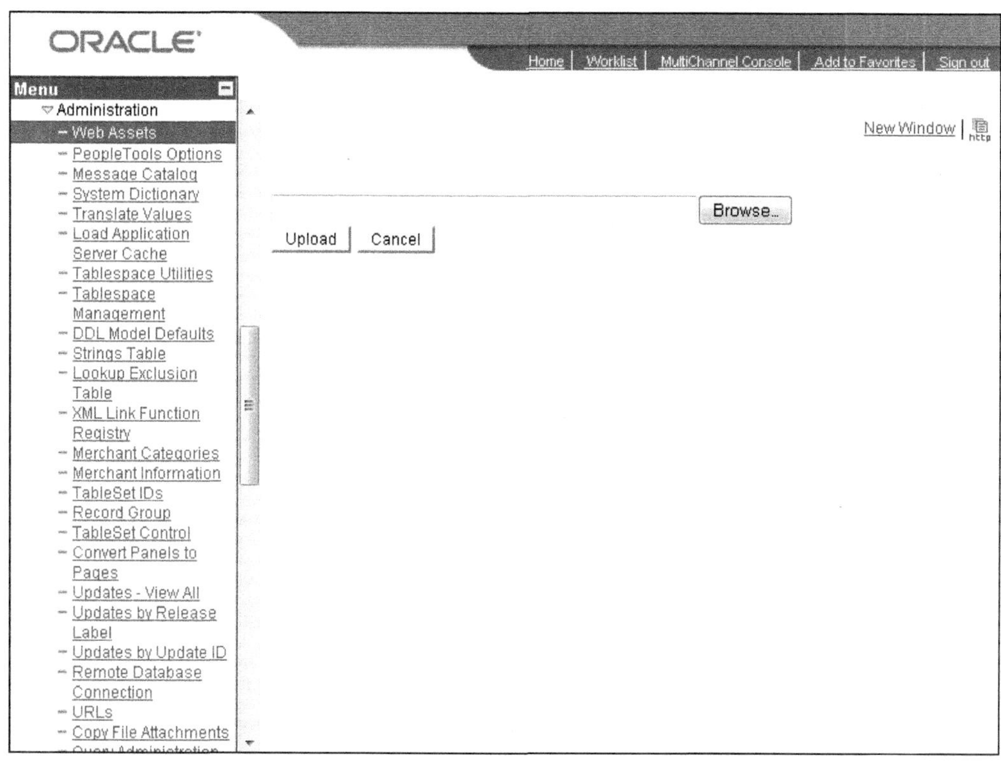

FIGURE 2-20. *File Attachment API upload page*

```
 *   &sys_dir        string   FTP server sub directory
 *   &sys_filename   string   On input, a prefix for files that will
 *                            be stored in the ftp or record storage
 *                            location. On return, the name of the
 *                            file in the storage location
 *   &user_filename  string   The name of the file uploaded by the
 *                            user. populated on return.
 *                            Output parameter only.
 *   &preserve_case  boolean  True to maintain the case of the file
 *                            name received from the user
 *   &html_header    string   HTML to display above the file input
 *                            text box on the attachment page. If this
 *                            value is empty, then this function will
 *                            use the HTML from the HTML definition
 *                            APT_FILE_ATTACH_HEADER
 *   &handle_errors  boolean  True to display errors, false to suppress
 *                            errors. If you choose false, you should
 *                            inspect the return value.
 *
```

```
 * Returns: return value of AddAttachment or -1 if &prefix_keys is
 *          true and user hasn't populated all the key fields.
 *
 */
Function APT_add_attachment(&url As string, &max_filesize As number,
      &prefix_keys As boolean, &key_rec As Record, &sys_dir As string,
      &sys_filename As string, &user_filename As string,
      &preserve_case As boolean, &html_header As string,
      &handle_errors As boolean) Returns number
   Local Field &field;
   Local string &key_string = "";
   Local number &field_idx = 1;
   Local number &retcode;

   If &prefix_keys Then
      For &field_idx = 1 To &key_rec.FieldCount
         &field = &key_rec.GetField(&field_idx);
         If (&field.IsKey = True) Then
            If (All(&field.Value) And
                  &field.IsRequired = True) Then
               If (&handle_errors) Then
                  /* display a message if prefix_keys is true, but
                   * user hasn't populated all the keys
                   */
                  MessageBox(0, "", 137, 28,
                        "Please attach the file after filling out " |
                        "the required fields on this page.");
               End-If;
               REM ** return our own custom error code;
               Return - 1;
            Else
               &key_string = &key_string | &field.Value;
            End-If;
         End-If;
      End-For;
      REM ** remove spaces from keys;
      &key_string = Substitute(&key_string, " ", "");
      /* PeopleBooks says the AddAttachment function URL must be 120
       * characters or less and &user_filename must be less than 64
       * characters. Furthermore, the ATTACHSYSFILENAME field is
       * defined as 128 characters. Therefore, we will limit the key
       * string to 64 characters: 64 for the keys and 64 for the name
       */
      &sys_filename = Left(&key_string | &sys_filename, 64);
   End-If;

   REM ** prefix sys_filename with the ftp file path;
   &sys_filename = &sys_dir | &sys_filename;

   If (None(&html_header)) Then
      &html_header = GetHTMLText(HTML.APT_FILE_ATTACH_HEADER);
   End-If;
```

```
&retcode = AddAttachment(&url, &sys_filename, "", &user_filename,
      &max_filesize, &preserve_case, &html_header);

/* AddAttachment returns the user_filename. sys_filename is a
 * combination of sys_filename and user_filename.
 */
&sys_filename = &sys_filename | &user_filename;

If (&retcode <> %Attachment_Success) Then
   REM ** set filename vars to "" on failure;
   &user_filename = "";
   &sys_filename = "";
End-If;

/* PeopleTools delivers message catalog entries for the file
 * attachment API. It sure would be nice if the entry number
 * matched the return code
 */
If (&handle_errors) Then
   Evaluate &retcode
   When %Attachment_Cancelled
      MessageBox(0, "", 137, 3, "AddAttachment cancelled");
      Break;
   When %Attachment_Failed
      MessageBox(0, "", 137, 2, "AddAttachment failed");
      Break;
   When %Attachment_FileTransferFailed
      MessageBox(0, "", 137, 4, "AddAttachment failed: " |
            "File Transfer did not succeed");
      Break;
   When %Attachment_NoDiskSpaceAppServ
      MessageBox(0, "", 137, 5, "AddAttachment failed: " |
            "No disk space on the app server");
      Break;
   When %Attachment_NoDiskSpaceWebServ
      MessageBox(0, "", 137, 6, "AddAttachment failed: " |
            "No disk space on the web server");
      Break;
   When %Attachment_FileExceedsMaxSize
      MessageBox(0, "", 137, 7, "AddAttachment failed: " |
            "File exceeds the max size");
      Break;
   When %Attachment_DestSystNotFound
      MessageBox(0, "", 137, 8, "AddAttachment failed: " |
            "Cannot locate destination system for ftp");
      Break;
   When %Attachment_DestSysFailedLogin
      MessageBox(0, "", 137, 9, "AddAttachment failed: " |
            "Unable to login into destination system for ftp");
      Break;
```

```
      When %Attachment_FileNotFound
         MessageBox(0, "", 137, 29, "The file was not found so " |
               "the operation could not be completed.");
         Break;
      When %Attachment_NoFileName
         MessageBox(0, "", 137, 38, "AddAttachment failed: " |
               "No File Name Specified.");
         Break;
      End-Evaluate;
   End-If;

   Return &retcode;
End-Function;
```

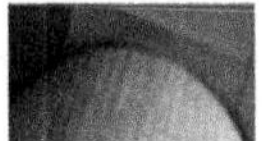

NOTE

Please ignore the interesting string concatenation and line breaks in the long strings of the preceding code. Those "interesting" line breaks exist for formatting purposes only. The code will execute as shown. Nevertheless, you should avoid this practice when writing your own code.

I placed several lines of documentation comments in the code for reference. Ignoring those for now, let's walk through the executable code, line by line, starting with the call specification:

```
Function APT_add_attachment(&url As string, &max_filesize As number,
      &prefix_keys As boolean, &key_rec As Record, &sys_dir As string,
      &sys_filename As string, &user_filename As string,
      &preserve_case As boolean, &html_header As string,
      &handle_errors As boolean) Returns number
```

The parameters to the `APT_add_attachment` function are similar to the original `add_attachment` function. Let's discuss the parameters that are different:

- `&RECNAME` We changed the `&RECNAME` parameter from a string to an actual record. As I previously mentioned, the `&RECNAME` parameter tells `add_attachment` where to find key values when creating a unique name in the chosen storage location. This change allows us to pass in a specific record from any level in the buffer without concern for context. In fact, if you prefer, you can even create a stand-alone record, populate the key values, and use that stand-alone record to provide key prefixes. If the key values plus the input value for `&sys_filename` are greater than 64 characters, this function will truncate `&sys_filename` at 64 characters prior to passing the value on to the native `AddAttachment` function.
- `&sys_dir` The parameter `&sys_dir` specifies a target directory on an FTP server. For example, if your FTP URL is defined as `ftp://hrms.example.com/psfiles` and the file needs to be stored in `ftp://hrms.example.com/psfiles/invoices`, then pass `invoices/` as the value for this parameter. If you are not using FTP storage, then pass an empty string as the value for this parameter ("").

- `&sys_filename` When calling `APT_add_attachment`, you may provide an additional prefix for `&sys_filename` by assigning a value to the `&sys_filename` parameter prior to calling the function. If you specify `&prefix_keys` and a value for `&sys_filename`, the final `&sys_filename` used to store the attachment will be a concatenation of the keys and the prefix specified in `&sys_filename`.
- `&preserve_case` The `&preserve_case` parameter tells the `AddAttachment` function to maintain the case of the original filename. This may be important when working with files on systems with case-sensitive filenames.
- `&html_header` The `&html_header` parameter allows us to add HTML to the File Attachment API upload page. This additional HTML may contain a basic header, some instructions, or even some JavaScript validation logic.
- `&handle_error` The `&handle_error` parameter replaces the `&MESSAGE_LVL` parameter from the original `add_attachment` function. A Boolean value to show or not show an error message is satisfactory. We'll leave the "show message on success" case to the code that actually called `APT_add_attachment`. While it would certainly be possible to leave error handling entirely up to the caller, I find the centralized evaluate statement and corresponding message catalog references to be very helpful.
- `&RETCODE` Unlike the delivered version, this version returns the `AddAttachment` return value as the function's return value. The delivered `add_attachment` function uses the input parameter `&RETCODE` to specify the `AddAttachment` return value.

Let's skip the variable declarations and move on to the first major block of code:

```
If &prefix_keys Then
   For &field_idx = 1 To &key_rec.FieldCount
      &field = &key_rec.GetField(&field_idx);
      If (&field.IsKey = True) Then
         If (All(&field.Value) And
               &field.IsRequired = True) Then
            If (&handle_errors) Then
               /* display a message if prefix_keys is true, but
                * user hasn't populated all the keys
                */
               MessageBox(0, "", 137, 28,
                     "Please attach the file after filling out " |
                     "the required fields on this page.");
            End-If;
            /* The user did not populate all required keys.
             * Return our own custom error code
             */
            Return - 1;
         Else
            &key_string = &key_string | &field.Value;
         End-If;
      End-If;
   End-For;
   REM ** remove spaces from keys;
   &key_string = Substitute(&key_string, " ", "");
   /* PeopleBooks says the AddAttachment function URL must be 120
```

```
     * characters or less and &user_filename must be less than 64
     * characters. Furthermore, the ATTACHSYSFILENAME field is
     * defined as 128 characters. Therefore, we will limit the key
     * string to 64 characters: 64 for the keys and 64 for the name
     */
   &sys_filename = Left(&key_string | &sys_filename, 64);
End-If;
```

This block is responsible for copying the key values from `&keys_rec` into the target filename. It does so by looping through the fields in `&keys_rec`. The code checks for a value in each required key field. If a required key field does not have a value, then it displays a message and returns `-1`.

The PeopleBooks documentation for the `AddAttachment` function says that the value passed into `AddAttachment` for the `UserFile` parameter cannot exceed 64 characters in length. It does not give guidance for the `DirAndFileName` parameter. However, looking at the `FILE_ATTACH_SBR` subrecord, we can see that the maximum value for `ATTACHSYSFILENAME` is 128 characters. Since the final value for `ATTACHSYSFILENAME` is a combination of the original `ATTACHSYSFILENAME` value and the `ATTACHUSERFILE` value, and if `ATTACHUSERFILE` can contain 64 characters, it stands to reason that any prefix given to `ATTACHSYSFILENAME` must be 64 characters or less. Therefore, the last executable line in this block truncates the `&sys_filename` value to a maximum of 64 characters. At this juncture, `&sys_filename` represents only the prefix we will pass into `AddAttachment`. `AddAttachment` will prefix the chosen filename with this value prior to sending it to the storage location (FTP or record).

As you can see from this code, we're prefixing `&sys_filename` with the keys, so, if you pass in a value for `&sys_filename` and specify `&prefix_keys`, then the key values will precede the prefix specified by `&sys_filename`. Of course, you could override this by either prefixing the keys yourself or changing the code in this function.

```
&sys_filename = &sys_dir | &sys_filename;
```

This is the final step required to prepare the `&sys_filename` variable for the `AddAttachment` function. If you specify an FTP URL and need to place the file in a subfolder of the URL, then pass that folder name into `APT_add_attachment` as the value for the parameter `&sys_dir`. The value must end in / because the filename will be appended to this value to derive the target path and file.

```
If (None(&html_header)) Then
   &html_header = GetHTMLText(HTML.APT_FILE_ATTACH_HEADER);
End-If;
```

This section provides default HTML for the header. This HTML will display in the File Attachment API upload page prior to the input field and Browse button. The following is the HTML definition of `APT_FILE_ATTACH_HEADER`. Create this HTML definition so the attachment function will be ready for testing.

```
<div class="PAPAGETITLE">Attach a file</div>
<p class="PSTEXT">
  Select a file using the <strong>Browse</strong> button and then
  click <strong>Upload</strong>
</p>
```

HTML Definitions

An HTML definition is a text definition maintained within App Designer. Using App Designer, you can create HTML definitions to store HTML, JavaScript, CSS, XML, or any other type of text. At runtime, you can extract that text using the `GetHTMLText()` PeopleCode function. HTML definitions can have bind variables and meta-HTML sequences. This makes HTML definitions an excellent choice for templates. Unfortunately, HTML definitions are available only to PeopleCode running online. I have often wished for the template capabilities of HTML definitions when writing web service handlers or App Engine programs.

When writing HTML in HTML definitions, be sure to use the same style class attributes as PeopleSoft does for similar items. For example, when creating hyperlinks, use the style class `PSHYPERLINK`. Notice that in the `APT_FILE_ATTACH_HEADER` HTML definition, we use `PAPAGETITLE` and `PSTEXT` to provide styling for HTML. Following this guideline will ensure that your custom HTML blends in with the rest of the PeopleSoft-generated HTML. Furthermore, if you change the style definitions for your PeopleSoft application, the visual appearance of your custom HTML will change accordingly.

We will make extensive use of HTML definitions in Part II of this book.

```
&retcode = AddAttachment(&url, &sys_filename, "", &user_filename,
      &max_filesize, &preserve_case, &html_header);

/* AddAttachment returns the user_filename. sys_filename is a
 * combination of sys_filename and user_filename.
 */
&sys_filename = &sys_filename | &user_filename;
```

This block calls `AddAttachment` and then sets the output parameter `&sys_filename` to the value that is used to identify the attachment within the chosen storage location (FTP or record).

```
If (&retcode <> %Attachment_Success) Then
   REM ** set filename vars to "" on failure;
   &user_filename = "";
   &sys_filename = "";
End-If;
```

If the attachment failed, then clear the output parameters `&user_filename` and `&sys_filename`.

```
/* PeopleTools delivers message catalog entries for the file
 * attachment API. It sure would be nice if the entry number
 * matched the return code
 */
If (&handle_errors) Then
   Evaluate &retcode
   When %Attachment_Cancelled
```

```
            MessageBox(0, "", 137, 3, "AddAttachment cancelled");
            Break;

            ...

         End-Evaluate;
   End-If;

   Return &retcode;
End-Function;
```

Finish the function by evaluating the return code for errors and display them as needed. Finally, return the `AddAttachment` result.

Let's update the `ATTACHADD` button PeopleCode to use our new function and then compare the difference in the File Attachment API upload page.

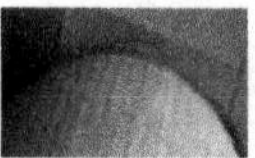

NOTE

The following code is a complete replacement for the `ATTACHADD` `FieldChange` PeopleCode we wrote earlier in this chapter.

```
Declare Function APT_add_attachment PeopleCode
      APT_ATTACH_FUNC.ATTACHADD FieldFormula;
Declare Function APT_set_buttons_state PeopleCode
      APT_ATTACH_FUNC.ATTACHADD FieldFormula;

Local number &retcode = APT_add_attachment(
      URL.APT_WEB_ASSET_ATTACHMENTS, 0, True,
      GetRecord(Record.APT_WEB_ASSETS), "",
      APT_WA_ATTACH.ATTACHSYSFILENAME,
      APT_WA_ATTACH.ATTACHUSERFILE, False, "", True);

If (&retcode = %Attachment_Success) Then
   APT_set_buttons_state(APT_WA_ATTACH.ATTACHUSERFILE,
         GetRecord(Record.FILE_ATTACH_WRK));
End-If;
```

Figure 2-21 shows the File Attachment API upload page after creating the HTML definition and updating the `ATTACHADD` PeopleCode.

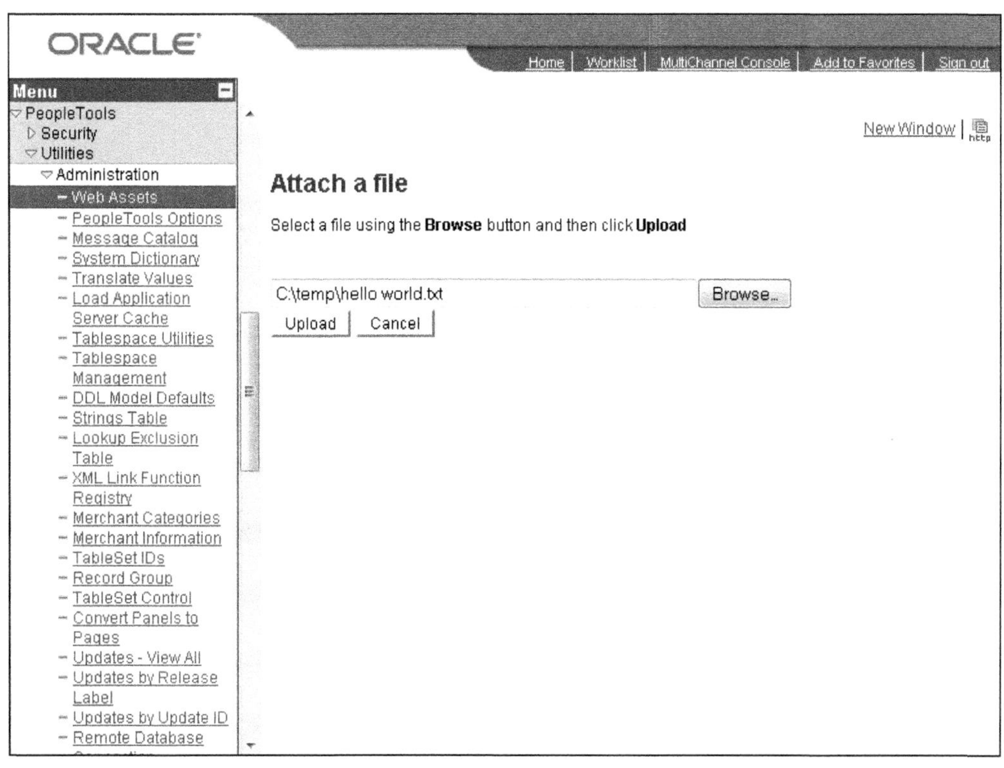

FIGURE 2-21. *File Attachment API upload page with custom HTML*

Moving to Level 1

Let's use the concepts learned thus far to add attachments to another component. Suppose that our human resources department requires photocopies of employees' driver's licenses. That department wants to attach scanned copies of driver's licenses to the Driver's License Data component in PeopleSoft. You can find the Driver's License component in the PeopleSoft HRMS application, by navigating to Workforce Administration | Personal Information | Biographical | Driver's License Data.

This request will require us to modify the Driver's License Data page, named `DRIVERS_LIC_GBL`. Following best practices, we want to keep modifications to a minimum. If we design the modification properly, this page is the only piece of the component we will need to modify.

Modifying the Page

Rather than adding the `ATTACHSYSFILENAME` and `ATTACHUSERFILE` fields to the `DRIVERS_LIC` record, which is the primary record at level 1, we will create a record with the same keys plus the `FILE_ATTACH_SBR` subrecord. Name this new record `APT_DL_ATTACH`. We will also need a record to store attachments, so create the record `APT_DL_ATTDET`, as shown in Figure 2-22.

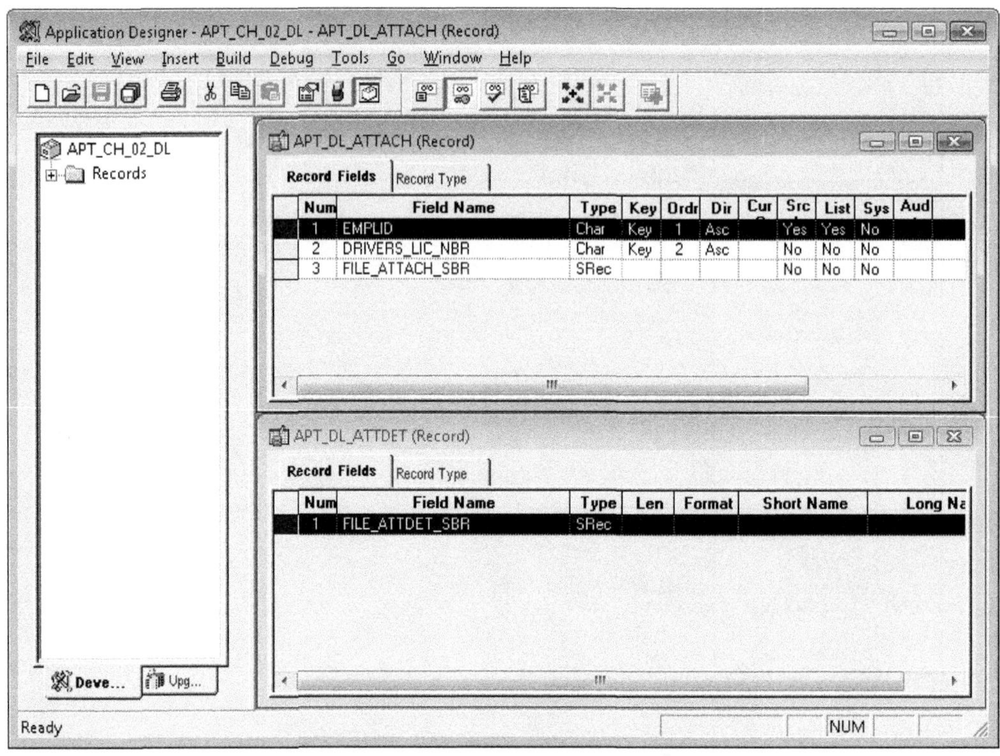

FIGURE 2-22. *Driver's License Data attachment records*

Next, we will add the attachment fields to the page `DRIVERS_LIC_GBL`. Our first step is to make some room on the Driver's License Data page by expanding the Driver's License Information scroll area and moving the License Type scroll area farther down the page. Next, we add the `ATTACHUSERFILE` field to the page, and then set the label, size, and display-only attributes.

When you save the page, App Designer will respond by presenting you with the error, "More than one data record in scroll—make fields from non-primary record related display," as shown in Figure 2-23. It turns out that adding `APT_DL_ATTACH.ATTACHUSERFILE` would place two data records inside the same scroll area. This is not allowed by App Designer.

The approach we took of adding a second data record to the buffer is similar to the approach we used with the Web Assets page example. What makes this different from the earlier example? In this example, we are trying to add another data record to a scroll area. The Web Assets page example added a second data record to level 0.

We can still add attachments to this component, but we need to modify our approach. Since we can have only one data record per scroll area, one option is to modify the existing data record by adding the `FILE_ATTACH_SBR` subrecord to that data record. In this case, that would require us to modify the `DRIVERS_LIC` record. Modifying delivered record definitions, however, is extremely risky. If you add or remove fields from a delivered record, then you may need to

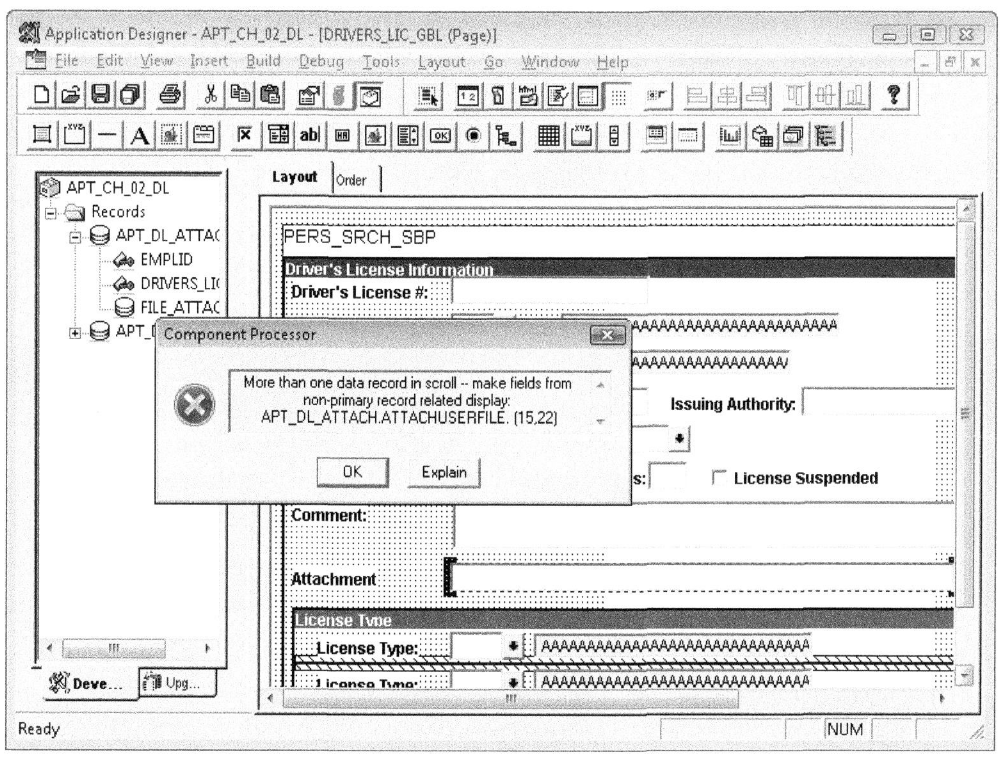

FIGURE 2-23. *Multiple data records in scroll error*

modify every view and SQL statement that uses that record. For example, if we add these two fields to `DRIVERS_LIC` and there is an App Engine program that inserts data into `DRIVERS_LIC`, then that App Engine will fail unless we add those two fields to the App Engine's SQL `INSERT` statements.

As an alternative, we can add the `ATTACHUSERFILE` and `ATTACHSYSFILENAME` fields to a derived/work record and display those derived/work fields on the page. After we put those fields on a page, we will need to figure out how to get those values into the database. Let's choose this alternative since it requires fewer modifications to delivered objects.

First, create a new derived/work record and add the fields `ATTACHSYSFILENAME` and `ATTACHUSERFILE`. Save the new record as `APT_DL_ATT_WRK`. Update the attachment field on the page `DRIVERS_LIC_GBL` to use this new derived/work record and save the page. (Note that changing a field's source resets its field label.) This resolves the "Multiple data records" error, because derived/work records are not data records. This derived/work record approach allows us to display data on a page, but we will need to use PeopleCode to save and load the derived/work record's data.

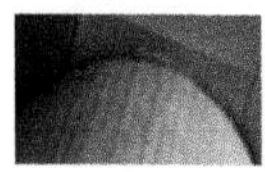

NOTE
We could have added `FILE_ATTACH_SBR` to `APT_DL_ATT_WRK`. However, we will later add PeopleCode to the `ATTACHSYSFILENAME` `RowInit` event. Using `FILE_ATTACH_SBR` would require us to modify the PeopleCode for that delivered record.

We also need to consider the Add, View, and Delete buttons. In the Web Assets page example, we added PeopleCode to the Web Assets component to provide attachment functionality. We could make the same change to the Driver's License Data component, but that would add one more item to the list of modified definitions. Fewer modified definitions simplifies patches and upgrades.

As an alternative to modifying the component, we could add `FieldChange` PeopleCode to the buttons' derived work record. In the Web Assets page example, the buttons' derived/work record was a delivered record. Adding code to those `FieldChange` events would add another definition to the list of modified definitions. To avoid modifying the `FILE_ATTACH_WRK` record, we can add the `ATTACHADD`, `ATTACHDELETE`, and `ATTACHVIEW` fields to `APT_DL_ATT_WRK`. Figure 2-24 shows the `APT_DL_ATT_WRK` record with the attachment data and button fields.

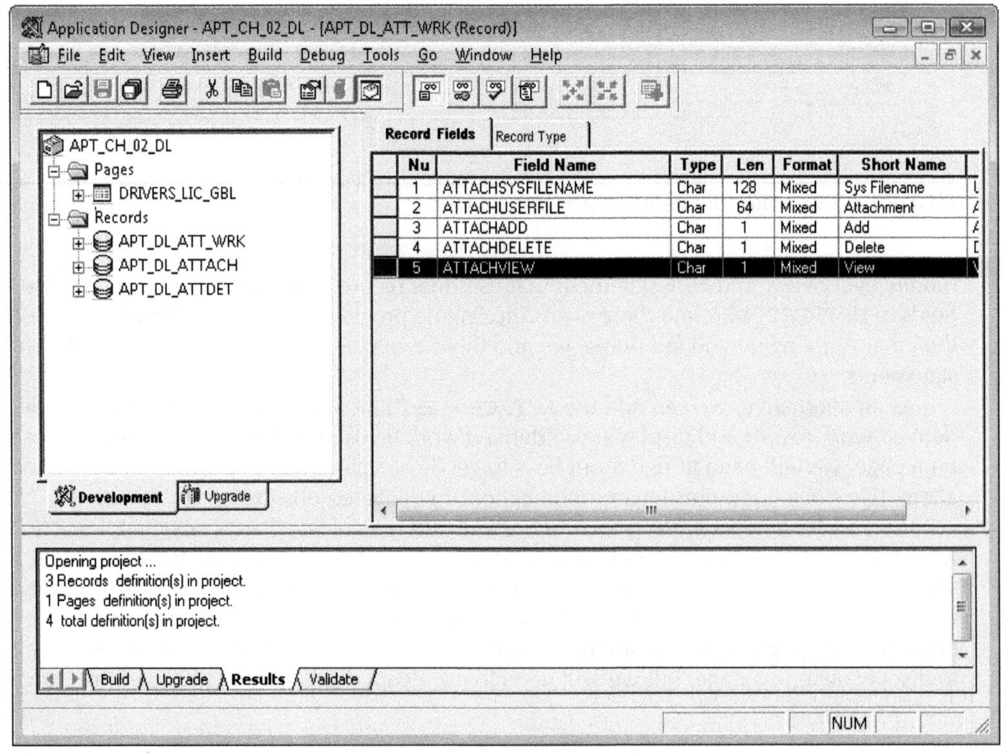

FIGURE 2-24. *The APT_DL_ATT_WRK derived/work record*

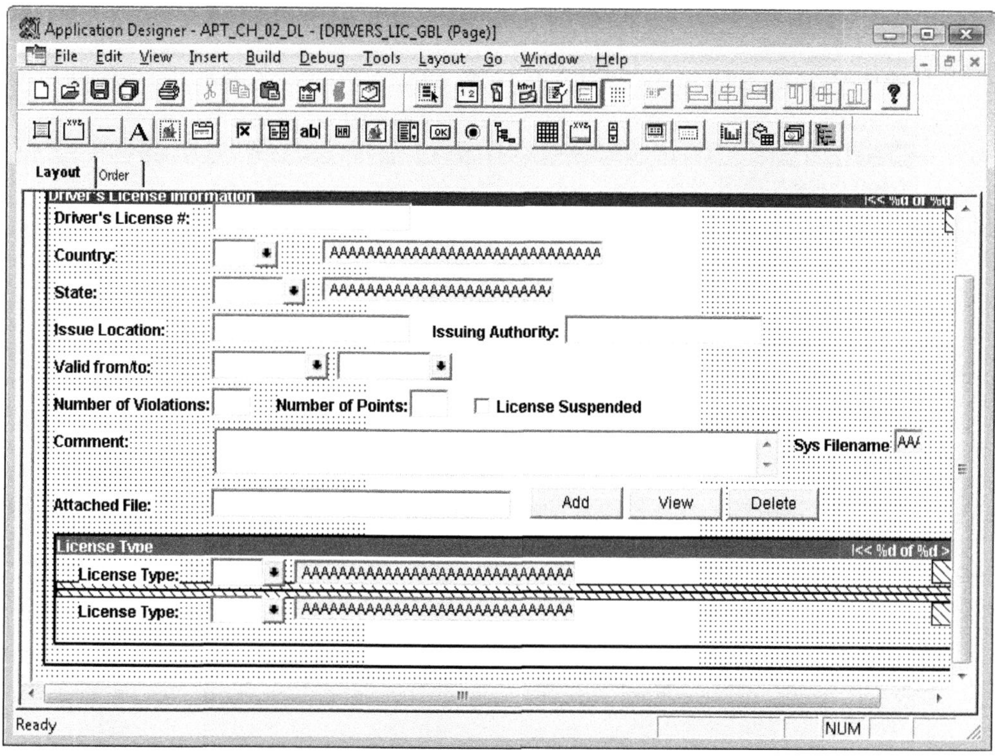

FIGURE 2-25. *Modified DRIVERS_LIC_GBL page in App Designer*

Add `APT_DL_ATT_WRK.ATTACHSYSFILENAME` to the page and make it invisible. Add three buttons and associate them with the `ATTACHADD`, `ATTACHVIEW`, and `ATTACHDELETE` fields of the `APT_DL_ATT_WRK` derived/work record. Figure 2-25 shows the lower portion of the modified `DRIVERS_LIC_GBL` page.

Test the page to make sure everything appears as expected. It should look like Figure 2-26. We have now completed the user interface modifications and can implement the three attachment buttons' `FieldChange` PeopleCode.

The PeopleCode for these buttons will require a URL definition for the attachment record. Just as you did for the Web Assets example, navigate to PeopleTools | Utilities | Administration | URLs. Add the URL definition `APT_DL_ATTACHMENTS` and give it the value `record://APT_DL_ATTDET`.

Adding the PeopleCode

It is time to add PeopleCode to this component. As I previously mentioned, we will break from the best practice of adding component-specific PeopleCode to component definitions for the purpose of avoiding another modification.

For the Add button, we can start with the final code for the Web Assets page `ATTACHADD` button and modify a copy of that code as necessary. The difference between this example and the Web

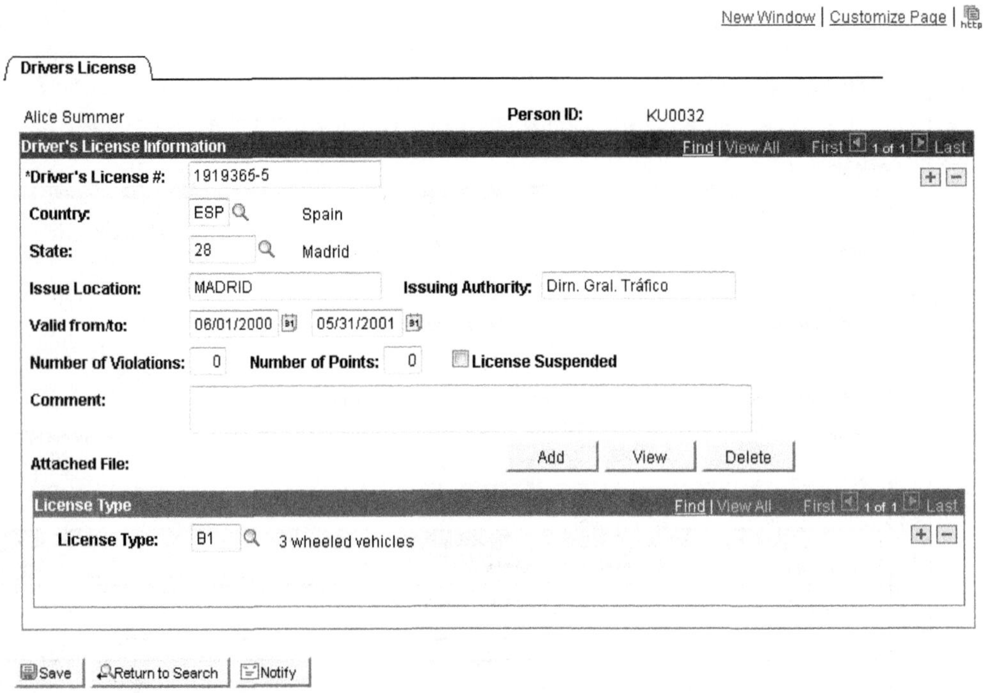

FIGURE 2-26. *Online view of the modified DRIVERS_LIC_GBL component*

Assets example is that we will need to update a derived/work record and a database table. In the Web Assets example, we were able to include the database table directly in the component buffer.

To implement the Add button, open the PeopleCode editor for the `APT_DL_ATT_WRK.ATTACHADD` field and switch to the `FieldChange` event. Add the following PeopleCode. Deviations from the Web Assets example are shown in bold.

```
Declare Function APT_add_attachment PeopleCode
      APT_ATTACH_FUNC.ATTACHADD FieldFormula;
Declare Function APT_set_buttons_state PeopleCode
      APT_ATTACH_FUNC.ATTACHADD FieldFormula;

Local Record &keys_rec = CreateRecord(Record.APT_DL_ATTACH);

&keys_rec.EMPLID.Value = DRIVERS_LIC.EMPLID;
&keys_rec.DRIVERS_LIC_NBR.Value = DRIVERS_LIC.DRIVERS_LIC_NBR;

Local number &retcode = APT_add_attachment(URL.APT_DL_ATTACHMENTS, 0,
      True, &keys_rec, "", APT_DL_ATT_WRK.ATTACHSYSFILENAME,
      APT_DL_ATT_WRK.ATTACHUSERFILE, False, "", True);
```

```
If (&retcode = %Attachment_Success) Then
   REM ** Populate original values. See Record.Save in PeopleBooks;
   &keys_rec.SelectByKey( False);

   &keys_rec.ATTACHSYSFILENAME.Value =
         APT_DL_ATT_WRK.ATTACHSYSFILENAME;
   &keys_rec.ATTACHUSERFILE.Value =
         APT_DL_ATT_WRK.ATTACHUSERFILE;

   If (&keys_rec.Save()) Then
      APT_set_buttons_state(APT_DL_ATT_WRK.ATTACHUSERFILE,
            GetRecord(Record.APT_DL_ATT_WRK));
   Else
      MessageBox(0, "", 0, 0,
            "Failed to save the attachment to the database");
      REM ** remove orphaned attachment from the database;
      &retcode = DeleteAttachment(URL.APT_DL_ATTACHMENTS,
            APT_DL_ATT_WRK.ATTACHSYSFILENAME);
   End-If;
End-If;
```

Before we go any further with this example, we should implement `RowInit` PeopleCode to enable and disable the attachment buttons. As part of this PeopleCode, we will load the `ATTACHSYSFILENAME` and `ATTACHUSERFILE` derived/work fields with data from the off-screen attachment table (`APT_DL_ATTACH`, the table we initially added to level 1, which resulted in a second record at level 1). As with the previous code listing, deviations from the Web Assets component are shown in bold.

```
Declare Function APT_set_buttons_state PeopleCode
      APT_ATTACH_FUNC.ATTACHADD FieldFormula;

Local Record &keys_rec = CreateRecord(Record.APT_DL_ATTACH);

&keys_rec.EMPLID.Value = DRIVERS_LIC.EMPLID;
&keys_rec.DRIVERS_LIC_NBR.Value = DRIVERS_LIC.DRIVERS_LIC_NBR;
&keys_rec.SelectByKey();

APT_DL_ATT_WRK.ATTACHSYSFILENAME = &keys_rec.ATTACHSYSFILENAME.Value;
APT_DL_ATT_WRK.ATTACHUSERFILE = &keys_rec.ATTACHUSERFILE.Value;

APT_set_buttons_state(APT_DL_ATT_WRK.ATTACHUSERFILE,
      GetRecord(Record.APT_DL_ATT_WRK));
```

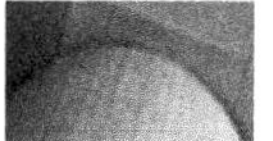

NOTE

The `RowInit` attachment button PeopleCode will have no effect until you add data to the `APT_DL_ATTACH` record through the component's new file attachment buttons.

Next, let's implement the View button. Copy the following code into the `FieldChange` event of record field `APT_DL_ATT_WRK ATTACHVIEW`. The only difference between this code and the Web Assets page View button attachment code is the name of the records.

```
Declare Function view_attachment PeopleCode
      FILE_ATTACH_WRK.ATTACHVIEW FieldChange;

Local number &retcode;

view_attachment(URL.APT_DL_ATTACHMENTS,
      APT_DL_ATT_WRK.ATTACHSYSFILENAME,
      APT_DL_ATT_WRK.ATTACHUSERFILE, 2, &retcode);
```

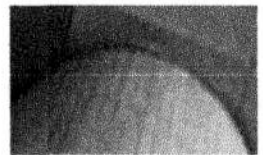

NOTE

Both examples in this chapter use `view_attachment`, a PeopleCode wrapper for the native `ViewAttachment` function. In Chapter 5 you will learn an alternative download method. The method described in Chapter 5 gives you complete control over the way PeopleSoft presents an attachment to the user.

We have one button left to implement: the Delete button. The code for the Delete button follows the same pattern as the Add button. We start with the code for the Web Assets page Delete button and then add code for the `APT_DL_ATTACH` record, since it is not in the buffer. Add the following code to the `FieldChange` event of the `ATTACHDELETE` field in the `APT_DL_ATT_WRK` record. The new code (shown in bold) creates a record object based on `APT_DL_ATTACH`, so we can delete data that does not exist in the component buffer.

```
Declare Function delete_attachment PeopleCode
      FILE_ATTACH_WRK.ATTACHDELETE FieldChange;
Declare Function APT_set_buttons_state PeopleCode
      APT_ATTACH_FUNC.ATTACHADD FieldFormula;

Local number &retcode;
Local Record &keys_rec;

delete_attachment(URL.APT_DL_ATTACHMENTS,
      APT_DL_ATT_WRK.ATTACHSYSFILENAME,
      APT_DL_ATT_WRK.ATTACHUSERFILE, 2, &retcode);

If (&retcode = %Attachment_Success) Then
   &keys_rec = CreateRecord(Record.APT_DL_ATTACH);

   &keys_rec.EMPLID.Value = DRIVERS_LIC.EMPLID;
   &keys_rec.DRIVERS_LIC_NBR.Value = DRIVERS_LIC.DRIVERS_LIC_NBR;
   &keys_rec.Delete();

   APT_set_buttons_state(APT_DL_ATT_WRK.ATTACHUSERFILE,
      GetRecord(Record.APT_DL_ATT_WRK));
End-If;
```

Attachments with Document Management Systems

The best place to store attachments is in a document management system like Oracle's Universal Content Management System (UCM). Document management systems support retention policies, indexing, searching, versioning, and many other valuable features.

Document management systems support a variety of integration protocols including WebDAV and web services. Integrating PeopleSoft with UCM, for example, can be as simple as generating the correct HTML links. Adding attachments to UCM can be facilitated by adding a link to the appropriate UCM folder and document upload page. You can display UCM attachments in PeopleSoft by consuming a UCM search web service, providing a transaction's keys as parameters. Opening attachments is just as trivial. The UCM search web service returns a document ID, and all you need to do is provide users with a link to that UCM document.

Another way to integrate with a document management system is to modify the File Attachment API. The File Attachment API offers only record and FTP repositories. As you have seen, however, we rarely call the native PeopleCode attachment functions directly. Rather, we wrap the native functions in custom functions that enhance the functionality of the native functions. This abstraction gives us a hook to create additional URL protocol handlers. For example, you could customize the `APT_add_attachment` function to handle URLs prefixed with webdav:// or ucm://.

You should now be able to add, view, and delete attachments from the Driver's License Data component.

Adding Multiple Attachments per Transaction

You can add multiple attachments to a transaction by deviating slightly from the Web Assets example. In the Web Assets example, we added the attachment fields and buttons to level 0. If you want to add multiple attachments to a transaction, create a new grid or scroll area within the level that will hold the attachments and add the attachment fields and buttons to that new grid or scroll area.

When you create the record containing the transaction's keys, make sure you have all the keys of the higher-level scroll area and don't add `FILE_ATTACH_SBR`. Instead, add `ATTACHSYSFILENAME` and `ATTACHUSERFILE` directly. By making `ATTACHSYSFILENAME` a key field, you will effectively make your attachment record a child record of the higher-level scroll area. Remember the rule for parent/child row sets:

> A child row set contains all of the key fields of the parent row set plus at least one additional field.

Processing Attachments

The ability to store records with transactions is of great value and can certainly expedite manual transaction processing when all supporting documentation is attached to the transaction. But there are other uses for attachments. For example, rather than requiring users to save imported files into specific directories or save them in specific formats, you can provide a friendlier user experience by offering users the ability to upload imported files to run control records.

Accessing Attachments

After a user uploads a file, we need a way to access that file. PeopleSoft provides the GetAttachment function for this specific purpose. The following listing contains the GetAttachment function signature:

```
GetAttachment(URL.URLID, &AttachSysFileName, &LocalFileName
      [, &LocalDirEnvVar[, &PreserveCase]])
```

Like the attachment functions we used earlier in this chapter, the GetAttachment function requires a URL, which identifies the attachment storage location. The function also requires a pointer to the attachment within that storage location (AttachSysFileName). The purpose of this function is to copy a file from the attachment repository into the local file system. The local file system is the app server, process scheduler server, or even your workstation (if you are running an App Engine locally). In order to copy the file to the local system, the GetAttachment function needs a local filename. Use the &LocalFileName parameter to specify the target filename on the local file system.

Rather than hard-code the local file path, the GetAttachment function allows you to specify an environment variable using the &LocalDirEnvVar parameter. For example, you could specify TEMP as the environment variable to have GetAttachment write files into your local temp directory.

Working Directories

Some file systems use / as the path delimiter, and some use \. Some file systems, like Windows, use drive letters; other file systems do not. Considering that a process may run on a Solaris app server, a Linux process scheduler server, or a Windows process scheduler server, how should you code the file path? The process scheduler actually maintains a table with file path information. For example, if you want GetAttachment to place files in a process's designated file location, then execute the following SQL:

```
SELECT PRCSOUTPUTDIR
  FROM PSPRCSPARMS
 WHERE PRCSINSTANCE = %ProcessInstance
```

Files placed in this directory by an App Engine will be available to the user through the View Log/Trace link in the Process Monitor.

Likewise, the application server has a couple of standard environment variables you can use to create files in specific locations. For example, PS_FILEDIR and PS_SERVDIR point to file storage locations on the application server. Your server administrator can create additional environment variables as needed.

Another method for creating parameterized file paths is to use a database table. The benefit of the environment variable approach over the table-driven approach is that multiple servers on various operating systems will share the same database.

Some file functions, such as GetFile, do not use environment variables. When using these functions, you can still access the value of environment variables by using the PeopleCode functions GetEnv and ExpandEnvVar.

Storing Attachments

PutAttachment is the non-user interface complement to AddAttachment. It allows you to add files to an attachment storage location in batch processes or even integrations. If you add attachments to transactions using PutAttachment and want users to be able to view those attachments online, be sure to update the transaction's ATTACHSYSFILENAME and ATTACHUSERFILE fields.

The PutAttachment function has syntax similar to the GetAttachment function:

```
PutAttachment(URL.URLID, &AttachSysFileName, &LocalFileName
      [, &LocalDirEnvVar[, &PreserveCase]])
```

PutAttachment is best used with integrations, implementations, and migrations.

Implementing File Attachment Validation

With the exception of file size constraints, the delivered File Attachment API offers little in the form of file attachment file type and content validation. Nevertheless, you can write your own file attachment validation routines.

Filename Validation

The attachment functionality we added to the Driver's License Data component expects image files. Therefore, it is appropriate to verify the uploaded file's type. Following a common file-validation technique, we can compare the attachment file's extension against a list of valid image file extensions.

The following code listing is a modified version of the Driver's License Data ATTACHADD FieldChange PeopleCode stored in the APT_DL_ATT_WRK record. Modifications are displayed in bold type. This listing verifies that the uploaded file's extension is within a list of acceptable image file extensions.

```
Declare Function APT_add_attachment PeopleCode
      APT_ATTACH_FUNC.ATTACHADD FieldFormula;
Declare Function APT_set_buttons_state
      PeopleCode APT_ATTACH_FUNC.ATTACHADD FieldFormula;

Local Record &keys_rec = CreateRecord(Record.APT_DL_ATTACH);
Local array of string &extensions;
Local string &ext;
Local string &file_name;
Local number &ext_idx = 0;
Local boolean &is_image_file = False;

&keys_rec.EMPLID.Value = DRIVERS_LIC.EMPLID;
&keys_rec.DRIVERS_LIC_NBR.Value = DRIVERS_LIC.DRIVERS_LIC_NBR;

Local number &retcode = APT_add_attachment(URL.APT_DL_ATTACHMENTS,
      0, True, &keys_rec, "", APT_DL_ATT_WRK.ATTACHSYSFILENAME,
      APT_DL_ATT_WRK.ATTACHUSERFILE, False, "", True);
```

```
If (&retcode = %Attachment_Success) Then

   REM ** Validate file name;
   &file_name = APT_DL_ATT_WRK.ATTACHUSERFILE;
   &extensions = Split("bmp gif jpeg jpg png tif tiff");

   While &extensions.Next(&ext_idx)
      &ext = &extensions [&ext_idx];
      If (&ext = Lower(Right(&file_name, Len(&ext)))) Then
         &is_image_file = True;
         Break;
      End-If;
   End-While;

   If (&is_image_file) Then

      REM ** Populate original values. See Record.Save in PeopleBooks;
      If ( Not &keys_rec.SelectByKey( False)) Then
         REM ** if row not found, SelectByKey will reset key values;
         &keys_rec.EMPLID.Value = DRIVERS_LIC.EMPLID;
         &keys_rec.DRIVERS_LIC_NBR.Value = DRIVERS_LIC.DRIVERS_LIC_NBR;
      End-If;

      &keys_rec.ATTACHSYSFILENAME.Value =
            APT_DL_ATT_WRK.ATTACHSYSFILENAME;
      &keys_rec.ATTACHUSERFILE.Value =
            APT_DL_ATT_WRK.ATTACHUSERFILE;

      If (&keys_rec.Save()) Then
         APT_set_buttons_state(APT_DL_ATT_WRK.ATTACHUSERFILE,
               GetRecord(Record.APT_DL_ATT_WRK));
      Else
         MessageBox(0, "", 0, 0,
               "Failed to save the attachment to the database");
         REM ** remove orphaned attachment from the database;
         &retcode = DeleteAttachment(URL.APT_DL_ATTACHMENTS,
               APT_DL_ATT_WRK.ATTACHSYSFILENAME);
      End-If;
   Else
      MessageBox(0, "", 0, 0,
            "This component only accepts image files. " |
            "Please attach an image file.");

      REM ** remove orphaned attachment from the database;
      &retcode = DeleteAttachment(URL.APT_DL_ATTACHMENTS,
            APT_DL_ATT_WRK.ATTACHSYSFILENAME);

      REM ** reset the file attachment work fields;
      APT_DL_ATT_WRK.ATTACHSYSFILENAME.SetDefault();
      APT_DL_ATT_WRK.ATTACHUSERFILE.SetDefault();
   End-If;
End-If;
```

This code provides minimal assurance as to the type of file uploaded. A full validation would involve reading and validating the contents of the attached image file.

Just like the file size constraint provided by the File Attachment API, the preceding filename validation code does not execute until after the image is transferred to the server. Depending on the file's size and network conditions, this could have a significant impact on the user's experience.

File Contents Validation

If the uploaded file is a text file, we can validate the contents of that file by copying the file to a temporary file and investigating its contents. For example, if you expect an XML file that conforms to a specific Document Type Definition (DTD), you can use the `GetAttachment` PeopleCode function to copy the attachment to a temporary file and then use the PeopleCode `XmlDoc` object to validate that XML.

Unfortunately, PeopleCode does not offer methods for reading binary files. The Java language, however, provides full support for binary files, as well as support for specific binary file formats. You will learn how to integrate Java with PeopleCode in Chapter 9. Many database platforms also contain functions for reading binary data from database tables. If your storage location is a database record definition, you may be able to use your database's procedural language to validate the contents of attachments.

Conclusion

This chapter walked through two File Attachment API examples and provided some file attachment and PeopleCode tips. Armed with this new understanding of the File Attachment API, you will be able to add attachments to any PeopleSoft component.

You will see references to this chapter in several chapters that follow. In Chapters 5, 6, and 7, we will add new web assets to the Web Assets component.

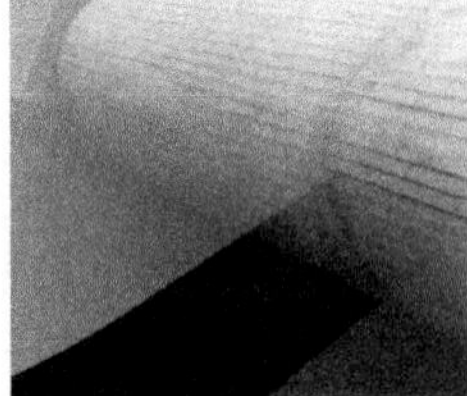

CHAPTER 3

Approval Workflow Engine

urchase requisitions, training requests, and employee transfers are some of the many enterprise transactions that require approval. Some transactions, such as training requests, may require a single-level manager or supervisor approval; other transactions may use complex routing rules to determine the approval path. For example, a purchase requisition for an item costing $10,000 or less may require no more than a manager's signature, whereas a purchase requisition for a single item costing $100,000 or more may require a senior vice president's approval. Prior to electronic workflow systems, the approval process consisted of signed forms routed from one approver to the next.

Prior to PeopleTools 8.48 and PeopleSoft 9.0, PeopleSoft applications used a PeopleTools approval framework called Virtual Approver. In PeopleTools 8.48, PeopleSoft introduced the Approval Workflow Engine (AWE). While some Financials and Supply Chain modules adopted AWE as early as version 8.8, the 9.0 version was the first to extensively use AWE.

AWE began as a custom workflow engine for PeopleSoft's Supply Chain Management module in version 8.8. The Supply Chain team continued to improve the workflow engine through release 8.9. In 9.0, many application development teams switched from Virtual Approver and legacy workflow to the new AWE. Since AWE is now a core component of PeopleTools 8.48, you can use it with any PeopleSoft application version.

At the time of this writing, the best available documentation for AWE is the "Approval Workflow Engine (AWE) for HCM 9.0" and the "Delegation Framework for HCM v. 9.0" red papers available from Oracle's support site, http://support.oracle.com. These red papers complement this chapter.

In this chapter, you will learn how to workflow-enable transactions, reduce your modification footprint, and use AWE from web services and batch processes.

The screenshots and navigation presented in this chapter were taken from a PeopleSoft HRMS 9.0 application. Even though AWE is a PeopleTools component that exists in every PeopleTools 8.48 and higher PeopleSoft application, the menu navigation for AWE metadata is application-specific. In HCM, the menu navigation for AWE is under Set Up HRMS | Common Definitions | Approvals. In Financials, it is under Set Up Financials | Supply Chain | Common Definitions | Approvals.

Workflow-Enabling Transactions

Workflow-enabling a transaction is a joint effort between developers and functional experts. Once a developer creates some supporting definitions, a functional expert can configure notifications and complex approval rules. This contrasts with the prior PeopleTools workflow engine, which required App Designer access to design and implement workflow activities, steps, rules, and routings.

Workflow-enabling a transaction consists of the following tasks:

- Create supporting definitions: record, SQL, and application class definitions.
- Configure metadata.
- Modify the source transaction.

In Chapter 2, we created a Web Asset component. Continuing that example, we want to add the requirement that prior to using a web asset, a member of the Portal Administrator group must approve the content and the web asset use case. In this chapter, we will use AWE to enhance the Web Assets page to ensure a web asset is approved before making it available for use.

Creating Supporting Definitions

AWE uses queries, SQL definitions, and application classes to provide data and business logic for routing and notifications. It also uses custom record definitions to store information about the state of an approval.

Cross-Reference Record

Transactions are composed of header and detail values. A *transaction* encompasses all of the data that represents a single unit. We identify a transaction through its header values. The level 0 scroll area, for example, is a transaction's header record. Level 1 and all the levels below it make up the transaction's detail records. Approving a transaction, therefore, requires approving the transaction header.

AWE maintains approval information in its own transaction tables. The link between AWE's transaction tables and the main transaction table is called the *cross-reference record* and is defined as containing the subrecord `PTAFAW_XREF_SBR` plus the transaction's keys. The cross-reference record is similar to the attachment repository record we used in the previous chapter, in that we create the record and point PeopleTools to the record, but we never actually modify data within the record.

Figure 3-1 shows our new web assets cross-reference record, named `APT_WA_AWE_XREF`. This will serve as the cross-reference record between web asset transactions and the corresponding AWE transaction. Save and build the `APT_WA_AWE_XREF` record.

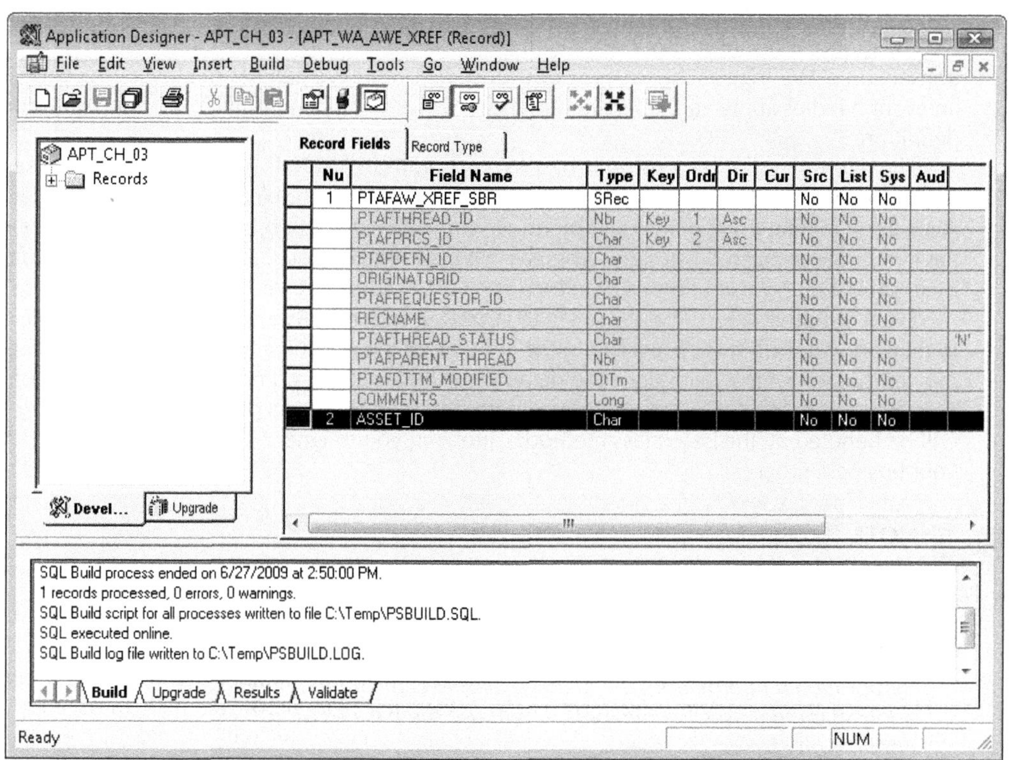

FIGURE 3-1. *Web assets cross-reference record*

Transaction Approval Thread ID

Each process has its own set of thread IDs. The AWE framework stores these thread IDs in a record named PTAFAW_IDS. Since we created a new cross-reference record, we will need to add a new row to the thread ID table, PTAFAW_IDS. AWE uses the thread ID as part of the cross-reference table's primary key. Since PeopleTools does not provide a user interface for maintaining thread IDs, we will need to add a new thread ID value using SQL. The following SQL inserts a new counter into the PTAFAW_IDS record:

```
INSERT INTO PS_PTAFAW_IDS(PTAFCOUNTERNAME, PTAFAWCOUNTER)
VALUES ('APT_WA_AWE_XREF', 1);
/
COMMIT
/
```

The value you provide for PTAFAWCOUNTER is the initial value to be used for thread IDs. Consider it similar to the first check number when opening a new checking account. Once you set the value, you can never go back and change it. For a new checking account, you might choose to start your checks with a number like 1000, so recipients won't question the integrity of your checking account. With thread IDs, the starting number doesn't matter as much. Therefore, it seems reasonable to start thread IDs at 1. After we create our first web asset approval transaction, the AWE framework will begin incrementing this value.

Approval Event Handlers

AWE triggers events throughout the approval cycle. For example, when a user submits a workflow transaction, AWE triggers the OnProcessLaunch event. We can handle these events by creating an event handler application class and registering the event handler with the approval process definition.

The event handler pattern used by AWE is common to OOP. Java, for example, uses registered event handler callbacks to notify listeners as events arise. The difference between the AWE implementation and a Java implementation is that a Java object that triggers events may have multiple registered listeners, whereas AWE allows only one. At the end of this chapter, I will show you how to add this functionality with a custom event handler.

Event handlers are subclasses of PTAF_CORE:ApprovalEventHandler. The AWE framework will call the appropriate event handler method as the event occurs during the course of a transaction's life cycle. Since the default handler methods do not contain any business logic, you need to implement only the events required for your business process. The rest of the events will be handled by the base class methods, allowing you to ignore events that are irrelevant to your business process.

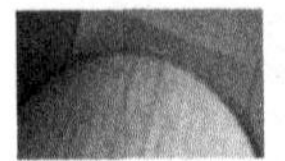

NOTE

The HRMS-specific documentation recommends subclassing the HMAF_AWE:Wrappers:ApprovalEventHandler class instead. Other modules and PeopleSoft applications may have similar recommendations. Consult your application-specific documentation for additional information. Since this example is meant to apply to any application that uses PeopleTools, it will use the base PTAF_CORE application classes.

The following code listing contains declarations for the common event handler methods. For a complete list, use App Designer to open the `PTAF_CORE:ApprovalEventHandler` application class's PeopleCode editor.

```
method OnProcessLaunch(&appInst As PTAF_CORE:ENGINE:AppInst);
method OnStepComplete(&stepinst As PTAF_CORE:ENGINE:StepInst);
method OnStepPushback(&userinst As PTAF_CORE:ENGINE:UserStepInst);
method OnStepReactivate(&stepinst As PTAF_CORE:ENGINE:StepInst);
method OnFinalHeaderDeny(&appinst As PTAF_CORE:ENGINE:AppInst);
method OnHeaderDeny(&userinst As PTAF_CORE:ENGINE:UserStepInst);
method OnHeaderApprove(&appinst As PTAF_CORE:ENGINE:AppInst);
```

Notice that each of these event handlers has some type of instance parameter. The type of instance depends on the type of event. An approval event, for example, will receive an approval instance. A step event, which occurs when an approval moves from one step to the next in the approval chain, will receive an approval step instance. The instance parameter contains properties and methods allowing you access to relevant AWE and transaction information. For example, each of the instance classes has a thread property. The thread property corresponds to the cross-reference record we created earlier. Since the cross-reference record contains transaction header key values, event handlers have full access to the underlying transaction.

In our example, we will implement approve and deny handlers. These handlers will update the status of a web asset. A web asset should not be available for use unless it is in approved status. Since AWE maintains approval history, it isn't necessary to maintain a transaction-specific approved or denied flag. Nevertheless, I recommend maintaining an approval flag for convenience. Whether you are writing reports, processes, or integration points, you may not want to join your transactions to the AWE tables just to determine the approval state of a transaction.

The only accurate way to maintain an approval flag is through an approval event handler. In this chapter, we will use the `OnHeaderApprove` and `OnHeaderDeny` event handler methods to maintain the transaction record's approval flag. This event-driven design contrasts with the legacy workflow strategy, which involved updating the approval flag within an approval component. A key difference between AWE and legacy workflow is that AWE does not require a component, whereas the legacy workflow engine required a component to update workflow transactions.

Let's create our web asset event handler. We'll need a new application package, as discussed in Chapter 1. Select File | New from the App Designer menu bar. When prompted for a definition type, select Application Package. Save this new application package with the name `APT_WA_AWE`. This new package will contain event handlers, user lists, criteria definitions, and many other AWE-related application classes. After saving the new application package, add a new class named `WebAssetAppr_EventHandler`. Add the following PeopleCode to this new class:

```
import PTAF_CORE:ApprovalEventHandler;

import PTAF_CORE:ENGINE:AppInst;
import PTAF_CORE:ENGINE:UserStepInst;
import PTAF_CORE:ENGINE:Thread;

class WebAssetAppr_EventHandler extends PTAF_CORE:ApprovalEventHandler
   method OnHeaderApprove(&appinst As PTAF_CORE:ENGINE:AppInst);
   method OnHeaderDeny(&userinst As PTAF_CORE:ENGINE:UserStepInst);
private
```

```
   method UpdateStatus(&thread As PTAF_CORE:ENGINE:Thread,
         &status As string);

end-class;

method OnHeaderApprove
   /+ &appinst as PTAF_CORE:ENGINE:AppInst +/
   /+ Extends/implements
      PTAF_CORE:ApprovalEventHandler.OnHeaderApprove +/
   %This.UpdateStatus(&appinst.thread, "A");
end-method;

method OnHeaderDeny
   /+ &userinst as PTAF_CORE:ENGINE:UserStepInst +/
   /+ Extends/implements
      PTAF_CORE:ApprovalEventHandler.OnHeaderDeny +/
   %This.UpdateStatus(&userinst.thread, "D");
end-method;

method UpdateStatus
   /+ &thread as PTAF_CORE:ENGINE:Thread, +/
   /+ &status as String +/

   /* &thread.recname contains the header record name, but we are
    * using a sibling record so we have to hard code the record name
    */
   Local Record &asset_rec = CreateRecord(Record.APT_WA_APPR);

   /* &thread.rec contains the cross reference record which has
    * header record keys
    */
   &thread.rec.CopyFieldsTo(&asset_rec);

   /* If we were updating the header record, then we could use the
    * following convenience method.
    */
   REM &thread.SetAppKeys(&asset_rec);

   &asset_rec.SelectByKey();
   &asset_rec.GetField(Field.APPR_STATUS).Value = &status;

   &asset_rec.Update();
end-method;
```

Let's walk through this code segment by segment, starting with the imports. We must import the base class, `PTAF_CORE:ApprovalEventHandler`. The *instance* imports, `PTAF_CORE:ENGINE:AppInst` and `PTAF_CORE:ENGINE:UserStepInst`, represent various parameters to the event handler's methods. The `PTAF_CORE:ENGINE:Thread` application class provides us with access to the transaction header.

The next segment represents our event handler's application class definition. This looks similar to the class definitions we created in Chapter 1. Of all the methods defined in the superclass, `PTAF_CORE:ApprovalEventHandler`, we declare only the methods (events) we want to handle.

Our approve and deny event handlers use the same PeopleCode and SQL to update the web asset header record. Rather than duplicate this code in each event, we centralize the code in a private method named `UpdateStatus`.

E-Mail Templates

When a developer adds a new value to the Web Assets component, we want the workflow engine to send an e-mail message to members of the Portal Administrator group. The message should look like this:

> Subject: Web Asset Approval
> I created a new web asset named EMPLOYEE_SHELF and would appreciate prompt approval at your earliest convenience. The web asset's details:
>
> Content Type: application/x-shockwave-flash
> Filename: empl-shelf.swf
> Description: The employee shelf is a Flex component based on the DisplayShelf Flex component. This component displays photos of a manager's direct reports in a fashion similar to iTunes cover art.
>
> You may approve this transaction at http://hrms.example.com/psp/hrms/EMPLOYEE/HRMS/c/APT_CUSTOM.APT_WEB_ASSETS.GBL?Page=APT_WEB_ASSETS&Action=U&ASSET_ID=EMPLOYEE_SHELF

This e-mail message contains several pieces of transaction-specific data. AWE allows us to use template bind variables to insert transaction data at runtime. AWE's templating system looks very similar to message catalog bind variables. The following text describes the same e-mail template as the preceding message, except that the transaction information is replaced with bind variables. We will add this template to the AWE metadata soon.

> Subject: Web Asset Approval
> I created a new web asset named `%2` and would appreciate prompt approval at your earliest convenience. The web asset's details:
>
> Content Type: `%3`
> Filename: `%4`
> Description: `%5`
>
> You may approve this transaction at `%1`

E-mail template bind variables correspond to selected fields from a SQL definition, with this difference: The `%1` bind variable is reserved for the approval page URL. Therefore, the SQL statement's column 1 equates to bind variable `%2`.

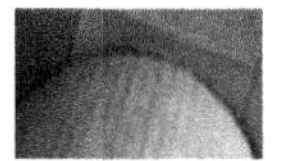

NOTE
Some workflow e-mail messages exist for notification purposes only. If you create a template that should not include a URL, you can leave the `%1` bind variable out of your template.

SQL Joins

PeopleSoft databases offer the following SQL join options:

- WHERE clause criteria joins
- ANSI join syntax

Which is better? It is really a matter of style and personal (or organizational) preference. I find that ANSI join syntax better clarifies the intent of a join by providing a separation between joins and actual criteria. It is easier for me to miss a join field when mixing join statements with actual filter criteria.

PeopleSoft's documentation and source code are full of WHERE clause join examples. Rarely do we see an ANSI join example. In this book, where appropriate, I have used ANSI joins instead of WHERE clause criteria joins to provide you with examples of this alternative join syntax.

The e-mail template identifies transactional data elements. AWE uses SQL definitions to provide data for each template variable except %1. An AWE e-mail template SQL definition must return a column for each bind variable except %1, and must contain SQL bind parameters for each transaction header key field.

The following SQL selects the transaction values required by this template. Create this SQL definition in App Designer and name it APT_WA_EMAIL_BIND.

```
SELECT WA.ASSET_ID
     , WA.MIMETYPE
     , ATT.ATTACHUSERFILE
     , WA.DESCR
  FROM PS_APT_WEB_ASSETS WA
 INNER JOIN PS_APT_WA_ATTACH ATT
    ON WA.ASSET_ID = ATT.ASSET_ID
 WHERE WA.ASSET_ID = :1
```

To create an e-mail template, open your browser and log in to your PeopleSoft application. Navigate to PeopleTools | Workflow | Notifications | Generic Templates and add the new value APT_WebAsset_AwaitingAppr. Use Figure 3-2 as a guide for creating this template.

After adding text to this template, fill in the Template Variables grid with a description of each of the bind variables. This will serve as documentation for you and others who may need to modify this template at a later time.

While we are here, let's create Approve and Deny notification templates.

For the approved request template, add the value APT_WebAsset_Approved and this message:

Sender: <person who approved web asset>
Subject: Web Asset Approved
I approved the new web asset named %2. You can view this transaction at %1.

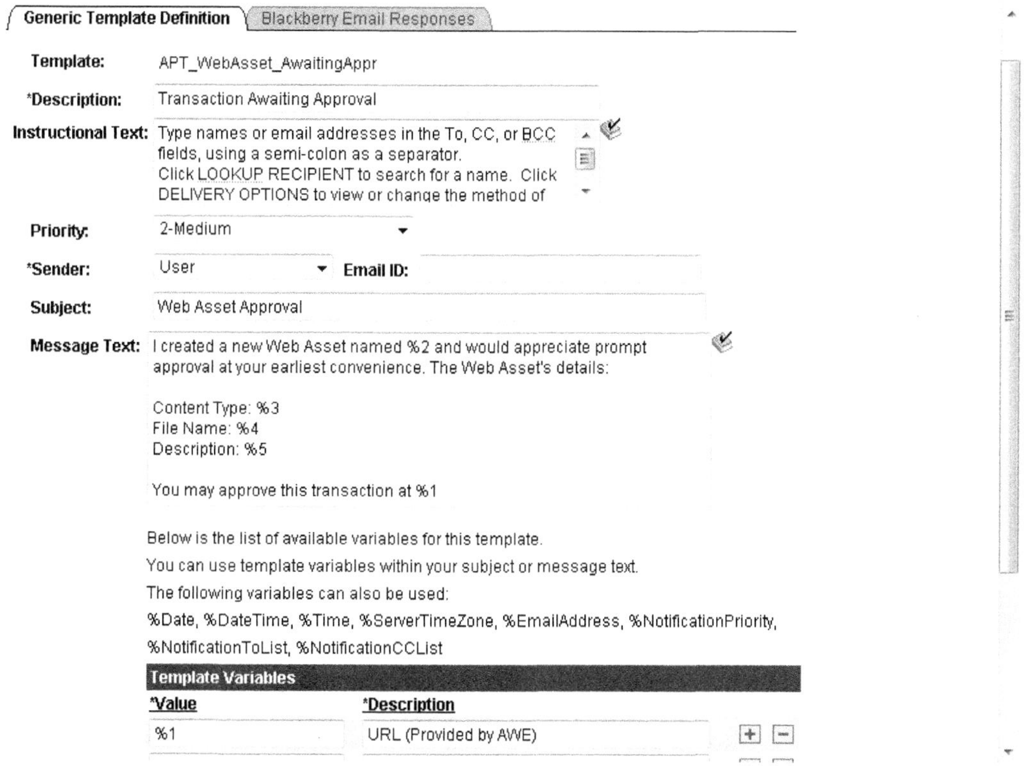

Generic Template Definition | Blackberry Email Responses

Template: APT_WebAsset_AwaitingAppr
*Description: Transaction Awaiting Approval
Instructional Text: Type names or email addresses in the To, CC, or BCC fields, using a semi-colon as a separator. Click LOOKUP RECIPIENT to search for a name. Click DELIVERY OPTIONS to view or change the method of
Priority: 2-Medium
*Sender: User Email ID:
Subject: Web Asset Approval
Message Text: I created a new Web Asset named %2 and would appreciate prompt approval at your earliest convenience. The Web Asset's details:

Content Type: %3
File Name: %4
Description: %5

You may approve this transaction at %1

Below is the list of available variables for this template.
You can use template variables within your subject or message text.
The following variables can also be used:
%Date, %DateTime, %Time, %ServerTimeZone, %EmailAddress, %NotificationPriority, %NotificationToList, %NotificationCCList

Template Variables

*Value	*Description
%1	URL (Provided by AWE)

FIGURE 3-2. *Web asset approval request e-mail template*

For the denied request template, add the value `APT_WebAsset_Denied` and this message:

Sender: <person who denied web asset>
Subject: Web Asset Denied
I denied your request to approve the new web asset named `%2`. Please feel free to contact me if you have questions.

You can view this transaction at `%1`.

Since both of these templates contain the same bind variables, they can share the same SQL definition. Create a SQL definition in App Designer named `APT_WA_EMAIL_NOTIFY_BIND` that has the following SQL:

```
SELECT :1
  FROM PS_INSTALLATION
```

Unlike the approval request template, our notification templates require only transaction keys. Rather than waste CPU cycles searching for values in transaction tables, we can move the transaction key bind values into the `SELECT` clause, and then specify PeopleSoft's common one-row table, `PS_INSTALLATION`, in the `FROM` clause.

User Lists

When a transaction is submitted to the AWE, it needs to know the intended recipients. We identify the intended recipient through a definition called a *user list*. User lists define a collection of operator IDs. Each application delivers a set of predefined user lists based on transaction data within that application. For example, the HRMS application delivers user lists generated from the organization's direct reports hierarchy.

We can create user lists from roles, SQL definitions, queries, or application classes. Roles provide the simplest configuration but the least flexibility (unless you are using dynamic roles). Queries and SQL definitions provide more flexibility because they allow you to use SQL logic to select a list of operator IDs. When using queries as user lists, be sure to save the query as a *process* query, rather than the standard *user* query.

Of the user list types, application classes offer the most flexibility. Through SQL and PeopleCode objects, application classes can combine and/or evaluate the results of the other three types of user lists. Application class user lists offer one more significant feature: a hook into the approval process. By using an application class, you can update other transactions, log information about the approval process, or even execute a web service. By convention, however, it is best to keep user lists as user lists, and use event handlers to perform other operations.

For demonstration purposes, we will use an application class user list. Application class user lists must conform to the following contract:

- They must extend the base class `PTAF_CORE:DEFN:UserListBase`.
- They must implement the method `GetUsers`.
- They must return an `array of string` (the array containing operator IDs).

Let's write a user list application class that returns members of the Portal Administrator role. For demonstration purposes, we will filter the results to even rows only.

To get started, create a new application class in the application package `APT_WA_AWE` and name it `WebAsset_ApprUserList`. The code for this class follows:

```
import PTAF_CORE:DEFN:UserListBase;

class WebAsset_ApprUserList extends PTAF_CORE:Defn:UserListBase
   method WebAsset_ApprUserList(&rec_ As Record);
   method GetUsers(&aryPrevOpr_ As array of string,
         &thread_ As Record) Returns array of string;
end-class;

method WebAsset_ApprUserList
   /+ &rec_ as Record +/
   %Super = create PTAF_CORE:DEFN:UserListBase(&rec_);
end-method;

method GetUsers
   /+ &aryPrevOpr_ as Array of String, +/
   /+ &thread_ as Record +/
```

```
   /+ Returns Array of String +/
   /+ Extends/implements PTAF_CORE:DEFN:UserListBase.GetUsers +/
   Local array of string &oprid_arr = CreateArrayRept("", 0);
   Local SQL &admin_sql = CreateSQL("SELECT ROLEUSER " |
         "FROM PSROLEUSER WHERE ROLENAME = 'Portal Administrator'");
   Local string &oprid;
   Local number &counter = 1;

   While &admin_sql.Fetch(&oprid)
      If (Mod(&counter, 2) = 0) Then
         &oprid_arr.Push(&oprid);
      End-If;
      &counter = &counter + 1;
   End-While;

   Return &oprid_arr;
end-method;
```

The `WebAsset_ApprUserList` constructor takes a record parameter. AWE will pass a pointer to the user list record definition at runtime. The record parameter is the `PTAFUSER_LIST` row containing the user list's AWE metadata. Generally speaking, you don't need to do anything with this record except pass it on to the superclass constructor.

The `GetUsers` method parameters provide you with transactional context. The `&aryPrevOpr_` parameter contains a list of all the user IDs that previously approved this transaction. The `&thread_` parameter contains a reference to the cross-reference record, `APT_WA_AWE_XREF`, providing you with access to the transaction's key values.

With our user list application class created, we can log in to PeopleSoft online and configure a user list definition. Navigate to Set Up HRMS | Common Definitions | Approvals | Maintain User Lists and add a new value named `APT_WebAsset_Approvers`. Figure 3-3 provides the rest of the details.

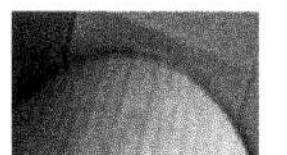

NOTE
Each of the PeopleSoft applications uses slightly different navigation, but most of them place user lists under Set Up [application name] *| Common Definitions | Approvals.*

As you will see later, the user list description will be displayed in the Approval Status Monitor. Therefore, it is important that the description be concise.

Notice the Include Users as Input check box and Transaction Keys as Input check box in Figure 3-3. When specifying an application class as a user list, you do not need to select these check boxes, because the AWE framework will automatically include these values as parameters to the `GetUers` method. If you choose SQL or query for the user list type, these values are passed to the SQL statement as bind parameters. The user passed to the SQL definition or query is the operator ID of the previous approver (or the requester if the approval was just initiated). When adding bind variables to queries or SQL statements, specify transaction keys in the same order in which they occur in the header transaction record. Whether you choose application class, query, or SQL, the previous approver on the first step is always the user who initiated the transaction.

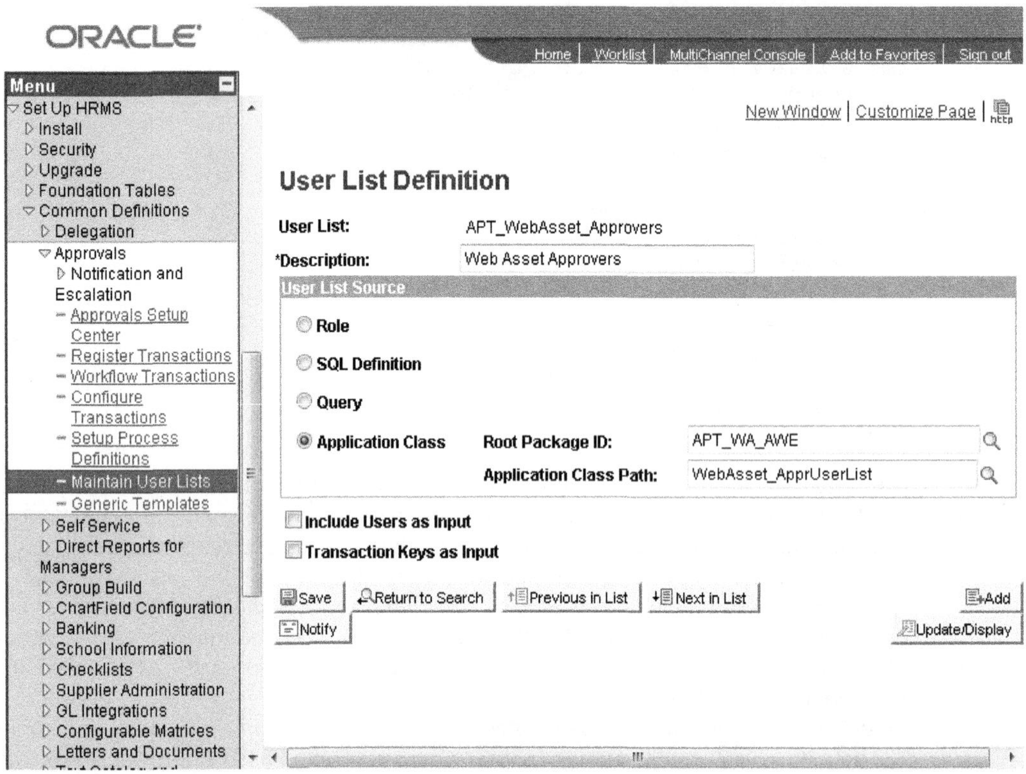

ORACLE
Home | Worklist | MultiChannel Console | Add to Favorites | Sign out
Menu
Set Up HRMS
Install
Security
Upgrade
Foundation Tables
Common Definitions
Delegation
Approvals
Notification and Escalation
Approvals Setup Center
Register Transactions
Workflow Transactions
Configure Transactions
Setup Process Definitions
Maintain User Lists
Generic Templates
Self Service
Direct Reports for Managers
Group Build
ChartField Configuration
Banking
School Information
Checklists
Supplier Administration
GL Integrations
Configurable Matrices
Letters and Documents
New Window | Customize Page |
User List Definition
User List: APT_WebAsset_Approvers
*Description: Web Asset Approvers
User List Source
Role
SQL Definition
Query
Application Class
Root Package ID: APT_WA_AWE
Application Class Path: WebAsset_ApprUserList
Include Users as Input
Transaction Keys as Input
Save | Return to Search | Previous in List | Next in List | Add
Notify | Update/Display

FIGURE 3-3. *`APT_WebAsset_Approvers` user list definition*

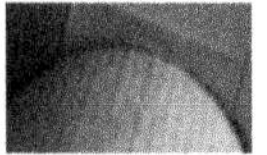

NOTE
The PeopleSoft documentation recommends that you select either Include Users as Input or Transaction Keys as Input, not both.

Configuring the AWE Metadata

Now that we have created the necessary supporting definitions, we can log in to the PeopleSoft application online and create our approval business process.

Registering the Transaction

Navigate to Set Up HRMS | Common Definitions | Approvals | Register Transactions and add a new process ID named `APT_WebAssets`. Specify the description **Web Asset Approval Transaction** and the cross-reference record we created earlier named `APT_WA_AWE_XREF`.

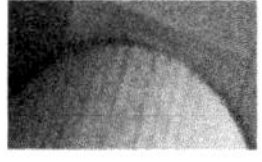

TIP
Many of the applications contain an AWE configuration shortcut collection. For example, in HRMS, navigate to Set Up HRMS | Common Definitions | Approvals | Approvals Setup Center for quick access to all online AWE configuration components.

Expand the Default Approval Component group box to expose its fields. Enter `APT_CUSTOM` for the menu and `APT_WEB_ASSETS` for the component.

Expand the Approval Event Handler Class group box. Set the root package ID to `APT_WA_AWE` and the path to `WebAssetAppr_EventHandler`.

Expand the Transaction Approval Levels group box to display its fields. For the level, choose Header. For this workflow, we want header-level approvals. If you were creating a workflow transaction for line-level approvals, you would choose Line for the level. In the Record (Table) Name field, enter `APT_WEB_ASSETS`. This is the name of our header record. After selecting a record name, the Level Record Key Field Label IDs grid will populate with the key fields from the chosen record. Select a label for each key field. Figure 3-4 shows the AWE process ID for this example.

New Window | Customize Page | http

Register Transactions

Process ID: APT_WebAssets
*Description: Web Asset Approval Transaction
Object Owner ID:
*Cross Reference Table: APT_WA_AWE_XREF

▸ Notification Options

▾ Default Approval Component
*Menu Name: APT_CUSTOM
*Approval Component: APT_WEB_ASSETS

▾ Approval Event Handler Class
Root Package ID: APT_WA_AWE
Path: WebAssetAppr_EventHandler

▸ Approval Status Monitor

▾ Transaction Approval Levels

	*Level	*Record (Table) Name
1	Header	APT_WEB_ASSETS

Level Record Key Field Label IDs

	Record (Table) Name	Field Name	*Field Label ID
1	APT_WEB_ASSETS	ASSET_ID	ASSET_ID

Expand/Collapse All

FIGURE 3-4. *`APT_WebAssets` AWE process ID*

Configuring the Transaction

Navigate to Set Up HRMS | Common Definitions | Approvals | Configure Transactions and select the `APT_WebAssets` process ID, which we created in the previous section.

This is the step where we identify the notification message sent to each participant in the approval process and the event that triggers that notification. The only item required at level 0 in this component is an Approval User Info View value. An Approval User Info View is a standard view that contains the `OPRID` field, as well as fields providing information about a user. AWE uses this information to display approver information in the AWE status monitor. Many PeopleSoft applications deliver application-specific user info views. An HRMS user info view, for example, may display a user's job title and manager. For our purposes, we can use the information provided by `PSOPRDEFN_VW`, a delivered view that derives a user's name from that user's security profile.

In the Events scroll area, we need to add a row for each event this workflow will trigger. Configure the Final Approval, Final Denial, and Route for Approval events as shown in Figures 3-5, 3-6, and 3-7.

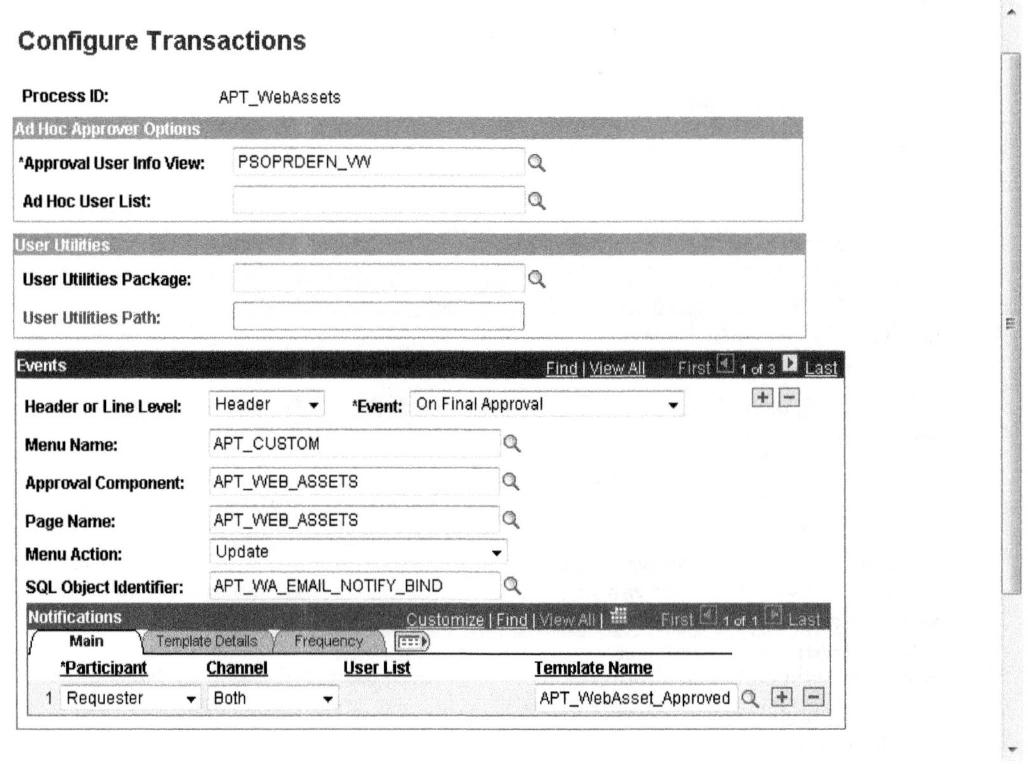

FIGURE 3-5. *Transaction configuration for On Final Approval event*

Configure Transactions

Process ID:	APT_WebAssets

Ad Hoc Approver Options

*Approval User Info View:	PSOPRDEFN_VW
Ad Hoc User List:	

User Utilities

User Utilities Package:	
User Utilities Path:	

Events — Find \| View All — First 2 of 3 Last

Header or Line Level:	Header	*Event:	On Final Denial
Menu Name:	APT_CUSTOM		
Approval Component:	APT_WEB_ASSETS		
Page Name:	APT_WEB_ASSETS		
Menu Action:	Update		
SQL Object Identifier:	APT_WA_EMAIL_NOTIFY_BIND		

Notifications — Customize \| Find \| View All \| — First 1 of 1 Last

Main | Template Details | Frequency

	*Participant	Channel	User List	Template Name
1	Requester	Both		APT_WebAsset_Denied

FIGURE 3-6. *Transaction configuration for On Final Denial event*

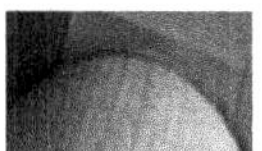

NOTE

For detailed information about the transaction events, see the "Approval Workflow Engine (AWE) for HCM 9.0" red paper available from Oracle's support site.

Setting Up Process Definitions

The next, and final, piece of AWE metadata to configure is the flow of approvals through AWE. This flow is called a *process definition*. A single process ID can contain multiple definitions. AWE provides two methods for differentiating between process definitions:

- Specify the definition ID when triggering the workflow process (hard-coded).
- Use definition criteria configured through the Setup Process Definitions page to determine which definition to apply.

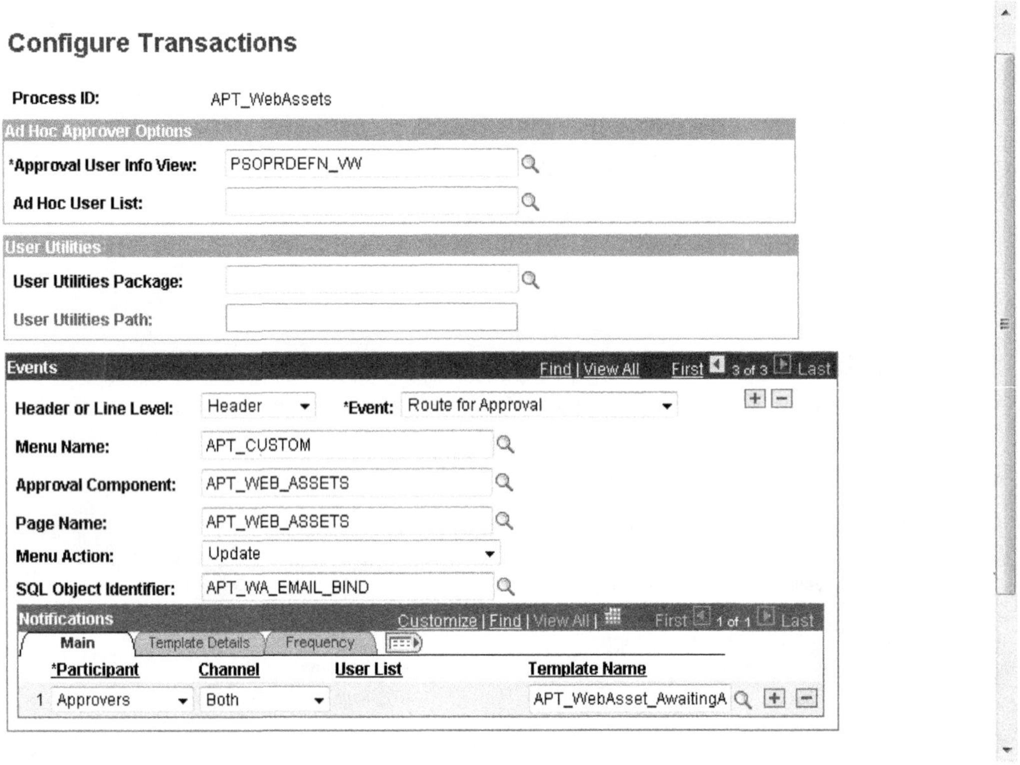

Configure Transactions

Process ID: APT_WebAssets

Ad Hoc Approver Options

***Approval User Info View:** PSOPRDEFN_VW

Ad Hoc User List:

User Utilities

User Utilities Package:

User Utilities Path:

Events Find | View All First 3 of 3 Last

Header or Line Level: Header ***Event:** Route for Approval

Menu Name: APT_CUSTOM

Approval Component: APT_WEB_ASSETS

Page Name: APT_WEB_ASSETS

Menu Action: Update

SQL Object Identifier: APT_WA_EMAIL_BIND

Notifications Customize | Find | View All | First 1 of 1 Last

Main | Template Details | Frequency

	*Participant	Channel	User List	Template Name
1	Approvers	Both		APT_WebAsset_AwaitingA

FIGURE 3-7. *Transaction configuration for Route for Approval event*

While still logged in to PeopleSoft through your web browser, navigate to Set Up HRMS | Common Definitions | Approvals | Setup Process Definitions and select the Add a New Value tab. Select `APT_WebAssets` as the process ID and enter `SHARE` for the definition ID. Ignoring the Details and Criteria links for now, add a description for each level and a user list for step 1. This approval has only one path and one step, as shown in Figure 3-8. If you were setting up an approval with multiple paths and steps, you would add those here. For example, an expense report may require supervisor, director, and auditor approval steps.

For the process definition, you can specify the following criteria:

- **Definition criteria** At runtime, if you don't specify a specific definition, AWE will use the definition criteria to determine which process definition to apply. Providing definition criteria is not required. When we write PeopleCode to submit a transaction to AWE, you will see how to hard-code definition criteria. By using definition criteria, however, you can configure different approvals based on transactional and environmental conditions. For example, you may need to create separate process definitions for different countries or business units.

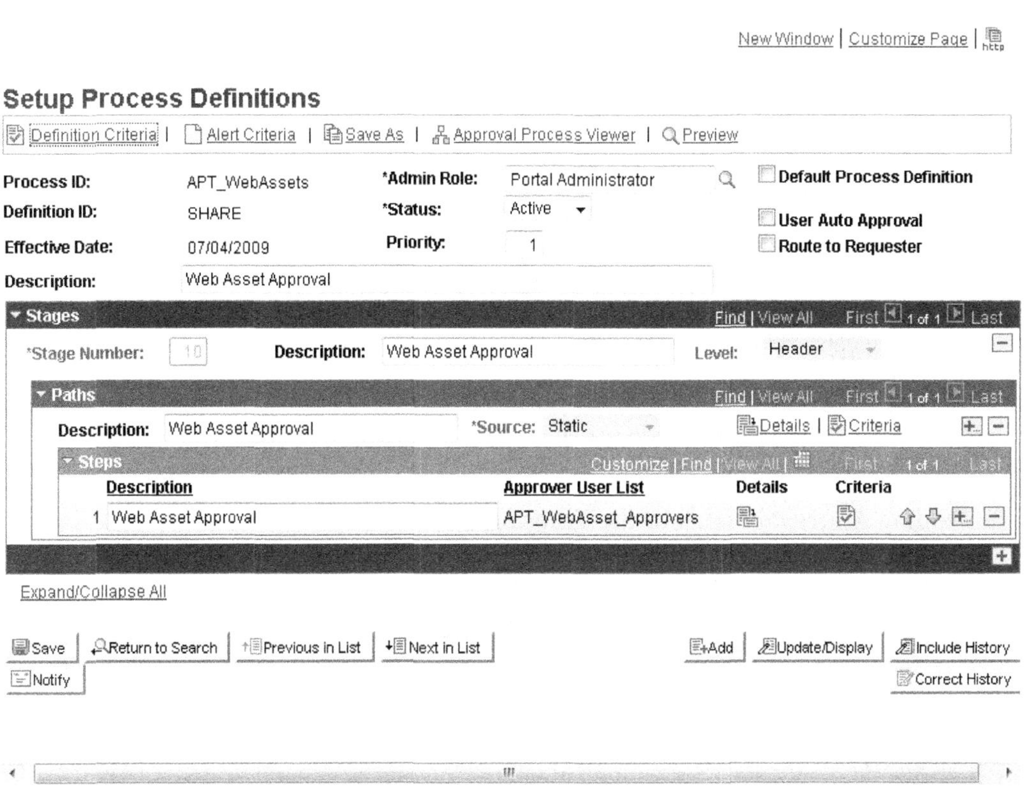

FIGURE 3-8. *`APT_WebAssets` `SHARE` process definition*

- **Path criteria** Some organizations use dollar limits to determine approval paths. For example, if your organization allows supervisors to approve expense reports under $50, requires manager approval for expense reports between $50 and $500, and requires director approval for anything over $500, you can configure those paths here by using path criteria to determine which path to apply.
- **Step criteria** You can use step criteria to determine whether or not to apply a particular step.

For this simple workflow approval, we have no criteria and only one process definition, path, and step. So, for our example, change the Criteria Type setting in the Definition, Paths, and Steps areas to Always True. Figure 3-8 shows a check mark over the criteria icon for each of the process definition's levels as an indicator that the definition, path, and step have criteria.

In addition to the Always True criteria type, AWE offers User Entered and Application Class types. The User Entered type provides a complex business rules editor that allows functional experts to configure criteria based on the state of the transaction. The Application Class type goes even further to provide unlimited criteria opportunities.

Modifying the Transaction

Even though adding workflow functionality to a transaction can be quite invasive, don't let this fact discourage you. When considering the maintenance cost of a modification versus the productivity benefit, be sure to include soft costs, such as how this modification will improve relations between your department and the rest of the organization. Information technology (IT) departments are often searching for ways to improve their reputation within an organization. Providing value-added system enhancements, such as workflow-enabling transactions, is a good place to start.

Even though we are adding workflow functionality to a custom transaction, we will treat it as if it were a delivered transaction to demonstrate techniques for reducing the impact of workflow modifications on delivered transactions.

Adding Approval Fields to the Transaction

By workflow-enabling the web asset transaction, we are saying that a web asset is not available for use until it is approved. Therefore, we will add an approval flag to the transaction to indicate the approval state of the transaction. Following the design pattern established in Chapter 2, we will create a sibling record to store the approval flag. Since we are adding the approval flag to the transaction's header, level 0, we won't have the "More than one data record" concern we experienced with the Driver's License Data component in Chapter 2.

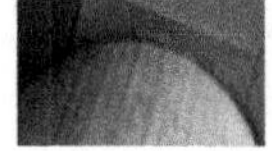

NOTE

As you recall from Chapter 2, we already have a sibling record for storing attachments. This is also a customization, and a suitable place to store the approval fields. For discussion purposes, we will add another sibling record to this transaction.

We will store the approval flag in a new record definition named `APT_WA_APPR`. Create this new record definition and add two fields: `ASSET_ID`, as the key field, and `APPR_STATUS`, with the default constant value P, as shown in Figure 3-9. Save and build the record.

Let's add the approval status field to the page now. Open the `APT_WEB_ASSETS` page in App Designer and drag the `APT_WA_APPR.APPR_STATUS` field from the project workspace onto the page canvas, as shown in Figure 3-10.

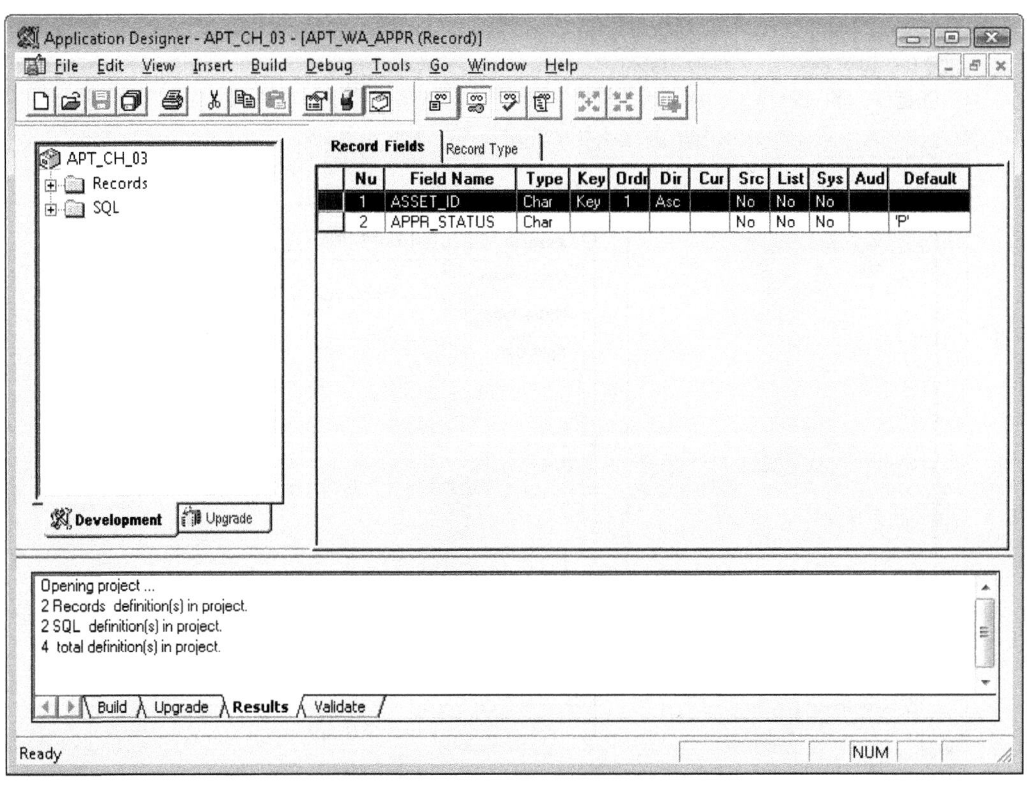

FIGURE 3-9. *`APT_WA_APPR` approval sibling record*

After adding the approval status field to this page, set the field to display only. Later, we will add buttons to this page to change the transaction's approval status. Also, shrink the Comment field to make room for the approval status. We will need to make additional layout changes to this page later when we add the Submit, Approve, and Deny buttons. Figure 3-11 shows the updated Web Assets page.

Do you still have a test transaction from Chapter 2? If so, with your test Web Asset definition open, change a value in one of the fields and then save. If you have database access to your system, select all the rows from the database table `PS_APT_WA_APPR`. Notice that your test asset isn't listed. In fact, if you haven't added any new web assets since adding the `APPR_STATUS` field

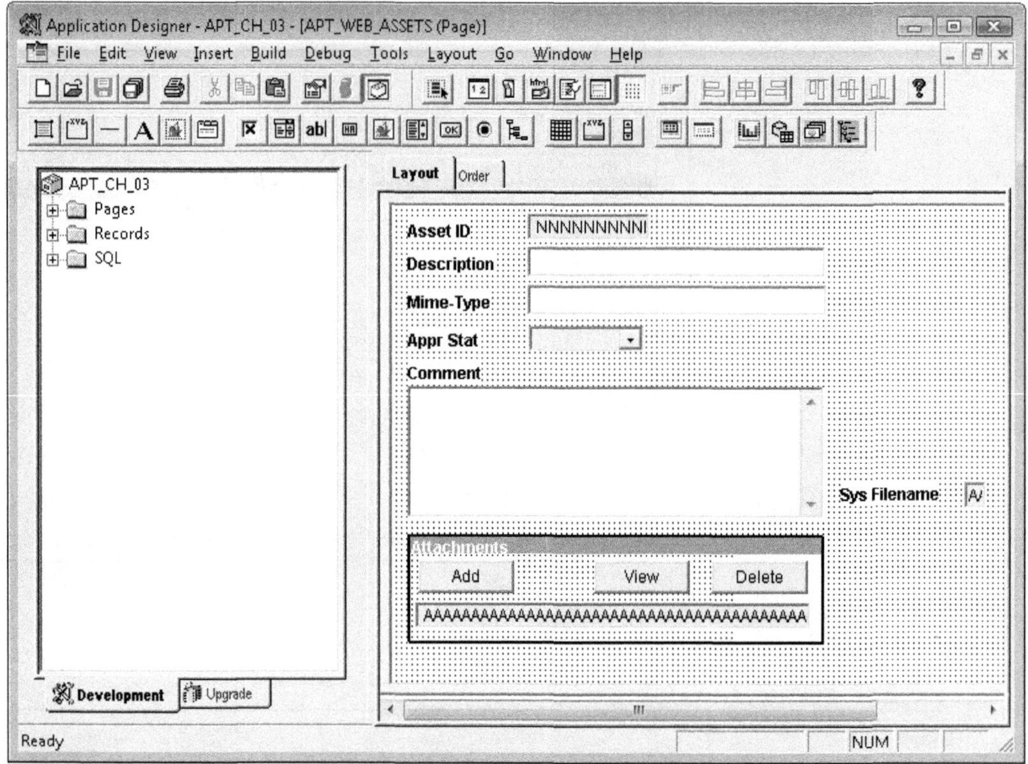

FIGURE 3-10. *`APT_WEB_ASSETS` page definition with the `APPR_STATUS` field*

to the page, there won't be any rows in the `PS_APT_WA_APPR` table. The component processor does not automatically insert new rows into `APT_WA_APPR` when saving existing transactions. It will, however, insert rows for new transactions. This is a bit misleading, because the page displays the `APPR_STATUS` default value of Pending. Therefore, when adding fields to a page in this manner, it is important to consider the impact on existing transactions.

Adding Approval Buttons

Next, let's add workflow buttons to this page. This page requires a Submit button for the transaction creator to initiate the workflow process, as well as Approve and Deny buttons for the approver. PeopleSoft delivers Submit, Approve, and Deny fields designed to be used as buttons, we just need to create a derived/work record to hold them.

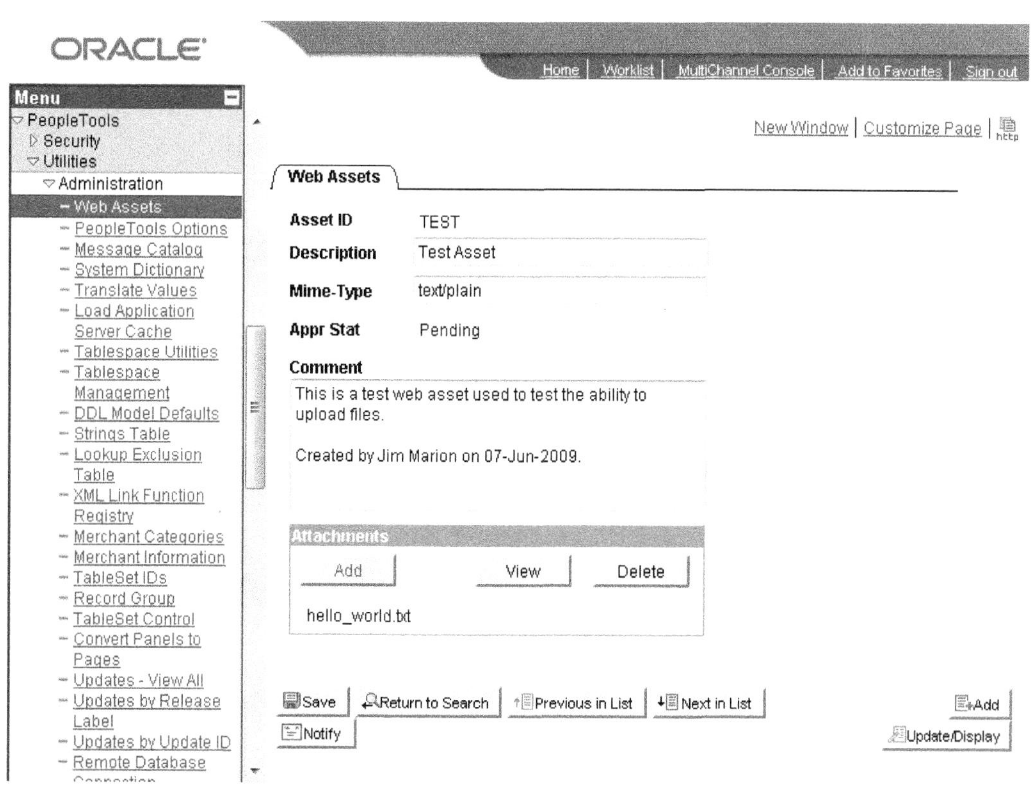

FIGURE 3-11. *`APT_WEB_ASSETS` page with `APPR_STATUS` field*

Open App Designer and create a new record by choosing File | New from the App Designer menu bar. Change the record type to derived/work. Add the fields `APPROVE_BTN`, `DENY_BTN`, and `SUBMIT_BTN`. Save the record as `APT_WA_APPR_WRK`. Figure 3-12 shows this new `APT_WA_APPR_WRK` record definition.

Now add three standard buttons to the page, and then set the buttons' record name to `APT_WA_APPR_WRK` and the field name to the appropriate field. Figure 3-13 is a design view of the page with the three approval buttons.

Later, we will add display logic to hide the Approve and Deny buttons if a viewer is not an approver. Also, we will want to show the Submit button when the transaction is created, but not after the transaction has already been submitted.

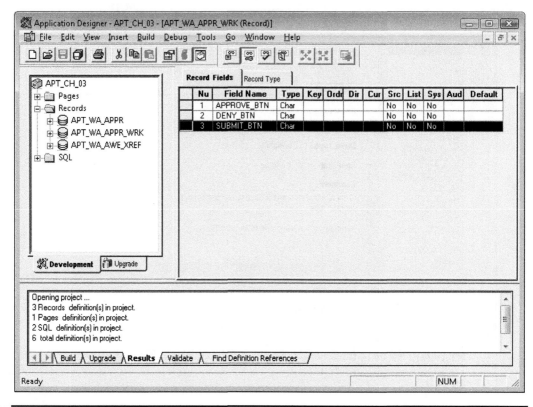

FIGURE 3-12. `APT_WA_APPR_WRK` *derived/work record*

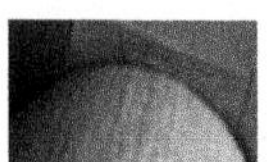

NOTE

In Chapter 2, we created a custom file attachment button state function to avoid hiding user interface elements. Now I am specifically hiding buttons. What's the difference? When using the file attachment buttons, the same user has access to all three buttons. With approvals, the submitting user should not be able to approve the transaction. Therefore, the Approve and Deny buttons are not user interface elements for the submitting user. Likewise, the user approving or denying the transaction is not the submitting user, and therefore should not have the Submit button. This differs from the file attachment example, in that the three buttons are for the file attachment user, whereas the Approve and Deny buttons are not for the submitting user.

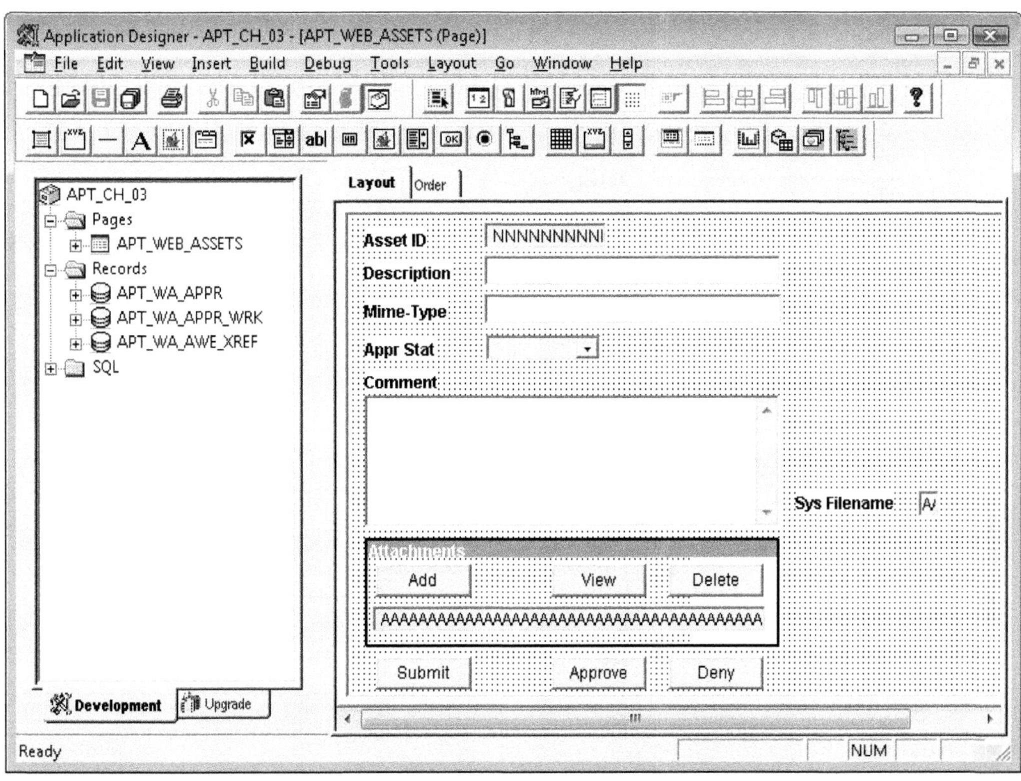

FIGURE 3-13. *Design view of the Web Assets page with approval buttons*

Adding the Approval Status Monitor

A new workflow feature made possible by the AWE framework is the Approval Status Monitor. We will cover several features of this monitor later in this chapter. Adding the Approval Status Monitor to a page is optional.

To make room for the Approval Status Monitor, we will need to rearrange a few more fields. The Approval Status Monitor resides in the subpage `PTAF_MON_SBP`. To add the monitor to a page, choose Insert | Subpage from the App Designer menu. When prompted for a subpage name, choose `PTAF_MON_SBP`. Figure 3-14 shows the `APT_WEB_ASSETS` page after rearranging fields and adding the Approval Status Monitor subpage.

When developing, I like to make small changes and view the results of those changes before moving on to the next change. It is much easier to find and resolve problems when making small, incremental changes, rather than after building an entire customization. Therefore, I encourage you to reload the Web Asset page in your browser after adding the Approval Status Monitor. Don't expect to see anything other than layout changes. The Approval Status Monitor won't display until we add initialization PeopleCode and submit a transaction.

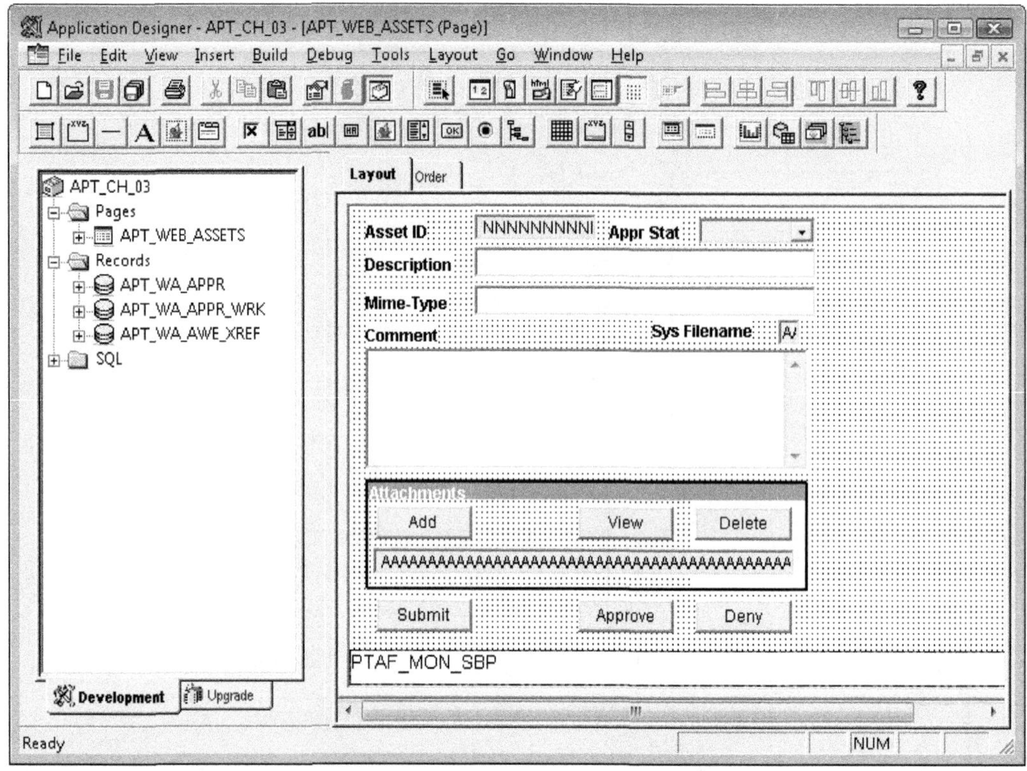

FIGURE 3-14. *Design view of the Web Assets page with the Approval Status Monitor*

We can now write some display logic to update the user interface and business logic to submit, approve, and deny web asset transactions.

Component Buffer Utilities

Users should be able to modify a web asset definition until that definition is submitted. Once submitted, the transaction should change to read-only. One method to disable fields at runtime is to drag each field from the App Designer project workspace outline onto the PeopleCode editor, and then set the `Enabled` property of that field to `False`, as follows:

```
APT_WEB_ASSETS.DESCR.Enabled = False;
APT_WEB_ASSETS.MIMETYPE.Enabled = False;
...
```

I have another technique. Rather than list each field individually, I have some shared FUNCLIB functions that iterate over the fields in a record or list of records and set the `Enabled` state of the field accordingly.

Create a new derived/work record named `APT_FIELD_FUNC` and insert the field `FUNCLIB`. Add the following code to the `FieldFormula` event of the `FUNCLIB` field.

```
/*
 * Set the enabled state of all the fields in &rec to &state. You
 * don't have to call this function directly. For convenience and for
 * clarity, call the enable_fields or disable_fields function.
 */
Function set_fields_state(&rec As Record, &state As boolean)
   Local number &fieldIndex = 1;

   For &fieldIndex = 1 To &rec.FieldCount
      &rec.GetField(&fieldIndex).Enabled = &state;
   End-For;
End-Function;


/*
 * Set the enabled state of all the fields in all the records in &recs
 * to &state. You don't have to call this function directly. For
 * convenience and for clarity, call the enable_records or
 * disable_records function.
 */
Function set_records_state(&recs As array of Record, &state As boolean)
   Local number &recIndex = 0;

   While &recs.Next(&recIndex)
      set_fields_state(&recs [&recIndex], &state);
   End-While;
End-Function;


/*
 * Enable each field in each record in &recsToEnable
 */
Function enable_records(&recsToEnable As array of Record)
   set_records_state(&recsToEnable, False);
End-Function;


/*
 * Disable each field in each record in &recsToDisable
 */
Function disable_records(&recsToDisable As array of Record)
   set_records_state(&recsToDisable, False);
End-Function;
```

```
/*
 * Enable each field in &rec
 */
Function enable_fields(&rec As Record)
   set_fields_state(&rec, True);
End-Function;


/*
 * Disable each field in &rec
 */
Function disable_fields(&rec As Record)
   set_fields_state(&rec, False);
End-Function;
```

Of the functions listed in the preceding code, we will call only the `disable_records` function. The call stack for `disable_records` looks like this:

```
disable_records
   set_records_state
      set_fields_state
```

Since the Web Assets component is relatively small, it would be more efficient to write 5 `RECORD.FIELD.Enabled = False` statements than to write 60 lines of reusable functions. A component with only five data-entry fields and buttons, however, is the exception. Imagine writing `RECORD.FIELD.Enabled = False` statements for all of the fields in the Purchase Order component buffer!

I like code that communicates clearly. The code's purpose should be self-evident. Yes, I did take 60 lines in a FUNCLIB to do what I could have done in 5 lines. But, these 60 lines will take a lot of "noise" out of my event handler code. Rather than writing code like this:

```
APT_WEB_ASSETS.ASSET_ID.Enabled = False
APT_WEB_ASSETS.DESCR.Enabled = False;
APT_WEB_ASSETS.MIMETYPE.Enabled = False;
APT_WEB_ASSETS.COMMENTS.Enabled = False;
FILE_ATTACH_WRK.ATTACHADD.Enabled = False;
FILE_ATTACH_WRK.ATTACHDELETE.Enabled = False;
```

I can write code that looks like this:

```
disable_records(CreateArray(
      GetRecord(Record.APT_WEB_ASSETS),
      GetRecord(Record.FILE_ATTACH_WRK)));
```

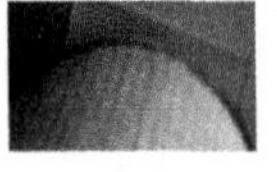

TIP

By combining recursion with the preceding functions, it is possible to disable all the fields in a row and the row's child rowsets regardless of the number of scroll levels.

The PostBuild PeopleCode

AWE provides two top-level application classes for submitting and managing workflow instances:

- `PTAF_CORE:LaunchManager` contains properties and methods for working with transactions prior to submission.
- `PTAF_CORE:ApprovalManager` contains properties and methods for administering submitted transactions.

We will use both application classes in this example.

The AWE developers recommend creating the `LaunchManager` and `ApprovalManager` application classes in the component `PostBuild` event, and then storing those objects as component-scoped variables. Since `PostBuild` happens after the rest of the component events, we can also use `PostBuild` to make any final, AWE-related user interface changes.

If you haven't already done so, log into App Designer and open the `APT_WEB_ASSETS` component. Choose View | View PeopleCode from the App Designer menu. We will start with some declarations:

```
/******** Declarations ********/
import PTAF_CORE:LaunchManager;
import PTAF_CORE:ApprovalManager;

Declare Function update_ui PeopleCode
      APT_WA_APPR_WRK.APPROVE_BTN FieldFormula;


/******** Component Scoped Variables ********/
REM ** Component scoped AWE Launch Manager for submitting;
Component PTAF_CORE:LaunchManager &c_aweLaunchManager;

REM ** Component scoped AWE Approval Manager for approve/deny;
Component PTAF_CORE:ApprovalManager &c_aweApprManager;
```

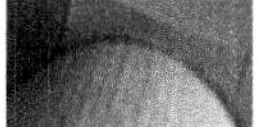

NOTE
I find it difficult to keep track of component- and global-scoped variables. To assist in differentiating local, component, and global variables, I've adopted the prefix c_ for component scope and g_ for global scope.

Our transaction has three workflow action buttons: Submit, Approve, and Deny. Even though a button click triggers a change in the workflow state, we won't update the workflow from the `FieldChange` event. Rather, we will wait until after save processing to submit, approve, or deny the transaction. It would be incorrect to submit a transaction that fails save processing validation (`SaveEdit` and deferred `FieldEdit`) because this would place an invalid transaction in the workflow system.

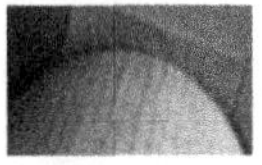

NOTE

Submitting transactions using the `SavePostChange` event is a recommendation that assumes the submitted transaction is loaded into the component buffer. If you write code that submits transactions to AWE using standalone records or transactions unrelated to the component buffer, it is not necessary to wait for `SavePostChange`.

We must keep track of the workflow button that was pressed so we can take the appropriate action in the `SavePostChange` event. We have three buttons and, therefore, three values to track. Since these values are mutually exclusive, we can use a single component-scoped variable to track the selected button. The following PeopleCode segment declares this component-scoped variable. We won't use this variable in the `PostBuild` event, so it is not necessary to declare it here. I do this as a convention only. I find component and global variables difficult to follow because there are so many events that can use a single variable.

```
/*
 * Possible approval actions (button click):
 *   S - submit
 *   A - approve
 *   D - deny
 *
 * Store chosen action in a component variable.
 */
Component string &c_apprAction;
```

Earlier in this chapter, we created a process ID when we registered the Web Assets component with AWE. We must pass this value to the AWE `LaunchManager` and `ApprovalManager` class constructors to identify the appropriate workflow process. The following code creates a constant to hold the process ID:

```
/******** Constants ********/

REM ** Process ID from Register Transactions;
Constant &PROCESS_ID = "APT_WebAssets";
```

With declarations out of the way, we can initialize the `LaunchManager` and `ApprovalManager` and then update the user interface elements.

```
/******** PostBuild mainline code ********/
REM ** pointer to transaction header;
Local Record &headerRec = GetRecord(Record.APT_WEB_ASSETS);


/* Initialize the launch and approval managers. ApprovalManager will
 * need reinitialization on submit
 */
&c_aweLaunchManager = create PTAF_CORE:LaunchManager(&PROCESS_ID,
      &headerRec, %OperatorId);
&c_aweApprManager = create PTAF_CORE:ApprovalManager(&PROCESS_ID,
      &headerRec, %OperatorId);
```

```
/* Uncomment the following line if you don't want AWE to choose the
 * Definition Id based on the preconfigured definition criteria.
 * Definition criteria is maintained using the "Setup Process
 * Definition" component.
 */
REM &c_aweLaunchManager.definition = "SHARE";

update_ui(GetLevel0(), &c_aweLaunchManager, &c_aweApprManager);

REM ** Turn on tracing after Defn ID is set (by AWE or hard coded);
REM &c_aweLaunchManager.appDef.trace_flag = True;
```

NOTE
Both the `ApprovalManager` and `LaunchManager` constructors have an operator ID parameter. It would be possible for AWE to determine the operator ID from the `%OperatorId` system variable (in fact, AWE does store the operator ID of the requesting user). By making the operator ID a constructor parameter, it is possible for users to submit approvals on behalf of other users.

In this example, we allow AWE to choose the appropriate process definition ID based on the criteria we configured in the Setup Process Definitions component. The `LaunchManager` class uses a technique called *lazy initialization* to initialize the process definition prior to using it. You can force AWE to select a process definition ID sooner by accessing the `hasAppDef` property.

The preceding code listing calls a function named `update_ui`. The `PostBuild` and `SavePostChange` events will contain the same user interface logic. To avoid redundancies, we centralize the common user interface code in a function named `update_ui`, which we will create in the next section.

The last line in the previous code listing is commented out. When executed, this line will cause AWE to trace the selection of process definition stages, paths, and steps. Since the AWE trace flag belongs to the `LaunchManager` class (`appDef` property), we must wait until one of the `LaunchManager` properties or methods selects the correct process definition. The `update_ui` function forces the `LaunchManager` to select a process definition by accessing the `submitEnabled` property.

Here is the complete listing of the component's `PostBuild` PeopleCode:

```
/******** Declarations ********/
import PTAF_CORE:LaunchManager;
import PTAF_CORE:ApprovalManager;

Declare Function update_ui PeopleCode
      APT_WA_APPR_WRK.APPROVE_BTN FieldFormula;


/******** Component Scoped Variables ********/
REM ** Component scoped AWE Launch Manager for submitting;
Component PTAF_CORE:LaunchManager &c_aweLaunchManager;
```

```
REM ** Component scoped AWE Approval Manager for approve/deny;
Component PTAF_CORE:ApprovalManager &c_aweApprManager;

/*
 * Possible approval actions a user can take (button clicked):
 *    S - submit
 *    A - approve
 *    D - deny
 *
 * Store chosen action in a component variable.
 */
Component string &c_apprAction;


/******** Constants ********/
REM ** Process ID from Register Transactions;
Constant &PROCESS_ID = "APT_WebAssets";

/******** PostBuild mainline code ********/
REM ** pointer to transaction header;
Local Record &headerRec = GetRecord(Record.APT_WEB_ASSETS);


/* Initialize the launch and approval managers. ApprovalManager will
 * need reinitialization on submit
 */
&c_aweLaunchManager = create PTAF_CORE:LaunchManager(&PROCESS_ID,
      &headerRec, %OperatorId);
&c_aweApprManager = create PTAF_CORE:ApprovalManager(&PROCESS_ID,
      &headerRec, %OperatorId);


/* Uncomment following line if you don't want AWE to choose the
 * Definition Id based on the preconfigured definition criteria.
 * Definition criteria is maintained using the "Setup Process
 * Definition" component.
 */
REM &c_aweLaunchManager.definition = "SHARE";

update_ui(GetLevel0(), &c_aweLaunchManager, &c_aweApprManager);

REM ** Turn on tracing after Defn ID is set (by AWE or hard coded);
REM &c_aweLaunchManager.appDef.trace_flag = True;
```

NOTE

The `LaunchManager` and `ApprovalManager` application classes form the external, top-level PeopleCode interface into AWE. For a complete listing of properties and methods, open the `PTAF_CORE` application package in App Designer, and then double-click the `LaunchManager` or `ApprovalManager` class to open it in a PeopleCode editor.

Common UI Code

You won't be able to save your `PostBuild` PeopleCode until you create the `update_ui` function, so now is a good time to create it. Add the following PeopleCode to the `FieldFormula` event of the `APPROVE_BTN` field in the `APT_WA_APPR_WRK` record. You can place shared functions in any event of any field attached to a record definition. By convention (it's not a requirement), we place them in the `FieldFormula` event of the first field in a record definition.

```
import PTAF_CORE:LaunchManager;
import PTAF_CORE:ApprovalManager;

Declare Function createStatusMonitor PeopleCode
      PTAFAW_MON_WRK.PTAFAW_FC_HANDLER FieldFormula;
Declare Function disable_records PeopleCode
      APT_FIELD_FUNC.FUNCLIB FieldFormula;

/*
 * Update the APT_WEB_ASSETS Page user interface based on the state
 * of the current workflow transaction.
 *
 * The parameter &rs0 is a rowset containing one row. That one row
 * must have the following records:
 *
 *    Record.APT_WEB_ASSETS
 *    Record.FILE_ATTACH_WRK
 *    Record.APT_WA_APPR_WRK
 *
 * &rs0 represents Level 0 for component APT_WEB_ASSETS
 */
Function update_ui(&rs0 As Rowset,
      &launchManager As PTAF_CORE:LaunchManager,
      &apprManager As PTAF_CORE:ApprovalManager)
   Local Row &row1 = &rs0.GetRow(1);
   Local Record &asset_rec = &row1.GetRecord(Record.APT_WEB_ASSETS);
   Local Record &attach_wrk_rec =
         &row1.GetRecord(Record.FILE_ATTACH_WRK);
   Local Record &appr_wrk_rec =
         &row1.GetRecord(Record.APT_WA_APPR_WRK);
   Local boolean &isApprover = False;

   /* If the transaction was submitted to AWE then:
    *    Create the status monitor
    *    Disable transaction fields
    */
   If (&apprManager.hasAppInst) Then
      &isApprover = &apprManager.hasPending;

      REM ** Initialize the AWE status monitor;
      createStatusMonitor(&apprManager.the_inst, "D", Null, False);
```

```
        REM ** Disable fields since transaction was submitted;
        disable_records(CreateArray(&asset_rec, &attach_wrk_rec));

        REM ** Reenable the View button;
        &attach_wrk_rec.ATTACHVIEW.Enabled = True;
    End-If;

    REM ** Set the state of buttons based on the state of the AWE Trx;
    &appr_wrk_rec.SUBMIT_BTN.Visible = &launchManager.submitEnabled;
    &appr_wrk_rec.APPROVE_BTN.Visible = &isApprover;
    &appr_wrk_rec.DENY_BTN.Visible = &isApprover;
End-Function;
```

The `update_ui` function uses an interesting pattern. The first parameter to this function is a rowset named `&rs0`. The zero in the name refers to level 0, which happens to be a rowset with one row. Throughout this book, I'm stressing the importance of writing code that is independent of its execution context. It is very difficult—sometimes even impossible—to unit test code that depends on the component processor to provide context. As we move into Parts II and III of this book, my reasons for stressing this fact should become evident.

The preceding code disables the component's data-entry fields and file attachment buttons. Once this transaction is submitted to the workflow framework, we don't want users to modify the attachment. We do, however, want users to be able to view the attachment. Therefore, after calling the generic field disabling routine, we must reenable the View button.

In Chapter 2, we wrote code in the `RowInit` event to enable or disable the file attachment buttons based on the state of the attachment field. By calling this shared function in the `PostBuild` event, we are actually overriding that `RowInit` PeopleCode. This happens because the `PostBuild` event executes after the `RowInit` event. Since everything in this component happens at level 0, and level 0 is guaranteed to have only one row, we could have written this code in `RowInit` and enabled only the file attachment buttons if the transaction didn't have an AWE transaction. For a multilevel component, however, that may not be an option because all of the data needed to initialize the workflow engine may not exist until all the rows are loaded. In `PostBuild`, with recursion and loops, we can disable every field at every level. Using `RowInit`, we would need to modify every record's `RowInit` event.

Enabling the Workflow Buttons

`LaunchManager` provides the `DoSubmit` method to submit transactions to the workflow engine. `ApprovalManager` has `DoApprove` and `DoDeny` methods for approving or denying transactions. We won't call these methods directly from `FieldChange` PeopleCode. Rather, we want the component processor to execute all component edits and save logic prior to submitting this transaction to the workflow engine. This ensures that we submit only saved transactions to the workflow engine.

Consider the scenario where a user creates a transaction, clicks a submit button, but then exits the transaction without saving, discarding the transaction as if it never happened. The workflow engine would now have a submitted workflow process with no corresponding transaction. To avoid this, we will use the `&c_apprAction` component variable we declared in the `PostBuild` event. The `FieldChange` event will update this variable and then call the `DoSave` PeopleCode function to execute save processing.

The final event in save processing is SavePostChange. We will call the appropriate workflow method from the SavePostChange event, using the &c_apprAction component variable to determine which method to call.

To add FieldChange PeopleCode to the Submit button, log in to App Designer and open the APT_WEB_ASSETS component. Choose View | View PeopleCode from the App Designer menu bar. In the PeopleCode editor, change the value in the upper-left drop-down list to the SUBMIT_BTN field of the APT_WA_APPR_WRK record. Change the value in the upper-right drop-down list to FieldChange and enter the following PeopleCode:

```
Component string &c_apprAction;

&c_apprAction = "S";
If ( Not GetRow().IsChanged) Then
   REM ** force save processing;
   SetComponentChanged();
End-If;

DoSave();
```

This FieldChange PeopleCode doesn't change any transaction data. Therefore, without a call to SetComponentChanged, the event won't trigger save processing. If save processing doesn't happen, our SavePostChange PeopleCode won't fire. We wrapped the call in an If statement so that we don't call SetComponentChanged if the component is already marked as changed.

Our APPROVE_BTN and DENY_BTN PeopleCode look similar. Switch to the APPROVE_BTN FieldChange event and add the following PeopleCode:

```
Component string &c_apprAction;

&c_apprAction = "A";
If ( Not GetRow().IsChanged) Then
   REM ** force save processing;
   SetComponentChanged();
End-If;

DoSave();
```

In the DENY_BTN FieldChange event, add the following:

```
Component string &c_apprAction;

&c_apprAction = "D";
If ( Not GetRow().IsChanged) Then
   REM ** force save processing;
   SetComponentChanged();
End-If;

DoSave();
```

The only difference between these three events is the value for &c_apprAction.

To add PeopleCode to the component SavePostChange event, with the component PeopleCode editor still open, change the value in the upper-left drop-down list to APT_WEB_ASSETS.GBL. Change the value in the upper-right drop-down list to SavePostChange and add the following PeopleCode:

```
import PTAF_CORE:LaunchManager;
import PTAF_CORE:ApprovalManager;

Declare Function update_ui PeopleCode
      APT_WA_APPR_WRK.APPROVE_BTN FieldFormula;

Component string &c_apprAction;
Component PTAF_CORE:LaunchManager &c_aweLaunchManager;
Component PTAF_CORE:ApprovalManager &c_aweApprManager;

Local Record &headerRec = GetRecord(Record.APT_WEB_ASSETS);
Local boolean &isApprover;

Evaluate &c_apprAction
When "S"
   &c_aweLaunchManager.DoSubmit();
   If (&c_aweLaunchManager.hasAppInst) Then
      REM ** Initialize Approval Manager if transaction was submitted;
      &c_aweApprManager = create PTAF_CORE:ApprovalManager(
            &c_aweLaunchManager.txn.awprcs_id,
            &headerRec, %OperatorId);
   End-If;
   Break;
When "A"
   &c_aweApprManager.DoApprove(&headerRec);
   Break;
When "D"
   &c_aweApprManager.DoDeny(&headerRec);
   Break;
End-Evaluate;

update_ui(GetLevel0(), &c_aweLaunchManager, &c_aweApprManager);

/* tracing options */
REM Local File &trace = GetFile("/tmp/apt_awe_trace.txt", "A", "A",
      %FilePath_Absolute);
REM &trace.WriteLine(&c_aweLaunchManager.appDef.trace);
REM &trace.Close();
```

This SavePostChange PeopleCode uses the LaunchManager and ApprovalManager that we initialized in the PostBuild event. The evaluate statement determines which manager to call based on the button that was pressed.

The commented code at the end of this event corresponds to the PostBuild tracing code you saw earlier. If you turned on tracing in PostBuild, use SavePostChange to write the trace value to a text file.

Tracing AWE

Since AWE is implemented entirely with PeopleCode, you can use the PeopleCode debugger and PeopleCode trace settings to debug and trace an approval as it moves through AWE. If your primary interest is in seeing how AWE applies criteria to choose stages, paths, and steps, you can turn on tracing in the `PTAF_CORE:DEFN:AppDef` class. For example, in our `PostBuild` code, we could turn on tracing by adding the following statement directly after setting the definition ID:

```
&c_aweLaunchManager.appDef.trace_flag = True;
```

To save this trace to a file, add PeopleCode similar to the following at the end of the `SavePostChange` event:

```
Local File &trace = GetFile("/tmp/awe_trace.txt", "A", "A", %FilePath_
Absolute);
&trace.WriteLine(&c_aweLaunchManager.appDef.trace);
&trace.Close();
```

The following trace file shows that AWE was not able to find a process definition path for the current transaction:

```
Instantiating [Process definition: 'APT_WebAssets',
    Definition ID: 'SHARE', Eff date: '2009-07-04']
    Header=(ASSET_ID=TEST9;)

  Found 1 stages.

    Instantiating stage 1: level = 0, descr = Web Asset Approval

      Found 1 paths.

        Defined Path 1: criteria check = False

      **** Skipping path 1

  **** Skipping stage 10
```

If your approver user list contains flawed logic, then you may see a trace that looks similar to this:

```
Instantiating [Process definition: 'APT_WebAssets',
    Definition ID: 'SHARE', Eff date: '2009-07-04']
    Header=(ASSET_ID=TEXT_FILE;)
  Found 1 stages.
    Instantiating stage 1: level = 0, descr = Web Asset Approval
      Found 1 paths.
        Defined Path 1: criteria check = True
        Found 1 steps.
          Step 1: criteria check=True
          Step instance 5135, step number 1
```

```
            Prev approvers (HCRUSA_KU0001)
            Approvers (<none>)
              Need 1 approvers, but found 0, requiring next
              Next (another) step is required
                (too few approvers in prev step),
                but not found: inserting error step!
```

The following trace file shows a web asset transaction without errors. You can see that AWE was able to find one path, one step, and two approvers:

```
Instantiating [Process definition: 'APT_WebAssets',
    Definition ID: 'SHARE', Eff date: '2009-07-04']
    Header=(ASSET_ID=TEXT_TEST;)
  Found 1 stages.
    Instantiating stage 1: level = 0, descr = Web Asset Approval
      Found 1 paths.
        Defined Path 1: criteria check = True
        Found 1 steps.
          Step 1: criteria check=True
          Step instance 5145, step number 1
            Prev approvers (HCRUSA_KU0001)
            Approvers (HCRUSA_KU0012,PSEM)
```

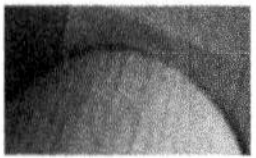

TIP
Use one of the clipboard copy commands (such as CTRL-C) to copy component-scoped variables from one PeopleCode event to another. The PeopleCode validator does not check for inconsistencies between component-scoped variable names. It assumes that two variables with different names are actually two different declarations.

Testing the Approval

We have enough code to submit a test transaction to AWE. If you test with a transaction you created in Chapter 2, be sure to add a corresponding row to the new `APT_WA_APPR` record. Prior to testing the Submit button, I ran the following SQL to add my Chapter 2 `TEST` web asset to the new `APT_WA_APPR` record:

```
INSERT INTO PS_APT_WA_APPR VALUES('TEST', 'P')
/
COMMIT
/
```

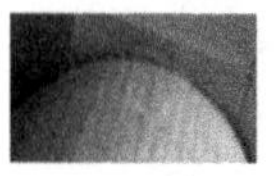

NOTE
Prior to testing the transaction's PeopleCode, you can verify your AWE configuration using the Preview Approval Process link on the AWE Process Definition configuration page.

In Chapter 2, after creating the Web Asset component, we created a role and permission list to provide access to this new component. We also added this role to a user profile so we could access and test the component. We can use that same user to add a new web asset and submit it for approval. Before submitting a transaction, however, we need an approver. When we created the user list, we wrote code to select even-numbered Portal Administrators. Before testing this new workflow, make sure you have at least two Portal Administrators that are also members of the `APT_CUSTOM` role.

Once you have a submitter and some approvers, create a new web asset. Prior to submitting a web asset, the Description, Mime-Type, and Comment fields should be enabled, and the Submit button should be visible. Once you submit it, the Submit button should disappear, the data-entry fields should change to disabled, and the Approval Status Monitor should appear. Figure 3-15 shows one of my many test web assets after submission.

Workflow-enabling a transaction requires a few new App Designer definitions, some PeopleCode, and some metadata configuration. Don't be discouraged if your first few tests fail. After Chapter 2, I had one web asset. By the end of this chapter, I had 38. It appears that it took me 37 tries to get it right!

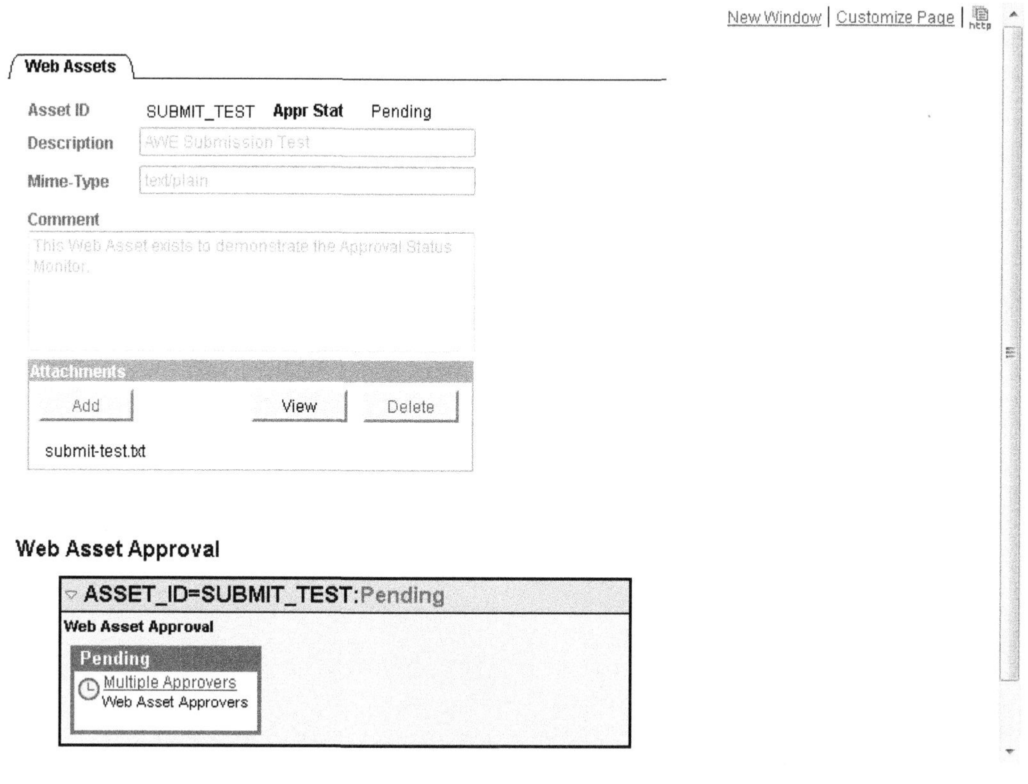

FIGURE 3-15. *Web asset after submission*

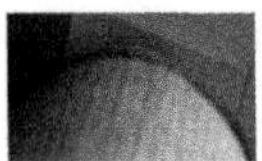

TIP

The Submit button is visible if the `LaunchManager.submitEnabled` property returns the value `True`. This property returns `True` only if the process ID and definition ID exist and the transaction wasn't previously submitted. Therefore, if your Submit button is invisible, compare your process ID with the process ID in the Register Transactions component. Also check your process definition criteria. It is possible that the `LaunchManager` was not able to find a definition matching your criteria. If you suspect your definition criteria is the problem, then try hard-coding the `LaunchManager.definition` property to your definition ID as shown in the component's `PostBuild` PeopleCode.

In my HRMS demo database, I submitted the web asset as user HCRUSA_KU0001. Two of the Portal Administrators, PSEM and HCRUSA_KU0012, received a notification e-mail, as shown in Figure 3-16.

From this e-mail message, I clicked the hyperlink to go directly to the web asset transaction, logged in as user HCRUSA_KU0012, and approved the transaction. Figure 3-17 shows this asset after approval.

Subject	Sender	Date
Web Asset Approval	hcrusa_ku0001@hrms.example.com	6:40 PM

Subject: Web Asset Approval
From: hcrusa_ku0001@hrms.example.com
Date: 6:40 PM
To: hcrusa_ku0012@hrms.example.com, psem@hrms.example.com

```
I created a new Web Asset named SUBMIT_TEST and would appreciate prompt approval at your
earliest convenience. The Web Asset's details:

Content Type: text/plain
File Name: submit-test.txt
Description: AWE Submission Test

You may approve this transaction at
http://hrms.example.com/psp/hrms/EMPLOYEE/HRMS/c/APT_CUSTOM.APT_WEB_ASSETS.GBL?Page=APT_WEB_ASS
```

FIGURE 3-16. *Web asset approval e-mail message*

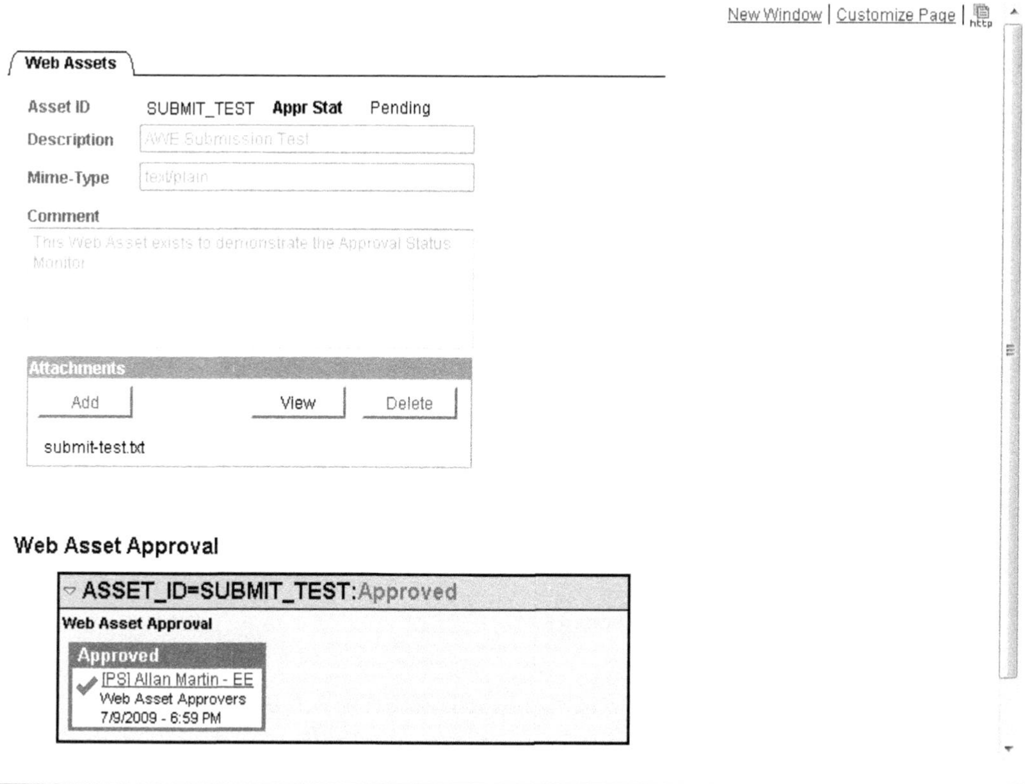

FIGURE 3-17. *Approved web asset*

Providing Custom Descriptions for the Approval Status Monitor

The text of the Approval Status Monitor is composed of descriptions and transaction key values. The Approval Status Monitor title comes from the process definition description, "Web Asset Approval." The group box header is composed of the transaction header key field names and values, `ASSET_ID=SUBMIT_TEST`. The text under the approver's name, "Web Asset Approvers," comes from the user list description.

AWE provides a mechanism to override the group box header and the approver's name in the Approval Status monitor. We do this by creating an application class that extends the class `PTAF_MONITOR:MONITOR:threadDescrBase`. Since `threadDescrBase` provides a default implementation for each of its methods, you only need to override the method representing the text you want to change. Besides text in the Approval Status Monitor, `threadDescrBase` contains a method that allows you to override the text displayed in the approver's worklist. The following code listing contains a sample implementation for each of the three `threadDescrBase` methods.

Add the class WebAsset_ThreadDescr to the application package APT_WA_AWE, and then insert the following code into the WebAsset_ThreadDescr class.

```
import PTAF_MONITOR:MONITOR:threadDescrBase;

class WebAsset_ThreadDescr extends PTAF_MONITOR:MONITOR:threadDescrBase
   method getThreadDescr(&keys As array of Field) Returns string;
   method getWorklistDescr(&recApplication As Record) Returns string;
   method getUserName(&OprId As string) Returns string;
end-class;

/* Set the group box header */
method getThreadDescr
   /+ &keys as Array of Field +/
   /+ Returns String +/
   /+ Extends/implements
         PTAF_MONITOR:MONITOR:threadDescrBase.getThreadDescr +/
   Local Field &field = &keys [1];
   Return &field.GetShortLabel(&field.Name) | ": " | &field.Value;
end-method;

/* Set the worklist transaction link description */
method getWorklistDescr
   /+ &recApplication as Record +/
   /+ Returns String +/
   /+ Extends/implements
      PTAF_MONITOR:MONITOR:threadDescrBase.getWorklistDescr +/

   &recApplication.SelectByKey();
   Return &recApplication.DESCR.Value;
end-method;

/* Provide a name for the approver */
method getUserName
   /+ &OprId as String +/
   /+ Returns String +/
   /+ Extends/implements
      PTAF_MONITOR:MONITOR:threadDescrBase.getUserName +/
   Local string &name = %Super.getUserName(&OprId);

   If (Left(&name, 4) = "[PS]") Then
      &name = Substitute(&name, "[PS] ", "");
   End-If;

   Return &name;
end-method;
```

The username in Figure 3-17 is `[PS] Allan Martin - EE`. This name comes from the user's security user profile and is the name given to user ID `HCRUSA_KU0012`. To make the name display a little friendlier, the `getUserName` method trims the `[PS]` portion from Allan's name.

We configure AWE to use `WebAsset_ThreadDescr` by updating the AWE process registration using the navigation Set Up HRMS | Common Definitions | Approvals | Register Transactions. Figure 3-18 shows the Approval Status Monitor settings, as well as an ad hoc package and class, which we will discuss in the next section.

Figure 3-19 shows an approval using the new `WebAsset_ThreadDescr` application class. Notice the group box header changed from `ASSET_ID=TESTWL` to `Asset ID: TESTWL`. Also, the approver's name no longer contains `[PS]`.

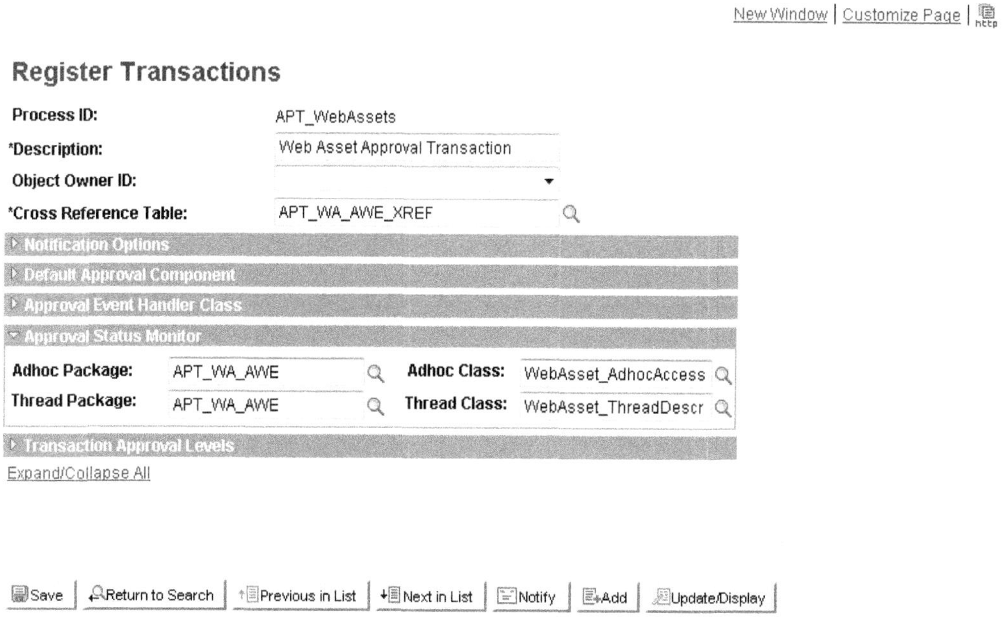

New Window | Customize Page | http

Register Transactions

Process ID:	APT_WebAssets
***Description:**	Web Asset Approval Transaction
Object Owner ID:	
***Cross Reference Table:**	APT_WA_AWE_XREF

▷ Notification Options

▷ Default Approval Component

▷ Approval Event Handler Class

▽ Approval Status Monitor

Adhoc Package:	APT_WA_AWE	**Adhoc Class:**	WebAsset_AdhocAccess
Thread Package:	APT_WA_AWE	**Thread Class:**	WebAsset_ThreadDescr

▷ Transaction Approval Levels

Expand/Collapse All

Save | Return to Search | Previous in List | Next in List | Notify | Add | Update/Display

FIGURE 3-18. *Registration of a custom Thread class*

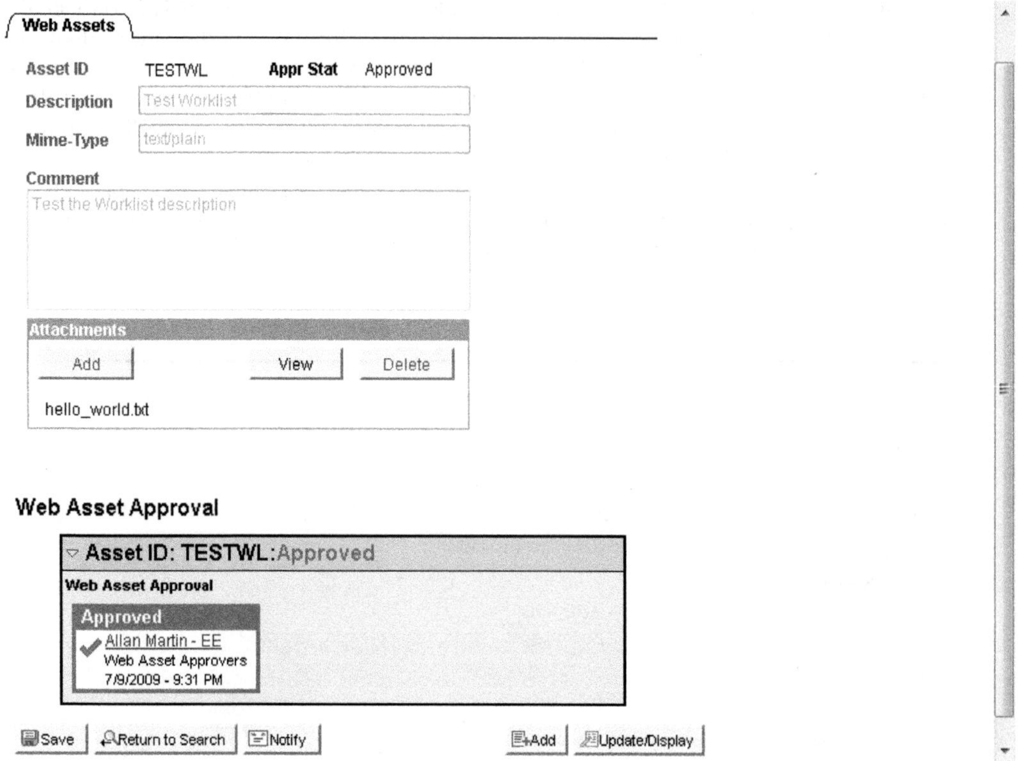

FIGURE 3-19. *Approval that uses the custom WebAsset_ThreadDescr class*

Allowing Ad Hoc Access

When designing a workflow, you will map out the approval path to the best of your ability. Nevertheless, you may find that you need additional approvers. Consider the example of a human resources employee who works primarily with the engineering department. If that employee requests to transfer out of the human resources department, the human resources manager may want to add the engineering manager to an approval path prior to approving this request. Figure 3-20 shows such an ad hoc approval process. Here, I added Charles Baran as a reviewer and the demo superuser, `PS`, as the final approver.

To enable ad hoc approvals, open the shared user interface PeopleCode we created earlier. You will find this code in the `FieldFormula` event of the `APT_WA_APPR_WRK.APPROVE_BTN` field. Locate the `createStatusMonitor` line that looks like this:

```
createStatusMonitor(&apprManager.the_inst, "D", Null, False);
```

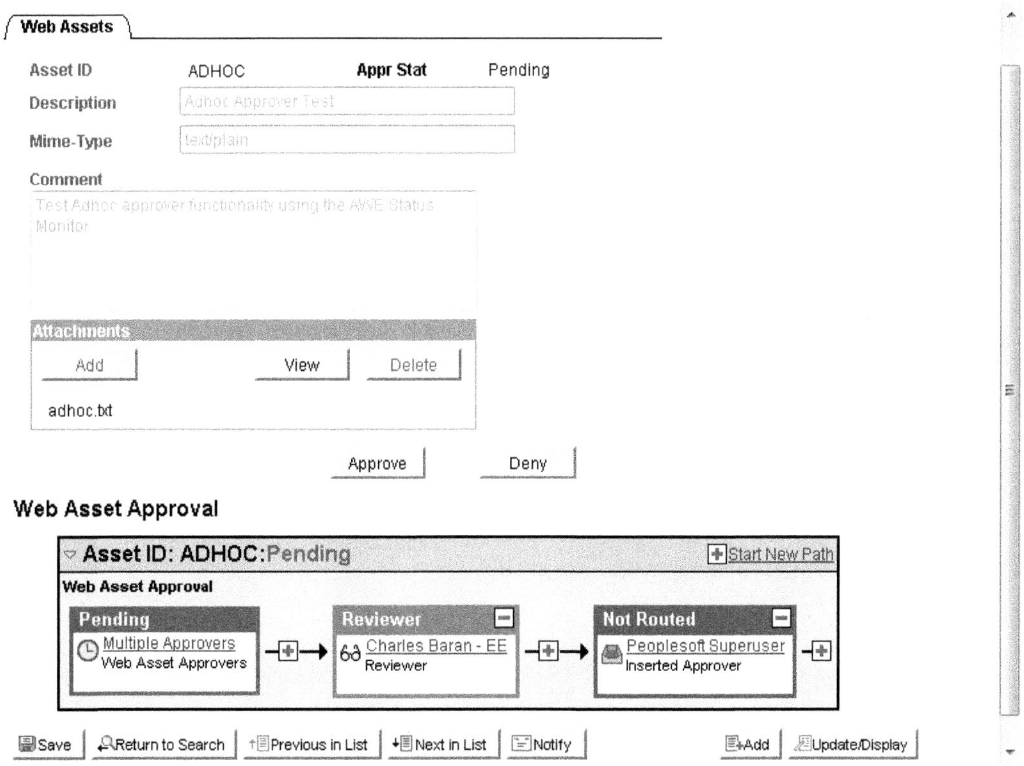

FIGURE 3-20. *Ad hoc approval process*

Replace the "D" with an "A":

```
createStatusMonitor(&apprManager.the_inst, "A", Null, False);
```

The "D" means display only, and the "A" is for ad hoc.

AWE contains default business logic to determine who can insert ad hoc approvers and ad hoc paths. As shown in Figure 3-18, I created a custom ad hoc approver application class to limit the number of ad hoc approvers. Ad hoc approver application classes extend the AWE-delivered application class `PTAF_MONITOR:ADHOC_OBJECTS:adhocAccessLogicBase`. The following code listing contains a basic ad hoc approver application class:

```
import PTAF_MONITOR:ADHOC_OBJECTS:adhocAccessLogicBase;
import PTAF_CORE:ENGINE:StepInst;
import PTAF_CORE:ENGINE:StageInst;

class WebAsset_AdhocAccess extends
      PTAF_MONITOR:ADHOC_OBJECTS:adhocAccessLogicBase
```

```
      method allowInsert(&oprid As string,
            &stepBefore As PTAF_CORE:ENGINE:StepInst,
            &stepAfter As PTAF_CORE:ENGINE:StepInst) Returns boolean;

      method allowDelete(&oprid As string,
            &currentStep As PTAF_CORE:ENGINE:StepInst) Returns boolean;

      method allowNewPath(&oprid As string,
            &stage As PTAF_CORE:ENGINE:StageInst) Returns boolean;

   private
      method isPortalAdmin(&oprid As string) Returns boolean;
   end-class;

   method allowInsert
      /+ &oprid as String, +/
      /+ &stepBefore as PTAF_CORE:ENGINE:StepInst, +/
      /+ &stepAfter as PTAF_CORE:ENGINE:StepInst +/
      /+ Returns Boolean +/
      /+ Extends/implements
         PTAF_MONITOR:ADHOC_OBJECTS:adhocAccessLogicBase.allowInsert +/
      Return %This.isPortalAdmin(&oprid);
   end-method;

   method allowDelete
      /+ &oprid as String, +/
      /+ &currentStep as PTAF_CORE:ENGINE:StepInst +/
      /+ Returns Boolean +/
      /+ Extends/implements
         PTAF_MONITOR:ADHOC_OBJECTS:adhocAccessLogicBase.allowDelete +/
      If (%Super.allowDelete(&oprid, &currentStep)) Then
         Return True;
      Else
         Return %This.isPortalAdmin(&oprid);
      End-If;
   end-method;

   method allowNewPath
      /+ &oprid as String, +/
      /+ &stage as PTAF_CORE:ENGINE:StageInst +/
      /+ Returns Boolean +/
      /+ Extends/implements
         PTAF_MONITOR:ADHOC_OBJECTS:adhocAccessLogicBase.allowNewPath +/
      Return %This.isPortalAdmin(&oprid);
   end-method;
```

```
method isPortalAdmin
   /+ &oprid as String +/
   /+ Returns Boolean +/
   Local string &is_admin;
   SQLExec("SELECT ROLENAME FROM PSROLEUSER WHERE ROLEUSER = :1 AND" |
         " ROLENAME='Portal Administrator'", &oprid, &is_admin);
   Return (All(&is_admin));
end-method;
```

The `allowInsert` and `allowNewPath` methods in this listing return `True` if the user identified by parameter `&oprid` is a member of the Portal Administrator role. The `allowDelete` method possesses a little more logic. The base class implementation for `allowDelete` permits deletions if the user identified by `&oprid` added the approval step, or if the user is an administrative user. The `allowDelete` override in the preceding code retains the default logic by calling the base class's `allowDelete` method and returning the same result. This example adds to the default logic by allowing Portal Administrators to delete paths and steps.

NOTE

The `AdhocAccess` class shown here uses SQL to determine whether a user is in a specific role. PeopleCode provides the `IsUserInRole` function for this purpose. Using `IsUserInRole` would have bound the `WebAsset_AdhocAccess` class to its execution context. Many of the approval framework methods contain an `OPRID` parameter. Use this parameter rather than assuming the approval is for the ID of the current user.

Workflow for Notifications

Workflow isn't just for approvals. Several years ago, I was working on my first PeopleTools 8.42 implementation. My team wrote a few App Engine batch process integrations to import data from external systems. If one of those batch processes failed, we wanted to notify an administrator who could resolve the issue and restart the integration process.

The easiest way to implement notifications from an App Engine program is to use the `SendMail` PeopleCode function. While it is true that this function is simple, it requires the developer to hard-code information about the recipient. To take advantage of features like workflow's alternate user ID, we decided to use the PeopleTools legacy workflow engine. The legacy workflow engine, unfortunately, is heavily dependent on the component processor. Therefore, to use the legacy workflow engine from a batch process, we needed to create a transaction record, page, and component, and then wrap that component in a component interface. As you have seen from this chapter, with AWE it is possible to submit and process a workflow transaction without the component buffer.

Creating an Event Handler Iterator

PeopleSoft applications deliver many transactions with workflow enabled. As an example, suppose that we have PeopleSoft Time and Labor and a non-PeopleSoft scheduling system, such as Oracle Workforce Scheduling. A scheduling system requires information about employees, including preferred working hours and absence requests. Using the `OnFinalApproval` workflow event, we could send approved absence information to a scheduling system. Looking at the AWE process IDs in the Register Transactions component, we see that the absence request process ID is `AbsenceManagement`. Opening that process ID, we see that the event handler is `GP_ABS_EVT_HANDLER:apprEventHandler`. To send an approved absence request to the scheduling program, we could modify the `OnHeaderApprove` event handler. As an alternative, we could create another handler, register it in AWE, and then call the delivered handler from the custom handler, effectively chaining handler implementations.

Building upon the object-oriented concepts discussed in Chapter 1, we will create a single, configurable handler that calls a collection of handlers. This approach requires some custom metadata tables and a few lines of code. The metadata tables will contain a list of event handlers for a given process. The custom event handler will iterate over that list, calling the appropriate event handler method.

Figure 3-21 shows the header and detail metadata records. I designed the metadata repository with online configuration in mind. I'll let you design the online page and component (define search keys as appropriate for your component). The header record, `APT_EVT_HNDLR`, contains the AWE process ID as the primary key. The detail record, `APT_EVT_HND_DTL`, uses the AWE process ID and `APP_CLASS` as key fields. I included a sequence number in the detail table to ensure that event handlers fire in the appropriate order.

After creating the metadata tables, create an application package named `APT_AWE` and add an application class named `EventHandlerIterator`. Add the following code to this new application class:

```
import PTAF_CORE:ApprovalEventHandler;
import PTAF_CORE:ENGINE:AdHocStepInst;
import PTAF_CORE:ENGINE:AppInst;
import PTAF_CORE:ENGINE:StepInst;
import PTAF_CORE:ENGINE:UserStepInst;
import PTAF_CORE:ENGINE:Thread;

class EventHandlerIterator extends PTAF_CORE:ApprovalEventHandler
   method OnProcessLaunch(&appInst As PTAF_CORE:ENGINE:AppInst);
   method OnHeaderApprove(&appinst As PTAF_CORE:ENGINE:AppInst);
   method OnHeaderDeny(&userinst As PTAF_CORE:ENGINE:UserStepInst);

private
   method callHandlers(&awprcs_id As string, &methodName As string,
         &parms As array of any);
end-class;

method OnProcessLaunch
   /+ &appInst as PTAF_CORE:ENGINE:AppInst +/
   /+ Extends/implements
      PTAF_CORE:ApprovalEventHandler.OnProcessLaunch +/
```

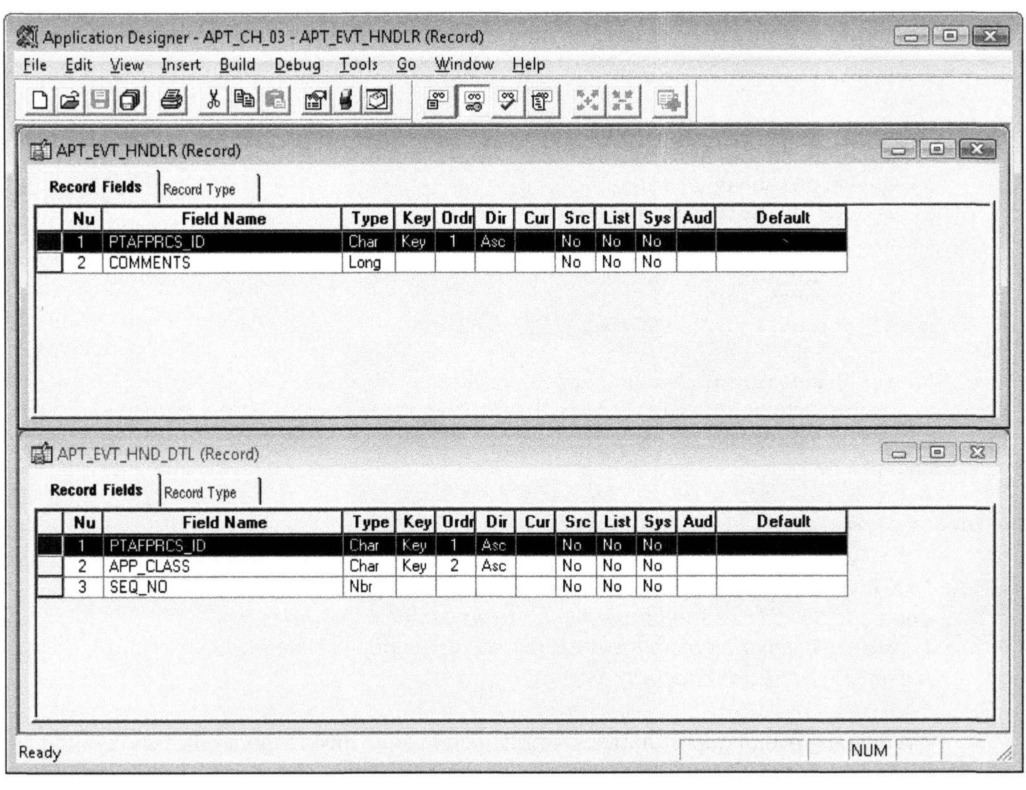

FIGURE 3-21. *Event handler iterator metadata repository*

```
   %This.callHandlers(&appInst.appDef.awprcs_id, "OnProcessLaunch",
         CreateArrayAny(&appInst));

end-method;

method OnHeaderApprove
   /+ &appinst as PTAF_CORE:ENGINE:AppInst +/
   /+ Extends/implements
      PTAF_CORE:ApprovalEventHandler.OnHeaderApprove +/
   %This.callHandlers(&appinst.appDef.awprcs_id, "OnHeaderApprove",
         CreateArrayAny(&appinst));

end-method;

method OnHeaderDeny
   /+ &userinst as PTAF_CORE:ENGINE:UserStepInst +/
   /+ Extends/implements
      PTAF_CORE:ApprovalEventHandler.OnHeaderDeny +/
```

```
    %This.callHandlers(&userinst.thread.txn.awprcs_id,
          "OnHeaderDeny", CreateArrayAny(&userinst));

end-method;

method callHandlers
   /+ &awprcs_id as String, +/
   /+ &methodName as String, +/
   /+ &parms as Array of Any +/
   Local SQL &handler_sql = CreateSQL("SELECT APP_CLASS FROM " |
         "PS_APT_EVT_HND_DTL WHERE PTAFPRCS_ID = :1 ORDER BY SEQ_NO",
         &awprcs_id);
   Local string &appClassName;

   While &handler_sql.Fetch(&appClassName);
      ObjectDoMethodArray(CreateObject(&appClassName), &methodName,
            &parms)
   End-While;

end-method;
```

NOTE
The `callHandlers` method in the preceding code uses one of the PeopleCode generic object methods to execute an object's method by name: `ObjectDoMethodArray`.

AWE offers several opportunities to apply patterns like this. For example, you could handle application class definition criteria in a similar manner. Unlike the event handler example that processed every application class in the list, a definition criteria handler would return as soon as one of the definition criteria classes returned false.

Using techniques similar to the `EventHandlerIterator` example described here, it is possible to add functionality to delivered applications without modifying delivered code.

Web Service-Enabling Approvals

One of the major benefits of AWE over PeopleSoft's legacy workflow engine is the ability to web service-enable approvals. The legacy workflow engine supported web services, but only through component interfaces. With AWE, you can submit, approve, deny, or push back a workflow transaction without a component interface.

Since legacy workflow required a component interface, web service-enabling approvals required a separate service operation handler for each approval process. Using AWE, you can write one service operation handler and pass the AWE process ID as part of the incoming message.

As you saw when we tested the web assets approval, the notification process generates a link to the target approval page to include in e-mail notifications. When submitting transactions online through your web browser, AWE is able to generate the correct transaction link using the PeopleCode `%Portal` and `%Node` system variables. Unfortunately, these system variables apply only to online PeopleCode. As a fallback method, AWE uses the `EMP_SERVLET` URL definition.

Set the URL value to the portion of your application's URL that includes the site name. In my case, that is http://hrms.example.com/psp/hrms.

The following is a PeopleCode fragment describing what a service operation handler might look like:

```
import PS_PT:Integration:IRequestHandler;
import PTAF_CORE:ApprovalManager;

class ApprovalHandler implements
      PS_PT:Integration:IRequestHandler
   method OnRequest(&MSG As Message) Returns Message;
   method OnError(&MSG As Message) Returns string;
end-class;

method OnRequest
   /+ &MSG as Message +/
   /+ Returns Message +/
   /+ Extends/implements
      PS_PT:Integration:IRequestHandler.OnRequest +/
   Local Message &resultMsg;
   Local Record &headerRec;
   Local PTAF_CORE:ApprovalManager &apprManager;
   Local string &processId;

   /*
    * TODO
    *    1. Authenticate the user (PS_TOKEN, WS-Security, etc) by
    *       calling SwitchUser
    *    3. Extract Process ID from &MSG
    *    2. Extract keys from &MSG to populate &headerRec
    */

   &apprManager = create PTAF_CORE:ApprovalManager(
         &processId, &headerRec, %OperatorId);

   If (&apprManager.hasAppInst) Then
      &apprManager.DoApprove(&headerRec);
   Else
      REM ** return error message;
   End-If;

   /*
    * TODO: Populate result message
    */

   Return &resultMsg;
end-method;

method OnError
   /+ &MSG as Message +/
```

```
   /+ Returns String +/
   /+ Extends/implements PS_PT:Integration:IRequestHandler.OnError +/
   Return "Error";
end-method;
```

When using web services, third-party systems can participate in the PeopleSoft workflow process.

Conclusion

In describing how to use AWE, this chapter made extensive use of concepts introduced in Chapter 1. The next chapter will continue this trend by showing how to use custom application classes to enhance the Pagelet Wizard.

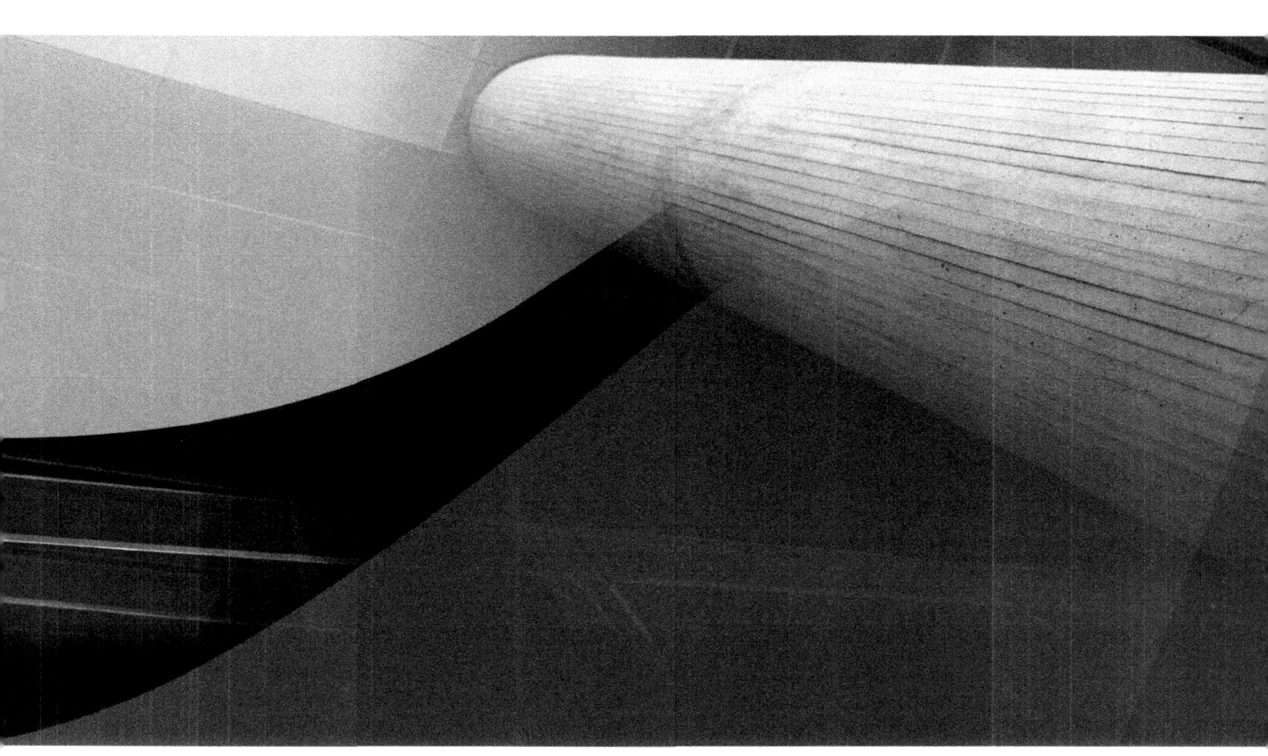

CHAPTER 4

Pagelet Wizard

As you work with PeopleSoft applications, you will notice the product's emphasis on configuration. ChartField configuration is an excellent example of the PeopleSoft development team's efforts to provide configuration opportunities. Besides reducing the number of modifications, configuration reduces the application users' dependence on their development team. Online configuration tools allow users to accomplish tasks that would normally require custom development. The Pagelet Wizard is one of these tools.

Pagelets Defined

Pagelets are modular, display-only, self-contained page fragments. Pagelets are most often associated with home pages, but they also can be inserted into standard pages. Just like other content displayed in PeopleSoft, pagelets must be registered in the portal registry in a subfolder of Portal Objects | Pagelets. Since pagelets are content references, you can create them from components, iScripts, or external URLs.

The Pagelet Wizard is a configuration tool that allows functional experts to create and share pagelets with various PeopleSoft users in their organization. In fact, since pagelets generated by the Pagelet Wizard support Web Services for Remote Portlets (WSRP), users of other portal products, such as Oracle WebCenter, can incorporate PeopleSoft pagelets into their third-party home pages.

A pagelet can be composed of anything a web browser can render, from standard HTML to rich AJAX, Flash, Scalable Vector Graphics (SVG), or JavaFX. Chapters 5, 6, and 7 will show you how to integrate rich Internet technologies with PeopleTools. And if you apply the concepts presented in Chapters 5 through 7 to the Pagelet Wizard, your users can create their own rich user experience.

I described pagelets as *display-only* because pagelets must not execute an event that causes the browser to submit the home page to the component processor. The component processor uses this submission technique, known as a *postback*, to maintain state between the online page and the component buffer. When a postback occurs, the component processor will transfer users from their home page to the component. In Chapter 7, you will learn how to use AJAX to overcome this limitation.

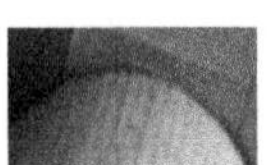

NOTE

PeopleTools 8.50 and higher use AJAX to reconcile differences between the component buffer and an online page, eliminating this postback issue. Nevertheless, I recommend that you use transaction pages to maintain data, and use pagelets to provide an alternative view of those transactions.

Pagelets can dramatically improve a user's experience because they bring relevant, user-centric transactional information to the top level of the application. For example, an accounts payable clerk must know the status of outstanding bills, as well as the amount of funds available to pay those bills. The clerk may want to pay some accounts within the discount period, but hold other bills until five days prior to their due date. Rather than requiring this clerk to sift through transactions, we can improve his experience by creating pagelets that list payables due in five days and payables due within the discount period. Since pagelets are composed of HTML, these lists can link directly to the PeopleSoft transactions they represent.

Creating a Pagelet

Figure 4-1 is an example of a home page with several pagelets. We are going to use the Pagelet Wizard to create the Salaries by Department pagelet shown in the center of Figure 4-1.

For our demonstration pagelet, we will create a pie chart pagelet from the query named DEPT_SALARIES__NVISION_, which is delivered with the HRMS demo database. Navigate to PeopleTools | Portal | Pagelet Wizard | Pagelet Wizard and add the new value APT_DEPT_SALARIES. After you add a new value, the Pagelet Wizard guides you through the steps required to create a pagelet, as shown in Figures 4-2 through 4-7:

- **Specify Pagelet Information** Step 1 prompts for a title (required) and a description (optional). PeopleSoft will display the pagelet's title on home pages.
- **Select Data Source** In step 2, you select a data type. For this pagelet, choose the PS Query type. After choosing a data type, the Pagelet Wizard will prompt you for the data type's settings. Since we chose PS Query as the type, the Pagelet Wizard prompts for the name of the query. When prompted, provide the name DEPT_SALARIES__NVISION_.

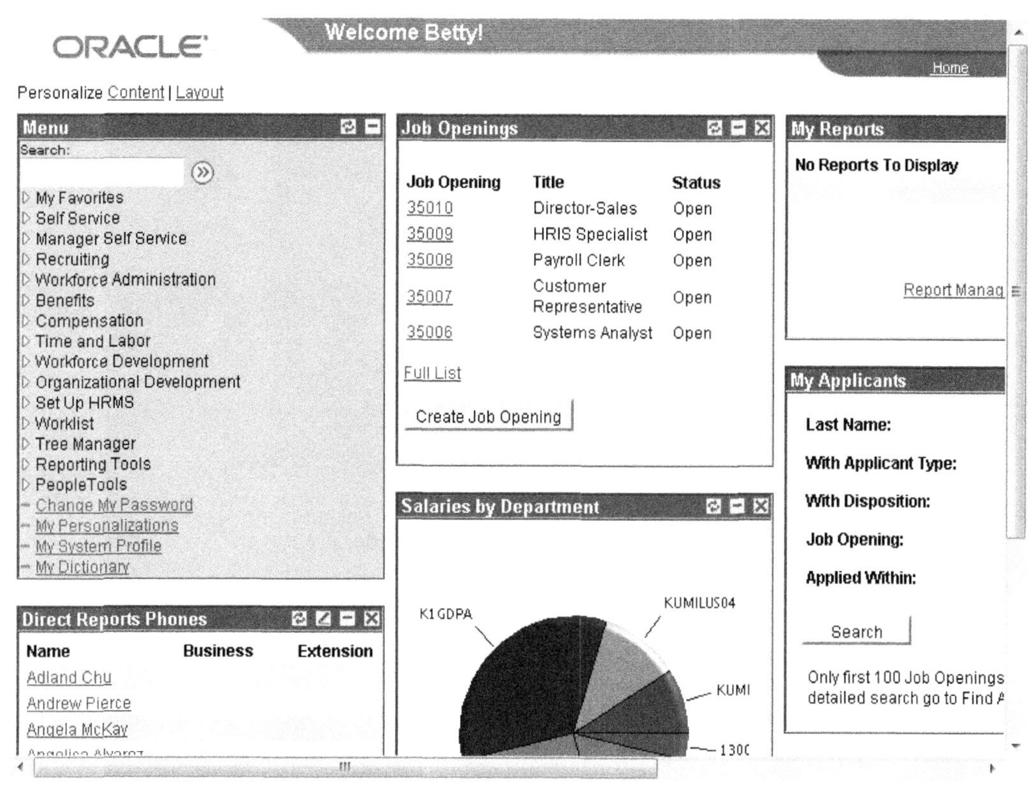

FIGURE 4-1. *Home page with pagelets*

New Window | Customize Page |

Pagelet Wizard

Step 1 of 6

Next >

Specify Pagelet Information

The following information will be used to identify and categorize your pagelet.

Pagelet Information

Pagelet ID: APT_DEPT_SALARIES

***Pagelet Title:** Salaries by Department

Description: Demonstration pagelet containing data for the first 10 departments.

Owner ID:

Category ID:

Save | Notify

FIGURE 4-2. *Pagelet Wizard step 1*

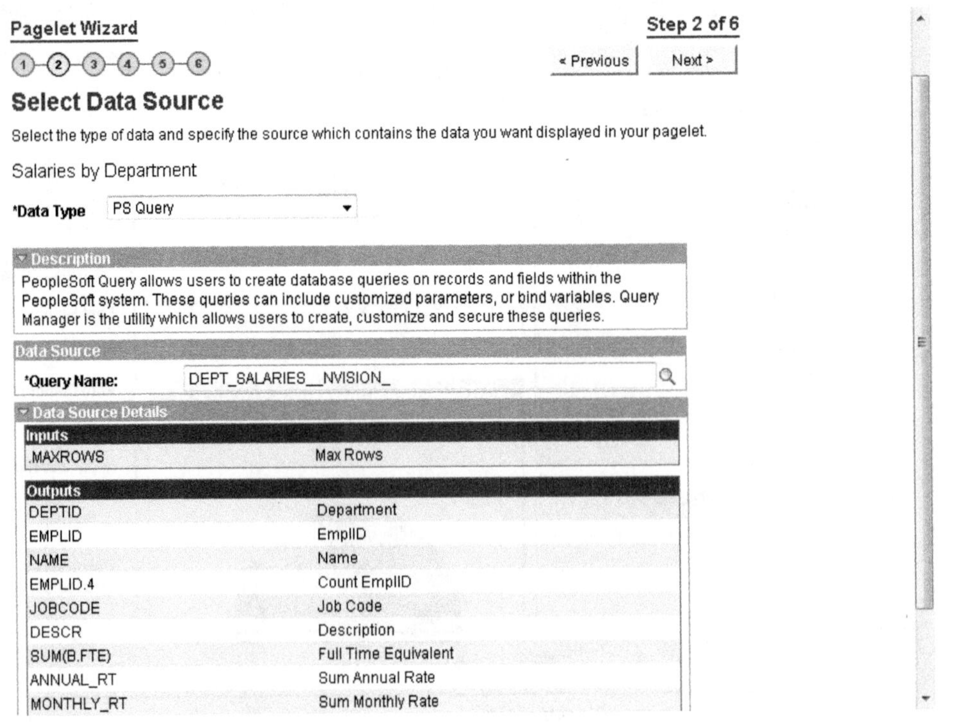

FIGURE 4-3. *Pagelet Wizard step 2*

New Window | Customize Page

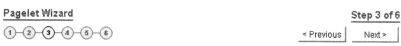

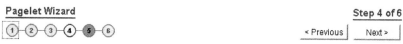

Specify Data Source Parameters

Specify the parameters and their associated options specific to the data source you have selected for your pagelet. Rows showing a selected 'Required' require a Default Value.

Salaries by Department

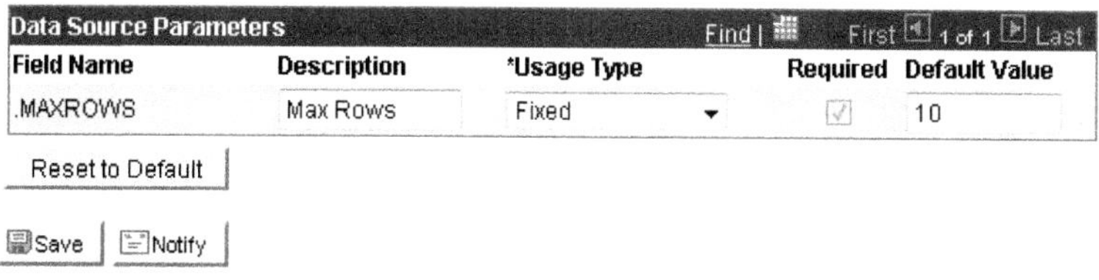

Find | First 1 of 1 Last

FIGURE 4-4. *Pagelet Wizard step 3*

Step 4 of 6

Select Display Format

Select the format in which you would like your pagelet data rendered.

Salaries by Department

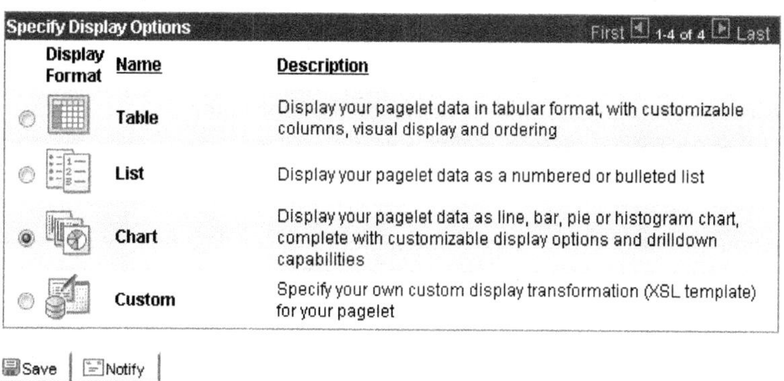

First 1-4 of 4 Last

Display your pagelet data in tabular format, with customizable columns, visual display and ordering

Display your pagelet data as a numbered or bulleted list

Display your pagelet data as line, bar, pie or histogram chart, complete with customizable display options and drilldown capabilities

Specify your own custom display transformation (XSL template) for your pagelet

Save | Notify

FIGURE 4-5. *Pagelet Wizard step 4*

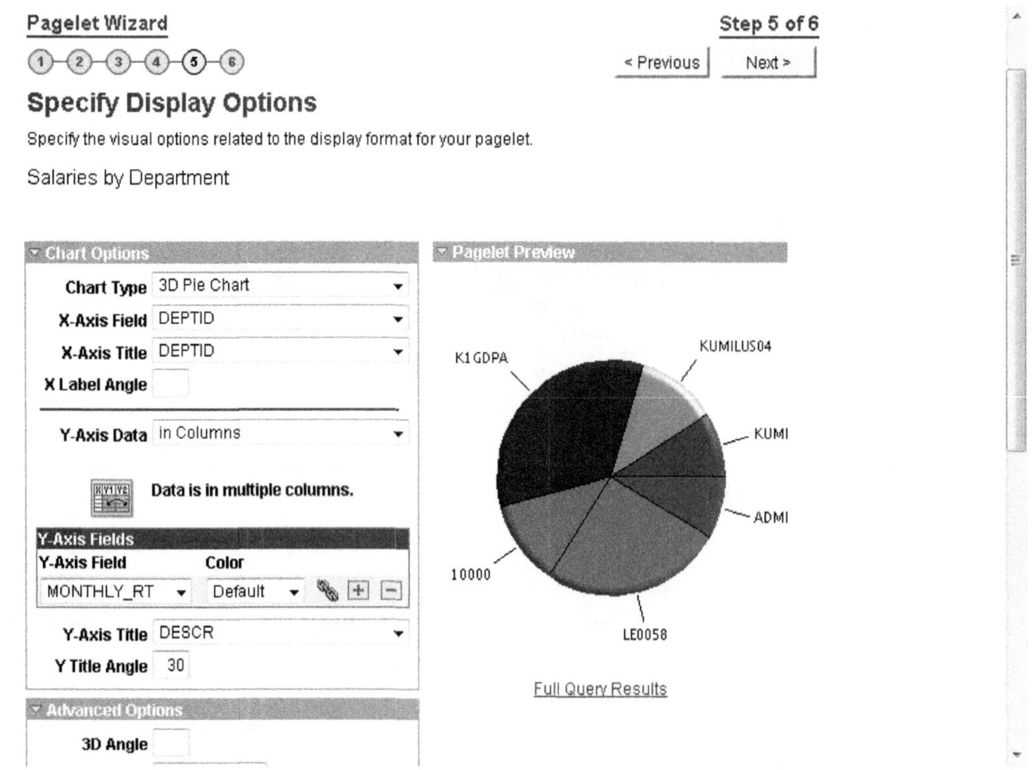

FIGURE 4-6. *Pagelet Wizard step 5*

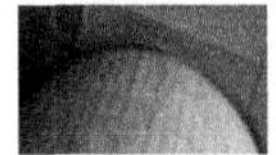

NOTE

If the `DEPT_SALARIES__NVISION_` *query is not available to you, then you may not have the query's base tables in your query security tree. I created this pagelet as a user with the PeopleSoft Administrator role, which gave me access to all records that exist in the various query security trees.*

- **Specify Data Source Parameters** Step 3 is enabled only for data types with parameters. Some data types, such as HTML, have only settings. Others, such as PS Query, have settings and parameters. Since the data type we selected in step 2 has parameters, step 3 prompts us for values. You can hard-code a value for a prompt, specify that the value is derived from a system variable, or let the user enter an appropriate value. In my HRMS demo database, the `DEPT_SALARIES__NVISION_` query returns about 2,300 rows, consisting of roughly 100 departments. If you were creating your own query for this pagelet, you would probably show the top 9 and lump the rest into a category titled "Other." To keep things simple, we will just specify the value 10 for the maximum number of rows and a usage type of Fixed.

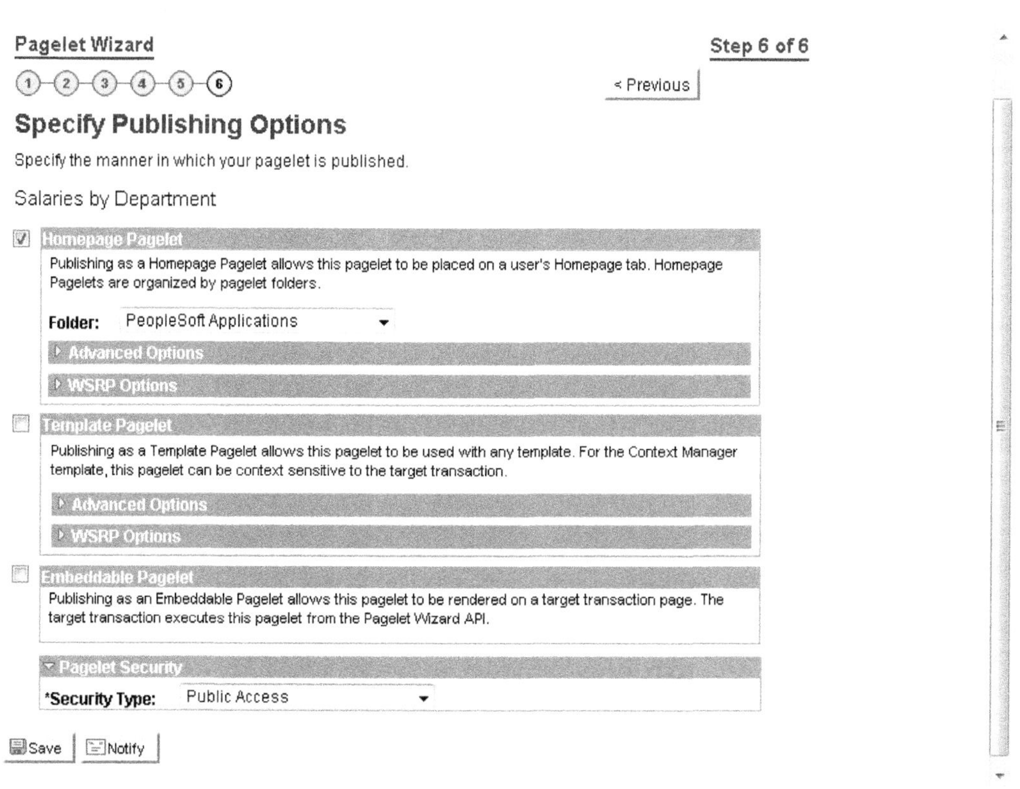
Pagelet Wizard
Step 6 of 6
1 2 3 4 5 6
< Previous
Specify Publishing Options
Specify the manner in which your pagelet is published.
Salaries by Department
Homepage Pagelet
Publishing as a Homepage Pagelet allows this pagelet to be placed on a user's Homepage tab. Homepage Pagelets are organized by pagelet folders.
Folder: PeopleSoft Applications
Advanced Options
WSRP Options
Template Pagelet
Publishing as a Template Pagelet allows this pagelet to be used with any template. For the Context Manager template, this pagelet can be context sensitive to the target transaction.
Advanced Options
WSRP Options
Embeddable Pagelet
Publishing as an Embeddable Pagelet allows this pagelet to be rendered on a target transaction page. The target transaction executes this pagelet from the Pagelet Wizard API.
Pagelet Security
*Security Type: Public Access
Save
Notify

FIGURE 4-7. *Pagelet Wizard step 6*

- **Select Display Format** In step 4, you choose a display format. Each data type has a predefined list of display formats. Choose the Chart display format for this example.
- **Specify Display Options** Step 5 allows you to configure a pagelet's display by providing values for the pagelet's display format. For example, the Chart display format requires you to declare the query field that contains data values.
- **Specify Publishing Options** Step 6 allows you to publish a pagelet as a home page pagelet, an Intelligent Context pagelet (template pagelets are Intelligent Context pagelets), or an embeddable transaction pagelet.

The Pagelet Wizard offers the easiest mechanism for creating a pagelet. As this example demonstrates, the Pagelet Wizard is a tool designed for functional experts. It doesn't require any coding or access to App Designer.

If you are new to the Pagelet Wizard, I encourage you to spend some time investigating its features before moving on to the next section of this chapter. After creating a few pagelets yourself, you will be ready to move to the next step: extending the Pagelet Wizard by creating new data types, transformers, and display formats.

Components of a Pagelet Wizard Pagelet

Just like AWE (discussed in the previous chapter), the Pagelet Wizard is an application class framework that we can extend through metadata configuration and the development of custom application classes.

Pagelets are composed of the following components:

- **Data types** A data type provides the source data for a pagelet. As you saw with the query pagelet we created in the previous section, data types have settings and parameters. For example, the URL data type has a URL setting and a Timeout parameter. At runtime, a data type uses these settings and parameters to retrieve the data that will be transformed and formatted according to the rest of the Pagelet Wizard's configuration steps.
- **Transformers** A display format determines how to transform and display the data provided by a data type. For example, the PS Query data type offers a variety of options for formatting query results. The most flexible option is the Custom display format because it allows you to transform a data type's results using XSL.
- **Display formats** The Pagelet Wizard uses transformers with display formats to transform a data type's return value into a format suitable for display in a user's browser. Transformers are independent of data types and display formats. Display formats, however, depend on transformers to generate results.

When registering a data type, you must specify which display formats are suitable for that data type. Similarly, when you create a display format, you specify the transformer used by that display format.

Pagelet Data Types

PeopleTools delivers the following data types:

- HTML
- URL
- Query
- Search Record
- Integration Broker
- Navigation Collection

The PeopleSoft Enterprise Portal includes additional data types for Enterprise Portal-specific modules.

The Pagelet Wizard also allows you to create your own data types. As an example, we will create an e-mail data type that returns e-mail header information in XML format.

Setup for the Custom Data Type Example

PeopleTools contains the MultiChannel Framework (MCF) application class framework for communicating with Post Office Protocol (POP) and Internet Message Access Protocol (IMAP) e-mail servers. These application classes depend on system objects that require some configuration prior to usage. For the following example to work, you will need to configure the delivered MCF_GETMAIL Integration Broker node and service operation routings. In the MCF_GETMAIL node, switch to the Connectors tab and set the MCF_Port and MCF_Protocol values to settings that are appropriate for your e-mail server. We will specify the server, username, and password as part of the data type, so you don't need to configure those connector values for this example.

After configuring the node's connector properties, ensure that the service operation routings and corresponding services and service operations are active. Since MCF uses Integration Broker to communicate with the e-mail server, be sure to configure your integration gateway and the application server's publication and subscription handlers (referred to as pub/sub handlers in psadmin, the application server administration utility). Chapters 12 and 14 make extensive use of Integration Broker, so now is a good time to make sure you have integration working. The viewlet http://blogs.oracle.com/peopletools/gems/ibsetupws.exe provides step-by-step instructions for configuring the Integration Broker. PeopleBooks provides additional documentation describing MCF and Integration Broker configuration.

Our objective is to create a data type that will fetch e-mail headers from a user's e-mail account and wrap those headers in XML. In order to connect to an e-mail server, PeopleSoft needs to know the target node name, the e-mail server, the user's e-mail account ID, and the user's password. Our criteria for determining whether a pagelet's variable is a setting or a parameter is the variability of the variable. If a variable varies by user, then it is a parameter. If it varies by pagelet, but is constant across users, then it is a setting. Since most companies have only one main e-mail server, and since we know the node name, we will make these two variables data type settings. The values for these settings may change from pagelet to pagelet, but not from user to user. We will create the username and password variables as data type parameters because they will vary from user to user.

Remember the query pagelet we created earlier? The query name is a setting; therefore, we set its value at design time at step 2. In step 3, we had the option of allowing users to configure the query data type's parameters or specifying values at design time.

Coding the Custom Data Type

Let's start coding this data type by creating a new application package named APT_PAGELET. Within this application class, add the subpackage DataSource. To the DataSource subpackage, add the application class EMailDataSource. After creating the application class structure, the fully qualified name for the EMailDataSource, will be APT_PAGELET:DataSource:EMailDataSource. Starting with imports and other definitions, we will step through the code required for this data type. You will find the full EMailDataSource code listing at the end of this section. I suggest you wait until reaching the full code listing before adding any code to the EMailDataSource.

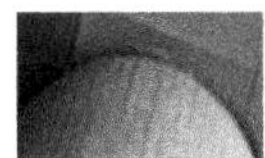

NOTE
The Pagelet Wizard does not enforce package and class naming conventions. Therefore, when creating your own data types, you can structure your application package in a manner that suits your needs.

```
import PTPPB_PAGELET:DataSource:DataSource;
import PTPPB_PAGELET:UTILITY:Collection;
import PTPPB_PAGELET:UTILITY:Setting;
```

```
/* All Pagelet Wizard Data Types must extend the abstract class
 * PTPPB_PAGELET:DataSource:DataSource
 */
class EMailDataSource extends PTPPB_PAGELET:DataSource:DataSource
   method EMailDataSource(&id_param As string);
   method initializeSettings(&NewSettings As
         PTPPB_PAGELET:UTILITY:Collection);
   method processSettingsChange();
   method execute() Returns string;
   method Clone() Returns object;
end-class;
```

The `PTPPB_PAGELET:DataSource:DataSource` contains four abstract methods. As you learned in Chapter 1, abstract methods are methods with a signature, but no implementation. These methods form a contract between the Pagelet Wizard and the developer. Since the `DataSource` base class provides default implementations for several of its methods, the only methods we need to declare are the constructor and the base class's abstract methods.

The DataSource Constructor

Let's implement the application class constructor.

```
method EMailDataSource
   /+ &id_param as String +/
   %Super = create PTPPB_PAGELET:DataSource:DataSource(&id_param);
   %This.setObjectSubType("APT_EMAIL");
   %This.setCanHaveParameters( True);
   %This.initializeSettings(%This.Settings);
   %This.hasSourceDataLinkHTML = False;
end-method;
```

Since the base class's constructor contains parameters, this class must also have a constructor that tells PeopleSoft how to create an instance of the base (`%Super`) class. The `&id_param` constructor parameter represents the metadata ID for this data type in the Pagelet Wizard metadata repository. After coding this data type, we will create an ID for this data type by registering it in the Pagelet Wizard's metadata repository. We won't use this value directly, but will pass it along to the base class constructor.

The rest of the method calls in the constructor configure default values for this data type. For example, setting `hasSourceDataLinkHTML` to `False` tells the Pagelet Wizard that this data type does not provide a link to the pagelet's underlying source data.

The initializeSettings Abstract Method

Data type constructors call the `initializeSettings` abstract method. The `initializeSettings` method is responsible for configuring the data type *setting* fields. Setting configuration consists of identifying the field type, prompt, and display order. The following `initializeSettings` method configures the server name and node name setting fields.

```
method initializeSettings
   /+ &NewSettings as PTPPB_PAGELET:UTILITY:Collection +/
   /+ Extends/implements
      PTPPB_PAGELET:DataSource:DataSource.initializeSettings +/
```

```
   Local PTPPB_PAGELET:UTILITY:Setting &server;
   Local PTPPB_PAGELET:UTILITY:Setting &node;
   Local string &nodeLabel;

   If &NewSettings = Null Then
      &NewSettings = create PTPPB_PAGELET:UTILITY:Collection(
            "APT_EMailDataSourceSettings");
   End-If;
   %This.setSettings(&NewSettings);

   &nodeLabel = CreateRecord(Record.PSMSGNODEDEFN)
         .MSGNODENAME.GetLongLabel("MSGNODENAME");

   &server = %This.initDefaultSetting(&SERVER_SETTING_,
         "E-mail Server");
   &node = %This.initDefaultSetting(&NODE_SETTING_, &nodeLabel);

   REM ** Set node prompt table;
   &node.EditType = &node.EDITTYPE_PROMPTTABLE;
   &node.PromptTable = "PSNODEDEFNVW";

   If (%This.settingHasAValue(&SERVER_SETTING_) And
         %This.settingHasAValue(&NODE_SETTING_)) Then
      %This.setSettingsComplete( True);
   End-If;

end-method;
```

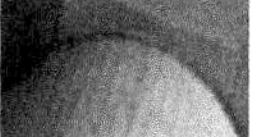

NOTE

The preceding code listing uses string literals for label text. PeopleSoft recommends storing strings in message catalog definitions. The message catalog offers multilingual support and online maintenance. The remainder of the code in this chapter uses string literals to simplify code examples. In practice, you should use message catalog definitions.

Let's break the `initializeSettings` method into manageable segments. The first segment contains the method signature and two setting declarations: `&server` and `&node`.

```
method initializeSettings
   /+ &NewSettings as PTPPB_PAGELET:UTILITY:Collection +/
   /+ Extends/implements
      PTPPB_PAGELET:DataSource:DataSource.initializeSettings +/
   Local PTPPB_PAGELET:UTILITY:Setting &server;
   Local PTPPB_PAGELET:UTILITY:Setting &node;
   Local string &nodeLabel;
```

The method signature has a parameter named `&NewSettings`. When we implement the abstract `Clone` method, we will call the `initializeSettings` method, providing settings from the original. When cloned, the `initializeSettings` method should use settings from the `&NewSettings` method parameter.

The next code segment creates a new settings collection if necessary, and then attaches that collection to this object instance by calling the `setSettings` method.

```
If &NewSettings = Null Then
   &NewSettings = create PTPPB_PAGELET:UTILITY:Collection(
         "APT_EMailDataSourceSettings");
End-If;
%This.setSettings(&NewSettings);
```

Here's the third segment:

```
&nodeLabel = CreateRecord(Record.PSMSGNODEDEFN)
      .MSGNODENAME.GetLongLabel("MSGNODENAME");
&server = %This.initDefaultSetting(&SERVER_SETTING_,
      "E-mail Server");
&node = %This.initDefaultSetting(&NODE_SETTING_, &nodeLabel);
```

This segment stands out from the rest because it uses a method we haven't created yet. As I was writing the `initializeSettings` method, I noticed each setting required similar initialization. Rather than write the same code for each setting, I chose to create a private *helper* method to create and initialize common setting values.

This section of the `initializeSettings` method also uses two variables we haven't declared: `&SERVER_SETTING_` and `&NODE_SETTING_`. These variables represent constants we will declare in the application class declaration. Rather than risk mistyping a setting name in the various code locations that refer to the setting by name, I chose to create a compiler checked constant. Unlike an unchecked string, if you incorrectly spell the constant, the PeopleCode compiler will throw an error. You will see the constant declaration in the final code listing at the end of this section.

The last item we will cover regarding this segment is the `&nodeLabel` variable. Whenever possible, we want to reuse existing configurations, object definitions, and so on. Rather than create a message catalog definition or hard-code a label for a well-used, well-known delivered field, I chose to reuse the existing node field label. This ensures that the label you use in the Pagelet Wizard is the same label a user would see when viewing nodes from the Integration Broker node configuration page.

The fourth segment of the code contains the following lines:

```
REM ** Set node prompt table;
&node.EditType = &node.EDITTYPE_PROMPTTABLE;
&node.PromptTable = "PSNODEDEFNVW";
```

The `&server` setting is a free-form text field with no validation. As such, the `initDefaultSetting` method performs the entire setting's configuration. The `&node` setting, on the other hand, represents a predefined Integration Broker node. Therefore, we can use a prompt table to identify and validate the user-chosen value. The lines in this segment further configure the `&node` setting by specifying the edit type and prompt table.

The final segment in this method calls the `setSettingsComplete` method, which is the method that controls the Pagelet Wizard step 2 Next button.

```
    If (%This.settingHasAValue(&SERVER_SETTING_) And
          %This.settingHasAValue(&NODE_SETTING_)) Then
       %This.setSettingsComplete( True);
    End-If;

end-method;
```

Since the server name and node name values are required by the MCF e-mail application classes, we don't want a user to move to step 3 until these fields contain valid values. This code executes a method named `settingHasAValue` to determine whether a setting has a value. This determination requires a couple of tests. Rather than code each test for each field in the `initializeSettings` method, and then again in the `processSettingsChange` method, I chose to centralize the logic in a single helper method. I believe this design decision helps the code read more like a sentence and less like obfuscated code. The following code listing describes the `settingHasAValue` method:

```
method settingHasAValue
   /+ &settingName as String +/
   /+ Returns Boolean +/
   Local PTPPB_PAGELET:UTILITY:Setting &setting;

   REM ** Look up the setting in the settings collection;
   &setting = %This.Settings.getItemByID(&settingName);

   REM ** Is it null? If so, then return False;
   If &setting = Null Then
      Return False
   End-If;

   REM ** Is it a zero length string? If so, then return False;
   If &setting.Value = "" Then
      Return False;
   End-If;

   REM ** The setting passed all the tests, so it must have a value;
   Return True;
end-method;
```

In the `initializeSettings` method, we test for the presence of a value (positive test). In the `processSettingsChange` method, we will test for the absence of a value (negative test). Rather than write `If` statements that use the `Not` operator, let's write a helper method that is the inverse of the `settingHasAValue` method, appropriately named `settingNeedsAValue`. Multicriteria positive tests are much easier to read than multicriteria tests for negative values.

```
method settingNeedsAValue
   /+ &settingName as String +/
   /+ Returns Boolean +/
   Return ( Not %This.settingHasAValue(&settingName));
end-method;
```

The `settingNeedsAValue` method is really just an alias for `Not %This.settingHasAValue`. It is my opinion that this alias is much easier to read than `If ((Not ...) Or (Not ...) Then`.

While we're on the subject of helper methods, here is the code for the `initDefaultSetting` method introduced a few paragraphs earlier:

```
method initDefaultSetting
   /+ &settingId as String, +/
   /+ &settingLabel as String +/
   /+ Returns PTPPB_PAGELET:UTILITY:Setting +/
   Local PTPPB_PAGELET:UTILITY:Setting &setting;
   &setting = %This.Settings.getItemByID(&settingId);

   If &setting = Null Then
      &setting = %This.createSettingProperty(&settingId, "");
   End-If;

   &setting.EditType = &setting.EDITTYPE_NOTABLEEDIT;
   &setting.FieldType = &setting.FIELDTYPE_CHARACTER;
   &setting.Enabled = True;
   &setting.Visible = True;
   &setting.RefreshOnChange = True;
   &setting.Required = True;
   &setting.LongName = &settingLabel;

   &setting.setObjectToRefreshOnValueChange(%This);

   Return &setting;
end-method;
```

When implementing the `initializeSettings` method, it is important to consider the case where a user creates, configures, saves, and closes a pagelet, only to reopen it later. When a user opens an existing pagelet definition, the Next button should be enabled, since all of the settings were previously set. Also, all the appropriate settings should be visible and enabled, just as they would be after finishing the Pagelet Wizard's second step.

The processSettingsChange Abstract Method

The next abstract method to implement is the `processSettingsChange` method. The Pagelet Wizard calls this method for each `FieldChange` event in step 2. This allows you to enable, disable, and redefine setting fields based on values chosen by the user. A good example of this is the Integration Broker data type, which is implemented in the `PTPPB_PAGELET:DataSource:IBDataSource` application class. After the user selects the Integration Broker data type in step 2, the Pagelet Wizard displays only the Service Operation prompt field. After the user selects a service operation, the Pagelet Wizard displays the Receiver Node Name prompt field.

The following code defines the `EMailDataSource processSettingsChange` method:

```
method processSettingsChange
   /+ Extends/implements
      PTPPB_PAGELET:DataSource:DataSource.processSettingsChange +/
```

```
   /* do nothing if no setting or if a setting is missing */
   rem Local PTPPB_PAGELET:UTILITY:Collection &outputs;
   Local PTPPB_PAGELET:DataSource:DataSourceParameter &parm;

   REM ** return if settings aren't valid;
   If (%This.settingNeedsAValue(&SERVER_SETTING_) Or
         %This.settingNeedsAValue(&NODE_SETTING_)) Then
      %This.setSettingsComplete( False);
      Return;
   End-If;

   /* We are finished with the Data Type settings. Show input and
    * output fields, if any, and then set up parameters for step 3.
    */
   rem &outputs = create PTPPB_PAGELET:UTILITY:Collection(
         "OutputFields");
   rem ... add output fields here...;
   rem %This.setOutputFields(&outputs);

   %This.initDefaultParameter(&USERNAME_PARM_,
         "User Name").Required = False;
   %This.initDefaultParameter(&PASSWORD_PARM_,
         "Password").Required = False;
   &parm = %This.initDefaultParameter(&MAXMSGCOUNT_PARM_,
         "Maximum Message Count");
   &parm.DefaultValue = "10";
   &parm.FieldType = &parm.FIELDTYPE_NUMBER;

   /* Add settings as internal parameters to save them with the
    * rest of the pagelet's data;
    */
   &parm = %This.initDefaultParameter(&SERVER_SETTING_, "");
   &parm.Value = %This.Settings.getItemByID(&SERVER_SETTING_).Value;
   &parm.UsageType = &parm.USAGETYPE_INTERNAL;

   &parm = %This.initDefaultParameter(&NODE_SETTING_, "");
   &parm.Value = %This.Settings.getItemByID(&NODE_SETTING_).Value;
   &parm.UsageType = &parm.USAGETYPE_INTERNAL;

   /* and set the ParameterCollection to be immutable */
   %This.getParameterCollection().setImmutable();

   %This.setSettingsComplete( True);
end-method;
```

A `processSettingsChange` method should start by validating the data type's settings. In our case, we want to validate the server and node name. For simplicity, we test only for the presence of a value. We could further verify the server setting by actually trying to connect to the e-mail server. If any data type setting is invalid or incorrect, it is important to call `%This.setSettingsComplete( False)` and then return without further processing. Once all settings have appropriate values, call `%This.setSettingsComplete( True)` to allow the user to move to step 3. The Pagelet Wizard will not enable the Next button until the `DataSource.SettingsComplete` property evaluates to `True`.

Some data types have input and output parameters that change based on the data type's settings. For example, the query pagelet we created earlier in this chapter had output fields that were determined by the query name chosen in step 2. The Pagelet Wizard shows the output fields to the user in step 2. If that query had prompts, those prompts would have appeared above the output fields as input fields. You set up the output fields collection after validating the data type's settings. The `processSettingsChange` code contains a declaration for an output field collection, but I commented it out since it isn't used by the `EMailDataSource`.

At this point in the wizard, the user is ready to move to step 3. This step displays the list of data type parameters that a home page user may want to modify. Parameters differ from settings. Parameters are pagelet instance-specific, whereas settings are common to all instances of a pagelet. In our case, we will have parameters for the user's e-mail username and password. Whereas the server name is common to all instances of the pagelet, the user's credentials are specific to the user. The next section of the `processSettingsChange` method initializes the step 3 parameters:

```
%This.initDefaultParameter(&USERNAME_PARM_,(
      "User Name").Required = False;
%This.initDefaultParameter(&PASSWORD_PARM_,
      "Password").Required = False;
&parm = %This.initDefaultParameter(
      &MAXMSGCOUNT_PARM_, "Maximum Message Count");
&parm.DefaultValue = "10";
&parm.FieldType = &parm.FIELDTYPE_NUMBER;
```

Just as with the setting initialization code in `initializeSettings`, I've taken the coding-by-exception approach. After writing 30 lines of common code, I centralized that common code into the `initDefaultParameter` private method, and then used my `processSettingsChange` code to set only the parameter properties that are exceptions to the default properties.

Coding by Exception and Other Antipatterns

Coding by exception is a pattern whereby programmers code only for exceptions. For example, the `initDefaultSetting` and `initDefaultParameter` methods set up defaults so that I code just for exceptional cases. The effect of applying this pattern to the `initializeSettings` and `processSettingsChange` methods is a reduction of 30 lines of code per method. However, it isn't the reduction in lines that I appreciate; it is the clarity of a code listing that is 30 lines shorter. Removing 60 lines of redundant code is like tuning in a fuzzy radio station. Communication is clearer without all that static.

Many programmers consider coding by exception to be an antipattern. By definition, an *antipattern* is a common but ineffective design pattern. Based on this definition, I'm sure every pattern becomes an antipattern when taken to extremes. Since my goal for using the pattern was to improve the clarity of my code, I consider the application of this pattern to be *effective*.

Another complaint raised by well-known design pattern enthusiasts is that coding by exception degrades performance. If you look closely at the `processSettingsChange` method and the `initDefaultParameter` method, you will notice some redundancy. For example, the `initDefaultParameter` method sets a parameter's required property to `True`. For some of the parameters, the `processSettingsChange` method immediately resets that property to `False`. This is a clear redundancy that may impact performance. The redundancy in this case, however, is no different from the redundancy involved in initializing many PeopleCode variables. Consider the following code:

```
Local number &maxValue = 10;
Local number &index;

For &index = 1 to &maxValue
   ...
End-For
```

At runtime, the variable `&index` has an initial value of `0`. That value is set when the variable is declared and is immediately available for use. However, as you can see from the code listing, I do not intend to use the value `0`. In fact, I don't actually set the value of `&index` to a meaningful number until I use it in the `For` loop. In this case, the redundant initialization of the `&index` variable is a necessary part of the PeopleCode language. It is not possible to declare a number, string, or Boolean variable without initializing it, because the PeopleCode runtime implicitly initializes primitive variable types at declaration. Does this have an impact on performance? Of course, but I doubt the impact is material.

Redundant initialization becomes important when dealing with constructed objects. Creating an in-memory instance of a record requires significantly more resources than setting the value of a numeric memory pointer. Instantiating a record, for example, may cause the PeopleCode runtime to execute SQL statements to collect the record's metadata. Therefore, I would think twice about using coding by exception to initialize object variables like records, application classes, and so on. I believe it is this type of exception coding that led to the modern assessment of coding by exception. This is no surprise, considering how modern languages focus on objects.

Patterns (design patterns or antipatterns) have a significant impact on the programs we create. Knowing them and using them effectively can have a dramatic positive impact. Unfortunately, the converse is also true. Using them ineffectively can have a dramatic negative impact.

As I previously mentioned, pagelets have two types of fields: settings and parameters. The Pagelet Wizard will save parameter values in the database, but not setting values. You are responsible for persisting setting values. Parameters can be stored in common field types, whereas data type settings may require special field specifications. For example, the HTML data type allows you to enter an unlimited amount of text in a setting field. With a setting like this, you may need to create a stand-alone record for storing that unlimited quantity of text.

After a pagelet's settings pass validation, you need to implement some form of persistence. You can find several examples of persistence methods in the `processSettingsChange` method of the delivered PTPPB_PAGELET:DataSource classes. One method is to copy settings into internal parameters. This is the approach I used in the processSettingsChange code. The following lines are an excerpt from that method and show how I used exception-based coding to change the usage type from *user-specified* to *internal*. Internal parameters are stored with regular pagelet parameters, but are not visible to the user.

```
/* Add settings as internal parameters to save them with the
 * rest of the pagelet's data;
 */
&parm = %This.initDefaultParameter(&SERVER_SETTING_, "");
&parm.Value = %This.Settings.getItemByID(&SERVER_SETTING_).Value;
&parm.UsageType = &parm.USAGETYPE_INTERNAL;

&parm = %This.initDefaultParameter(&NODE_SETTING_, "");
&parm.Value = %This.Settings.getItemByID(&NODE_SETTING_).Value;
&parm.UsageType = &parm.USAGETYPE_INTERNAL;
```

The processSettingsChange method executes a private method named initDefaultParameter. The initDefaultParameter method is similar to the initDefaultSetting method described earlier, but with one key difference. Since the Pagelet Wizard stores parameter information, including the usage type, we don't need to reinitialize these properties. The following listing contains the code for the initDefaultParameter method:

```
method initDefaultParameter
   /+ &parmId as String, +/
   /+ &parmLabel as String +/
   /+ Returns PTPPB_PAGELET:DataSource:DataSourceParameter +/
   Local PTPPB_PAGELET:DataSource:DataSourceParameter &parm;
   Local PTPPB_PAGELET:UTILITY:Collection &coll;

   &coll = %This.getParameterCollection();
   &parm = &coll.getItemByID(&parmId);

   REM ** Create parameter and set default values;
   If (&parm = Null) Then
      &parm = create PTPPB_PAGELET:DataSource:DataSourceParameter(
            &parmId);

      &parm.LongName = &parmLabel;
      &parm.FieldType = &parm.FIELDTYPE_CHARACTER;
      &parm.UsageType = &parm.USAGETYPE_USERSPECIFIED;
      &parm.Required = True;

      &coll.Insert(&parm);
   End-If;

   Return &parm;
end-method;
```

The Clone Abstract Method

The `Clone` method is supposed to create an exact copy of the current object. Cloning involves more than just copying values from one object to the next. If an object contains objects, then the nested object must be cloned as well. The following code listing demonstrates a `Clone` method implementation:

```
method Clone
   /+ Returns Object +/
   /+ Extends/implements PTPPB_PAGELET:DataSource:DataSource.Clone +/
   Local APT_PAGELET:DataSource:EMailDataSource &copy =
         create APT_PAGELET:DataSource:EMailDataSource(%This.ID);
   &copy.PageletID = %This.PageletID;
   &copy.ParameterCollection = %This.ParameterCollection.Clone();
   REM ** If you have output fields, then uncomment next line;
   rem &copy.OutputFields = %This.OutputFields.Clone();
   &copy.initializeSettings(%This.Settings.Clone());
   Return &copy;
end-method;
```

Notice that the `Clone` method *deep* clones object properties like the `Settings` property. A *shallow* clone would cause the main object's properties and the new cloned object's properties to point to the same in-memory objects.

I commented out the deep clone for `OutputFields`. If you create a data type that uses output fields, be sure to clone the `OutputFields` as well.

The execute Abstract Method

The `execute` method is responsible for collecting data from its source and returning it in string form so the Pagelet Wizard can format the data for display. In our example data type, this means the data type must read parameters from the pagelet's parameters collection, connect to the e-mail server using the MCF application classes, and then format the returned e-mail headers as XML.

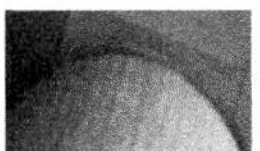

NOTE
Pagelet Wizard data types generally return XML because XML can be formatted in a variety of ways using XSL. For example, using XSL, you can convert XML into SVG or Flash charts, RTF, or standard HTML. XSL is a very powerful transformation language. If you aren't already familiar with XSL, I encourage you to learn it.

```
method execute
   /+ Returns String +/
   /+ Extends/implements
         PTPPB_PAGELET:DataSource:DataSource.execute +/
   Local PTPPB_PAGELET:UTILITY:Collection &paramColl;
   Local PT_MCF_MAIL:MCFGetMail &getMail;
   Local PT_MCF_MAIL:MCFInboundEmail &email;
   Local array of PT_MCF_MAIL:MCFInboundEmail &emailArr;
   Local XmlDoc &xmlDoc;
   Local XmlNode &xmlDocNode;
   Local XmlNode &rowNode;
```

```
Local XmlNode &dataNode;
Local string &userNameValue;
Local string &passwordValue;
Local string &server;
Local string &nodeName;
Local string &dttmSent;
Local number &maxMsgCount;
Local number &msgIndex = 0;

&paramColl = %This.getParameterCollection();

REM ** Read parameters from saved collection;
&maxMsgCount = Value(&paramColl.getItemByID(
      &MAXMSGCOUNT_PARM_).evaluatedValue());
&server = &paramColl.getItemByID(
      &SERVER_SETTING_).evaluatedValue();
&nodeName = &paramColl.getItemByID(
      &NODE_SETTING_).evaluatedValue();
&userNameValue = &paramColl.getItemByID(
      &USERNAME_PARM_).evaluatedValue();
&passwordValue = &paramColl.getItemByID(
      &PASSWORD_PARM_).evaluatedValue();

REM ** Fetch e-mails;
&getMail = create PT_MCF_MAIL:MCFGetMail();
&getMail.SetMCFEmail(&userNameValue, &passwordValue, &server,
      &nodeName);
&emailArr = &getMail.ReadEmails(&maxMsgCount);

REM ** Create an XML Document containing e-mails;
&xmlDoc = CreateXmlDoc(
      "<?xml version='1.0' standalone='yes'?><messages/>");
&xmlDocNode = &xmlDoc.DocumentElement;
If (&getMail.Status <> 0) Then
   &rowNode = &xmlDocNode.AddElement("error");
   &rowNode.AddAttribute("status", String(&getMail.Status));
Else
   While &emailArr.Next(&msgIndex)
      &email = &emailArr [&msgIndex];

      REM ** Human readable date format;
      &dttmSent = DateTimeToLocalizedString(
            &email.DttmSent, "EEE, MMM d, yyyy 'at' HH:mm:ss");

      &rowNode = &xmlDocNode.AddElement("message");
      &rowNode.AddAttribute("id", &email.UID);

      &dataNode = &rowNode.AddElement(
            "from").AddText(&email.From);
```

```
        &dataNode = &rowNode.AddElement(
              "to").AddText(&email.NotifyTo);
        &dataNode = &rowNode.AddElement(
              "cc").AddText(&email.NotifyCC);
        &dataNode = &rowNode.AddElement(
              "subject").AddText(&email.Subject);
        &dataNode = &rowNode.AddElement(
              "date-sent").AddText(&dttmSent);
     End-While;
  End-If;

  Return &xmlDoc.GenXmlString();
end-method;
```

Following the variable declarations in the preceding code are five lines of code that read parameter values into local variables. Notice that I use the `evaluatedValue` property of each parameter. As you saw in step 3 of the Pagelet Wizard, parameter values can be derived from system variables. The `evaluatedValue` property takes this into account and returns the correct value for the parameter, regardless of the parameter's `UsageType`.

The next three lines use the `MCFGetMail` application class to read messages from the e-mail server. The MCF classes abstract the details of working with the Integration Broker `GETMAILTARGET` target connector. For more information about the `MCFGetMail` application class, see the *PeopleCode API Reference*.

The rest of the code in this method uses the PeopleCode XML classes to generate an XML document from an array of e-mail messages.

Templates

The `execute` method used by the Pagelet Wizard generates the same document structure every time it runs. The detail values and row count may differ between executions, but the structure is always the same. With careful study, it is possible to infer the structure of the generated XML document, but the actual structure is not readily discernible. Unfortunately, the easiest way to determine the shape of the XML document is to run the `execute` method and view its results.

Templates, on the other hand, look like the result document, but with variables. An HTML definition is an example of a template. HTML definitions contain all the markup required to create a result document and may have bind variables to insert dynamic, runtime-evaluated information. Since the Pagelet Wizard always executes online, we could mock up the resultant XML document in an HTML definition. HTML definitions, however, don't support *control flow statements* (loops, conditional logic, and so on). One workaround is to create two HTML definitions: one main document template and one row template. Another alternative is to use a Java template engine. In Chapter 9, you will learn how to use the Apache Velocity template engine to generate structured documents from PeopleCode objects.

The EMailDataSource Code Listing

The complete code listing for our APT_PAGELET:DataSource:EMailDataSource follows. This code listing contains a few details that were missing from the previous listings. For example, the previous listings used constants that were never declared. The following listing contains those declarations.

```
import PTPPB_PAGELET:DataSource:DataSourceParameter;
import PTPPB_PAGELET:DataSource:DataSource;
import PTPPB_PAGELET:UTILITY:Collection;
import PTPPB_PAGELET:UTILITY:Setting;

import PT_MCF_MAIL:MCFGetMail;
import PT_MCF_MAIL:MCFInboundEmail;

/* All Pagelet Wizard Data Types must extend the abstract class
 * PTPPB_PAGELET:DataSource:DataSource
 */
class EMailDataSource extends PTPPB_PAGELET:DataSource:DataSource
   method EMailDataSource(&id_param As string);
   method initializeSettings(
         &NewSettings As PTPPB_PAGELET:UTILITY:Collection);
   method processSettingsChange();
   method execute() Returns string;
   method Clone() Returns object;

private
   method initDefaultSetting(&settingId As string,
         &settingLabel As string)
         Returns PTPPB_PAGELET:UTILITY:Setting;
   method initDefaultParameter(&parmId As string,
         &parmLabel As string)
         Returns PTPPB_PAGELET:DataSource:DataSourceParameter;
   method settingHasAValue(&settingName As string) Returns boolean;
   method settingNeedsAValue(&settingName As string) Returns boolean;

   REM ** Step 2 setting names;
   Constant &SERVER_SETTING_ = "server";
   Constant &NODE_SETTING_ = "node";

   REM ** Step 3 parameters;
   Constant &USERNAME_PARM_ = "username";
   Constant &PASSWORD_PARM_ = "password";
   Constant &MAXMSGCOUNT_PARM_ = ".MAXMSGCOUNT";
end-class;

/* Constructor */
method EMailDataSource
   /+ &id_param as String +/
   %Super = create PTPPB_PAGELET:DataSource:DataSource(&id_param);
   %This.setObjectSubType("APT_EMAIL");
```

```
   %This.setCanHaveParameters( True);
   %This.initializeSettings(%This.Settings);
   %This.hasSourceDataLinkHTML = False;
end-method;

method initializeSettings
   /+ &NewSettings as PTPPB_PAGELET:UTILITY:Collection +/
   /+ Extends/implements
      PTPPB_PAGELET:DataSource:DataSource.initializeSettings +/
   Local PTPPB_PAGELET:UTILITY:Setting &server;
   Local PTPPB_PAGELET:UTILITY:Setting &node;
   Local string &nodeLabel;

   If &NewSettings = Null Then
      &NewSettings = create PTPPB_PAGELET:UTILITY:Collection(
            "APT_EMailDataSourceSettings");
   End-If;
   %This.setSettings(&NewSettings);

   &nodeLabel = CreateRecord(Record.PSMSGNODEDEFN)
         .MSGNODENAME.GetLongLabel("MSGNODENAME");

   &server = %This.initDefaultSetting(&SERVER_SETTING_,
         "E-mail Server");
   &node = %This.initDefaultSetting(&NODE_SETTING_, &nodeLabel);

   REM ** Set node prompt table;
   &node.EditType = &node.EDITTYPE_PROMPTTABLE;
   &node.PromptTable = "PSNODEDEFNVW";

   If (%This.settingHasAValue(&SERVER_SETTING_) And
         %This.settingHasAValue(&NODE_SETTING_)) Then
      %This.setSettingsComplete( True);
   End-If;

end-method;

method processSettingsChange
   /+ Extends/implements
      PTPPB_PAGELET:DataSource:DataSource.processSettingsChange +/
   /* do nothing if no setting - or if a setting is missing */
   rem Local PTPPB_PAGELET:UTILITY:Collection &outputs;
   Local PTPPB_PAGELET:DataSource:DataSourceParameter &parm;

   REM ** return if settings aren't valid;
   If (%This.settingNeedsAValue(&SERVER_SETTING_) Or
         %This.settingNeedsAValue(&NODE_SETTING_)) Then
      %This.setSettingsComplete( False);
      Return;
   End-If;
```

```
   /* We are finished with the Data Type settings, show input and
    * output fields, if any, and then set up parameters for step 3.
    */
   rem &outputs = create PTPPB_PAGELET:UTILITY:Collection("OutputFields");
   rem ... add output fields here...;
   rem %This.setOutputFields(&outputs);

   %This.initDefaultParameter(&USERNAME_PARM_,
         "User Name").Required = False;
   %This.initDefaultParameter(&PASSWORD_PARM_,
         "Password").Required = False;

   &parm = %This.initDefaultParameter(&MAXMSGCOUNT_PARM_,
         "Maximum Message Count");
   &parm.DefaultValue = "10";
   &parm.FieldType = &parm.FIELDTYPE_NUMBER;

   /* Add settings as internal parameters to save them with the
    * rest of the pagelet's data;
    */
   &parm = %This.initDefaultParameter(&SERVER_SETTING_, "");
   &parm.Value = %This.Settings.getItemByID(&SERVER_SETTING_).Value;
   &parm.UsageType = &parm.USAGETYPE_INTERNAL;

   &parm = %This.initDefaultParameter(&NODE_SETTING_, "");
   &parm.Value = %This.Settings.getItemByID(&NODE_SETTING_).Value;
   &parm.UsageType = &parm.USAGETYPE_INTERNAL;

   /* and set the ParameterCollection to be immutable */
   %This.getParameterCollection().setImmutable();

   %This.setSettingsComplete( True);
end-method;

method execute
   /+ Returns String +/
   /+ Extends/implements
         PTPPB_PAGELET:DataSource:DataSource.execute +/
   Local PTPPB_PAGELET:UTILITY:Collection &paramColl;
   Local PT_MCF_MAIL:MCFGetMail &getMail;
   Local PT_MCF_MAIL:MCFInboundEmail &email;
   Local array of PT_MCF_MAIL:MCFInboundEmail &emailArr;
   Local XmlDoc &xmlDoc;
   Local XmlNode &xmlDocNode;
   Local XmlNode &rowNode;
   Local XmlNode &dataNode;
   Local string &userNameValue;
   Local string &passwordValue;
   Local string &server;
   Local string &nodeName;
```

```
Local string &dttmSent;
Local number &maxMsgCount;
Local number &msgIndex = 0;

&paramColl = %This.getParameterCollection();

REM ** Read parameters from saved collection;
&maxMsgCount = Value(&paramColl.getItemByID(
      &MAXMSGCOUNT_PARM_).evaluatedValue());
&server = &paramColl.getItemByID(
      &SERVER_SETTING_).evaluatedValue();
&nodeName = &paramColl.getItemByID(
      &NODE_SETTING_).evaluatedValue();
&userNameValue = &paramColl.getItemByID(
      &USERNAME_PARM_).evaluatedValue();
&passwordValue = &paramColl.getItemByID(
      &PASSWORD_PARM_).evaluatedValue();

REM ** Fetch e-mails;
&getMail = create PT_MCF_MAIL:MCFGetMail();
&getMail.SetMCFEmail(&userNameValue, &passwordValue, &server,
      &nodeName);
&emailArr = &getMail.ReadEmails(&maxMsgCount);

REM ** Create an XML Document containing e-mails;
&xmlDoc = CreateXmlDoc(
      "<?xml version='1.0' standalone='yes'?><messages/>");
&xmlDocNode = &xmlDoc.DocumentElement;
If (&getMail.Status <> 0) Then
   &rowNode = &xmlDocNode.AddElement("error");
   &rowNode.AddAttribute("status", String(&getMail.Status));
Else
   While &emailArr.Next(&msgIndex)
      &email = &emailArr [&msgIndex];

      REM ** Human readable date format;
      &dttmSent = DateTimeToLocalizedString(&email.DttmSent,
            "EEE, MMM d, yyyy 'at' HH:mm:ss");

      &rowNode = &xmlDocNode.AddElement("message");
      &rowNode.AddAttribute("id", &email.UID);

      &dataNode = &rowNode.AddElement(
            "from").AddText(&email.From);
      &dataNode = &rowNode.AddElement(
            "to").AddText(&email.NotifyTo);
      &dataNode = &rowNode.AddElement(
            "cc").AddText(&email.NotifyCC);
      &dataNode = &rowNode.AddElement(
            "subject").AddText(&email.Subject);
```

```
        &dataNode = &rowNode.AddElement(
              "date-sent").AddText(&dttmSent);
      End-While;
   End-If;

   Return &xmlDoc.GenXmlString();
end-method;

/* Returns an exact duplicate of this EMailDataSource */
method Clone
   /+ Returns Object +/
   /+ Extends/implements PTPPB_PAGELET:DataSource:DataSource.Clone +/
   Local APT_PAGELET:DataSource:EMailDataSource &copy =
         create APT_PAGELET:DataSource:EMailDataSource(%This.ID);
   &copy.PageletID = %This.PageletID;
   &copy.ParameterCollection = %This.ParameterCollection.Clone();
   REM ** If you have output fields, then uncomment next line;
   rem &copy.OutputFields = %This.OutputFields.Clone();
   &copy.initializeSettings(%This.Settings.Clone());
   Return &copy;
end-method;

method initDefaultSetting
   /+ &settingId as String, +/
   /+ &settingLabel as String +/
   /+ Returns PTPPB_PAGELET:UTILITY:Setting +/
   Local PTPPB_PAGELET:UTILITY:Setting &setting;
   Local PTPPB_PAGELET:DataSource:DataSourceParameter &parm;

   &setting = %This.Settings.getItemByID(&settingId);

   REM ** Create setting;
   If &setting = Null Then
      &setting = %This.createSettingProperty(&settingId, "");
   End-If;

   REM ** Set default values;
   &setting.EditType = &setting.EDITTYPE_NOTABLEEDIT;
   &setting.FieldType = &setting.FIELDTYPE_CHARACTER;
   &setting.Enabled = True;
   &setting.Visible = True;
   &setting.RefreshOnChange = True;
   &setting.Required = True;
   &setting.LongName = &settingLabel;

   &setting.setObjectToRefreshOnValueChange(%This);

   Return &setting;
end-method;
```

```
method initDefaultParameter
   /+ &parmId as String, +/
   /+ &parmLabel as String +/
   /+ Returns PTPPB_PAGELET:DataSource:DataSourceParameter +/
   Local PTPPB_PAGELET:DataSource:DataSourceParameter &parm;
   Local PTPPB_PAGELET:UTILITY:Collection &coll;

   &coll = %This.getParameterCollection();
   &parm = &coll.getItemByID(&parmId);

   REM ** Create parameter and set default values;
   If (&parm = Null) Then
      &parm = create PTPPB_PAGELET:DataSource:DataSourceParameter(
            &parmId);

      &parm.LongName = &parmLabel;
      &parm.FieldType = &parm.FIELDTYPE_CHARACTER;
      &parm.UsageType = &parm.USAGETYPE_USERSPECIFIED;
      &parm.Required = True;

      &coll.Insert(&parm);
   End-If;

   Return &parm;
end-method;

method settingHasAValue
   /+ &settingName as String +/
   /+ Returns Boolean +/
   Local PTPPB_PAGELET:UTILITY:Setting &setting;

   REM ** Look up the setting in the settings collection;
   &setting = %This.Settings.getItemByID(&settingName);

   REM ** Is it null? If so, then return False;
   If &setting = Null Then
      Return False
   End-If;

   REM ** Is it a zero length string? If so, then return False;
   If &setting.Value = "" Then
      Return False;
   End-If;

   REM ** The setting passed all the tests, so it must have a value;
   Return True;
end-method;

method settingNeedsAValue
   /+ &settingName as String +/
```

```
    /+ Returns Boolean +/
    Return ( Not %This.settingHasAValue(&settingName));
end-method;
```

Other DataSource Properties and Methods

The DataSource abstract class contains a few other methods you can override to implement additional behavior. For example, you can override the getSourceDataLinkHTML method to provide a link to the pagelet's source data. You can see a demonstration of this in the PTPPB_PAGELET:DataSource:QueryDataSource application class.

%This.personalizationInstructions and %This.configurizationInstructions are examples of properties you can set to customize the behavior of the Pagelet Wizard.

If you look back at the EMailDataSource constructor, you will see the code: %This.setObjectSubType("APT_EMAIL"). The Pagelet Wizard uses this value to display the object type's DTD. A DTD describes the structure of an XML document, including the document's elements and attributes. The DTD is stored as an HTML definition with the name:

```
PTPPB_" | %This.ObjectSubType | "DTD"
```

You are not required to create a DTD for custom data types. If you choose to create a DTD, you can view that DTD online from PeopleTools | Portal | Pagelet Wizard | Define Data Types. Providing a DTD helps other developers create display formats, transformers, and XSL templates for your data type.

Registering the Data Type

The Pagelet Wizard needs some information about this data type before we can use it to create pagelets. To configure the data type's metadata, navigate to PeopleTools | Portal | Pagelet Wizard | Define Data Types and add a new value named APT_EMAIL. When defining a data type, we must specify the data type's application class, as well as the display formats that are compatible with this data type, as shown in Figure 4-8.

Creating a Test Pagelet

When you click the Personalize Content or Personalize Layout links on your PeopleSoft home page, you will see a list of available pagelets. To help organize the Personalize Content page, pagelets are listed under headings. Before we create a test pagelet, let's create a new heading.

Adding a New Pagelet Heading

Headings are actually subfolders of the Portal Objects | Pagelets portal registry folder. To create a new subfolder, open the portal registry by navigating to PeopleTools | Portal | Structure and Content. Within the portal registry, open the folder Portal Objects and then the folder Pagelets. While viewing the contents of the Pagelets portal registry folder, click the Add Folder hyperlink. Figure 4-9 is a partial screen shot of the folder we will use for custom pagelets. Create and save this folder. We will refer to it when we create an e-mail pagelet.

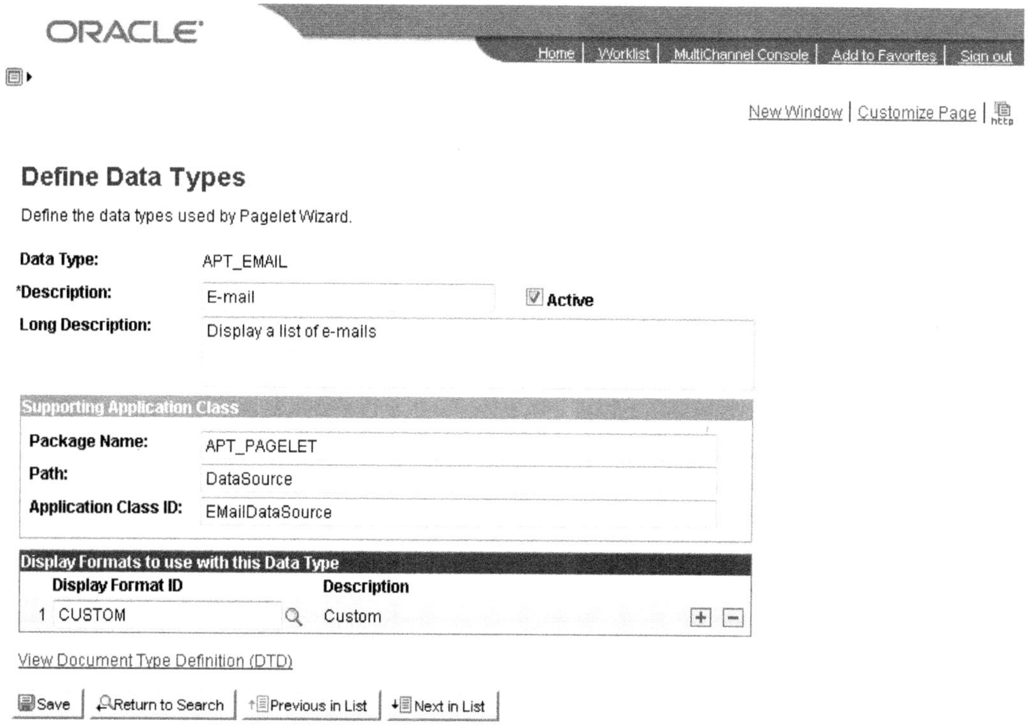

ORACLE

Home | Worklist | MultiChannel Console | Add to Favorites | Sign out

New Window | Customize Page | http

Define Data Types

Define the data types used by Pagelet Wizard.

Data Type: APT_EMAIL

***Description:** E-mail ☑ **Active**

Long Description: Display a list of e-mails

Supporting Application Class

Package Name: APT_PAGELET

Path: DataSource

Application Class ID: EMailDataSource

Display Formats to use with this Data Type

	Display Format ID	Description
1	CUSTOM	Custom

View Document Type Definition (DTD)

Save | Return to Search | Previous in List | Next in List

FIGURE 4-8. *Pagelet Wizard data type metadata*

Creating the E-Mail Pagelet

Navigate to PeopleTools | Portal | Pagelet Wizard | Pagelet Wizard and create a new pagelet using the `EMailDataSource` data type (see Figures 4-10 through 4-15), as follows:

1. On the Specify Pagelet Information page (step 1), add the value `APT_TEST_EMAIL`.
2. On the Select Data Source page (step 2), select the E-mail data type. After selecting the data type, the server and message node fields should appear. These fields appear in response to the `initializeSettings` method that is called by the `EMailDataSource` constructor. The Pagelet Wizard constructs a new instance of the `EMailDataSource` from the data type `FieldChange` event. Figure 4-11 shows my `EMailDataSource` with my server. After you enter values for the server and node, the Pagelet Wizard enables the Next button in the upper-right corner. The Pagelet Wizard enables this button in response to the `%This .setSettingsComplete( True)` call in our `processSettingsChange` method.

Customize Page | http

Folder Administration | Folder Security

Root >Portal Objects >Pagelets >Demo Pagelets

Folder Administration

Name: APT_DEMO
Parent Folder: Pagelets
*Label: Demo Pagelets
Copy object
Select New Parent Folder
Long Description: (254 Characters)
Product:
*Valid from date: 07/22/2009
Creation Date: 07/22/200
Sequence number:
Valid to date:
Author: PS
Object Owner ID
Hide from portal navigation
Hide from MSF navigation
Add Folder

Folder Navigation
Is Folder Navigation Disabled
Folder Navigation Object Name:

Folder Attributes
Delete
Name:
Translate
Label:
Attribute value:

FIGURE 4-9. *`APT_DEMO` pagelet portal registry folder*

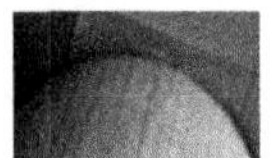

NOTE
Unless you are familiar with Integration Broker and MCF, I suggest you use the `MCF_GETMAIL` node, as shown Figure 4-11.

3. On the Specify Data Source page (step 3), you see the data type parameters we configured in the `processSettingsChange` method. Since we provided a default value for the only required parameter, the Pagelet Wizard automatically enables the Next button. As you recall from the query pagelet we created earlier, step 5 will generate a preview of the pagelet we are designing. Therefore, for design purposes, we will specify a username and password for the default values here. We will delete them before saving the pagelet, because we don't want to pass these default values along to the user, since they will contain our e-mail server credentials. Figure 4-12 shows step 3 with the parameters populated.

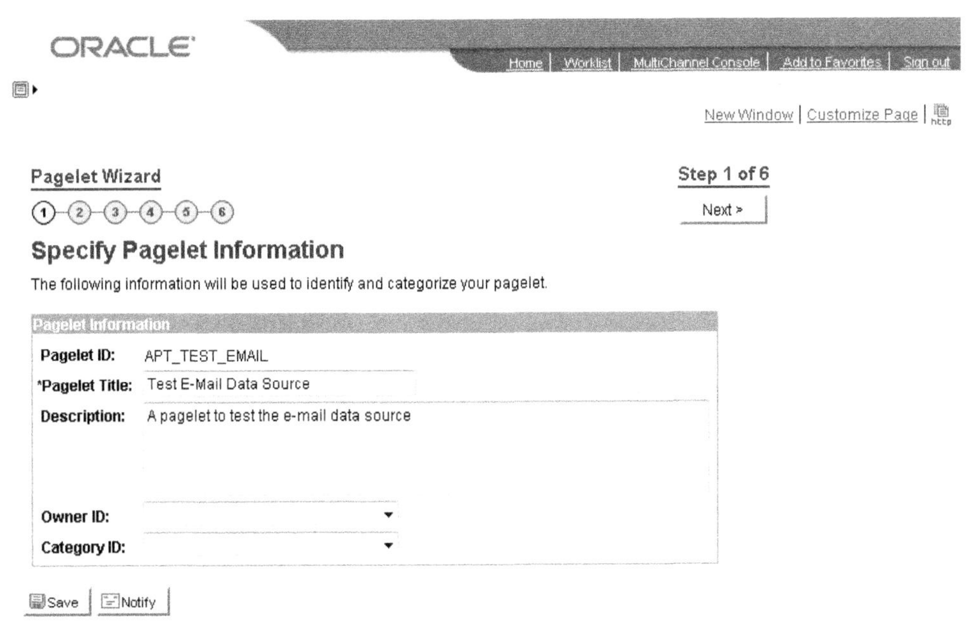

FIGURE 4-10. *Pagelet Wizard step 1 for the e-mail pagelet*

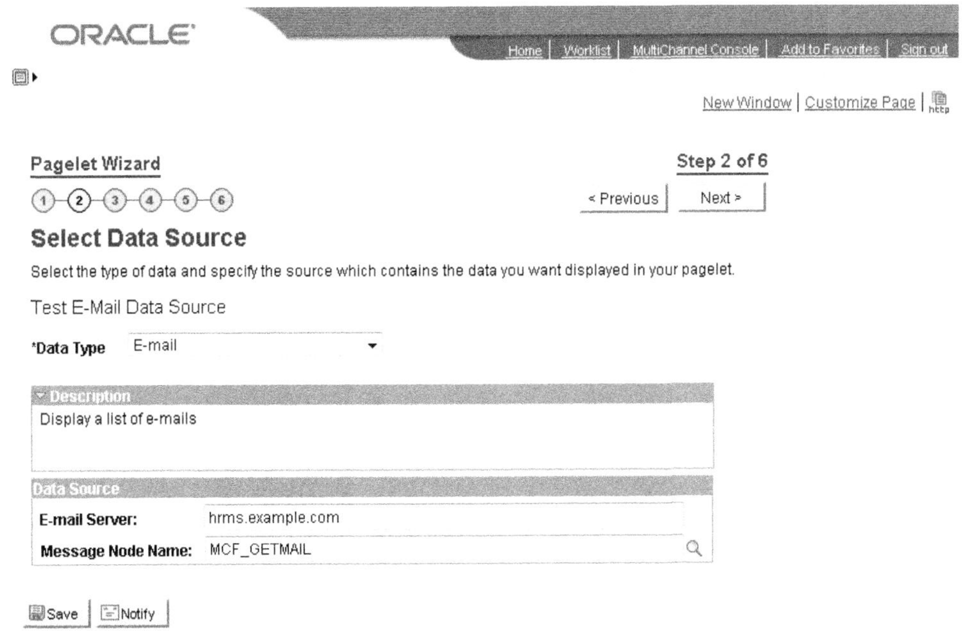

ORACLE
Home | Worklist | MultiChannel Console | Add to Favorites | Sign out
New Window | Customize Page | http

Pagelet Wizard
Step 2 of 6
1 2 3 4 5 6
< Previous
Next >

Select Data Source

Select the type of data and specify the source which contains the data you want displayed in your pagelet.

Test E-Mail Data Source

*Data Type E-mail

Description
Display a list of e-mails

Data Source
E-mail Server: hrms.example.com
Message Node Name: MCF_GETMAIL

Save
Notify

FIGURE 4-11. *Pagelet Wizard step 2 for the e-mail pagelet*

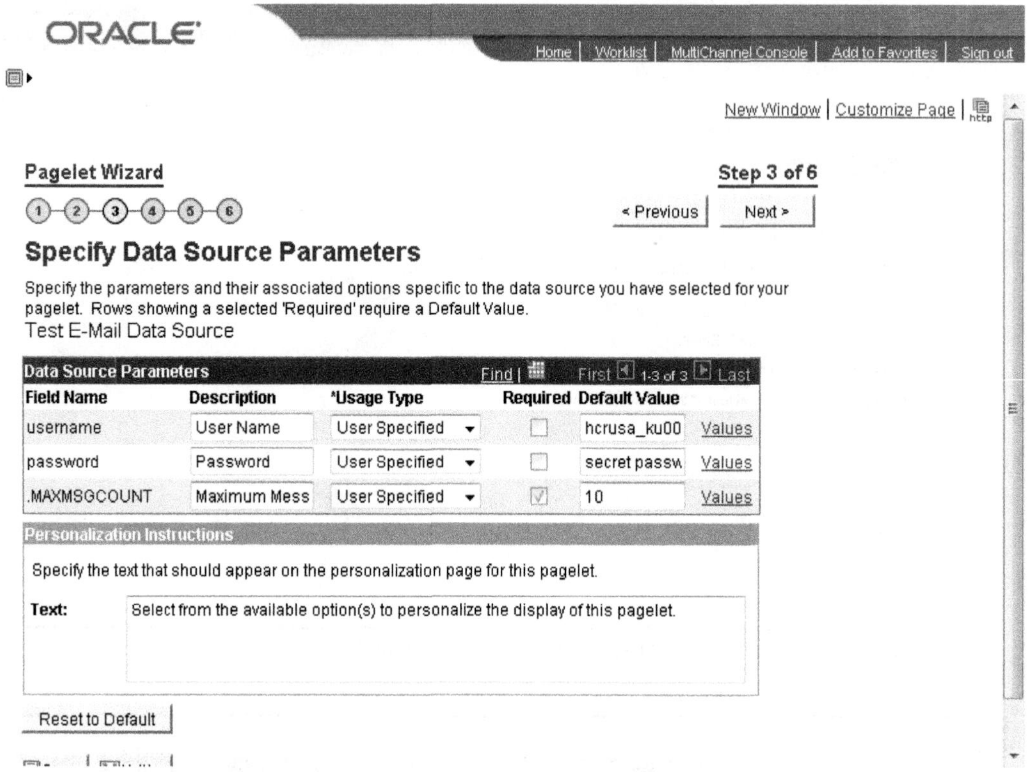

ORACLE

Home | Worklist | MultiChannel Console | Add to Favorites | Sign out

New Window | Customize Page | http

Pagelet Wizard **Step 3 of 6**

1 2 3 4 5 6 « Previous Next »

Specify Data Source Parameters

Specify the parameters and their associated options specific to the data source you have selected for your pagelet. Rows showing a selected 'Required' require a Default Value.

Test E-Mail Data Source

Data Source Parameters — Find | First 1-3 of 3 Last

Field Name	Description	*Usage Type	Required	Default Value	
username	User Name	User Specified	☐	hcrusa_ku00	Values
password	Password	User Specified	☐	secret passw	Values
.MAXMSGCOUNT	Maximum Mess	User Specified	☑	10	Values

Personalization Instructions

Specify the text that should appear on the personalization page for this pagelet.

Text: Select from the available option(s) to personalize the display of this pagelet.

Reset to Default

FIGURE 4-12. *Pagelet Wizard step 3 for the e-mail pagelet*

NOTE

I'm sure you noticed that PeopleSoft does not mask your e-mail password as you type. The Pagelet Wizard does not have a password field type. This is important to note, as some organizations may not allow passwords to be displayed on the screen in plain text. Additionally, this example stores passwords in the database without encrypting them. We chose to persist parameter values using the standard Pagelet Wizard persistence mechanism, which doesn't allow for encryption. With a little rework and PeopleSoft's pluggable encryption[1], you can easily remedy this situation.

4. On the Select Display Format page (step 4), we have only one option, the Custom display format. Therefore, just click Next to move on to step 5.

ORACLE

Home | Worklist | MultiChannel Console | Add to Favorites | Sign out

Pagelet Wizard

Step 5 of 6

1 2 3 4 5 6

< Previous | Next >

Specify Display Options

Specify the visual options related to the display format for your pagelet.

Test E-Mail Data Source

Custom Options

XSL Template

Generate

XML <?xml version="1.0"?> <messages><message id="21">

XSL <?xml version="1.0"?> <xsl:stylesheet version="1.0" xmlns:xsl="http://www.w3.org/1999/XSL/Transform">

Pagelet Preview

Enter the XSL or generate the XSL from an existing template.

Additional_text

Header

Opening Text

Closing Text

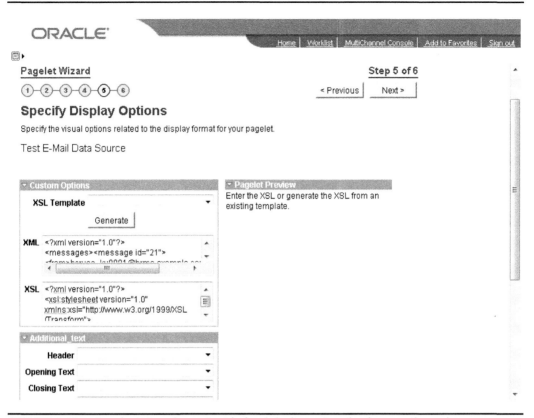

FIGURE 4-13. *Pagelet Wizard step 5 with the default preview for the e-mail pagelet*

5. On the Specify Display Options page (step 5), you will be greeted by a very anticlimatic pagelet preview that says, "Enter the XSL or generate the XSL from an existing template," as shown in Figure 4-13. The Custom display format allows us to transform an XML data type into something meaningful using XSL. The next item to note in step 5 is the XML text box, which contains the XML generated by our data type.

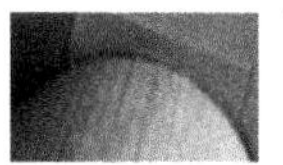

TIP

Take a look at the XML in the XML text box. Do you see a list of messages or an error message? The error handling in the `EMailDataSource execute` *method returns the same message, regardless of the error returned by* `MCFGetMail`. *Before continuing, make sure you specified the correct server name, username, and password in steps 2 and 3. If those are correct, then verify that your application server can connect to your e-mail server.*

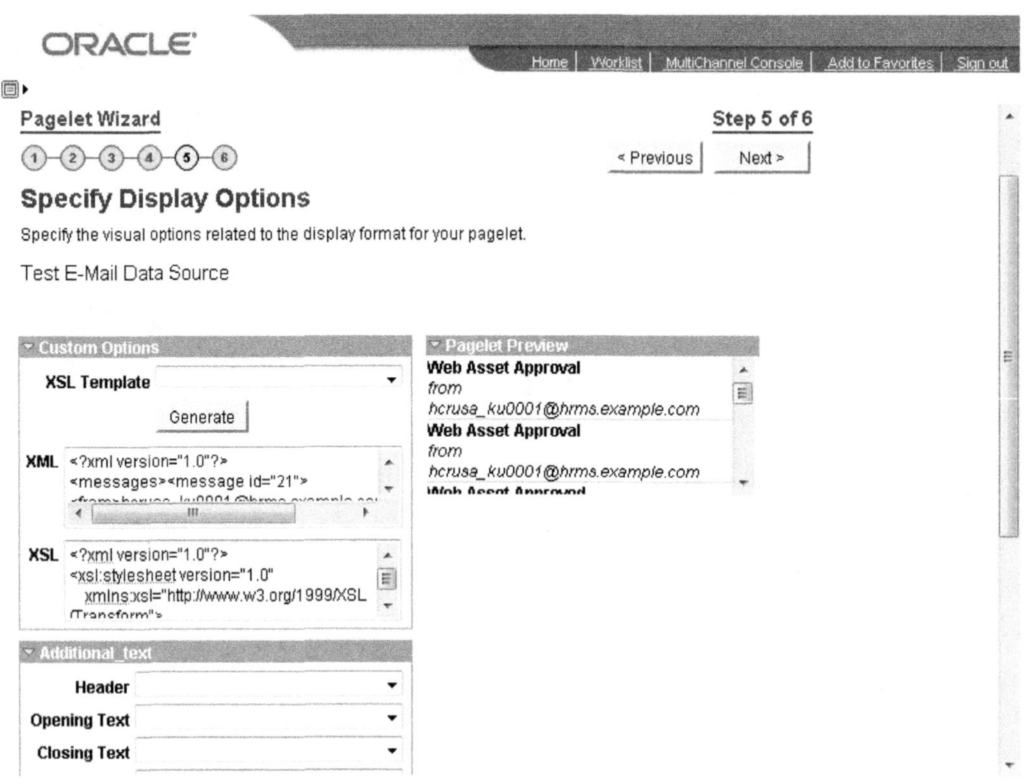

FIGURE 4-14. *Pagelet Wizard step 5 with custom XSL for the e-mail pagelet*

So we can generate something meaningful from this data type, replace the existing XSL with the following code:

```
<?xml version="1.0"?>
<xsl:stylesheet version="1.0"
    xmlns:xsl="http://www.w3.org/1999/XSL/Transform">
  <xsl:template match="/">
    <html dir='ltr'>
      <body>
        <div style="height: 100px; overflow: auto;">
          <xsl:apply-templates/>
        </div>
      </body>
    </html>
  </xsl:template>
```

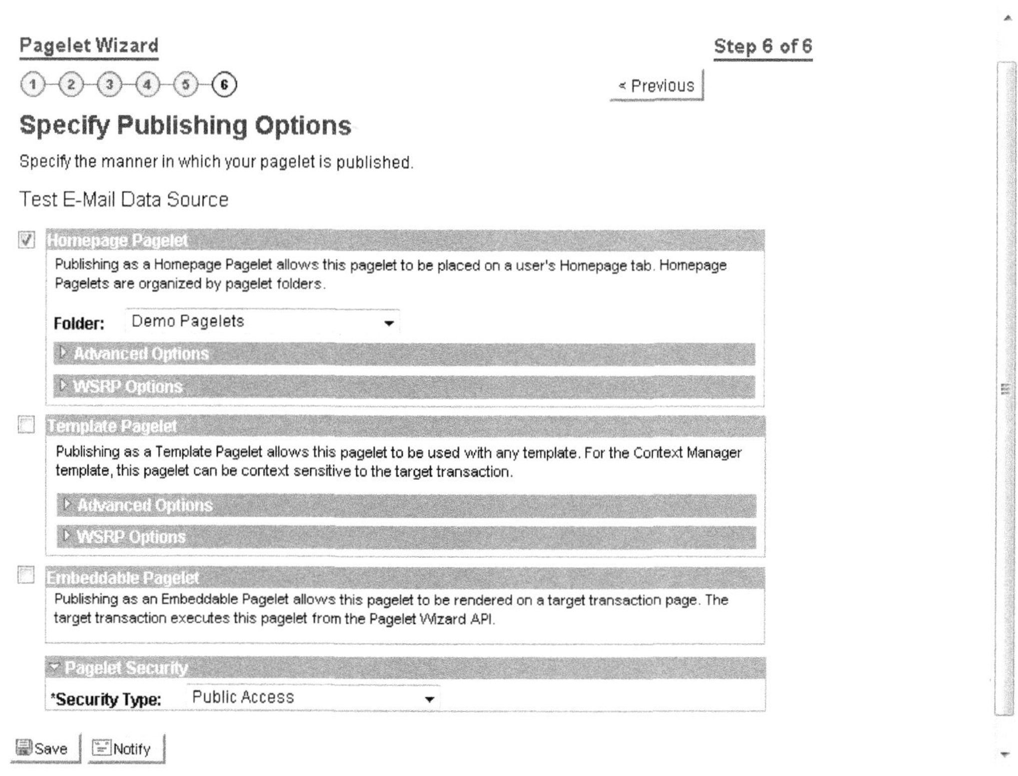

FIGURE 4-15. *Pagelet Wizard step 6*

```
<xsl:template match="messages/message">
  <div style="border-bottom: 1px solid #dfdfdf;">
    <div style="font-weight: bold;">
      <xsl:value-of select="subject"/>
    </div>
    <div style="font-style: italic;">
      from
      <xsl:value-of select="from"/>
    </div>
  </div>
</xsl:template>
```

```
<xsl:template match="messages/error">
  <div style="font-weight: bold; color: #990000">
    Unable to connect to the e-mail server. Please check your user
    name and password settings.
    Error code: <xsl:value-of select="@status"/>
  </div>
</xsl:template>

</xsl:stylesheet>
```

After updating the XSL field with this XSL, you should see a pagelet preview that resembles Figure 4-14. Of course, if you want to see a list of e-mail messages, your inbox must contain messages.

6. When you are satisfied with your pagelet, move on to step 6 and choose to publish this pagelet as a Homepage Pagelet, in the new Demo Pagelets folder, as shown in Figure 4-15.
7. Before saving your pagelet, be sure to go back to step 3 and delete your e-mail username and password. We set these default values just so we could generate a pagelet preview in step 6. If you leave your username and password in step 3, these default values will be provided to every PeopleSoft user in your organization!

   We must make only one more change before we can add this pagelet to a home page.

Adding the Pagelet to the Home Page Tab List

PeopleSoft applications can have multiple home page tabs. PeopleSoft allows an administrator to determine which pagelets should be available to each tab. Before users can add this new pagelet to a home page, we need to add the pagelet to a home page tab's list of available content.

To make this pagelet (and any other pagelet in the Demo Pagelets folder) available on the home page, follow these steps:

1. Open the portal registry by navigating to PeopleTools | Portal | Structure and Content.
2. In the portal registry, navigate to Portal Objects | Homepage | Tabs.
3. In the Tabs folder, click the edit link next to the content reference labeled My Page.
4. From the Content Ref Administration page, switch to the Tab Content tab.
6. Select the Include All check box in the Demo Pagelets group box, as shown in Figure 4-16.

You now have a working pagelet created from a custom data type. Feel free to add it to your home page.

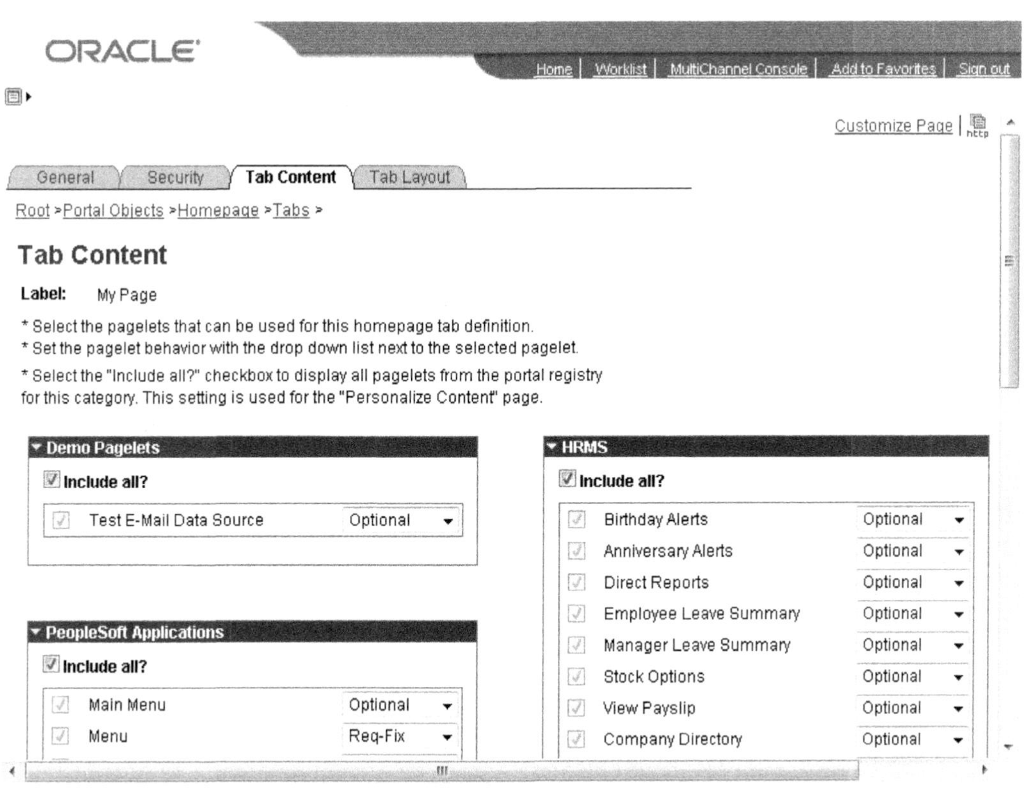

FIGURE 4-16. *My Page content reference tab content*

Pagelet Transformers

As previously discussed, the Pagelet Wizard uses data types, display formats, and transformers. When we create pagelets, the Pagelet Wizard asks us to select a data type and a display format, but it doesn't ask us about a transformer.

A transformer is actually an assistant to a display format. After generating a display template for a given data source, a display format applies that display template to the data source using a transformer.

PeopleSoft applications come with two configured transformers:

- The PASSTHRU transformer doesn't modify the data in any way. It just passes the data type's result along to the display format without any modifications.
- The XSL transformer uses XSL to transform the data type's XML.

Just like a data source, a transformer has stored parameters. The XSL transformer, for example, expects one parameter named XSL. A display format, such as the Chart display format, generates XSL based on configuration options chosen in step 5 of the Pagelet Wizard, and then updates the transformer's parameter collection.

Generally speaking, transformers should be independent of the data type and display format. Neither the XSL or PASSTHRU transformer has knowledge of its data types and display formats.

Transformers extend the abstract class `PTPPB_PAGELET:Transformer:Transformer` and must implement the abstract `execute` method as well as the `Clone` method. The `PTPPB_PAGELET:Transformer:PassthroughTransformer` is the simplest example of a transformer because it just returns the data type's data without transformation.

If your transformer has parameters, you must implement the additional `getParameterCollection` method. The `PTPPB_PAGELET:Transformer:XSLTransformer` class is an example of a transformer with parameters.

In Chapter 9, we will use Java and regular expressions to create a custom meta-HTML resolver. The following pseudo code is a prototype for a meta-HTML transformer based on that Chapter 9 meta-HTML resolver:

```
import PTPPB_PAGELET:EXCEPTION:InvalidValueException;
import PTPPB_PAGELET:Transformer:Transformer;
import PTPPB_PAGELET:UTILITY:Collection;
import PTPPB_PAGELET:UTILITY:Parameter;

/* All Transformers extend PTPPB_PAGELET:Transformer:Transformer */
class MetaHTMLTransformer
      extends PTPPB_PAGELET:Transformer:Transformer
   method MetaHTMLTransformer(&ID_param As string);
   method getParameterCollection()
         Returns PTPPB_PAGELET:UTILITY:Collection;
   method execute(&pageletID As string) Returns string;
   method Clone() Returns PTPPB_PAGELET:Transformer:Transformer;
end-class;

/* Required constructor */
method MetaHTMLTransformer
   /+ &ID_param as String +/
   %Super = create PTPPB_PAGELET:Transformer:Transformer(&ID_param);
end-method;

/* If your transformer has parameters, then implement the
 * getParameterCollection method. An example parameter is the XSL
 * parameter required by the XSLTransformer.
 */
method getParameterCollection
   /+ Returns PTPPB_PAGELET:UTILITY:Collection +/
   /+ Extends/implements
      PTPPB_PAGELET:Transformer:Transformer.getParameterCollection +/
   If %This.ParameterCollection <> Null Then
      Return %This.ParameterCollection;
   End-If;
```

```
   /* Initialize collection since it doesn't exist (lazy
    * initialization)
    */

   Local PTPPB_PAGELET:UTILITY:Parameter &parm;

   REM ** addParameter will create an empty collection;
   &parm = %This.addParameter("PARM1", "");
   &parm = %This.addParameter("PARM2", "");

   %This.ParameterCollection.setImmutable();
   Return %This.ParameterCollection;
end-method;

/* The execute method is declared abstract in the base class. This
 * means you are required to implement the execute method.
 *
 * The execute method returns the transformed result
 */
method execute
   /+ &pageletID as String +/
   /+ Returns String +/
   /+ Extends/implements
      PTPPB_PAGELET:Transformer:Transformer.execute +/

   REM ** Source data comes from %This.DataToTransform.Value;
   Local string &sourceText = %This.DataToTransform.Value;
   Local string &transformedText;

   REM ** Validate input;
   If (None(&sourceText)) Then
      throw create
            PTPPB_PAGELET:EXCEPTION:InvalidValueException(
            "Source Text", "");
   End-If;

   REM ** Validate parameters, if any;
   Local string &parm1 = %This.ParameterCollection.getItemByID(
            "PARM1").Value;
   If (None(&parm1)) Then
      throw create PTPPB_PAGELET:EXCEPTION:InvalidValueException(
            "PARM1", "");
   End-If;

   Local string &parm2 = %This.ParameterCollection.getItemByID(
            "PARM2").Value;
   If (None(&parm2)) Then
      throw create PTPPB_PAGELET:EXCEPTION:InvalidValueException(
            "PARM2", "");
   End-If;
```

```
   REM ** TODO: transform sourceText into &transformedText;

   Return &transformedText;
end-method;

/* Make a copy of this object. */
method Clone
   /+ Returns PTPPB_PAGELET:Transformer:Transformer +/
   /+ Extends/implements
      PTPPB_PAGELET:Transformer:Transformer.Clone +/
   Local APT_PAGELET:Transformer:MetaHTMLTransformer &t;
   &t = create APT_PAGELET:Transformer:MetaHTMLTransformer(%This.ID);

   If (%This.DataToTransform <> Null) Then
      &t.DataToTransform = %This.DataToTransform.Clone();
   End-If;

   If (%This.ParameterCollection <> Null) Then
      &t.ParameterCollection = %This.ParameterCollection.Clone();
   End-If;
   Return &t;
end-method;
```

Just like data types, transformers need to be registered with the Pagelet Wizard metadata repository.

XSL Templates

As you may have noticed, XML and XSL are central to the Pagelet Wizard. Many of the Pagelet Wizard's components expect data types to return data in XML format. For example, the PS Query data type returns query results as an XML document. A URL data type can return an RSS feed's XML document.

When we registered the `EMailDataSource`, we chose the Custom display format. This allowed us to write a custom XSL template to transform the e-mail message headers into HTML. Since we may use this same XML for another pagelet that connects to a different e-mail server, we may want to save it for reuse. You can register an XSL template for use with a particular data type by adding a new value to PeopleTools | Portal | Pagelet Wizard | Define XSL.

Display Formats

Display formats convert a data type into a formatted pagelet. As you saw in the "Data Types" section, you must tell the Pagelet Wizard which display formats are acceptable for a data type.

PeopleTools delivers seven display formats. Most of the display formats dynamically generate XSL and then use the XSL transformer to create HTML. The simplest display format is the PASSTHRU format, which complements the PASSTHRU transformer. Its purpose is to pass the results of the data type through the Pagelet Wizard without modification. This is the preferred display format for the HTML and URL data types when those types return plain HTML. Since it is possible for either of those two data types to return XML, the PASSTHRU display format is not always appropriate, but it usually provides the best fit.

Display formats follow a pattern similar to data types, but with the major difference that they require custom pages. These custom pages contain several delivered subpages plus any setting fields required for the custom display format. If you navigate to PeopleTools | Portal | Pagelet Wizard | Define Display Formats, you can see the names of the pages used for each of the display formats. If you create your own display format, I recommend cloning an existing display format page and modifying your copy accordingly.

Display formats are application classes that extend the abstract class `PTPPB_PAGELET:TransformBuilder:TransformBuilder`. The code for a custom display format might look something like this:

```
import PTPPB_PAGELET:TransformBuilder:TransformBuilder;
import PTPPB_PAGELET:Transformer:Transformer;
import PTPPB_PAGELET:UTILITY:Collection;
import PTPPB_PAGELET:UTILITY:Parameter;
import PTPPB_PAGELET:UTILITY:Setting;
import PTPPB_PAGELET:XSL:XSLDoc;

class MyCustomBuilder
      extends PTPPB_PAGELET:TransformBuilder:TransformBuilder
   method MyCustomBuilder(&id_param As string);

   method genTransformParameterCollection()
         Returns PTPPB_PAGELET:UTILITY:Collection;
   method initializeSettings(
         &NewSettings As PTPPB_PAGELET:UTILITY:Collection);
   method updateSettings();
   method Clone()
         Returns PTPPB_PAGELET:TransformBuilder:TransformBuilder;

private
   method generateXSL() Returns PTPPB_PAGELET:XSL:XSLDoc;
end-class;

method MyCustomBuilder
   /+ &id_param as String +/
   %Super = create
         PTPPB_PAGELET:TransformBuilder:TransformBuilder(&id_param);

   %This.initializeSettings(%This.Settings);

   %This.Transformer = %This.getAssociatedTransformer();
end-method;

method initializeSettings
   /+ &NewSettings as PTPPB_PAGELET:UTILITY:Collection +/
   /+ Extends/implements
      PTPPB_PAGELET:TransformBuilder:
      TransformBuilder.initializeSettings +/
   Local PTPPB_PAGELET:UTILITY:Setting &setting;
```

```
      %This.setSettings(&NewSettings);

      &setting = %This.Settings.getItemByID("MYSETTING1");
      If &setting = Null Then
         &setting = %This.createSettingProperty("MYSETTING1",
               "default value");
      End-If;

      &setting = %This.Settings.getItemByID("LONG_TEXT");
      If &setting = Null Then
         &setting = %This.createSettingProperty("LONG_TEXT", "");
      End-If;
      &setting.FieldType = &setting.FIELDTYPE_LONGCHARACTER;
   end-method;

   /* Update internal settings on save */
   method updateSettings
      /+ Extends/implements
         PTPPB_PAGELET:TransformBuilder:
         TransformBuilder.updateSettings +/
      REM ** code to update settings;
   end-method;

   /* This Display Format assumes the transformer is the XSLTransformer,
    * or, at least a transformer with an XSL parameter.
    */
   method genTransformParameterCollection
      /+ Returns PTPPB_PAGELET:UTILITY:Collection +/
      /+ Extends/implements
         PTPPB_PAGELET:TransformBuilder:
         TransformBuilder.genTransformParameterCollection +/
      Local string &xsl;
      Local PTPPB_PAGELET:Transformer:Transformer &trx;
      Local PTPPB_PAGELET:UTILITY:Parameter &parm;

      &trx = %This.Transformer;
      &parm = &trx.getParameterCollection().getItemByID("XSL");
      &xsl = %This.generateXSL().GenXmlString();

      If &parm = Null Then
         &parm = &trx.addParameter("XSL", &xsl);
      Else
         &parm.Value = &xsl;
      End-If;

      Return &trx.getParameterCollection();
   end-method;

   method generateXSL
      /+ Returns PTPPB_PAGELET:XSL:XSLDoc +/
```

```
   Local PTPPB_PAGELET:XSL:XSLDoc &xslDoc;
   &xslDoc = create PTPPB_PAGELET:XSL:XSLDoc();
   REM ** TODO: Add XSL element nodes to &xslDoc;

   Return &xslDoc;
end-method;

/* Copy this object */
method Clone
   /+ Returns PTPPB_PAGELET:TransformBuilder:TransformBuilder +/
   /+ Extends/implements
      PTPPB_PAGELET:TransformBuilder:TransformBuilder.Clone +/
   Local APT_PAGELET:TransformBuilder:MyCustomBuilder &b;
   &b = create APT_PAGELET:TransformBuilder:MyCustomBuilder(%This.ID);

   &b.Descr = %This.Descr;
   &b.LongDescr = %This.LongDescr;
   &b.Transformer = %This.Transformer.Clone();
   &b.initializeSettings(%This.Settings.Clone());

   Return &b;
end-method;
```

Conclusion

Just like AWE, the Pagelet Wizard is a well-designed user configuration tool built entirely from common App Designer definitions. The design of the Pagelet Wizard, driven by application classes and metadata, makes it as extensible as it is flexible. In the hands of a functional expert, the delivered Pagelet Wizard is an effective tool for enhancing the user experience. The predefined data types, transformers, and display formats offer a variety of ways to select and format data. In the hands of a developer, the Pagelet Wizard offers unlimited possibilities.

The material in this chapter just scratches the surface of the Pagelet Wizard's extensibility. If you are interested in extending the Pagelet Wizard, review the application classes in the `PTPPB_PAGELET` application package. In that package, you will find several well-written data types, transformers, and display formats.

The Pagelet Wizard enables PeopleSoft users to rapidly create page fragments that rival the best designed pages of expert PeopleSoft developers. Given the ease of use and flexibility of the Pagelet Wizard, the next time a user asks you for a custom page to view transactional information, consider the Pagelet Wizard.

Notes

1. Oracle Corporation, *Enterprise PeopleTools 8.49 PeopleBook: Security Administration*, Securing Data with Pluggable Cryptography [online]; available from http://download.oracle.com/docs/cd/E13292_01/pt849pbr0/eng/psbooks/tsec/book.htm?File=tsec/htm/tsec13.htm%23g037ee99c9453fb39_ef90c_10c791ddc07_633.

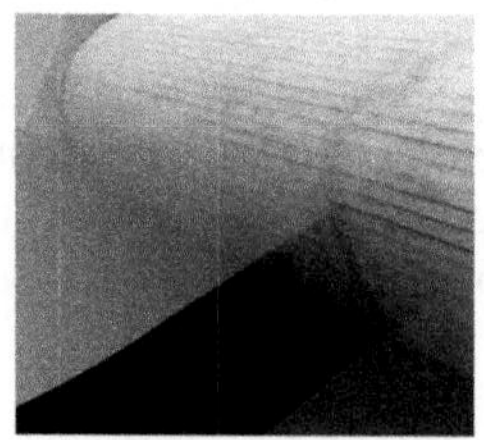

PART II

Extend the User Interface

CHAPTER 5

Understanding and Creating iScripts

y now, you should be familiar with page and component development. Using App Designer, you can design a data bound page in true "what you see is what you get" (WYSIWYG) fashion, and then view that page at runtime through PeopleSoft's Pure Internet Architecture (PIA). The PIA is responsible for every aspect of a component's life cycle. It converts a design-time display into HTML and JavaScript, responds to user-initiated events, marshals data between the database and the display, and manages relationships between header and detail rows.

iScripts offer an alternative to pages and components. They are similar to those items, in that you access them from a web browser, but that is where the similarities end. Unlike PeopleSoft page development, which uses drag and drop, iScript development requires coding. It is impossible to create an iScript without writing code.

In this chapter, you will learn how to use iScripts to extend your browser's feature set through bookmarklets, integrate with desktop applications such as Microsoft Outlook, and build rich user interfaces using Flex.

iScripts Defined

iScripts are the PeopleCode equivalent of Active Server Pages (ASP) or Java Server Pages (JSP). iScripts are PeopleCode functions that have access to the HTTP request and response entities through the PeopleCode `Request` and `Response` objects. iScripts provide full access to the PeopleSoft application database using standard PeopleCode data access objects and functions, as well as managed definitions like HTML definitions, SQL definitions, application classes, and FUNCLIBs.

An iScript does not have a component processor. It has no event handlers. It does not have a page assembler. It doesn't even have a component buffer or any sort of data binding architecture. What does an iScript have? Freedom! At runtime, a page created in App Designer is just a page. iScripts, on the other hand, can become whatever you want them to be. You can write an iScript that becomes a calendar appointment, a spreadsheet, or even synthesized speech! What's more, an iScript may be a calendar appointment for one HTTP request and a spreadsheet the next.

iScripts follow a few basic rules. By definition, iScripts are FUNCLIB functions, which means they are PeopleCode functions defined in record field PeopleCode. Just as with FUNCLIB functions, developers generally create iScripts in the `FieldFormula` event, but this is not required. iScripts differ from FUNCLIB functions in the following ways:

- An iScript *must* be defined in a record, known as WEBLIB whose name starts with `WEBLIB`.
- An iScript function name *must* start with `IScript_`.
- An iScript function has no parameters.
- An iScript function does not return a value.

PeopleSoft uses the `WEBLIB_` naming convention to differentiate WEBLIBs from standard FUNCLIBs. Also, PeopleSoft uses the `IScript_` naming convention to differentiate private, internal functions from public iScript functions. This required naming convention presents a challenge to organizations that have naming convention standards for custom definitions. They cannot prefix custom web libraries with their custom identification text to differentiate delivered web libraries from custom libraries.

As you will see later in this chapter, iScripts gather parameters through the `Request` object and return a value through the `Response` object.

Our First iScript

We will start with the traditional Hello World example. Since iScripts are record field PeopleCode functions, create a new record in App Designer. Switch to the Record Type tab and change the type to derived/work.

Next, we need to add a field to this record. PeopleSoft applications come with several iScript fields. You can use any field to identify an iScript. I generally use the field `ISCRIPT1`. For this example, insert the field `ISCRIPT1` into the record definition and save the record. When prompted, name the record `WEBLIB_APT_HW`. Figure 5-1 shows the new WEBLIB record definition.

Coding the iScript

After saving the record, switch to the record's PeopleCode view and double-click the `FieldFormula` event. (As noted earlier, you can write iScript code in any event, but by convention, PeopleSoft developers use the `FieldFormula` event.) Type the following code into the PeopleCode editor and save the script:

```
Function IScript_HelloWorld()
   %Response.Write("Hello World");
End-Function;
```

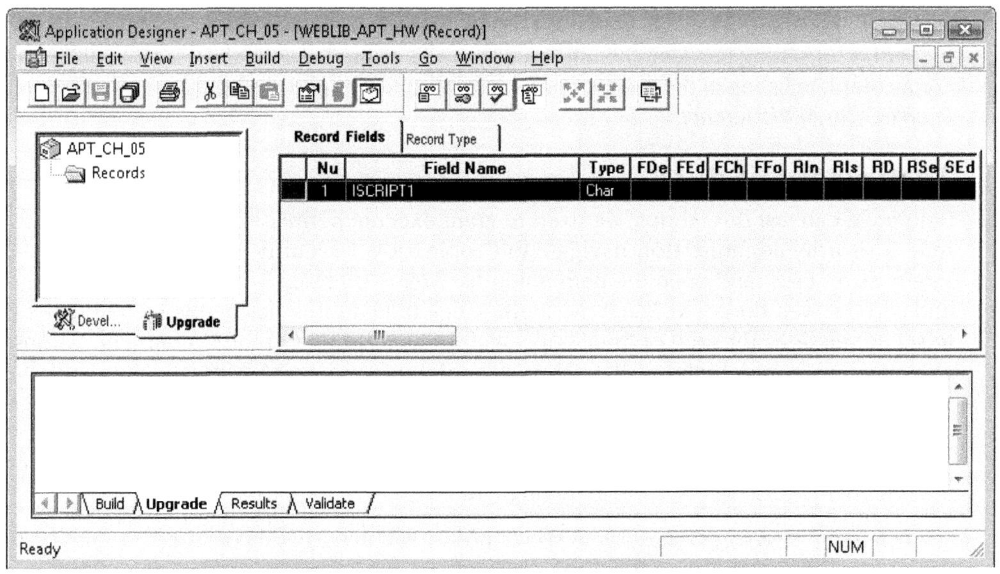

FIGURE 5-1. *WEBLIB_APT_HW derived/work record definition*

WEBLIB Naming Conventions

When naming App Designer definitions, it is a best practice to use a site-specific prefix. For example, each definition in this book uses the `APT_` prefix. This helps you, as the reader, differentiate between delivered definitions and the definitions created in this book's examples. Similarly, a site-specific prefix helps developers differentiate between delivered definitions and custom definitions.

Some definitions, like WEBLIBs, however, must conform to a naming convention that violates this site-specific recommendation. In this case, it is customary to place the site-specific prefix after the PeopleTools required prefix. Therefore, WEBLIBs created in this book will always begin with `WEBLIB_APT_`. Unfortunately, this naming convention leaves only four characters for identifying the purpose of a WEBLIB. It is rare that you find a four-letter word that summarizes the purpose of a WEBLIB. With that said, expect very cryptic WEBLIB names. If I am not able to identify a four-letter word that describes a WEBLIB, I generally resort to an abbreviation.

Notice the code looks similar to any other FUNCLIB function. iScripts follow the same patterns and utilize the same concepts.

This code listing introduces the `%Response` system variable. `%Response` is a system variable that is available to any online PeopleCode event. For example, you may see `%Response.RedirectURL` in a `FieldChange` event, but most of the `Response` object's properties and methods are relevant only for iScripts.

The `Response` object encapsulates methods and properties for generating an appropriate HTTP response to return to the client browser. Our iScript uses the `Response` object's `Write` method to generate the HTTP response body. The `Response` object also includes methods and properties for setting headers, the return code, and even redirecting the user to a different page. For a complete listing of the `Response` object's properties and methods, refer to the PeopleBooks *PeopleCode API Reference*.

Testing the iScript

Before we can test this iScript, we need to grant execute permission to a permission list. Log in as a security administrator, navigate to PeopleTools | Security | Permissions & Roles | Permission Lists, and open the permission list `APT_CUSTOM`. Switch to the Web Libraries tab and add the web library `WEBLIB_APT_HW`. Click the Edit link beside the web library's name to set permissions for each of the iScripts within that library. On the Weblib Permssions page, click the Full Access button. Click OK to accept the iScript permission changes, and then save the permission list. You can read more about web libraries and security in the *Security Administration* PeopleBook.

Now you can execute this iScript. While logged in to a web browser with a user containing the role `APT_CUSTOM`, enter the following URL:

> http://<server>/psp/<site>/EMPLOYEE/HRMS/s/WEBLIB_APT_HW.ISCRIPT1.FieldFormula .IScript_HelloWorld

Replace <server> with your PeopleSoft server name and <site> with your PeopleSoft site name. When you load this URL, you should see a web page that resembles Figure 5-2.

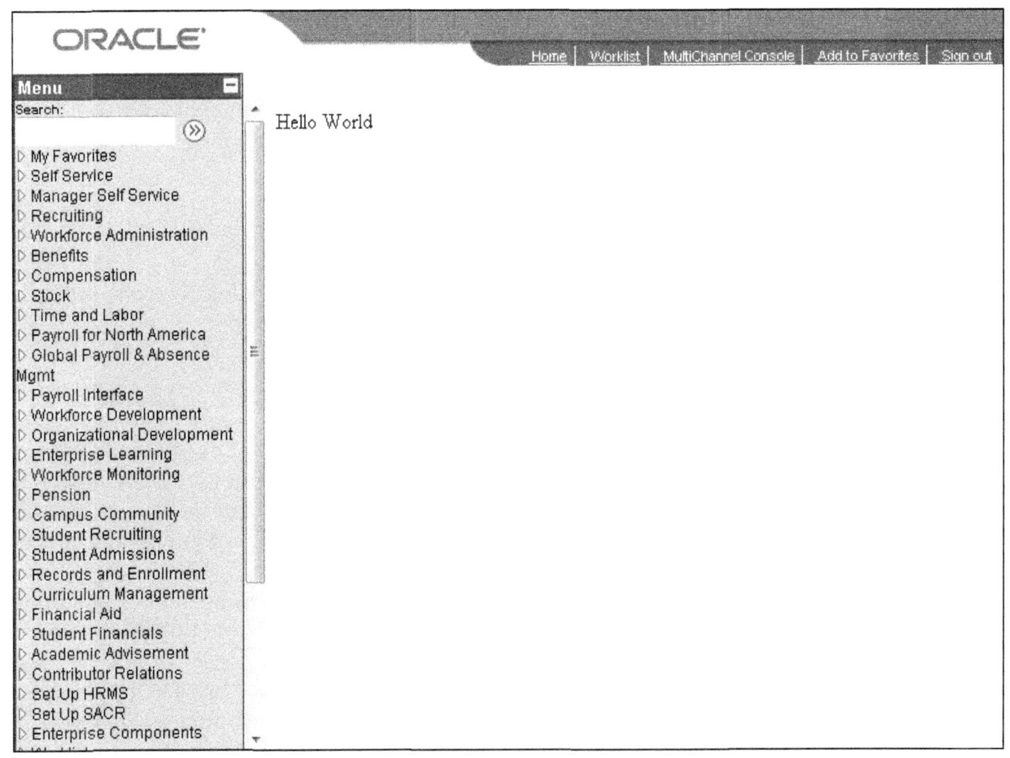

FIGURE 5-2. *Running the Hello World iScript*

NOTE
Replacing psp with psc in the URL for this example will render the same iScript result, but with the PeopleSoft header and menu removed.

Modifying the iScript

Browsers have default fonts for various document types. For example, when displaying HTML, your browser will use a serif font such as Times New Roman, and it will use a fixed-width font, like Courier, for plain text. Since our iScript prints plain text, we would expect the web browser to interpret it as such and display it with a fixed-width font. Notice, however, that the text is displayed using your browser's default HTML font.

Using your browser's view source command, you can verify that the content returned by the iScript contains no HTML. Since the content isn't telling the browser to display this text as HTML, something else is. The web server, in this case, is telling the browser how to interpret the iScript's content.

A web server sends the `Content-Type` header as part of the HTTP response so that browsers appropriately interpret the response's content. PeopleSoft defaults the `Content-Type` header to `text/html`. You can confirm this with an HTTP debugging proxy or packet sniffer like Fiddler or Wireshark.

Let's modify the iScript to set the header to a more appropriate content type, as follows:

```
Function IScript_HelloWorld()
   %Response.SetContentType("text/plain");
   %Response.Write("Hello World");
End-Function;
```

Reload the iScript in your browser. Did you notice the font change? Correctly setting HTTP headers can have a significant impact on the behavior of your browser.

A Bookmarklet to Call an iScript

With the basics of IScripts identified, let's move onto a more practical example: the browser bookmarklet. A browser bookmark, sometimes referred to as a favorite, provides a mechanism for storing a URL. We typically think of bookmarks in relation to web page addresses, but bookmarks can store any type of URL. For example, you could create a bookmark to an e-mail address using the `mailto` protocol.

A *bookmarklet* is a bookmark that uses the JavaScript protocol.[1] You can think of a bookmarklet as a bookmark to a tiny JavaScript program. Through bookmark toolbar buttons, bookmarklets offer a means of extending the browser's user interface.

I first learned about bookmarklets from my friend and colleague Chris Heller. At OpenWorld, Chris presented a very practical iScript/bookmarklet example: using a bookmarklet to turn tracing on or off. I find that I regularly trace SQL to troubleshoot prompts, so a bookmarklet should help significantly.

Before bookmarklets, this was my nine-step approach to tracing:

1. Navigate to the transaction that contained the prompt.
2. Click the new window link.
3. In the new window, navigate to PeopleTools | Utilities | Debug | Trace SQL.
4. Turn on tracing in that new window.
5. Switch back to the previous window, the transaction window.
6. Click the prompt.
7. Switch back to the trace window.
8. Turn off trace.
9. Review the trace file.

Using the PeopleCode `SetTraceSQL` function, we can turn tracing on and off from an iScript. Using a bookmarklet, we can call this iScript from a browser toolbar button.

Writing the SetTraceSQL iScript

Let's define the iScript. Since WEBLIBs contain collections of iScripts, we could add this iScript to the previously defined WEBLIB record. However, because we may have multiple trace iScripts (`SetTracePC`, `SetTraceSQL`, and so on), it seems more appropriate to create a new record called `WEBLIB_APT_DBG` to store all of our trace functions.

Just as with the Hello World iScript, our first step is to create a derived/work record with a single field named `ISCRIPT1`. Rather than create a new record, add the field, and so on, let's clone the `WEBLIB_APT_HW` record by saving it as `WEBLIB_APT_DBG`. When prompted, do not copy the record's PeopleCode.

NOTE

When you're copying record definitions, App Designer will ask you if you want to save a copy of the source record's PeopleCode. Unless you specifically want to copy the source record's PeopleCode, say no. Saying yes will cause App Designer to loop through every event of every field (even if the record has no PeopleCode). Depending on the size of the record, this can take a considerable amount of time.

After creating `WEBLIB_APT_DBG`, open the `ISCRIPT1 FieldFormula` PeopleCode event editor and add the following PeopleCode:

```
Function IScript_SetSQLTrace
   Local number &level = Value(%Request.GetParameter("level"));
   SetTraceSQL(&level);

   %Response.Write("Trace level set to " | &level);
End-Function;
```

This code introduces the `%Request` system variable. This variable is available to all online PeopleCode and represents the HTTP request received by the application server. The `GetParameter` method provides access to URL query string parameters as well as form post data. By creating the WEBLIB function with a `level` parameter, we make the function generic enough to turn tracing on and off. To turn on tracing, we call the iScript with a value greater than zero. To turn off tracing, we call the iScript with a value of zero.

Add this new iScript to the `APT_CUSTOM` permission list and follow these steps to test it:

1. Navigate to http://hrms.example.com/psp/hrms/EMPLOYEE/HRMS/s/WEBLIB_APT_DBG.ISCRIPT1.FieldFormula.IScript_SetSQLTrace?level=7.
2. Look at the size of the log file in your App Server's log file directory.
3. Click the home link at the top of the PeopleSoft application.
4. Recheck the trace file's size (it should be larger).
5. Navigate to http://hrms.example.com/psp/hrms/EMPLOYEE/HRMS/s/WEBLIB_APT_DBG.ISCRIPT1.FieldFormula.IScript_SetSQLTrace?level=0.
6. Recheck the trace file's size (it should be even larger).
7. Click the home link at the top of the PeopleSoft application.
8. Recheck the trace file's size (the size should be the same as step 6).

TIP

You may see the text, "Authorization Error -- Contact your Security Administrator," even after adding the iScript to the correct permission list. PeopleSoft displays this error message if you mistype the URL. For example, if you typed the field name as `ISCRIPT` instead of `ISCRIPT1`, PeopleSoft will display this authorization error message. Also, PeopleSoft URLs are case-sensitive. Therefore, you will see the same error message if you defined the function as `IScript_SetSQLTrace`, but called it with a lowercase `i`, as in `iScript_SetSQLTrace`.

Creating a Bookmarklet

Now let's write some JavaScript to call this URL. As you saw, we can call our SQL trace iScript from a standard URL, and, therefore, could use a regular bookmark. The problem with this approach is that activating a standard bookmark will cause the browser to navigate away from the transaction page. Instead, we will craft a JavaScript URL that opens the iScript in a new window. Here is the URL:

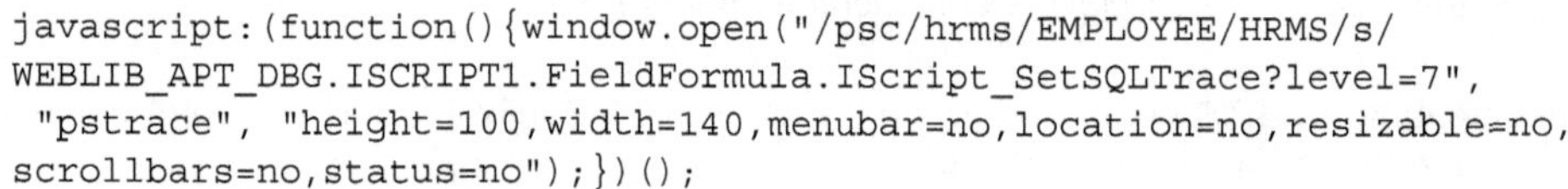

```
javascript:(function(){window.open("/psc/hrms/EMPLOYEE/HRMS/s/
WEBLIB_APT_DBG.ISCRIPT1.FieldFormula.IScript_SetSQLTrace?level=7",
 "pstrace", "height=100,width=140,menubar=no,location=no,resizable=no,
scrollbars=no,status=no");})();
```

NOTE

The JavaScript for this example hard-codes the site, portal, and node names into the URL. Considering that you may use multiple sites, debug multiple portals, and run multiple applications, hard-coding these components of the URL is not a good idea. For example, along with the HRMS production system noted in this URL, you may also have HCMDMO, HCMDEV, HCMTST, and so on. In Chapter 6, we will rewrite this bookmarklet using JavaScript regular expressions to parse the site, node, and portal values from the current URL.

Don't worry about the details of this JavaScript. We will cover JavaScript in detail in Chapter 6. For now, it is enough to know that the `window` object has an `open` method, which has three parameters: URL, window name, and options. If you log in to PeopleSoft and type this URL into your browser, you will see the iScript open in a new window, as depicted in Figure 5-3.

Before adding this bookmarklet to the browser's toolbar, let's embellish it a little. First, we will add a button to turn off tracing. Since adding a button will require some HTML, create a new App Designer HTML definition named `APT_TRACE_BOOKMARKLET`. Add the following HTML to `APT_TRACE_BOOKMARKLET`:

```
<html>
  <head>
    <title>Trace Bookmarklet</title>
    <style type="text/css">
      body {
        font-family: Arial, sans-serif;
        font-size: small;
      }
```

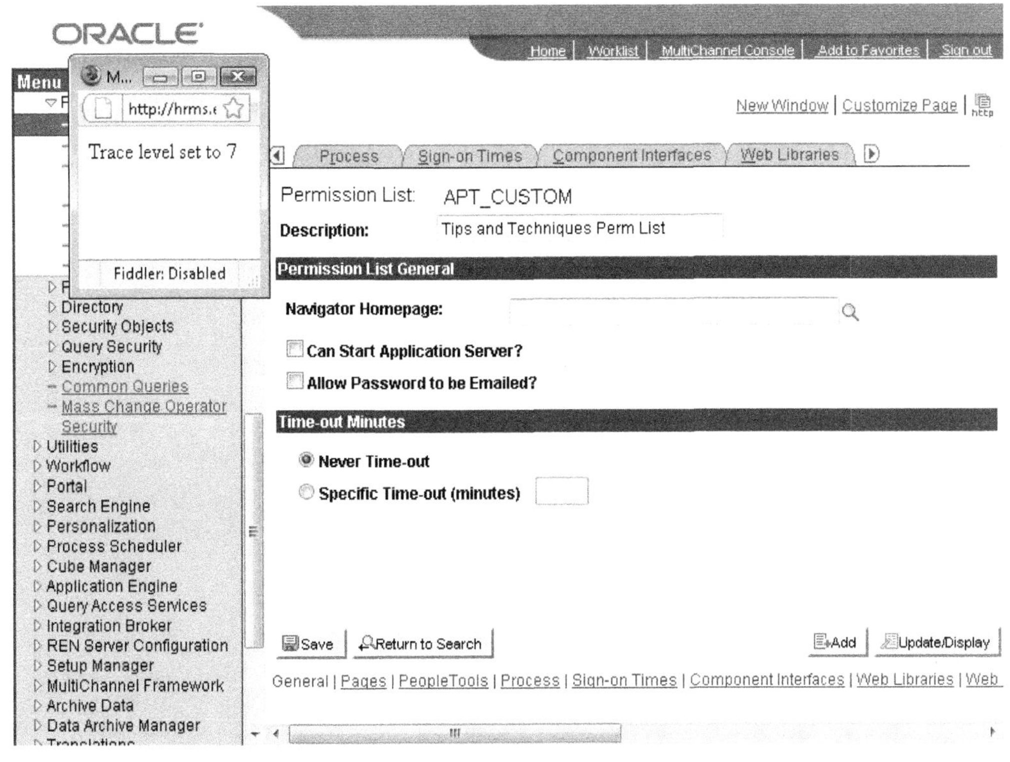

FIGURE 5-3. *Trace SQL bookmarklet*

```
    </style>
  </head>
  <body>
    <form action="%Bind(:1)" method="GET">
      <p>Trace level is now <b>%Bind(:2)</b></p>
      <input type="hidden" name="level" value="0"/>
      <input type="submit" value="Trace off"/>
    </form>
  </body>
</html>
```

This HTML contains two bind variables. The first parameter, `%Bind(:1)`, is the iScript's URL. Rather than hard-code the URL, as we did in the bookmarklet, we can use the `GenerateIScriptContentURL` PeopleCode function. The second parameter, `%Bind(:2)`, is the new trace level.

After turning off tracing, let's have the pop-up window close automatically. This will require two steps. First, when the user clicks the Trace Off button, the browser will send a request to the trace iScript to turn off tracing. Next, the response from the PeopleSoft server will send a response containing JavaScript to close the pop-up window. The following code listing contains HTML and

JavaScript for closing the pop-up window. Save this HTML definition with the name APT_TRACE_BOOKMARKLET_CLOSE.

```
<html>
  <head>
    <title>Trace Bookmarklet</title>
    <script type="text/javascript">
      window.close();
    </script>
  </head>
  <body>
    <!-- Users will likely never see this HTML. The browser should
         close the window before displaying this content -->
    You may close this browser window.
  </body>
</html>
```

Next, let's update the iScript's PeopleCode. Here is the next iteration:

```
Function IScript_SetSQLTrace
   Local number &level = Value(%Request.GetParameter("level"));
   Local string &url;
   Local string &html;

   /* This function accesses the database. We don't want this
    * function's database access to add to the size of the trace file.
    * Therefore, if &level is 0, then trace is on, so don't look up
    * values in the database until tracing is turned off. Otherwise,
    * look up all values before turning on tracing.
    */
   If (&level = 0) Then
      SetTraceSQL(&level);
      &html = GetHTMLText(HTML.APT_TRACE_BOOKMARKLET_CLOSE);
   Else
      &url = GenerateScriptContentURL(%Portal, %Node,
            Record.WEBLIB_APT_DBG, Field.ISCRIPT1,
            "FieldFormula", "IScript_SetSQLTrace");
      &html = GetHTMLText(HTML.APT_TRACE_BOOKMARKLET, &url, &level);
      SetTraceSQL(&level);
   End-If;

   %Response.Write(&html);
End-Function;
```

Once you have a working bookmarklet, you may add it to your browser's toolbar. The easiest way to get a bookmarklet onto a toolbar is to get the bookmarklet's JavaScript into a hyperlink. Numerous sites offer bookmarklet creators that generate hyperlinks from bookmarklet URLs. I prefer the Bookmarklet Builder at http://www.subsimple.com/bookmarklets/jsbuilder.htm. After you have a bookmarklet in a hyperlink, you can use your mouse to drag the hyperlink to your browser's bookmark/links toolbar.

Figure 5-4 shows the new trace SQL pop-up window and my trace SQL toolbar button (in the upper-left corner).

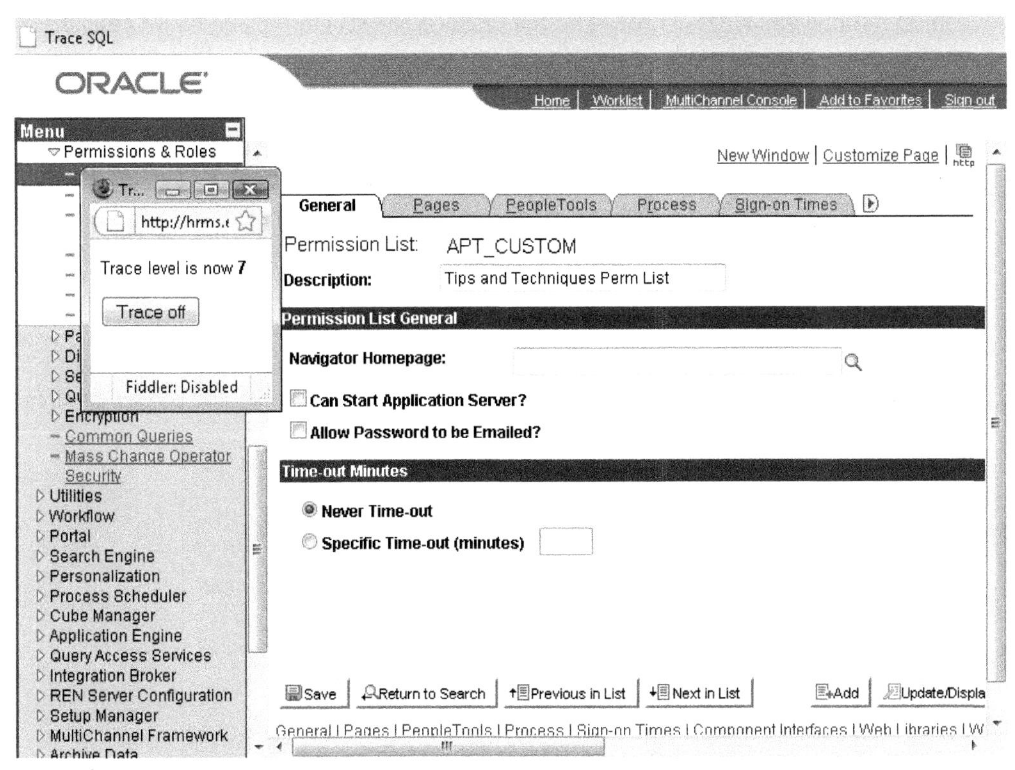

FIGURE 5-4. *Trace SQL bookmarklet window and toolbar button*

For additional information about bookmarklets, take a look at http://www.bookmarklets.com and http://www.subsimple.com/bookmarklets/default.asp. The Subsimple site contains excellent tips and tools for building your own bookmarklets.

Desktop Integration

Using iScripts, we can generate files in a variety of file formats and serve those files to users. If we set the `Response` object's HTTP headers appropriately, the user's web browser will open the file with the correct desktop application. For example, RTF files (a file format used by Microsoft Word) are plain text files containing RTF format character sequences. Through careful inspection, it is possible to insert database values into an RTF file. Prior to XML Publisher, I combined RTF with XSL to generate mail-merge letters. Desktop spreadsheet programs such as Microsoft Excel or OpenOffice Calc have XML file formats that we can generate and serve from iScripts.

Another productive desktop application integration point we can satisfy through iScripts is personal information management (PIM) system integration. Desktop applications such as Microsoft Outlook, Mozilla's Thunderbird/Sunbird, and Yahoo! Zimbra allow users to store tasks, contacts, and events, as well as other important personal information. PeopleSoft applications contain several areas of overlap with PIM applications. For example, CRM contains prospect contact information, HRMS contains recruiting interview schedules, and FSCM contains payables tasks. Using iScripts, we can integrate this information with the desktop PIM application of our choice. As an example, we will use iScripts to integrate calendar information.

Creating an iScript to Serve Calendar Content

Many PeopleSoft transactions are date-centric. For example, payables have due dates, and interviews have schedule dates. It would be nice to have an automated way to add these events to your calendar. We could add these events to calendars using the server-side integration points offered by most enterprise calendar systems. As an alternative, we can use iScripts to create iCalendar files.

iCalendar files are plain text files containing text conforming to IETF RFC 5545.[2] The text of an iCalendar file describes an event in a format understood by most desktop calendar applications. Since iCalendar files contain plain text, we can generate and serve them from iScripts.

NOTE
IETF stands for Internet Engineering Task Force. RFC stands for Request for Comment. An IETF-published RFC is considered a standard. Therefore, IETF RFC 5545 is the standard defining iCalendar files.

The following are the contents of a sample iCalendar file:

```
BEGIN:VCALENDAR
VERSION:2.0
PRODID:-//PT Tips and Techniques//PeopleCode vCal 1.0//EN
BEGIN:VEVENT
DTSTART:20090814T160000Z
DTEND:20090814T180000Z
SUMMARY:Interview Stewart Johannsen
DESCRIPTION:Interview Stewart Johannsen with Vicky Adler
LOCATION:Conf Rm 1
CATEGORIES:Business,Interviews,Administration
END:VEVENT
END:VCALENDAR
```

We will create an iScript to serve this content. First, place the iCalendar content above in an HTML definition named `APT_ICAL_TEMPLATE`. Next, create a derived/work record named `WEBLIB_APT_CAL`. Add the field `ISCRIPT1` to this record, and then add the following PeopleCode to the `FieldFormula` event:

```
Function IScript_Calendar
   %Response.SetContentType("text/calendar");
   %Response.SetHeader("Content-Disposition",
         "attachment;filename=PSEvent.ics");
   %Response.Write(GetHTMLText(HTML.APT_ICAL_TEMPLATE));
End-Function;
```

The first line of this function tells the browser that this is an iCalendar file that should be rendered by a calendar program, rather than by a web browser.

When downloading dynamically generated files from the Internet, unless instructed otherwise, your browser will use the name of the program that generated the file. For example, when generating files from the calendar iScript, the browser will suggest the name `WEBLIB_APT_CAL.ISCRIPT1.FieldFormula.IScript_Calendar`. Using the `Content-Disposition` header allows us to provide a user-friendly name for the downloaded file.

Besides providing a friendly name, the `Content-Disposition` header assists the browser in determining how to handle the iScript's response. Some file types don't have registered MIME content handlers. If your computer does not have an application registered to handle the `text/calendar` MIME type, your browser will look for a default file type handler using the file's extension.

Add this WEBLIB to the `APT_CUSTOM` permission list and call it from the URL http://hrms.example.com/psc/hrms/EMPLOYEE/HRMS/s/WEBLIB_APT_CAL.ISCRIPT1.FieldFormula.IScript_Calendar. Your browser should respond by prompting you to open or save the downloaded file. If you have a modern calendar software program, such as Microsoft Outlook 2007, saving this calendar entry will automatically add it to your calendar. Figure 5-5 is a screenshot of my Mozilla Firefox browser suggesting that I open this calendar file with Microsoft Outlook.

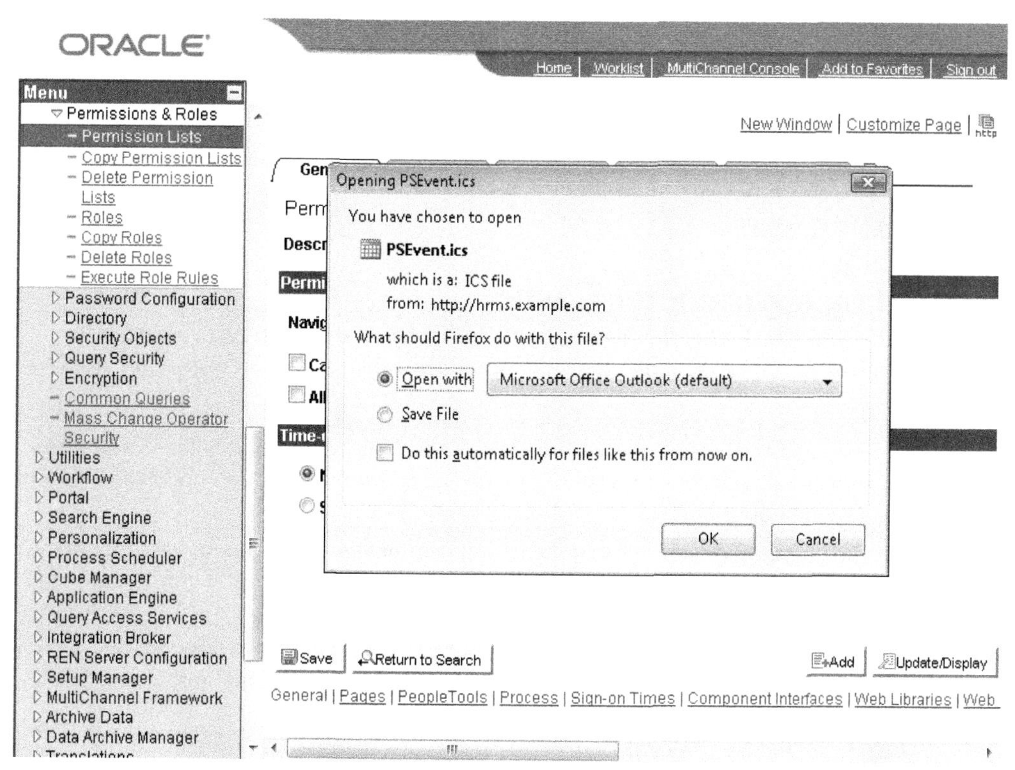

FIGURE 5-5. *iCalendar file download prompt*

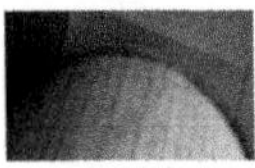

NOTE
Client application support for the iCalendar format varies widely by application and version. The screenshots in this chapter utilize Microsoft Outlook 2007, which supports multiple-event iCalendar files.

Now let's make this iCalendar dynamic by replacing each of the values in the template HTML definition with an HTML bind variable. Update your copy of the `APT_ICAL_TEMPLATE` file with the following (basically, just replace each value with a bind variable of the form `%Bind(:n)`):

```
BEGIN:VCALENDAR
VERSION:2.0
PRODID:-//PT Tips and Techniques//PeopleCode vCal 1.0//EN
BEGIN:VEVENT
DTSTART:%Bind(:1)
DTEND:%Bind(:2)
SUMMARY:%Bind(:3)
DESCRIPTION:%Bind(:4)
LOCATION:%Bind(:5)
CATEGORIES:%Bind(:6)
END:VEVENT
END:VCALENDAR
```

NOTE
If you plan to generate iCalendar files in batch mode, store your template in a message catalog definition rather than an HTML definition. HTML definitions are available only to online PeopleCode. For a more robust templating solution, see the discussion of templating PeopleCode in Chapter 9.

Building a Parameter Cache

We need to add the HTML definition's bind variables to the iScript. Also, we need to parameterize the iScript so that it doesn't always serve the same iCalendar event. There are a few ways to do this:

- Specify all values as query string parameters. This method turns the iScript into a formatting web service. The iScript reads data from the request and marks it up in iCalendar format.
- Specify transaction keys as query string parameters. This reduces the amount of data sent to the iScript, but tightly couples the iScript to a specific transaction.
- Use a parameter cache. With a parameter cache, we create a record to hold all of the parameters required by this iScript. We then populate the record from the originating transaction and add the cache ID to the iScript's URL as a query string parameter.

Specifying all the parameters in a query string won't work for us, because the length of the parameters can exceed the maximum length of a URL. Additionally, since we may use this same iScript for multiple transactions within a PeopleSoft application, it's best to keep the iScript transaction-agnostic. Therefore, we will take the parameter cache approach.

The cache pattern consists of PeopleCode in the source transaction that inserts values into a cache and then supplies the user with a link to this iScript. The link will need to uniquely identify the row in the cache record. We can use a Globally Unique Identifier (GUID) to provide uniqueness. (A GUID is a system-generated character sequence commonly used as a unique identifier.)

Our cache consists of a single record definition that stores parameters by row, with each row identified by a GUID. Let's create the cache record now. Name it `APT_CAL_CACHE`. This record is defined as a standard SQL table. Figure 5-6 shows the record's fields. Be sure to make the GUID field a key field. After adding all of the fields, save and build the record.

Next, we will modify the iScript function to read a GUID from the `%Request` object and then populate the iCalendar bind variables from values in the cache table. Replace the `IScript_Calendar` function you created earlier with the following PeopleCode:

```
Function IScript_Calendar
   Local Record &cache = CreateRecord(Record.APT_CAL_CACHE);
   Local string &dtstart;
   Local string &dtend;
   Local datetime &tempTime;
```

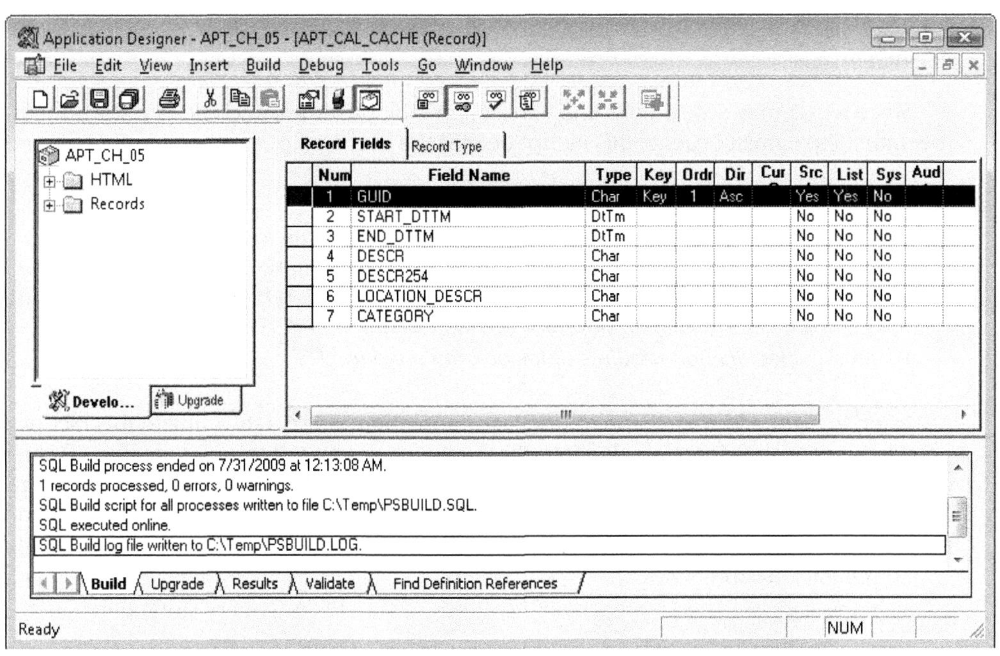

FIGURE 5-6. *iCalendar cache record definition*

```
   &cache.GUID.Value = %Request.GetParameter("id");
   If (&cache.SelectByKey()) Then

      %Response.SetContentType("text/calendar");
      %Response.SetHeader("Content-Disposition",
            "attachment;filename=PSEvent.ics");

      REM ** Format dates;
      &tempTime = DateTimeToTimeZone(&cache.START_DTTM.Value, "Local",
            "UTC");
      &dtstart = DateTimeToLocalizedString(&tempTime,
            "yyyyMMdd'T'HHmmss'Z'");
      &tempTime = DateTimeToTimeZone(&cache.END_DTTM.Value, "Local",
            "UTC");
      &dtend = DateTimeToLocalizedString(&tempTime,
            "yyyyMMdd'T'HHmmss'Z'");

      %Response.Write(GetHTMLText(HTML.APT_ICAL_TEMPLATE,
            &dtstart, &dtend, &cache.DESCR.Value,
            &cache.DESCR254.Value, &cache.LOCATION_DESCR.Value,
            &cache.CATEGORY.Value));
      &cache.Delete();
   Else
      %Response.Write("Event not found. Please revisit the " |
            "original transaction");
   End-If;
End-Function;
```

Since a user may access the same transaction multiple times, and each access will insert a row into the parameter cache, this iScript deletes the cache entry after serving it to the browser.

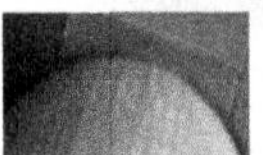

NOTE

The previous code listing uses the UTC time zone. Navigate to PeopleTools | Utilities | International | Time Zones[3] *and make sure your system has a UTC time zone. UTC is similar to GMT, but PeopleSoft's GMT metadata observes daylight saving time (DST). The iCalendar specification requires dates be converted to UTC.*

Later, we will add some PeopleCode to a transaction to generate a link to this iScript. For now, let's use SQL to insert a value into the cache so we can test this iScript. Since GUIDs consist of cryptic 36-character string, we won't want to type one into the SQL insert and then again into a URL. Instead, let's use our own identifier: `CACHE_TEST`. Use the following SQL statements to populate the cache.

For Oracle, use this SQL:

```
INSERT INTO PS_APT_CAL_CACHE
VALUES('CACHE_TEST'
     , TO_DATE('2010-07-23 09:00', 'YYYY-MM-DD HH24:MI')
     , TO_DATE('2010-07-23 11:00', 'YYYY-MM-DD HH24:MI')
```

```
      , 'Interview Stewart (cache)'
      , 'Interview Stewart Johannsen with Vicky Adler'
      , 'Conf Rm 1'
      , 'Inter')
```

For SQL Server, use this SQL:

```
INSERT INTO PS_APT_CAL_CACHE
VALUES('CACHE_TEST'
      , '2010-07-23 09:00'
      , '2010-07-23 11:00'
      , 'Interview Stewart (cache)'
      , 'Interview Stewart Johannsen with Vicky Adler'
      , 'Conf Rm 1'
      , 'Inter')
```

Load this iScript in your browser. You should see an iCalendar entry that is similar to the one you saw with the previous iScript. However, we changed the description so we could see that this file came from the `APT_CAL_CACHE` record. Here is the iScript's URL with the new ID query string parameter:

http://hrms.example.com/psc/hrms/EMPLOYEE/HRMS/s/WEBLIB_APT_CAL.ISCRIPT1
.FieldFormula.IScript_Calendar?id=CACHE_TEST

TIP
You may want to comment out the `&cache.Delete()` statement in the iScript until you have the iScript working successfully.

Modifying the Transaction

It is time to integrate a transaction with our scheduling system. Using the delivered HRMS demo data, I scheduled an interview, as shown in Figure 5-7. Let's add a download link just to the right of the Location column in the Interview Schedule grid.

To add the download link, we will need a derived/work record and some PeopleCode. To reduce the impact of this customization, we will add the PeopleCode to the derived/work record rather than the component.

The download button will need a field for its PeopleCode. Create a new field named `APT_DOWNLOAD_PB`, as shown in Figure 5-8.

Next, create a derived/work record and add the `APT_DOWNLOAD_PB` field to this new record, as shown in Figure 5-9. Save the record as `APT_INTERVW_WRK`.

With our supporting definitions created, we can add a new hyperlink to the interview page. Open the page `HRS_INT_SCHED`. Scroll down to the Interview Schedule grid and add a new button as the last column in the grid. Double-click the new button to reveal its properties and change the button's type to Hyperlink. Set the button's record name to `APT_INTERVW_WRK` and its field name to `APT_DOWNLOAD_PB`. Check Enable When Page is Display Only. On the Label tab, change the Type to Text. Figure 5-10 is a partial screenshot of the modified page in App Designer. Notice the Add to Calendar column on the right within the grid. Save the page.

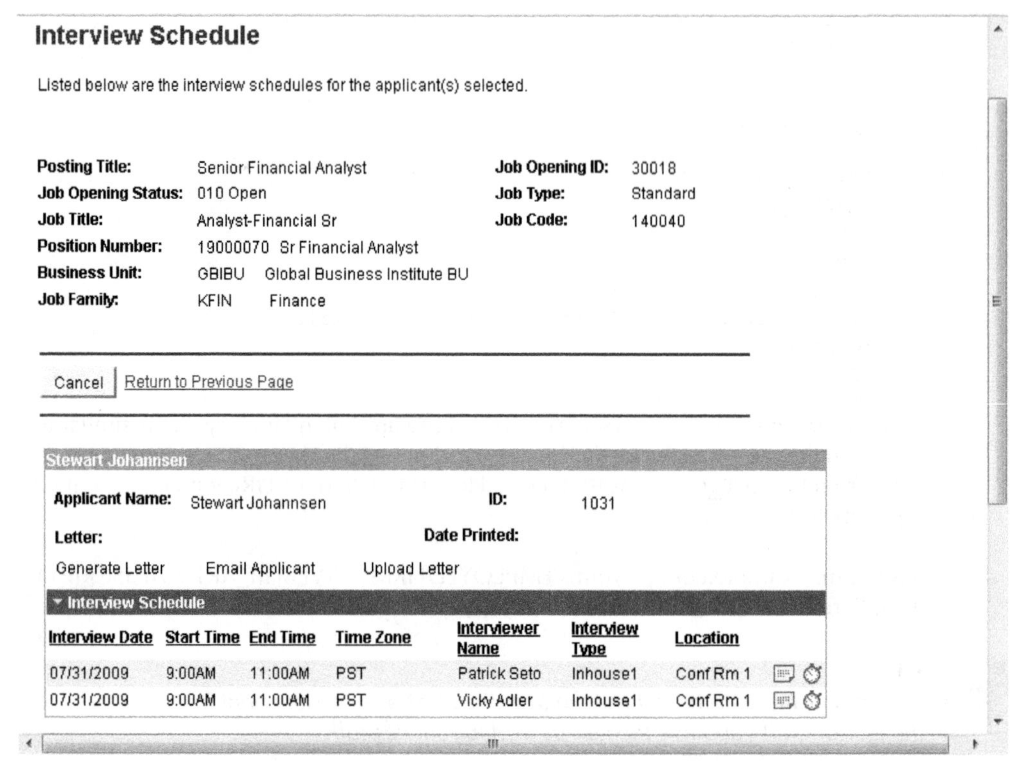

FIGURE 5-7. *Interview schedule before customization*

We will add PeopleCode after reviewing the visual appearance of the page. To view this page online, navigate to Self Service | Recruiting Activities | Interview Team Schedule. Since I am using the delivered HRMS demo database, I logged in as HCRUSA_KU0011. On the Interview Team Schedule page, select the View Schedule link next to any of the job openings.

The next step is to make the hyperlink active by adding some `FieldChange` PeopleCode. Open the `APT_INTERVW_WRK` record, and then open the `APT_DOWNLOAD_PB FieldChange` PeopleCode event editor. Add the following PeopleCode:

```
Local Record &cache = CreateRecord(Record.APT_CAL_CACHE);
Local string &guid;
Local string &url;
Local string &dateStr = DateTimeToLocalizedString(
      HRS_INT_SCHED.HRS_INT_DT, "MM/dd/yyyy");
```

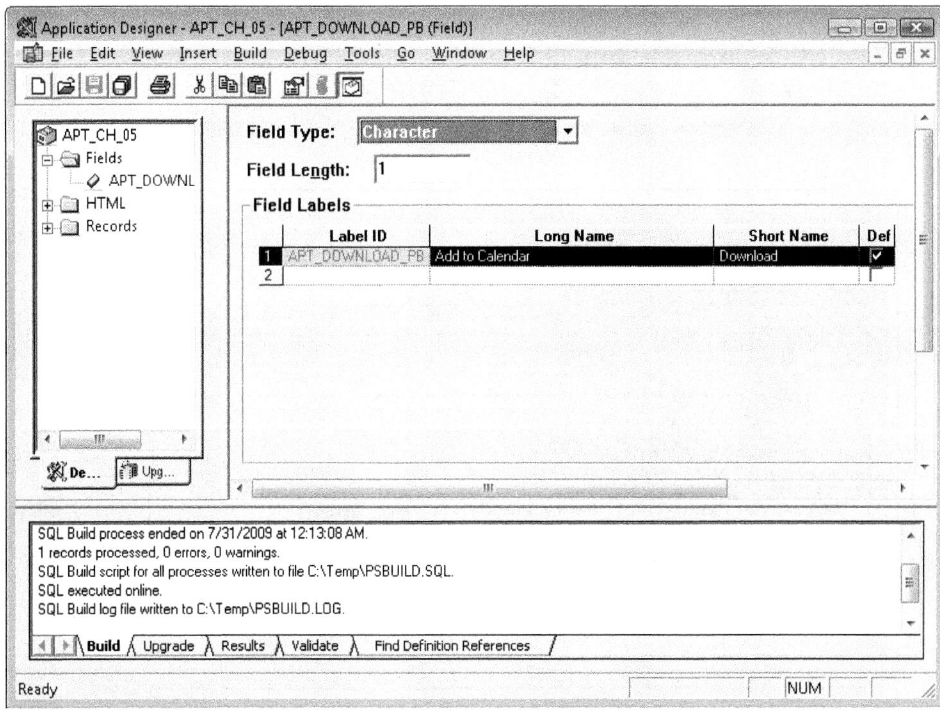

FIGURE 5-8. *New APT_DOWNLOAD_PB field definition*

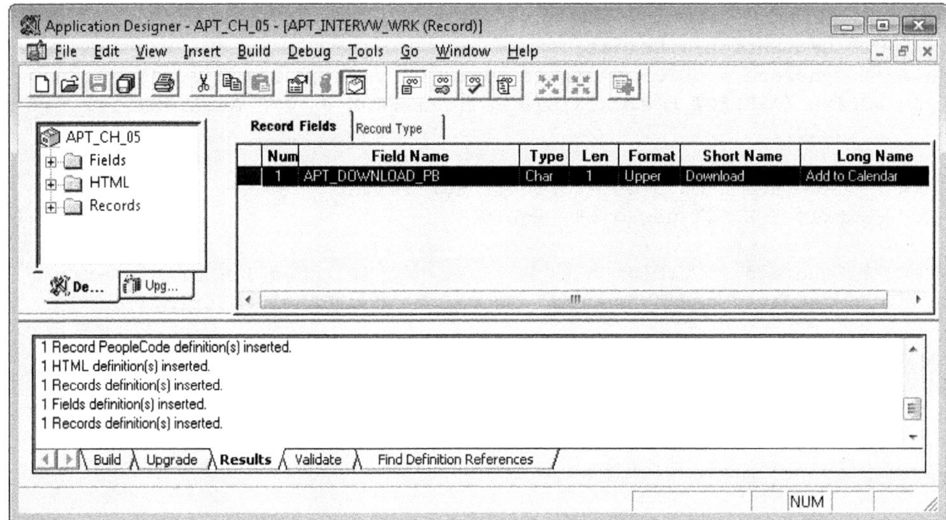

FIGURE 5-9. *APT_INTERVW_WRK record definition*

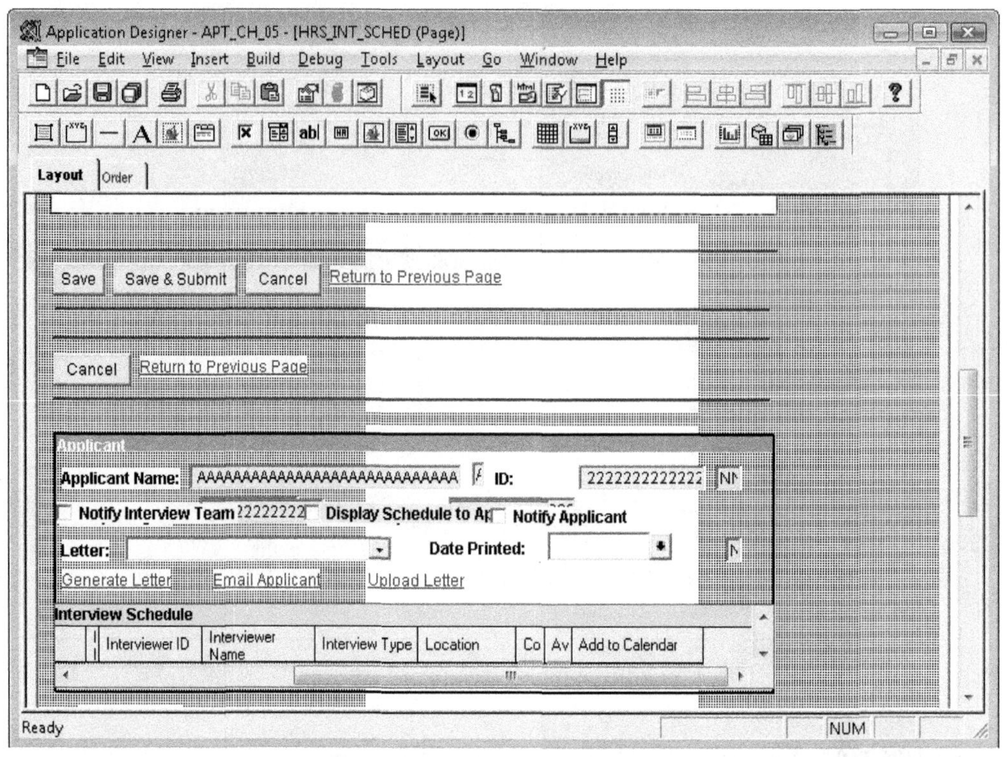

FIGURE 5-10. *HRS_INT_SCHED page online*

```
/* GUID generation alternatives */
REM ** Generate a GUID on Oracle DB on PT version below 8.49;
REM SQLExec("SELECT RAWTOHEX(SYS_GUID()) FROM PS_INSTALLATION",
      &guid);

REM ** Generate a GUID on Microsoft SQL Server
REM SQLExec("SELECT newid()", &guid);

REM ** Generate a GUID with PT 8.49 or higher (Java 1.5 or higher);
&guid = GetJavaClass("java.util.UUID").randomUUID().toString();

&cache.GUID.Value = &guid;
&cache.START_DTTM.Value = DateTimeValue(&dateStr |
      HRS_INT_SCHED.HRS_START_TM);
```

```
&cache.END_DTTM.Value = DateTimeValue(&dateStr |
      HRS_INT_SCHED.HRS_END_TM);

&cache.DESCR.Value = "Interview " | HRS_APP_NAME_I.NAME_DISPLAY;
&cache.DESCR254.Value = "You are scheduled to interview " |
      HRS_APP_NAME_I.NAME_DISPLAY | " for the " |
      HRS_JOBCODE_I.DESCR | " position.";

&cache.CATEGORY.Value = "Interview";

&cache.Insert();

&url = GenerateScriptContentURL(%Portal, %Node,
      Record.WEBLIB_APT_CAL, Field.ISCRIPT1, "FieldFormula",
      "IScript_Calendar") | "?id=" | &guid;

ViewContentURL(&url);
```

This code copies selected transaction values into our iCalendar cache record using a GUID as a key. Our first dilemma is determining how to create a GUID.[4] Since PeopleBooks does not contain documentation for a GUID generation function, we will turn to the PeopleTools infrastructure.

From the operating system to the database, we have several options for creating a GUID. The preceding code presents two of those options: SQL or Java. If you are using PeopleTools 8.49 or higher, you can take advantage of the database and platform-independent GUID-generation capabilities provided by Java 1.5. If you are using an earlier version of PeopleTools, you can call on the strength of your database to generate a GUID. This example contains GUID-generation SQL for Oracle and SQL Server. If neither of these fits your environment, take a look at the Apache Commons Id[5] project, which provides a UUID object that is very similar to the Java 1.5 UUID object.

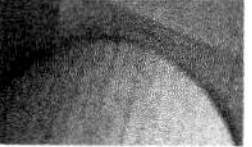

NOTE
Java offers a variety of ways to extend PeopleCode. Part III of this book is devoted to Java.

Reload the Interview Schedule page and test the new Add to Calendar hyperlink. When you click this link, your browser should prompt you to open or save a file named PSEvent.ics. Figure 5-11 shows the Interview Schedule page with a browser download prompt, and Figure 5-12 shows that same interview in Microsoft Outlook.

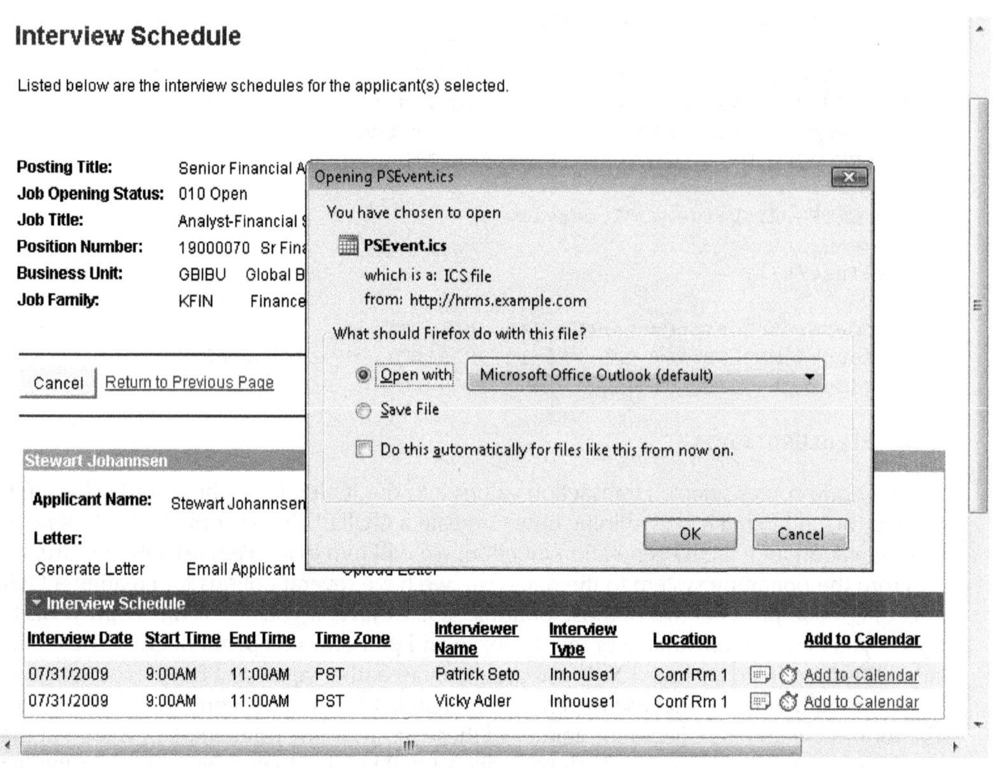

FIGURE 5-11. *Interview Schedule page with download prompt*

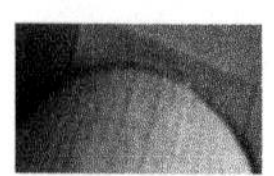

NOTE

If you receive an authorization error after clicking the Add to Calendar hyperlink, verify that your logged-in user is a member of the `APT_CUSTOM` *role (or a member of another role that has access to the* `IScript_Calendar` *function from the* `WEBLIB_APT_CAL` *web library).*

The interview scenario presented here is just one example of using iScripts to integrate with PIM systems. You can use the same approach to integrate CRM contacts as vCards or ESA action items as VTODO's (to-do's).

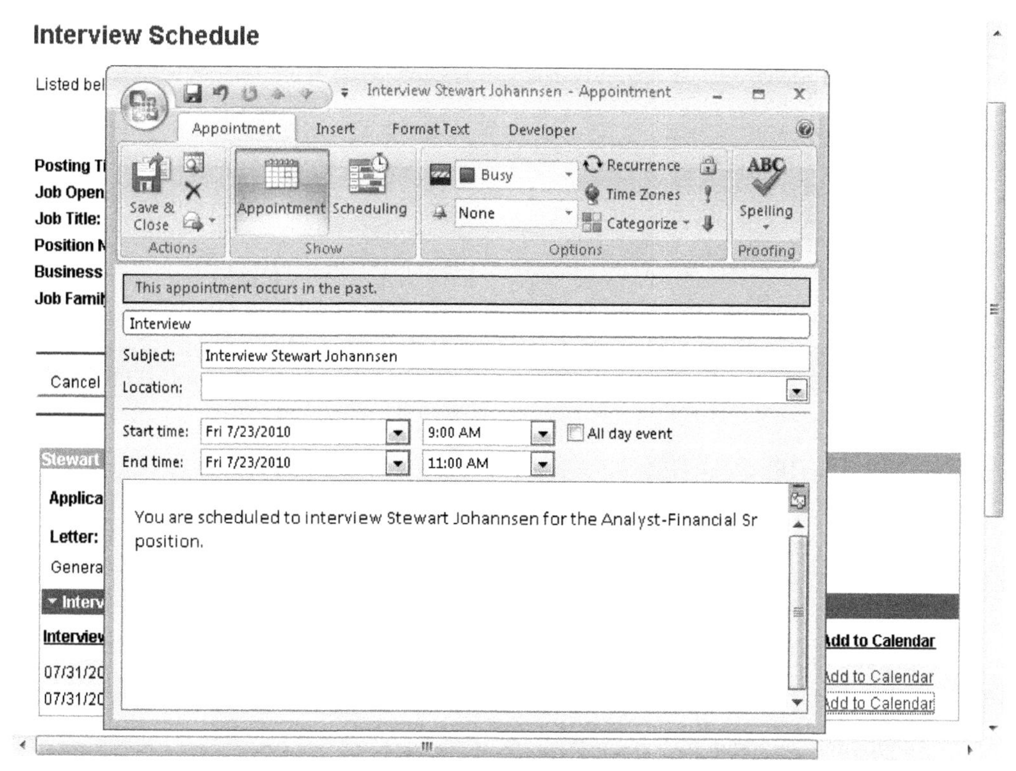

FIGURE 5-12. *Interview details in Microsoft Outlook*

Serving File Attachments

In the next section of this chapter, we are going to incorporate Adobe Flex with PeopleSoft pages. Flex uses the binary SWF file format. We need a way to store those binary files and then serve them upon request. If you have access to your web server, I recommend storing static content, such as Flex SWF files, on your web server. If you don't have access to your web server's file system, you can use the Web Assets component we created in Chapter 2. Before you can use the Web Assets component, however, you will need to create a method to serve assets, just as the web server would if the files were stored on the web server's file system.

Through customizations in Chapter 3, we added an attachment record and an approval record to our Web Assests component. We will need an SQL statement to join these three records so we only select approved web assets that have attachments. Create a new SQL definition in App Designer. Name it APT_APPROVED_ASSET_DETAILS and add the following SQL:

```
SELECT A.MIMETYPE
     , B.ATTACHSYSFILENAME
  FROM PS_APT_WEB_ASSETS A
 INNER JOIN PS_APT_WA_ATTACH B
    ON A.ASSET_ID = B.ASSET_ID
 INNER JOIN PS_APT_WA_APPR C
    ON A.ASSET_ID = C.ASSET_ID
 WHERE C.APPR_STATUS = 'A'
   AND A.ASSET_ID = :1
```

Next, create a new derived/work record that contains the field ISCRIPT1. Name this new record WEBLIB_APT_WA. Open the ISCRIPT1 FieldFormula event and add the following PeopleCode:

```
Function IScript_GetWebAsset()
   Local any &data;
   Local string &id = %Request.GetParameter("id");
   Local string &file_name;
   Local string &content_type;
   Local SQL &cursor;

   SQLExec(SQL.APT_APPROVED_ASSET_DETAILS, &id, &content_type,
         &file_name);

   %Response.SetContentType(&content_type);

   &cursor = CreateSQL("SELECT FILE_DATA FROM PS_APT_WA_ATTDET " |
         "WHERE ATTACHSYSFILENAME = :1 ORDER BY FILE_SEQ",
         &file_name);
   While &cursor.Fetch(&data);
      %Response.WriteBinary(&data);
   End-While;
End-Function;
```

As always, add this new WEBLIB to the APT_CUSTOM permission list before testing the iScript. Here is the URL I used to test this iScript:

http://hrms.example.com/psc/hrms/EMPLOYEE/HRMS/s/WEBLIB_APT_WA.ISCRIPT1
.FieldFormula.IScript_GetWebAsset?id=SUBMIT_TEST

When adding workflow to the Web Assets component in Chapter 3, I created an asset with the ID SUBMIT_TEST, which is the ID that I passed to the iScript as a query string parameter. Replace this value with an approved asset from your Web Asset's component.

iScripts as Data Sources

Rich Internet technologies change the way we interact with web-based applications. PeopleTools 8.4 used the traditional, highly visible HTTP Request/Response cycle to implement web-based applications. Using this model, a FieldChange event or prompt submitted the entire page to the PeopleSoft server, requiring the user to wait for the browser to "repaint" the page. The rich Internet approach, on the other hand, uses transparent mechanisms to send HTTP requests to the web server, process the web server's response, and then update the page accordingly. PeopleTools 8.5 uses AJAX to implement this rich experience. AJAX makes extensive use of iScripts. AJAX is the subject of Chapter 7. Here, we will cover another rich Internet technology: Adobe's Flex.

Because iScripts allow you to define the structure of the returned data without the additional HTML generated by the component processor and the page assembler, iScripts make excellent data source providers. For example, Adobe's Flex allows programmers to create rich user interfaces that read from and write to web resources. We can use iScripts to implement those web resources.

Flex Requirements

Flex is a popular technology for generating rich Internet applications. It uses the ubiquitous Adobe Flash Player to display rich components. By combining Flex with iScripts, we can create a rich user experience bound to PeopleSoft data.

Flex requires the following tools:

- Text editor
- Flex SDK command-line compiler
- The latest copy of Adobe's Flash Player

You can download the open source Flex SDK, including the Flex command-line compiler, from http://opensource.adobe.com. Installation is a matter of expanding the zip file into the directory of your choice. For convenience, I recommend adding the Flex SDK bin directory to your `PATH` environment variable.

Flex programs are defined in XML, which means you can edit them with any text editor. PeopleSoft developers use text editors to create SQR programs, modify COBOL programs, or even write database-specific T-SQL and PL/SQL programs. Even though you can use any text editor, I recommend downloading one of the syntax-highlighting text editors, such as jEdit (my preference), Textpad, or Notepad++. Each of these text editors has syntax highlighting for the common PeopleSoft text file formats: SQR, COBOL, SQL, and XML. In addition to syntax highlighting, jEdit has a variety of plug-ins to support common development tasks. You can find a jEdit Data Mover and PeopleCode syntax file, as well as all my public jEdit syntax files, at http://www.box.net/jimjmarion.

If you are interested in a full-featured Flex development environment, you may want to try Adobe's Flex Builder. For a middle-of-the-road approach that balances cost (free) with productivity, you can configure Eclipse to use an XML schema for code completion and Apache Ant for build support. While this solution is free, it may not be as productive as Adobe's Flex Builder. For the examples in this chapter, we will use a standard text editor and the Flex command-line compilers.

Say Hello to Flex

Let's start with a Hello World sample application. In Chapter 1, we created the `UserGreeter` application class. We will create a Flex component that fetches its data from a PeopleSoft iScript.

Figure 5-13 is a screenshot of what we are trying to create. The box in the center of the page containing the text "Hello [PS] PeopleSoft Superu…" is a Flex component. The Flex component is static, but the text is dynamic. The greeting "Hello…" actually comes from an iScript, and shows a different value for each logged-in user.

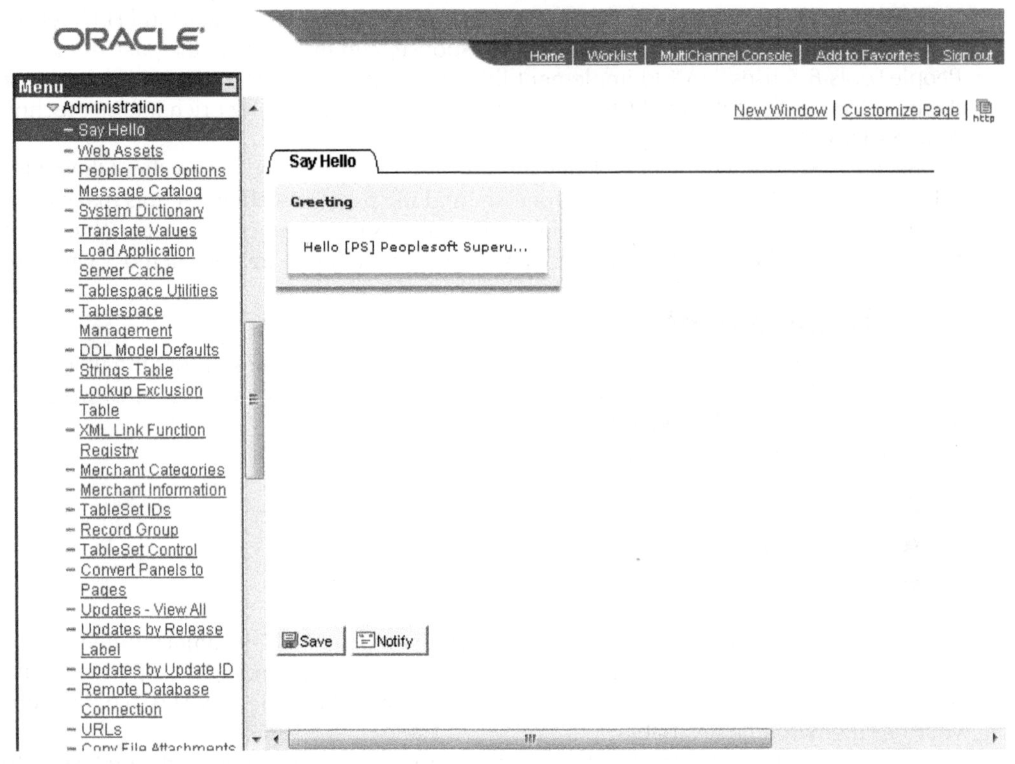

FIGURE 5-13. *PeopleSoft page with a Flex component*

Creating SayHello.mxml

Using your favorite text editor, create a text file named SayHello.mxml and add the following contents:

```
<?xml version="1.0" encoding="utf-8"?>
<mx:Application xmlns:mx="http://www.adobe.com/2006/mxml" width="100%"
    height="310" creationComplete="configureApp();" styleName="plain"
    horizontalAlign="left">
  <mx:Script>
    <![CDATA[
    import flash.external.*;
    import mx.controls.Alert;

    public function configureApp():void {
      try {
        if (ExternalInterface.available) {
          var url:String = ExternalInterface.call("getServiceURL");
```

```
          dataService.url = url;
          dataService.send();
        } else {
          Alert.show("Unable acquire service URL: " +
              "ExternalInterface not available");
        }
      } catch (e:Error) {
        Alert.show("Error: " + e.message);
      }
    }
  ]]>
  </mx:Script>
  <mx:HTTPService id="dataService" method="GET"></mx:HTTPService>

  <mx:Panel
      title="Greeting" horizontalAlign="center"
      paddingTop="10" paddingBottom="10" paddingLeft="10"
      paddingRight="10">

    <mx:Label id="greeting" width="180"
        text="{dataService.lastResult.message}"/>

  </mx:Panel>
</mx:Application>
```

Open a command window (type **cmd.exe** at the Windows Run prompt) and navigate to the directory containing your text file (`cd <path to mxml file>`). Compile this text file into a SWF file using the command line:

```
mxmlc -keep-generated-actionscript=true -incremental=true SayHello.mxml
```

If you added the Flex SDK bin directory to your `PATH` environment variable, you can issue the `mxmlc` command directly from the command line. If you didn't, then you will need to use the full path to `mxmlc`. For example, if you installed the Flex SDK at C:\flex_sdk_3, you would issue this command:

```
C:\flex_sdk_3\bin\mxmlc -keep-generated-actionscript=true -incremental=true
SayHello.mxml
```

Check the compiler's output for errors and resolve any identified errors before continuing.

TIP

For build automation, try Apache Ant. Flex fully integrates with Ant through custom Ant tasks. This allows you to create reusable project build files. As you know, development is iterative. This means you will recompile the same file several times. Ant's build system automates mundane operating system tasks such as compiling, copying files, and deploying files. Many full-featured development environments offer Apache Ant integration. JDeveloper, Eclipse, and even jEdit offer full Ant integration, as well as XML syntax highlighting and formatting.

Uploading the SWF File

The `mxmlc` Flex compiler used SayHello.mxml to generate SayHello.swf. Now we need to move this file to a location where our PeopleSoft users can download it as part of a standard PeopleSoft page request. If you have access to your PeopleSoft web server, you will achieve the best performance by placing SayHello.swf in a folder on your PeopleSoft web server. This allows your web browser to take advantage of the web server's cache headers.

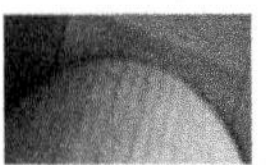

CAUTION

Before using your PeopleSoft web server for anything beyond what is delivered by PeopleSoft, make sure you are familiar with your license agreement. Serving additional files, such as SWF files, may require a full web server license, rather than the restricted use license included with PeopleSoft applications.

Assuming you don't have access to your PeopleSoft web server's file system, we will use the Web Assets component from Chapter 2 and the iScript we created earlier in this chapter to serve SayHello.swf.

Using your web browser, log in to PeopleSoft and navigate to PeopleTools | Utilities | Administration | Web Assets. Add the new value `APT_FLEX_HW`, as shown in Figure 5-14.

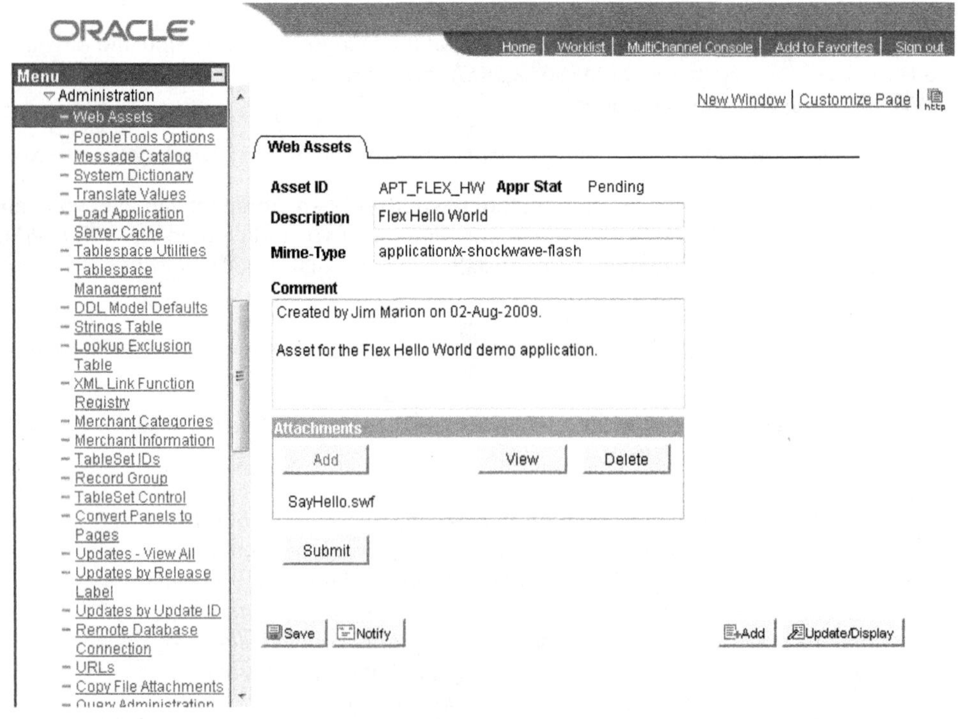

FIGURE 5-14. *APT_FLEX_HW web asset definition*

Notice the Mime-Type field is set to `application/x-shockwave-flash` and the attachments group box contains the file SayHello.swf.

Before you try downloading this new web asset, I suggest that you modify the `APT_APPROVED_ASSET_DETAILS` SQL definition. As written, the SQL requires you to approve a web asset before you can serve it. As you recall from Chapter 3, once a web asset is approved, it can't be modified. You may find yourself recompiling and reuploading SayHello.swf several times as you resolve issues. To make this process simpler, comment out `C.APPR_STATUS = 'A'` in the `APT_APPROVED_ASSET_DETAILS` SQL definition. By making this change, you will be able to modify and test the same web asset multiple times. If you decide not to change the SQL, be sure to run through the web asset approval cycle before continuing.

You can verify your web browser loads this web asset correctly using this URL:

http://hrms.example.com/psp/hrms/EMPLOYEE/HRMS/s/WEBLIB_APT_WA.ISCRIPT1
.FieldFormula.IScript_GetWebAsset?id=APT_FLEX_HW

Figure 5-15 shows the new SayHello Flex web asset. In the next step, we will write PeopleCode to provide real-time data to the Flex `HTTPService`.

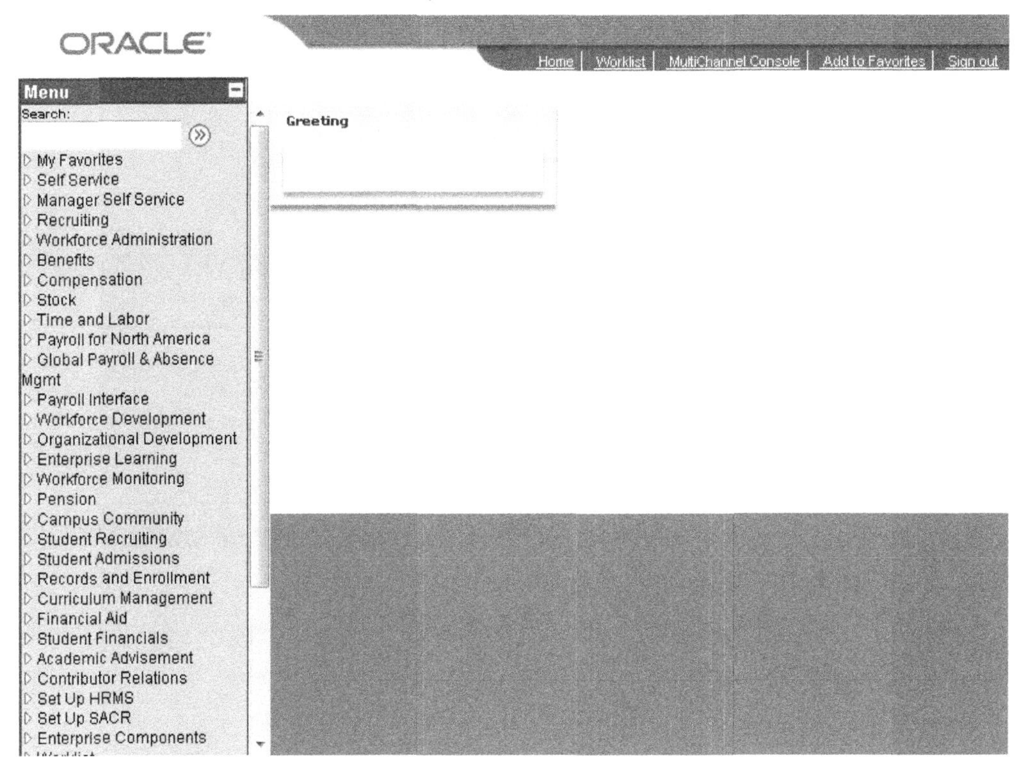

FIGURE 5-15. *Downloaded APT_FLEX_HW Web Asset*

Creating the Say Hello HTTPService iScript

The SayHello Flex definition includes an HTTPService element. The intent is to create a static SWF file that reads dynamic content from the PeopleSoft application. We can provide data to Flex using iScripts or Integration Broker. Since we are using Flex in the context of a PeopleSoft application, we can reuse the existing PeopleSoft authenticated session by serving data from an iScript.

We want our iScript to serve XML that has a certain format. Using the template concept demonstrated earlier, we can use an HTML definition to create an XML template for this iScript.

Create a new HTML definition with the name APT_SAY_HELLO_TEMPLATE and add the following code:

```
<?xml version="1.0"?>
<message>%Bind(:1)</message>
```

To define the SayHello HTTPService iScript, use App Designer to create a new derived/work record. Add the field ISCRIPT1 and save the record as WEBLIB_APT_HI. Figure 5-16 shows this new WEBLIB in App Designer.

Next, switch to the record's PeopleCode display and open the ISCRIPT1 FieldFormula event PeopleCode editor. Add the following code to this event:

```
import APT_GREETERS:UserGreeter;

Function IScript_SayHelloService
   Local APT_GREETERS:UserGreeter &greeter =
         create APT_GREETERS:UserGreeter();
   Local string &message = &greeter.sayHello();
   Local string &xml = GetHTMLText(HTML.APT_SAY_HELLO_TEMPLATE,
         &message);

   %Response.SetContentType("text/xml");
   %Response.WriteLine(&xml);
End-Function;
```

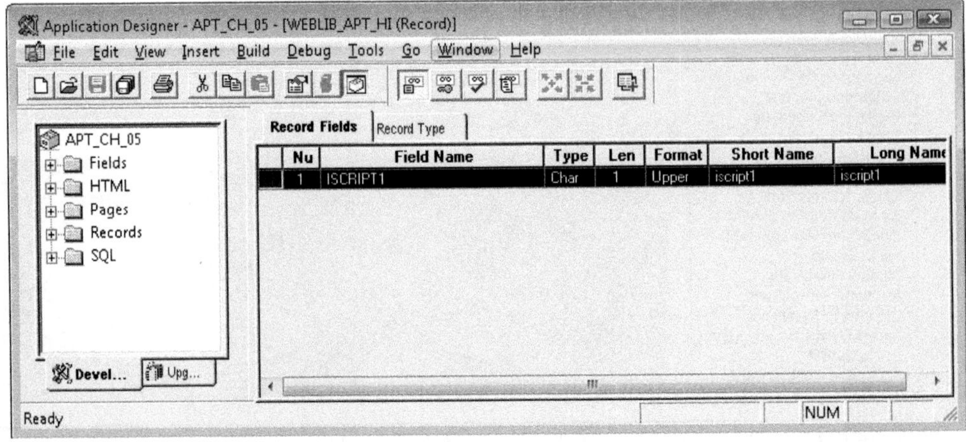

FIGURE 5-16. *WEBLIB_APT_HI Derived/Work record definition*

As always, after creating the iScript, be sure to add it to the `APT_CUSTOM` permission list. You can test this new iScript by navigating to this URL:

http://hrms.example.com/psc/hrms/EMPLOYEE/HRMS/s/WEBLIB_APT_HI.ISCRIPT1.FieldFormula.IScript_SayHelloService

Logged in as demo user `PS`, I get the following results:

```
<?xml version="1.0"?>
<message>Hello [PS] Peoplesoft Superuser</message>
```

Supporting App Designer Definitions

Besides fetching data from PeopleSoft, we want to embed Flex content in a PeopleSoft page. To do this, we need to create the following objects in App Designer:

- An HTML definition that will contain JavaScript and HTML for inserting the SWF file into a PeopleSoft page
- A derived/work record used to add the HTML definition to a page
- A PeopleSoft page
- A PeopleSoft component

Create a new HTML definition named `APT_SAY_HELLO_FLEX` and add the following HTML.

NOTE
This HTML contains a few lines of JavaScript (covered in Chapters 6 through 8), which uses the Google AJAX Libraries API (http://code.google.com/apis/ajaxlibs/) to serve the SWFObject JavaScript library. I highly recommend using the SWFObject JavaScript library to simplify embedding SWF files in HTML, but do have some concerns about the security ramifications of allowing a third-party site to inject[6] uncontrolled JavaScript into highly confidential PeopleSoft pages. As an alternative to using the Google AJAX Libraries API, you can download the SWFObject JavaScript library (http://code.google.com/p/swfobject/) and then place it on your web server, serve it from a JavaScript HTML definition, or serve it as a web asset. Chapter 6 explains these options in greater detail.

```
<script type="text/javascript"
src="http://ajax.googleapis.com/ajax/libs/swfobject/2.2/swfobject.js">
</script>

<script language="javascript" type="text/javascript">
  function getServiceURL() {
    return "%Bind(:1)";
  }
</script>
```

```
<div id="APT_flashContent">
  <p>Your browser does not support Flash</p>
</div>

<script type="text/javascript">
  (function() {
    var params = {
      allowscriptaccess: "always"
    };
    swfobject.embedSWF("%Bind(:2)", "APT_flashContent", "250", "150",
        "9.0.0", "", false, params);
  })();
</script>
```

The HTML definition shown in this code listing contains bind variables for the SWF file's location and the iScript `HTTPService` location. Rather than hard-code these URLs, we will use the PeopleCode `GenerateScriptContentURL` function to create URLs at runtime. This ensures that the URLs point to the correct servers as you promote your code from DEV to TST to PRO.

HTML that is generated at runtime must be associated with a derived/work record. Create a new derived/work record named `APT_FLEX_HI_WRK` and add the field `HTMLAREA`, as shown in Figure 5-17.

With all the supporting definitions created, we can build a new PeopleSoft page for the Flex content. Create a new page named `APT_FLEX_SAY_HELLO`. Add an HTML Area control to the top of the page and set its properties as follows:

- Value: Field
- Record Name: `APT_FLEX_HI_WRK`
- Field Name: `HTMLAREA`

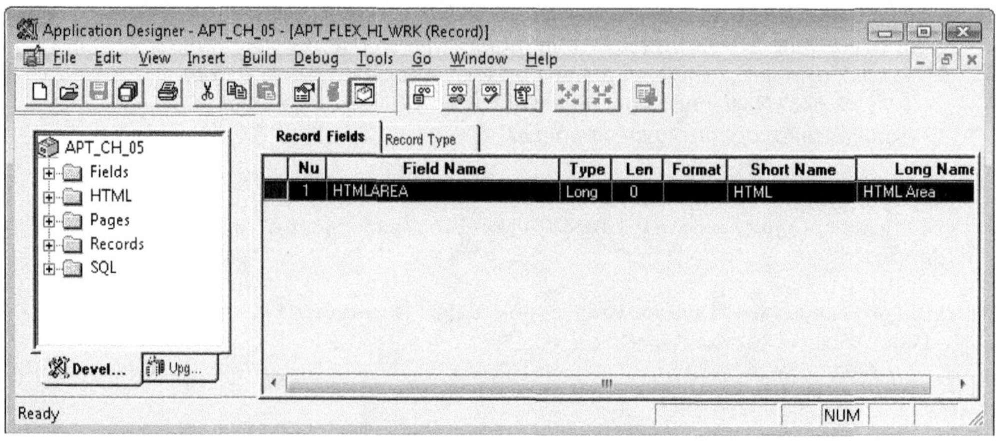

FIGURE 5-17. *APT_FLEX_HI_WRK Derived/Work record definition*

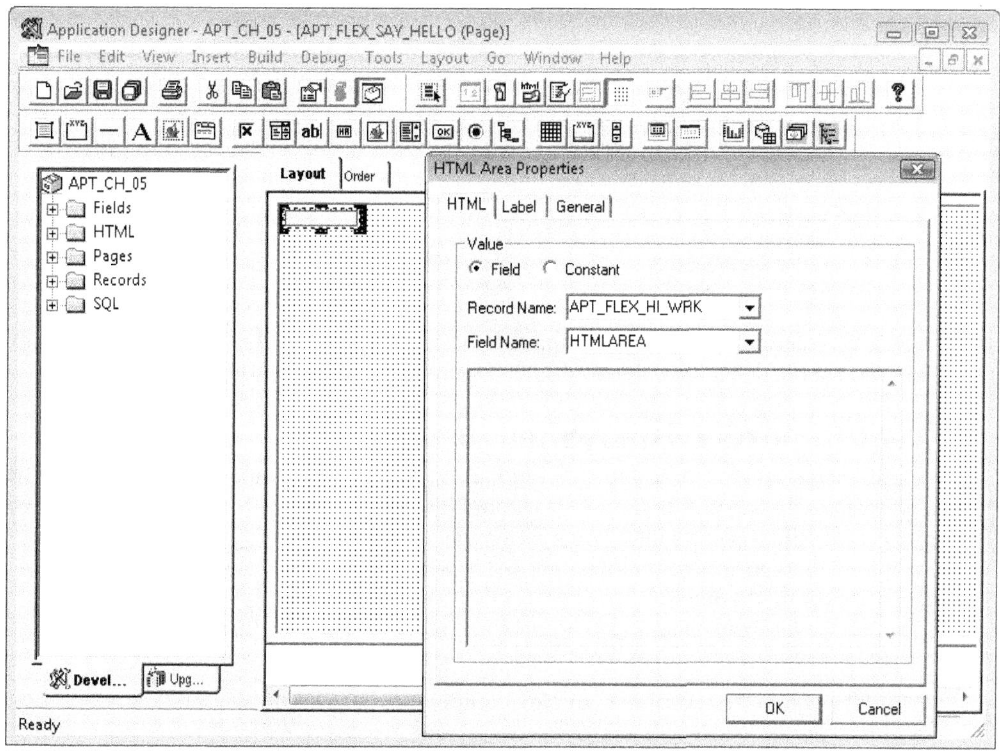

FIGURE 5-18. *HTML Area properties*

Figure 5-18 shows the HTML Area control's properties. You can see the HTML Area control on the page in the background. Save this page after configuring the HTML Area control.

Before we can view this example online, we need to create a component and register it with the PeopleTools portal. Create a new component named `APT_FLEX_SAY_HELLO`. Add the `APT_FLEX_SAY_HELLO` page to this component and set the search record to `INSTALLATION`. Save this component and register it using the following details:

- Menu: `APT_CUSTOM`
- Folder: PT_ADMINISTRATION
- Content reference label: **Say Hello**
- Long description: **Say Hello from Flex**
- Permission list: `APT_CUSTOM`

Be sure to update the new menu item's label after registration.

For our final step before testing this example, we will add PeopleCode to the `APT_FLEX_SAY_HELLO` component. Open the `APT_FLEX_SAY_HELLO` component and switch to the Structure tab. Navigate to Scroll - Level 0 | APT_FLEX_HI_WRK. Highlight this item in the outline, right-click the item, and then select View PeopleCode from the context menu. The RowInit event editor should appear. Add the following PeopleCode to this event:

```
Local string &swfUrl = GenerateScriptContentURL(%Portal, %Node,
      Record.WEBLIB_APT_WA, Field.ISCRIPT1, "FieldFormula",
      "IScript_GetWebAsset") | "?id=APT_FLEX_HW";
Local string &serviceUrl = GenerateScriptContentURL(%Portal, %Node,
      Record.WEBLIB_APT_HI, Field.ISCRIPT1, "FieldFormula",
      "IScript_SayHelloService");

APT_FLEX_HI_WRK.HTMLAREA = GetHTMLText(HTML.APT_SAY_HELLO_FLEX,
      &serviceUrl, &swfUrl);
```

Save the component and test it by navigating to PeopleTools | Utilities | Administration | Say Hello. You should see a page that looks like Figure 5-13, shown earlier in this chapter.

Direct Reports DisplayShelf

Let's take the concepts learned thus far and apply them to something a little more practical. In this next example, we will combine a custom Flex component with an iScript and a PeopleSoft page to create the Apple iTunes Cover Flow[7] effect to display employee photos. In Chapter 7, we will add AJAX to show employee attributes when a user selects an image. Figure 5-19 is a screenshot of the PeopleSoft/Flex component we will create.

The 3D Cover Flow effect is provided by the sample DisplayShelf ActionScript component. You can download the DisplayShelf's source files from the blog post:

http://www.quietlyscheming.com/blog/components/tutorial-displayshelf-component/

Creating the Employee Photo iScript

This example will require an iScript to serve employee photos. Create a new derived/work record containing the field ISCRIPT1. Save this record with the name WEBLIB_APT_EPIC.

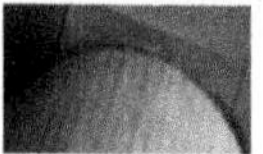

NOTE

The WEBLIB name WEBLIB_APT_EPIC is not to be confused with Epoch. Combined, the PeopleTools required WEBLIB prefix and the typical site specific prefix do not leave many characters available for describing the intent of a WEBLIB. The EPIC in the record name is actually an abbreviation for Employee PICture.

Open the ISCRIPT1 FieldFormula PeopleCode event editor and add the following PeopleCode. This code listing selects image data from the HR employee photo table. It assumes those photos are stored in JPEG format. Notice that it contains the query string parameter EMPLID.

```
Function IScript_EmployeePhoto
   Local string &emplid = %Request.GetParameter("EMPLID");
   Local any &data;

   SQLExec("SELECT EMPLOYEE_PHOTO FROM PS_EMPL_PHOTO " |
         "WHERE EMPLID = :1", &emplid, &data);
   %Response.SetContentType("image/jpeg");
   %Response.WriteBinary(&data);
End-Function;
```

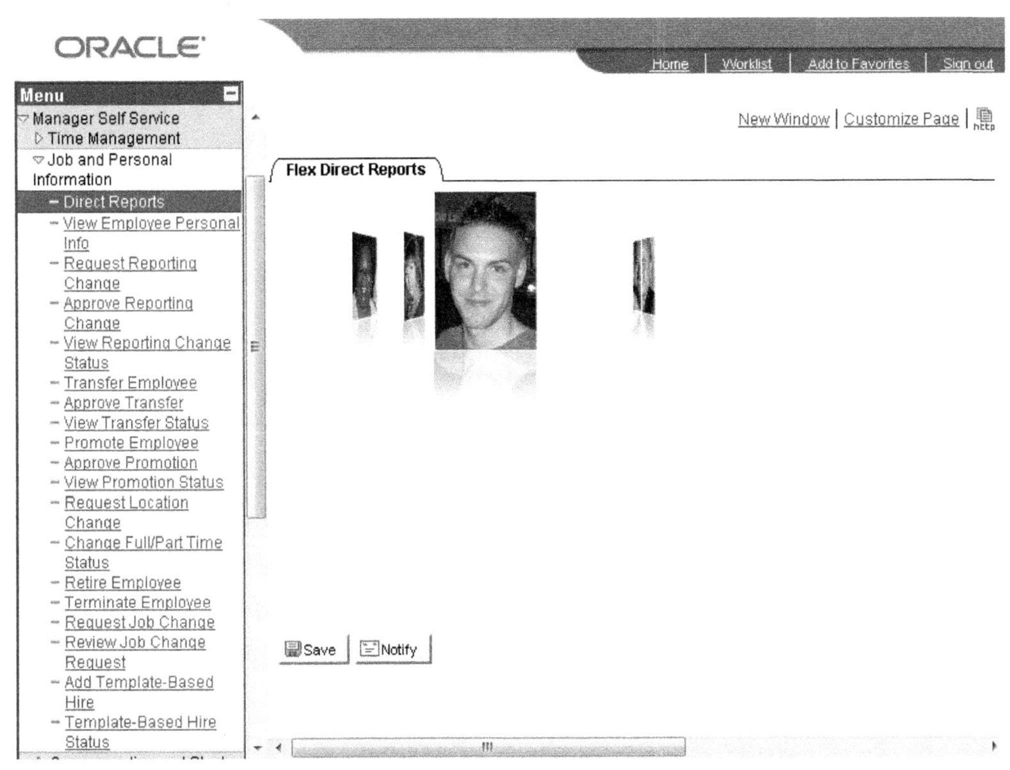

FIGURE 5-19. *Employee photos Cover Flow effect*

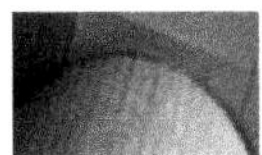

CAUTION

The iScript to serve employee photos accepts an employee's ID and then returns information about that employee without first verifying that the requesting user has access to the requested employee's information. Depending on the nature of the requested information, this may present a security risk. When building your own iScripts, be sure to verify that the user has access to the requested information.

After adding this iScript to the `APT_CUSTOM` permission list, you can test it with this URL:

http://hrms.example.com/psc/hrms/EMPLOYEE/HRMS/s/WEBLIB_APT_EPIC.ISCRIPT1
.FieldFormula.IScript_EmployeePhoto?EMPLID=KU0054

ImageCoverFlow.mxml Source Code

Just as we did with the `SayHello` Flex example, we need to create a Flex MXML file. Create a new text file and name it ImageCoverFlow.mxml. Add the following Flex code to this new text file:

```
<?xml version="1.0" encoding="utf-8"?>
<mx:Application xmlns:mx="http://www.adobe.com/2006/mxml"
    xmlns:local="*" height="100%" width="100%"
    creationComplete="configureApp()" styleName="plain">

  <mx:Script>
    <![CDATA[
    import flash.external.ExternalInterface;
    import mx.controls.Image;
    import mx.controls.Alert;

    public function configureApp():void {
      try {

        var imageRenderer:ClassFactory = new ClassFactory(Image);
        imageRenderer.properties = {width: 160, height: 120};
        shelf.itemRenderer = imageRenderer;

        if (ExternalInterface.available) {
          imgService.url = ExternalInterface.call("getServiceURL");
          imgService.send();
        } else {
          Alert.show("Unable acquire service URL: " +
              "ExternalInterface not available");
        }
      } catch (e:Error) {
        Alert.show("Error: " + e.message);
      }
    }
  ]]>
  </mx:Script>

  <mx:HTTPService id="imgService" method="GET" resultFormat="e4x"/>

  <local:DisplayShelf id="shelf" horizontalCenter="0"
    verticalCenter="0" borderThickness="0" borderColor="#FFFFFF"
    dataProvider="{imgService.lastResult.image.url}"
    enableHistory="false" width="100%" />

</mx:Application>
```

After creating the ImageCoverFlow.mxml file and downloading the `DisplayShelf` source code, place the DisplayShelf.as and TiltingPanel.as files in the same directory as the ImageCoverFlow.mxml file. Compile the ImageCoverFlow.mxml file from the command line using the following command:

```
mxmlc -keep-generated-actionscript=true -incremental=true ImageCoverFlow.mxml
```

Just as you did with the `SayHello` example, resolve any compile errors before continuing.

Uploading ImageCoverFlow.swf

Using your web browser, log in to PeopleSoft and navigate to PeopleTools | Utilities | Administration | Web Assets. Add the new value `APT_IMG_CF`, as shown in Figure 5-20. Be sure to attach the ImageCoverFlow.swf file to the web asset.

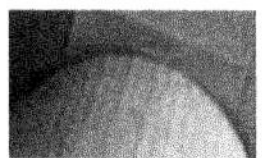

NOTE

You could test this web asset using the URL http://hrms.example.com/psc/hrms/EMPLOYEE/HRMS/s/WEBLIB_APT_WA.ISCRIPT1.FieldFormula.IScript_GetWebAsset?id=APT_IMG_CF, just as we did with the `SayHello` *example. This time, however, the Flex component has a white background color. Therefore, until we provide a data service, the Image Cover Flow web asset will not be visible.*

Writing the Image URL HTTPService iScript

The `DisplayShelf` component needs a list of image URLs. It will load these images into the user interface at runtime. Using an iScript, we can generate a list of a manager's employees by `EMPLID` and use the employee photo iScript we created earlier to serve photos to the `DisplayShelf` component.

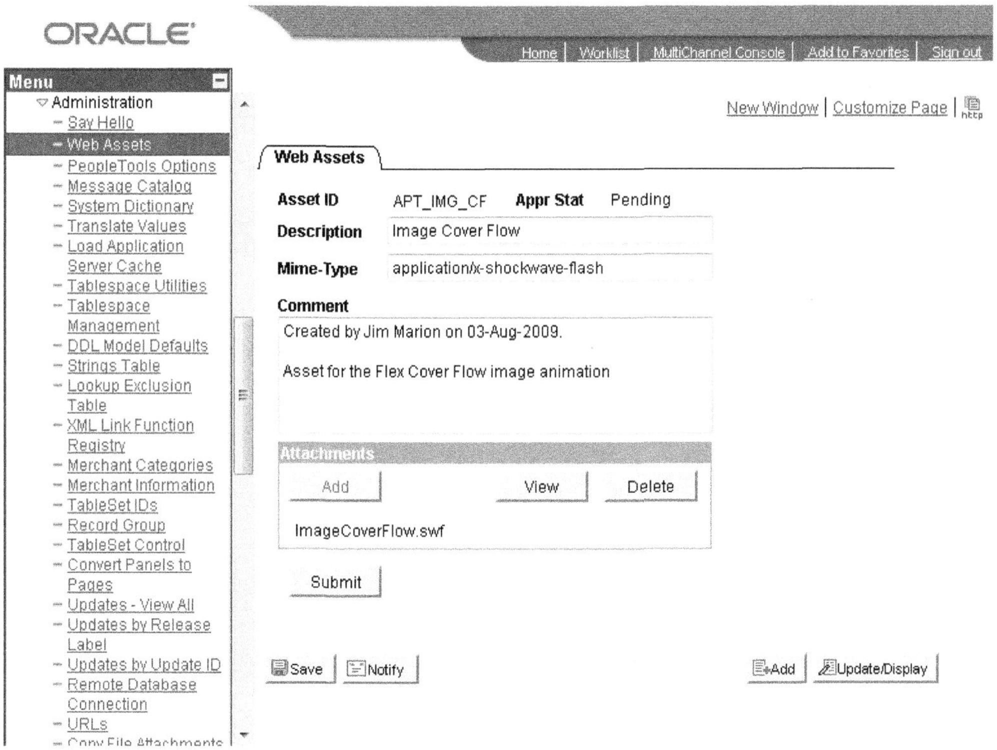

FIGURE 5-20. *APT_IMG_CF web asset definition*

We will start with an SQL statement that selects a supervisor's direct reports. Create an SQL statement named APT_SUPERVISOR_DIRECTS and add the following SQL:

```
SELECT J.EMPLID
  FROM PS_JOB J
 INNER JOIN PS_EMPL_PHOTO P
    ON P.EMPLID = J.EMPLID
 WHERE J.EFFDT = (
SELECT MAX(J_ED.EFFDT)
  FROM PS_JOB J_ED
 WHERE J_ED.EMPLID = J.EMPLID
   AND J_ED.EMPL_RCD = J.EMPL_RCD
   AND J_ED.EFFDT <= %CurrentDateIn )
   AND J.EFFSEQ = (
SELECT MAX(J_ES.EFFSEQ)
  FROM PS_JOB J_ES
 WHERE J_ES.EMPLID = J.EMPLID
   AND J_ES.EMPL_RCD = J.EMPL_RCD
   AND J_ES.EFFDT = J.EFFDT )
   AND SUPERVISOR_ID = :1
```

NOTE
The inner join in the APT_SUPERVISOR_DIRECTS SQL statement will limit the number of returned employees to only employees with photos. The demo database does not contain photos for every employee, and, therefore, will not show an image for each of a supervisor's employees. For a production system, it would be appropriate to use a left outer join and display placeholder images for employees without photos.

Following the same pattern we used for the SayHello HTTPService, we will create an HTML template for image details. Create the HTML definition APT_DIRECT_RPTS_TEMPLATE and add the following XML fragment:

```
<image>
  <url>%Bind(:1)</url>
</image>
```

Next, we will create an iScript to serve image parameters to the Flex ImageCoverFlow component. The iScript will use the preceding XML template to generate a full XML document containing a URL for each employee photo. Create a new derived/work record, add the field ISCRIPT1, and name the record WEBLIB_APT_DRI (DRI is an abbreviation for Direct Reports Information). Open the ISCRIPT1 FieldFormula event editor and add the following PeopleCode:

```
Function IScript_DirectReportsService()
   Local SQL &emplCursor = GetSQL(SQL.APT_SUPERVISOR_DIRECTS,
         %EmployeeId);
   Local string &emplid;
```

```
   Local string &baseUrl = GenerateScriptContentURL(%Portal, %Node,
         Record.WEBLIB_APT_EPIC, Field.ISCRIPT1, "FieldFormula",
         "IScript_EmployeePhoto") | "?EMPLID=";
   Local string &rowXml;

   %Response.SetContentType("text/xml");
   %Response.WriteLine("<?xml version=""1.0""?>");
   %Response.WriteLine("<images>");

   While &emplCursor.Fetch(&emplid)
      &rowXml = GetHTMLText(HTML.APT_DIRECT_RPTS_TEMPLATE,
            &baseUrl | &emplid);
      %Response.WriteLine(&rowXml);
   End-While;

   %Response.WriteLine("</images>");
End-Function;
```

Add the new WEBLIB and iScript to the `APT_CUSTOM` permission list, and then test it. If you are using the PeopleSoft HRMS demo database, you can test this iScript by adding the `APT_CUSTOM` role to the user profile `HCRUSA_KU0007`, logging in as `HCRUSA_KU0007`, and then navigating to this URL:

http://hrms.example.com/psc/hrms/EMPLOYEE/HRMS/s/WEBLIB_APT_DRI.ISCRIPT1
.FieldFormula.IScript_DirectReportsService

TIP

Notice that the iScript's PeopleCode doesn't ask for the user's EMPLID (query string parameter). Instead, the iScript uses the `%EmployeeId` PeopleCode system variable. When creating iScripts, it is critical that you derive as much information as possible on the application server and prompt only for information you can't derive. Prompting for certain types of information, such as an employee's ID, may allow a malicious user to access confidential data.

Supporting App Designer Definitions

Just like the `SayHello` Flex example we previously created, this example will require an HTML definition, derived/work record, page, and component. Create a new HTML definition and name it `APT_DIRECT_REPORTS_FLEX`. Add the following HTML to this new definition. You will notice the HTML in this definition is nearly identical to the `APT_SAY_HELLO_FLEX` HTML definition. In fact, by replacing a couple of static items with bind variables, both examples could share the same HTML definition.

```
<script type="text/javascript"
src="http://ajax.googleapis.com/ajax/libs/swfobject/2.2/swfobject.js">
</script>

<script language="javascript" type="text/javascript">
  function getServiceURL() {
    return "%Bind(:1)";
```

```
  }
</script>

<div id="APT_flashContent">
  <p>Your browser does not support Flash</p>
</div>

<script type="text/javascript">
  (function() {
    var params = {
      allowscriptaccess: "always"
    };
    swfobject.embedSWF("%Bind(:2)", "APT_flashContent", "400", "200",
        "9.0.0", "", false, params);
  })();
</script>
```

Next, we need a derived/work record for the page's HTML Area control. Create a new derived/work record named APT_FLX_DRI_WRK and add the field HTMLAREA to this new record.

After creating the APT_FLX_DRI_WRK record, clone the APT_FLEX_SAY_HELLO page: open that page in App Designer, choose File | Save As, and save it as APT_FLEX_DIR_RPTS. Double-click the page's HTML Area to reveal its properties. Change the record name to APT_FLX_DRI_WRK and set the field name to HTMLAREA.

Create a new component named APT_FLEX_DIR_RPTS. Add the APT_FLEX_DIR_RPTS page to this component and change the page's Item Label to **Flex Direct Reports**. Set the component's search record to INSTALLATION. Register this new component using the following details:

- Menu: APT_CUSTOM
- Folder: HC_JOB_PERSONAL_INFO
- Content reference label: **Direct Reports**
- Long description: **Direct Reports Flex Cover Flow**
- Permission list: APT_CUSTOM

Be sure to update the new menu item's label after registration.

Before closing the component, open the component's PeopleCode editor and add the following PeopleCode to the APT_FLX_DRI_WRK record's RowInit event:

```
Local string &swfUrl = GenerateScriptContentURL(%Portal, %Node,
      Record.WEBLIB_APT_WA, Field.ISCRIPT1, "FieldFormula",
      "IScript_GetWebAsset") | "?id=APT_IMG_CF";
Local string &serviceUrl = GenerateScriptContentURL(%Portal, %Node,
      Record.WEBLIB_APT_DRI, Field.ISCRIPT1, "FieldFormula",
      "IScript_DirectReportsService");

APT_FLX_DRI_WRK.HTMLAREA = GetHTMLText(HTML.APT_DIRECT_REPORTS_FLEX,
      &serviceUrl, &swfUrl);
```

You can test this new component by logging in to PeopleSoft through your web browser and then navigating to Manager Self Service | Job and Personal Information | Direct Reports. You should see a page that appears similar to Figure 5-19, shown earlier in this chapter.

Conclusion

In this chapter, we created several iScripts. As part of the exercises in this chapter, we created one WEBLIB for each iScript. PeopleTools allows you to create multiple iScripts in a single WEBLIB. It just so happened that the iScripts we created in this chapter were unique enough to warrant their own WEBLIBs. We will use iScripts extensively in Chapter 7. In that chapter we will add multiple, related iScripts to the same WEBLIB.

We also covered some of the details of iScript security. When writing iScripts, it is critical that security be your first thought. Always validate iScript parameters and verify the user's ability to access the requested data, and *never* ask a user for information you can derive (user's employee ID, operator ID, and so on).

Notes

1. Wikipedia, "Bookmarklet" [online]; available from http://en.wikipedia.org/wiki/Bookmarklet; Internet; accessed 29 July 2009.
2. IETF, Internet Calendaring and Scheduling Core Object Specification (iCalendar)" [online]; available from http://tools.ietf.org/html/rfc5545; Internet; accessed 25 March 2010.
3. Oracle Corporation, *Enterprise PeopleTools 8.49 PeopleBook: Global Technology*, "Maintaining Time Zones" [online]; available from http://download.oracle.com/docs/cd/E13292_01/pt849pbr0/eng/psbooks/tgbl/htm/tgbl06.htm#g037ee99c9453fb39_ef90c_10c791ddc07__69e6; Internet; accessed 31 July 2009.
4. Jim Marion, "HOWTO: Generate GUID from PeopleCode" [online]; available from http://jjmpsj.blogspot.com/2009/07/howto-generate-guid-from-peoplecode.html; Internet; accessed 31 July 2009.
5. Apache Commons, "The Id Component" [online]; available from http://commons.apache.org/sandbox/id/; Internet; accessed 31 July 2009.
6. Open Web Application Security Project (OWASP), "Top 10 2007-Injection Flaws" [online]; available from http://www.owasp.org/index.php/Top_10_2007-A2; Internet; accessed 3 August 2009.
7. Wikipedia, "Cover Flow" [online]; available from http://en.wikipedia.org/wiki/Cover_Flow; Internet; accessed 3 August 2009.

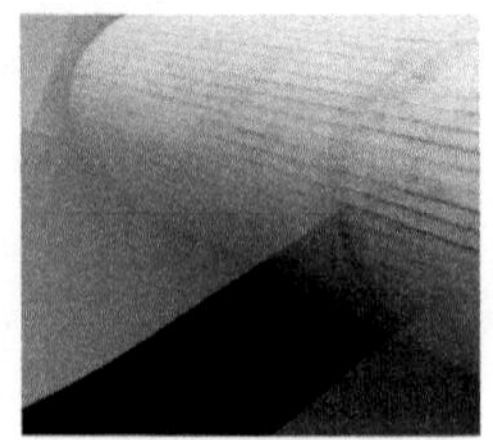

CHAPTER 6

JavaScript for the PeopleSoft Developer

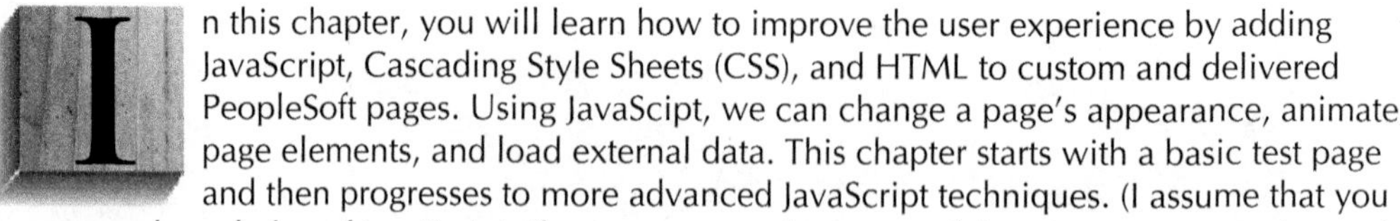

In this chapter, you will learn how to improve the user experience by adding JavaScript, Cascading Style Sheets (CSS), and HTML to custom and delivered PeopleSoft pages. Using JavaScipt, we can change a page's appearance, animate page elements, and load external data. This chapter starts with a basic test page and then progresses to more advanced JavaScript techniques. (I assume that you have some knowledge of JavaScript; if not, you can refer to any of the many resources devoted to the subject.)

A Static JavaScript Example

To demonstrate JavaScript features in PeopleSoft, let's start with a blank page. Create a new page by choosing File | New from the App Designer menu bar and selecting Page as the definition type. Just so we have a field to interact with, add a text field to the page. For the text field's record, choose `INSTALLATION`. For the field, choose `COMPANY`. Save the page using the name `APT_JSINTRO`. Figure 6-1 shows this new page.

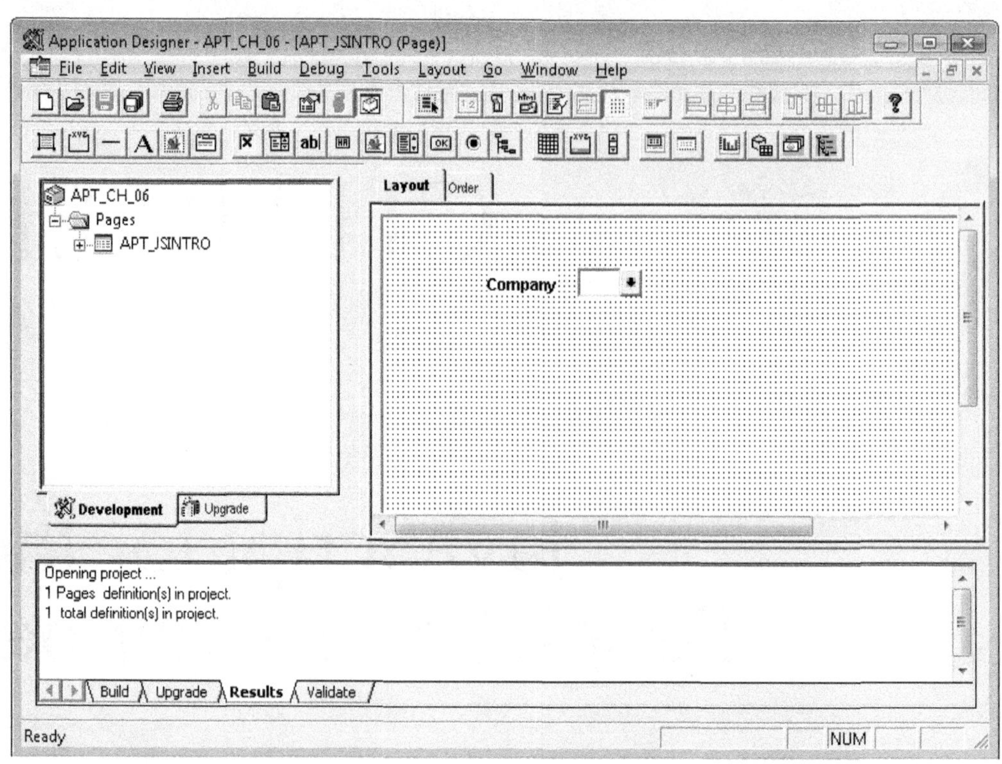

FIGURE 6-1. *APT_JSINTRO page*

Create a new component and add the APT_JSINTRO page. Set the search record to INSTALLATION. Change the page label to **JavaScript intro**. Save the component as APT_JSINTRO. Use the following values to register the component:

- Menu: APT_CUSTOM
- Folder: PT_ADMINISTRATION
- Content reference label: **JavaScript Intro**
- Long description: **Introduction to JavaScript**
- Permission list: APT_CUSTOM

After registering the component, open the menu APT_CUSTOM and set the label for the APT_JSINTRO menu item. Test this page in your browser by navigating to PeopleTools | Utilities | Administration | JavaScript Intro. Your purpose for testing at this stage is to make sure the page opens in your browser as expected.

CAUTION
It is possible to use this custom page to change the value for the Company field. This is by design. If you make the Company field display-only, our JavaScript won't be able to interact with it as a text field. But be careful not to change the company or save this page online.

If all is well, open the page in App Designer and add an HTML Area page control. The size and location of the HTML Area control does not matter, because it will contain only JavaScript, which doesn't affect the visual display of the page. Figure 6-2 shows a design view of this page. Notice the HTML Area page control in the upper-left corner of the page.

Double-click the HTML Area control to reveal its properties. Change the Value property to Constant, and then enter the following code into the Properties window:

```
<script type="text/javascript">
  alert("Hello from JavaScript!");
</script>
```

This code listing is a mixture of HTML and JavaScript. The first and last lines are HTML directives that tell the browser to interpret the code between the directives as JavaScript. The line in the middle tells the browser to display a message box.

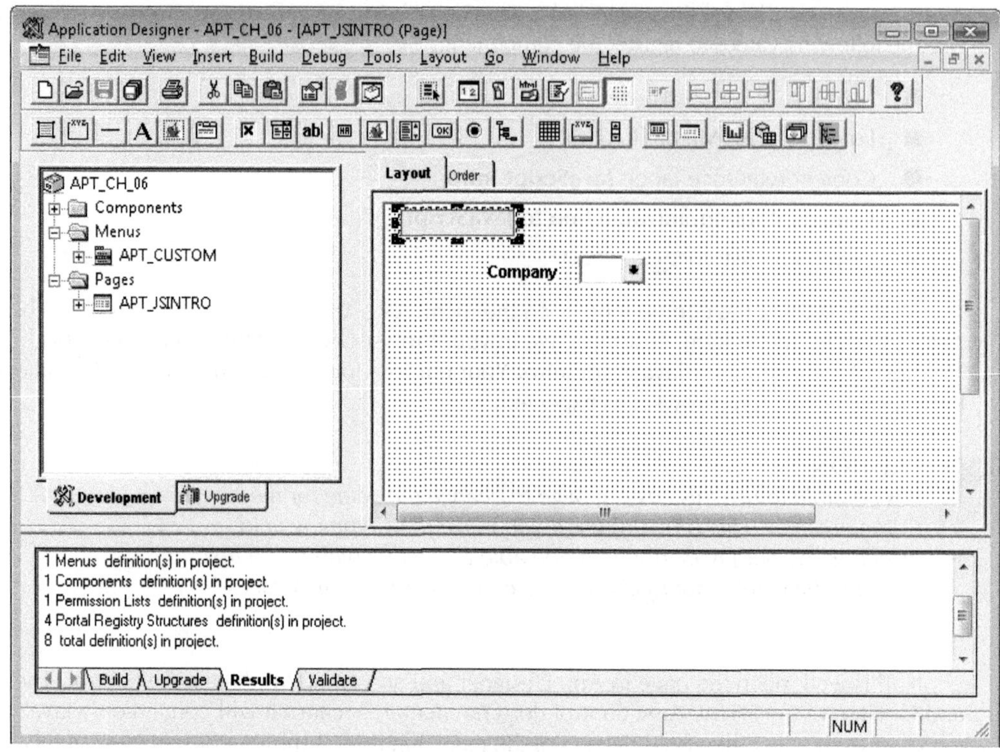

FIGURE 6-2. *APT_JSINTRO in design view*

Browsers interpret JavaScript immediately. This is similar to the way the PeopleCode runtime interprets PeopleCode. Just as the PeopleCode runtime executes each command as it is encountered, the browser executes each JavaScript line as it is read. Just as with PeopleCode, you can defer execution of specific lines by wrapping them in a function. The browser does not execute code inside a function until the function is called.

When you reload this page in your browser, your browser should display a message box containing the text "Hello from JavaScript!" as shown in Figure 6-3.

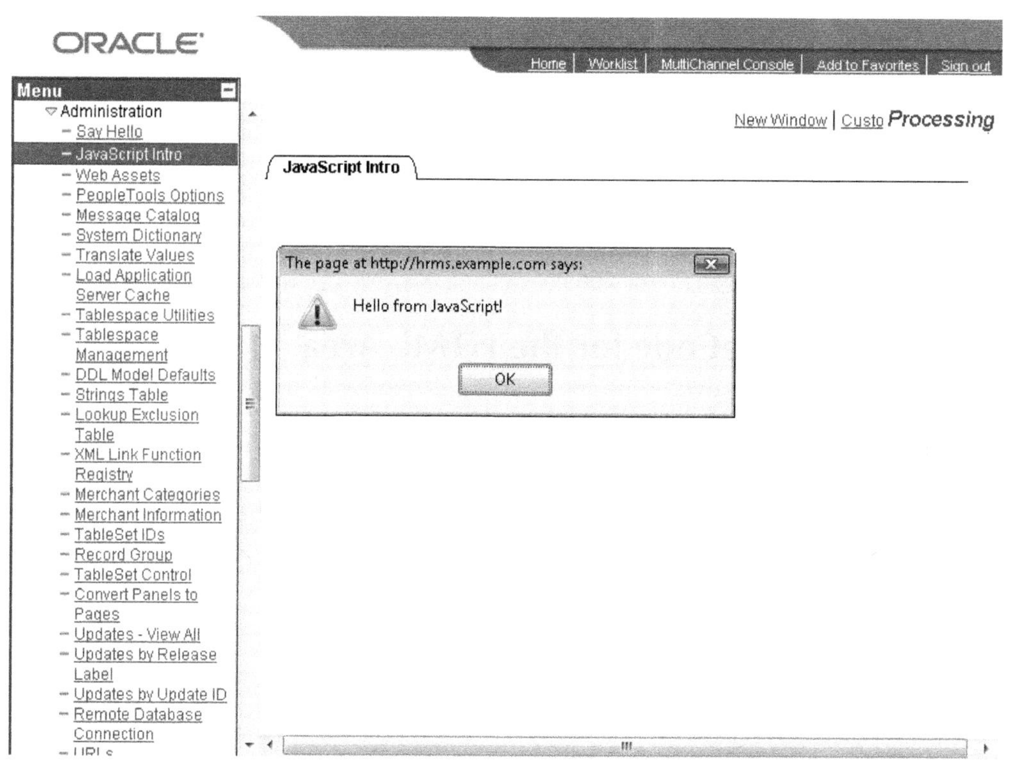

FIGURE 6-3. *Runtime view of APT_JSINTRO with a JavaScript message box*

A Dynamic JavaScript Example

The previous example contained an impersonal greeting. Let's use the `UserGreeter` class we created in Chapter 1 to add a second HTML Area control with a personal touch.

You saw how to create dynamic HTML Area controls in Chapter 5, when we added a Flex component to a PeopleSoft page. Rather than hard-code the HTML and JavaScript into an HTML Area control, you specify dynamic HTML by setting the value of a derived/work record's field. You can set the value of an HTML Area control from any PeopleCode event. Generally, you initialize HTML Area controls in `RowInit`, and then, if necessary, change the value from other events, such as `FieldChange`.

Creating the Derived/Work Record for Dynamic HTML

Create a new derived/work record and add the field HTMLAREA. Save the record as APT_JS_WRK.

I generally use the field named HTMLAREA because it is a long character field. When designing your own customizations, be sure to pick a field that is long enough to hold the amount of HTML you plan to provide. The component processor will actually truncate the value of a derived/work record field if the supplied value is longer than the length of the field's definition.

Add a new HTML Area control to the APT_JSINTRO page. The Value property will default to Field. Set the Record Name property to APT_JS_WRK and the Field Name property to HTMLAREA. When the component processor and page assembler construct the APT_JSINTRO page, they will populate the HTML Area control with the value of the APT_JS_WRK.HTMLAREA field.

Adding PeopleCode for the HTML Area

Since the value for our HTMLAREA comes from a derived/work record, and derived/work record fields have no data, we will use PeopleCode to set its value. Open the RowInit event of the APT_JS_WRK.HTMLAREA record field and add the following PeopleCode:

```
import APT_GREETERS:UserGreeter;

Local string &html;
Local APT_GREETERS:UserGreeter &g = create APT_GREETERS:UserGreeter();

&html = "<script type='text/javascript'>";
&html = &html | "alert('" | &g.sayHello() | "') ";
&html = &html | "</script>";

APT_JS_WRK.HTMLAREA.Value = &html;
```

This example uses the RowInit event to initialize our HTML Area control. When designing JavaScript customizations, the event you choose will depend on the purpose of your JavaScript. If you want to add an HTML Area control to a grid, as we did with the iCalendar download in Chapter 5, then you will use the RowInit event to initialize the HTML Area control within each row. On the other hand, if you want to change the JavaScript based on changes to the component's buffer, then you may use the FieldChange event.

Before testing this page, let's comment out the first message box. Change the JavaScript in the static HTML Area control to read as follows:

```
<script type="text/javascript">
  // alert("Hello from JavaScript!");
</script>
```

Notice the // characters before the call to alert. The // character sequence is the JavaScript single-line comment. Placing this sequence anywhere on any line hides the rest of the text on that line from the JavaScript interpreter. Multiline comments are marked just like the PeopleSoft multiline comment sequence: /* */. Anything between the asterisks is hidden from the JavaScript interpreter.

Reload this page in your web browser. You should see a new message box containing a personalized greeting, as shown in Figure 6-4.

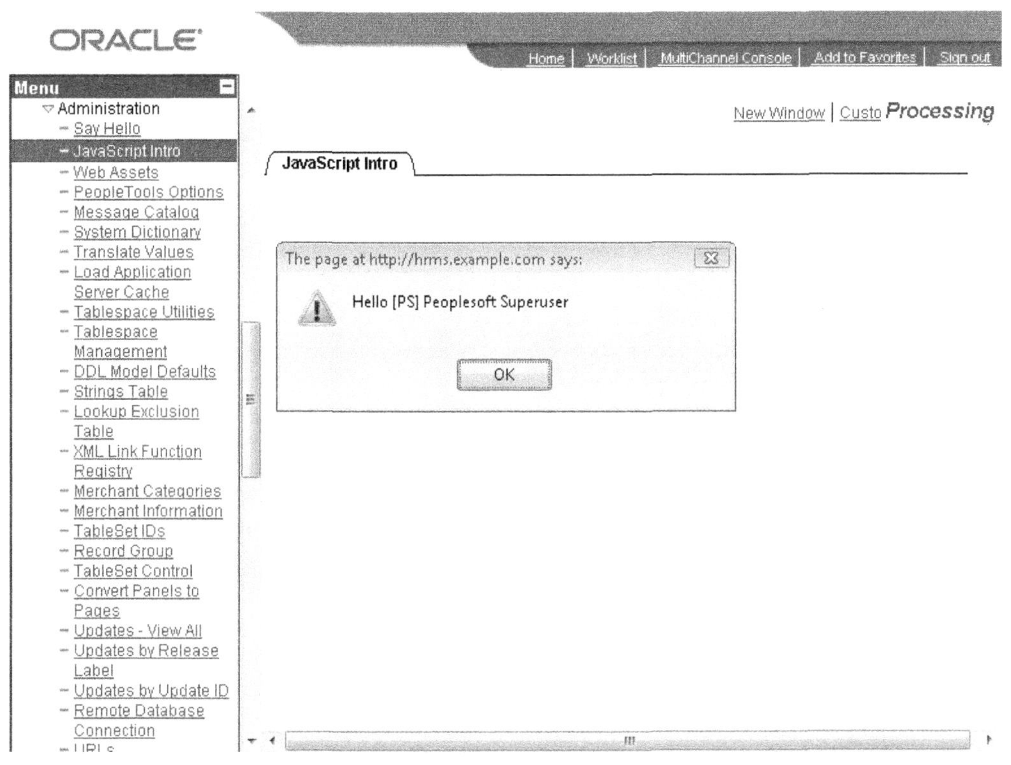

FIGURE 6-4. *APT_JSINTRO with PeopleCode-generated JavaScript*

Creating an HTML Definition

All that embedded HTML and JavaScript make the PeopleCode quite messy. Let's move that HTML out of the PeopleCode editor and into an HTML definition.

Create a new HTML definition by choosing File | New from the App Designer menu bar and choosing HTML for the definition type. Enter the following code into this new HTML definition:

```
<script type="text/javascript">
  alert("Template says, \"%Bind(:1)\"");
</script>
```

This code listing is very similar to our initial Hello World example. Rather than hard-coding the greeting, however, we use PeopleSoft HTML definition bind variables. Save the HTML definition as `APT_JS_GREETING`.

Modify the `APT_JS_WRK.HTMLAREA.RowInit` event PeopleCode so that it resembles the following listing:

```
import APT_GREETERS:UserGreeter;

Local string &html;
Local APT_GREETERS:UserGreeter &g = create APT_GREETERS:UserGreeter();

&html = GetHTMLText(HTML.APT_JS_GREETING, &g.sayHello());

APT_JS_WRK.HTMLAREA.Value = &html;
```

Inspecting PeopleSoft's User Interface with Firebug

Firebug, a Mozilla Firefox browser plug-in, is a popular web development tool. It has features for investigating, debugging, and manipulating web pages. The Mozilla Firefox web browser and Firebug browser plug-in are both available for download from Mozilla's web site.

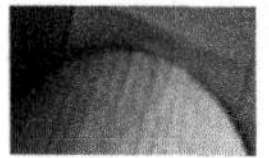

NOTE
Internet Explorer has a tool called IE Developer Toolbar. Unfortunately, IE Developer Toolbar has far fewer features than Firebug.

Before using JavaScript to change the appearance of a field on a page, we must be able to identify that field through JavaScript. Firebug's inspection tool allows you to use your mouse to select a page element and see the HTML that defines that element. If we use Firebug to inspect the `COMPANY` field element, we see that the element's ID attribute has the value `INSTALLATION_COMPANY`. Generally speaking, PeopleSoft page field IDs use the convention *`RECORD_FIELD`*.

Using Firebug's Console

Firebug's console allows you to execute JavaScript within the context of the current page. You can display the Firebug console by selecting View | Firebug from the Firefox menu bar.

Unfortunately, the current page context is a frameset, not the main content window. Therefore, to test code fragments in the console window, we will prefix all context-specific references with `window.frames["TargetContent"]`. Type the following into the console command line:

```
window.frames["TargetContent"].document
    .getElementById("INSTALLATION_COMPANY");
```

When you run this command, the console output window will display the HTML that defines this element. Moving your mouse over the HTML displayed in the output window will highlight the element within the page. The console is an excellent tool for prototyping JavaScript.

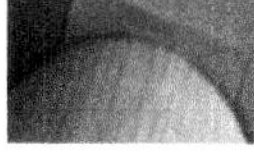

NOTE

PeopleSoft serves content through two primary servlets: `psp` *and* `psc`*. By switching the URL in the address bar from psp to psc, it is possible to test JavaScript in the Firebug console within the context of the transaction page, rather than the context of the PeopleSoft portal frameset. Using the psc URL, you can type* `document.getElementById("INSTALLATION_COMPANY")`*, rather than the full preceding* `window.frames[...]` *code.*

Using Firebug to Enhance the Trace Bookmarklet

In Chapter 5, we wrote some JavaScript in the form of a bookmarklet. The JavaScript hard-coded certain portions of the URL that may change from one application instance to another. Using regular expressions,[1] we can make that JavaScript work with any PeopleSoft instance. (In Chapter 9, you will learn how to add regular expression support to PeopleCode.)

Let's use the Firebug console to test some JavaScript fragments to see if they give us the results we desire. First, we need some JavaScript that will give us the URL of the current component. To find this, we need to know a little about the browser's Document Object Model (DOM).[2] The top-level object is a `window` object and is exposed to JavaScript as the global variable named `window`. While reviewing the `window` object's properties and methods with an online JavaScript reference,[3] we see that the `window` object's `location` property contains the page's URL. Here is a JavaScript fragment you can test in the Firebug console that returns the relative URL for a component:

```
window.frames["TargetContent"].location.pathname
```

If you're still viewing the `APT_JSINTRO` page, Firebug prints the following text to the console:

```
"/psc/hrms/EMPLOYEE/HRMS/c/APT_CUSTOM.APT_JSINTRO.GBL"
```

Using regular expressions, we can parse the site name, portal, and node names from this URL. Enter the following expression into the Firebug console command line:

```
window.frames["TargetContent"].location.pathname.match(
    /^\/ps[pc]\/(.+?\/)(.+?\/)(.+?\/)/);
```

Firebug will respond by displaying something similar to the following (your values may differ slightly):

```
["/psc/hrms/EMPLOYEE/HRMS/", "hrms/", "EMPLOYEE/", "HRMS/"]
```

Firebug printed an array containing four elements. The first element is the full path we saw earlier. The second, third, and fourth elements contain portions of the URL that matched capture sequences in the regular expression.

Modify the previously executed Firebug statement by adding `[1]` to the end of the command:

```
window.frames["TargetContent"].location.pathname.match(
    /^\/ps[pc]\/(.+?\/)(.+?\/)(.+?\/)/)[1];
```

Notice that the Firebug console printed the second element in the array. Unlike PeopleCode arrays, which always start with the index numbered 1, JavaScript arrays start with index 0.

Let's modify our bookmarklet so it derives portions of the trace iScript URL from the current PeopleSoft page. By doing so, our bookmarklet will work with any PeopleSoft instance. Here is the uncompressed JavaScript URL. Replace your trace bookmarklet with the following JavaScript code:

```
javascript:
(function(){
  var v1 = window.frames["TargetContent"].location.pathname.match(
      /^\/ps[pc]\/(.+?\/)(.+?\/)(.+?\/)/);
  window.open("/psc/" + v1[1] + v1[2] + v1[3] +
      "s/WEBLIB_APT_DBG.ISCRIPT1.FieldFormula.IScript_SetSQLTrace?" +
      "level=7", "pstrace", "height=100,width=140,menubar=no," +
      "location=no,resizable=no,scrollbars=no,status=no");
})();
```

The following is the reformatted bookmarklet JavaScript, with the long text strings replaced with placeholders:

```
(function(){
  var v1 = [array, of, regular, expression, matches];
  window.open("url", "window name", "options");
})();
```

The first line of this code creates a new function. We could execute this code directly, without placing it in a function. However, in the absence of a function, the browser would add the `v1` variable to the current page's global namespace. Wrapping the JavaScript in a function scopes the variables to the function only.

Here is the specification for a JavaScript function:

```
function functionName(parm1, parm2) {
  // do something with parm1 and parm2
  // return a value if desired
  return true;
}
```

Notice that our bookmarklet's function declaration does not match this specification. For example, our function declaration is missing a name. A function declaration without a name is an anonymous function. You will see many examples of anonymous functions throughout the chapters in Part II of this book.

The function begins and ends with a parenthesis, and is followed by a second set of parentheses. By wrapping the anonymous function in parentheses and then following it with parentheses, we instruct the JavaScript interpreter to execute this code immediately. This type of anonymous function declaration is known as a *self-invoking function*.[4] Why not just declare the function and then execute it? When you declare a function, you add a name to the global namespace. In this case, the global namespace happens to belong to the current page, not the bookmarklet. If the function were a named function, calling the bookmarklet would actually add another function to the current page. Using an anonymous function avoids potential name collisions.

Another important fact about bookmarklets is that they should not return a value.[5] The `window.open` method we executed returns a value. Without an anonymous function, the browser would actually navigate away from the current PeopleSoft page and open a blank page containing the text result returned by `window.open`.

Styling an Element

Let's add some JavaScript to the `APT_JSINTRO` page we created earlier to add some styling. We will change the background color of the `INSTALLATION_COMPANY` field.

Switch back to App Designer and add another HTML Area control to the page. Place this HTML Area control below the `COMPANY` field, as shown in Figure 6-5.

In this example, we are writing JavaScript that interacts with the HTML DOM. It is critical that the JavaScript not execute until after the browser interprets the element's HTML tags. Since browsers build the DOM in memory while reading a document, placing our code after the corresponding HTML element ensures the element is available for JavaScript interaction.

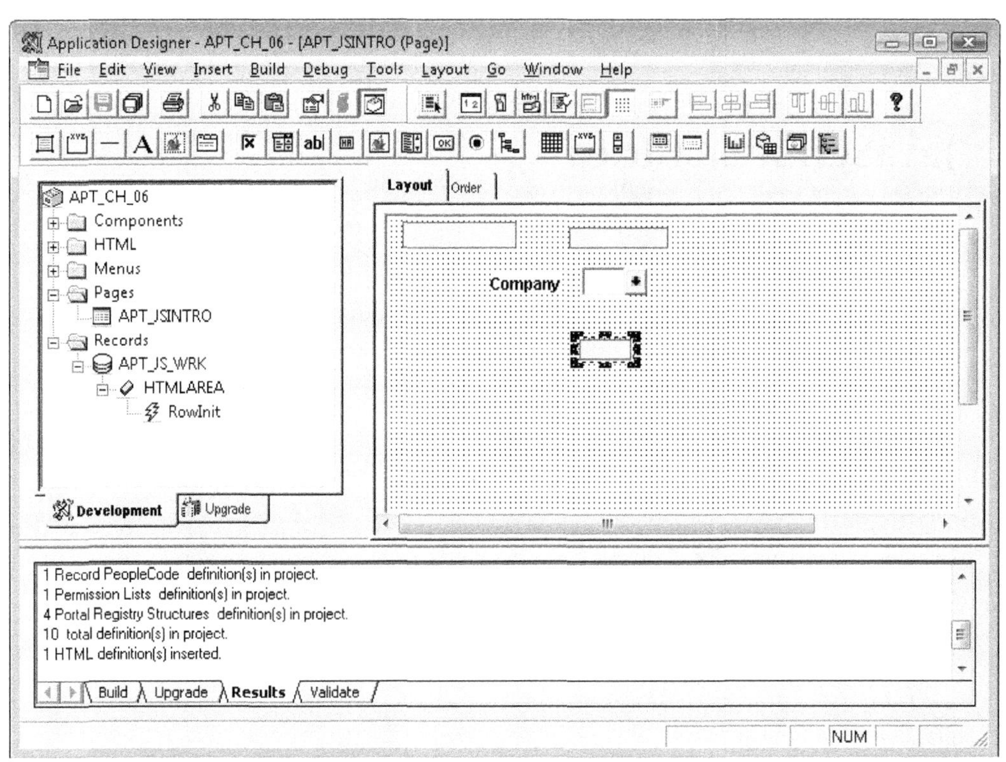

FIGURE 6-5. *APT_JSINTRO page with a new HTML Area*

Double-click the new empty HTML Area control, select Constant, and add the following HTML and JavaScript:

```
<script type="text/javascript">
  document.getElementById("INSTALLATION_COMPANY").style
      .backgroundColor = "PaleGreen";
</script>
```

Switch back to your browser and reload the page. The background color of the company field should have changed to a pale green.

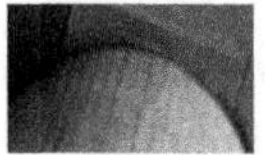

NOTE
The CSS specification provides support for several named colors. Besides names, you can also use an RGB macro to specify red, green, and blue values, or you can use the common HTML hexadecimal RGB representation. For example, `PaleGreen` in hexadecimal is represented as `#98FB98`. In hexadecimal format, the first and second characters represent the red value, the third and fourth represent the green value, and the fifth and sixth represent the blue value. Using the RGB macro, we could also specify this color as `rgb(152, 251, 152)`. The RGB macro uses decimal notation, rather than hexadecimal.

JavaScript Libraries

The JavaScript language is a dialect of the ECMAScript[6] standard. Because the language is standardized, all browsers interpret the core language components the same way. For example, curly braces, `for` loops, and `if` statements mean the same thing in Microsoft's Internet Explorer as they do in Apple's Safari. Unfortunately, that is where the similarities end.

Most of the JavaScript we write with PeopleSoft applications involve HTML DOM interactions. Even though there is a standards body that governs web development, browsers interpret the DOM differently. For example, just a few years ago, the style code presented in the previous section would work only in Internet Explorer. Just as Meta-SQL provides an SQL abstraction from the underlying database implementation, JavaScript libraries abstract the idiosyncrasies between web browser implementations.

JavaScript libraries also provide shortcuts for common tasks. This is similar to Meta-SQL's SQL shortcuts, such as `%InsertSelect`. For example, animating an HTML object may require several lines of JavaScript. However, using a JavaScript library such as jQuery, you can animate an object with a single line of JavaScript.

In Chapter 5, we used the SWFObject JavaScript library to provide a cross-browser method for inserting Flex components. You can find a list of the most common JavaScript libraries on the Google AJAX Libraries API[7] project site. While there are many JavaScript libraries to choose from, jQuery is my personal favorite. The jQuery JavaScript library is fast, lightweight, well maintained, and very well written.

Serving JavaScript Libraries

JavaScript libraries are composed of one or more plain text files containing JavaScript code. One of the challenges we face is selecting a JavaScript library storage location that a web browser can access. Several storage options are available:

- If you are using PeopleTools 8.50 or later, you can store all your JavaScript libraries as HTML definitions. This is the approach used by the PeopleTools team, which stores PeopleSoft JavaScript libraries in HTML definitions, and then uses the `%JavaScript` meta-HTML and `Response.GetJavaScriptURL` method to serve JavaScript libraries. This approach is best because it provides all the benefits of managed definitions—migration support and text searching—as well as the web server benefits of caching and compression. You can store a library like the jQuery JavaScript library in a single HTML definition. Unfortunately, prior releases of PeopleTools limited the size of HTML definitions, and that size varied by release. If you are using an earlier version of PeopleTools, you will need an alternative.
- Another storage location is the web server's file system. This approach offers caching and compression, just like the HTML definition approach, but without the ability to migrate JavaScript libraries as projects. Furthermore, this approach requires your system administrator to grant you access to the web server's file system. This approach will not work without access. It may require you to redeploy your JavaScript files after each PeopleTools upgrade. And, depending on your web server and deployment mode, you may need to restart your web server each time you change a JavaScript file that is stored on the web server.

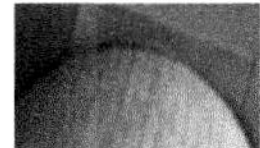

NOTE
It is possible to deploy and change files on a development web server without restarting that web server instance. If you prefer to store files on your web server, you should discuss this option with your application system administrator.

- If neither of the preceding storage options will work in your environment, you can store JavaScript libraries as message catalog entries and then serve them from iScripts. The reason I mention this option last is because iScripts do not support caching, and, therefore, require an HTTP request, including the web server, app server, and database server for each request. In a well-tuned environment, the overhead of such a request is minimal. Nevertheless, this approach can't compete with the speed of parsing a file the browser already has in its cache.

The remainder of this book will use the iScript/message catalog approach. Here, we will use this approach with jQuery, a JavaScript library we will explore in the next section. To begin, go to http://jquery.com and download the latest minified version of jQuery.

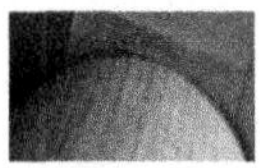

NOTE
The jQuery library is available in two forms: minified and uncompressed. The uncompressed version is useful for JavaScript debugging. The minified version is a smaller file, which provides better download performance. Unfortunately, the minification process obfuscates the source code in a manner that makes it very difficult to read.

Next, create a message catalog entry to store the contents of the jQuery JavaScript library. Launch your web browser, sign in to PeopleSoft, and navigate to PeopleTools | Utilities | Administration | Message Catalog. Create a new message set numbered 25000 and give this message set the description **JavaScript Libraries**. In message number 1, set the message text to **jQuery JavaScript library**, and paste the text of the jQuery JavaScript library into the Explanation field, as shown in Figure 6-6.

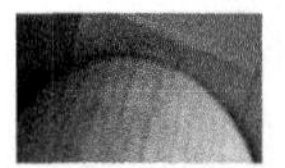

NOTE
If you already have a message set defined for 25000, use a different number. Just be sure to reference the correct number in the rest of this chapter's examples.

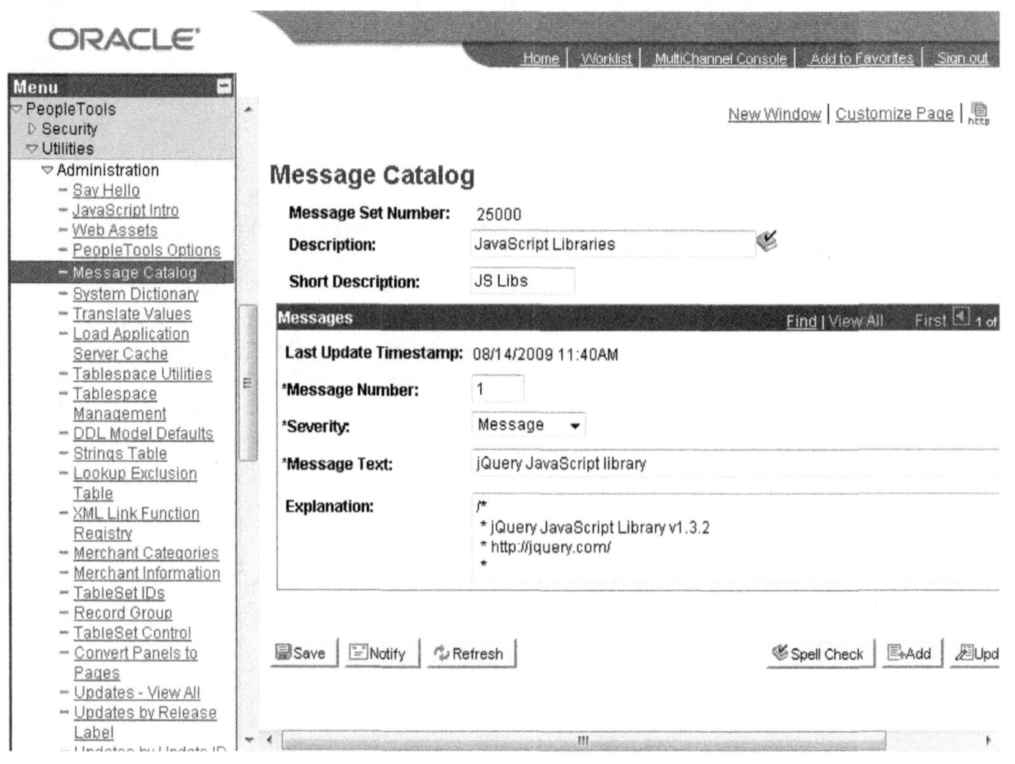

FIGURE 6-6. *jQuery message catalog entry*

Next, create a derived/work record and add the field ISCRIPT1. Name the new record WEBLIB_APT_JSL (an abbreviation for JavaScript Libraries). Double-click the FieldFormula event of the field ISCRIPT1 and enter the following PeopleCode:

```
Function IScript_jQuery
   local string &js = MsgGetExplainText(25000, 1, "alert('The " |
         "jQuery JavaScript library message catalog entry does " |
         "not exist.');");

   %Response.SetContentType("text/javascript");
   %Response.Write(&js);
End-Function;
```

Save the record and add this WEBLIB/iScript to the permission list APT_CUSTOM.

I considered making this function more generic, so it could serve any JavaScript message catalog entry. By creating a separate function for each library, however, you can control access on a per-library basis through permission lists. If you would prefer a generic, single iScript function, use the following code instead:

```
Function IScript_GetJSLib()
   Local number &libId = Value(%Request.GetParameter("id"));
   local string &js = MsgGetExplainText(25000, &libId, "alert('The " |
         "requested JavaScript library message catalog entry does " |
         "not exist.');");

   %Response.SetContentType("text/javascript");
   %Response.Write(&js);
End-Function;
```

This more generic function hard-codes the message set, but this is not necessary. You could make the set number a parameter instead. However, changing the function in this manner would make it possible for a user to view any message catalog entry. While this may not pose a security threat, it certainly opens possibilities.

Using jQuery

jQuery is my favorite cross-browser JavaScript library. It fits well with PeopleSoft, is actively maintained, and is widely used among developers.

JavaScript must wait for the web browser to load the DOM prior to interacting with page elements. In the previous styling example, we handled this by placing our JavaScript after the COMPANY field. A more effective approach is to queue JavaScript that interacts with the DOM to execute after the DOM is available. Browsers have various methods for communicating the state of the DOM. Using jQuery, you can write cross-browser JavaScript to queue your code to run after the DOM is available.

Let's modify the APT_JSINTRO page so that it uses jQuery to change the COMPANY field's style after the DOM is available. Inserting the jQuery JavaScript library into this page will require an HTML definition and some PeopleCode. Create a new HTML definition and add the following HTML:

```
<script type="text/javascript" src="%Bind(:1)"></script>
```

Save this HTML definition as APT_JS_LIB.

This HTML definition uses a bind variable for the jQuery library's URL. We could hard-code the path to the jQuery iScript, but that would tightly couple this HTML definition to the current PeopleSoft instance. Hard-coding the URL would make it impossible to migrate this definition as part of a proper change control policy. As an alternative, we will use the `GenerateScriptContentURL` function to determine the iScript's URL at runtime.

Open the `RowInit` event of the `APT_JS_WRK.HTMLAREA` record field. Replace the existing `RowInit` PeopleCode with the following:

```
Local string &html;
Local string &url;

&url = GenerateScriptContentURL(%Portal, %Node, Record.WEBLIB_APT_JSL,
      Field.ISCRIPT1, "FieldFormula", "IScript_jQuery");
&html = GetHTMLText(HTML.APT_JS_LIB, &url);

APT_JS_WRK.HTMLAREA.Value = &html;
```

Open the `APT_JSINTRO` page in App Designer. Double-click the HTML Area control that is below the `COMPANY` field, and replace the existing HTML with the following HTML:

```
<script type="text/javascript">
  $(document).ready(function() {
    $("#INSTALLATION_COMPANY").css(
        "background-color", "PaleGreen");
  });
</script>
```

While this code resembles the JavaScript we've seen in other examples, it has some differences. One new item is the `$`, which is a variable created by the jQuery JavaScript library. It is a synonym for the `jQuery` global function. The `jQuery`, or `$`, function takes a selector as an argument. A selector can be as simple as a JavaScript object or as complex as a CSS selector or XPath expression. The first line uses a JavaScript object as a selector: `$(document)`. The result of this function call is a jQuery collection.

Next on the call stack is the `ready` method. The statement `$(document).ready` uses the `jQuery` function to return a jQuery collection containing the JavaScript `document` object, and then executes the `ready` method against that collection. The `ready` method queues functions and then executes them after the browser finishes loading the HTML DOM. Browsers identify this event differently, and jQuery provides a browser-independent method for registering a callback for the DOM `ready` event. By waiting until the DOM is fully loaded, we ensure that the target element exists prior to any interaction.

Inside the call to the `ready` method, you see an anonymous function declaration. The jQuery JavaScript library makes extensive use of anonymous functions. By using an anonymous function, we avoid polluting the global namespace with a function name that is used only once. The code inside this anonymous function performs the actual JavaScript operation. Our purpose for wrapping this code in an anonymous function is to delay execution of the code until a specific event happens. The `ready` method will receive a pointer to this anonymous function.

Moving on to the code inside the anonymous function, you see some significant changes to the previous background color example. The first example includes this line:

```
document.getElementById("INSTALLATION_COMPANY").style
      .backgroundColor = "PaleGreen";
```

and our current jQuery example contains this line:

```
$("#INSTALLATION_COMPANY").css("background-color", "PaleGreen");
```

Notice that these examples differ in the manner used to select an element, as well as the method used to change the background color.

The first example used W3C standard DOM[8] methods to select the target element. The second example used jQuery's CSS selectors to accomplish the same task. jQuery's selectors offer a flexible alternative to DOM selection methods. In contrast to jQuery, the DOM offers two selection methods: `getElementsByTagName` and `getElementById`. For example, if we wanted a collection of input elements, we could execute `document.getElementsbyTagName("input")`. The input element, however, is actually a generic element for many types of data-entry controls. What if we wanted to select only text input elements? jQuery has support for CSS attribute selectors as well as XPath selectors. A common CSS selector use case is selecting all elements with a particular style class that are children of another element.

Next, notice the difference in the method used to change the background color. The `css` method is unique to jQuery collections, whereas the `style` property is common to many browsers. The `style` object has properties that must be set one by one. The `css` method allows you to specify multiple CSS settings with a single method call. For example, we could change the border, background, font, and foreground with the following line of jQuery JavaScript:

```
$("#INSTALLATION_COMPANY").css(
    {backgroundColor: "green",
     fontWeight: "bold",
     color: "white",
     border: "1px solid #c0c0c0"});
```

Making Global User Interface Changes

When entering data into a transactional system, users tab between several fields. The tab order of those fields may not be intuitive. It is possible for users to lose their place after tabbing from one field to the next. Let's create a customization that highlights the active text field, making it very clear to users which data-entry field is active.

With each enhancement request, a developer must weigh the benefit of a modification against the cost of maintaining that modification. While some modifications may offer benefits for any page, the cost of physically changing every page is too great to merit the modification. However, if we identify an App Designer definition that is used by all PeopleSoft pages, then we can implement a global enhancement with a single modification.

Identifying Common Definitions

Many of the elements that compose the PeopleSoft user interface exist as definitions in App Designer. If you could modify one PeopleSoft definition that affects every page within PeopleSoft, then the cost of the modification may be fairly low in comparison to the associated benefits.

For example, the header used on every PeopleSoft page is an HTML definition that is modifiable from App Designer.

The PeopleSoft user interface is a combination of HTML, CSS, and JavaScript. We know that some of that HTML is stored in App Designer as HTML definitions. We also know that CSS is stored in App Designer style sheet definitions. What about JavaScript?

Since PeopleSoft application developers use the same design tools as customer developers, let's assume that JavaScript definitions are stored in App Designer. App Designer, however, doesn't have a JavaScript definition type. Therefore, we must consider other types of definitions that are capable of storing JavaScript. Looking through the PeopleBooks *PeopleCode API* reference, we see that the `Response` object contains a method named `GetJavaScriptURL`, and the method's parameter is an HTML definition. Given this information, we can conclude that JavaScript files are stored in App Designer as HTML definitions.

Let's use the Firebug plug-in to test this hypothesis. When you select the Firebug Script tab, the first thing you will see is the HTML source for the current page. Just above that text, and below Firebug's other tabs, you see the name of the script file currently displayed in the Firebug script panel. The script name is actually a button. Click the script name to reveal a list of all the JavaScript files used on this page. In this list, you should see names like `PT_ISCROSSDOMAIN`, `PT_PAGESCRIPT`, `PT_COPYURL`, and so on. You can confirm that these files represent HTML definitions by opening them in App Designer. If you open them in App Designer, be sure to only use the file's base name, not the entire name. The base name is the name of the file up to the last underscore (_). For example, `PT_ISCROSSDOMAIN_1.js` represents the HTML definition `PT_ISCROSSDOMAIN`. The remaining _# represents the HTML definition's version number. To ensure your web browser maintains a fresh copy, PeopleSoft applications use the convention *`NAME_VERSION`* for JavaScript files, images, and style sheets.

NOTE
If you don't see a list of JavaScript files containing the names mentioned here, check your web profile. The default DEV web profile places the contents of these JavaScript HTML definitions inside the current HTML document. The PROD profile caches them as separate files on the web server.

If we find a common HTML definition that we can edit with App Designer, then we can add new HTML, JavaScript, and CSS. Likewise, if we can find some common JavaScript, then we can add new JavaScript to create CSS and HTML. Since both JavaScript and HTML exist in App Designer as HTML definitions, all we need to find is a common HTML definition. Looking at the list, `PT_PAGESCRIPT` sounds like a good candidate. If you are using PeopleTools 8.50, then this definition is an excellent candidate. `PT_PAGESCRIPT`, however, contains a lot of code. In PeopleTools 8.4*x*, HTML definitions had a maximum size limitation that varied by release. PeopleTools 8.50 removed the maximum size limitation for HTML definitions. Therefore, we not only need to find a common HTML definition, but we also must find one with enough available space for us to add HTML, JavaScript, and CSS.

My favorite HTML definition to modify is `PT_COPYURL`, which is included in every PeopleSoft page. The only exception to this rule is iScripts. Since iScripts are not assembled by the PeopleSoft architecture, they do not include the common PeopleSoft HTML definitions. As you saw in Chapter 5, we can use iScripts to serve nonbrowser documents. Therefore, it would not make sense to add JavaScript to iScript content.

Minimizing the Impact

If we are going to modify a delivered definition, we want to minimize the impact of that modification. Writing several hundred lines of code, or even worse, interweaving custom code with delivered code, is not considered "minimizing the impact." Rather, we can apply the FUNCLIB minimization technique used when modifying delivered PeopleCode.

With the FUNCLIB technique you write your code in a custom FUNCLIB function, and then call that FUNCLIB function from the delivered code. The net effect is that you add only two lines to the delivered code, rather than potentially several hundred lines of code. We can apply this same technique to JavaScript libraries by writing our code in a separate definition, and then using JavaScript to insert our code into the delivered JavaScript.

Coding the Solution

With our modification strategy and target objects loosely identified, we are ready to write some code.

Bootstrap Code

When you turn on your computer, a small program searches your hard drive for a boot partition, and then launches your operating system according to the instructions located in that boot partition. This process is called *bootstrapping*.[9] We will follow a similar pattern. Our solution will load a couple of JavaScript libraries and CSS files. Before we can load these resources, however, we need to write a few lines of code to bootstrap our solution. In this chapter, we will write just enough bootstrapping code to highlight the active data-entry field. In Chapter 7, we will extend this solution to bootstrap JavaScript functionality on a per-component basis.

We will add our bootstrap code to the `PT_COPYURL` HTML definition. Since we will review the bootstrap code section by section, I recommend waiting for the complete listing before modifying `PT_COPYURL`.

In the earlier bookmarklet example, we used an anonymous function to avoid polluting the global namespace. We want to continue in this good-citizen spirit by minimizing the number of items we add to the global namespace. We can accomplish this by creating one object in the global namespace, and then adding all of our required functionality to that object as properties and methods. In a sense, this custom object provides a secondary namespace similar to the global namespace.

The following code tests for the existence of a single global object, and then creates it if it doesn't exist.

```
if(!window.apt) {
  apt = {/* code goes here */};

  // Additional code will go here
}
```

We first test for the existence of our global object, because it is possible for the same JavaScript file to be included twice. Redefining the object may remove functionality that was added by another custom JavaScript module.

It would also be wise to keep our custom namespace clean by organizing custom objects in child namespaces, similar to the way Java uses packages to organize code. The following JavaScript defines a namespace-creation JavaScript function. We will place this code below the `apt` object creation line so that it is inside the `if` statement (the previous `apt` creation line is repeated for reference).

```
if(!window.apt) {
  apt = {
    namespace: {
      create: function (ns) {
        var arr = ns.split(".");
        var level = window;
        var item;

        while (item = arr.shift()) {
          if(!level[item]) {
            level[item] = {};
          }
          // Move to the next level in the namespace
          level = level[item];
        }
      }
    }
  }
}
```

Loading iScripts as JavaScript files will require us to parse the current URL and generate a new iScript URL. If our code was executed on the server, we would use the `GenerateScriptContentURL` PeopleCode function. Since our code is executing in the browser, however, we don't have access to this function. Fortunately, we can use regular expressions to write our own version of `GenerateScriptContentURL`. To keep our namespaces organized, let's place this function in the `files` namespace.

```
apt.namespace.create("apt.files");
/* function: generateIScriptContentUrl
 * parameter: object containing the following properties:
 *   record, field, event, IScript_function
 * example:
 *   apt.files.generateScriptContentUrl({record: "WEBLIB_APT_JSL",
 *       field: "ISCRIPT1", event: "FieldFormula",
 *       script: "IScript_jQuery"});
 */
apt.files.generateScriptContentUrl = (function() {
  var re = /ps[pc]\/(.+?\/)(.+?\/)(.+?\/)/;
  var buffer = window.location.pathname.match(re);
  buffer[0] = "/psc/";
  buffer[4] = "s/";
  buffer[6] = buffer[8] = buffer[10] = ".";
  // Use a closure to avoid string construction and
  // regular expression evaluation on each execution
  return (function(parms) {
    buffer[5] = parms.record;
    buffer[7] = parms.field;
    buffer[9] = parms.event;
```

```
      buffer[11] = parms.script;
      var result = buffer.join("");
      buffer[5] = buffer[7] = buffer[9] = buffer[11] = "";
      return result;
    });
  })();
```

We may call this JavaScript version of the `generateScriptContentUrl` function multiple times within a page. With each call, the base URL will remain static. Rather than evaluate the current document's URL with each execution, the preceding code uses a JavaScript closure[10] to initialize the base URL and save it in a string array buffer for future executions. This requires a few extra lines of code, but reduces the code's execution time.

The final portion of our bootstrap code contains function declarations for importing JavaScript and CSS files:

```
  /* function: importScript
   * parameters: object with the following properties:
   *   id, url
   * example:
   *   apt.files.importScript({id: "jq",
   *       url: "/url/to/javascript/file"});
   */
  apt.files.importScript = function(parms) {
    document.write("<scr" + "ipt id='" + parms.id + "' " +
        "type='text/javascript' src='" + parms.url + "'><\/script>");

  }
}
```

Highlighting the active data-entry field involves changing the background color. The background color of an HTML element is determined by CSS. As you saw with the background color example earlier, it is possible to set display styles inline. In this example, we want to set the background color when the user enters a data-entry field, and then reset the background color when the user exits that field. Therefore, if we set the element's style as we did before, we will need to create a variable to hold the original background color so we can reset the color when the user exits the data-entry field. As an alternative, we can use CSS style classes. With a style class, we can add the highlighting class on entrance and remove it on exit. In order to use a style class, however, we must define it in CSS.

CSS files are referenced in the header section of an HTML page. When editing pages in App Designer, however, it is not possible to modify the page's HTML header. But we can modify the header at runtime through JavaScript. Therefore, we will add the following code inside the `if(!window.apt) {...}` curly braces to define a CSS style sheet import function.

```
  /* function: importStylesheet
   * parameters:
   *   url
   * example:
   *   apt.files.importStylesheet("/url/to/css/file"});
   */
```

```
apt.files.importStylesheet = function (url) {
  var ss = document.createElement("link");
  ss.rel = "stylesheet";
  ss.type = "text/css";
  ss.href = url;
  document.getElementsByTagName("head")[0].appendChild(ss);
}
```

The following is the entire bootstrap code listing. Add this code to the end of the delivered PT_COPYURL HTML definition.

```
//% APT_CH_06, JavaScript global mod Bootstrap code follows
if(!window.apt) {
  apt = {
    namespace: {
      create: function (ns) {
        var arr = ns.split(".");
        var level = window;
        var item;

        while (item = arr.shift()) {
          if(!level[item]) {
            level[item] = {};
          }
          // Move to the next level in the namespace
          level = level[item];
        }
      }
    }
  }

  apt.namespace.create("apt.files");
  /* function: generateIScriptContentUrl
   * parameter: object containing the following properties:
   *   record, field, event, IScript_function
   * example:
   *   apt.files.generateScriptContentUrl({record: "WEBLIB_APT_JSL",
   *       field: "ISCRIPT1", event: "FieldFormula",
   *       script: "IScript_jQuery"});
   */
  apt.files.generateScriptContentUrl = (function() {
    var re = /ps[pc]\/(.+?\/)(.+?\/)(.+?\/)/;
    var buffer = window.location.pathname.match(re);
    buffer[0] = "/psc/";
    buffer[4] = "s/";
    buffer[6] = buffer[8] = buffer[10] = ".";
    // Use a closure to avoid string construction and
    // regular expression evaluation on each execution
    return (function(parms) {
      buffer[5] = parms.record;
      buffer[7] = parms.field;
```

```
      buffer[9] = parms.event;
      buffer[11] = parms.script;
      var result = buffer.join("");
      buffer[5] = buffer[7] = buffer[9] = buffer[11] = "";
      return result;
    });
  })();

  /* function: importScript
   * parameters: object with the following properties:
   *   id, url
   * example:
   *   apt.files.importScript({id: "jq",
   *       url: "/url/to/javascript/file"});
   */
  apt.files.importScript = function(parms) {
    document.write("<scr" + "ipt id='" + parms.id + "' " +
        "type='text/javascript' src='" + parms.url + "'><\/script>");

  }

  /* function: importStylesheet
   * parameters:
   *   url
   * example:
   *   apt.files.importStylesheet("/url/to/css/file"});
   */
  apt.files.importStylesheet = function (url) {
    var ss = document.createElement("link");
    ss.rel = "stylesheet";
    ss.type = "text/css";
    ss.href = url;
    document.getElementsByTagName("head")[0].appendChild(ss);
  }
}
```

Our bootstrap code is a little on the long side. In Chapters 7 and 8, we will shorten this code by moving some of it to an external library, and then loading that library through AJAX.

The Highlighting Code

We will use an iScript/HTML definition combination to serve the JavaScript required for the active text field customization. Create a new HTML definition and add the following JavaScript:

```
apt.namespace.create("apt.ui");

if(!window.apt.ui.highlight) {
  /* Create a conditional execution flag to avoid redefining this
   * object.
   */
  apt.ui.highlight = true;
```

```
  $(document).ready(function(){
    $("input[type='text'], input[type='password'], " +
        "select, textarea").focus(function(e) {
      // Add a style class when activated
      $(this).addClass("APT_hasFocus");
    }).blur(function(e) {
      // Remove a style class when not active
      $(this).removeClass("APT_hasFocus");
    });
  });
}
```

Save the HTML definition as APT_HIGHLIGHT_ACTIVE_JS.

The preceding JavaScript references the APT_hasFocus style class. Before testing this JavaScript enhancement, we need to create a style sheet containing a definition for APT_hasFocus. Create a new HTML definition and add the following CSS:

```
.APT_hasFocus {
  background-color: #99FF99;
  border: 2px solid black;
}
```

Save this HTML definition as APT_HIGHLIGHT_ACTIVE_CSS.

We will serve both of these HTML definitions from the WEBLIB_APT_JSL derived/work record. Open the FieldFormula event of the WEBLIB_APT_JSL.ISCRIPT1 field. Add the following PeopleCode to the end of this event's existing PeopleCode:

```
Function IScript_HighlightActiveJs
   %Response.SetContentType("text/javascript");
   %Response.Write(GetHTMLText(HTML.APT_HIGHLIGHT_ACTIVE_JS));
End-Function;

Function IScript_HighlightActiveCss
   %Response.SetContentType("text/css");
   %Response.Write(GetHTMLText(HTML.APT_HIGHLIGHT_ACTIVE_CSS));
End-Function;
```

After saving the WEBLIB, be sure to add its iScripts to the APT_CUSTOM permission list.

With all of our JavaScript libraries defined, we can add them to PT_COPYURL and test this customization. Add the following JavaScript to the end of PT_COPYURL:

```
//% import scripts
if(!window.jQuery) {
  apt.files.importScript({
      id:  "jq",
      url: apt.files.generateScriptContentUrl({
          record: "WEBLIB_APT_JSL",
          field:  "ISCRIPT1",
          event:  "FieldFormula",
          script: "IScript_jQuery"})
  });
}
```

```
apt.files.importScript({
    id:  "apt_ui_ha",
    url: apt.files.generateScriptContentUrl({
        record: "WEBLIB_APT_JSL",
        field:  "ISCRIPT1",
        event:  "FieldFormula",
        script: "IScript_HighlightActiveJs"
    })
});

apt.files.importStylesheet(
    apt.files.generateScriptContentUrl({
        record: "WEBLIB_APT_JSL",
        field:  "ISCRIPT1",
        event:  "FieldFormula",
        script: "IScript_HighlightActiveCss"
    })
);
```

NOTE

The preceding code imports iScripts into the `PT_COPYURL` HTML definition. iScripts imported into common HTML definitions must *be accessible to all PeopleSoft users. If they are not accessible, users will receive authorization errors. Even after granting access to all users, you can still secure the contents of iScripts by using the `IsUserInRole` and `IsUserInPermissionList` PeopleCode functions. For testing and demonstration purposes, we will add these iScripts to the `APT_CUSTOM` permission list. You should work with your security administrator to determine the appropriate permission list for global access.*

Because we need the browser to interpret each file before moving to the next file, we needed to add them directly to `PT_COPYURL`. In Chapter 7, you will learn how to use AJAX to load a component's libraries at runtime, eliminating the need to add them to `PT_COPYURL`.

Figure 6-7 shows the `APT_CUSTOM` permission list that demonstrates the highlight active text field modification. The background color of the Description field is a pale green, and the border is extra thick.

Test several pages. As you navigate through the application, notice that this customization even appears on search pages.

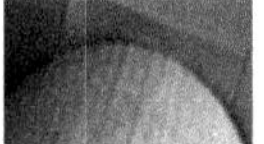

TIP

Developers often ask me how to change the default search page criteria operator from begins with *to* contains. *Combining the techniques shown in this chapter with the AJAX techniques shown in Chapter 7, it is possible to write component-specific JavaScript to change this behavior without actually modifying the component.*

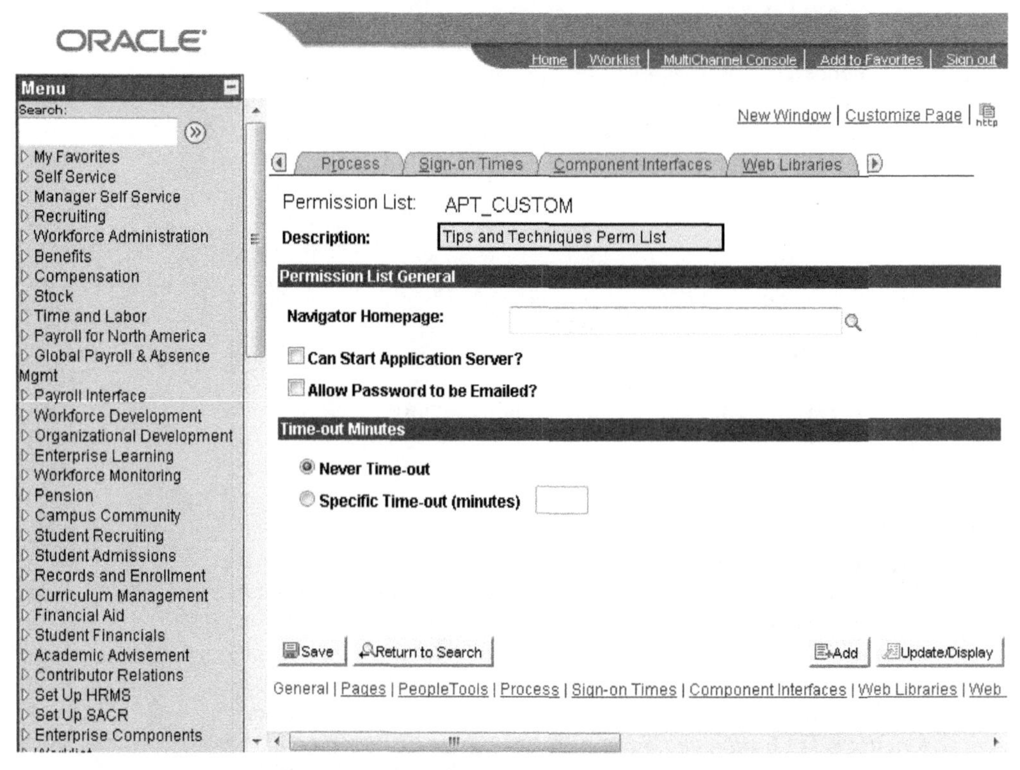

FIGURE 6-7. *PeopleSoft page with active field highlighted*

Using jQuery Plug-ins

The jQuery JavaScript library offers many visual effects. We will cover some of them in Chapter 7. Besides the delivered features and effects, developers have created a very long list of plug-ins. jQuery plug-ins allow you to change the tooltip style, provide a right-click context menu, add drag-and-drop support, create dialog windows, validate user input, and so on. You can browse the list at http://plugins.jquery.com/.

Thickbox

My favorite jQuery plug-in is Thickbox. It is similar to Lightbox,[11] but with less animation.

Before you begin working with Thickbox, I suggest you visit http://jquery.com/demo/thickbox/ to review the examples. As you work with the examples, notice that there is an animated graphic that appears while the modal dialog is loading its content.

Let's add Thickbox to our `APT_JSINTRO` page. Thickbox requires three files:

- A JavaScript file to expose the Thickbox API, load content, and respond to events
- A CSS file that defines the background colors, dialog frames, and transparency settings
- An image file that is displayed while Thickbox is loading content

Go to http://jquery.com/demo/thickbox/ and download thickbox.js, thickbox.css, and loadingAnimation.gif. We will create a web asset for the GIF and save the other two files as HTML definitions.

Creating Supporting Definitions

Let's begin with the image. Navigate to PeopleTools | Utilities | Administration | Web Assets and create a new asset named `APT_LOAD_IMG`. In the Description field, enter **Thickbox loading animation**, and set the Mime-Type field to image/gif. Attach the file, save the web asset, and then run it through the approval process. After creating and approving this new web asset, you should be able to view the file in your browser by navigating to a URL that is similar to this (change the server and node names to match your environment):

http://hrms.example.com/psc/hrms/EMPLOYEE/HRMS/s/WEBLIB_APT_WA.ISCRIPT1
.FieldFormula.IScript_GetWebAsset?id=APT_LOAD_IMG

Next, open the thickbox.js file in a text editor. Just after the copyright notice, you will see a line containing the following text:

```
var tb_pathToImage = "images/loadingAnimation.gif";
```

Update the quoted image path so the line looks like this:

```
var tb_pathToImage = apt.files.generateScriptContentUrl({
    record: "WEBLIB_APT_WA",
    field:  "ISCRIPT1",
    event:  "FieldFormula",
    script: "IScript_GetWebAsset"}) + "?id=APT_LOAD_IMG";
```

Since we are serving this image from an iScript, rather than a hard-coded path, we will use the `generateScriptContentUrl` method we created earlier. We won't need to import this function into our page, because it is part of the bootstrap code we added to `PT_COPYURL`. The browser will process `PT_COPYURL` prior to the Thickbox library, because `PT_COPYURL` is included in the HTML head element, whereas the Thickbox library is part of the HTML body.

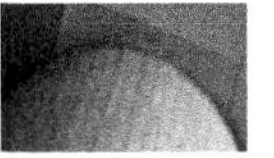

NOTE
Since we are serving the HTML definition from an iScript, we could actually use an HTML bind variable and the PeopleCode `GenerateScriptContentURL` function, rather than our custom JavaScript `generateScriptContentUrl` function.

Create a new HTML definition and insert the text of the modified thickbox.js file. Save the HTML definition as `APT_JQ_THICKBOX_JS`.

Create another HTML definition, add the contents of the thickbox.css file, and save the HTML definition as `APT_JQ_THICKBOX_CSS`. As before, open the `FieldFormula` event of the record field `WEBLIB_APT_JSL ISCRIPT1` and add the following PeopleCode:

```
Function IScript_JqThickboxJs
   %Response.SetContentType("text/javascript");
   %Response.Write(GetHTMLText(HTML.APT_JQ_THICKBOX_JS));
End-Function;
```

```
Function IScript_JqThickboxCss
   %Response.SetContentType("text/css");
   %Response.Write(GetHTMLText(HTML.APT_JQ_THICKBOX_CSS));
End-Function;
```

Add these two new iScripts to the `APT_CUSTOM` permission list, and access them by URL to make sure the iScripts serve the correct content. Here are the two URLs from my server:

http://hrms.example.com/psc/hrms/EMPLOYEE/HRMS/s/WEBLIB_APT_JSL.ISCRIPT1.FieldFormula.IScript_JqThickboxCss

http://hrms.example.com/psc/hrms/EMPLOYEE/HRMS/s/WEBLIB_APT_JSL.ISCRIPT1.FieldFormula.IScript_JqThickboxJs

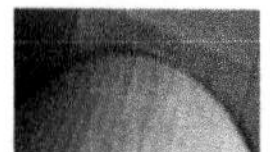

NOTE

You can see the results of the `IScript_JqThickBoxCss` function (the CSS function) by using your web browser to access your site's version of the URL shown here. If you test the `IScript_JqThickBoxJs` URL (the JavaScript function), however, your web browser will prompt you to download, save, or run the JavaScript contents. You can then save the iScript's results to a file and review those results with a text editor.

Adding Thickbox to a Page

Now that we can effectively serve Thickbox from our web server, let's add the Thickbox plug-in to the `APT_JSINTRO` page. We will start by displaying the Oracle home page in a Thickbox frame. Next, we will open a PeopleSoft query in a Thickbox frame.

Since we added jQuery to our bootstrap code, we can remove it from the `APT_JSINTRO` page. Open the `RowInit` event of the record field `APT_JS_WRK HTMLAREA` and delete the event's PeopleCode. Delete the corresponding HTML Area control (the HTML Area depicted in Figure 6-5, directly above the `COMPANY` field) and add a new HTML Area control below the rest of the controls on this page. Set the new HTML Area's value to Field, set the record to `APT_JS_WRK`, and set the field to `HTMLAREA`. Save the page. Figure 6-8 shows the modified page.

Create a new HTML definition named `APT_JSINTRO_THICKBOX` and add the following HTML:

```
<script type="text/javascript">
  apt.files.importScript({
      id:  "apt_ui_tb",
      url: apt.files.generateScriptContentUrl({
          record: "WEBLIB_APT_JSL",
          field:  "ISCRIPT1",
          event:  "FieldFormula",
          script: "IScript_JqThickboxJs"
      })
  });

  apt.files.importStylesheet(
      apt.files.generateScriptContentUrl({
          record: "WEBLIB_APT_JSL",
```

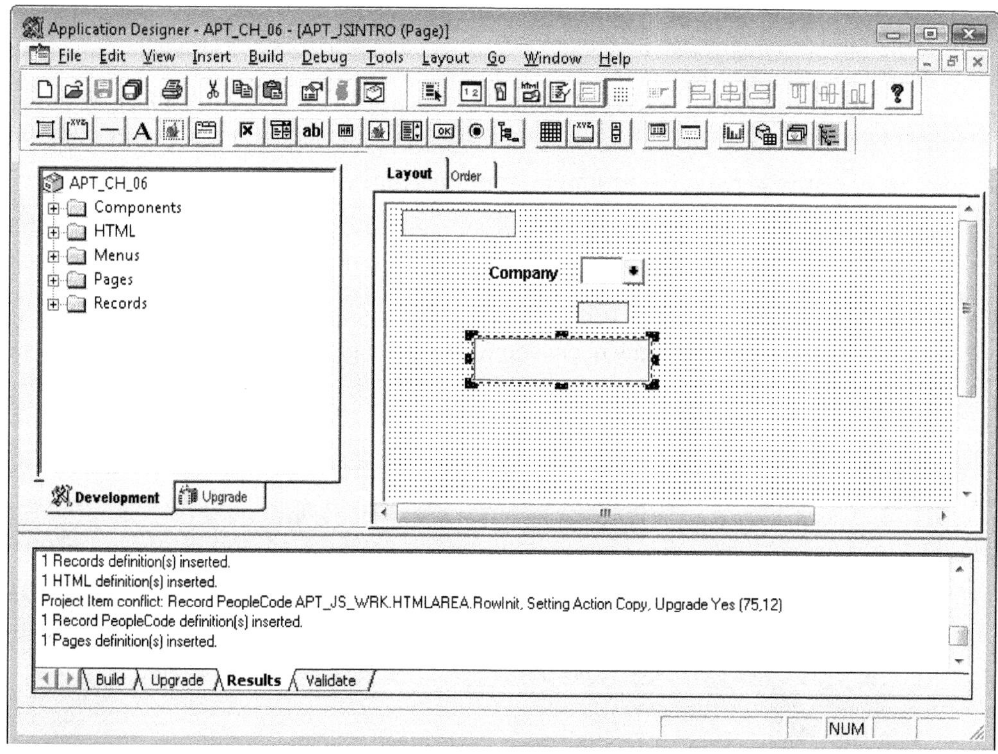

FIGURE 6-8. *APT_JSINTRO page after modifications*

```
            field:  "ISCRIPT1",
            event:  "FieldFormula",
            script: "IScript_JqThickboxCss"
        })
    );
</script>

<a href="#" onclick="tb_show('Oracle Homepage',
    'http://www.oracle.com?TB_iframe=true&height=300&width=500',
    false);return false;" class="PSHYPERLINK">View Oracle Homepage</a>
```

The first two segments of this HTML definition should look very familiar by now. They import our JavaScript and CSS libraries. The third component is an HTML hyperlink. The `onclick` event calls the Thickbox show method, `tb_show`, to open the Thickbox dialog. The second parameter to `tb_show` is a URL that contains Thickbox-specific query string parameters. The `TB_iframe` parameter tells Thickbox to display the contents of the URL in an `iframe` HTML element. The `width` and `height` query string parameters specify the width and height for the Thickbox dialog frame.

Notice that the HTML hyperlink uses the PSHYPERLINK style class. This is the PeopleSoft default style class for hyperlinks. By creating HTML elements with the same style classes as delivered HTML elements, we can be sure that our custom elements will match delivered elements, even if PeopleSoft changes the style class's definition.

Now we need to insert this HTML definition into page APT_JSINTRO. Open the RowInit event of the record field APT_JS_WRK HTMLAREA and add the following PeopleCode:

```
APT_JS_WRK.HTMLAREA = GetHTMLText(HTML.APT_JSINTRO_THICKBOX);
```

If you reload the APT_JSINTRO page in your browser, you should see a new hyperlink below the COMPANY data-entry field. Clicking this hyperlink should display the Oracle home page in a Thickbox dialog frame, as shown in Figure 6-9.

Let's add a second hyperlink to this HTML definition and have the hyperlink open the current user's role query. This is the same query you would execute if you opened a user profile, switched

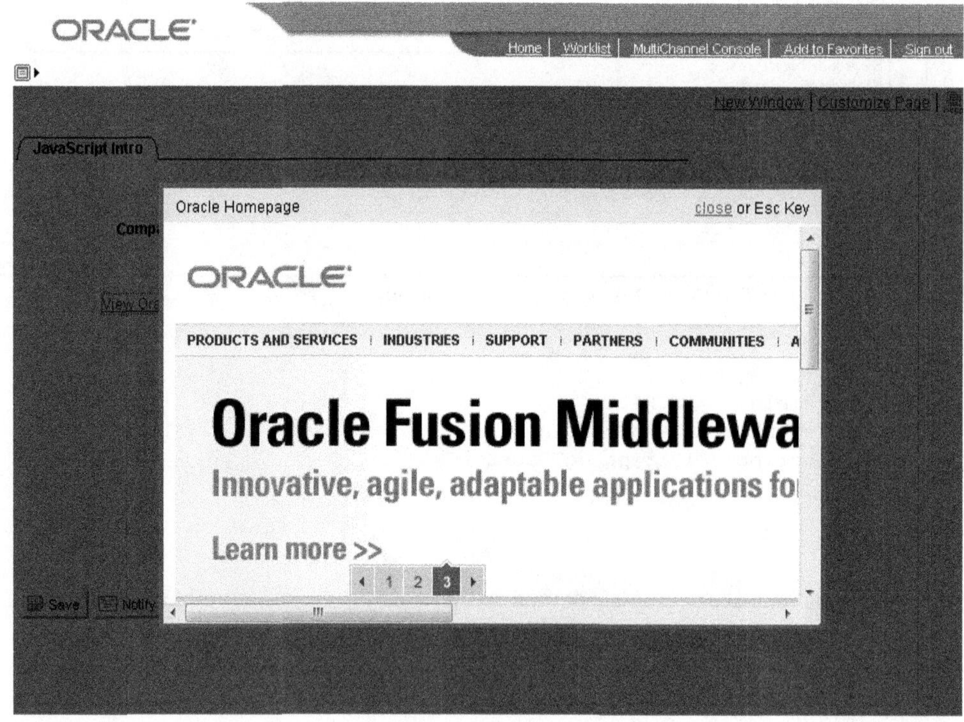

FIGURE 6-9. *APT_JSINTRO page with Thickbox*

to the User ID Queries tab, and clicked the User ID's Roles hyperlink. Add the following code to the end of the APT_JSINTRO_THICKBOX HTML definition:

```
<br/>
<a href="#" onclick="tb_show('User\'s Roles',
    '%Bind(:1)',
    false);return false;" class="PSHYPERLINK">View User's Roles</a>
```

Open the RowInit event of the record field APT_JS_WRK HTMLAREA and replace the existing PeopleCode with the following:

```
Local string &url = GenerateQueryContentURL(%Portal, %Node,
      "PT_SEC_USER_ROLES", True) | "&BIND1=" | %OperatorId |
      "&TB_iframe=true&height=300&width=500";


APT_JS_WRK.HTMLAREA = GetHTMLText(HTML.APT_JSINTRO_THICKBOX, &url);
```

After reloading the APT_JSINTRO page online, you should see a page that resembles Figure 6-10. Figure 6-11 shows the APT_JSINTRO page with the user role query open in a Thickbox dialog.

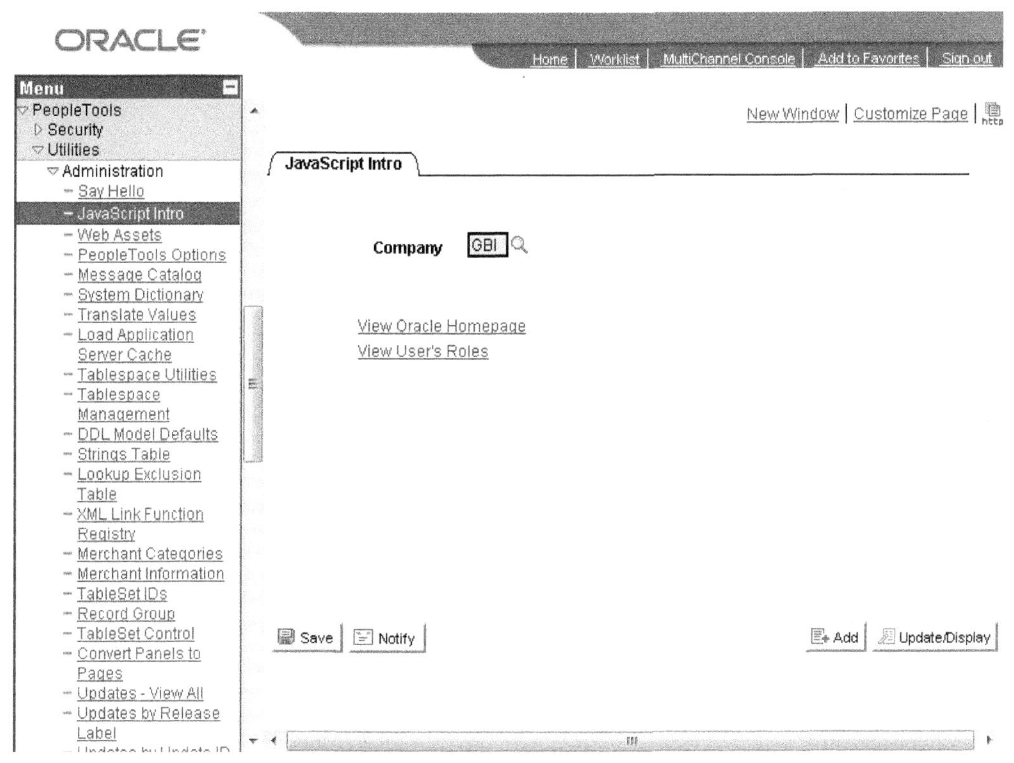

FIGURE 6-10. *APT_JSINTRO with View User's Roles hyperlink*

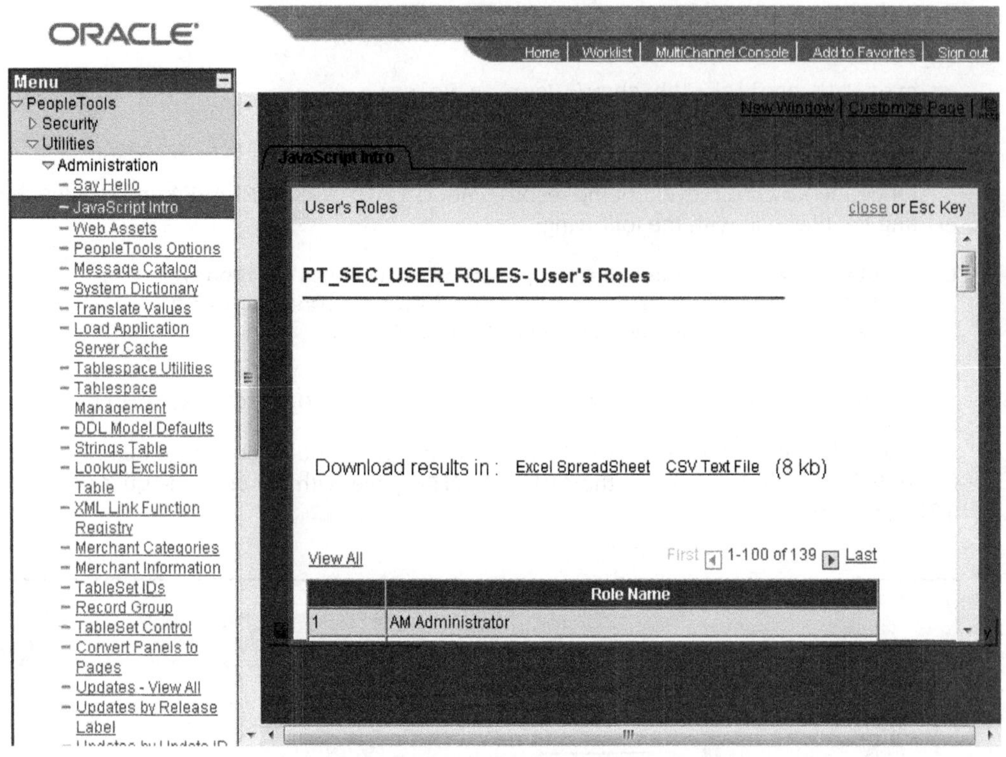

FIGURE 6-11. *APT_JSINTRO with role query open in Thickbox*

WEBLIB_APT_JSL iScript Code

Through the course of this chapter, we have added several iScripts to the WEBLIB_APT_JSL WEBLIB. The following is a complete listing of the WEBLIB_APT_JSL.ISCRIPT1 .FieldFormula event.

```
Function IScript_jQuery
   Local string &js = MsgGetExplainText(25000, 1, "alert('The " |
         "jQuery JavaScript library message catalog entry does " |
         "not exist.');");

   %Response.SetContentType("text/javascript");
   %Response.Write(&js);
End-Function;

Function IScript_HighlightActiveJs
   %Response.SetContentType("text/javascript");
   %Response.Write(GetHTMLText(HTML.APT_HIGHLIGHT_ACTIVE_JS));
End-Function;
```

```
Function IScript_HighlightActiveCss
   %Response.SetContentType("text/css");
   %Response.Write(GetHTMLText(HTML.APT_HIGHLIGHT_ACTIVE_CSS));
End-Function;

Function IScript_JqThickboxJs
   %Response.SetContentType("text/javascript");
   %Response.Write(GetHTMLText(HTML.APT_JQ_THICKBOX_JS));
End-Function;

Function IScript_JqThickboxCss
   %Response.SetContentType("text/css");
   %Response.Write(GetHTMLText(HTML.APT_JQ_THICKBOX_CSS));
End-Function;
```

Performance Issues

Serving JavaScript and CSS from iScripts, as we did in this chapter, suffers from two significant performance issues:

- JavaScript and CSS served by iScripts are not cached on the web server, and, therefore, require an app server and database server request for each iScript request.
- PeopleSoft ignores caching header values set in iScripts, forcing the browser to request a new copy of the JavaScript or CSS on each request.

In Chapter 13, you will learn how to use servlet filters to mitigate these performance issues.

Conclusion

In this chapter, you learned how to add JavaScript, CSS, and HTML to existing PeopleSoft pages, as well as globally, to all pages. You saw multiple ways to store and serve JavaScript, HTML, and CSS, and also acquired some valuable reusable JavaScript libraries. The next two chapters will build on this chapter by adding AJAX and animations. In Chapter 7, you will learn how to make page-specific JavaScript and HTML modifications without touching delivered pages. In Chapter 8, we will use the techniques covered in Chapters 6 and 7 to create a custom PeopleSoft administration toolbar.

Notes

1. Mozilla Developer Center, *Core JavaScript 1.5 Guide*, "Regular Expressions" [online]; available from https://developer.mozilla.org/en/Core_JavaScript_1.5_Guide/Regular_Expressions; Internet; accessed 19 August 2009.
2. Wikipedia, "Document Object Model" [online]; available from http://en.wikipedia.org/wiki/Document_Object_Model; Internet; accessed 10 August 2009.
3. Mozilla Developer Center, *Gecko DOM Reference* [online]; available from https://developer.mozilla.org/en/Gecko_DOM_Reference; Internet; accessed 18 August 2009.

4. Mike Girouard, "A Week in JavaScript Patterns: Self-Invocation" [online]; available from http://www.lovemikeg.com/blog/2008/08/17/a-week-in-javascript-patterns-self-invocation/; Internet; accessed 17 August 2009.
5. Troels Jakobsen, *Bookmarklets - Browser Power*, "Rules for Bookmarklets" [online]; available from http://www.subsimple.com/bookmarklets/rules.asp#ReturnValues; Internet; accessed 10 August 2009.
6. Wikipedia, "ECMAScript" [online]; available from http://en.wikipedia.org/wiki/ECMAScript; Internet; accessed 10 August 2009.
7. Google Code, "Google AJAX Libraries API" [online]; available from http://code.google.com/apis/ajaxlibs/; Internet; accessed 10 August 2009.
8. W3Schools, *JavaScript and HTML DOM Reference* [online]; available from http://www.w3schools.com/HTMLDOM/dom_reference.asp; Internet; accessed 18 August 2009.
9. Wikipedia, "Bootstrapping (computing)" [online]; available from http://en.wikipedia.org/wiki/Bootstrapping_%28computing%29; Internet; accessed 17 August 2009.
10. Robert Nyman, "Explaining JavaScript Scope And Closures" [online]; available from http://robertnyman.com/2008/10/09/explaining-javascript-scope-and-closures/; Internet; accessed 17 August 2009.
11. Leandro Vieria Pinho, "jQuery lightBox plugin" [online] available from http://leandrovieira.com/projects/jquery/lightbox/; Internet; accessed 18 August 2009.

CHAPTER 7

AJAX and PeopleSoft

JAX is an acronym for Asynchronous JavaScript and XML. The term was coined to describe the technique of using JavaScript to asynchronously send, load, or process external XML. While the fundamentals are the same, the term now encompasses all transparent HTTP requests initiated from JavaScript, regardless of the threading model or data format. The key is that the browser sends a transparent request to a service over HTTP.

JavaScript libraries dramatically simplify AJAX by providing several methods and configuration options for AJAX requests, as well as abstracting the differences between implementing web browsers. This chapter builds on the previous two chapters by using JavaScript (Chapter 6) to request and process data served from iScripts (Chapter 5). We will continue to use the jQuery JavaScript library introduced in the previous chapter.

Hello AJAX

To be pedagogically correct, we will start with a Hello World example. We will create an iScript that uses `UserGreeter` to generate an HTML greeting, and then we will modify a page so that it uses AJAX to asynchronously load this greeting.

Creating the AJAX Request Handler

Since iScripts have full PeopleCode support and can be run from a URL, they make excellent AJAX server-side request handlers. Create a new derived/work record and add the field `ISCRIPT1`. Save the record as `WEBLIB_APT_HWA` (for Hello World AJAX). Next, open the `FieldFormula` event of the field `ISCRIPT1` and add the following PeopleCode:

```
import APT_GREETERS:UserGreeter;

Function IScript_SayHelloRequestHandler
   Local APT_GREETERS:UserGreeter &greeter =
         create APT_GREETERS:UserGreeter();
   Local string &message = &greeter.sayHello();
   Local string &result = "<p>" | &message | "</p>";

   %Response.SetContentType("text/html");
   %Response.WriteLine(&result);
End-Function;
```

This code generates an HTML fragment. Next, we will write some JavaScript to call this iScript and insert its response into a page. Be sure to add this WEBLIB and iScript to the `APT_CUSTOM` permission list.

Ajaxifying a Page

Let's now Ajaxify[1] a page. Open the page `APT_JSINTRO`, which we created in Chapter 6, and add a new HTML Area control. The location of the HTML Area doesn't matter. As shown in Figure 7-1, I placed it beneath the other page controls.

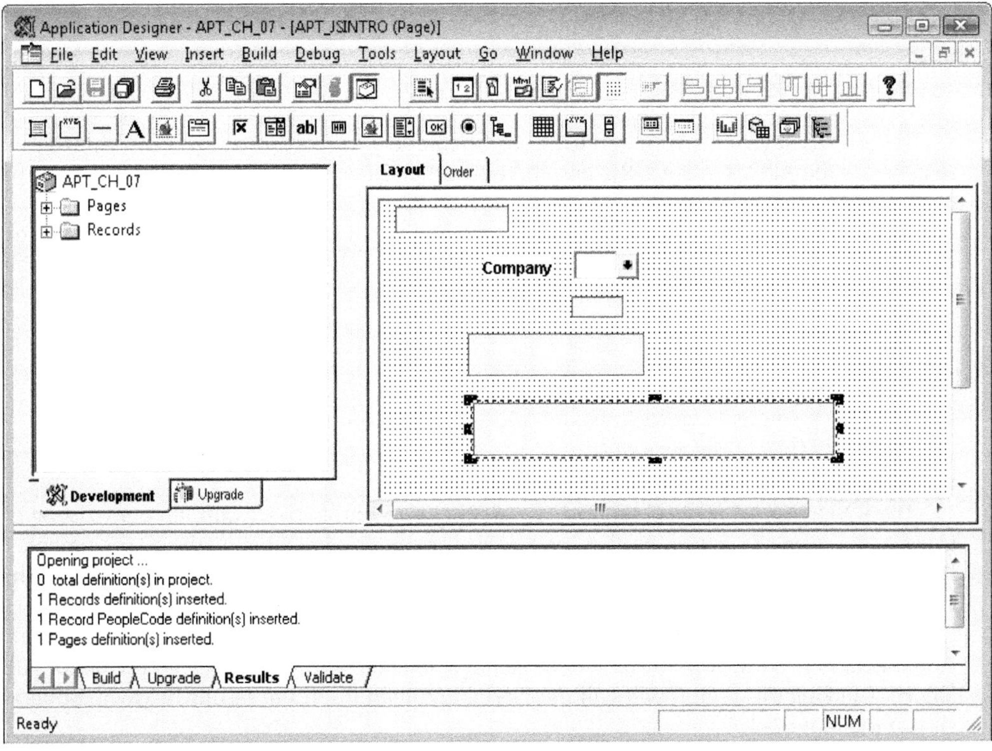

FIGURE 7-1. *APT_JSINTRO with a new HTML Area control*

Let's write some JavaScript and HTML to define a new button and handle the button's `onclick` event. Double-click this new HTML Area, set the Value to Constant, and add the following HTML:

```
<script type="text/javascript">
  // note: our bootstrap code from chapter 06 creates the apt object
  apt.ch07 = {
    sayHi: function() {
      var url = apt.files.generateScriptContentUrl({
          record: "WEBLIB_APT_HWA",
          field:  "ISCRIPT1",
          event:  "FieldFormula",
          script: "IScript_SayHelloRequestHandler"
      });
      $("#APT_greeting").load(url);
    }
  }
</script>
```

```
<input type="button" class="PSPUSHBUTTON" onclick="apt.ch07.sayHi()"
    value="Say Hi"/>
<br/>
<br/>
<div id="APT_greeting"><!-- empty --></div>
```

The sayHi JavaScript function uses our Chapter 6 generateScriptContentUrl function to generate the AJAX service URL, and then uses the jQuery load method to insert external content into an HTML element.

Below the script HTML element, you see the additional HTML used to implement this example. To ensure the custom HTML button maintains the same look and feel as the PeopleSoft application, we've used the delivered CSS class PSPUSHBUTTON.

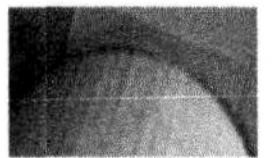

NOTE

Button styles changed in PeopleTools 8.5. PeopleTools 8.5 uses CSS and HTML to create buttons that are more visually appealing than the standard HTML input element.

The jQuery load method requires an existing element. In this example, our existing element is the APT_greeting div. Notice the HTML comments nested inside the div element. The PeopleSoft page assembler removes empty div elements from the resultant document. The HTML comments provide content, which keeps the page assembler from removing the empty div.

Log in to PeopleSoft through your web browser and navigate to PeopleTools | Utilities | Administration | JavaScript Intro. When the page appears, you should see a new button labeled Say Hi. Clicking this button will call the iScript and then insert the results below the button, as shown in Figure 7-2.

Adding Animation

The jQuery load method accepts three parameters: the service URL, an object containing the service's parameters, and a callback method. We can use the callback parameter to implement some basic animation. Let's add an effect that causes the greeting to fade in when it is loaded. While we are at it, let's add another effect that causes the greeting to fade out if a user clicks the Say Hi button again.

First, double-click the APT_JSINTRO AJAX HTML Area control so you can edit its contents. Add a style attribute to the APT_greeting div so that it matches the following:

```
<div id="APT_greeting" style="display: none;"><!-- empty --></div>
```

Change the load JavaScript method call from this:

```
    $("#APT_greeting").load(url);
```

to this:

```
    $("#APT_greeting").fadeOut("fast", function() {
        $("#APT_greeting").load(url, function() {
            $("#APT_greeting").fadeIn("fast");
        })
    });
```

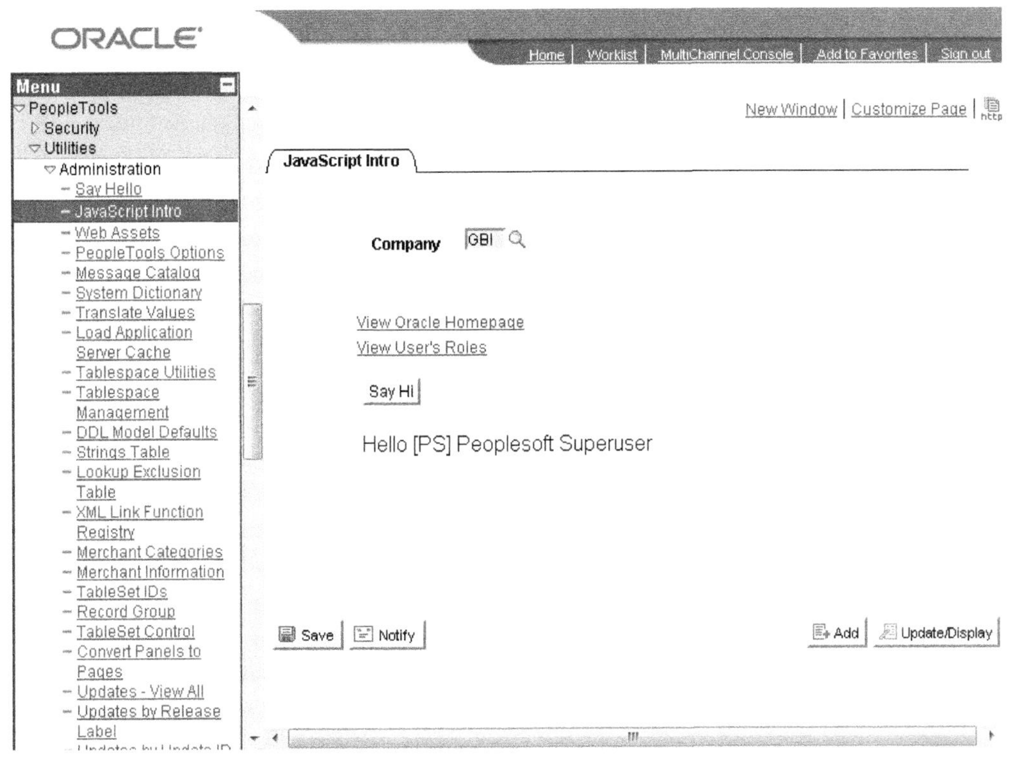

FIGURE 7-2. *APT_JSINTRO with AJAX content*

The complete code listing follows:

```
<script type="text/javascript">
  apt.ch07 = {
    sayHi: function() {
      var url = apt.files.generateScriptContentUrl({
          record: "WEBLIB_APT_HWA",
          field:  "ISCRIPT1",
          event:  "FieldFormula",
          script: "IScript_SayHelloRequestHandler"
      });
      $("#APT_greeting").fadeOut("fast", function() {
          $("#APT_greeting").load(url, function() {
              $("#APT_greeting").fadeIn("fast");
          })
      });
    }
  }
</script>
```

Security Concerns

Our Hello World AJAX example injects HTML into the current PeopleSoft page. Injecting HTML in this manner is the simplest means of implementing AJAX. It requires very little client-side processing. The server generates the content, and the client just inserts the content at the appropriate location. As long as the application has complete control over the generated HTML, this approach is acceptable. This approach ceases to be acceptable, however, when the HTML is generated by a mechanism other than a design-time, hard-coded HTML template.

For example, if you create an online page that contains an HTML editor, it is possible to allow users to enter HTML markup online, and then store that HTML within the database. If you then use AJAX to serve this user-generated content, without any server-side validation, you may open your system to security vulnerabilities.

The Open Web Application Security Project (OWASP) lists cross-site scripting[2] (XSS) as the number one security vulnerability. There are three types of cross-site scripting:

1. A *reflected* XSS attack is where a site collects information and then displays it to the user as HTML.
2. A *stored* XSS attack is similar to the reflected attack, except it stores the malicious HTML in the database, where it can be served to multiple users.
3. *DOM injection* is exactly what our Hello World AJAX example accomplishes. The key difference is that our AJAX example is not malicious.

Online HTML editors are not the only way to collect malicious HTML. If you have a comment field on a data-entry page, and use AJAX to inject the contents of that field, make sure you use the `EscapeHTML` PeopleCode function to encode the contents of the comment field.

```
<input type="button" class="PSPUSHBUTTON" onclick="apt.ch07.sayHi()"
    value="Say Hi"/>
<br/>
<br/>
<div id="APT_greeting" style="display: none;"><!-- empty --></div>
```

Save the page in App Designer, and then switch back to your browser. Reload the page and click the Say Hi button. Now, instead of appearing instantly after you click the Say Hi button, the iScript response fades in quickly. If you click the button multiple times, you will notice that it fades out prior to making the HTTP request, and then fades back in when it is complete.

Ajaxifying the Direct Reports DisplayShelf

In Chapter 5, we created a Flex `DisplayShelf` component that shows a manager's direct reports. Let's add AJAX to that page to load an employee's detail information when the display shelf's selection changes.

Modifying the Flex Source

The Flex source code for our direct reports' Cover Flow effect does a great job of consuming an iScript XML service, but it doesn't trigger any events. Before we can use AJAX to respond to selection changes, we must modify the Flex source code. The following code contains a complete listing for the ImageCoverFlow.mxml file. The new additions are in bold.

```
<?xml version="1.0" encoding="utf-8"?>
<mx:Application xmlns:mx="http://www.adobe.com/2006/mxml"
    xmlns:local="*" height="100%" width="100%"
    creationComplete="configureApp()" styleName="plain">

  <mx:Script>
    <![CDATA[
    import flash.external.ExternalInterface;
    import mx.controls.Image;
    import mx.controls.Alert;
    import mx.rpc.events.ResultEvent;

    public function configureApp():void {
      try {

        var imageRenderer:ClassFactory = new ClassFactory(Image);
        imageRenderer.properties = {width: 160, height: 120};
        shelf.itemRenderer = imageRenderer;

        if (ExternalInterface.available) {
          imgService.url = ExternalInterface.call("getServiceURL");
          imgService.send();
        } else {
          Alert.show("Unable acquire service URL: " +
              "ExternalInterface not available");
        }
      } catch (e:Error) {
        Alert.show("Error: " + e.message);
      }
    }

    public function dataRetrieved(e:ResultEvent):void {
      try {
        fireShelfChange(0);
      } catch (e:Error) {
        Alert.show("Error: dataRetrieved: " + e.message);
      }

    }

    public function fireShelfChange(imageIndex:Number):void {
      try {
        if (ExternalInterface.available) {
          var emplid:String =
```

```
                imgService.lastResult.image[imageIndex].emplid;
            ExternalInterface.call("employeeChanged", emplid);
          } else {
            Alert.show("Unable to update employee details: " +
                "ExternalInterface not available");
          }
        } catch (e:Error) {
          Alert.show("Error: " + e.message);
        }
      }
    ]]>
    </mx:Script>

    <mx:HTTPService id="imgService" method="GET"
        result="dataRetrieved(event)" resultFormat="e4x"/>

    <local:DisplayShelf id="shelf" horizontalCenter="0"
      verticalCenter="0" borderThickness="0" borderColor="#FFFFFF"
      dataProvider="{imgService.lastResult.image.url}"
      enableHistory="false" width="100%"
      change="fireShelfChange(shelf.selectedIndex);" />

</mx:Application>
```

The preceding code adds two new functions to our Flex. The first function, `dataRetrieved`, is an event handler for the `HTTPService` element. The primary purpose for this function is to call an externally defined JavaScript function after the `HTTPService` loads its data. The second new function, `fireShelfChange`, notifies the containing HTML document when the `DisplayShelf` component's selection changes.

Save this source code in a text file named ImageCoverFlow.mxml, and compile it using the same command line you used in Chapter 5.

After compiling the source, upload the generated SWF file into a web asset named `APT_EMP_CF`. Set the Description field to **Employee CoverFlow** and the Mime-Type field to `application/x-shockwave-flash`. Upload ImageCoverFlow.swf, save the transaction, and run it through the approval process.

NOTE
If you commented out the approval flag as recommended in Chapter 5, then you don't need to approve this transaction.

Modifying the Direct Reports Service

Our Direct Reports iScript service serves only an image URL. Our Flex component, however, now expects to find a corresponding employee ID. Open the `FieldFormula` event of the record field `WEBLIB_APT_DRI ISCRIPT1` and add `&emplid` as a second bind parameter to the `GetHTMLText` function call. The following code listing contains the service's full PeopleCode listing. The single addition is in bold.

```
Function IScript_DirectReportsService()
   Local SQL &emplCursor = GetSQL(SQL.APT_SUPERVISOR_DIRECTS,
         %EmployeeId);
```

```
   Local string &emplid;
   Local string &baseUrl = GenerateScriptContentURL(%Portal,
         %Node, Record.WEBLIB_APT_EPIC, Field.ISCRIPT1,
         "FieldFormula", "IScript_EmployeePhoto") | "?EMPLID=";
   Local string &rowXml;

   %Response.SetContentType("text/xml");
   %Response.WriteLine("<?xml version=""1.0""?>");
   %Response.WriteLine("<images>");

   While &emplCursor.Fetch(&emplid)
      &rowXml = GetHTMLText(HTML.APT_DIRECT_RPTS_TEMPLATE,
            &baseUrl | &emplid, &emplid);
      %Response.WriteLine(&rowXml);
   End-While;

   %Response.WriteLine("</images>");
End-Function;
```

Since the service is now passing an additional bind variable to the HTML definition, we need to add some more XML to this template. Open the APT_DIRECT_RPTS_TEMPLATE definition and update it as follows. The new line is in bold.

```
<image>
  <url>%Bind(:1)</url>
  <emplid>%Bind(:2)</emplid>
</image>
```

Creating a New HTML AJAX Service

The details about our direct reports reside in the database. Therefore, we will need to write some SQL to extract this information. The following SQL retrieves a few employee details. After running through this example, you can extend this SQL to suit your needs. Save this new SQL definition as APT_DIRECT_DETAILS.

```
SELECT J.DEPTID
     , P.NAME_DISPLAY
  FROM PS_JOB J
 INNER JOIN PS_PERSON_NAME P
    ON P.EMPLID = J.EMPLID
 WHERE J.EFFDT = (
 SELECT MAX(J_ED.EFFDT)
  FROM PS_JOB J_ED
 WHERE J_ED.EMPLID = J.EMPLID
   AND J_ED.EMPL_RCD = J.EMPL_RCD
   AND J_ED.EFFDT <= %CurrentDateIn )
   AND J.EFFSEQ = (
 SELECT MAX(J_ES.EFFSEQ)
  FROM PS_JOB J_ES
 WHERE J_ES.EMPLID = J.EMPLID
   AND J_ES.EMPL_RCD = J.EMPL_RCD
```

```
AND J_ES.EFFDT = J.EFFDT )
AND J.EMPLID = :1
AND J.SUPERVISOR_ID = :2
```

This SQL contains a supervisor ID bind variable. We will populate this bind variable with the employee ID of the logged-in user. Technically, we need only the employee ID to extract the details we are interested in seeing. But consider that a curious user may be tempted to use this service to view details about another employee. By adding the supervisor ID criteria, a technique known as *row-level security,* we eliminate this potential vulnerability.

We want to load the selected employee's details into the current page when the display shelf selection changes. Therefore, we will need to create a new AJAX request handler that returns HTML. Create a new HTML definition, name it `APT_DIRECT_RPT_DETAILS`, and add the following HTML:

```
<div>
  <div class="PSEDITBOXLABEL" style="float: left; width: 100px;">
    Employee ID
  </div>
  <div class="PSEDITBOX_DISPONLY">%Bind(:1)</div>
  <div class="PSEDITBOXLABEL" style="float: left; width: 100px;">
    Name
  </div>
  <div class="PSEDITBOX_DISPONLY">%Bind(:2)</div>
  <div class="PSEDITBOXLABEL" style="float: left; width: 100px;">
    Dept ID
  </div>
  <div class="PSEDITBOX_DISPONLY">%Bind(:3)</div>
  <div style="float:clear;"></div>
</div>
```

Open the `FieldFormula` event of record field `WEBLIB_APT_DRI ISCRIPT1` and add the following PeopleCode to the end of this event:

```
Function IScript_DirectReportsHandler()
   Local string &emplid = %Request.GetParameter("id");
   Local string &deptid;
   Local string &name;

   SQLExec(SQL.APT_DIRECT_DETAILS, &emplid, %EmployeeId, &deptid,
         &name);
   %Response.SetContentType("text/html");
   %Response.Write(GetHTMLText(HTML.APT_DIRECT_RPT_DETAILS,
         &emplid, &deptid, &name));
End-Function;
```

Be sure to add this new iScript to the `APT_CUSTOM` permission list.

Modifying the Container Page

The Flex `DisplayShelf` component uses the `ExternalInterface` object to call a container function named `employeeChanged`. However, our HTML container does not contain an `employeeChanged` function. Therefore, we need to add that function. Open the `APT_DIRECT_REPORTS_FLEX` HTML definition and update the contents to match the following listing (additions are in bold).

```
<script type="text/javascript"
src="http://ajax.googleapis.com/ajax/libs/swfobject/2.2/swfobject.js">
</script>

<script language="javascript" type="text/javascript">
  function getServiceURL() {
    return "%Bind(:1)";
  }

  function employeeChanged(emplid) {
    $("#APT_employeeDetails").fadeOut("fast", function() {
      $("#APT_employeeDetails").load("%Bind(:3)", {id: emplid},
        function() {
          $("#APT_employeeDetails").fadeIn("fast");
        });
    });
  }
</script>

<div id="APT_flashContent">
  <p>Your browser does not support Flash</p>
</div>

<div id="APT_employeeDetails"
    style="display: none; margin-top: 20px;">
  <!-- placeholder -->
</div>

<script type="text/javascript">
  (function() {
    var params = {
      allowscriptaccess: "always"
    };
    swfobject.embedSWF("%Bind(:2)", "APT_flashContent", "400", "200",
        "9.0.0", "", false, params);
  })();
</script>
```

Open the page `APT_FLEX_DIR_RPTS` and expand the HTML Area control so that it spans from left to right. PeopleSoft will allow the content to grow in height, but not in width.

Next, open the `APT_FLEX_DIR_RPTS` component and switch to the structure tab. Expand the Scroll–Level 0 item, right-click the `APT_FLX_DRI_WRK` item (which should have a lightning bolt next to it to signify that this item has PeopleCode), and select View PeopleCode.

In the PeopleCode editor, we need to add another variable for a third iScript URL, and then pass that variable to the GetHTMLText function. We also need to tell this component to use our new Flex web asset. The following PeopleCode contains these modifications (changes are in bold).

```
Local string &swfUrl = GenerateScriptContentURL(%Portal, %Node,
      Record.WEBLIB_APT_WA, Field.ISCRIPT1, "FieldFormula",
      "IScript_GetWebAsset") | "?id=APT_EMP_CF";
Local string &serviceUrl = GenerateScriptContentURL(%Portal, %Node,
      Record.WEBLIB_APT_DRI, Field.ISCRIPT1, "FieldFormula",
      "IScript_DirectReportsService");
Local string &ajaxUrl = GenerateScriptContentURL(%Portal, %Node,
      Record.WEBLIB_APT_DRI, Field.ISCRIPT1, "FieldFormula",
      "IScript_DirectReportsHandler");

APT_FLX_DRI_WRK.HTMLAREA = GetHTMLText(HTML.APT_DIRECT_REPORTS_FLEX,
      &serviceUrl, &swfUrl, &ajaxUrl);
```

You can test your code now by logging in as a manager (HCRUSA_KU0007 in the demo database) and navigating to Manager Self Service | Job and Personal Information | Direct Reports. Notice that the details, which are below the DisplayShelf component, change as you scroll through the images. Figure 7-3 shows this modified page.

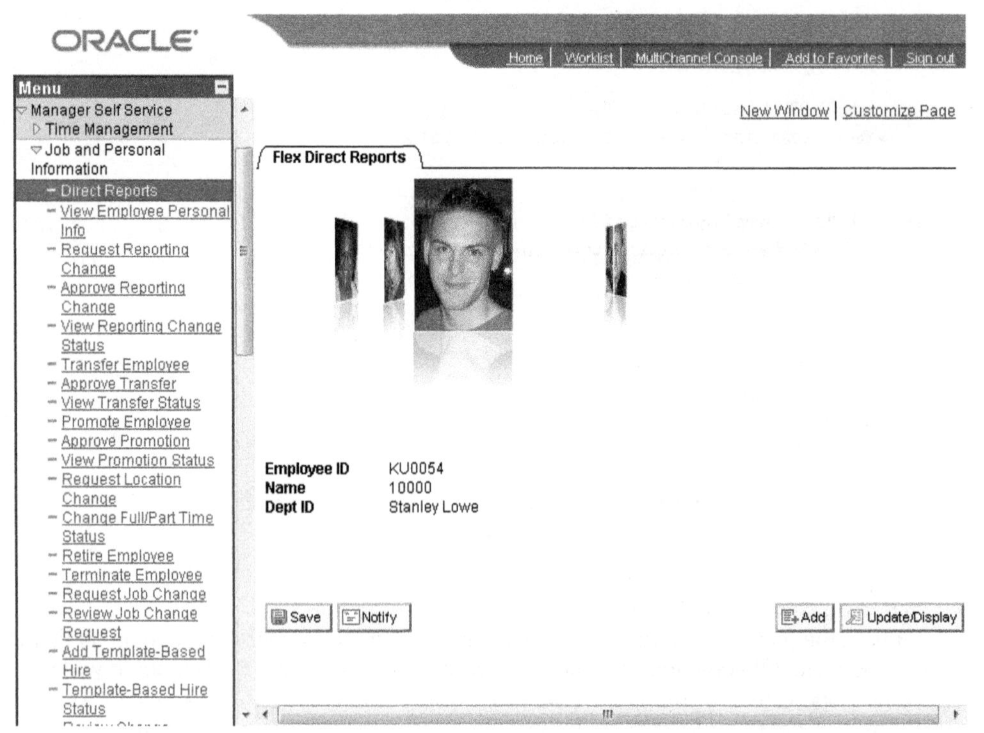

FIGURE 7-3. *Flex Direct Reports page with AJAX details*

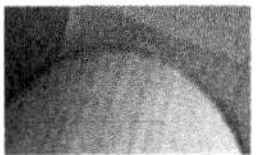

NOTE

When I wrote this chapter, the latest version of Firefox was 3.6. That version of Firefox appears to reload plug-in content if the page interacts with the plug-in before the plug-in is fully loaded. The AJAX shown in this example, combined with the Firefox reloading bug, causes Firefox to infinitely reload the Flex component. Both Microsoft's Internet Explorer and Google Chrome loaded the content without issue.

A Configurable User Interface

The total cost of a modification includes the expense of maintaining that modification across patches, bundles, maintenance packs, and upgrades. The less invasive a modification is, the lower its cost. Now that you understand how to insert rich Internet features into PeopleSoft pages, we can look for ways to reduce the number of objects touched by a modification.

Using a Metadata Repository

We already discussed how to apply global customizations by modifying a single HTML definition. Now let's see if we can find a way to reduce all page-specific JavaScript enhancements, regardless of the page, to a single modification, and then use a metadata-driven approach to determine which modification to apply to each page.

Remember the `generateScriptContentUrl` function we created in Chapter 6? That function parsed the site, portal, and node names from the current URL. We can use a similar approach to determine a page's menu, component, market, and page name. With this information, we can use AJAX to download page-specific JavaScript, HTML, and CSS customizations.

The solution should be flexible enough to allow us to specify a script for all items in a menu, a component regardless of the menu, a page regardless of the component, or any combination of these three items. This solution should also allow us to specify generic scripts that should exist for all navigations, as well as search page-specific scripts. This means that when a developer specifies a menu, component, and market, the associated script should be used on every page within that component, including the search page. If a developer specifies the same criteria and selects a search type of search page only, then the associated script should appear on only the search page. If a developer selects a page name, and no other criteria, then the associated script should appear on every instance of that page, regardless of the component.

For our scripts to execute correctly, we will also want an *inclusion* sequence. A library, such as jQuery, should be included prior to other scripts. Therefore, we will process global scripts first and page-specific scripts second. Within this classification of global versus page-specific, we will insert scripts according to a sequence number. For example, scripts with a sequence of 0 should be added to the page prior to scripts with a sequence of 1.

Creating the Metadata Repository

If this is going to be a metadata-driven solution, we need to create a metadata repository. Based on our stated requirements, our metadata record will have the following fields:

- APT_SCRIPT_ID
- `MENUNAME`

- PNLGRPNAME
- MARKET
- PNLNAME
- APT_SEARCH_PG_FLAG
- SEQ_NBR
- APT_APPEND_TO
- HTMLAREA

This metadata repository definition includes three custom fields: APT_SCRIPT_ID, APT_SEARCH_PG_FLAG, and APT_APPEND_TO. Let's create these fields now so we can use them to create our metadata record definition.

Create a new field of type character with a length of 30. Set the label ID to APT_SCRIPT_ID, the long name to **Script ID**, and the short name to **Script**. Save the field as APT_SCRIPT_ID.

Create another field of type character with a length of 4. Set the label ID to APT_SEARCH_PG_FLAG, the long name to **Search Page Behavior**, and the short name to **Search Page**. Add the following translate values:

- BOTH, with a long name and short name of **Both**
- NS, with a long name of **All except search** and a short name of **Not search**
- SO, with a long name of **Search page only** and a short name of **Srch only**

The third custom field identifies the target location for custom HTML and JavaScript. Create it as type character with a length of 4. Set the label ID to APT_APPEND_TO, the long name to **Append Location**, and the short name to **Append To**. Save the field as APT_APPEND_TO. Add translate values as follows:

- BODY, with a long name and short name of **Body**
- HEAD, with a long name and short name of **Head**

Create a new record definition and add the nine fields listed at the beginning of this section. Save the record as APT_UI_SCRIPTS. For the field APT_SEARCH_PG_FLAG, set the default value to BOTH and select the Required flag. For the field APT_APPEND_TO, select the Required flag and set the default value to BODY. Create the record's keys as shown in Figure 7-4, and then build the record definition.

Maintaining the Metadata Repository

Next, let's create a page and component to maintain this metadata repository. Create a new page and name it APT_UI_SCRIPTS. Add all of the fields from the APT_UI_SCRIPTS record definition. Figure 7-5 shows these fields arranged on the page. Make the APT_SCRIPT_ID field display-only and resize the MENUNAME field.

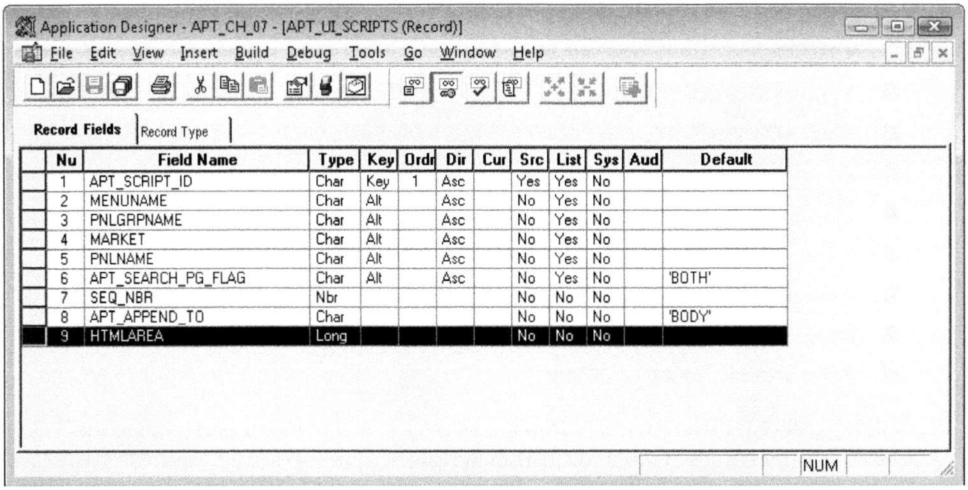

FIGURE 7-4. *APT_UI_SCRIPTS metadata repository record keys*

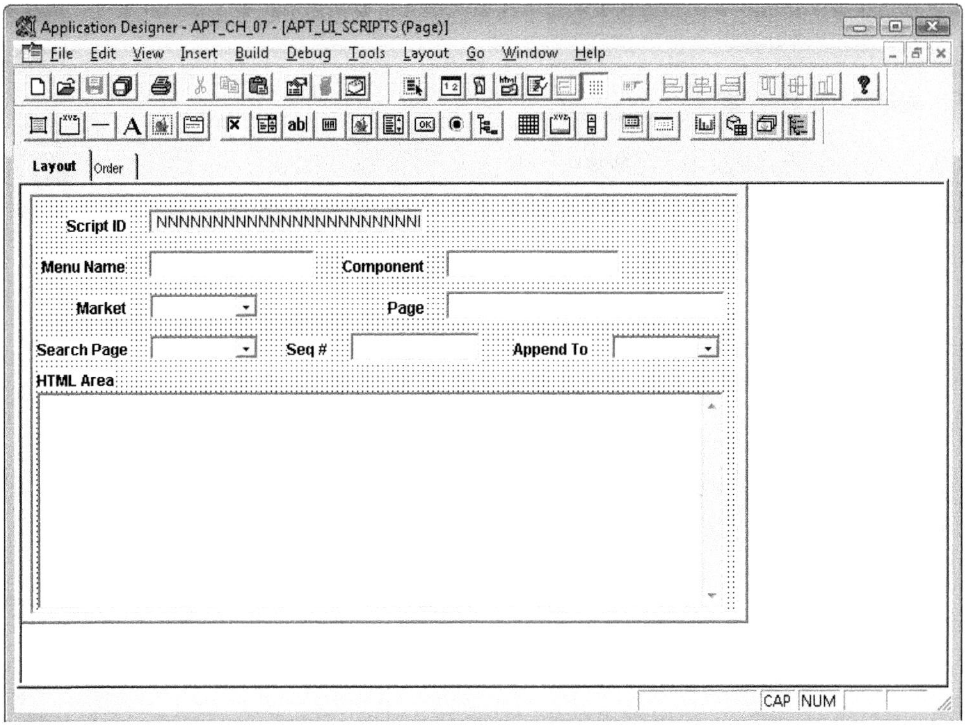

FIGURE 7-5. *APT_UI_SCRIPTS metadata repository page*

Create a new component and set the search record to APT_UI_SCRIPTS. Add the APT_UI_SCRIPTS page and set its item label to **Custom Scripts**. Register the component using the following values:

- Menu: APT_CUSTOM
- Bar: CUSTOM
- Portal: EMPLOYEE
- Folder: PT_ADMINISTRATION
- Content reference: APT_UI_SCRIPTS_GBL
- Content reference label: **Custom Scripts**
- Long description: **Custom user interface scripts**
- Permission list: APT_CUSTOM

After registering the component, open the APT_CUSTOM menu and change the APT_UI_SCRIPTS_GBL menu item label to **Custom Scripts**. Figure 7-6 shows the APT_UI_SCRIPTS page online.

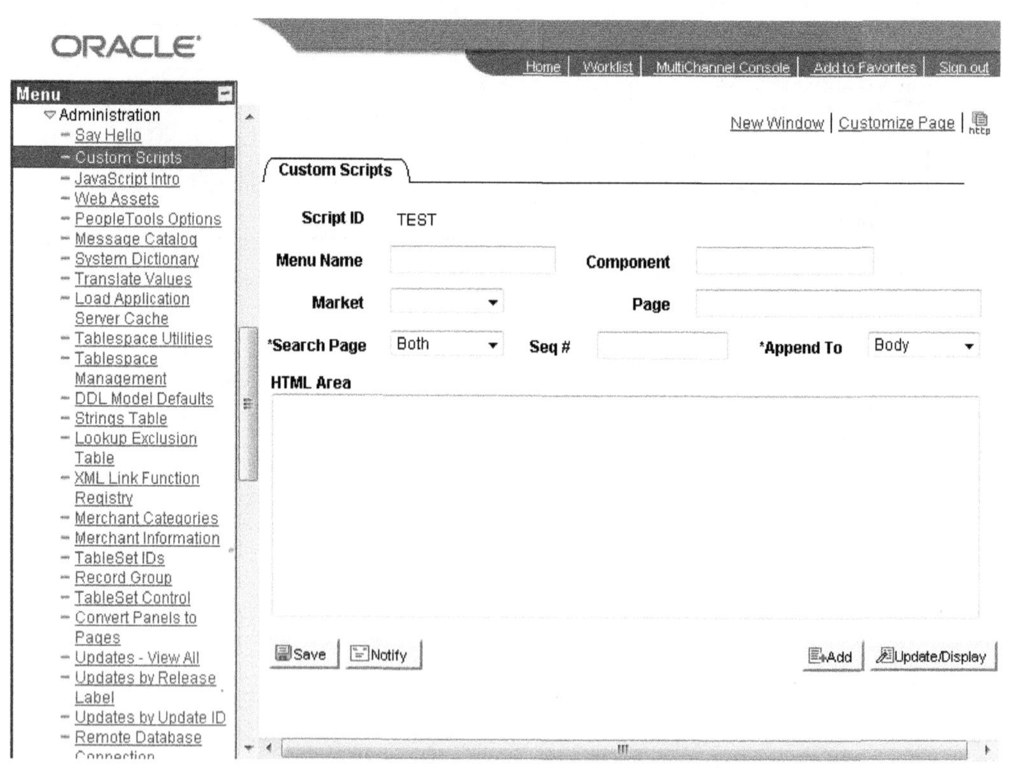

FIGURE 7-6. *APT_UI_SCRIPTS page online*

Let's add some data to this repository so we have something to test. Navigate to PeopleTools | Utilities | Administration | Custom Scripts and add values as shown in Figures 7-7 through 7-11. Each of these scripts will display a different message box.

Serving Scripts

Now that we have data in our metadata repository, we will create an SQL statement to extract the appropriate data based on the current navigation. Create a new SQL definition and add the following SQL:

```
SELECT APT_APPEND_TO
     , HTMLAREA
  FROM PS_APT_UI_SCRIPTS S
 WHERE MENUNAME IN(' ', :1)
   AND PNLGRPNAME IN(' ', :2)
   AND MARKET IN (' ', :3)
   AND PNLNAME IN (' ', :4)
   AND APT_SEARCH_PG_FLAG IN ('BOTH', :5)
 ORDER BY
```

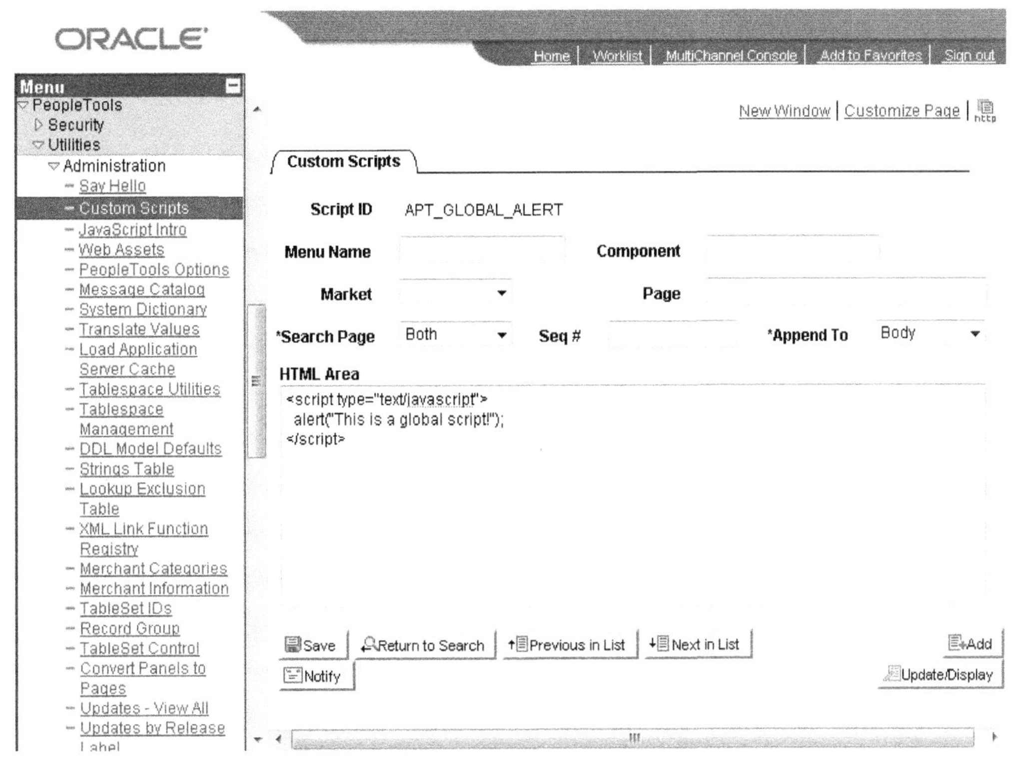

FIGURE 7-7. *APT_GLOBAL_ALERT global test data*

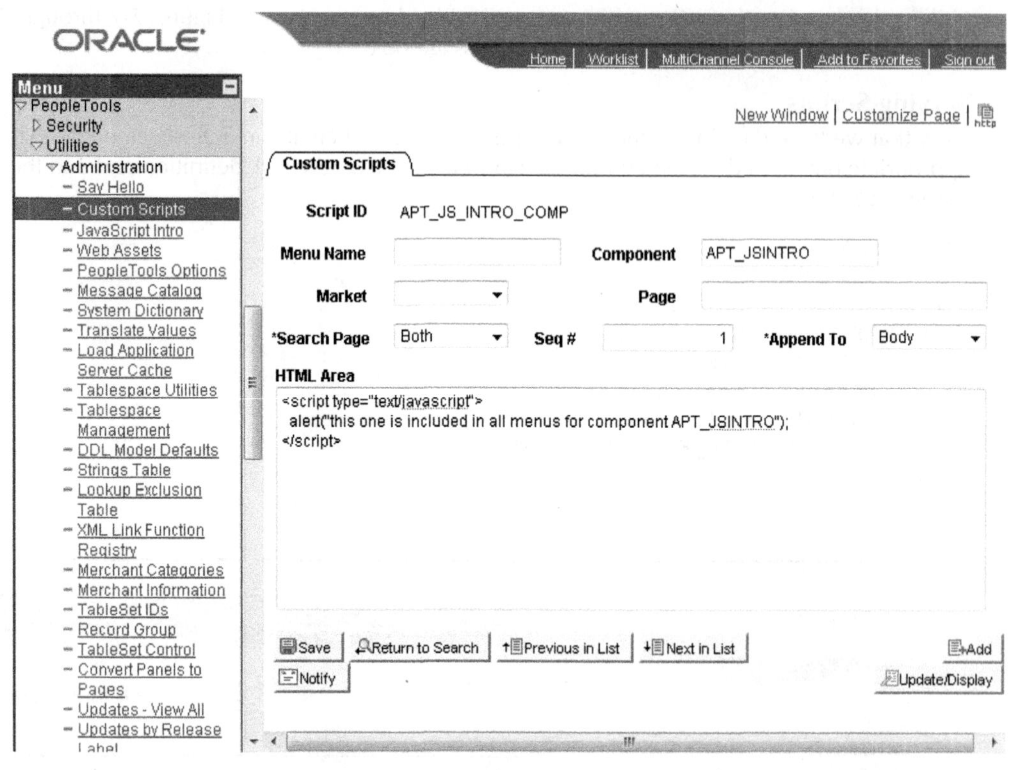

FIGURE 7-8. *APT_JSINTRO_COMP component test data*

```
CASE
   WHEN MENUNAME %Concat PNLGRPNAME %Concat MARKET %Concat
         PNLNAME = '    ' THEN 0
   ELSE 1
END
   , SEQ_NBR
```

Save this SQL as `APT_GET_UI_SCRIPTS`. The `IN(' ', :n)` allows us to select all items that are either blank (space) or match the requested value. For example, if the menu is `APT_CUSTOM` and the component is `APT_WEB_ASSETS`, then we want to match all rows that have a blank for every key value except menu, as well as every row that has a blank for all keys except component. Furthermore, we want to match those rows that uniquely identify the menu `APT_CUSTOM` and component `APT_WEB_ASSETS`.

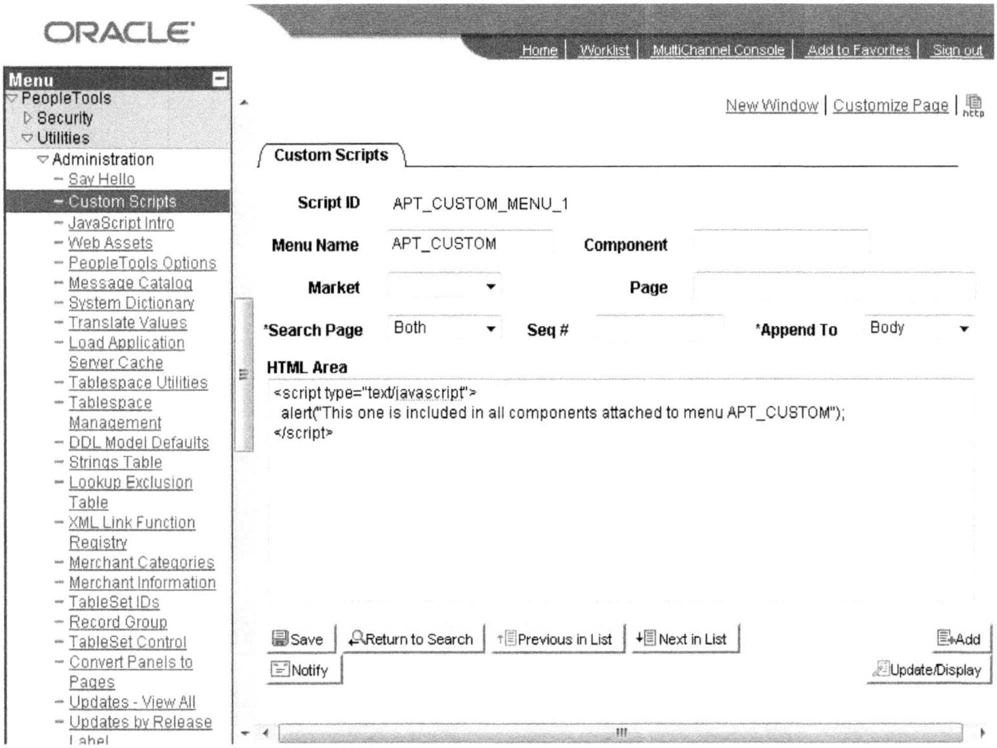

FIGURE 7-9. *APT_CUSTOM_MENU_1 menu test data*

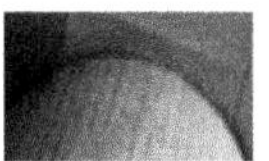

NOTE

After adding the SQL to an SQL definition, right-click inside the SQL editor and choose Resolve Meta SQL. This will display database-specific SQL in the output window.

Next, we will create an iScript to serve the SQL's results to a web browser. Some of the scripts will be inserted into the HTML `head` element, and some will go into the `body` element. Therefore, we need to structure the iScript's results so the bootstrap code can differentiate one script from the next. For this example, we will use JavaScript Object Notation (JSON)[3] to structure our data. JSON is a JavaScript native data format. Unlike XML, which requires a special parser, web browsers can interpret JSON without additional plug-ins. You'll see how to use JSON when we modify the bootstrap code.

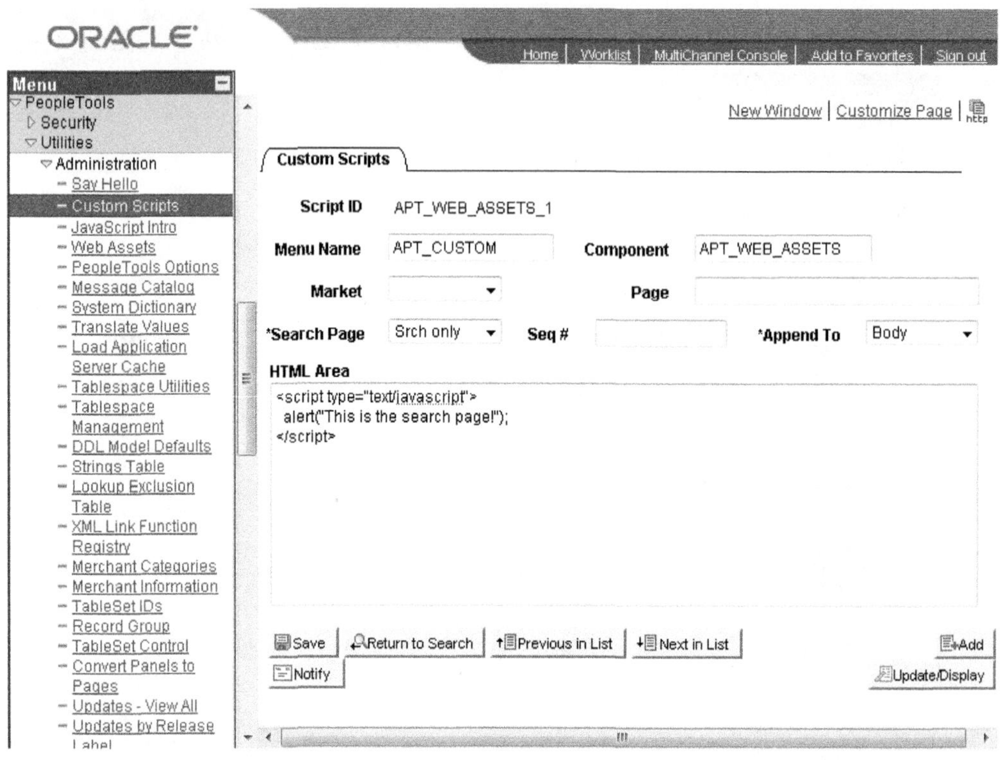

FIGURE 7-10. *APT_WEB_ASSETS_1 web assets search page test data*

To create this iScript, open the `FieldFormula` event of the record field `WEBLIB_APT_JSL ISCRIPT1` and add the following PeopleCode:

```
Function IScript_UI()
   Local SQL &scriptsCursor;
   Local string &menu = %Request.GetParameter("m");
   Local string &component = %Request.GetParameter("c");
   Local string &market = %Request.GetParameter("mk");
   Local string &page = %Request.GetParameter("p");
   Local number &isSearch = Value(%Request.GetParameter("s"));
   Local string &searchOption;

   Local string &location;
   Local string &data;
   Local string &jsonRow;
   Local string &html;
   Local boolean &needsComma = False;
```

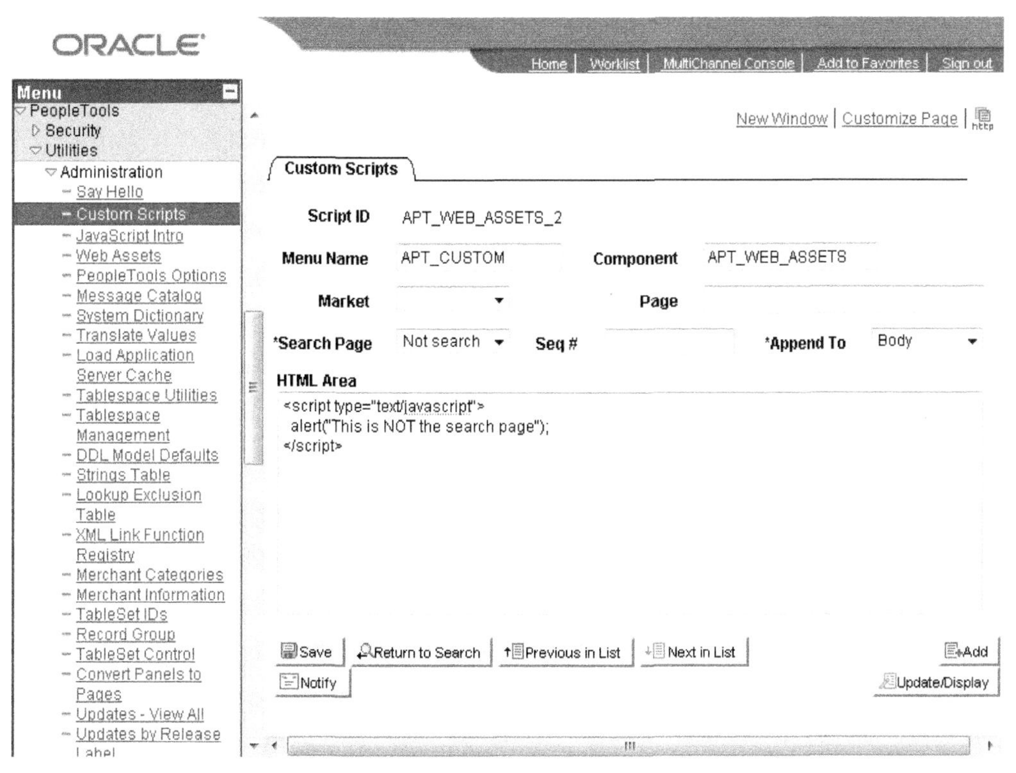

FIGURE 7-11. *APT_WEB_ASSETS_2 web assets transaction page test data*

```
REM ** If this is a search page, then look for Search Only scripts;
If (&isSearch = 1) Then
   &searchOption = "SO";
Else
   &searchOption = "NS";
End-If;
%Response.SetContentType("text/plain");

%Response.WriteLine("[");
&scriptsCursor = GetSQL(SQL.APT_GET_UI_SCRIPTS, &menu, &component,
      &market, &page, &searchOption);
While &scriptsCursor.Fetch(&location, &data);
   REM ** re-initialize row data -- only use comma after first row;
   If (&needsComma) Then
      &jsonRow = ", ";
   Else
      &needsComma = True;
      &jsonRow = "";
   End-If;
```

```
        REM ** JSON doesn't allow \' (JavaScript does, JSON doesn't);
        &html = EscapeJavascriptString(&data);
        &html = Substitute(&html, "\'", "'");

        &jsonRow = &jsonRow | "{""appendTo"": """ | &location |
              """, ""data"": """ | &html | """}";
        %Response.WriteLine(&jsonRow);
    End-While;
    %Response.WriteLine("]");

End-Function;
```

The function contains standard PeopleCode. The PeopleCode declares some variables, opens an SQL cursor, and then iterates over the results of that cursor, converting the data into JSON format. The only function call that may seem extraordinary is the call to `EscapeJavaScriptString`. In this iScript, we are using the `EscapeJavaScriptString` function to convert the contents of the `HTMLAREA` database field into content that is compatible with JavaScript strings. The `HTMLAREA` field may contain quotation marks, newline characters, and a variety of other characters that must be escaped prior to placing them in quotation marks.

Immediately following the call to `EscapeJavaScriptString`, you can see the `Substitute` function used to replace `\'` with `'`. JavaScript allows `\'`, but JSON does not. The substitution here is simplistic, but it will suit our purposes for this chapter. The problem with this substitution is that it doesn't account for `\\'`, which is valid for JSON and JavaScript. In fact, if the substitution in this code saw `\\'`, it would replace those characters with `\'`, which would be invalid. In Chapter 9, you will learn how to use a server-side JSON parser to generate JSON. The JSON parser contains logic to account for these string idiosyncrasies.

Be sure to add this new iScript to the `APT_CUSTOM` permission list.

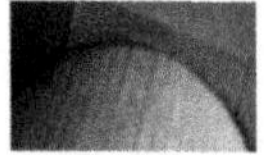

NOTE
We could clean up this code a bit by creating an HTML definition for the JSON row data and calling `GetHTMLText` for each row.

Test this new iScript by navigating to the following URL:

http://hrms.example.com/psc/hrms/EMPLOYEE/HRMS/s/WEBLIB_APT_JSL.ISCRIPT1
.FieldFormula.IScript_UI?&m=APT_CUSTOM&c=APT_WEB_ASSETS&mk=GBL&p=&s=1.

The query string parameters are prefilled to simulate the request that would be made from the Web Assets component search page.

NOTE
You can validate the JSON results of this iScript by copying the text and pasting it into the text field at http://www.jsonlint.com/.

The following code listing contains the results generated by the iScript and reformatted for print.

```
[
  {
      "appendTo": "BODY",
      "data": "<script type=\"text/javascript\">\n  " +
          "alert(\"This is a global script!\");\n</script>"
  },
```

```
    {
        "appendTo": "BODY",
        "data": "<script type=\"text/javascript\">\n  " +
            "alert(\"This one is included in all components " +
            "attached to menu APT_CUSTOM\");\n</script>"
    },
    {
        "appendTo": "BODY",
        "data": "<script type=\"text/javascript\">\n  " +
            "alert(\"This is the search page!\");\n</script>"
    }
]
```

The iScript `IScript_UI` sets the `Content-Type` header to `text/plain`. The actual content type for JSON data is `application/json`. If you change the content type to `application/json`, however, the browser will prompt you to download this file. While this is perfectly acceptable, that response makes it difficult to review the iScript's result. Once you finish the reviewing process, I recommend updating `IScript_UI` so that it returns the correct content type.

Modifying the Bootstrap Code

In Chapter 6, we hard-coded some of our custom JavaScript libraries in the bootstrap code. We now have a configurable mechanism for adding global features like those we hard-coded. Therefore, we can remove those hard-coded libraries and add them to our metadata. To use this new mechanism, however, we will need to modify the bootstrap code.

Parsing JSON

Our iScript returns JSON data. Since JSON is native JavaScript, we could use the JavaScript `eval` function to convert JSON from plain text into a JavaScript object. This is considered unsafe, however, because the data interpreted by `eval` may contain any JavaScript, including malicious functions. In other words, the `eval` function does not require the JSON to contain JSON data.

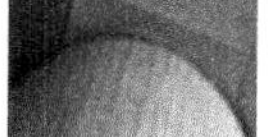

NOTE

When I wrote this chapter, Microsoft Internet Explorer 8 and Mozilla Firefox 3.5 supported native JSON parsing. Other browsers, such as Google Chrome, were building JSON support, but had not yet released it. jQuery, the AJAX library demonstrated here, had not yet implemented support for native JSON, and was still using the `eval` *function. By the time you read this chapter, I anticipate jQuery will support the native JSON parser. Nevertheless, if your browser doesn't support JSON parsing, it is expected that jQuery will fall back to the JavaScript* `eval` *function.*

As a safe alternative, we can use a JavaScript JSON parser. Download the JSON parser from http://www.json.org/json2.js and open it in a text editor. Just like the jQuery JavaScript library, the json2.js file size exceeds the maximum size PeopleTools 8.4*x* allows for HTML definitions. Using PeopleTools 8.4*x* necessitates the creation of a new message catalog definition. Create a new message catalog definition for message set 25000, message number 2. Set the definition's message text to **JSON2 parser from json.org**; and paste the contents of json2.js into the Explanation field.

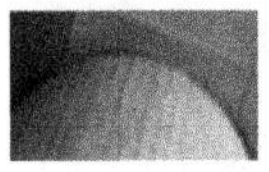

TIP

Using a JavaScript minification program, like the one available from http://www.crockford.com/javascript/jsmin.html, will reduce the size of the json2.js by 80%. This will make the file small enough to fit inside a PeopleTools 8.4x HTML definition.

Open the `FieldFormula` event for record field `WEBLIB_APT_JSL ISCRIPT1` and add the following PeopleCode to the end of this event:

```
Function IScript_JSON2
   Local string &js = MsgGetExplainText(25000, 2, "alert('The " |
         "JSON2 JavaScript library message catalog entry does " |
         "not exist.');");

   %Response.SetContentType("text/javascript");
   %Response.Write(&js);
End-Function;
```

Be sure to add this new iScript to the `APT_CUSTOM` permission list.

Next, we need to get jQuery to use a JSON parser rather than its own `eval` alternative. To accomplish this, we can use a jQuery `dataFilter`. A `dataFilter` is a function with two parameters: the response data and the data's type. It scrubs, sanitizes, and otherwise modifies response data, and returns the modified response data. So, a `dataFilter` is a function that has an opportunity to modify response data before jQuery executes the AJAX `success` callback function.

We register a `dataFilter` function with jQuery by listing it as an optional parameter to the `$.ajax` method at execution time. This means that we must pass a custom `dataFilter` to jQuery every time we call `$.ajax`. Since we plan to use JSON and AJAX in a variety of places within the application, let's create another JavaScript library to encompass this functionality. Create a new HTML definition, name it `APT_AJAX_JS`, and add the following code:

```
(function($) {
  if(!window.apt.ajax) {
    apt.namespace.create("apt.ajax");
    apt.ajax.getJSON = function(options) {
      // add data filter to use native JSON parser rather than eval
      // see http://bit.ly/sMHt0
      options.dataFilter = function(data) {
        return JSON.parse(data);
      }
      return $.ajax(options);
    }
  }
})(jQuery);
```

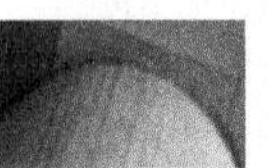

NOTE

This code is an adaptation from Dave Ward's post, "Improving jQuery's JSON performance and security," available from http://encosia.com/2009/07/07/improving-jquery-json-performance-and-security/.

This code creates a new namespaced function called `apt.ajax.getJSON` and is actually a wrapper around jQuery's `$.ajax` method. Our code will call this method whenever we expect JSON data, to ensure that the data is parsed safely.

This `dataFilter` uses the `JSON.parse` method. Later, we will modify our bootstrap code so that it imports the JSON2 JavaScript library if the browser does not offer native JSON support. This will ensure the JSON object exists before `apt.ajax.getJSON` attempts to use it.

The previous JavaScript code listing uses the self-executing function technique introduced in the previous chapter. This time, the self-executing function requires a parameter named `$`. There are other JavaScript libraries that use the `$` alias. By wrapping the contents of a library in an anonymous function and passing in the global `jQuery` variable, we ensure that the `$` alias used within this code points to jQuery, and not some other library.[4]

Now let's create an iScript function to serve this HTML definition. Open the `FieldFormula` event of the record field `WEBLIB_APT_JSL ISCRIPT1` and add the following PeopleCode to the end of this event:

```
Function IScript_Ajax
   %Response.SetContentType("text/javascript");
   %Response.Write(GetHTMLText(HTML.APT_AJAX_JS));
End-Function;
```

Be sure to add this new iScript to the `APT_CUSTOM` permission list.

You can test this iScript by navigating to your server's version of this URL:

http://hrms.example.com/psc/hrms/EMPLOYEE/HRMS/s/WEBLIB_APT_JSL.ISCRIPT1
.FieldFormula.IScript_Ajax

The iScript should return the contents of the `APT_AJAX_JS` HTML definition.

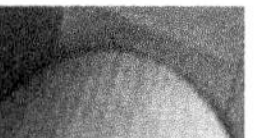

NOTE
Considering the content type of the `IScript_Ajax` iScript, your browser may prompt you to save the results to a file. If this occurs, save the result to a file, and then verify the contents by opening the new file in a text editor.

Downloading Custom Scripts

We now have a JSON parser and a custom AJAX wrapper to ensure jQuery uses the JSON parser. Next, we need to write some JavaScript to download a JSON array of per-page JavaScripts. Create a new HTML definition and add the following code:

```
// PART 1
$(document).ready(function() {
  apt.namespace.create("apt.ui");

  if(!apt.ui.uiLoader) {
    // single run flag
    apt.ui.Loader = true;

    // PART 2
    (function(url) {
      if(!url) {
```

```
      return;
    }
    // PART 3
    var re =
/\/c\/([\w_]+?)\.([\w_]+?)\.([\w_]+?)(?:\?.+?PAGE=([\w_]+?))?\b/;

    var parts = url.match(re);

    if(parts[4] == undefined) {
      // reset page var to blank if it isn't in the URL
      parts[4] = "";
    }

    var parms = {
        m:  parts[1], // menu
        c:  parts[2], // component
        mk: parts[3], // market
        p:  parts[4]  // page name
    };

    // PART 4
    /* if the current page contains a button named #ICSsearch, then
     * this is a search page
     */
    if($("#\\#ICSearch").length > 0) {
      parms["s"] = 1;
    } else {
      parms["s"] = 0;
    }

    // PART 5
    // Place AJAX call to download scripts
    apt.ajax.getJSON({
        async: false,
        data: parms,
        dataType: "text",
        url: apt.files.generateScriptContentUrl({
            record: "WEBLIB_APT_JSL",
            field:  "ISCRIPT1",
            event:  "FieldFormula",
            script: "IScript_UI"
        }),
        error: function (XMLHttpRequest, textStatus, errorThrown) {
          var message = textStatus || errorThrown;
          alert("Error loading enhancements: " + message);
        },
        success: function(data, status) {
          // PART 6
          for(var idx = 0; idx < data.length; idx++) {
            var script = data[idx];
            $(script.appendTo + ":first").append(script.data);
          }
```

```
            }
         });
      })(window.strCurrUrl);
   }
});
```

Name this new HTML definition APT_UI_LOADER_JS.

This JavaScript begins with the same code as many of our other libraries. It declares a namespace, and then it sets a flag to ensure the library is executed only once (part 1). Next, the library declares a self-executing function that takes one parameter: a URL (part 2). The first half of this self-executing function parses the menu, component, page, and so on from the URL parameter (part 3). The next segment uses the jQuery selector `$("#\\#ICSearch")` to determine if the current page is a search page (part 4). `#ICSearch` is the name of the search page's search button. If the button exists, then the current page is a search page. The final segment of this code calls our AJAX wrapper function (part 5) and appends the result to the appropriate location (part 6).

As usual, we must create an iScript to serve this JavaScript library. Open the `FieldFormula` event of the record field `WEBLIB_APT_JSL ISCRIPT1` and add the following PeopleCode:

```
Function IScript_UILoader
   %Response.SetContentType("text/javascript");
   %Response.Write(GetHTMLText(HTML.APT_UI_LOADER_JS));
End-Function;
```

Be sure to add this new iScript to the `APT_CUSTOM` permission list.

You can test the iScript by navigating to this URL:

http://hrms.example.com/psc/hrms/EMPLOYEE/HRMS/s/WEBLIB_APT_JSL.ISCRIPT1
.FieldFormula.IScript_UILoader

NOTE

It is a good idea to test your JavaScript library iScripts. A PeopleCode error in an iScript may go undetected after the JavaScript library is integrated into an application. When you run one of these iScripts, you expect it to return the contents of your JavaScript library.

Importing Scripts

The following code listing contains the new import scripts section of our bootstrap code. Open the `PT_COPYURL` HTML definition and scroll through the listing until you see the text `//% import scripts`. Replace the remaining definition contents with the code presented in the following listing.

```
//% import scripts
if(!window.jQuery) {
  apt.files.importScript({
      id:  "jq",
      url: apt.files.generateScriptContentUrl({
          record: "WEBLIB_APT_JSL",
          field:  "ISCRIPT1",
```

```
            event:  "FieldFormula",
            script: "IScript_jQuery"})
    });
  }

  if (!window.JSON) {
    // Native JSON not available, so import it
    apt.files.importScript({
        id:  "json2",
        url: apt.files.generateScriptContentUrl({
            record: "WEBLIB_APT_JSL",
            field:  "ISCRIPT1",
            event:  "FieldFormula",
            script: "IScript_JSON2"})
    });
  }

  apt.files.importScript({
      id:  "apt_ajax",
      url: apt.files.generateScriptContentUrl({
          record: "WEBLIB_APT_JSL",
          field:  "ISCRIPT1",
          event:  "FieldFormula",
          script: "IScript_Ajax"
      })
  });

  apt.files.importScript({
      id:  "apt_ui_loader",
      url: apt.files.generateScriptContentUrl({
          record: "WEBLIB_APT_JSL",
          field:  "ISCRIPT1",
          event:  "FieldFormula",
          script: "IScript_UILoader"
      })
  });

  /* Redefine import function after load. IE doesn't like this
   * version prior to load, but the other version doesn't work after
   * the document is loaded
   */
  apt.files.importScript = function(parms) {
    var s = document.createElement("script");
    s.type = "text/javascript";
    s.src = parms.url;
    s.id = parms.id;
    s.defer = (parms.defer) ? parms.defer : false;
    document.getElementsByTagName("head")[0].appendChild(s);
  }
```

In this iteration of the import scripts section, we removed the active field highlighting code and inserted the JSON parser library, our new AJAX library, and the UI loader library.

The JSON2 JavaScript library conditionally creates the JSON object if the browser doesn't provide a native implementation. We've taken this one step further—the code doesn't even import the JSON2 JavaScript library if the browser provides native JSON support.

Making this change will remove the active highlighting code. In a few paragraphs, we will add it back in using our new Custom Scripts component.

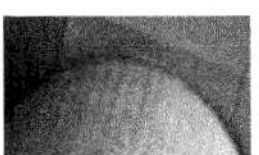

NOTE

The last code block in the preceding listing redefines the `importScript` function. The original `importScript` function works only while the page is loading. Once the page is loaded, the `document.write` method functions differently. The alternative presented in the last code block uses the DOM to insert a script node. I originally used this second `importScript` function instead of the `document.write` version demonstrated in Chapter 6. After testing in Microsoft Internet Explorer, however, I noticed that it exhibited erratic loading behavior when using the DOM. When using `document.write`, Internet Explorer loaded external scripts in the order in which they were listed. When using the DOM, however, Internet Explorer executed scripts in a random order.

Testing the Custom Scripts Component

Remember all that test data we created earlier in this chapter? We created a global script, scripts for the menu `APT_CUSTOM` and the component `APT_JSINTRO`, and separate scripts for the `APT_WEB_ASSETS` component search page and transaction page. If you navigate to PeopleTools | Utilities | Administration | Web Assets, you should see three message boxes on the search page. The first will tell you that it is from the global script. The second will tell you it exists because you are on a component attached to the `APT_CUSTOM` menu. The third will tell you that you are on the Web Assets search page. If you select a web asset, you will see three more message boxes, with the last one telling you that you are not on a search page.

After verifying that this new feature works, delete the test data by running the following SQL:

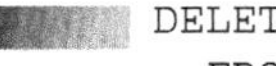

```
DELETE
  FROM PS_APT_UI_SCRIPTS
```

Be sure to commit your changes, if required by your database.

Highlight Active Field Revisited

When we modified the bootstrap code, we removed the JavaScript and CSS that highlight the active data-entry field. Let's add that enhancement back to our application through our new Custom Scripts component.

Navigate to PeopleTools | Utilities | Administration | Custom Scripts and add the new value `APT_HIGHLIGHT_ACTIVE`. Leave the criteria fields blank and accept the default values for the Search Page and Append To fields. Add the following code to the HTML Area data-entry field:

```
<script type="text/javascript">
  apt.files.importScript({
      id:  "apt_ui_ha",
      url: apt.files.generateScriptContentUrl({
          record: "WEBLIB_APT_JSL",
          field:  "ISCRIPT1",
          event:  "FieldFormula",
          script: "IScript_HighlightActiveJs"
      })
  });

  apt.files.importStylesheet(
      apt.files.generateScriptContentUrl({
          record: "WEBLIB_APT_JSL",
          field:  "ISCRIPT1",
          event:  "FieldFormula",
          script: "IScript_HighlightActiveCss"
      })
  );
</script>
```

Figure 7-12 shows the Custom Scripts page with the appropriate values.

Since our `APT_UI_LOADER_JS` code appends the contents of the HTML Area field to an existing HTML element, similar to our `importScript` and `importStylesheet` functions, we could have placed the contents of the `APT_HIGHLIGHT_ACTIVE_JS` and `APT_HIGHLIGHT_ACTIVE_CSS` HTML definitions directly into the Custom Scripts HTML Area. This would save the browser from the expense of making two additional requests. However, although this would reduce the number of connections, it would have increased the size of the JSON download. In Chapter 9, we will extend this example with a custom meta-HTML resolver that will allow us to take advantage of web server and browser caching to eliminate the download altogether. Using the approach presented in Chapter 9, the user will download the contents of `APT_HIGHLIGHT_ACTIVE_JS` and `APT_HIGHLIGHT_ACTIVE_CSS` once, and then access them from the web browser's cache thereafter.

After you save this new Custom Script definition, your web browser will automatically highlight the active data-entry field. To verify this, return to the Custom Scripts search page.

NOTE

I tested this example in Google Chrome 2, Mozilla Firefox 3.5, and Microsoft Internet Explorer 8. On Chrome and Firefox, this example worked flawlessly. Internet Explorer, however, does not add the `APT_hasFocus` CSS class to the active element until after the first active element loses the focus. I believe this is because the highlight jQuery code does not execute until after the DOM is ready. Unfortunately, this occurs after the PeopleSoft-delivered JavaScript sets the focus to a particular field. Importing the highlighting code directly from `PT_COPYURL`, rather than from the Custom Scripts component, resolved this issue.

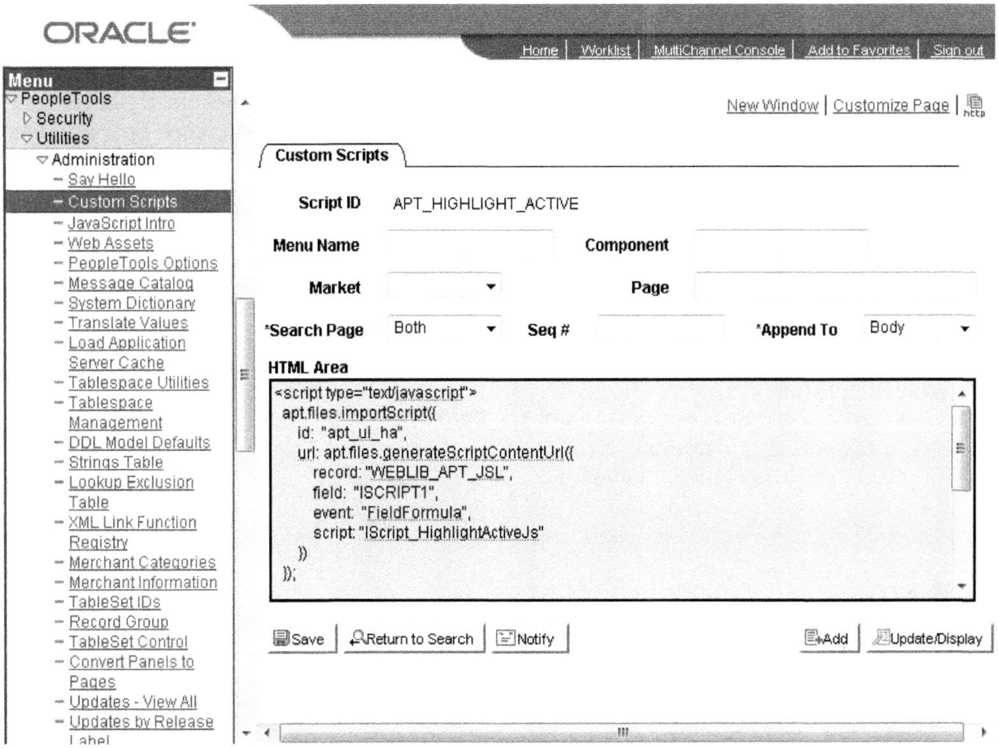

FIGURE 7-12. *Custom Scripts page with highlighting code*

Changing Search Operators

A frequent question posed in forums is how to change the search page operator from the default value "begins with" to a different value, such as "contains." I have searched for a delivered solution, but can't find one. With a little JavaScript, however, we can compose our own solution.

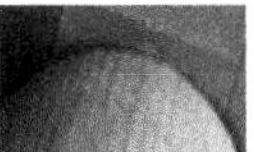

NOTE

The following JavaScript makes assumptions about the PeopleTools search page HTML. These assumptions were true of PeopleTools 8.49 and PeopleTools 8.50, but may not be true with other releases. Nevertheless, the concept is the same. If this JavaScript does not work with your PeopleTools release, use Firebug to investigate your search page's HTML. You may find that the operator field's name or value list differs from the one presented here.

The Custom Scripts component's Advanced Search page has six fields, each with its own operator. Using Firebug's inspector, highlight the Menu Name operator field. In the Firebug panel, you will see that the Menu Name operator field is an HTML `select` element that has the name `APT_UI_SCRIPTS_MENUNAME$op`. It is my observation that Advanced Search page operator names use the convention *`RECNAME_FIELDNAME$op`*. Also notice that the `select` element has an `onchange` JavaScript event handler. Upon further inspection, observe that the `select` element has ten options. Those ten options are key/value pairs that describe the ten possible search operators. If we want to change the value of the menu name operator, then we can look up the operator's value based on the option's contents. For example, the not = operator has a value of 3. Therefore, to change the operator from begins with to not =, we will need to change the operator's value from 1 to 3.

Using JavaScript, we can select the appropriate search field operator, choose a different `select` option, and then call the operator's field change event. Here is some JavaScript to accomplish this task:

```
$(document).ready(function() {
  var newValue = 9;
  var coll = $("select[name='APT_UI_SCRIPTS_MENUNAME$op']");
  if(coll.val() != newValue) {
    coll.val(newValue).change();
  }
});
```

NOTE
The preceding code uses `$(document).ready` to ensure the code doesn't execute before the document finishes loading. Since we will be executing this code from the UI loader code, and the UI loader code doesn't execute until `$(document).ready` fires, this second `$(document).ready` is redundant. This redundant call, however, is immaterial because jQuery will execute the code immediately. It is better to add safeguards like this than to assume they already exist.

In this code listing, after the `document.ready()` method call, we see another jQuery selector:

```
$("select[name='APT_UI_SCRIPTS_MENUNAME$op']")
```

This selector searches for all `select` HTML elements that have the name `APT_UI_SCRIPTS_MENUNAME$op`. Since the document contains only one element by that name, jQuery will return a collection with one element. We will refer to this collection multiple times, so the code stores the collection in a variable named `coll`.

In Chapter 1, I mentioned fluent interface design and the role of method chaining in composing fluent code. jQuery makes significant use of method chaining. Many jQuery method calls return a jQuery collection. In the preceding code, the `val(newValue)` call returns the collection that is currently stored in `el`. We then chain a call to `change()` to the end of `val()`. This is the same as the following:

```
el.val(newValue)
el.change();
```

To test this code, follow these steps:

1. Navigate to PeopleTools | Utilities | Administration | Custom Scripts.
2. When the page loads, change the URL in your browser's address bar from /psp/ to /psc/.
3. Select the Advanced Search link.
4. Type the preceding full JavaScript listing into the Firebug console.
5. Click the Run button.

When you run this code, the menu name search operator should change from begins with to between, and two new fields should appear.

When we add this code to the Custom Scripts component, we will set the search only flag. Since our Custom Scripts module does not include a flag for differentiating between the Advanced Search page and the Basic Search page, we should make sure this code executes properly on the Basic Search page.

Select the Basic Search hyperlink and run this code again. This time, the code will execute, but not do anything. Since the Basic Search page does not have search operators, the jQuery selector will return a collection with zero elements. The method calls that follow this selector, `val()` and `change()`, have no effect on an empty collection.

Let's create an entry in the Custom Scripts component for this JavaScript. Navigate to PeopleTools | Utilities | Administration | Custom Scripts and add the value `APT_UI_SCRIPTS_SRCH_DEFAULTS`. Set the menu name to `APT_CUSTOM`, the component to `APT_UI_SCRIPTS`, and the search page to `Srch Only`. Add the following code and save the script.

```
<script type="text/javascript">
  if(!window.apt.setSearchOp) {
    window.apt.setSearchOp = function () {
        // The value for "between" is 9. Change this to your desired
        // search operator value.
        var newValue = 9;

        // The name of the search key field is APT_UI_SCRIPTS_MENUNAME.
        // Generally speaking, PeopleSoft creates HTML element names by
        // combining record and field names with an underscore as in
        // RECORD_FIELD. Change the following value to the name of your
        // search key record_field
        var coll = $("select[name='APT_UI_SCRIPTS_MENUNAME$op']");

        if(coll.val() != newValue) {
          coll.val(newValue).change();
        }
      };
```

```
    if(window.net) {
      // PeopleTools 8.50 specific code
      // Place in a closure so variables will have a local
      // scope, but be accessible from net.ContentLoader.
      (function() {
        var originalContentLoader = net.ContentLoader;

        net.ContentLoader = function(url, form, name, method, onload,
            onerror, params, contentType, bAjax, bPrompt) {
          var originalOnLoad = onload;

          if(name == "#ICAdvSearch") {
            onload = function() {
              if (typeof originalOnLoad == "undefined" ||
                  !originalOnLoad) {
                this.processXML();
              } else {
                originalOnLoad.call(this);
              }

              setSearchOp();
            }
          }
        };
      })();

    } else {
      // PeopleTools 8.4x; the code below will handle the pt 8.4x case
    }

    $(document).ready(function() {
        window.apt.setSearchOp();
    });
  }
</script>
```

Figure 7-13 shows the `APT_UI_SCRIPTS_SRCH_DEFAULTS` metadata.

Return to the search page and click Advanced Search. The page should automatically change the menu name search operator to between and add from and to fields, as shown in Figure 7-14.

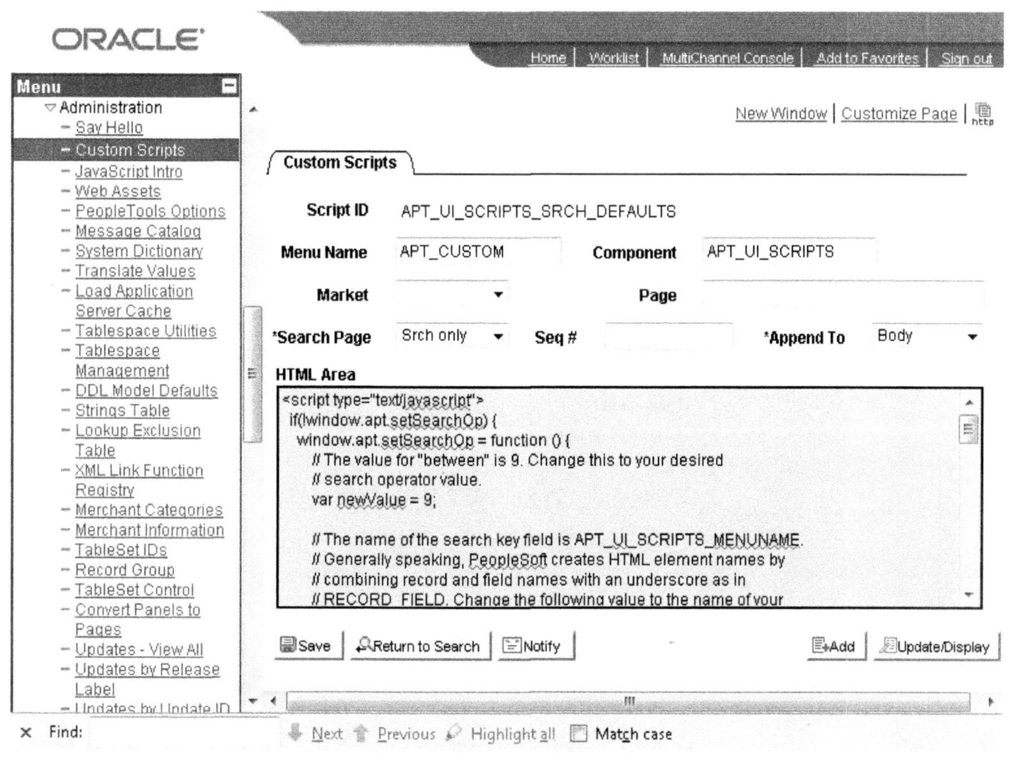

FIGURE 7-13. *APT_UI_SCRIPTS_SRCH_DEFAULTS metadata*

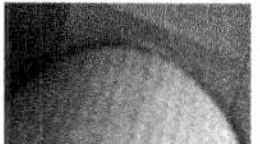

NOTE

While the Custom Scripts utility fills a significant gap in user interface development, it may not satisfy all of your user interface customization requirements. The contents of these scripts do not have access to the component buffer, and therefore cannot access data that exists only in the buffer. They can, however, access all the data on the given page. If you need to pass values to JavaScript, and those values exist only in the component buffer, you may still require a page modification.

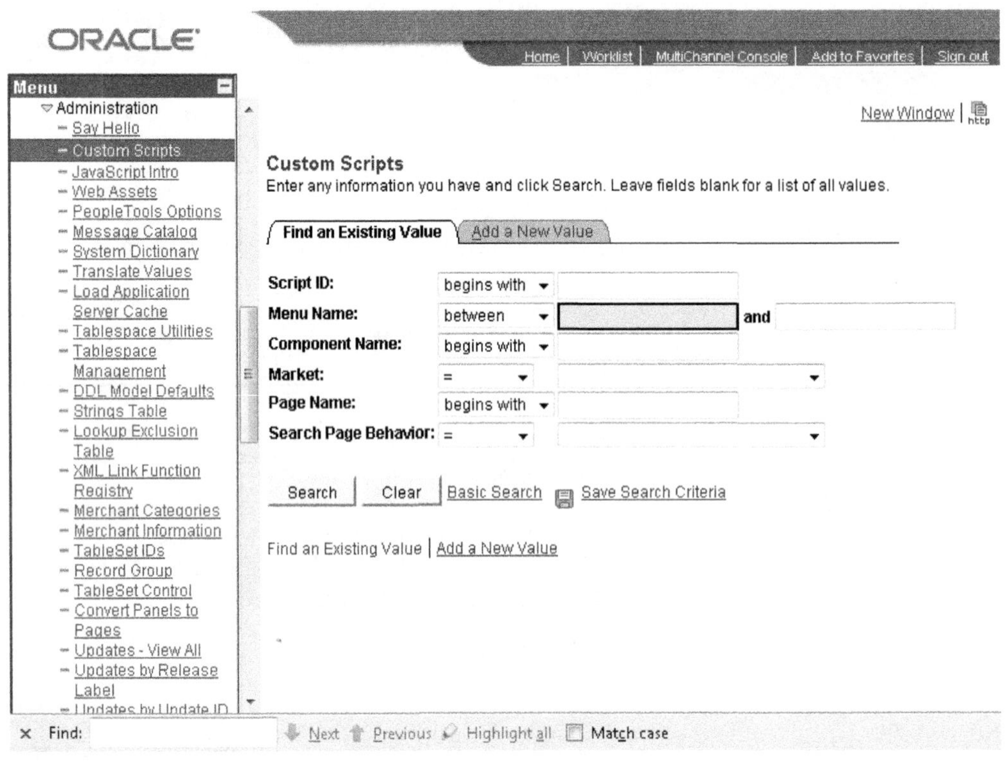

FIGURE 7-14. *Custom Scripts Advanced Search page*

Fiddler

Fiddler is an HTTP proxy for debugging web applications, and it is one of my favorite tools. It allows you to inspect HTTP requests and responses, set breakpoints, and generate new HTTP requests. It is very handy for coding and debugging JavaScript and AJAX code.

Unlike standard web browser HTTP requests, AJAX requests are transparent, meaning that the data is sent to an HTTP server, and then processed without any notification to the user. Without a debugging proxy like Fiddler, it would be very difficult to see the data that was sent to the HTTP server or the response that was received from the HTTP AJAX request handler.

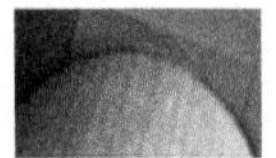

NOTE

Firebug, introduced in Chapter 6, is also useful with AJAX. The Firebug console shows AJAX requests and responses. After creating the global custom scripts modification described in this chapter, if you open the Firebug console and navigate to any PeopleSoft page, you will see an iScript URL appear in the Firebug console.

To get started, download and install Fiddler from http://www.fiddlertool.com/. After installation, you can launch Fiddler from your Microsoft Windows Start menu or from Internet Explorer.

To see Fiddler in action, log in to PeopleSoft through your web browser (if you use Firefox, you can either use the Firefox FiddlerHook[5] extension or manually set your HTTP proxy to the address used by Fiddler). In Fiddler, you will see each HTTP request, along with its form parameters and response data.

Any HTTP interaction that causes the browser to automatically submit a new request can be difficult to debug. For example, both web server redirect responses and documents containing redirect JavaScript submit a request before the user has a chance to respond. Because the interaction may happen transparently, it is not possible to view the contents of the files generated by this process. Using Fiddler, however, you have a complete record of the HTTP request response history. Figure 7-15 is a screenshot of Fiddler showing the PeopleSoft login HTTP redirect, along with the form data that was sent as part of the original login request.

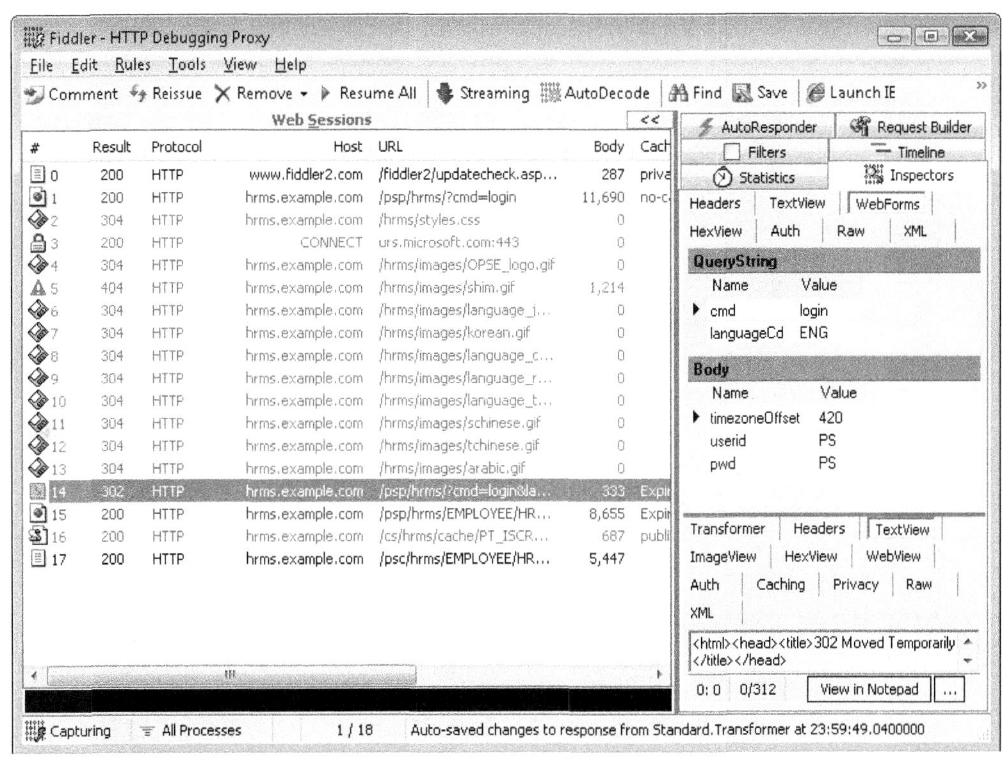

FIGURE 7-15. *Fiddler showing HTTP redirect*

In your web browser, navigate to PeopleTools | Utilities | Administration | Custom Scripts, and then switch back to Fiddler. You will see several new entries in Fiddler. Select one of the rows with a green background, and then select the Inspectors tab on the right. The upper panel of the pane on the right contains request information, and the lower panel contains response information. In the lower, response panel, click the Headers button. Notice the `Content-Type` header has a value of `text/javascript`. This is the value we set in our iScript when we used the `%Response.SetContentType` method.

You can view the contents of the downloaded JavaScript file by selecting the TextView button. If you have compression turned on in your web profile, however, you may see a warning message telling you that the response is encoded and must be decoded before inspection. In this case, select the Transformer button and then the No Compression radio button. After turning off compression, return to text view to see the contents of the downloaded file. Figure 7-16 shows the `APT_AJAX_JS HTML` definition displayed in Fiddler.

Scrolling down the Fiddler list a little further, you should see a row in black text. This row represents the JSON AJAX request. Looking at the Request Inspector, you can see the form data that was posted to the WEBLIB function `IScript_UI`. In the Response Inspector, you see the results returned by the `IScript_UI`, as shown in Figure 7-17.

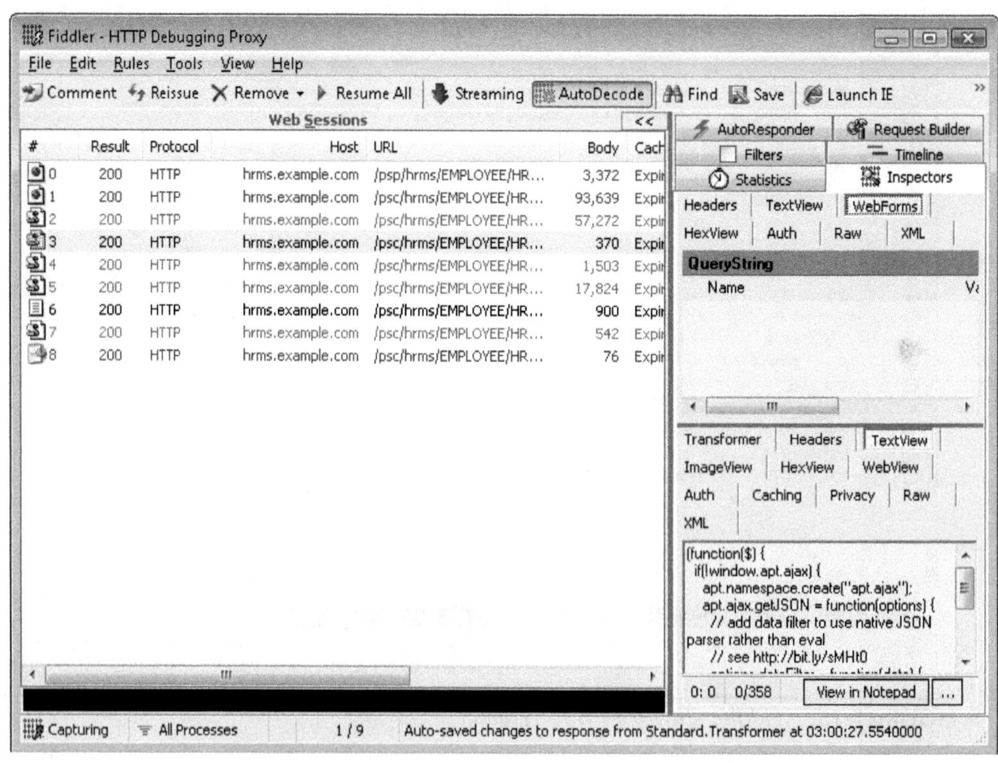

FIGURE 7-16. *Downloaded JavaScript file in Fiddler*

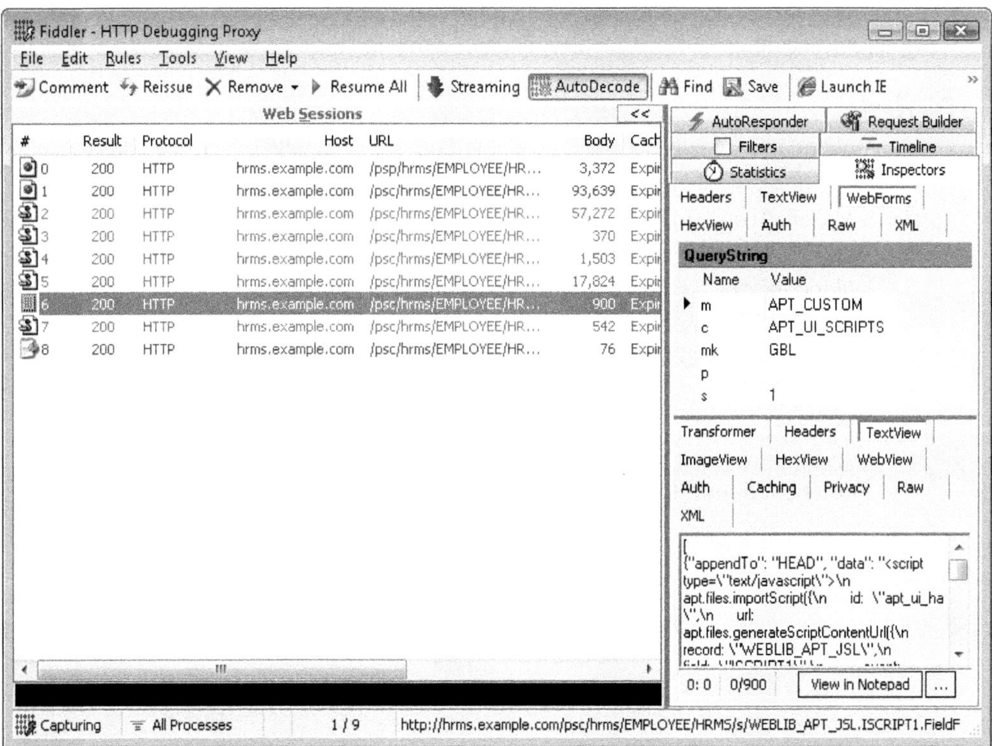

FIGURE 7-17. *JSON response in Fiddler*

Conclusion

As you saw with the Direct Reports display shelf example in this chapter, AJAX allows you to load HTML into a page without reloading the entire page. AJAX also allows you to load related data into a page without affecting the component buffer. Using JavaScript, we added visual effects to the Direct Reports display shelf page. With a small amount of code, we were able to present a very smooth transition effect.

With the Custom Scripts example, you used a new data format: JSON. Using structured data in the form of JSON or XML, you can iterate over the data and insert its contents into the appropriate location within a page.

Chapter 8 builds on this chapter by showing you how to create a custom administration toolbar that exists on every page, without requiring page modifications. Chapter 9 will show you how to create a custom meta-HTML resolver that allows you to add placeholder tokens to the Custom Scripts HTML Area control. At runtime, the iScript JSON data source will replace those tokens with data. This will allow you to insert HTML definitions as JavaScripts, App Designer style sheets as CSS style sheets, and App Designer image definitions as image URLs. In fact, the solution is extensible, so you will be able to use it to insert and resolve any token you can imagine.

If you are a seasoned JavaScript programmer and web developer, you will recognize that the examples presented here suffer from some minor performance issues—specifically, that iScripts don't support caching. But don't worry, because we will resolve this in Chapters 9 and 14.

Notes

1. Wiktionary, "Ajaxify"[online]; available from http://en.wiktionary.org/wiki/Ajaxify; Internet; accessed 19 August 2009.
2. OWASP, "Top 10 2007-Cross Site Scripting" [online]; available from http://www.owasp.org/index.php/Top_10_2007-A1; Internet; accessed 20 August 2009.
3. Wikipedia, "JSON" [online]; available from http://en.wikipedia.org/wiki/JSON; Internet; accessed 21 August 2009.
4. jQuery Project, *jQuery JavaScript Library*, "Plugins/Authoring" [online]; available from http://docs.jquery.com/Plugins/Authoring#Custom_Alias; Internet; accessed 22 August 2009.
5. Microsoft Corporation, "FiddlerHook" [online]; available from http://www.fiddler2.com/fiddler2/addons/fiddlerhook/; Internet; accessed 18 January 2010.

CHAPTER 8

Creating Custom Tools

Chapter 5 described how to expose server-side logic as services that could be consumed by the client-side user interface. In Chapter 6, you learned how to write JavaScript to create and interact with user interface elements. In Chapter 7, we tied the information in Chapters 5 and 6 together by calling server-side logic from the client-side user interface. In this chapter, we will use the concepts presented in Chapters 5 through 7 to create a custom administration toolbar. To make this toolbar configurable, we will create a toolbar button metadata repository. Then we will use the Custom Scripts module from Chapter 7 to make this toolbar accessible from all PeopleSoft pages.

The Toolbar Button Metadata Repository

Our toolbar requirements call for a configurable, secured list of buttons. These buttons have an image, tooltip text, and a command. Each tool also requires a tool identifier (key field).

The metadata repository for the toolbar should contain the following:

- Security so that specific tools are available only to authorized users
- A button image for each command
- A tooltip to describe the button's function
- A long text field for the JavaScript and HTML that implements the button's behavior.

NOTE
PeopleTools comes with several images that have a width and height of 16 pixels, a size that fits our toolbar. In this chapter, we will use the standard 16-by-16 images that are delivered with your PeopleSoft application.

Setting Up the Repository Tables

Our metadata repository requires a couple of fields that don't exist yet. Let's create those fields before creating the repository. Create the field `APT_TOOL_ID`, as shown in Figure 8-1. Then define the field `APT_TOOLTIP` as shown in Figure 8-2.

Since the toolbar's button images, represented by the `IMAGE_NAME` field, will come from App Designer image definitions, we can use PeopleTools metadata to create a prompt table for the `IMAGE_NAME` field. Create a new SQL view and define the fields and keys as shown in Figure 8-3. Save the record definition as `APT_IMAGE_SRCH`.

Set the view's SQL to the following, and then build the record definition.

```
SELECT DISTINCT CONTNAME
  , DESCR
  FROM PSCONTDEFN
 WHERE CONTTYPE = 1
```

With the fields and prompt tables defined, we can now create the repository's tables. Define the fields and key structure for the repository's header record, named `APT_TOOL_DEFN`, as shown in Figure 8-4. Create the `APT_TOOL_DEFN` record definition's prompt table as shown in Figure 8-5.

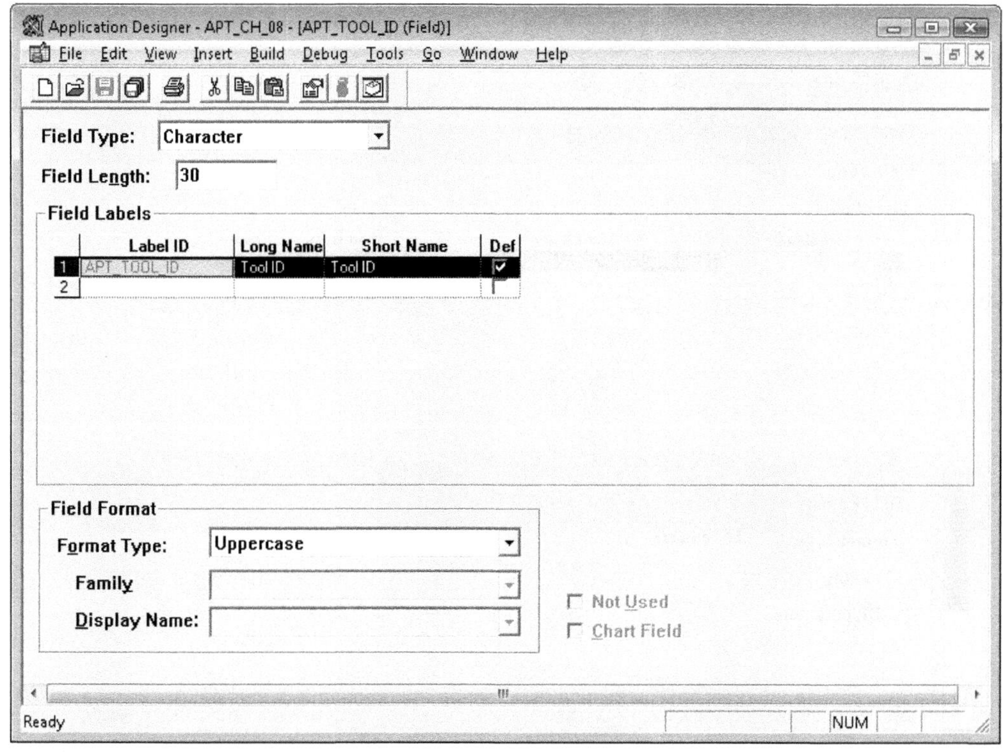

FIGURE 8-1. *APT_TOOL_ID field definition*

Each toolbar button will have a collection of permission lists to define the button's access. Figure 8-6 describes the field and key structure of the permission list detail record named `APT_TOOL_PERMS`, and Figure 8-7 shows the prompt table properties for this record. After defining these fields and record definitions, build your project.

Later, we will write an iScript to serve the toolbar's button metadata. Now let's create an SQL statement to select buttons based on the current user's permission lists. Add the following SQL to a new SQL definition and save it as `APT_TOOLBAR_BUTTONS`.

```
SELECT TOOL.APT_TOOL_ID
  , TOOL.APT_TOOLTIP
  , TOOL.IMAGE_NAME
  , TOOL.HTMLAREA
  FROM PS_APT_TOOL_DEFN TOOL
 WHERE EXISTS (
SELECT 'X'
  FROM PS_APT_TOOL_PERMS PERMS
 INNER JOIN PSUSERCLASSVW PL
    ON PERMS.CLASSID = PL.CLASSID
 WHERE PL.OPRID = :1
   AND PERMS.APT_TOOL_ID = TOOL.APT_TOOL_ID)
```

Application Designer - APT_CH_08 - [APT_TOOLTIP (Field)]
File Edit View Insert Build Debug Tools Go Window Help
Field Type: Character
Field Length: 50
Field Labels

	Label ID	Long Name	Short Name	Def
1	APT_TOOLTIP	Tooltip Text	Tooltip	✔
2				

Field Format
Format Type: Mixedcase
Family
Display Name:
Not Used
Chart Field
Ready
NUM

FIGURE 8-2. *APT_TOOLTIP field definition*

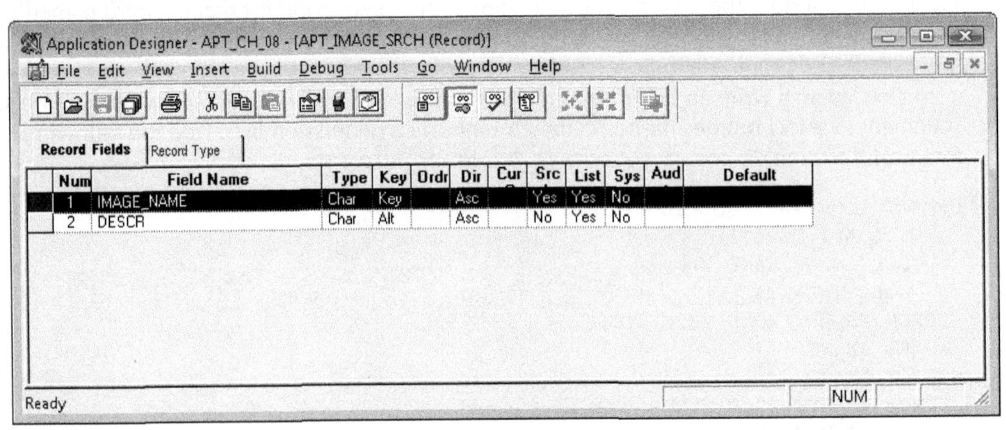

FIGURE 8-3. *APT_IMAGE_SRCH prompt table definition*

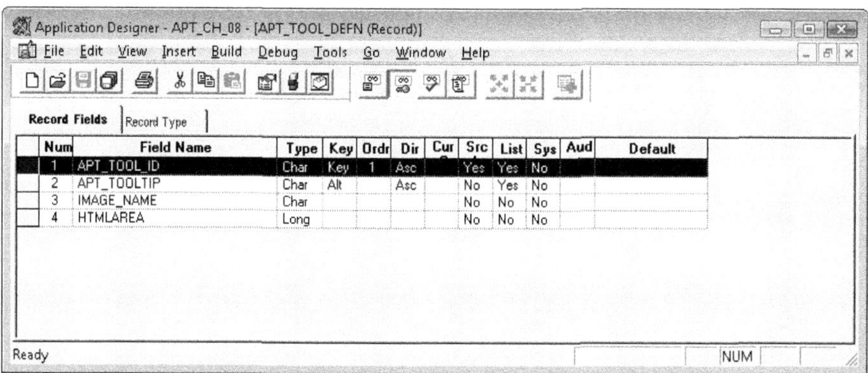

FIGURE 8-4. *APT_TOOL_DEFN field order and key structure*

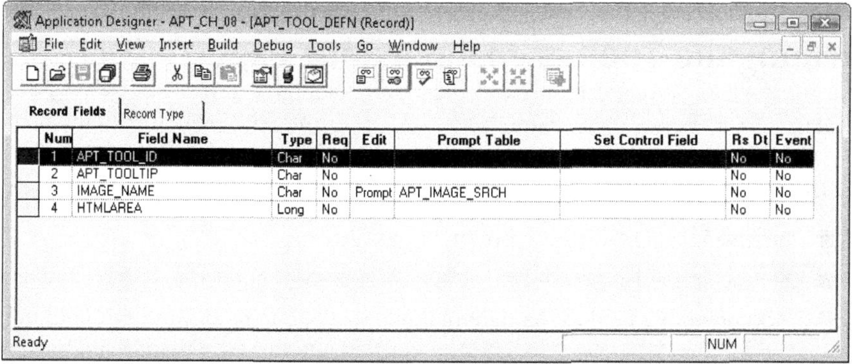

FIGURE 8-5. *APT_TOOL_DEFN prompt table properties*

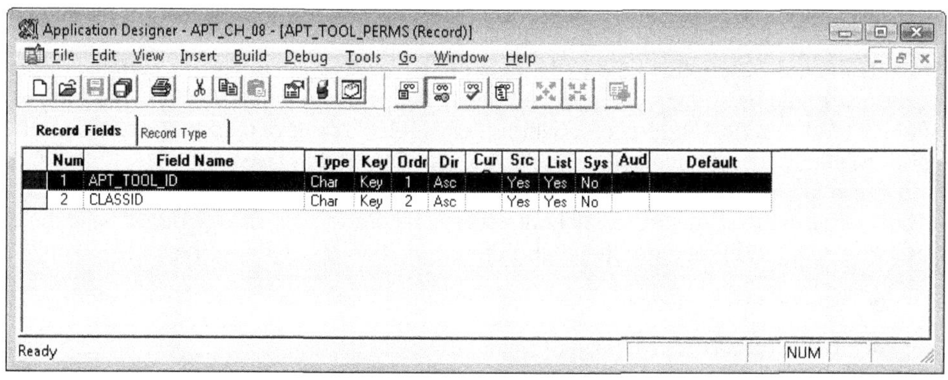

FIGURE 8-6. *APT_TOOL_PERMS fields and key structure*

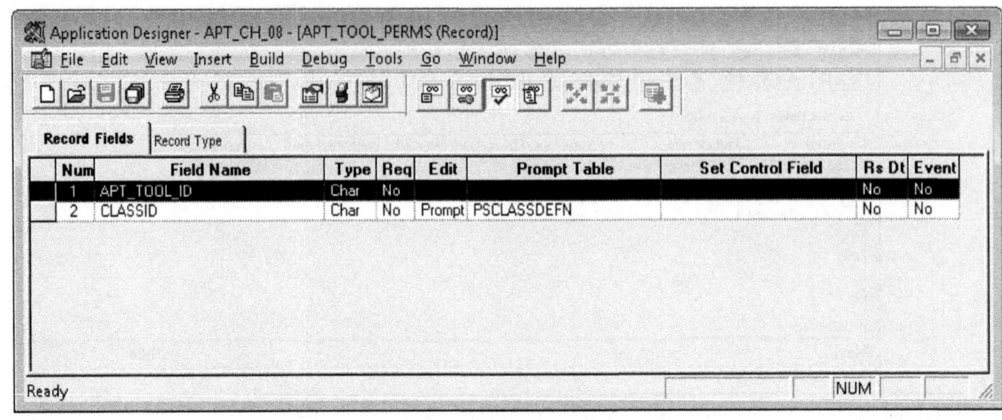

FIGURE 8-7. *APT_TOOL_PERMS fields prompt table properties*

Creating the Toolbar Maintenance Page

Now that we have a metadata repository, let's create a page and component to maintain that metadata. Create a new page, name it `APT_TOOL_DEFN`, and then add all the fields from record `APT_TOOL_DEFN` to this page. Lay out the fields as shown in Figure 8-8.

After positioning the fields, make the following field changes:

- Set the Tool ID field's use option to display-only.
- Set the Image Name field's size option to custom and make it a display control field.
- Add an empty field to the right of the Image Name field. Bind this field to the `DESCR` field of the `APT_IMAGES_SRCH` record. Relate this new field to the Image Name display control field.
- Edit the HTML Area field's label by setting the label type to text and the label text to **Tool Command**.

The Permission Lists grid in Figure 8-8 contains the `CLASSID` (permission list) field from `APT_TOOL_PERMS`. Open the `CLASSID` field's properties and make it a display control field. The Permission List Description field to the right of the Permission List field is a related display field. Create this field by adding an empty text box to the page, and then bind it to the `CLASSDEFNDESC` field of the `PSCLASSDEFN` record. Set this field's related control field to Permission List. For the grid, enable its display title and set the title text to **Permission Lists**.

Create a new component and add the `APT_TOOL_DEFN` page. Change the page's item label to **Tool Definition**, and set the component's search record to `APT_TOOL_DEFN`. Save the component as `APT_TOOL_DEFN` and use the Registration Wizard to register it, using the following values:

- Menu: `APT_CUSTOM`
- Bar: `CUSTOM`
- Portal: `EMPLOYEE`

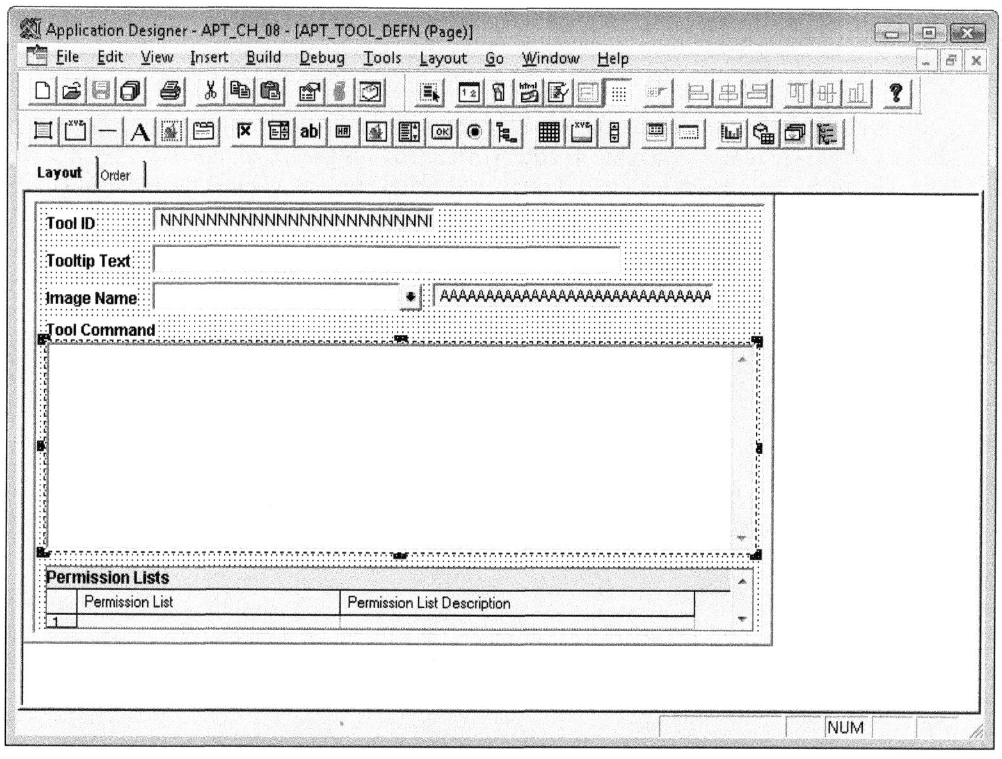

FIGURE 8-8. *APT_TOOL_DEFN page in App Designer*

- Folder: PT_ADMINISTRATION
- Content reference: `APT_TOOL_DEFN_GBL`
- Content reference label: **Toolbar Tools**
- Long description: **Toolbar tool definitions**
- Permission list: `APT_CUSTOM`

After registering the component, open the menu definition and set the `APT_TOOL_DEFN` menu item to Toolbar Tools.

Test this page online by navigating to PeopleTools | Utilities | Administration | Toolbar Tools. Add the new value `APT_SAY_HELLO`. When the page appears, set the Tooltip Text field to **Say hello tool** and the image name to `PS_ALT_DESCRIPTION_ICN`. Add the following code to the Tool Command edit field:

```
<script type="text/javascript">
  $(document).ready(function() {
    $("#APT_SAY_HELLO").click(function() {
```

```
      alert("Hello World!");
    });
  });
</script>
```

This code begins with the usual HTML script declaration. By designing this component to accept HTML, we make it possible to add HTML elements to a page. For example, a toolbar button may require a hidden `div` to display additional content when activated. Inside the `$(document).ready` event handler, we have the jQuery selector `#APT_SAY_HELLO`. Later, we will write an iScript that uses the tool ID as the toolbar button's HTML element ID. The call to `click` adds an HTML `onclick` event handler and binds it to the command `alert("Hello World!")`.

Add the permission list `APT_CUSTOM` to the Permission Lists grid, and then save the transaction. Figure 8-9 shows this page with the specified values.

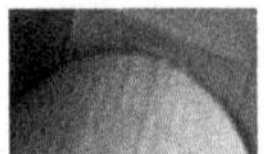

TIP
If you want to create a prompt page for the image field that shows images, not just names, take a look at the Navigation Collection component's image search page: `PTPP_SCIMGSRCH`.

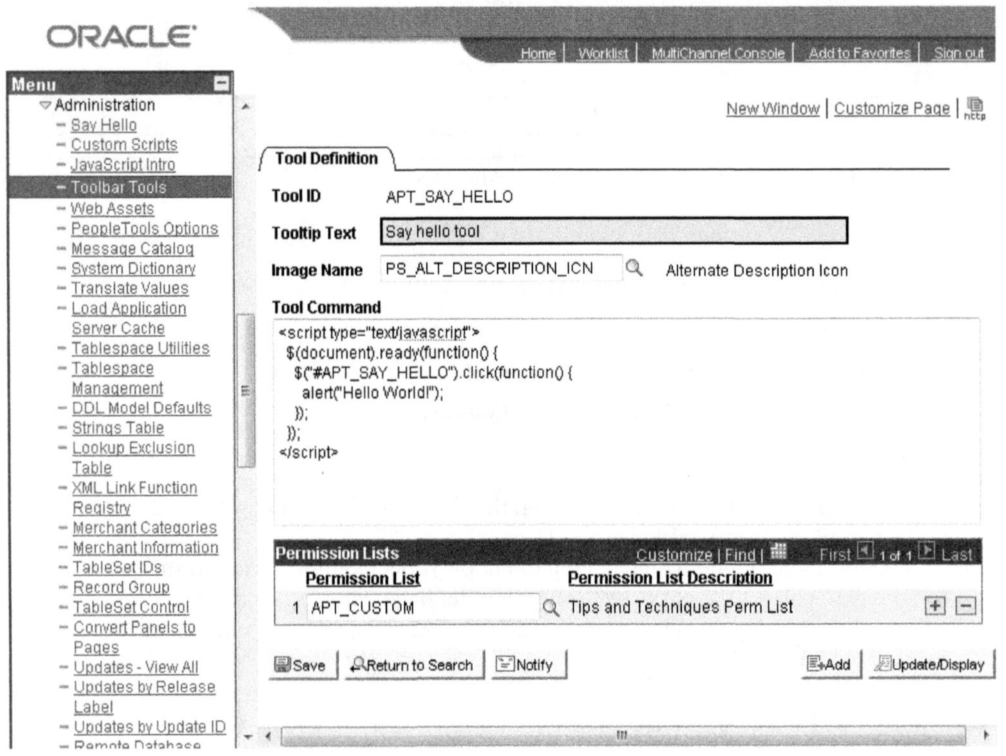

FIGURE 8-9. *APT_TOOL_DEFN page online*

Defining the Toolbar's HTML

The preceding metadata defined a single button. Before we show this button on a page, we need to define the button's toolbar. The toolbar's HTML is composed of a container HTML definition and a per-button HTML definition.

The following HTML describes the toolbar container:

```
<div id="APT_toolbar" class="container">
%Bind(:1)
</div>
<div style="clear: both;"/>
```

Save this HTML definition as APT_TOOLBAR.

The following code listing contains the code for the per-button HTML. Add this HTML to a new HTML definition and save it as APT_TOOLBAR_BUTTON.

```
<span id="%Bind(:1)"><img src="%Bind(:2)"
    alt="%Bind(:3)" title="%Bind(:3)"/>%Bind(:4)</span>
```

We will use CSS to make this HTML look like a toolbar with buttons. Create another HTML definition and add the following CSS:

```
#APT_Toolbar.container {
  background-color: #f0f0f0;
  border-style: solid none solid solid;
  border-color: #c0c0c0 #fff #c0c0c0 #c0c0c0;
  border-width: 1px 0px 1px 1px;
  float: left;
}

#APT_Toolbar.container span {
  float: left;
  padding: 1px;
  border-style: solid solid none solid;
  border-color: #fff #c0c0c0 #fff #fff;
  border-width: 1px 1px 0px 1px;
  padding: 1px;
  width: 16px;
  height: 16px;
  text-align: center;
  vertical-align: middle;
  cursor: pointer;
}
```

Save this definition as APT_TOOLBAR_CSS.

Next, define two iScripts: one to serve CSS and another to serve the button HTML. Open the FieldFormula event of the record field WEBLIB_APT_JSL ISCRIPT1. Add the following code to the end of this event:

```
Function IScript_ToolbarCss()
   %Response.SetContentType("text/css");
   %Response.Write(GetHTMLText(HTML.APT_TOOLBAR_CSS));
End-Function;
```

```
Function IScript_Toolbar()
   Local SQL &buttonCursor = GetSQL(SQL.APT_TOOLBAR_BUTTONS,
         %OperatorId);
   Local string &toolId;
   Local string &toolTip;
   Local string &imageName;
   Local string &toolCmd;

   Local string &imageUrl;
   Local array of string &buttons = CreateArrayRept("", 0);

   While &buttonCursor.Fetch(&toolId, &toolTip, &imageName, &toolCmd)
      &imageUrl = %Response.GetImageURL(@("Image." | &imageName));
      &buttons.Push(GetHTMLText(HTML.APT_TOOLBAR_BUTTON, &toolId,
            &imageUrl, &toolTip, &toolCmd));
   End-While;

   %Response.Write(GetHTMLText(HTML.APT_TOOLBAR,
         &buttons.Join("", "", "")));
End-Function;
```

The first function in this listing, `IScript_ToolbarCss`, looks similar to many of the other iScripts we have written. Its purpose is to serve an HTML definition as a CSS file. The second iScript, `IScript_Toolbar`, however, is a bit unique. This function selects the tools for the current user based on the user's permission lists, and then inserts the button's HTML into an array. At the end of the function, the code converts the array to a string, and then writes it to the client browser. Notice that this function uses the metadata SQL definition we created earlier, as well as the two HTML definitions we just created.

Attaching the Toolbar to Pages

We are now ready to attach this toolbar to our PeopleSoft pages. We will use the Custom Scripts component from Chapter 7 to attach this toolbar to every PeopleSoft page. Then we will add another button to the toolbar.

Defining a Custom Script for the Toolbar

Log in to your PeopleSoft application online and navigate to PeopleTools | Utilities | Administration | Custom Scripts. Add the new value `APT_TOOLBAR` and define a new custom script. Leave all the main header fields blank and set the search page behavior to Not search. Add the following code in the HTML Area edit box:

```
<script type="text/javascript">
  apt.files.importStylesheet(apt.files.generateScriptContentUrl({
          record: "WEBLIB_APT_JSL",
          field:  "ISCRIPT1",
          event:  "FieldFormula",
          script: "IScript_ToolbarCss"})
    );
```

```
  $(document).ready(function() {
    var url = apt.files.generateScriptContentUrl({
          record: "WEBLIB_APT_JSL",
          field:  "ISCRIPT1",
          event:  "FieldFormula",
          script: "IScript_Toolbar"});
    $.get(url, function(data){
        $("#PAGEBAR TD:first").append(data);
    });
  });
</script>
```

Figure 8-10 shows this custom script definition.

Once you save the new custom script, your browser will automatically download the new toolbar. In the upper-left corner of the page in Figure 8-10, you can see the new toolbar with one button. Clicking the toolbar button displays a message box, as shown in Figure 8-11.

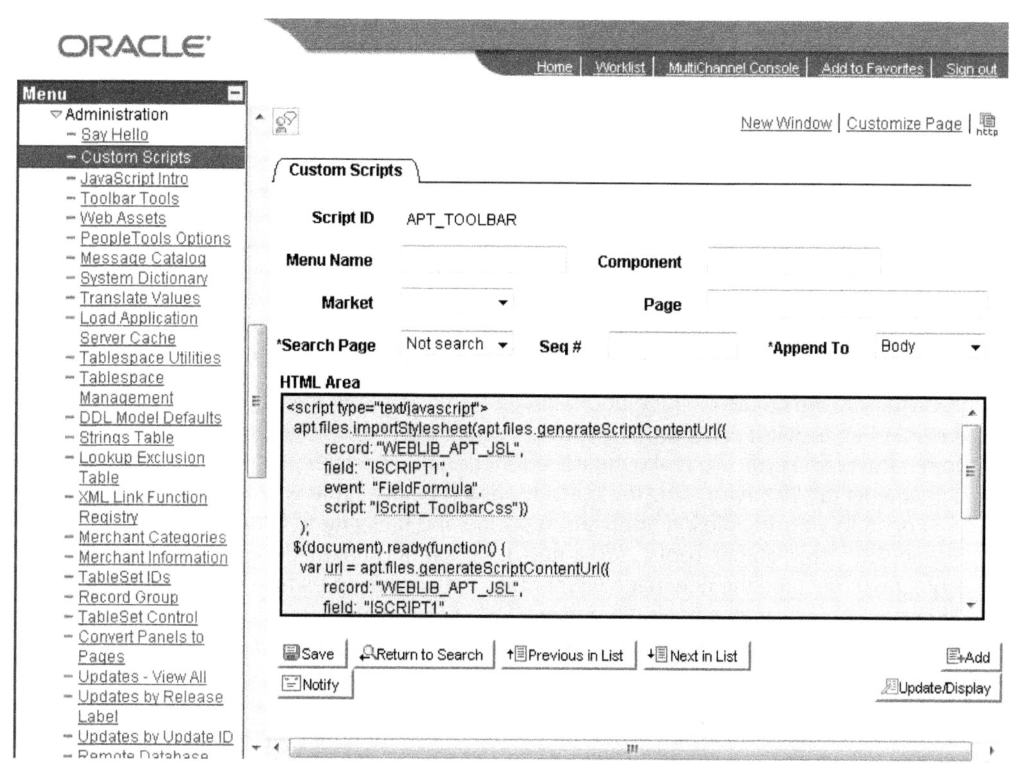

FIGURE 8-10. *APT_TOOLBAR custom script*

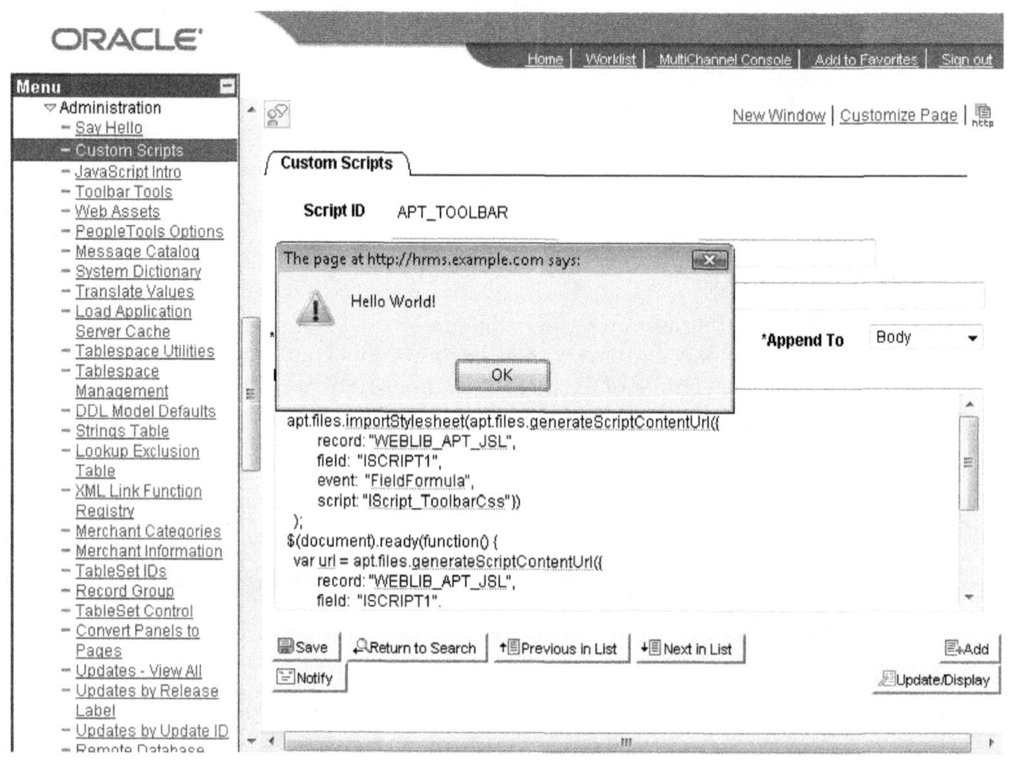

FIGURE 8-11. *APT_SAY_HELLO button in action*

Adding the Trace Toolbar Button

In Chapter 5, we created a trace bookmarklet to turn on SQL tracing. One drawback of a bookmarklet is that it exists only in your computer's web browser. Unfortunately, bookmarklets do not travel with you. To make the trace functionality portable, let's create a toolbar button that implements this behavior. This toolbar button will be available wherever you run PeopleSoft.

Log in to your PeopleSoft application online and navigate to PeopleTools | Utilities | Administration | Toolbar Tools. Add a new tool definition named `APT_TRACE_SQL`. Since the tool ID will become the new page element ID, I recommend using a site-specific prefix. As with all custom objects in this book, I am using `APT`. Set the tooltip text to **Trace SQL** and choose the `PT_APP_REVIEWER_ICN` image. This is a 16-by-16 image of a pair of glasses. (I chose the glasses because we use a trace file to *look* into a process.)

The following code defines our toolbar button's action. First, the JavaScript waits until the document is loaded, and then binds an `onclick` handler to the button. Add this code in the Tool Command edit box:

```
<script type="text/javascript">
  $(document).ready(function(){
    $("#APT_TRACE_SQL").click(function() {
```

```
      var url = apt.files.generateScriptContentUrl({
          record: "WEBLIB_APT_DBG",
          field:  "ISCRIPT1",
          event:  "FieldFormula",
          script: "IScript_SetSQLTrace"});

      window.open(url + "?level=7", "pstrace",
          "height=100,width=140,menubar=no,location=no," +
          "resizable=no,scrollbars=no,status=no");
    });
  });
</script>
```

Add the permission list APT_CUSTOM to the Permission Lists grid at the bottom of the page, and then save this new definition, which is shown in Figure 8-12. As you can see in the figure, our toolbar now has a second button. Clicking this button opens the new trace window you saw in Chapter 5.

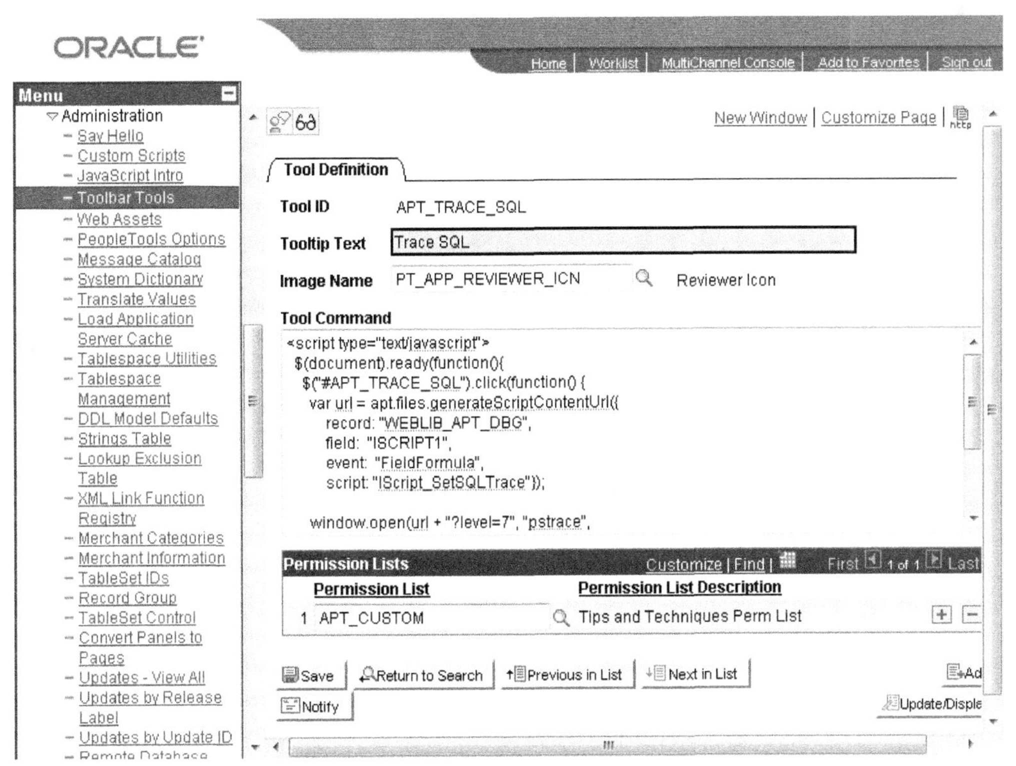

FIGURE 8-12. *APT_TRACE_SQL tool definition*

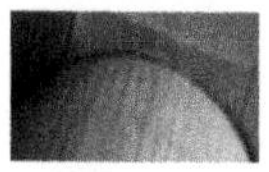

NOTE
How do you know which permission list to choose? When you create toolbar buttons, choose permission lists that are required to execute the functions/features targeted by the button. The code for the trace tool button calls an iScript that is secured by the `APT_CUSTOM` *permission list. Therefore, in order for the toolbar button to work correctly, the user must have the permissions provided by that permission list.*

Modifying the Bootstrap Code

In Chapter 6, we wrote a `generateScriptContentUrl` function to create iScript URLs. Later in this chapter, we will use a similar approach to generate component and query URLs. Since the code for each generate function is relatively similar, we will implement the component and query functions by modifying the `generateScriptContentUrl` function so that all three functions share similar base code.

Separating Common Code from Bootstrap Code

The `generateScriptContentUrl` function is located in our bootstrap code. Our bootstrap code is already nearly 100 lines long. Looking at the code, you can see several functions that seem more like library functions than bootstrap code. The intent is to write as little code as possible to load our customizations. Let's see if we can shrink the bootstrap code back down to ten lines and load the additional lines as a library. This will make our modification (`PT_COPYURL`) easier to manage by reducing our modification footprint.

Reset `PT_COPYURL` to its original state by copying our customization into a new HTML definition named `APT_COMMON_LIB_JS`. The customized code starts with this line:

```
//% APT_CH_06, JavaScript global mod Bootstrap code follows
```

With `PT_COPYURL` reset to its original state, add the following code to the end of the `PT_COPYURL` HTML definition:

```
//% APT_CH_08, JavaScript global mod Bootstrap code follows
(function(path) {
  var buffer = path.match(
      /ps[pc]\/(.+?)(?:_\d)*?\/(.+?)\/(.+?)\//
    );
  var url = "/psc/" + buffer[1] + "/" + buffer[2] + "/" +
      buffer[3] +
      "/s/WEBLIB_APT_JSL.ISCRIPT1.FieldFormula.IScript_CommonLib";
  document.write("<scr" + "ipt id='APT_common_lib' " +
      "type='text/javascript' src='" + url + "'><\/script>");
})(window.location.pathname);
```

We did it! These ten lines (well, ten lines plus one comment) contain just enough code to load our entire customization from an iScript. Some of the preceding code, such as the regular expression, is redundant to code contained in the common JavaScript library it imports. Even though this is a violation of the Don't Repeat Yourself (DRY) principle, it is worth repeating ourselves to reduce the modification footprint.

The preceding JavaScript references an iScript named IScript_CommonLib, which does not exist yet. We will need to create it before testing our work online. To create the iScript, open the FieldFormula event of the record field WEBLIB_APT_JSL ISCRIPT1 and add the following PeopleCode:

```
Function IScript_CommonLib()
   %Response.SetContentType("text/javascript");
   %Response.Write(GetHTMLText(HTML.APT_COMMON_LIB_JS));
End-Function;
```

Be sure to add this new iScript to the APT_CUSTOM permission list. Next, ensure that your common code continues to function properly by logging in to PeopleSoft through your web browser and navigating to PeopleTools | Utilities | Administration | Custom Scripts. On the Basic Search page, the active data-entry field should have a green background. Switching to the Advanced Search tab, you should see the menu search operator change from "begins with" to "between."

Adding New URL-Generation Functions

With our common library code separated from the delivered PT_COPYURL HTML definition, let's define the generateComponentContentUrl and generateQueryContentUrl functions. While we are at it, let's enhance the generateScriptContentUrl function. Here, we'll look at the code for these functions. The full code listing is presented in the next section.

The following code provides the declaration for these functions:

```
apt.files.generateScriptContentUrl = function(options, data)
apt.files.generateComponentContentUrl = function(options, data)
apt.files.generateQueryContentUrl = function(options, binds)
```

Each of these functions requires two parameters. The first parameter is an object named options that contains function-specific properties, as well as some properties that are common to all three generation functions. The following code listing contains examples of the options object for each of the three URL-generation functions:

```
// generateScriptContentUrl option parameter
{
  record: "WEBLIB_APT_JSL",
  field:  "ISCRIPT1",
  event:  "FieldFormula",
  script: "IScript_jQuery"
}

// generateComponentContentUrl option parameter
{
  menu:      "APT_CUSTOM",
  component: "APT_TOOL_DEFN",
  market:    "GBL",
  page:      "APT_TOOL_DEFN", /* optional */
  action:    "U"              /* optional */
}
/* NOTE: see the PeopleBooks GenerateComponentContentURL function for
```

```
 * a list of valid values for the action property.
 */

// generateQueryContentUrl option parameter
{
  query:     "PT_SEC_PLIST_CREF",
  isPublic: true
}
```

For each of these functions, the `options` object may contain an additional `isNewWindow` property. If set to `true`, the URL-generation function will return a URL that causes the application server to create a separate state block for transactions occurring on that new URL. This is similar to clicking the New Window link in a standard component.

NOTE
We could further extend the `options` object to allow for portal and node parameters. For our purposes, however, we are working in only a single node and portal, so we will avoid cluttering our code with these optional parameters. You can implement them later if necessary.

The second parameter of each generation function provides a convenience mechanism for generating URL query strings. The `generateScriptContentUrl data` parameter is an optional object that contains key/value pairs, with the property name representing the key. The `generateComponentContentUrl` data parameter is similar. Use it to specify search keys and values when generating a component URL to open a specific transaction, bypassing the component's search page. The `generateQueryContentUrl` function differs in that it doesn't require key/value pairs. It requires only bind variable values. Therefore, rather than pass an object to this function, you specify bind variable values as items in an array. The following code listing demonstrates how to create data parameters for each of these functions.

```
// generateScriptContentUrl data parameter
{EMPLID: "KU0001"}

// generateComponentContentUrl data parameter
{APT_TOOL_ID: "APT_SAY_HELLO"}

// generateQueryContentUrl data parameter
["APT_CUSTOM", "EMPLOYEE"]
```

Notice that the first two declarations in this code use JavaScript object definition syntax, whereas the third uses array definition syntax.

Writing the New Common Code

The `generateScriptContentUrl` function we wrote in Chapter 6 used a JavaScript closure to parse the current URL once, and then save the URL's segments for reuse on each call to `generateScriptContentUrl`. We want to follow a similar approach, but make those values available to all the generate functions. This will require us to move the closure from the function definition to the `apt.files` object definition. Then, any function defined inside the object definition will be able to share values by retaining pointers to the object's variables.

The following code listing contains a rewrite of the `apt.files` namespace. Since the generate functions share similar logic, the `apt.files` namespace (or object) begins by declaring several helper methods that only members of the `apt.files` namespace can access (private methods) and finishes by declaring a handful of public methods. The following code listing is a full rewrite of the `APT_COMMON_LIB_JS` HTML definition. I recommend deleting the existing code in `APT_COMMON_LIB_JS` prior to inserting this new code.

```
// create our global object if it doesn't exist
if(!window.apt) {
  apt = {
    namespace: {
      create: function (ns) {
        var arr = ns.split(".");
        var level = window;
        var item;

        while (item = arr.shift()) {
          if(!level[item]) {
            level[item] = {};
          }
          // Move to the next level in the namespace
          level = level[item];
        }
      }
    }
  }

  /* !! Chapter 8 changes begin here !! */
  apt.files = (function() {
    // Perform common processing first, and then use a closure to
    // store pointers to the results.
    var buffer = window.location.pathname.match(
        /ps[pc]\/(.+?)(?:_\d)*?\/(.+?)\/(.+?)\//);

    /* ** initialize private fields ** */
    // generate base URL for current request
    var baseUrl = "/psc/" + buffer[1] + "/" + buffer[2] + "/" +
        buffer[3];

    // generate base URL for new window request
    var baseUrlNew = "/psc/" + buffer[1] + "_newwin" + "/" +
        buffer[2] + "/" + buffer[3];

    /* ** private methods ** */
    // determine if obj is an array
    // see http://bit.ly/1Mo5
```

```
function isArray(obj) {
  return (Object.prototype.toString.call(obj) ===
      "[object Array]");
}

// Each generate method has an isNewWindow option. The
// generate method calls getBaseUrl to determine the correct
// base URL given the caller's options.
function getBaseUrl(options) {
  return (options.isNewWindow) ? baseUrlNew : baseUrl
}

// Convert a data object into a query string and append each
// item to arr array
function dataToString(arr, data) {
  if(!isArray(arr)) {
    // shift args; fn called with data in arr location
    data = arr;
    arr = [];
  }

  if(data) {
    for (var key in data) {
      arr.push(encodeURIComponent(key) + '=' +
          encodeURIComponent(data[key]));
    }
  }
  return arr;
}

// Create a URL query string by joining arr with "&" separator
// and prefixing with "?"
function toQueryString(arr) {
  if(arr.length > 0) {
    return "?" + arr.join("&");
  } else {
    return "";
  }
}

/* ** public methods are inside this closure **/

/* Each of the following generate methods follows the same
 * pattern.
 *
 * Each has its own set of parameters (record, field, menu, etc).
 *
 * Each includes options.isNewWindow to get app server to generate
 * a new state block.
 *
```

```
 * Each includes a data parameter that is either an array or a
 * key/value object.
 *
 */
return {
  /* function: generateIScriptContentUrl
   * parameter: object containing the following properties:
   *   record, field, event, IScript_function
   * example:
   *   apt.files.generateScriptContentUrl({
   *       record: "WEBLIB_APT_JSL",
   *       field:  "ISCRIPT1",
   *       event:  "FieldFormula",
   *       script: "IScript_jQuery"});
   */
  generateScriptContentUrl: function(options, data) {
    return getBaseUrl(options) + "/s/" +
        options.record + "." + options.field + "." +
        options.event + "." + options.script +
        toQueryString(dataToString(data));
  },
  /* function: generateComponentContentUrl
   * parameter: object containing the following properties:
   *   menu, component, market, page (optional),
   *   action (optional)
   * example:
   *   apt.files.generateComponentContentUrl({
   *       menu:      "APT_CUSTOM",
   *       component: "APT_TOOL_DEFN",
   *       market:    "GBL"});
   */
  generateComponentContentUrl: function(options, data) {
    var url = getBaseUrl(options) + "/c/" +
        options.menu + "." + options.component + "." +
        options.market;
    var qsArray = [];

    if(options.page) {
      qsArray.push("Page=" + options.page);
    }

    if(options.action) {
      qsArray.push("Action=" + options.action);
    }

    return url + toQueryString(dataToString(qsArray, data));
  },
  /* function: generateQueryContentUrl
   * parameter: object containing the following properties:
```

```
     *   query, isPublic
     * example:
     *   apt.files.generateQueryContentUrl({
     *          isPublic: true,
     *          isNewWindow: true,
     *          query: "PT_SEC_PLIST_PAGES"
     *        },
     *        ["APT_CUSTOM"]);
     */
    generateQueryContentUrl: function(options, binds) {
      var visibility = (options.isPublic) ? "PUBLIC" : "PRIVATE";
      var url = getBaseUrl(options) +
          "/q/?ICAction=ICQryNameURL=" +
          visibility + "." + options.query

      if(binds) {
        for (var idx = 0; idx < binds.length; idx++) {
          url += "&BIND" + (idx+1) + "=" + binds[idx];
        }
      }

      return url;
    },
    /* function: importScript
     * parameters: object with the following properties:
     *   id, url
     * example:
     *   apt.files.importScript({id: "jq",
     *       url: "/url/to/javascript/file"});
     */
    importScript: function(parms) {
      document.write("<scr" + "ipt id='" + parms.id + "' " +
          "type='text/javascript' src='" + parms.url +
          "'><\/script>");
    },
    /* function: importStylesheet
     * parameters:
     *   url
     * example:
     *   apt.files.importStylesheet("/url/to/css/file"});
     */
    importStylesheet: function (url) {
      var ss = document.createElement("link");
      ss.rel = "stylesheet";
      ss.type = "text/css";
      ss.href = url;
      document.getElementsByTagName("head")[0].appendChild(ss);
    }
  };
})();
```

```
  /* !! Chapter 8 changes end here !! */
}

//% import scripts
if(!window.jQuery) {
  apt.files.importScript({
      id:  "jq",
      url: apt.files.generateScriptContentUrl({
          record: "WEBLIB_APT_JSL",
          field:  "ISCRIPT1",
          event:  "FieldFormula",
          script: "IScript_jQuery"})
  });
}

// import JSON parser if no native support
if (!window.JSON) {
  // Native JSON not available, so import it
  apt.files.importScript({
      id:  "json2",
      url: apt.files.generateScriptContentUrl({
          record: "WEBLIB_APT_JSL",
          field:  "ISCRIPT1",
          event:  "FieldFormula",
          script: "IScript_JSON2"})
  });
}

// import AJAX customization to force JSON parsing
apt.files.importScript({
    id:  "apt_ajax",
    url: apt.files.generateScriptContentUrl({
        record: "WEBLIB_APT_JSL",
        field:  "ISCRIPT1",
        event:  "FieldFormula",
        script: "IScript_Ajax"
    })
});

// import Custom Scripts module code
apt.files.importScript({
    id:  "apt_ui_loader",
    url: apt.files.generateScriptContentUrl({
        record: "WEBLIB_APT_JSL",
        field:  "ISCRIPT1",
        event:  "FieldFormula",
        script: "IScript_UILoader"
    })
});
```

```
/* Redefine import function after load. This importScript function
 * uses DOM rather than document.write. The document.write approach
 * does not work after the HTML document is loaded. We can't use the
 * DOM approach, however, before the DOM is loaded. Therefore, we
 * must have two importScript functions: one for preload and one for
 * post load.
 */
apt.files.importScript = function(parms) {
  var s = document.createElement("script");
  s.type = "text/javascript";
  s.src = parms.url;
  s.id = parms.id;
  s.defer = (parms.defer) ? parms.defer : false;
  document.getElementsByTagName("head")[0].appendChild(s);
}
```

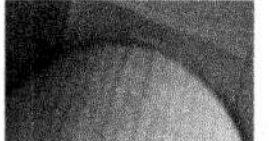

NOTE

Depending on your PeopleTools release, the size of the preceding code may be dangerously close to the maximum length of an HTML definition. Most of that space, fortunately, is formatting that exists to make the code easier to read and can be removed by a minification program. To that end, I included a minified copy of this file, named `bootstrap.min.js`, with the Chapter 8 source code.

Launching Another Component

The PeopleTools folder contains several tools that are useful within the context of a given component. For example, the portal registry contains display attributes for a PeopleSoft component. It would be helpful to be able to open a component's portal registry definition (known as a content reference, or CREF) directly from a component. Using our new toolbar module, we can create a toolbar button to open the CREF. Using the jQuery Thickbox plug-in, we can show the portal registry entry in context within the current component.

Creating an iScript to Get CREF Information

To open a specific component in the portal registry, we need to specify certain key values in the URL used to access the portal registry. Specifically, we need to specify the current component's CREF name and parent folder name. Unfortunately, these values are not available within the component's HTML. We can, however, derive them with PeopleCode in an iScript. Using AJAX, we can acquire this information from the iScript without disturbing the user. We can then parse the iScript's response and open the portal registry component.

Rather than hard-code the JSON markup in our PeopleCode, create an HTML definition named APT_HTML_CREF_EDIT_ATTRS_JSON and add the following JSON template:

```
{"name": "%Bind(:1)", "parent": "%Bind(:2)"}
```

The following code uses the portal registry PeopleCode classes to determine the CREF name and parent name given a component's URL:

```
Function IScript_GetCrefEditAttrs()
   Local string &url = %Request.GetParameter("url");
   Local ApiObject &portal = %Session.GetPortalRegistry();
   Local ApiObject &cref;

   &portal.Open(%Portal);
   &cref = &portal.FindCRefByURL(&url);

   %Response.SetContentType("application/json");
   If (All(&cref)) Then
      %Response.Write(GetHTMLText(HTML.APT_HTML_CREF_EDIT_ATTRS_JSON,
            &cref.name, &cref.parentname));
   End-If;

   &portal.Close();
End-Function;
```

So that we can call this code from JavaScript, create a new derived/work record and add the field `ISCRIPT1`. Save the record as `WEBLIB_APT_TOOL`. Open the `ISCRIPT1 FieldFormula` event and add the preceding code. Save this record and add it to the Web Library section of the `APT_CUSTOM` permission list. You can test this iScript by calling this URL:

http://hrms.example.com/psc/hrms/EMPLOYEE/HRMS/s/WEBLIB_APT_TOOL.ISCRIPT1.FieldFormula.IScript_GetCrefEditAttrs?url=http%3A%2F%2Fhrms.example.com%2Fpsp%2Fhrms%2FEMPLOYEE%2FHRMS%2Fc%2FMAINTAIN_SECURITY.ACCESS_CNTRL_LISTX.GBL

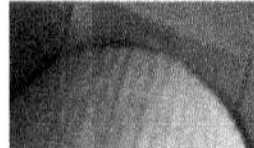

NOTE
The query string `url` parameter in this URL is a fully qualified component URL encoded to hide the special HTTP characters embedded within the URL. When we generate this URL from JavaScript, our AJAX library will automatically encode this parameter.

Calling this URL should return contents similar to the following:

```
{"name": "PT_ACCESS_CNTRL_LISTX_GBL", "parent": "PT_PERMISSIONS_ROLES"}
```

Adding the Edit CREF Toolbar Button

Now we can create a toolbar button that calls the iScript we just created and then opens the appropriate component portal registry entry. Within your browser, navigate to PeopleTools | Utilities | Administration | Toolbar Tools and add the new value `APT_EDIT_CREF`. Set the tooltip text to **Open CREF for editing** and the image to `PTTREE_EDITDATA`. Add the following JavaScript in the Tool Command edit box:

```
<script type="text/javascript">
  /* ** Import dependencies ** */
  // import thickbox... only if not already loaded
  if(!window.tb_show) {
    apt.files.importScript({
```

```
        id:  "apt_ui_tb",
        url: apt.files.generateScriptContentUrl({
            record: "WEBLIB_APT_JSL",
            field:  "ISCRIPT1",
            event:  "FieldFormula",
            script: "IScript_JqThickboxJs"
        })
    });

    apt.files.importStylesheet(
        apt.files.generateScriptContentUrl({
            record: "WEBLIB_APT_JSL",
            field:  "ISCRIPT1",
            event:  "FieldFormula",
            script: "IScript_JqThickboxCss"
        })
    );
}

// bind toolbar button
$(document).ready(function() {
  $("#APT_EDIT_CREF").click(function() {
    var compUrl = location.protocol + "//" + location.host;
    if(location.port) {
      compUrl += ":" + location.port;
    }
    compUrl += location.pathname;
    var serviceUrl = apt.files.generateScriptContentUrl({
        record: "WEBLIB_APT_TOOL",
        field:  "ISCRIPT1",
        event:  "FieldFormula",
        script: "IScript_GetCrefEditAttrs"});

    var options = {
      url: serviceUrl,
      data: {url: compUrl},
      dataType: "text",
      success: function(data, status) {
        var editUrl = apt.files.generateComponentContentUrl({
              isNewWindow: true,
              menu:      "PORTAL_ADMIN",
              component: "PORTAL_CREF_ADM",
              market:    "GBL",
              action:    "C"
            }, {
              PORTALPARAM_PNAME: data.parent,
              PORTALPARAM_CNAME: data.name
            });
        tb_show('Edit Content Reference',
            editUrl + '&TB_iframe=true&height=400&width=600',
            false);
```

```
        }
      };

      apt.ajax.getJSON(options);
    })
  });
</script>
```

This code imports the jQuery Thickbox plug-in, and then binds some JavaScript to the `onclick` event of the `APT_EDIT_CREF` toolbar button. When clicked, this button's JavaScript calls `IScript_GetCrefEditAttrs` to determine the current component's CREF name and parent folder name. It then generates a URL for the portal registry and opens that URL in Thickbox.

The `generateComponentContentUrl` function call in this listing uses the optional `isNewWindow` parameter to generate a new application server state block. This will generate a URL that is similar to the URL used by the New Window hyperlink. Generating a new state block allows a user to have two separate components open at the same time.

Finish the toolbar button definition by adding the permission list `PTPT1300`. This permission list identifies users with access to the portal registry. Figure 8-13 shows this tool's metadata.

After saving the tool definition, a new toolbar button with a pencil icon will appear in your custom toolbar. Clicking that button will open the portal registry entry for the current component (Toolbar Tools in this case). Figure 8-14 shows the portal registry entry open with the toolbar button definition in the background.

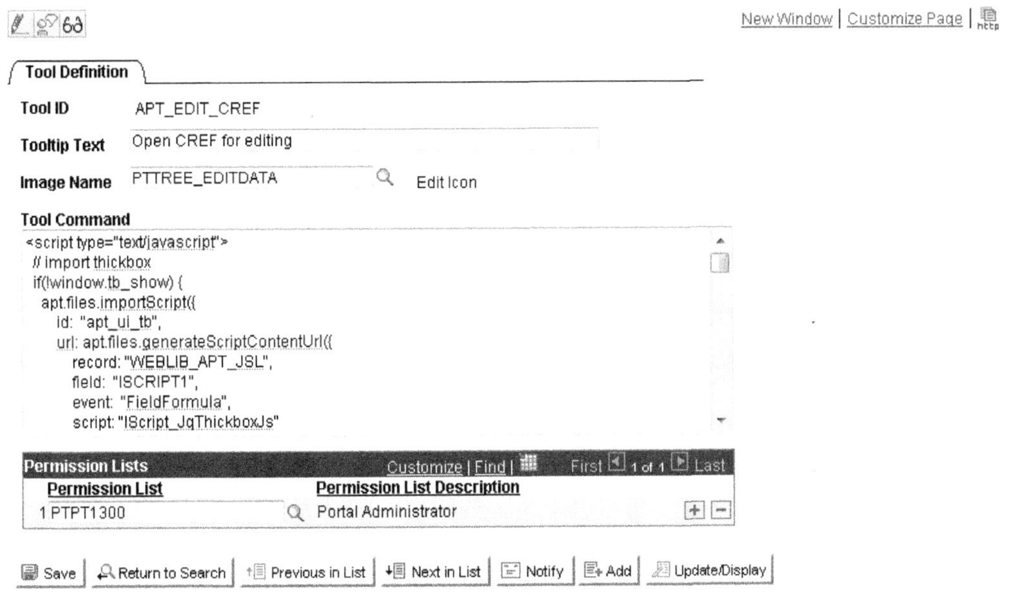

FIGURE 8-13. *APT_EDIT_CREF tool metadata*

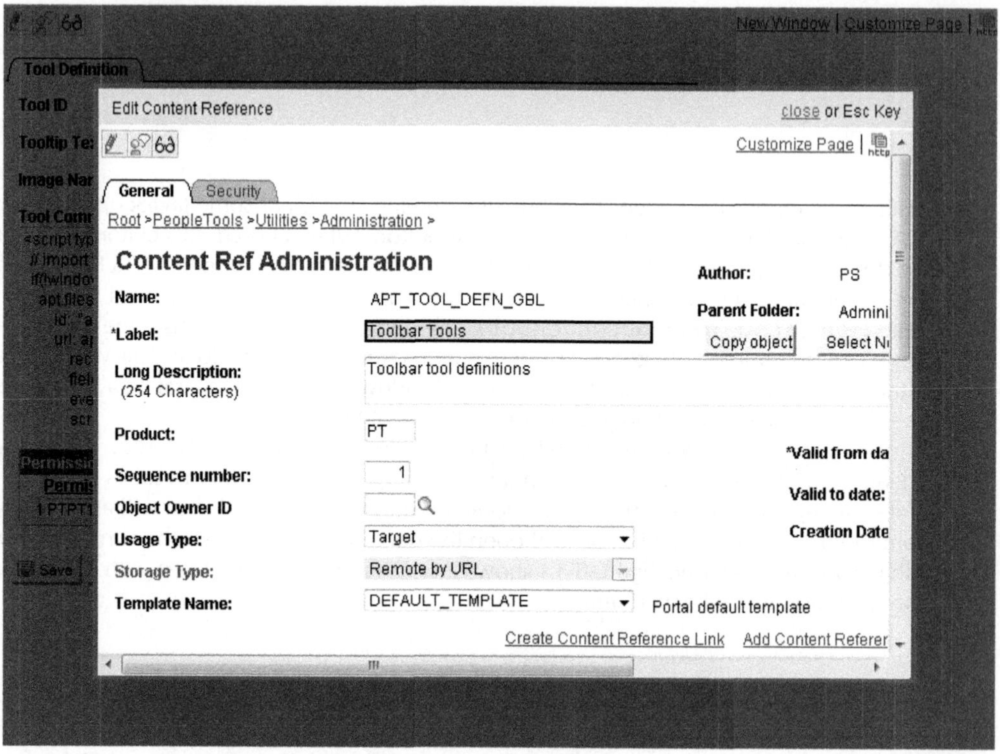

FIGURE 8-14. *Portal registry editor open in Thickbox*

Viewing Query Results

While queries aren't necessarily tools, they do provide valuable information about a given component or transaction.

From the PeopleTools Permission List component, we can run queries that show pages and components for which the permission list provides access. Let's reverse that. We will create a query that shows which permission lists provide access to the given component, and add a button to our toolbar to run that query.

Creating a Query to Get a Page's Permission Lists

Navigate to Reporting Tools | Query | Query Manager and create a new query. Define the query so that it contains SQL similar to the following:

```
SELECT A.CLASSID, A.CLASSDEFNDESC
  FROM PSCLASSDEFN A, PSPRSMDEFN B, PSPRSMPERM C
  WHERE B.PORTAL_NAME = C.PORTAL_NAME
     AND B.PORTAL_REFTYPE = C.PORTAL_REFTYPE
     AND B.PORTAL_OBJNAME = C.PORTAL_OBJNAME
     AND A.CLASSID = C.PORTAL_PERMNAME
```

```
AND B.PORTAL_REFTYPE = 'C'
AND B.PORTAL_URI_SEG1 = :1
AND B.PORTAL_URI_SEG2 = :2
AND B.PORTAL_URI_SEG3 = :3
AND B.PORTAL_NAME = :4
AND B.PORTAL_CREF_USGT = 'TARG'
```

The order of the columns, records, and criteria is irrelevant (although the four bind variables must be in the order represented above). The four bind variables represent menu, component, market, and portal, in that order. Save the query as a public query and give it the name `APT_COMPONENT_PERMS`.

Adding the Query Toolbar Button

Now we can create a toolbar tool definition for this query. Navigate to PeopleTools | Utilities | Administration | Toolbar Tools and add the new value `APT_PL_QUERY`. Set the tooltip text to **Component's permission lists** and the image to `PT_QUERY_ADD_CRITERIA`. In the Tool Command edit box, add the following code:

```
<script type="text/javascript">
  // import thickbox if not already imported
  if(!window.tb_show) {
    apt.files.importScript({
        id:  "apt_ui_tb",
        url: apt.files.generateScriptContentUrl({
            record: "WEBLIB_APT_JSL",
            field:  "ISCRIPT1",
            event:  "FieldFormula",
            script: "IScript_JqThickboxJs"
        })
    });

    apt.files.importStylesheet(
        apt.files.generateScriptContentUrl({
            record: "WEBLIB_APT_JSL",
            field:  "ISCRIPT1",
            event:  "FieldFormula",
            script: "IScript_JqThickboxCss"
        })
    );
  }

  // bind toolbar button
  $(document).ready(function() {
    $("#APT_PL_QUERY").click(function() {
      var matches = window.location.pathname.match(
        /ps[pc]\/.+?(?:_\d)*?\/(.+?)\/.+?\/c\/(.+?)\.(.+?)\.(.+?)$/);
      var portal    = matches[1];
      var menu      = matches[2];
      var component = matches[3];
      var market    = matches[4];
```

```
        var url = apt.files.generateQueryContentUrl(
            {
              isNewWindow: true,
              isPublic:    true,
              query:       "APT_COMPONENT_PERMS"
            },
            [menu, component, market, portal]
          );

        tb_show('Permission Lists',
            url + '&TB_iframe=true&height=400&width=600',
            false);
    })
  });
</script>
```

This JavaScript is similar to the JavaScript we created for the other buttons. First, we import any dependencies, and then we bind some JavaScript to the toolbar button's `onclick` event.

Add the permission list `PTPT1100`, which identifies security administrators, and save the new definition. Now you will see a new toolbar button with a query filter icon (a funnel with a plus sign). Figure 8-15 shows this tool's metadata.

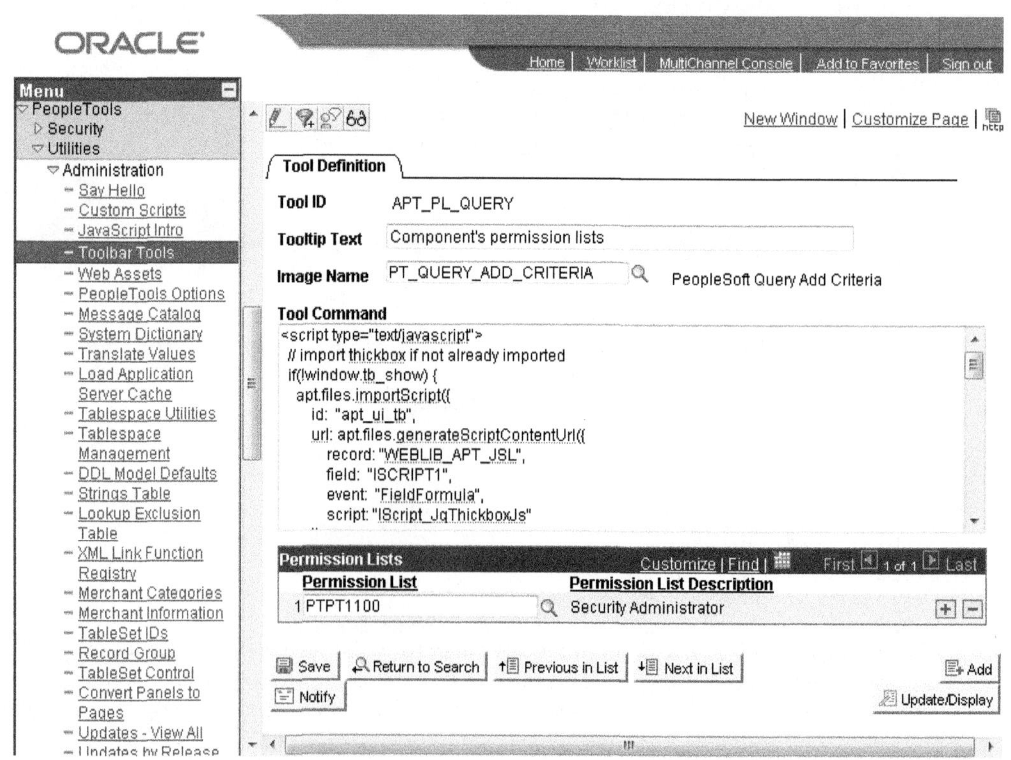

FIGURE 8-15. *APT_PL_QUERY toolbar button metadata*

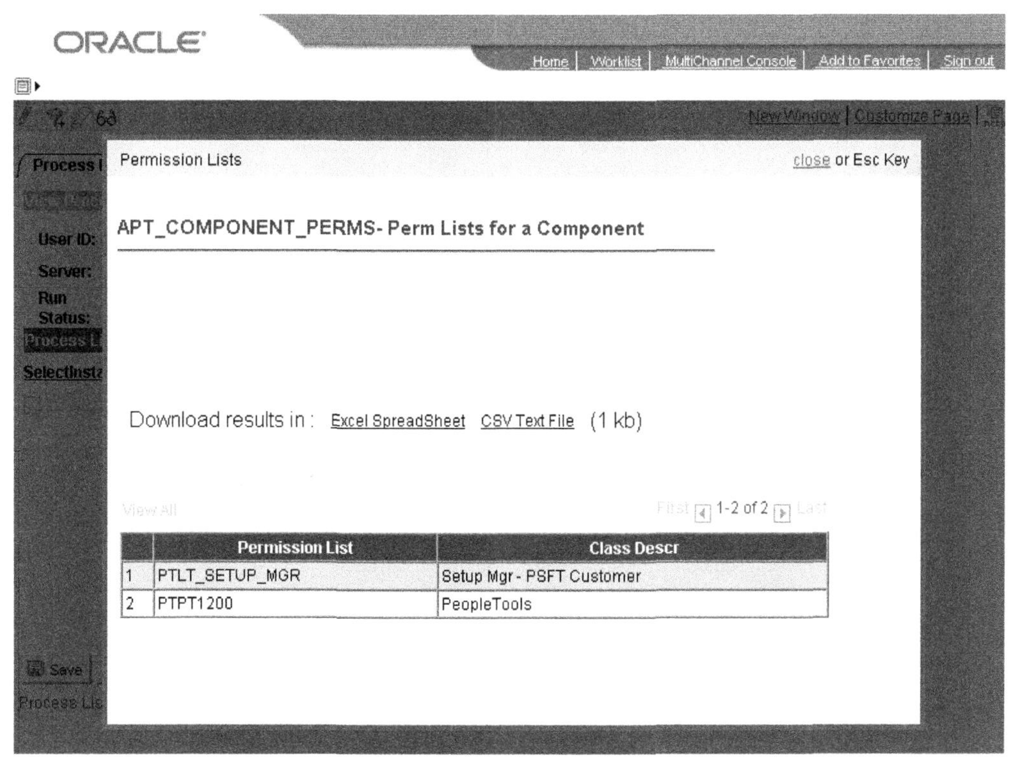

FIGURE 8-16. *Clicking the query toolbar button shows the Process Monitor permission lists.*

To test this button, navigate to PeopleTools | Process Scheduler | Process Monitor. On the Process Monitor page, click the query button. Your web browser should respond by opening the new permission list query in Thickbox, as shown in Figure 8-16.

The JavaScript Complement to PeopleCode Globals

The query toolbar button example uses a regular expression that should look vaguely familiar. The first half of the expression comes from our `apt.files` common library code. The result of this regular expression is an array containing elements that represent PeopleCode global variables. It parses the site, node, and portal elements of a component's URL. The regular expression is restated in the query example because the `apt.files` code in the `APT_COMMON_LIB_JS` HTML definition does not expose the results of the regular expression.

Rather than extracting these same variables multiple times or exposing them from the `apt.files` namespace, we can execute this regular expression early in our library code, and then reference the results just as we would if we were writing PeopleCode. For example, we could add the following JavaScript near the beginning of the APT_COMMON_LIB_JS HTML definition:

```
(function() {
  var matches = window.location.pathname.match(
    /ps[pc]\/(.+?)(?:_\d)*?\/(.+?)\/(.+?)\/c\/(.+?)\.(.+?)\.(.+?)$/);

  apt.sysVars = {
    site: matches[1],
    portal: matches[2],
    node: matches[3],
    menu: matches[4],
    component: matches[5],
    market: matches[6]
  }
})();
```

Using this code, if we want to reference the current component by name, we can use apt.sysVars.component, which is a JavaScript complement to the PeopleCode %Component variable.

The preceding apt.sysVars code suffers from one minor flaw that could have a significant impact. The code creates an object named apt.sysVars with six read/write properties. Since we don't want developers writing code that modifies the values of these properties, we should modify this code to make these properties read-only. Enter JavaScript closures.

Using a JavaScript closure, we can refactor this code to provide read-only accessors to privately scoped data:

```
apt.sysVars = (function(url) {
  var matches = url.match(
    /ps[pc]\/(.+?)(?:_\d)*?\/(.+?)\/(.+?)\/c\/(.+?)\.(.+?)\.(.+?)$/);
  return {
    getSite: function() {
      return matches[1];
    },
    getPortal: function() {
      return matches[2];
    },
    getNode: function() {
      return matches[3];
    },
    getMenu: function() {
      return matches[4];
    },
    getComponent: function() {
      return matches[5];
```

```
    },
    getMarket: function() {
      return matches[6];
    }
  }
})(window.location.pathname);
```

Using this modified version, we can determine the name of the current component from the expression `apt.sysVars.getComponent()`.

If you consider yourself to be fluent with JavaScript, you may want to incorporate this final listing into the `APT_COMMON_LIB_JS` HTML definition.

Leaving the Portal

Let's create one more tool—a button for leaving the portal.

I rely heavily on the Firebug console when creating JavaScript enhancements. From the console, it is possible to reference variables and functions defined in a page's JavaScript, as long as you prefix that reference with the page's frame name. For example, the following code prints the current page's URL to the Firebug console:

```
frames["TargetContent"].strCurrUrl
```

To make it easier to test code, I usually navigate to a component, and then change the URL in the browser's address bar so that it references the content servlet (psc) rather than the portal servlet (psp). Unfortunately, this action takes me back to the search page, rather than to the previously selected transaction. As an alternative, we can create a toolbar button that changes the top-level URL to the current component's URL, including the page, edit mode, and transaction.

Navigate to PeopleTools | Utilities | Administration | Toolbar Tools and add the value `APT_LEAVE_PORTAL`. Set the tooltip text to **Leave Portal** and set the image to `PT_CREATE_ICN`. Add the `PTPT1200` permission list to the Permission Lists grid, and then add the following code to the Tool Command edit box:

```
<script type="text/javascript">
  // bind toolbar button
  $(document).ready(function() {
    $("#APT_LEAVE_PORTAL").click(function() {
      if(window != top) {
        saveWarning(window, null, "_top",
            strCurrUrl.replace(/psp/, "psc"));
      }
    })
  });
</script>
```

This code looks similar to many of the other buttons we've implemented, except for one function call. Prior to navigating away from the current page, we should check to see if any of the data in the component has changed since the user last saved. The preceding code accomplishes this by calling the undocumented PeopleSoft- delivered `saveWarning` JavaScript function.

PeopleSoft delivers a handful of undocumented JavaScript functions that allow you to determine if a page or component changed since the last save. I blogged about some of these functions at http://jjmpsj.blogspot.com/2006/10/leveraging-peoplesofts-javascript-save.html.

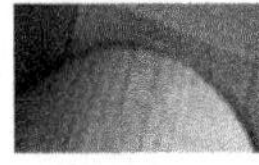

WARNING

The JavaScript presented here uses an undocumented PeopleSoft function. Since this function is not documented, it may change in future releases. Be sure to keep a list of every location where you use this and all other undocumented functions, so you can test their usage after each PeopleTools patch and/or upgrade.

Conclusion

In this chapter, we created a toolbar for our PeopleSoft pages. There are many uses for this toolbar. The tools we created in this chapter are just a sampling to get you started. Here are some other tools you might consider adding:

- Generic file attachment functionality
- Database session tracing with TKPROF results
- PeopleCode tracing
- Export of page fields to XML

Furthermore, the custom toolbar you created in this chapter can serve end users just as well as developers and administrators. Even though the tools described here were intended for developers, it is possible to create end-user tools to perform actions such as opening queries, running XML Publisher reports, and so on.

This chapter concludes this book's user interface section, but many of the remaining chapters contain examples that reference JavaScript and PeopleCode presented in Chapters 5 through 8. For example, in Chapter 9, we will create a custom meta-HTML resolver and then use it with the Custom Scripts module from Chapter 7 and the Toolbar Tools component from this chapter.

PART III

Java

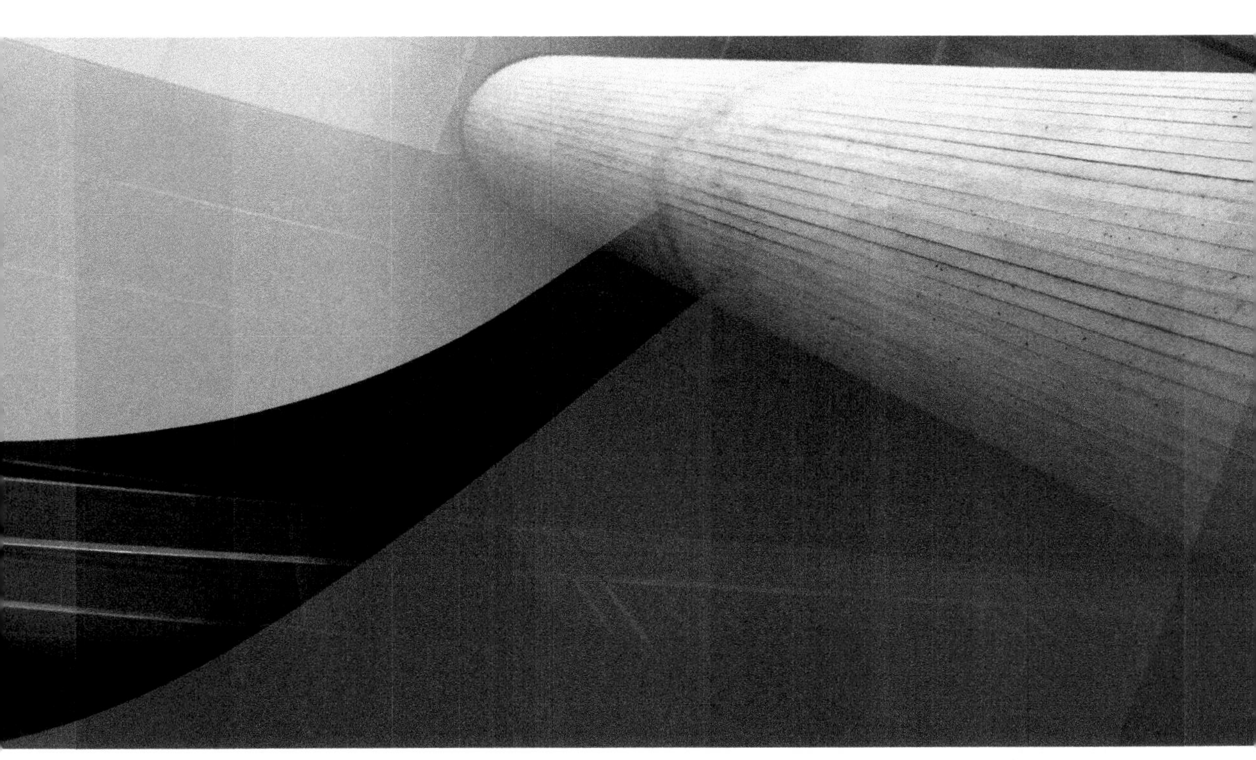

CHAPTER 9

Extending PeopleCode with Java

his chapter begins a six-chapter journey into the Java language. In this chapter, you will create an extensible meta-HTML processor, a template processor using the Apache Velocity Engine, and a server-side JSON parser that uses the JSON.simple Java-based JSON parser.

Through these examples you will learn when and how to use Java, how to deploy and use third-party Java classes, and strategies for dealing with Java *upcasting* from PeopleCode. *Upcasting* and *downcasting* are OOP terms used to describe the process of referencing an object as a type higher or lower in the inheritance hierarchy. The term *upcasting* is used when storing an object in a variable declared as a super type of the given object. To *downcast* an object is to reference that object as if it were a subclass of the given object. In our Chapter 1 logging framework, we upcasted `MessageBoxLogger` and `FileLogger` to the base class `Logger` at creation. Near the end of this chapter, you will see how Java's upcasting affects our ability to use Java objects from PeopleCode.

Java Overview

Java, not to be confused with JavaScript, is an OOP language. Similar to PeopleCode objects, Java objects have constructors, properties, and methods. However, Java objects have several differences from PeopleCode objects. We will discuss these differences throughout this chapter.

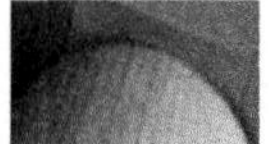

NOTE

We wrote a lot of JavaScript in Part II of this book. Considering names only, one would think that JavaScript was a scripted version of the Java language. However, Java and JavaScript are not even related. For more details, see the article "JavaScript: How Did We Get Here?" by Steve Champeon (http://www.oreillynet.com/pub/a/javascript/2001/04/06/js_history.html) and the Wikipedia definition of JavaScript (http://en.wikipedia.org/wiki/JavaScript#History_and_naming).

Just as PeopleCode objects are defined in class definitions, Java objects are defined in Java class definitions. An instance of a Java definition is called an *object*, and the definition itself is called a *class*.

Why Java?

Before we start writing PeopleCode that uses Java, let's consider why you might want to use Java with PeopleCode. Here are some of the advantages:

- **Leverage Java's robust language** The Java language contains functionality that doesn't exist in PeopleCode. For example, with Java, you can manipulate strings using regular expressions, structure data with hashtables, and even manipulate images.
- **Reuse existing libraries** The Java community is prolific, offering innumerable resources. You can find Java packages to perform just about any task. With third-party Java libraries, you can template content, process JSON, evaluate XQuery queries, generate PDF files, and even process binary Microsoft Excel files. Besides third-party libraries, your organization

may have its own collection of Java classes that contain integration and business logic code. Rather than rewrite that logic or those integrations in PeopleCode, SQL, and SQR, you may be able to reuse it with your PeopleSoft application.

- **Utilize existing skill sets** Due to Java's great popularity, finding Java programmers is much easier than finding PeopleCode programmers. One reason to use Java is to redistribute your organization's workload by offloading some of your enterprise resource planning (ERP) system programming tasks from your PeopleCode programmers to your Java programmers.

Why Not C++ or .NET or ...?

Considering that PeopleCode can execute native operating system functions, you might ask, "Why use Java instead of [insert your favorite language here]?" One reason to choose Java over another language is the support the PeopleSoft application server offers for Java through PeopleCode native types and functions.

Another reason to choose Java is portability. PeopleSoft applications can run on multiple operating systems. You may develop code in a Windows VMware image, and then deploy that code to a production Oracle Enterprise Linux server. If you use native libraries, the code you write for your Window's development instance will not run on your production instance. When using Java, however, it is possible to run the same code on both your Window's development instance and the Oracle Enterprise Linux server.

Java and PeopleCode 101

Next, we are going to look at some sample Java programs. To run Java from PeopleSoft, you need a PeopleCode interpreter. For testing and demonstration purposes, the two most logical places are App Engine PeopleCode and iScripts. Since iScripts require special security settings, whereas we can run App Engine PeopleCode directly from App Designer, we will use an App Engine.

To begin, create a new App Engine program and add a new action. Set the step's action to PeopleCode, and then save the program as APT_JAVA_TST. Next, choose File | Definition Properties from the App Designer menu bar. In the Program Properties window, select the Advanced tab, and then select Disable Restart. Save the program again.

Java Strings

As always, we will start with a Hello World example. Practically speaking, this first example is irrelevant. Pedagogically, however, it has value. Add the following code to your APT_JAVA_TST program's PeopleCode action:

```
REM ** Create a Java object
Local JavaObject &jString;

&jString = CreateJavaObject("java.lang.String", "Hello World");

REM ** Use some of the Java object' methods
MessageBox(0, "", 0, 0, "Contents: " | &jString.toString());
MessageBox(0, "", 0, 0, "Length: " | &jString.length());
MessageBox(0, "", 0, 0, "indexOf('o'): " | &jString.indexOf("o"));
MessageBox(0, "", 0, 0, "charAt: " | &jString.charAt(1));
```

```
REM ** case sensitive
MessageBox(0, "", 0, 0, "Equals 'HELLO WORLD': " |
      &jString.equals("HELLO WORLD"));
MessageBox(0, "", 0, 0, "Equals 'hello world': " |
      &jString.equals("hello world"));
MessageBox(0, "", 0, 0, "Equals 'Hello World': " |
      &jString.equals("Hello World"));
```

The reason I said this example has no practical value is because we are using objects and methods that already exist in the PeopleCode language. However, since you are already familiar with strings and the many PeopleCode functions you can use with strings, this example offers an excellent learning opportunity.

Starting at the top, you see a variable declaration:

```
Local JavaObject &jString
```

What makes this declaration unique is the variable type: `JavaObject`. All Java variables have the type `JavaObject`.

Next, we call the PeopleCode `CreateJavaObject` function:

```
&jString = CreateJavaObject("java.lang.String", "Hello World");
```

This code instructs the PeopleCode runtime to create a Java object of type `java.lang.String`.

In Chapters 6 through 8, we used a custom JavaScript namespacing function to avoid cluttering the global browser namespace with our custom JavaScript variables. Java has a similar feature. In the preceding sample, `java.lang` represents the namespace—or *package*, as we call it in Java—and `String` represents the actual object name. Besides offering organization and structure, packages avoid naming collisions. If we wanted to, we could create an object named `String` and place it in our own namespace.

The first parameter to `CreateJavaObject` is the fully qualified name of the class to instantiate. The second parameter to `CreateJavaObject` is the constructor's arguments. When the PeopleCode runtime executes this line of code, it will call the `java.lang.String` constructor that has a `String` parameter. In Java, strings are immutable. Therefore, any data contained within a `String` must be passed to the `String`'s constructor.

The remainder of the code executes various `String` methods.

Run this program by selecting Edit | Run Program from the App Designer menu bar. In the Run Request dialog, select the Output Log to File option and note the log filename. Click the OK button to close the dialog box. App Designer will respond by opening a command prompt window and running this App Engine program. When the command prompt window disappears, open the log file that was referenced in the Run Request dialog. Here is the content of my log file:

```
PeopleTools 8.49 - Application Engine
Copyright (c) 1988-2009 PeopleSoft, Inc.
All Rights Reserved


Contents: Hello World (0,0)
 Message Set Number: 0
 Message Number: 0
 Message Reason: Contents: Hello World (0,0) (0,0)
```

```
Length: 11 (0,0)
 Message Set Number: 0
 Message Number: 0
 Message Reason: Length: 11 (0,0) (0,0)

indexOf('o'): 4 (0,0)
 Message Set Number: 0
 Message Number: 0
 Message Reason: indexOf('o'): 4 (0,0) (0,0)

charAt: 101 (0,0)
 Message Set Number: 0
 Message Number: 0
 Message Reason: charAt: 101 (0,0) (0,0)

Equals 'HELLO WORLD': False (0,0)
 Message Set Number: 0
 Message Number: 0
 Message Reason: Equals 'HELLO WORLD': False (0,0) (0,0)

Equals 'hello world': False (0,0)
 Message Set Number: 0
 Message Number: 0
 Message Reason: Equals 'hello world': False (0,0) (0,0)

Equals 'Hello World': True (0,0)
 Message Set Number: 0
 Message Number: 0
 Message Reason: Equals 'Hello World': True (0,0) (0,0)
Application Engine program APT_JAVA_TST ended normally
```

Java supports inheritance in a manner similar to PeopleCode application classes. The base class for all Java classes is `java.lang.Object`. The `Object` class implements methods that are guaranteed to exist for all Java classes, the most common being `toString()`. Therefore, we can call `toString()` on any `JavaObject` variable, and we will always receive a string result.

Notice that `&jString.indexOf("o")` returns 4, even though *o* is the fifth letter in the string "Hello World." Java collections and arrays begin with an index of 0, whereas PeopleCode uses the first index value of 1.

The preceding output contains the text `charAt: 101`, which corresponds to the code `&jString.charAt(1)`. The `101` result is the actual numeric code for the letter *e*, the second letter in "Hello World."

It is important to note that Java is a case-sensitive language. This is confirmed by the preceding output, which contains three different equality tests.

Regular Expressions

This is where Java strings get interesting. The PeopleCode language contains functions for parsing and searching strings. Writing a string-manipulation routine, however, requires several lines of PeopleCode and, possibly, even iterating over every character in the string. Java offers us an alternative: regular expressions.[1]

Regular expressions help us identify patterns within strings. Let's continue with the "Hello World" string from the previous example by writing some regular expression patterns and running tests against that string. If you would like to follow along, create a new step and PeopleCode action in the App Engine program `APT_JAVA_TST`. Name the new step `Regex`. With this first example, we will test for the existence of the letter *o* within the string "Hello World."

```
Local JavaObject &pattern;
Local JavaObject &matcher;
Local JavaObject &greeting;

&greeting = CreateJavaObject("java.lang.String", "Hello World");
&pattern = GetJavaClass("java.util.regex.Pattern").compile("o");
&matcher = &pattern.matcher(&greeting);

If (&matcher.find()) Then
   MessageBox(0, "", 0, 0, &greeting | " contains an 'o'");
Else
   MessageBox(0, "", 0, 0, &greeting | " does not contain an 'o'");
End-If;
```

Along with all of the output from the previous step, this step should print the following additional message:

```
java.lang.String contains an 'o' (0,0)
 Message Set Number: 0
 Message Number: 0
 Message Reason: java.lang.String contains an 'o' (0,0) (0,0)
```

Let's refactor this example to count the number of *o* characters. Since the input string "Hello World" contains two *o* characters, we expect the result to be 2. Replace the existing `if/else/end-if` construct with the following `while` loop (changes are in bold).

```
Local JavaObject &pattern;
Local JavaObject &matcher;
Local JavaObject &greeting;
Local number &count = 0;

&greeting = CreateJavaObject("java.lang.String", "Hello World");
&pattern = GetJavaClass("java.util.regex.Pattern").compile("o");
&matcher = &pattern.matcher(&greeting);

While &matcher.find()
   &count = &count + 1;
End-While;

MessageBox(0, "", 0, 0, "Found " | &count | " o's");
```

Running this code will produce the output (emphasis added):

```
...
Found 2 o's (0,0)
 Message Set Number: 0
 Message Number: 0
 Message Reason: Found 2 o's (0,0) (0,0)
...
```

Regular expression pattern matching is case-sensitive. We can change this behavior through flags. The regular expression in the next example uses the `i` flag to specify a case-insensitive match for *O* (uppercase) characters. Replace the code in your `Regex` step with the following (changes are in bold).

```
Local JavaObject &pattern;
Local JavaObject &matcher;
Local JavaObject &greeting;
Local number &count = 0;

&greeting = CreateJavaObject("java.lang.String", "Hello World");
&pattern = GetJavaClass("java.util.regex.Pattern").compile("(?i)O");
&matcher = &pattern.matcher(&greeting);

While &matcher.find()
   &count = &count + 1;
End-While;

MessageBox(0, "", 0, 0, "Found " | &count | " o's");
```

Even though our string does not contain uppercase *O*s, running this code will produce the same results as the previous code listing. This is because we specified the case-insensitive pattern matching flag.

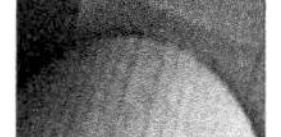

NOTE
With step 1 still active in our App Engine, the program generates several lines that are irrelevant to this example. You can turn off that step by unselecting the step's Active check box.

We can use quantifiers to specify how often a character should appear:

- ? matches once or not at all.
- * matches zero or more times.
- \+ matches one or more times.

We can also specify exactly how many times to match a pattern using `{n}`, and even add upper limits to the match using `{n, m}`, which says, "Match at least `n` times, but no more than `m` times." The following example matches the combination *ll* in "Hello" by specifying the quantifier for matching *l* exactly two times (changes to the `Regex` PeopleCode action are shown in bold).

```
Local JavaObject &pattern;
Local JavaObject &matcher;
Local JavaObject &greeting;
Local number &count = 0;

&greeting = CreateJavaObject("java.lang.String", "Hello World");
&pattern = GetJavaClass("java.util.regex.Pattern").compile("l{2}");
&matcher = &pattern.matcher(&greeting);
```

```
While &matcher.find()
   &count = &count + 1;
End-While;

MessageBox(0, "", 0, 0, "Found ll " | &count | " time(s)");
```

When run, this code prints the following (emphasis added):

```
Found ll 1 time(s) (0,0)
 Message Set Number: 0
 Message Number: 0
 Message Reason: Found ll 1 time(s) (0,0) (0,0)
```

We can also use character classes to specify the characters to match. The following example matches word boundaries (space, newline, tab, and so on) by using the word boundary character class `\b`.

```
Local JavaObject &pattern;
Local JavaObject &matcher;
Local JavaObject &greeting;
Local number &count = 0;

&greeting = CreateJavaObject("java.lang.String", "Hello World");
&pattern = GetJavaClass("java.util.regex.Pattern").compile("\b");
&matcher = &pattern.matcher(&greeting);

While &matcher.find()
   &count = &count + 1;
End-While;

MessageBox(0, "", 0, 0, "Found " | &count | " word boundaries");
```

Running this code produces the following results (emphasis added):

```
Found 4 word boundaries (0,0)
 Message Set Number: 0
 Message Number: 0
 Message Reason: Found 4 word boundaries (0,0) (0,0)
Application Engine program APT_JAVA_TST ended normally
```

Is that correct—four word boundaries? Yes, actually it is correct. Where are all of these boundaries?

- Position 0, immedately before the *H* in "Hello"
- After the *o* in "Hello"
- Before the *W* in "World"
- After the *d* in "World"

We can also use regular expressions to capture pattern matches by placing pattern sequences in parentheses:

```
Local JavaObject &pattern;
Local JavaObject &matcher;
Local JavaObject &greeting;
Local number &count = 0;

&greeting = CreateJavaObject("java.lang.String", "Hello World");
&pattern = GetJavaClass("java.util.regex.Pattern").compile("(\w+)\b");
&matcher = &pattern.matcher(&greeting);

While &matcher.find()
   &count = &count + 1;
   MessageBox(0, "", 0, 0, "Sequence " | &count | ": '" |
         &matcher.group() | "'");
End-While;

MessageBox(0, "", 0, 0, "Found " | &count | " matches");
```

This regular expression uses two character classes (`\w` and `\b`), a quantifier (+), and a capturing group (parentheses). The `\w` character class matches any word character. By pairing that with +, we are asking for a sequence of one or more word characters. The preceding code produces the following output (emphasis added):

```
Sequence 1: 'Hello' (0,0)
 Message Set Number: 0
 Message Number: 0
 Message Reason: Sequence 1: 'Hello' (0,0) (0,0)

Sequence 2: 'World' (0,0)
 Message Set Number: 0
 Message Number: 0
 Message Reason: Sequence 2: 'World' (0,0) (0,0)

Found 2 matches (0,0)
 Message Set Number: 0
 Message Number: 0
 Message Reason: Found 2 matches (0,0) (0,0)
```

Look again at the regular expression: `(\w+)\b`. The `\b` word boundary is actually redundant. The match will stop automatically when it reaches the first nonword character. I point this out because regular expressions can be very tricky to write.

As you saw with the JavaScript regular expressions examples in prior chapters, regular expressions can be quite complex. Later in this chapter, we will create regular expressions that are applicable as well as more complicated.

Formatting Strings

Another benefit of Java is robust string formatting. PeopleCode provides all of the components to develop a custom, robust string-formatting routine, but nothing out of the box.

For example, many other languages contain a `printf` function. Using `printf`, you specify a parameterized format string as well as a list of values. The function returns a string with all of the parameters replaced by the corresponding list of values.

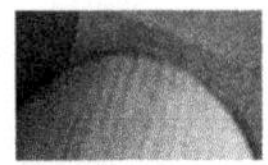

NOTE
The example in this section uses the `format` method of the Java `String` object. The `format` method did not exist prior to Java 1.5. Therefore, this example requires PeopleTools 8.49 or later. Versions of PeopleTools prior to 8.49 used Java 1.4.

Add a new step and PeopleCode action to the App Engine `APT_JAVA_TST`. Name this new step `format`, and then add the following PeopleCode:

```
Function printf(&language As string, &country As string,
      &message As string, &parms As array of any) Returns string
   Local JavaObject &jLocale = CreateJavaObject("java.util.Locale",
         &language, &country);
   Local JavaObject &jParms = CreateJavaArray("java.lang.Object[]",
         &parms.Len);

   CopyToJavaArray(&parms, &jParms);
   Return GetJavaClass("java.lang.String").format(&jLocale, &message,
         &jParms);
End-Function;

Local string &message = "Amount gained or lost since last statement " |
      "dated %1$tc: $ %2$(,.2f";
Local array of any &parms = CreateArrayAny();
&parms.Push(%Datetime);
&parms.Push(252356.69);

MessageBox(0, "", 0, 0, printf("en", "us", &message, &parms));
MessageBox(0, "", 0, 0, printf("es", "es", &message, &parms));
```

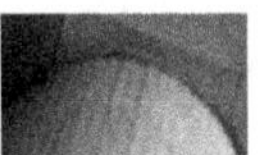

NOTE
This code is also listed on my blog at http://jjmpsj.blogspot .com/2008/09/printf-for-peoplesoft.html.

The preceding code declares a function named `printf`. A more appropriate place for a reusable function like this function is a FUNCLIB. For demonstration purposes, however, I placed it directly in the App Engine step.

This code introduces the `GetJavaClass` PeopleCode function. Unlike `CreateJavaObject`, which creates an in-memory instance of a Java class, `GetJavaClass` returns a pointer to the actual class definition. We can use this pointer to execute static methods and access static properties (called *fields*). Static members differ from instance members in that you can access static members without first creating an instance of the class definition.

When you run the sample code, you will see output similar to the following (emphasis added):

```
Amount gained or lost since last statement dated Thu Sep
      03 00:41:57 PDT 2009: $ 252,356.69 (0,0)
 Message Set Number: 0
 Message Number: 0
 Message Reason: Amount gained or lost since last statement dated
      Thu Sep 03 00:41:57 PDT 2009: $ 252,356.69 (0,0) (0,0)

Amount gained or lost since last statement dated jue sep
      03 00:41:57 PDT 2009: $ 252.356,69 (0,0)
 Message Set Number: 0
 Message Number: 0
 Message Reason: Amount gained or lost since last statement dated
      jue sep 03 00:41:57 PDT 2009: $ 252.356,69 (0,0) (0,0)
```

Look closely at the output. We called the function twice: once with US English locale and once with Spain Spanish locale. The Java runtime used this locale information to set the date and number format. Notice the day of the week format differs between the English and Spanish versions. Also, the currency formats differ: the English currency values use a comma as the thousands separator, whereas the Spanish currency uses the decimal.

Java Arrays

Java and PeopleCode both have arrays. Both use the same bracket syntax to access elements within an array. In PeopleCode, Java arrays appear as Java objects, not as arrays. Since a Java array appears to PeopleCode as a Java object, you might wonder how to access the elements of a Java array.

PeopleCode has the built-in `CopyFromJavaArray` function for copying Java arrays into PeopleCode arrays. Once the contents of a Java array are copied to a PeopleCode array, you can access the contents in the same way as with any other PeopleCode array—even if the array contains `JavaObject` items.

Java's `String` object has a `split` method that is very similar to the PeopleCode `Split` function. The Java version, however, allows you to split strings using regular expressions, whereas the PeopleCode version allows you to specify only string delimiters. The following example uses the nonword character class (`\W`) to split a multiline phrase into an array of words. Here is the string we want to split:

```
Hello PS.
Welcome to PeopleSoft.
```

We can use the regular expression "`\W+`" to split this phrase into an array of words. This regular expression removes spaces, punctuation, and newline characters. To run this example, add another step to the App Engine `APT_JAVA_TST` and name the step `Array`. In this new step, add a PeopleCode action, and then add the following code:

```
Local JavaObject &greeting;
Local JavaObject &javaWords;
Local array of any &pcWords = CreateArrayAny();
Local number &index;
Local string &result = "";
```

```
REM ** create string;
&greeting = CreateJavaObject("java.lang.String", "Hello " |
      %OperatorId | "." | Char(13) | Char(10) |
      "Welcome to PeopleSoft.");

MessageBox(0, "", 0, 0, &greeting.toString());

REM ** split string into array of words;
&javaWords = &greeting.split("\W+");
```

With our phrase split into words, let's use the `CopyFromJavaArray` function to copy those words into a PeopleCode array. Add the following code to the end of the prior listing:

```
REM ** resize the PeopleCode array to match the Java Array;
&pcWords [&javaWords.length] = Null;

REM ** copy the Java array into a PeopleCode array;
CopyFromJavaArray(&javaWords, &pcWords);

REM ** print results;
&result = "[";
While &pcWords.Next(&index)
   If (&index > 1) Then
      &result = &result | ", ";
   End-If;
   &result = &result | "'" | &pcWords [&index] | "'";
End-While;

&result = &result | "]";
MessageBox(0, "", 0, 0, &result);
```

Running this example produces the following output. Notice that the `\b` regular expression character class matches punctuation as well as spaces.

```
Hello PS.

Welcome to PeopleSoft. (0,0)
 Message Set Number: 0
 Message Number: 0
 Message Reason: Hello PS.

Welcome to PeopleSoft. (0,0) (0,0)

['Hello', 'PS', 'Welcome', 'to', 'PeopleSoft'] (0,0)
 Message Set Number: 0
 Message Number: 0
 Message Reason: ['Hello', 'PS', 'Welcome', 'to', 'PeopleSoft'] (0,0) (0,0)
```

Notice that the new PeopleCode array contains words only—no punctuation, whitespace characters, and so on. I can't even imagine trying to accomplish this with just PeopleCode.

Java Collections

PeopleCode's support for collections begins and ends with arrays. Java, on the other hand, has extensive support for collections including maps (`Hashtable`, `HashMap`, and so on), lists (`LinkedList`, `ArrayList`, and so on), and iterators.

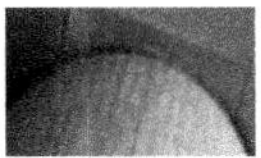

NOTE

As noted in Chapter 1, some of the PeopleTools team created collection app classes in the `EOIU:Common` application package. Looking at the code, however, you will see that these collection classes are actually implemented using PeopleCode arrays.

The `Hashtable` class lends itself to many uses within PeopleCode. A hashtable is a collection of key/value pairs. Unlike an array, which is indexed by number, hashtables are indexed by objects. To retrieve a value from a hashtable, you specify the value's key. You can think of a hashtable as similar to a record definition. A field's name is similar to a hashtable key, and a field's value is similar to the hashtable key's value.

Let's write some PeopleCode that uses Java hashtables. Open the `APT_JAVA_TST` App Engine program, and add a new step and PeopleCode action. Name the new step `hashtable` and add the PeopleCode from the following listing. The code in this listing creates a hashtable containing restaurants and daily specials. The restaurant name serves as the key, and the value is an array of menu items on special.

```
Local JavaObject &hashtable = CreateJavaObject("java.util.Hashtable");

REM ** Add special's to menu;
&hashtable.put("Luigi's Pizzeria",
      CreateArray("Pizza", "Pasta", "Salad"));
&hashtable.put("Bob's drive-in",
      CreateArray("1/2 lb Burger",
            "Root Beer Float", "Onion Rings"));

REM ** Print Bob's specials;
Local array of string &specials = &hashtable.get("Bob's drive-in");

MessageBox(0, "", 0, 0, &specials.Join());
```

When run, this code prints the following results:

```
(1/2 lb Burger,Root Beer Float,Onion Rings) (0,0)
 Message Set Number: 0
 Message Number: 0
 Message Reason: (1/2 lb Burger,Root Beer Float,
       Onion Rings) (0,0) (0,0)
```

Writing a Meta-HTML Processor

Meta-HTML offers a mechanism for inserting information into HTML at runtime. Whether or not a meta-HTML sequence is resolved at runtime depends on the meta-HTML usage context. For example, the meta-HTML `%Image` is resolved when it is used with a static HTML Area control on a PeopleSoft page. When used from an iScript, however, the PeopleCode runtime will not resolve `%Image`. With iScripts, developers are expected to use `%Response.GetImageURL` along with HTML bind variables. For each meta-HTML sequence, PeopleBooks describes when and where you can use it.

Regardless of PeopleSoft's meta-HTML resolution rules, we must consider the fact that some of our HTML is served from custom database tables, not from standard PeopleSoft HTML definitions. Therefore, we need an alternative for meta-HTML sequence resolution.

To write a string-parsing routine in PeopleCode to process meta-HTML sequences sounds like a daunting task. With regular expressions, however, we can do it with just a few lines of code.

Let's create a new application class for our meta-HTML processor. First, create a new application package named `APT_META_HTML`. Then add a new class named `Processor` to this package, and save the package. Add the following code to the `Processor` application class:

```
class Processor
   method process(&html As string) Returns string;

private
   REM ** Meta-HTML helper/resolver definitions go here;
end-class;

method process
   /+ &html as String +/
   /+ Returns String +/
   REM ** Calls to Meta-HTML helpers/resolvers go here;
   Return &html;
end-method;
```

This code defines the shell of our `Processor` application class. Since it doesn't do anything yet, we won't bother testing it.

We will now proceed to write meta-HTML helpers, or *resolvers*, as I call them. With each resolver, we will expand the new `Processor` class and then modify some of our code from Chapters 6 and 7. If you prefer, you can skip to the complete `Processor` class code listing presented at the end of this section, and enter that code prior to working through the examples. Otherwise, follow along and I'll show you were to place each resolver.

Implementing %Image

In Chapter 6, we implemented Thickbox, a jQuery plug-in for displaying content in an HTML dialog window. Prior to using Thickbox, I gave instructions for setting the file location of the `loadingAnimation` graphic distributed with Thickbox. At that time, our only solution for storing graphics was to upload them to the database as web assets and serve them from iScripts.

The problem with this approach is that iScripts don't support caching. Since the loadingAnimation.gif graphic doesn't change, it would improve performance if a user's browser downloaded the image only once, rather than downloading it for each page. As an alternative, it would be nice to take advantage of App Designer's image definitions and the caching functionality available to image definitions. By implementing our own version of `%Image`, we can achieve these results.

While still in the `Processor` class PeopleCode editor, add the following private method declaration to the end of the class definition (additions are in bold; context is provided for clarity):

```
Private
   REM ** Meta-HTML helper/resolver definitions go here;
   method processImages(&html As string) Returns string;
end-class;
```

Next, add the following to the `process` method (additions are in bold; context is provided for clarity):

```
method process
   /+ &html as String +/
   /+ Returns String +/
   REM ** Calls to Meta-HTML helpers/resolvers go here;
   Return %This.processImages(&html);
end-method;
```

Finally, let's implement the method responsible for converting `%Image` tokens into URLs. Add the following code to the end of the class's PeopleCode:

```
method processImages
   /+ &html as String +/
   /+ Returns String +/
   Local JavaObject &pattern;
   Local JavaObject &matcher;
   Local string &imgUrl;

   REM ** Resolve %Image(IMAGE_NAME) tags;
   &pattern = GetJavaClass("java.util.regex.Pattern").compile(
         "(?i)%Image\((\w+)\)");

   &matcher = &pattern.matcher(
         CreateJavaObject("java.lang.String", &html));

   While &matcher.find()
      &imgUrl = %Response.GetImageURL(
            @("Image." | &matcher.group(1)));
      &html = Substitute(&html, &matcher.group(), &imgUrl);
   End-While;

   Return &html;
end-method;
```

The first segment of this code looks very similar to our earlier regular expression examples. Like the earlier examples, this code declares some Java variables, creates a regular expression object, and then loops through the results, processing each match.

Let's break down the regular expression: `(?i)%Image\((\w+)\)`. Our objective is to match `%Image(NAME_OF_IMAGE)` and replace it with `/the/url/to/NAME_OF_IMAGE_113.gif`. For convenience, we also want to match `%image`, `%IMAGE`, or any other uppercase/lowercase combination. The `(?i)` at the beginning of the regular expression tells Java to ignore case when evaluating matches. The next portion of the regular expression, `%Image`, tells Java what text to locate. The entire text we want to replace contains parentheses. Since parentheses have a special meaning in regular expressions, we are required to escape them with a backslash as shown here: `\(`. Next, we want to capture all word characters found before the closing parenthesis.

The preceding code uses `%Response.GenerateImageURL` to determine the URL for an App Designer-managed image definition.

If you have access to your web server, you can achieve the same performance benefit without this code by placing your image directly on the web server. The web server approach, however, has several drawbacks:

- Web server files must be manually migrated. They are not part of a project, as App Designer-managed definitions are.
- For many web servers, changes to the web server's directory are not reflected until after the web service is restarted.
- The browser doesn't always reload its cache when a file changes on the server. App Designer ensures that the web browser always has the most recent copy of an image by incrementing the image's version number, and then generating a corresponding link.

We will use the loadingAnimation.gif file from Thickbox to test this new processor. Since our meta-HTML processor depends on image definitions, let's create an image definition for loadingAnimation.gif. Choose File | New from the App Designer menu bar. In the New Definition dialog, select Image. As the path to the image file, provide the path to where you downloaded Thickbox, which includes the loadingAnimation.gif file. The file will not appear at first, because the file type is set to JPG. Change this filter item to GIF. After clicking OK, App Designer will prompt you for a second image file. Ignore this second request by clicking the No button. Since App Designer cannot display GIF files, it allows you to upload a BMP or JPG representation of the GIF file. Save the image as `APT_TB_LOADING_ANIMATION`.

Now that we have our image file in App Designer, let's modify the Thickbox JavaScript so it can use this image definition. Open the `APT_JQ_THICKBOX_JS` HTML definition. Near the top of the file, you should see the following code:

```
var tb_pathToImage = apt.files.generateScriptContentUrl({
    record: "WEBLIB_APT_WA",
    field:  "ISCRIPT1",
    event:  "FieldFormula",
    script: "IScript_GetWebAsset"}) + "?id=APT_LOAD_IMG";
```

This is the code we wrote to generate a URL to the Web Assets iScript and download the image. Replace this code with the following:

```
var tb_pathToImage = "%Image(APT_TB_LOADING_ANIMATION)";
```

We also need to modify our iScript to get it to use the meta-HTML processor application class. Open the `FieldFormula` event of the record field `WEBLIB_APT_JSL ISCRIPT1`. Add the following line to the very top of this event's PeopleCode:

```
import APT_META_HTML:Processor;
```

Next, we need to create an instance of the `Processor` class and call its `process` method. Replace the function `IScript_JqThickboxJs` with the following code:

```
Function IScript_JqThickboxJs
   Local APT_META_HTML:Processor &p =
         create APT_META_HTML:Processor();
   Local string &html = GetHTMLText(HTML.APT_JQ_THICKBOX_JS);

   &html = &p.process(&html);

   %Response.SetContentType("text/javascript");
   %Response.Write(&html);
End-Function;
```

To test this, navigate to the following URL:

http://hrms.example.com/psc/hrms/EMPLOYEE/HRMS/s/WEBLIB_APT_JSL.ISCRIPT1.FieldFormula.IScript_JqThickboxJs

After calling this URL, you should see a line of code similar to the following near the beginning of the downloaded file:

```
var tb_pathToImage = "/cs/hrms/cache/APT_TB_LOADING_ANIMATION_492.gif";
```

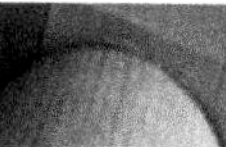

NOTE
In Chapter 8, we created a toolbar with images. The iScript that serves the toolbar uses `%Response.GetImageURL` to cache toolbar images in a manner very similar to the `%Image` resolver presented here. Rather than use `%Image`, however, the toolbar button HTML definition, `APT_TOOLBAR_BUTTON`, uses `%Bind(:2)` as a placeholder for the image location. I believe it would make the HTML easier to understand and maintain if it said `%Image(%Bind(:2))`. Then it would be clear that the intent of `%Bind(:2)` is to display an image.

Implementing %JavaScript

Another area we can improve performance for our Chapter 6 and 7 customizations is by caching JavaScript HTML definitions. Let's write a `%JavaScript` meta-HTML resolver, and then update some of our Chapter 6 and 7 code to use that resolver.

Add the following `processJavaScript` declaration to the private section of the `Processor` class declaration (additions are in bold; context is provided for clarity).

```
Private
   REM ** Meta-HTML helper/resolver definitions go here;
   method processImages(&html As string) Returns string;
   method processJavaScript(&html As string) Returns string;
end-class;
```

Next, modify the `process` method as follows (additions are in bold; context is provided for clarity):

```
method process
   /+ &html as String +/
   /+ Returns String +/
   REM ** Calls to Meta-HTML helpers/resolvers go here;
   &html = %This.processImages(&html);
   Return %This.processJavaScript(&html);
end-method;
```

Implement the `processJavaScript` method as follows. Place this code at the end of the `Processor` class's existing PeopleCode.

```
method processJavaScript
   /+ &html as String +/
   /+ Returns String +/
   Local JavaObject &pattern;
   Local JavaObject &matcher;
   Local string &jsUrl;

   REM ** Resolve %JavaScript(HTML_DEFN) tags;
   &pattern = GetJavaClass("java.util.regex.Pattern").compile(
         "(?i)%JavaScript\((\w+)\)");

   &matcher = &pattern.matcher(
         CreateJavaObject("java.lang.String", &html));

   While &matcher.find()
      &jsUrl = %Response.GetJavaScriptURL(@("HTML." | &matcher.group(1)));
      &html = Substitute(&html, &matcher.group(), &jsUrl);
   End-While;

   Return &html;
end-method;
```

Now let's plug this custom meta-HTML processor into an existing HTML and PeopleCode definition. Open the HTML definition `APT_COMMON_LIB_JS` and find the code near the end of the definition that looks like the following (look for `IScript_Ajax`):

```
// import AJAX customization to force JSON parsing
apt.files.importScript({
    id:  "apt_ajax",
    url: apt.files.generateScriptContentUrl({
        record: "WEBLIB_APT_JSL",
        field:  "ISCRIPT1",
        event:  "FieldFormula",
        script: "IScript_Ajax"
    })
});
```

Replace the url property value shown in this code with the following code. (Both the original code to replace and the new code are shown in bold; the additional code is shown for context.)

```
// import AJAX customization to force JSON parsing
apt.files.importScript({
    id:  "apt_ajax",
    url: "%JavaScript(APT_AJAX_JS)"
});
```

Do the same for the next importScript call in APT_COMMON_LIB_JS (look for IScript_UILoader):

```
// import Custom Scripts module code
apt.files.importScript({
    id:  "apt_ui_loader",
    url: apt.files.generateScriptContentUrl({
        record: "WEBLIB_APT_JSL",
        field:  "ISCRIPT1",
        event:  "FieldFormula",
        script: "IScript_UILoader"
    })
});
```

Replace the url property value shown in this code with the following code.

```
// import Custom Scripts module code
apt.files.importScript({
    id:  "apt_ui_loader",
    url: "%JavaScript(APT_UI_LOADER_JS)"
});
```

Our last step is to modify the iScript that serves APT_COMMON_LIB_JS to make it use the new meta-HTML Processor application class. Open the FieldFormula event of record field WEBLIB_APT_JSL ISCRIPT1 and scroll to the very end of the PeopleCode editor. The end of the event contains the function IScript_CommonLib. Replace the code for this function with the following:

```
Function IScript_CommonLib()
   Local APT_META_HTML:Processor &p =
         create APT_META_HTML:Processor();
   Local string &html = GetHTMLText(HTML.APT_COMMON_LIB_JS);

   &html = &p.process(&html);

   %Response.SetContentType("text/javascript");
   %Response.Write(&html);
End-Function;
```

After making these modifications, use your web browser to navigate to this URL:

http://hrms.example.com/psc/hrms/EMPLOYEE/HRMS/s/WEBLIB_APT_JSL.ISCRIPT1.FieldFormula.IScript_CommonLib

When the page loads, scroll to the end and look for some code that resembles the following:

```
// import AJAX customization to force JSON parsing
apt.files.importScript({
    id:  "apt_ajax",
    url: "/cs/hrms/cache/APT_AJAX_JS_383.js"
});

// import Custom Scripts module code
apt.files.importScript({
    id:  "apt_ui_loader",
    url: "/cs/hrms/cache/APT_UI_LOADER_JS_467.js"
});
```

Implementing %GenerateQueryContentURL

Let's implement one more meta-HTML tag before moving on to the next Java topic. This time, we will create a meta-HTML equivalent of the PeopleCode function `GenerateQueryContentURL`. Our client-side JavaScript version of `generateQueryContentUrl` works if the query is served by the current node. But what if you are using an application like PeopleSoft's Enterprise Portal, where some of the content is served by a different node? The URL would be different. By using PeopleCode instead of JavaScript, we can leverage the PeopleCode `GenerateXxxContentUrl` functions. These functions know how to generate the correct URL regardless of the node providing the content

After we create this new resolver, we will implement meta-HTML resolution in our new common scripts and toolbar modules.

Add the `processGenerateQueryContentUrl` method declaration to the private section of the `Processor` class declaration as follows (additions are in bold; context is provided for clarity):

```
Private
   REM ** Meta-HTML helper/resolver definitions go here;
   method processImages(&html As string) Returns string;
   method processJavaScript(&html As string) Returns string;
   method processGenerateQueryContentUrl(&html As string) Returns string;
end-class;
```

Next, modify the `process` method as follows (additions are in bold; context is provided for clarity):

```
method process
   /+ &html as String +/
   /+ Returns String +/
   REM ** Calls to Meta-HTML helpers/resolvers go here;
   &html = %This.processImages(&html);
   &html = %This.processJavaScript(&html);
   Return %This.processGenerateQueryContentUrl(&html);
end-method;
```

Implement the processJavaScript method as follows. Place this code at the end of the Processor class's existing PeopleCode.

```
method processGenerateQueryContentUrl
   /+ &html as String +/
   /+ Returns String +/
   Local JavaObject &pattern;
   Local JavaObject &matcher;
   Local string &qryUrl;

   Local boolean &isPublic = False;
   Local boolean &isNewWindow = False;

   /* Resolve %GenerateQueryContentUrl(PORTAL_NAME, NODE_NAME,
    *       QUERY_NAME, IS_PUBLIC, IS_NEWWIN) tags
    */
   &pattern = GetJavaClass("java.util.regex.Pattern").compile(
         "(?i)%GenerateQueryContentUrl\(" |
         "(\w+), ?(\w+), ?(\w+), ?(\w+), ?(\w+)\)");

   &matcher = &pattern.matcher(
         CreateJavaObject("java.lang.String", &html));

   While &matcher.find()
      If (&matcher.group(4) = "True") Then
         &isPublic = True;
      End-If;

      If (&matcher.group(5) = "True") Then
         &isNewWindow = True;
      End-If;

      &qryUrl = GenerateQueryContentURL(&matcher.group(1),
            &matcher.group(2), &matcher.group(3), &isPublic,
            &isNewWindow);
      &html = Substitute(&html, &matcher.group(), &qryUrl);
   End-While;

   Return &html;
end-method;
```

Next, let's modify the Common Scripts and Toolbar Tools components so that they use our new meta-HTML processor. Open the FieldFormula event of record field WEBLIB_APT_JSL ISCRIPT1 and find the function IScript_UI. Modify the function's code so that it matches the following code listing. This change requires you to add two lines and modify one line (modifications are shown in bold).

```
Function IScript_UI()
   Local APT_META_HTML:Processor &p = create APT_META_HTML:Processor();
```

```
   Local SQL &scriptsCursor;
   Local string &menu = %Request.GetParameter("m");
   Local string &component = %Request.GetParameter("c");
   Local string &market = %Request.GetParameter("mk");
   Local string &page = %Request.GetParameter("p");
   Local number &isSearch = Value(%Request.GetParameter("s"));
   Local string &searchOption;

   Local string &location;
   Local string &data;
   Local string &jsonRow;
   Local string &html;
   Local boolean &needsComma = False;

   REM ** If this is a search page, then look for Search Only scripts;
   If (&isSearch = 1) Then
      &searchOption = "SO";
   Else
      &searchOption = "NS";
   End-If;
   %Response.SetContentType("application/json");

   %Response.WriteLine("[");
   &scriptsCursor = GetSQL(SQL.APT_GET_UI_SCRIPTS, &menu, &component,
         &market, &page, &searchOption);
   While &scriptsCursor.Fetch(&location, &data);
      REM ** re-initialize row data -- only use comma after first row;
      If (&needsComma) Then
         &jsonRow = ", ";
      Else
         &needsComma = True;
         &jsonRow = "";
      End-If;

      REM ** JSON doesn't allow \' (JavaScript does, JSON doesn't);
      &html = &p.process(&data);
      &html = EscapeJavascriptString(&html);
      &html = Substitute(&html, "\'", "'");

      &jsonRow = &jsonRow | "{""appendTo"": """ | &location |
            """, ""data"": """ | &html | """}";
      %Response.WriteLine(&jsonRow);
   End-While;
   %Response.WriteLine("]");

End-Function;
```

While we are at it, let's make the same change to the `IScript_Toolbar` function. I presented the entire code listing here for context. Add the lines that are in bold.

```
Function IScript_Toolbar()
   Local APT_META_HTML:Processor &p = create APT_META_HTML:Processor();
```

```
    Local SQL &buttonCursor = GetSQL(SQL.APT_TOOLBAR_BUTTONS,
          %OperatorId);
    Local string &toolId;
    Local string &toolTip;
    Local string &imageName;
    Local string &toolCmd;

    Local string &imageUrl;
    Local array of string &buttons = CreateArrayRept("", 0);

    While &buttonCursor.Fetch(&toolId, &toolTip, &imageName, &toolCmd)
       &toolCmd = &p.process(&toolCmd);
       &imageUrl = %Response.GetImageURL(@("Image." | &imageName));
       &buttons.Push(GetHTMLText(HTML.APT_TOOLBAR_BUTTON, &toolId,
             &imageUrl, &toolTip, &toolCmd));
    End-While;

    %Response.Write(GetHTMLText(HTML.APT_TOOLBAR,
          &buttons.Join("", "", "")));
End-Function;
```

To test this code, log in to your PeopleSoft application through your web browser and navigate to PeopleTools | Utilities | Administration | Custom Scripts. Open the script with the ID `APT_HIGHLIGHT_ACTIVE`. The HTML Area edit box for this script uses JavaScript functions to import a JavaScript file and a CSS file, both of which are served by iScripts. We can take advantage of caching and eliminate one JavaScript file by replacing the `apt.files.importScript` call with `%JavaScript`. Here is the modified code for the HTML Area edit box:

```
<script type="text/javascript"
    src="%JavaScript(APT_HIGHLIGHT_ACTIVE_JS)"></script>
<script type="text/javascript">
  apt.files.importStylesheet(
      apt.files.generateScriptContentUrl({
          record: "WEBLIB_APT_JSL",
          field:  "ISCRIPT1",
          event:  "FieldFormula",
          script: "IScript_HighlightActiveCss"
      })
  );
</script>
```

This code adds one script HTML element and removes the call to `apt.files.importScript`. We can verify that `%JavaScript(APT_HIGHLIGHT_ACTIVE_JS)` is replaced with a URL to a cached file by using Firebug or Fiddler to view the contents of the `IScript_UI` download. Figure 9-1 shows Fiddler with the `APT_HIGHLIGHT_ACTIVE_JS.js` file highlighted. Prior to returning to the search page, I launched Fiddler and verified that the my Firefox status bar contained the text `Fiddler: On` (Internet Explorer uses Fiddler automatically and does not require any additional configuration). After returning to the search page, I highlighted the `IScript_UI` row in Fiddler, selected Inspectors from the right sidebar, and then TextView in the lower panel. If you are using Firebug instead, switch to the Scripts tab and use the filename drop-down list to select `IScript_UI`.

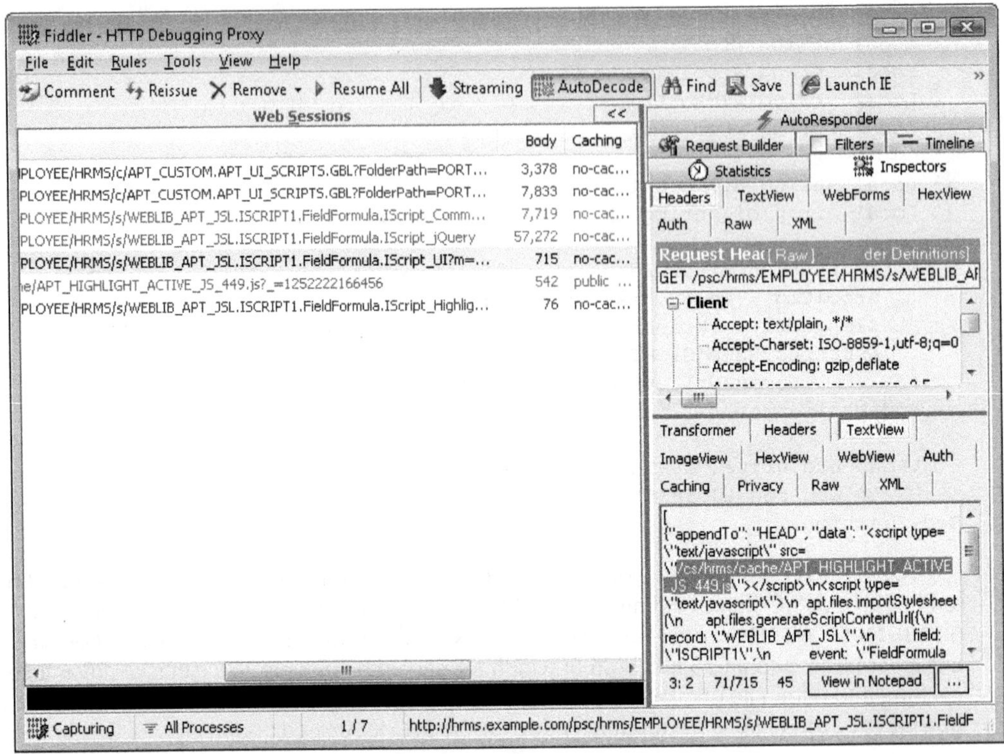

FIGURE 9-1. *IScript_UI contents in Fiddler*

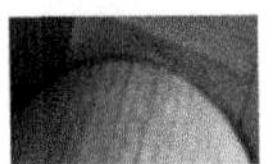

NOTE

Since the highlight CSS is also stored in an HTML definition, we could use `%JavaScript(APT_HIGHLIGHT_ACTIVE_CSS)` *to create the URL for the CSS file. This would reduce our code by a few lines and take advantage of browser caching. While browsers seem to interpret this without issue, the problem with this approach is that* `%JavaScript` *creates a file with the extension .js. When a web server serves a static .js file, it sets the* `Content-Type` *header to* `text/javascript`*. A better alternative is to combine the free-form style sheets that are part of PeopleTools 8.50 with a* `%Stylesheet` *custom meta-HTML tag.*

To test our `%GenerateQueryContentUrl` meta-HTML resolver, we can modify the component permission list toolbar tool we created in Chapter 8. Navigate to PeopleTools | Utilities | Administration | Toolbar Tools and open the tool named `APT_PL_QUERY`. Scroll through the Tool Command edit box until you come to a block that reads as follows:

```
var url = apt.files.generateQueryContentUrl(
    {
      isNewWindow: true,
      isPublic:    true,
      query:       "APT_COMPONENT_PERMS"
    },
    [menu, component, market, portal]
  );
```

Replace this block with the following, and then save your changes.

```
var url = "%GenerateQueryContentURL(EMPLOYEE, HRMS,
 APT_COMPONENT_PERMS, True, True)&BIND1=" + menu +
    "&BIND2=" + component + "&BIND3=" + market +
    "&BIND4=" + portal;
```

NOTE
To fit the page, I broke the meta-HTML line to go in the Tool Command edit box into two lines. When you enter this code, be sure to place it on a single line. Failure to do so will result in a JavaScript error.

As before, we can view the resulting URL through Fiddler. Figure 9-2 is a screenshot of Fiddler with the query's URL highlighted in the `IScript_Toolbar` response.

Complete Code for the Meta-HTML Processor

The following is the complete code listing for the meta-HTML processor.

```
class Processor
   method process(&html As string) Returns string;

private
   REM ** Meta-HTML helper/resolver definitions go here;
   method processImages(&html As string) Returns string;
   method processJavaScript(&html As string) Returns string;
   method processGenerateQueryContentUrl(&html As string)
         Returns string;
end-class;

method process
   /+ &html as String +/
   /+ Returns String +/
   REM ** Calls to Meta-HTML helpers/resolvers go here;
   &html = %This.processImages(&html);
```

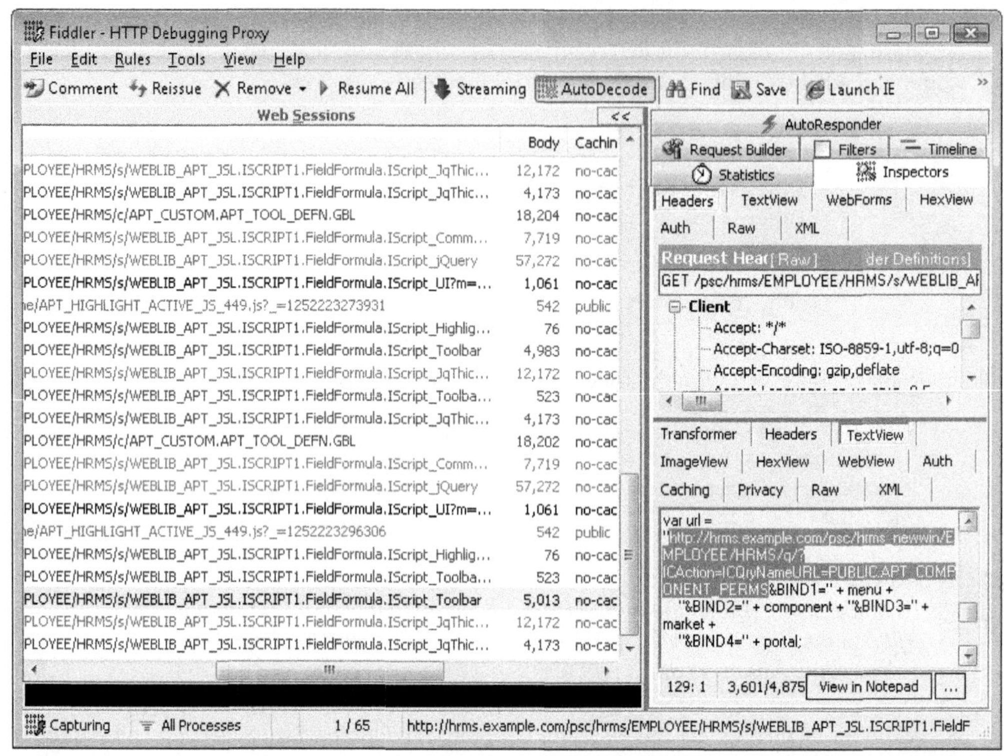

FIGURE 9-2. *Fiddler showing the query's URL*

```
   &html = %This.processJavaScript(&html);
   Return %This.processGenerateQueryContentUrl(&html);
end-method;

method processImages
   /+ &html as String +/
   /+ Returns String +/
   Local JavaObject &pattern;
   Local JavaObject &matcher;
   Local string &imgUrl;

   REM ** Resolve %Image(IMAGE_NAME) tags;
   &pattern = GetJavaClass("java.util.regex.Pattern").compile(
         "(?i)%Image\((\w+)\)");

   &matcher = &pattern.matcher(
         CreateJavaObject("java.lang.String", &html));
```

```
   While &matcher.find()
      &imgUrl = %Response.GetImageURL(
            @("Image." | &matcher.group(1)));
      &html = Substitute(&html, &matcher.group(), &imgUrl);
   End-While;

   Return &html;
end-method;

method processJavaScript
   /+ &html as String +/
   /+ Returns String +/
   Local JavaObject &pattern;
   Local JavaObject &matcher;
   Local string &jsUrl;

   REM ** Resolve %JavaScript(HTML_DEFN) tags;
   &pattern = GetJavaClass("java.util.regex.Pattern").compile(
         "(?i)%JavaScript\((\w+)\)");

   &matcher = &pattern.matcher(
         CreateJavaObject("java.lang.String", &html));

   While &matcher.find()
      &jsUrl = %Response.GetJavaScriptURL(@("HTML." |
            &matcher.group(1)));
      &html = Substitute(&html, &matcher.group(), &jsUrl);
   End-While;

   Return &html;
end-method;

method processGenerateQueryContentUrl
   /+ &html as String +/
   /+ Returns String +/
   Local JavaObject &pattern;
   Local JavaObject &matcher;
   Local string &qryUrl;

   Local boolean &isPublic = False;
   Local boolean &isNewWindow = False;

   /* Resolve %GenerateQueryContentUrl(PORTAL_NAME, NODE_NAME,
    *       QUERY_NAME, IS_PUBLIC, IS_NEWWIN) tags
    */
   &pattern = GetJavaClass("java.util.regex.Pattern").compile(
         "(?i)%GenerateQueryContentUrl\(" |
         "(\w+), ?(\w+), ?(\w+), ?(\w+), ?(\w+)\)");

   &matcher = &pattern.matcher(
         CreateJavaObject("java.lang.String", &html));
```

```
    While &matcher.find()
      If (&matcher.group(4) = "True") Then
         &isPublic = True;
      End-If;

      If (&matcher.group(5) = "True") Then
         &isNewWindow = True;
      End-If;

      &qryUrl = GenerateQueryContentURL(&matcher.group(1),
            &matcher.group(2), &matcher.group(3), &isPublic,
            &isNewWindow);
      &html = Substitute(&html, &matcher.group(), &qryUrl);
   End-While;

   Return &html;
end-method;
```

As you worked through the code presented for the `APT_META_HTML:Processor` application class, I hope you recognized several patterns. The `process`*`XXX`* methods contain several redundancies. For example, the only differences between the `processImages` method and the `processJavaScript` method are the regular expression and the `%Response` method call. Additionally, many of our iScripts share the same code. If you compare the `IScript_JqThickboxJs` function with the `IScript_CommonLib` function, you will notice the only difference is the HTML definition name. Such redundancies beg for refactoring. We will refactor much of this code in Chapter 15.

With our new meta-HTML resolver in place, we are not using several of the iScripts in `WEBLIB_APT_JSL`. Now is a good time to delete those unused iScripts. Here is a list of the iScripts we no longer need:

- `IScript_Ajax`
- `IScript_UILoader`
- `IScript_HighlightActiveJs`

What about `IScript_JqThickboxJs`? It seems that it would be possible to replace uses of `IScript_JqThickboxJs` with `%JavaScript(APT_JQ_THICKBOX_JS)`. Unfortunately, the HTML definition served by `IScript_JqThickboxJs` contains meta-HTML that uses `APT_META_HTML:Processor`. In this instance, the iScript provides meta-HTML resolution that would not exist without the iScript. If we reverted the `APT_JQ_THICKBOX_JS` HTML definition to its Chapter 6 state, we could use our custom meta-HTML resolver to cache the Thickbox HTML definition. As it is now, however, it caches the Thickbox loading image. With this scenario, we need to choose which file to cache: the image or the JavaScript definition—we can't cache both.

Using Third-Party Libraries

In addition to the Java API and the Java libraries delivered with PeopleTools, you can use other, third-party Java libraries. Here, we'll take a look at using Apache Commons, the Apache Velocity Engine, and JSON.

To use a third-party library, you need to add it to PeopleSoft's Java class path. The method for adding Java classes to an installation's class path differs by operating system and installation. Generally, you make third-party Java libraries available to PeopleCode by placing them in your `$PS_HOME/class` directory. This applies to your application server, process scheduler server, and App Designer home directory.

Java libraries can be distributed as class or JAR files. A JAR file is a standard zip file containing a Java package hierarchy and Java class files. If your library is distributed as class files, you can deploy those class files without restarting PeopleSoft. On the other hand, if your Java library is distributed as a JAR file or collection of JAR files, you will need to restart PeopleSoft after deploying the library. What part of PeopleSoft do you need to restart? If you deployed the library to your application server, you need to restart your application server; this is also the case with your process scheduler server or local App Designer installation. You must restart PeopleSoft after deploying a JAR file because PeopleSoft iterates over the JAR files in the class directory at startup, adding each JAR file to the class path.

Apache Commons

The Apache Commons project[2] contains some of my favorite Java utility libraries. Much of the functionality in these libraries already exists in PeopleCode in some form or another, but I've found a few features in the Commons libraries that either are missing from PeopleCode or are much easier to accomplish using these Java classes.

The Commons library is divided into three sections:

- The Commons Proper section contains active, maintained subprojects. There is little risk associated with these libraries.
- The Commons Sandbox section contains prototype subprojects that are in active development but haven't graduated to Commons Proper.
- The Commons Dormant subprojects are inactive sandbox projects.

Java's fundamental classes belong to a package named `java.lang`. This includes classes such as `Class`, `Object`, `String`, and `Thread`, as well as many others. These classes form the foundation of the Java language. The Apache Commons Lang project offers an extension to these `java.lang` classes.

Prior to running the following examples, download Commons Lang from the Apache Commons web site (http://commons.apache.org/lang/). After downloading and verifying the download, expand it and copy the commons-lang-*.jar file into your local App Designer %PS_HOME%\class directory. We will run our examples from an App Engine within App Designer, so you don't need to copy this file to the PeopleSoft server.

NOTE
If you plan to deploy a solution using Commons Lang, you will need to copy the JAR file to your PeopleSoft application server's $PS_HOME directory.

To follow along, add a new step and PeopleCode action to the App Engine program `APT_JAVA_TST`. The step's name is not important; you can keep the default name provided by App Designer. You may also want to inactivate prior steps in this program so that your tests run only the current example.

String Utilities

The Commons Lang `StringUtils` class contains several utility methods for working with strings. Some of these methods already exist as part of the PeopleCode language; others don't. For example, the `StringUtils.split` and `StringUtils.join` methods already have PeopleCode equivalents. Other functionalities—such as abbreviate, capitalize, and center— don't have native PeopleCode implementations. Rather than write our own PeopleCode implementations, we can *borrow* from `StringUtils`.

The `StringUtils.abbreviate` method shortens strings by first determining if a string exceeds a specified length. If it does, the method creates a new string that is three characters smaller than the specified length, and then places an ellipsis at the end of the string. Here is some code to demonstrate `StringUtils.abbreviate`:

```
Local JavaObject &stringUtils =
      GetJavaClass("org.apache.commons.lang.StringUtils");
Local array of string &names =
      CreateArray("Charles Baran", "PeopleSoft Super User");
Local string &abbrName;
Local number &maxLength = 15;
Local number &index = 0;

While &names.Next(&index)
   &abbrName = &stringUtils.abbreviate(&names [&index], &maxLength);
   MessageBox(0, "", 0, 0, &abbrName);
End-While;
```

Running this code produces the following (emphasis added):

```
Charles Baran (0,0)
 Message Set Number: 0
 Message Number: 0
 Message Reason: Charles Baran (0,0) (0,0)

PeopleSoft S... (0,0)
 Message Set Number: 0
 Message Number: 0
 Message Reason: PeopleSoft S... (0,0) (0,0)
```

In this output, the string "Charles Baran" is printed without an ellipsis because the string's length is less than 15 characters. The string "PeopleSoft Super User" is abbreviated because it is longer than 15 characters.

String-Escaping Utilities

The PeopleCode language includes functions for escaping HTML, JavaScript, and WML. What about XML, CSV, SQL, or even Java? For that matter, what about *un*escaping strings? Enter Commons Lang `StringEscapeUtils`. The following code uses the PeopleCode `EscapeJavaScript` function to print a string that is safe to use with JavaScript. Next, it uses `StringEscapeUtils .unescapeJavaScript` to convert the escaped string back to its original form.

```
Local JavaObject &escUtils =
      GetJavaClass("org.apache.commons.lang.StringEscapeUtils");
```

```
Local string &original = "alert(""Hello World"");" |
      Char(13) | Char(10) | "return true;";
Local string &escaped = &escUtils.escapeJavaScript(&original);
Local string &unescaped = &escUtils.unescapeJavaScript(&escaped);

MessageBox(0, "", 0, 0, "Original: " | &original);
MessageBox(0, "", 0, 0, "Escaped: " | &escaped);
MessageBox(0, "", 0, 0, "Unescaped: " | &unescaped);

If (&original = &unescaped) Then
   MessageBox(0, "", 0, 0, "Strings equal");
Else
   MessageBox(0, "", 0, 0, "Strings NOT equal");
End-If;
```

This code produces the following output (emphasis added):

```
Original: alert("Hello World");
return true; (0,0)
 Message Set Number: 0
 Message Number: 0
 Message Reason: Original: alert("Hello World");
return true; (0,0) (0,0)

Escaped: alert(\"Hello World\");\r\nreturn true; (0,0)
 Message Set Number: 0
 Message Number: 0
 Message Reason: Escaped: alert(\"Hello World\");\r\n
     return true; (0,0) (0,0)

Unescaped: alert("Hello World");
return true; (0,0)
 Message Set Number: 0
 Message Number: 0
 Message Reason: Unescaped: alert("Hello World");
return true; (0,0) (0,0)

Strings equal (0,0)
 Message Set Number: 0
 Message Number: 0
 Message Reason: Strings equal (0,0) (0,0)
```

Perhaps a more relevant example is escaping XML for use with web services. The following example is similar to the previous one, but uses the `escapeXml` method to convert currency symbols into XML entities.

```
Local JavaObject &escUtils =
      GetJavaClass("org.apache.commons.lang.StringEscapeUtils");
Local string &original = "$, £, €";
Local string &escaped = &escUtils.escapeXml(&original);
Local string &unescaped = &escUtils.unescapeXml(&escaped);
```

```
MessageBox(0, "", 0, 0, "Original: " | &original);
MessageBox(0, "", 0, 0, "Escaped: " | &escaped);
MessageBox(0, "", 0, 0, "Unescaped: " | &unescaped);

If (&original = &unescaped) Then
   MessageBox(0, "", 0, 0, "Strings equal");
Else
   MessageBox(0, "", 0, 0, "Strings NOT equal");
End-If;
```

This code produces the following output (emphasis added):

```
Original: $, £, € (0,0)
 Message Set Number: 0
 Message Number: 0
 Message Reason: Original: $, £, € (0,0) (0,0)

Escaped: $, &#163;, &#8364; (0,0)
 Message Set Number: 0
 Message Number: 0
 Message Reason: Escaped: $, &#163;, &#8364; (0,0) (0,0)

Unescaped: $, £, € (0,0)
 Message Set Number: 0
 Message Number: 0
 Message Reason: Unescaped: $, £, € (0,0) (0,0)

Strings equal (0,0)
 Message Set Number: 0
 Message Number: 0
 Message Reason: Strings equal (0,0) (0,0)
```

Apache Velocity

Several chapters in this book use HTML definitions (and even just plain-old strings) to generate structured content. For example, in Chapter 5, we used an HTML definition to generate an iCalendar file. In Chapter 8, we used a per-row HTML definition as well as a header HTML definition to generate HTML for toolbar buttons.

An alternative to static HTML definitions is a template engine. Besides offering parameterized templates, like HTML definitions, template engines usually include decision and control-flow statements. There are several template engines for Java. Here, we will look at using the Apache Velocity Engine.

To use Apache Velocity from PeopleCode, you will need to download a copy from http://velocity.apache.org/ and place the following JAR files in your %PS_HOME%\class directory:

- commons-collections-*.jar
- commons-lang-*.jar
- velocity-*.jar

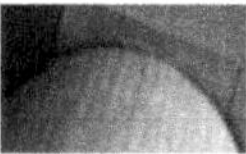

NOTE
When I wrote this chapter, Velocity was distributed as two JAR files: velocity-1.6.2.jar and velocity-1.6.2-dep.jar. The velocity-dep.jar file contains commons-collections, commons-lang, and oro. If you use velocity*-dep, you do not need to copy commons-collections and commons-lang.*

As an example, we will use this template engine to generate an iCalendar with multiple events. This example uses Velocity in an App Engine run locally from App Designer. To follow along, create a new App Engine named `APT_VEL_TST` and then add a new step (the name isn't important) and PeopleCode action. You may also want to inactivate prior steps.

To run the Apache Velocity Engine, you need the following:

- A Velocity configuration file
- A log4j configuration
- A template defined using the Velocity Template Language (VTL)
- PeopleCode to load Velocity, create objects, and apply a template

NOTE
The following code is for illustrative purposes only. For reusability, I recommend wrapping the Velocity Engine in an application class.

Configuring Velocity

You can configure Velocity through PeopleCode or through a configuration file. To keep our code as clean as possible, we will use a configuration file. Create a file named velocity.properties and save it in your %PS_HOME%\class directory. Add the following to this file:

```
resource.loader=file
file.resource.loader.class=org.apache.velocity.runtime.resource\
.loader.FileResourceLoader
file.resource.loader.path=c:/velocity/templates
file.resource.loader.cache=true
# check every five minutes
file.resource.loader.modificationCheckInterval=300

runtime.log.logsystem.log4j.logger=velocity
```

NOTE
The velocity.properties file does not need to exist in PS_HOME. If you place it somewhere else, however, be sure to update the PeopleCode shown in a later listing.

Configuring Logging

PeopleSoft uses log4j for various portions of the application. We will discuss log4j in detail in Chapter 10. For now, we need to modify the delivered log4j.properties file to properly initialize the Velocity Engine. Add the following to the end of your %PS_HOME%\class\log4j.properties file.

```
# Velocity log4j configuration
log4j.logger.velocity=WARN, stdout
log4j.appender.stdout=org.apache.log4j.ConsoleAppender
log4j.appender.stdout.layout=org.apache.log4j.PatternLayout
log4j.appender.stdout.layout.ConversionPattern=%5p [%c] %m%n
```

TIP

The logging configuration here tells log4j to print warning messages only. To print all information, including debug information, replace `WARN` *with* `ALL`*. This is very helpful if you are having trouble with your Velocity Engine configuration or template file.*

Creating a Template

Velocity templates use VTL. You can find a complete VTL reference on the Velocity web site. Here is a very basic template that iterates over the events in a collection to generate a multiple-event iCalendar entry (VTL-specific language is in bold):

```
BEGIN:VCALENDAR
VERSION:2.0
PRODID:-//PT Tips and Techniques//Velocity vCal 1.0//EN
#foreach ($event in $events)
BEGIN:VEVENT
DTSTART:$event.start
DTEND:$event.end
SUMMARY:$event.summary
DESCRIPTION:$event.descr
LOCATION:$event.location
CATEGORIES:$event.categories
END:VEVENT
#end
END:VCALENDAR
```

For testing purposes, create the folder structure c:\velocity\templates on your workstation's file system and add the preceding template code to a new file named c:\velocity\templates\icalendar.vm.

NOTE

You may place templates in a different location if you prefer. The configuration file in this example expects templates to exist in c:\velocity\templates. If you place templates in a different location, be sure to update the `file.resource.loader.path` *property of the velocity.properties file.*

In Chapter 5, you learned that iCalendar files expect dates in a particular format. VTL is robust enough to convert a PeopleSoft date into an acceptable date format. Also, the `CATEGORIES` key in this example expects `$event.categories` to be a comma-delimited string. We could have written the template so that it received an array of categories and joined them into a comma-delimited string.

Writing PeopleCode to Process the Template

Assuming that the data for our template comes from a PeopleSoft transaction, we need to write some PeopleCode to collect data, and then process that data with the Velocity Engine. Here is a PeopleCode sample (I hard-coded the data for simplicity). To test this sample, in `APT_VEL_TST`, add a PeopleCode action to the first step and insert the following PeopleCode. Prior to running this code, be sure to disable the Restart property.

```
REM ** Create the Velocity Template Engine object;
Local JavaObject &engine = CreateJavaObject(
      "org.apache.velocity.app.VelocityEngine");
REM ** Get a pointer to the class loader;
REM **  we will use it to load the configuration file;
Local JavaObject &cl = &engine.getClass().getClassLoader();
REM ** Load the configuration file;
Local JavaObject &configStream =
      &cl.getResourceAsStream("velocity.properties");
Local JavaObject &configProps = CreateJavaObject(
      "org.apache.commons.collections.ExtendedProperties");
REM ** The context contains the template's variables;
Local JavaObject &context;
REM ** A variable for the actual template instance;
Local JavaObject &template;

REM ** Each event will be a separate hashtable (key/value pairs);
Local JavaObject &event1 = CreateJavaObject("java.util.Hashtable");
Local JavaObject &event2 = CreateJavaObject("java.util.Hashtable");

REM ** The collection of events used in the #foreach is an ArrayList;
Local JavaObject &eventList = CreateJavaObject("java.util.ArrayList");

REM ** Velocity will write results to a java.io.Writer;
Local JavaObject &result = CreateJavaObject("java.io.StringWriter");

REM ** Initialize Velocity from the config file;
&configProps.load(&configStream);
&engine.setExtendedProperties(&configProps);
&engine.init();

REM ** Create a context for our template data;
&context = CreateJavaObject("org.apache.velocity.VelocityContext");

REM ** populate our data;
&event1.put("start", "20090813T160000Z");
&event1.put("end", "20090813T180000Z");
&event1.put("summary", "Event One");
&event1.put("descr", "This is event number one");
&event1.put("location", "Conference room 1");
&event1.put("categories", "Business,Conferences");
```

```
&event2.put("start", "20090814T160000Z");
&event2.put("end", "20090814T180000Z");
&event2.put("summary", "Event Two");
&event2.put("descr", "This is event number two");
&event2.put("location", "Conference room 2");
&event2.put("categories", "Business,Conferences");

&eventList.add(&event1);
&eventList.add(&event2);

&context.put("events", &eventList);

REM ** Merge the template;
&template = &engine.getTemplate("icalendar.vm");
&template.merge(&context, &result);

REM ** print the results;
MessageBox(0, "", 0, 0, &result.toString());
```

Running this code produces the following output (the `BEGIN` and `END` event tags are in bold for clarity). Because we used the `MessageBox` statement, you should see the same output printed twice. The following listing shows only the relevant results.

```
BEGIN:VCALENDAR
VERSION:2.0
PRODID:-//PT Tips and Techniques//Velocity vCal 1.0//EN
BEGIN:VEVENT
DTSTART:20090813T160000Z
DTEND:20090813T180000Z
SUMMARY:Event One
DESCRIPTION:This is event number one
LOCATION:Conference room 1
CATEGORIES:Business,Conferences
END:VEVENT
BEGIN:VEVENT
DTSTART:20090814T160000Z
DTEND:20090814T180000Z
SUMMARY:Event Two
DESCRIPTION:This is event number two
LOCATION:Conference room 2
CATEGORIES:Business,Conferences
END:VEVENT
END:VCALENDAR
```

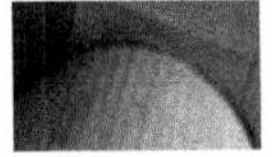

NOTE

If you run this from App Designer, you may see a log4j error at the top of the file stating it can't find the PSJChart.log file. Ignore this error. It is caused by the delivered configuration in log4j.properties and has no impact on this example.

Using JSON

JSON is a language-independent data-interchange format based on a subset of the JavaScript programming language.[3] As you saw in Chapter 7, you can create JSON by stringing together data with JSON markup.

The http://json.org web site maintains a list of JSON parsers by language. Looking at the list of Java implementations, you can see you have a lot of options. The examples in this section use JSON.simple, which is available from http://code.google.com/p/json-simple/. Many of the JSON Java libraries require Java 1.5 or higher. This is fine if you are using PeopleTools 8.49 or higher. The JSON.simple Java library works with Java 1.2 and later. Another important consideration when choosing a Java library is overloading, a topic we will discuss later. The JSON.simple library uses method overloading in a manner that is safe for PeopleCode.

As with any Java library, download the JSON.simple library and place it in your %PS_HOME%\class directory prior to use.

Producing JSON

JSON is gaining in popularity. Google, Yahoo, Flickr, and many other sites offer JSON services as an alternative to XML-based web services. As demonstrated in Chapter 7, you can serve JSON from PeopleSoft.

In Chapter 7, we wrote an iScript named `IScript_UI`. In that function, we used the PeopleCode `Substitute` function to replace `\'` with `'`. Our purpose for substituting particular characters was to make the output safe for JavaScript usage. This substitution satisfies most cases, but what about the case where the code contains `\\'` (two backslashes and a single quote)? If the `\\` is inside quotes, then this could be valid JSON. As an alternative, let's use JSON.simple to build proper JSON strings.

TIP
Using the techniques described in this section, it is possible to write an `OnRequest` synchronous handler that returns JSON from a web service.

The JSON.simple Java library provides support for the Java `Map` and `List` interfaces. We used both maps (`Hashtable`) and lists (`ArrayList`) in various examples in this chapter. The Apache Velocity example used both.

The following code takes the hashtable collection example presented at the beginning of this chapter and converts the hashtable's contents into JSON. Since the JSON.simple library does not support PeopleCode arrays, I converted the original example's PeopleCode arrays into `ArrayLists`. (I also modified the example slightly to make it more appropriate for JSON.)

```
Local JavaObject &restaurants =
      CreateJavaObject("java.util.ArrayList");
Local JavaObject &bobs = CreateJavaObject("java.util.Hashtable");
Local JavaObject &luigis = CreateJavaObject("java.util.Hashtable");
Local JavaObject &luigisSpecials =
      CreateJavaObject("java.util.ArrayList");
Local JavaObject &bobsSpecials =
      CreateJavaObject("java.util.ArrayList");
Local JavaObject &json = GetJavaClass("org.json.simple.JSONValue");
Local string &jsonString;
```

```
&luigisSpecials.add("Pizza");
&luigisSpecials.add("Pasta");
&luigisSpecials.add("Salad");

&luigis.put("name", "Luigi's Pizzeria");
&luigis.put("specials", &luigisSpecials);

&bobsSpecials.add("1/2 lb Burger");
&bobsSpecials.add("Root Beer Float");
&bobsSpecials.add("Onion Rings");

&bobs.put("name", "Bob's drive-in");
&bobs.put("specials", &bobsSpecials);

&restaurants.add(&luigis);
&restaurants.add(&bobs);

&jsonString = &json.toJSONString(&restaurants);

MessageBox(0, "", 0, 0, &jsonString);
```

Running this code from our test App Engine, `APT_JAVA_TST`, produces the following results:

```
[
    {
        "specials": [
            "Pizza",
            "Pasta",
            "Salad"
        ],
        "name": "Luigi's Pizzeria"
    },
    {
        "specials": [
            "1\/2 lb Burger",
            "Root Beer Float",
            "Onion Rings"
        ],
        "name": "Bob's drive-in"
    }
]
```

NOTE

The actual JSON returned by JSON.simple is optimized for data transfer, and, therefore, doesn't contain any whitespace. To make it easier to read, I formatted the preceding output using an online JSON formatter and validator, available at http://www.jsonlint.com/.

Our Custom Scripts module generates JSON data that contains custom scripts separated by insert location. Some of our scripts contain quotes and other characters that we cannot embed in

JSON directly. We attempted to make our scripts safe by using the `EscapeJavaScriptString` PeopleCode function. Using `EscapeJavaScriptString` had the unfortunate side effect of changing `'` (single quote) characters into `\'`, an escape sequence that is valid for JavaScript, but not for JSON. Let's modify the Custom Scripts iScript to generate JSON using the JSON.simple Java library.

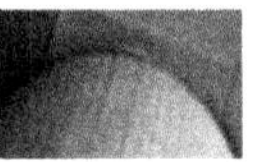

NOTE
The following modification requires the json-simple JAR file to be in your app server's class path (typically $PS_HOME/class). After adding this file to your app server's file system, reboot your app server to make the JAR file accessible to PeopleCode.

Open the `FieldFormula` event of the record field `WEBLIB_APT_JSL ISCRIPT1`. Search for the `IScript_UI` function and replace it with the following code. Most of the changes to this function are in bold. By using JSON.simple, I was able to delete several lines of code (the deleted lines are not shown). Rather than try to reconcile the differences, it might be easier to replace the entire function.

```
Function IScript_UI()
   Local APT_META_HTML:Processor &p = create APT_META_HTML:Processor();

   Local SQL &scriptsCursor;
   Local string &menu = %Request.GetParameter("m");
   Local string &component = %Request.GetParameter("c");
   Local string &market = %Request.GetParameter("mk");
   Local string &page = %Request.GetParameter("p");
   Local number &isSearch = Value(%Request.GetParameter("s"));
   Local string &searchOption;

   Local string &location;
   Local string &data;

   Local JavaObject &json = GetJavaClass("org.json.simple.JSONValue");
   Local JavaObject &scripts = CreateJavaObject("java.util.ArrayList");
   Local JavaObject &scriptProps;

   REM ** If this is a search page, then look for Search Only scripts;
   If (&isSearch = 1) Then
      &searchOption = "SO";
   Else
      &searchOption = "NS";
   End-If;

   &scriptsCursor = GetSQL(SQL.APT_GET_UI_SCRIPTS, &menu,
         &component, &market, &page, &searchOption);

   While &scriptsCursor.Fetch(&location, &data);
      &scriptProps = CreateJavaObject("java.util.Properties");
      &scriptProps.setProperty("appendTo", &location);
```

```
        &scriptProps.setProperty("data", &p.process(&data));
        &scripts.add(&scriptProps);
    End-While;

    %Response.SetContentType("application/json");
    %Response.WriteLine(&json.toJSONString(&scripts));
End-Function;
```

After making the changes shown in the preceding code, navigate to this URL:

http://hrms.example.com/psc/hrms/EMPLOYEE/HRMS/s/WEBLIB_APT_JSL.ISCRIPT1 .FieldFormula.IScript_UI?m=APT_CUSTOM&c=APT_UI_SCRIPTS&mk=GBL&p=&s=1

Save the result, and open the resultant file in a text editor. You will see that the JSON.simple string escape routine is more aggressive than the PeopleCode `EscapeJavaScriptString`. All the slashes (/) were replaced with \/. If all is well, the Custom Scripts module should continue to highlight the active text field, display the custom administration toolbar, and modify the Custom Scripts Advanced Search page.

Consuming JSON

With the major public web services offering services in JSON format, it is good to consider the possibilities for consuming JSON from PeopleSoft. Consuming JSON directly from PeopleCode, however, is a little awkward. When parsing a JSON string, we expect either an array (`List`) or an object (`Map`). The JSON.simple parse methods, however, return `java.lang.Object`, the Java base class for all objects. Even though the actual return value is an instance of either `org.json.simple.JSONObject` or `org.json.simple.JSONArray`, PeopleCode offers no method for converting the `Object` to its underlying type. Therefore, it is not possible to call methods belonging to the results' implementing class. We can still call methods of the underlying class; we just can't call them directly. Our options are to use Java reflection or to write a custom Java helper class. Here, we'll look at using reflection. In Chapter 12, we will discuss creating and deploying custom Java classes.

Reflection is used by Java to inspect and manipulate objects, especially when the object type is unknown. In our case, we know the object type, but the PeopleCode runtime doesn't.

Let's start with some code that uses the Google AJAX Search API to search news listings for the phrase "Oracle Corporation." To follow along, add another step and PeopleCode action to the `APT_JAVA_TST` App Engine program (the step's name is not important) and then add the following code.

```
Local string &data =
      %IntBroker.ConnectorRequestUrl(
      "http://ajax.googleapis.com/ajax/services/search/news?v=1.0" |
      "&q=Oracle+Corporation");
```

Next, let's add some code to parse the Google JSON response into an object tree:

```
Local JavaObject &json = GetJavaClass("org.json.simple.JSONValue");
Local JavaObject &obj = &json.parse(&data);
```

Since the top-level element in a JSON data structure is either an object or an array, the variable `&obj` either points to an instance of `org.json.simple.JSONArray` or `org.json.simple.JSONObject`. The actual implementation class for `&obj` is determined by the type of data returned by the JSON response. If the JSON response begins with `[` (left square bracket), then `&obj` is a `JSONArray`. If the response begins with { (left curly bracket), then `&obj` is a `JSONObject`. We can test this by adding one more line of PeopleCode:

```
MessageBox(0, "", 0, 0, "&obj: " | &obj);
MessageBox(0, "", 0, 0, "&obj.getClass().getName(): " |
      &obj.getClass().getName());
```

Didn't I say one more line? The preceding code contains two lines. While I was printing the name of the class represented by `&obj`, I thought I would throw in an additional line to print what PeopleSoft thinks `&obj` is. The first line prints PeopleCode's perception of `&obj`, and the second line prints the actual class represented by `&obj`.

Here is a complete listing of the previous code segments:

```
Local string &data = %IntBroker.ConnectorRequestUrl(
      "http://ajax.googleapis.com/ajax/services/search/news?v=1.0" |
      "&q=Oracle+Corporation");
Local JavaObject &json = GetJavaClass("org.json.simple.JSONValue");
Local JavaObject &obj = &json.parse(&data);

MessageBox(0, "", 0, 0, "&obj: " | &obj);
MessageBox(0, "", 0, 0, "&obj.getClass().getName(): " |
      &obj.getClass().getName());
```

Running this code prints the following (emphasis added):

```
&obj: java.lang.Object (0,0)
 Message Set Number: 0
 Message Number: 0
 Message Reason: &obj: java.lang.Object (0,0) (0,0)

&obj.getClass().getName(): org.json.simple.JSONObject (0,0)
 Message Set Number: 0
 Message Number: 0
 Message Reason: &obj.getClass().getName(): org.json.simple.JSONObject
      (0,0) (0,0)
```

This output confirms that PeopleCode thinks `&obj` is a `java.lang.Object`, but the Java Virtual Machine (JVM) knows it is really `org.json.simple.JSONObject`.

The following code listing is a partial mockup of the results returned by the Google News AJAX Search API.

```
{
  "responseData": {
    "results": [
      {
        ...
        "content": "Content of search result",
        "unescapedUrl": "URL to result article",
```

```
          ...
          "title": "Title of Article"
          ...
        }
      ]
    }
}
```

Assuming that this JSON is stored in a variable named `jsonData`, the following object/array notation would return the value of the `unescapedUrl` property:

```
jsonData.responseData.results[0].unescapedUrl
```

Let's use PeopleCode and Java reflection to print the title (`title`) and URL (`unescapedUrl`) of each search result.

The first order of business is to access the `responseData` property of the JSON response. Since the `JSONObject` class implements the `java.util.Map` interface, we will use `Map.get("responseData")` to access the `responseData` object.

Just as a PeopleCode application class defines the properties and methods for a PeopleCode object, a Java class defines the properties and methods for a Java object. We can query those properties and methods by accessing the object's `Class`. (We actually already accessed the `Class` object for `&obj` when we printed the implementation class name using `&obj.getClass().getName()`.) We can get a pointer to a class's method by calling `Class.getMethod()`.

The following PeopleCode fragment finds and prints the `get` method of the root JSON object. If you would like to follow along, add a new step and PeopleCode action to `APT_JAVA_TST` and add the following PeopleCode. Note that the complete code listing for printing the title and URL is presented at the end of this section.

```
Local string &data = %IntBroker.ConnectorRequestUrl(
      "http://ajax.googleapis.com/ajax/services/search/news?v=1.0" |
      "&q=Oracle+Corporation");
Local JavaObject &json = GetJavaClass("org.json.simple.JSONValue");
Local JavaObject &obj = &json.parse(&data);

Local JavaObject &mapGetMethodParms =
      CreateJavaObject("java.lang.Class[]",
      GetJavaClass("java.lang.Object"));
Local JavaObject &mapGetMethod = &obj.getClass().getMethod("get",
      &mapGetMethodParms);

MessageBox(0, "", 0, 0, "&mapGetMethod: " | &mapGetMethod.toString());
```

To acquire a pointer to an object's method, we start with the object and access its declaring class, which is always an instance of `java.lang.Class`. The `java.lang.Class` object has a method named `getMethod`, which returns a pointer to a specific method. This method requires two parameters: the name of the method you want to retrieve and the array containing the method's parameter types. Unlike PeopleCode application class methods, Java class methods can have multiple declarations, each with a different number and/or type of parameters. This Java feature is called *overloading*, and it applies to methods and constructors (method overloading by parameter type presents another challenge to PeopleCode).

In the preceding code, we first create a Java array containing the `get` method's parameters (`&mapGetMethodParms`), and then we call `getMethod()` to retrieve a pointer to the `get` method that has one parameter of type `java.lang.Object`.

When run, this PeopleCode prints the following:

```
&mapGetMethod: public java.lang.Object java.util.HashMap.get(java.lang.Object)
(0,0)
 Message Set Number: 0
 Message Number: 0
 Message Reason: &mapGetMethod: public java.lang.Object
      java.util.HashMap.get(
      java.lang.Object) (0,0) (0,0)
```

From this output, you see that the `get` method returns an `Object`, not a `JSONObject` or `JSONArray`. Therefore, if we want to execute any method against the `Object` returned by `get` other than the methods declared by `java.lang.Object` (mainly `toString()`), then we will need to use reflection on the return value as well. Also notice the `get` method declaration here says that `get` is declared by `java.util.HashMap`, not `JSONObject`.

A `java.lang.reflect.Method` object points to the class's method, not the object's method. This means that the method pointer `&mapGetMethod` can be used with multiple instances of `JSONObject`.

The following PeopleCode executes the `get` method against the JSON result, and then prints what PeopleCode thinks the `get` method returned, as well as the actual implementing class name of the return value.

```
Local string &data = %IntBroker.ConnectorRequestUrl(
      "http://ajax.googleapis.com/ajax/services/search/news?v=1.0" |
      "&q=Oracle+Corporation");
Local JavaObject &json = GetJavaClass("org.json.simple.JSONValue");
Local JavaObject &obj = &json.parse(&data);

Local JavaObject &mapGetMethodParms =
      CreateJavaObject("java.lang.Class[]",
      GetJavaClass("java.lang.Object"));
Local JavaObject &mapGetMethod = &obj.getClass().getMethod("get",
      &mapGetMethodParms);

Local JavaObject &responseData = &mapGetMethod.invoke(&obj,
      CreateJavaObject("java.lang.Object[]", "responseData"));

MessageBox(0, "", 0, 0, "&responseData: " | &responseData);
MessageBox(0, "", 0, 0, "&responseData.getClass().getName(): " |
      &responseData.getClass().getName());
```

This PeopleCode prints the following:

```
&responseData: java.lang.Object (0,0)
 Message Set Number: 0
 Message Number: 0
 Message Reason: &responseData: java.lang.Object (0,0) (0,0)
```

```
&responseData.getClass().getName(): org.json.simple.JSONObject (0,0)
 Message Set Number: 0
 Message Number: 0
 Message Reason: &responseData.getClass().getName():
      org.json.simple.JSONObject (0,0) (0,0)
```

Notice that we are once again dealing with a `JSONObject`, but PeopleCode thinks it is a `java.lang.Object`.

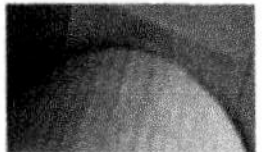

NOTE
The Java language allows you to cast an object from one type to another as long as the target type is in the source object's inheritance hierarchy. Casting eliminates the need for reflection as used in the example here. Unfortunately, PeopleCode does not support Java casting.

As you can see from the preceding code, we will be invoking `&mapGetMethod` often. Let's write a function so we can nest `get` calls together in a fashion that might be easier to read when compared to several `invoke` statements. The following PeopleCode contains a new function declaration as well as a call to the next `Map get` method.

```
REM Local JavaObject &mapGetMethod;

Function mapGet(&map As JavaObject, &key As string) Returns JavaObject
   /* NOTE: The &mapGetMethod variable is intentionally NOT declared.
    * I want to use this variable as local to the PeopleCode event,
    * not local to the function. In events, PeopleCode does not allow
    * you to declare local variables above function declarations.
    * Declaring it below the function declaration would result in the
    * error: Duplicate temporary variable declaration.
    */
   Return &mapGetMethod.invoke(&map,
         CreateJavaObject("java.lang.Object[]", &key));
End-Function;

Local string &data = %IntBroker.ConnectorRequestUrl(
      "http://ajax.googleapis.com/ajax/services/search/news?v=1.0" |
      "&q=Oracle+Corporation");
Local JavaObject &json = GetJavaClass("org.json.simple.JSONValue");
Local JavaObject &obj = &json.parse(&data);

Local JavaObject &mapGetMethodParms =
      CreateJavaObject("java.lang.Class[]",
      GetJavaClass("java.lang.Object"));
&mapGetMethod = &obj.getClass().getMethod("get", &mapGetMethodParms);

Local JavaObject &results =
      mapGet(mapGet(&obj, "responseData"), "results");
```

```
MessageBox(0, "", 0, 0, "&results: " | &results);
MessageBox(0, "", 0, 0, "&results.getClass().getName(): " |
      &results.getClass().getName());
```

At the top of this code listing, you see the new function declaration. Near the bottom of this listing, you see the actual function call. Notice how I nested the calls to `mapGet`. The inside call returns the outer `responseData` object, and the outside call returns the inner `results` object. This is the object hierarchy in reverse. I don't think I like this syntax. It is better than writing `invoke(...)` for each call, but the inside-out approach seems a little confusing. As an alternative, we could declare a variable for each JSON element.

The preceding code generates the following results (emphasis added):

```
&results: java.lang.Object (0,0)
 Message Set Number: 0
 Message Number: 0
 Message Reason: &results: java.lang.Object (0,0) (0,0)

&results.getClass().getName(): org.json.simple.JSONArray (0,0)
 Message Set Number: 0
 Message Number: 0
 Message Reason: &results.getClass().getName():
      org.json.simple.JSONArray (0,0) (0,0)
```

Let's keep working our way down the JSON data. Our next hurdle is to call the `size` and `get` methods of the `JSONArray` returned by the previous code. This will allow us to iterate over the contents of the `JSONArray`.

```
Function mapGet(&map As JavaObject, &key As string) Returns JavaObject
   /* NOTE: The &mapGetMethod variable is intentionally NOT declared.
    * I want to use this variable as local to the PeopleCode event,
    * not local to the function. In events, PeopleCode does not allow
    * you to declare local variables above function declarations.
    * Declaring it below the function declaration would result in the
    * error: Duplicate temporary variable declaration.
    */
   Return &mapGetMethod.invoke(&map,
         CreateJavaObject("java.lang.Object[]", &key));
End-Function;

Function listGet(&list As JavaObject, &index As number) Returns JavaObject
   /* NOTE: The &listGetMethod variable is intentionally NOT declared.
    * See mapGet function for details
    */
   Return &listGetMethod.invoke(&list,
         CreateJavaObject("java.lang.Object[]", &index));
End-Function;

Local string &data = %IntBroker.ConnectorRequestUrl(
      "http://ajax.googleapis.com/ajax/services/search/news?v=1.0" |
      "&q=Oracle+Corporation");
Local JavaObject &json = GetJavaClass("org.json.simple.JSONValue");
Local JavaObject &obj = &json.parse(&data);
```

```
Local JavaObject &mapGetMethodParms = CreateJavaObject(
      "java.lang.Class[]", GetJavaClass("java.lang.Object"));
&mapGetMethod = &obj.getClass().getMethod("get", &mapGetMethodParms);

Local JavaObject &responseData = mapGet(&obj, "responseData");
Local JavaObject &results = mapGet(&responseData, "results");

Local JavaObject &listGetMethodParms = CreateJavaObject(
      "java.lang.Class[]", GetJavaClass("java.lang.Integer").TYPE);
&listGetMethod =
      &results.getClass().getMethod("get", &listGetMethodParms);
Local JavaObject &listSizeMethod =
      &results.getClass().getMethod("size", Null);
Local number &resultSize = Value(&listSizeMethod.invoke(
      &results, Null).toString());

MessageBox(0, "", 0, 0, "&results[0].getClass().getName(): " |
      listGet(&results, 0).getClass().getName());
MessageBox(0, "", 0, 0, "&results.size(): " | &resultSize);
```

The get method of JSONObject has a parameter of type java.lang.Object. Finding the get method is a matter of creating a java.lang.Class array that contains a pointer to the java.lang.Object class. Finding the get method of JSONArray is a different story. The get method of JSONArray has an int parameter. The int type is a primitive Java type that does not inherit from java.lang.Object, the base class for java.lang.Class. Since int is not an Object, it cannot be added to a Class array. To work around this, Java provides the TYPE property (also known as a field) of the java.lang.Integer Java class. The java.lang.Integer class is an object wrapper for the primitive int Java type.

The preceding code produces the following results (emphasis added):

```
&results[0].getClass().getName(): org.json.simple.JSONObject (0,0)
 Message Set Number: 0
 Message Number: 0
 Message Reason: &results[0].getClass().getName():
      org.json.simple.JSONObject (0,0) (0,0)

&results.size(): 4 (0,0)
 Message Set Number: 0
 Message Number: 0
 Message Reason: &results.size(): 4 (0,0) (0,0)
```

We are almost there. The final element in the Google News AJAX Search API is an object containing the title and unescapedUrl properties. With Java reflection helper methods defined, this last part is as easy as writing a For loop.

The following listing contains the final code for this reflection example. Additions are in bold.

```
REM Local JavaObject &mapGetMethod;

Function mapGet(&map As JavaObject, &key As string) Returns JavaObject
   /* NOTE: The &mapGetMethod variable is intentionally NOT declared.
    * I want to use this variable as local to the PeopleCode event,
```

```
     * not local to the function. In events, PeopleCode does not allow
     * you to declare local variables above function declarations.
     * Declaring it below the function declaration would result in the
     * error: Duplicate temporary variable declaration.
     */
   Return &mapGetMethod.invoke(&map,
         CreateJavaObject("java.lang.Object[]", &key));
End-Function;

Function listGet(&list As JavaObject, &index As number)
      Returns JavaObject
   /* NOTE: The &listGetMethod variable is intentionally NOT declared.
    * See mapGet function for details
    */
   Return &listGetMethod.invoke(&list,
         CreateJavaObject("java.lang.Object[]", &index));
End-Function;

Local string &data = %IntBroker.ConnectorRequestUrl(
      "http://ajax.googleapis.com/ajax/services/search/news?v=1.0" |
      "&q=Oracle+Corporation");
Local JavaObject &json = GetJavaClass("org.json.simple.JSONValue");
Local JavaObject &obj = &json.parse(&data);

Local JavaObject &mapGetMethodParms =
      CreateJavaObject("java.lang.Class[]",
            GetJavaClass("java.lang.Object"));
&mapGetMethod = &obj.getClass().getMethod("get", &mapGetMethodParms);

Local JavaObject &responseData = mapGet(&obj, "responseData");
Local JavaObject &results = mapGet(&responseData, "results");

Local JavaObject &listGetMethodParms =
      CreateJavaObject("java.lang.Class[]",
            GetJavaClass("java.lang.Integer").TYPE);
&listGetMethod = &results.getClass().getMethod("get",
      &listGetMethodParms);

Local JavaObject &listSizeMethod =
      &results.getClass().getMethod("size", Null);
Local number &resultSize =
      Value(&listSizeMethod.invoke(&results, Null).toString());
Local number &resultIndex = 0;

For &resultIndex = 0 To (&resultSize - 1)
   Local JavaObject &resultItem = listGet(&results, &resultIndex);
   Local string &url = mapGet(&resultItem, "unescapedUrl").toString();
   Local string &title = mapGet(&resultItem, "title").toString();
   MessageBox(0, "", 0, 0, &title | ": " | &url);
End-For;
```

Using JSON.simple in this manner to process a variety of JSON services will result in a lot of redundant code. An alternative approach that brings us closer to `&json.responseData.results[0].unescapedUrl` is to wrap JSON.simple in an application package. Using an application package, I was able to write the entire parse code as follows:

```
import APT_JSON_SIMPLE:JSONArray;
import APT_JSON_SIMPLE:JSONObject;
import APT_JSON_SIMPLE:JSONValue;

Local string &json = %IntBroker.ConnectorRequestUrl(
      "http://ajax.googleapis.com/ajax/services/search/news?v=1.0" |
      "&q=Oracle+Corporation");
Local APT_JSON_SIMPLE:JSONValue &parser =
      create APT_JSON_SIMPLE:JSONValue();
Local APT_JSON_SIMPLE:JSONArray &results =
      &parser.parseAsObject(&json)
      .getObject("responseData")
      .getArray("results");

Local number &resultSize = &results.getSize();
Local number &resultIndex = 0;

For &resultIndex = 0 To (&resultSize - 1)
   Local APT_JSON_SIMPLE:JSONObject &resultItem =
         &results.getObject(&resultIndex);
   Local string &url = &resultItem.getValue("unescapedUrl").toString();
   Local string &title = &resultItem.getValue("title").toString();
   MessageBox(0, "", 0, 0, &title | ": " | &url);
End-For;
```

While this syntax—`json.getObject().getObject().getArray()`—is not as elegant as `object.property.property[0].unencodedUrl`, it is fairly close.

How Do I Know What Is Available?

As with any language, Java's features change between versions. Therefore, it is important to know which version your application uses. Most of the PeopleTools 8.4*x* releases used one of the Java 1.4 versions. PeopleTools 8.49, however, made the leap to Java 1.5. PeopleTools 8.50 moved to Java 1.6.

To determine your Java version, open a command prompt (shell in Linux), and execute the command `%PS_HOME%\jre\bin\java -version`. This will tell you the Java version used by your PeopleSoft application. Armed with this information, you can find the features available to your Java version in the API documentation at http://java.sun.com.

Besides the delivered Java API, you can take advantage of the libraries available from numerous open source projects. My favorite Java libraries exist at http://www.apache.org/. You can also find good Java libraries on many other sites, including http://www.eclipse.org and http://www.java.net.

Conclusion

As you saw in this chapter, Java has a lot to offer the PeopleCode developer. The next chapters will further demonstrate how to leverage the Java programming language to supplement PeopleCode development. In Chapter 10, we will use Java to create a logging framework for PeopleCode. In Chapter 11 you will learn additional strategies for working with Java from PeopleCode, including how to write and deploy your own Java classes.

Notes

1. Wikipedia, "Regular expression" [online]; available from http://en.wikipedia.org/wiki/Regular_expression; Internet; accessed 2 September 2009.
2. Apache Software Foundation, "Apache Commons" [online]; available from http://commons.apache.org/; Internet; accessed 6 September 2009.
3. Wikipedia, "JSON" [online]; available from http://en.wikipedia.org/wiki/JSON; Internet; accessed 7 September 2009.

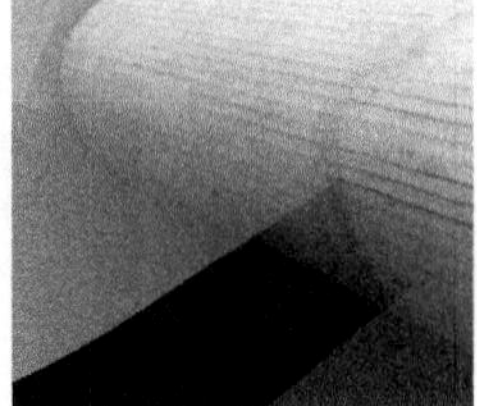

CHAPTER 10

A Logging Framework for PeopleCode

inding and resolving application irregularities is a daily task for most programmers. Some irregularities are caused by users entering inaccurate data or running processes incorrectly. Other irregularities stem from computer programming issues. Whatever the cause, it is our job to find the problem and propose a solution.

Finding and resolving problems involves detective work. We need to reconstruct the scene of the crime. So grab your hat and fingerprinting kit—the game is afoot.

Investigating Problems

To reconstruct the crime scene, we look for clues. When taking a statement from the user who reported the problem (the victim), we seek the following information:

- Who did it—description of the perpetrator (the application, process, and so on)
- What happened to the victim—the process failed, data was corrupted, and so on
- When the incident occurred
- Where the user was in the system—what component was being used
- How the incident happened—running a process, entering data, and so on
- Why the incident took place (from the victim's perspective)
- What the victim may have done to provoke the attack
- If the application (perpetrator) provided any error messages
- Any other information that may lead to the capture of this criminal

With the information acquired from the victim and various witnesses, we head back to our forensics lab (cubicle) to analyze the facts. This involves making phone calls, researching other cases, digging through the perpetrator's history (log files), and then trying to reconstruct the crime scene to see if we can replicate the experience of the victim. Once we discover the series of events triggering the attack, we can dig deeper to uncover the reason the perpetrator behaves the way it does.

Our greatest weapon in the fight for justice is the log file. For discussion purposes, I am lumping tracing and logging together. Both provide vital information about a crime scene.

Delivered Logging Tools

PeopleSoft applications include facilities for tracing PeopleCode and SQL. Both of these facilities trace every statement, offering an exceptional level of detail. Another benefit of PeopleSoft's tracing facilities is that they are configurable. You can turn tracing on and off at the session level or application level. At runtime, you can change trace settings.

The problem with trace files is that they rapidly grow to a size that is impossible to manage. It is quite common for PeopleSoft's configurable trace facilities to generate files that are too large to open using a standard text editor. Unfortunately, PeopleSoft's configurable trace facilities do not allow you to select the data or routine that is traced. In other words, you cannot target a block of code or specific variable. Tracing in PeopleSoft is an all or nothing proposition. Trace files are configurable, but not targeted.

The MessageBox statement can serve a function similar to tracing, but takes an opposite approach. With a MessageBox statement, you determine exactly what gets traced—a targeted approach. The problem with MessageBox-style tracing is that it is not configurable. To use MessageBox, you must modify code. In development, this is acceptable. Here is a short list of the problems associated with MessageBox-style tracing:

- If we add a MessageBox trace statement, we must remember to remove it. We cannot leave MessageBox trace statements in PeopleCode, because they will display every time a user executes the modified code.
- Finding the correct combination of MessageBox trace statements may require a significant amount of effort. Deleting these statements once the problem is resolved is a waste of this effort. You may need to debug this same code later and will need to reinvest the same amount of time and effort.
- Modifying code in production to trace production issues is not acceptable.

Adding File.WriteLine statements to code is another common targeted tracing technique. Unfortunately, it suffers the same problems as the MessageBox statement.

Employing the SetTracePC and SetTraceSQL functions is a highly effective method for generating targeted trace files. However, just like the MessageBox and File alternatives, this approach is not configurable. Since it is not configurable, any statements added during a debugging session must be removed at the end of the debugging session. Removing these statements erases your investment in the debugging session.

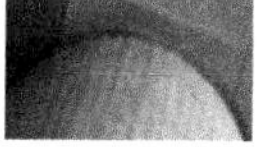

NOTE

I demonstrate how to turn MessageBox-style debugging into a configurable solution in the Oracle wiki entry at http://wiki.oracle.com/page/Introducing+PSUnit. You can use this same approach to make any one of these targeted PeopleCode solutions a configurable solution.

The log4j Java Logging Framework

In Chapter 1, we started writing our own logging framework. Rather than continue to extend that code, let's leverage what already exists. In your %PS_HOME%\class (or $PS_HOME/appserv/classes) directory, you will see a file named log4j*.jar. log4j[1] is a popular logging framework for Java. It is configurable, meaning you can turn on logging through configuration, and it is targeted, meaning you determine what to log. Because it is a targeted solution, you must write code to see logging output.

Hello log4j

Let's get started with a Hello log4j program. Create a new App Engine program named APT_LOG4JTST. Name the first step hw_log4j. Open the App Engine's properties and disable the Restart property. Add a new action to step hw_log4j and set the action's type to PeopleCode. Save the App Engine, and then add the following PeopleCode to step hw_log4j:

```
Local JavaObject &logger = GetJavaClass(
      "org.apache.log4j.Logger").getLogger(
      "AE.APT_LOG4JTST.MAIN.hw_log4j");
```

```
Local JavaObject &layout = CreateJavaObject(
      "org.apache.log4j.PatternLayout",
      "%-4r %d [%t] %-5p %c [%x] - %m%n");
Local JavaObject &appender = CreateJavaObject(
      "org.apache.log4j.ConsoleAppender", &layout);

&logger.addAppender(&appender);
&logger.setLevel(GetJavaClass("org.apache.log4j.Level").DEBUG);
&logger.debug("Hello log4j.");
```

Running the App Engine from App Designer produces a log file that contains the following text:

```
267  2010-07-23 01:03:22,146 [Thread-0]
    DEBUG AE.APT_LOG4JTST.MAIN.hw_log4j  [] - Hello log4j.
```

The log4j framework prints a single line of text formatted according to the pattern provided to the `PatternLayout` constructor. Contrast this against the four lines of output generated by the `MessageBox` statement. I find the four lines of output generated by the `MessageBox` statement a little annoying. As you recall from prior examples, when called from an App Engine, the `MessageBox` function prints the message as well as three additional lines describing the parameters passed to the `MessageBox` function. Notice the preceding log4j output consists of one line. If you find that one line of text to be too verbose, you can change the trace output format by modifying the pattern provided to the `PatternLayout` constructor.

NOTE

When run locally, log4j will try to initialize itself from the log4j .properties file that exists in %PS_HOME%\class. During initialization, it may attempt to create a logger for a file named .\LOGS\PSJChart .log. If so, you will see errors in your App Engine log file telling you that log4j could not find the PSJChart.log file. Ignore these errors. Since we are not using the PeopleSoft Java charting class in this example, the log4j error message is irrelevant.

Let's take a closer look at the code in this example to see how the log4j framework works.

Loggers

The first line of `hw_log4j` creates a logger:

```
Local JavaObject &logger = GetJavaClass(
      "org.apache.log4j.Logger").getLogger(
      "AE.APT_LOG4JTST.MAIN.hw_log4j");
```

The `Logger` class is the top level-interface to the log4j framework. The `Logger` class's constructor is *protected*, which means you cannot create instances of `Logger` directly. Notice that we use the `Get` Java function rather than the `Create` Java function. Calling `CreateJavaObject()` on the `Logger` class will generate an error. To acquire an instance of a `Logger`, we call the static `getLogger` method and provide the name of the `Logger` we want to access.

Loggers have names and inherit properties from other loggers based on a naming convention. The ancestral relationship of loggers is determined by a . (dot) delimited list of names, where the first name represents the top of the hierarchy and the last name represents the bottom of the hierarchy. For example, the logger in the preceding code listing is named `AE.APT_LOG4JTST.MAIN.hw_log4j`. If we define a logger named `AE`, then any `Logger` instance created that has a name that begins with `AE.` will inherit its settings from the predefined logger named `AE`. Furthermore, if we define a logger with the name `AE.APT_LOG4JTST`, then all loggers below `AE.APT_LOG4JTST` will inherit the settings of `AE.APT_LOG4JTST`. Therefore, it is important to consider your log4j logger naming convention. Note that log4j logger names are case-sensitive.

NOTE
The `AE` in the logger name is an abbreviation for App Engine. This allows me to define a logger for all App Engine programs, and then add additional loggers for specific process definitions as needed.

Loggers exist for the duration of the JVM in which they were created. In our example, since we are running an App Engine program, the logger exists for the life of the App Engine. When using log4j online, however, once a logger is loaded, it exists until the application server is shut down. With loggers cached in memory, subsequent uses do not require the same creation overhead.

Layouts

A log event contains a description of the event, the date and time of the event, a level describing the urgency of the event, and many other pertinent facts. A layout is responsible for formatting this information into a message suitable for writing to a log destination. The log4j library contains layouts for generating HTML, XML, and unstructured, single-line log statements. The following code uses the `PatternLayout`[2] to format a logging event according to a specified pattern:

```
Local JavaObject &layout = CreateJavaObject(
      "org.apache.log4j.PatternLayout",
      "%-4r %d [%t] %-5p %c [%x] - %m%n");
```

The `PatternLayout` class contains a variety of conversion characters that are replaced at runtime with data from the logging event. For example, `%d` will be replaced with the date the logging event occurred. Conversion characters can have modifiers. A modifier changes the format of the conversion's output. In the example, `%-4r` left-aligns the output of `%r` and sets the minimum width of the output to four characters (`%r` prints the number of elapsed milliseconds since the creation of the layout). For the `%d` conversion character, we can specify the date and time format using `java.text.SimpleDateFormat`[3] conversion characters, or as a named format such as `%d{ISO8601}`.

When selecting a layout, choose one that matches your destination. For example, if you are printing to an XML file, choose the `XMLLayout` class.

Appenders

Each `Logger` instance contains a collection of appenders. An appender specifies the target for log statements. An appender can be as simple as the console window or as complex as a Telnet server (`TelnetAppender`). One logger can have several appenders, allowing you to print the same log statement to multiple destinations. Furthermore, considering the logger name in our example, if we define a logger named `AE` that uses the `ConsoleAppender` and then define a logger named `AE.APT_LOG4JTST` with a `FileAppender`, the Logger `AE.APT_LOG4JTST.MAIN.hw_log4j` will print to the console and to a file.

Each appender has its own layout that is used to format statements written to the appender. In the `hw_log4j` step, we used the following code to create the `ConsoleAppender`:

```
Local JavaObject &appender = CreateJavaObject(
      "org.apache.log4j.ConsoleAppender", &layout);

&logger.addAppender(&appender);
```

Levels

Log and trace messages can be categorized as errors, warnings, debug statements, and so on. A logger's level determines which types of statements are written to its appenders. The level acts as a filter for the logger, allowing only messages within a specific threshold to be written to its appenders. A logger's level is inclusive, with `ALL` being the highest level of verbosity and `FATAL` providing the least amount of output. For example, when a logger's level is set to `DEBUG`, a logger will print all messages to its appenders. When the level is set to `ERROR`, however, it will print only `ERROR` and `FATAL` messages. In `hw_log4j`, we specified the logger's level using the following code:

```
&logger.setLevel(GetJavaClass("org.apache.log4j.Level").DEBUG);
```

Logger Methods

After a logger is configured, you can call one of its logging methods to add information to the log target (appender). The `Logger` class includes one method for each of the predefined log levels: `all`, `debug`, `info`, `warn`, `error`, and `fatal`, as well as a generic method named `log`. You can call any one of these methods without concern for the logger's log level. If your code encounters a condition that is acceptable, but not recommended, then call the `warn` method. At runtime, if the logger is configured for `debug`, `info`, or `warn`, then it will send `warn` statements to the target appender. In the `hw_log4j` example, we called the `debug` method as follows:

```
&logger.debug("Hello log4j.");
```

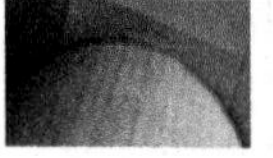

NOTE

The `Logger.error` method is a little interesting. We cannot call the `error` method directly, because `error` is a PeopleCode reserved word. Unlike some reserved words, it cannot even be used as a method name. Later in this chapter, we will discuss strategies for dealing with `Logger.error`.

Tracing log4j

As you work through the examples in this chapter, you may find it beneficial to have log4j trace its internal workings. To enable log4j's internal tracing, open your application server's psappsrv.cfg file and search for the `JavaVM Options` key. When you find it, append `-Dlog4j.configDebug=true` to the end of the configuration line. Here is an example of my application server's `JavaVM Options` key:

```
JavaVM Options=-Xrs
     -Dxdo.ConfigFile=%PS_HOME%/appserv/xdo.cfg
     -Dlog4j.configDebug=true
```

NOTE
When setting the `JavaVM Options` key, be sure to enter the entire statement on a single line.

When the `log4j.configDebug` system property is enabled, log4j writes internal tracing statements to your application server's stdout file. When debugging configuration issues, I find this logged output to be invaluable.

Configuring log4j

The log4j logging framework offers a handful of methods for configuration: the Java properties file, an XML file, and from an API.

The Java properties file, log4j.properties, is the method used by PeopleSoft to configure log4j. This method consists of a properties file identifying logger configurations, including levels, appenders, and layouts.

The XML configuration file, log4j.xml, is my preferred configuration option. Since PeopleSoft delivers a log4j.properties file, however, I recommend configuring log4j through the log4j.properties file. But if you prefer the log4j.xml file format, you can copy the delivered log4j.properties configuration information into your own log4j.xml file. In fact, if you create a log4j.xml file, you can leave the delivered log4j.properties file in place. When log4j loads, it searches for the XML configuration file before searching for the properties file. If it finds the XML file, it stops searching and configures its loggers.

There are many good online tutorials and even some books showing how to configure log4j from a configuration file. Unfortunately, few of them show how to configure a logger from PeopleCode. Our `hw_log4j` example uses PeopleCode to configure a logger. Let's configure a couple more loggers and appenders.

NOTE
You can disable the previous steps in the App Engine to avoid creating extraneous output.

Add a new step to `APT_LOG4JTST` named `cfg_lg4j`, and then add the following code:

```
REM ** Configure a logger for all App Engines;
Local JavaObject &aeLogger = GetJavaClass(
      "org.apache.log4j.Logger").getLogger("AE");
Local JavaObject &aeLayout = CreateJavaObject(
      "org.apache.log4j.PatternLayout",
      "%-4r %d [%t] %-5p %c [%x] - %m%n");
Local JavaObject &aeAppender = CreateJavaObject(
      "org.apache.log4j.ConsoleAppender", &aeLayout);
```

```
&aeLogger.addAppender(&aeAppender);
&aeLogger.setLevel(GetJavaClass("org.apache.log4j.Level").WARN);

REM ** Configure first Appender;
Local JavaObject &xmlLayout = CreateJavaObject(
      "org.apache.log4j.xml.XMLLayout");
Local JavaObject &fileAppender = CreateJavaObject(
      "org.apache.log4j.RollingFileAppender", &xmlLayout,
      "c:\temp\APT_LOG4J.ent");

rem Roll when log file reaches 5 Megabytes;
&fileAppender.setMaxFileSize("5MB");
rem Keep the previous five log files;
&fileAppender.setMaxBackupIndex(5);

REM ** Configure second Appender;
Local JavaObject &htmlLayout = CreateJavaObject(
      "org.apache.log4j.HTMLLayout");
Local JavaObject &htmlAppender = CreateJavaObject(
      "org.apache.log4j.RollingFileAppender", &htmlLayout,
      "c:\temp\APT_LOG4J.html");

rem Roll when log file reaches 5 Megabytes;
&htmlAppender.setMaxFileSize("5MB");
rem Keep the previous five log files;
&htmlAppender.setMaxBackupIndex(5);

REM ** Configure logger for this program;
Local JavaObject &logger = GetJavaClass(
      "org.apache.log4j.Logger").getLogger(
      "AE.APT_LOG4JTST.MAIN.cfg_lg4j");
&logger.setLevel(GetJavaClass("org.apache.log4j.Level").DEBUG);
&logger.addAppender(&fileAppender);
&logger.addAppender(&htmlAppender);

REM ** Write several statements to the log file;
&logger.debug("This is a debug statement.");
&logger.info("This is an info statement.");
&logger.warn("This is a warning statement.");
&logger.log(
      GetJavaClass("org.apache.log4j.Level").toLevel("ERROR"),
      "This is an error statement.");
&logger.fatal("This is a fatal statement.");

REM ** Write to higher level AE log file;
&aeLogger.debug("This is a debug statement.");
&aeLogger.info("This is an info statement.");
&aeLogger.warn("This is a warning statement.");
&aeLogger.log(
```

```
    GetJavaClass("org.apache.log4j.Level").toLevel("ERROR"),
    "This is an error statement.");
&aeLogger.fatal("This is a fatal statement.");
```

This code creates two loggers and three appenders. The first logger is named `AE` and has one appender that writes to the console (App Engine output file). The second logger is named `AE.APT_LOG4JTST.MAIN.cfg_lg4j` and has two appenders. The first appender writes to an XML file, and the second appender writes to an HTML file. Let's look at these output files.

The APT_LOG4J.ent File

Notice that we gave the XML file the extension *.ent rather than *.xml. After running the preceding code, APT_LOG4J.ent contains the following text:

```
<log4j:event logger="AE.APT_LOG4JTST.MAIN.hw_log4j"
    timestamp="1252902459184" level="DEBUG" thread="Thread-0">
<log4j:message><![CDATA[This is a debug statement.]]></log4j:message>
</log4j:event>

<log4j:event logger="AE.APT_LOG4JTST.MAIN.cfg_lg4j"
    timestamp="1252902459192" level="INFO" thread="Thread-0">
<log4j:message><![CDATA[This is an info statement.]]></log4j:message>
</log4j:event>

<log4j:event logger="AE.APT_LOG4JTST.MAIN.cfg_lg4j"
    timestamp="1252902459192" level="WARN" thread="Thread-0">
<log4j:message><![CDATA[This is a warning statement.]]></log4j:message>
</log4j:event>

<log4j:event logger="AE.APT_LOG4JTST.MAIN.cfg_lg4j"
    timestamp="1252902459193" level="ERROR" thread="Thread-0">
<log4j:message><![CDATA[This is an error statement.]]></log4j:message>
</log4j:event>

<log4j:event logger="AE.APT_LOG4JTST.MAIN.cfg_lg4j"
    timestamp="1252902459193" level="FATAL" thread="Thread-0">
<log4j:message><![CDATA[This is a fatal statement.]]></log4j:message>
</log4j:event>
```

The output file `APT_LOG4J.ent` is not a valid XML file. Rather, it is only an XML fragment. To be a valid XML file, it must have an XML declaration and a root element. Therefore, trying to manipulate the output of the `XMLLayout` using an XML parser or XSLT processor will result in an error.

To process this file as an XML file, we can treat it as an external XML entity. The following XML file references `APT_LOG4J.ent` as an external entity and will allow us to parse or process log4j XML output. Create a new file named `APT_LOG4J.xml` in the same folder as `APT_LOG4J.ent` and add the following XML:

```
<?xml version="1.0" ?>

<!DOCTYPE log4j:eventSet SYSTEM "log4j.dtd"
    [<!ENTITY data SYSTEM "APT_LOG4J.ent">]>
```

```
<log4j:eventSet version="1.2"
    xmlns:log4j="http://jakarta.apache.org/log4j/">
  &data;
</log4j:eventSet>
```

The APT_LOG4J4J.html File

The logger `AE.APT_LOG4JTST.MAIN.cfg_lg4j` has another appender and layout, `HTMLLayout`, which produces an HTML file named `APT_LOG4J.html`. Figure 10-1 shows this log file in a web browser.

The APT_LOG4J4JTST.log File

The logger `&logger` created an XML file and an HTML file. Our third file was produced by the logger `&aeLogger`, which wrote to the `ConsoleAppender`. When running an App Engine through App Designer, console output goes to the App Engine log file. Our APT_LOG4JTST.log output file contains entries that look like the following:

```
353  2010-07-23 08:27:39,184 [Thread-0] DEBUG
   AE.APT_LOG4JTST.MAIN.cfg_lg4j [] - This is a debug statement.
361  2010-07-23 08:27:39,192 [Thread-0] INFO
   AE.APT_LOG4JTST.MAIN.cfg_lg4j [] - This is an info statement.
361  2010-07-23 08:27:39,192 [Thread-0] WARN
   AE.APT_LOG4JTST.MAIN.cfg_lg4j [] - This is a warning statement.
362  2010-07-23 08:27:39,193 [Thread-0] ERROR
   AE.APT_LOG4JTST.MAIN.cfg_lg4j [] - This is an error statement.
362  2010-07-23 08:27:39,193 [Thread-0] FATAL
   AE.APT_LOG4JTST.MAIN.cfg_lg4j [] - This is a fatal statement.
363  2010-07-23 08:27:39,194 [Thread-0] WARN
   AE [] - This is a warning statement.
363  2010-07-23 08:27:39,194 [Thread-0] ERROR
   AE [] - This is an error statement.
363  2010-07-23 08:27:39,194 [Thread-0] FATAL
   AE [] - This is a fatal statement.
```

You see that the App Engine log file contains output for two loggers: `AE.APT_LOG4JTST.MAIN.cfg_lg4j` and `AE`. In our PeopleCode, however, we configured only `AE` to write to the `ConsoleAppender`. The `cfg_lg4j` logger inherits the `ConsoleAppender` from its ancestor, `AE`.

Log session start time Fri Jul 23 08:27:39 PDT 2010

Time	Thread	Level	Category	Message
353	Thread-0	DEBUG	AE.APT_LOG4JTST.MAIN.hw_log4j	This is a debug statement.
361	Thread-0	INFO	AE.APT_LOG4JTST.MAIN.hw_log4j	This is an info statement.
361	Thread-0	WARN	AE.APT_LOG4JTST.MAIN.hw_log4j	This is a warning statement.
362	Thread-0	ERROR	AE.APT_LOG4JTST.MAIN.hw_log4j	This is an error statement.
362	Thread-0	FATAL	AE.APT_LOG4JTST.MAIN.hw_log4j	This is a fatal statement.

FIGURE 10-1. *APT_LOG4J.html viewed in a web browser*

If you want to change this behavior, add the following PeopleCode immediately after creating the Logger instance:

```
&logger.setAdditivity(False);
```

The cfg_lg4j code logs error messages, but does not use the &logger.error method. As I mentioned earlier, &logger.error cannot be called directly because error is a PeopleCode reserved word. Instead, the code calls &logger.log using the appropriate log level (special thanks to Corey Pedersen from the University of Utah for pointing this out to me).

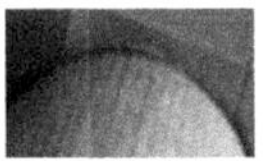

NOTE
The code in this example sets the log level on the logger. Some appenders support a Threshold property that allows you to set the log level for specific appenders. This gives you the ability to specify different log levels for appenders attached to the same logger.

Improving Logging Performance

The examples presented thus far log static, predefined strings. Real-life use cases, however, will involve concatenating variables to produce meaningful debugging statements. This type of string construction can be quite costly. You should avoid constructing log message strings when logging is disabled. Besides standard string construction overhead, debug statements may involve loops as well as property and method calls that exist for the purpose of logging information.

To avoid calling properties and methods when logging is disabled, use the &logger.is*Xxx*Enabled methods. The following code is an example of using the isDebugEnabled() method:

```
if(&logger.isDebugEnabled()) then
   &logger.debug("This is a debug statement.");
end-if;
```

Avoiding Logger Reconfiguration

When using PeopleCode to configure loggers, it is difficult to know if a logger is already initialized. You don't want to waste CPU cycles creating loggers, appenders, and layouts for a preconfigured logger. Furthermore, appenders that bind to listening ports, like the TelnetAppender, will fail if you try to reconfigure them using the same port information (because the JVM is already bound to the listening port).

As an alternative to reconfiguration, use code like the following to determine if a logger already exists:

```
Local string &name = "my.peoplecode.logger";
Local JavaObject &manager = GetJavaClass(
      "org.apache.log4j.LogManager");
Local JavaObject &logger = &manager.exists(&name);

If (&logger = Null) Then
   &logger = GetJavaClass("org.apache.log4j.Logger").getLogger(&name);
   REM ** Configure Appenders and Layouts;
End-If;
```

Using log4j in the Process Scheduler

When run from the Process Scheduler, the `ConsoleAppender` does not print to any of the Process Scheduler's output files. With the following PeopleCode, you can send the `ConsoleAppender`'s output to a file:

```
/*
 * Redirect stdout to file
 */
Function redirect_stdout(&fileName as string)
   Local JavaObject &jSystem = GetJavaClass("java.lang.System");
   Local JavaObject &jfos_out = CreateJavaObject(
         "java.io.FileOutputStream", &fileName, True);
   Local JavaObject &jps_out = CreateJavaObject(
         "java.io.PrintStream", &jfos_out, True);
   &jSystem.setOut(&jps_out);
End-Function;
```

Use the following SQL to acquire the App Engine's output directory. Placing files in this location will make them available through the Process Scheduler's View Log/Trace link.

```
SELECT PRCSOUTPUTDIR
  FROM PSPRCSPARMS
 WHERE PRCSINSTANCE = %ProcessInstance
```

An Integrated Logging Framework

Let's wrap the log4j Java objects in some PeopleCode application classes to make them easier to use. Besides adding simplicity, our application classes will do the following:

- Load configuration information from someplace other than an application server configuration file
- Allow for per-user, per-session configuration
- Work across *think-time* functions (app server is stateless; Java is not)
- Provide a mechanism to reload the configuration

In this section, we will create three application classes: `Level`, `Logger`, and `LogManager`. To prepare for creating these classes, create a new application package and name it `APT_LOG4J`.

NOTE
The application classes used in this example implement a limited subset of the log4j logging framework. Feel free to extend these classes to satisfy your specific requirements.

Creating the Level Class

The `Level` class is the most basic of the log4j wrapper classes. It exists to provide a type-safe parameter for the `Logger.isEnabledFor` method we will create later. Add the class `Level` to the `APT_LOG4J` application package and enter the following PeopleCode:

```
/**
 * Represents an org.apache.log4j.Level JavaObject
 */
class Level
   method Level(&name As string);
   method getLevel() Returns JavaObject;

private
   instance string &name_;
   instance JavaObject &level_;
end-class;

method Level
   /+ &name as String +/
   &name_ = &name;
end-method;

method getLevel
   /+ Returns JavaObject +/

   /* Lazy initialization makes this object stateless. If Level is
    * accessed across App Server calls, then &level will get
    * reinitialized.
    */
   If (&level_ = Null) Then
      &level_ = GetJavaClass("org.apache.log4j.Level").toLevel(&name_);
   End-If;

   Return &level_;
end-method;
```

It is not possible to access a `JavaObject` on both sides of a think-time function. Consider the following PeopleCode:

```
Local JavaObject &logger = GetJavaClass(
      "org.apache.log4j.Logger").getLogger(
      "my.online.logger");

&logger.debug("Beginning transaction.");

Local number &result = MessageBox(%MsgStyle_YesNoCancel,
      "Continue processing", 0, 0, "Would you like to continue?");
```

```
if (&result = %MsgResult_Yes) Then
   REM ** Throws a null pointer exception;
   &logger.debug("Continuing with transaction.");
End-If;
```

In this code, `&logger` is initialized prior to calling a think-time function. When the think-time function returns, `&logger` will be set to `null`. Our `APT_LOG4J:Level` class protects against this type of exception by maintaining its internal state with PeopleCode types rather than `JavaObjects`. The `&level_ JavaObject` instance variable exists for caching purposes only. If the PeopleCode that uses a particular `APT_LOG4PC:Level` instance does not execute a think-time function, then `&level_` will be initialized only once.

Creating the Logger Class

Add another application class to the `APT_LOG4J` application package. Name this new class `Logger`. The `Logger` class follows the same lazy initialization/stateless pattern as the `Level` class. Add the following code to this new application class:

```
/**
 * Represents an org.apache.log4j.Logger JavaObject
 *
 * Implements the basic print methods only.
 */
import APT_LOG4J:Level;

class Logger
   method Logger(&name As string);

   method debug(&message As string);
   method info(&message As string);
   method warn(&message As string);
   method err(&message As string);
   method fatal(&message As string);

   method isDebugEnabled() Returns boolean;
   method isInfoEnabled() Returns boolean;
   method isEnabledFor(&level As APT_LOG4J:Level) Returns boolean;

private
   method getLogger() Returns JavaObject;
   method getThisLogger() Returns JavaObject;

   instance JavaObject &logger_;
   instance JavaObject &thisLogger_;
   instance string &name_;

end-class;

method Logger
   /+ &name as String +/
   &name_ = &name;
end-method;
```

```
method debug
   /+ &message as String +/
   %This.getLogger().debug(&message);
end-method;

method info
   /+ &message as String +/
   %This.getLogger().info(&message);
end-method;

method warn
   /+ &message as String +/
   %This.getLogger().warn(&message);
end-method;

method err
   /+ &message as String +/
   %This.getLogger().log(
         GetJavaClass("org.apache.log4j.Level").toLevel("ERROR"),
               &message);
end-method;

method fatal
   /+ &message as String +/
   %This.getLogger().fatal(&message);
end-method;

method isDebugEnabled
   /+ Returns Boolean +/
   Return %This.getLogger().isDebugEnabled();
end-method;

method isInfoEnabled
   /+ Returns Boolean +/
   Return %This.getLogger().isInfoEnabled();
end-method;

method isEnabledFor
   /+ &level as APT_LOG4J:Level +/
   /+ Returns Boolean +/
   Return %This.getLogger().isEnabledFor(&level.getLevel());
end-method;


/***********************
 * private methods follow
 */

method getLogger
   /+ Returns JavaObject +/
```

```
    /* Lazy initialization ensures that this object is stateless and
     * protects against Null pointer exceptions.
     */
    If (&logger_ = Null) Then
       Local JavaObject &manager = GetJavaClass(
             "org.apache.log4j.LogManager");

       /* Implement per-user configurations
        */
       REM ** First test for user specific logger;
       &logger_ = &manager.exists(&name_ | ".oprid." | %OperatorId);

       REM ** If no user specific logger, get instance from &name;
       If (&logger_ = Null) Then
          If (%This.getThisLogger().isDebugEnabled()) Then
             %This.getThisLogger().debug("Logger " | &name_ |
                   ".oprid." | %OperatorId |
                   " does not exist; using base name.");
          End-If;
          rem &logger_ = &manager.exists(&name_);
          &logger_ = GetJavaClass(
                "org.apache.log4j.Logger").getLogger(&name_);
       End-If;
    End-If;

    Return &logger_;
 end-method;

 method getThisLogger
    /+ Returns JavaObject +/
    If (&thisLogger_ = Null) Then
       &thisLogger_ = GetJavaClass(
             "org.apache.log4j.Logger").getLogger("APT_LOG4J.Logger");
    End-If;

    Return &thisLogger_;
 end-method;
```

The `getLogger` method in this code does more than just return the log4j `Logger` instance with the given name. It first tests for the existence of a logger named `&name | ".oprid." | %OperatorId`. This allows us to configure *user-specific* loggers. For example, let's say user `HCRUSA_KU0001` receives an error when entering expense reports. Rather than turn on system-wide tracing, we could configure a logger for that specific user. Assuming we have a logger named `PS.EXPENSE_MENU.EXPENSE_COMPONENT`, we could define an additional logger and appender named `PS.EXPENSE_MENU.EXPENSE_COMPONENT.oprid.HCRUSA_KU0001`.

The `APT_LOG4J:Logger` class emits its own logging statements. To see these statements, you need to configure either a logger named `APT_LOG4J.Logger` or the ancestral logger `APT_LOG4J`.

The LogManager Class

The default behavior of the log4j library is to initialize itself from a file on the application server's or Process Scheduler server's class path. If you run your PeopleSoft applications using a load-balanced configuration, then changing the log4j configuration file will require you to touch each application server's configuration file. The following code presents a method for loading a log4j configuration from a message catalog definition. Using a message catalog definition offers the following benefits:

- Configuration changes exist in one location, so you get centralized management.
- Developers can make changes without access to the application server's file system.

Now we'll create the `LogManager` class for our example. We'll look at this code in pieces. The complete application class code is presented at the end of this section. To prepare for the following code listings, add a new class named `LogManager` to the `APT_LOG4PC` application package.

The LogManager Declaration

The following declaration describes the public and private methods and instance variables for the `LogManager` application class.

```
/**
 * Class for ensuring log4j is initialized.
 */
import APT_LOG4J:Level;
import APT_LOG4J:Logger;

class LogManager
   method getLogger(&name As string) Returns APT_LOG4J:Logger;
   method reloadConfig();

private
   method initialize();
   method isInitialized() Returns boolean;
   method isNotInitialized() Returns boolean;
   method getThisLogger() Returns JavaObject;

   instance JavaObject &thisLogger_;
   Constant &THIS_LOGGER_NAME = "APT_LOG4J";
end-class;
```

The `LogManager` application class has two public methods: `getLogger()` and `reloadConfig()`.

The `Logger` class we previously created assumes log4j is already initialized. Since we are loading the log4j configuration from a message catalog entry, we need a mechanism to satisfy this assumption. We will satisfy this assumption by retrieving `Logger` instances from the `LogManager` rather than creating them directly. The `LogManager`, therefore, will be able to verify that the log4j framework is initialized prior to creating a `Logger`.

Using the getLogger method described in the class declaration, creating a Logger will look similar to:

```
&logger = create APT_LOG4J:LogManager().getLogger("My.Logger.Name");
```

Once the log4j framework is initialized, the LogManager class will not reconfigure log4j until the application server is restarted. It is preferable, however, to have the LogManager class reconfigure log4j after a user modifies the log4j message catalog definition. The reloadConfig method provides this functionality. In our test cases described later, we will write an iScript that uses reloadConfig to reload the log4j configuration.

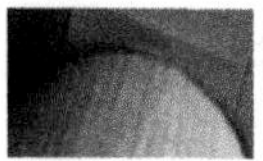

NOTE
If you use a custom page and record definition rather than a message catalog definition, you could use the record's or component's SavePostChange event to automatically reload the log4j configuration.

Moving down the class declaration to the private instance variables, you see a JavaObject variable named &thisLogger. Just like the APT_LOG4J:Logger class, this class will use an instance variable to cache a pointer to an internal logger. When we write code for this internal logger, we will ensure that the variable is initialized, just in case the variable is used across think-time functions.

The getLogger() Method Implementation Code

The following code listing initializes the log4j framework, if necessary, and then creates an instance of an APT_LOG4J:Logger. The code for the isNotInitialized() and initialize() methods will be described later.

```
method getLogger
   /+ &name as String +/
   /+ Returns APT_LOG4J:Logger +/
   If (%This.isNotInitialized()) Then
      %This.initialize();
   End-If;

   Return create APT_LOG4J:Logger(&name);
end-method;
```

From this code, it is clear that multiple calls to getLogger from the same LogManager instance will require only one call to initialize. What isn't clear is what happens when multiple users (or the same user but from different components) call getLogger. It is my experience that the application server loads the JVM upon first use, and then never fully releases it until the application server is shut down. Since log4j stores Logger instances in a static collection, preconfigured Logger instances remain for the duration of the application server. Therefore, once initialize is called, it will not be called again until the application server is restarted, regardless of the user.

The reloadConfig() Method Implementation Code

As you can see from the following code listing, the method `reloadConfig()` is an alias to the `initialize` method discussed next.

```
method reloadConfig
   %This.initialize();
end-method;
```

Unlike `getLogger`, which first confirms log4j is initialized, `reloadConfig` forces the `LogManager` to reload the log4j message catalog configuration.

The initialize Private Method Implementation Code

The `LogManager's` primary reason for existence is to configure the log4j framework prior to use. The `initialize` method is the mechanism used by `LogManager` to perform this configuration step. The following code listing contains the PeopleCode for the `initialize` method:

```
method initialize
   /* Create test logger used to verify system initialized.
    * Note: This is just the default config. If you want to see
    * debug statements, then create a configuration for a logger
    * named APT_LOG4J.
    */
   &thisLogger_ = GetJavaClass(
         "org.apache.log4j.Logger").getLogger(&THIS_LOGGER_NAME);
   Local JavaObject &appender =
         CreateJavaObject("org.apache.log4j.varia.NullAppender");

   &thisLogger_.addAppender(&appender);
   &thisLogger_.setLevel(GetJavaClass("org.apache.log4j.Level").OFF);

   /* Initialize loggers from a Message Catalog Entry.
    * See http://bit.ly/439d4T
    */
   Local string &config = MsgGetExplainText(26000, 1, "");
   Local JavaObject &configString =
         CreateJavaObject("java.lang.String", &config);
   Local JavaObject &in = CreateJavaObject(
         "java.io.ByteArrayInputStream", &configString.getBytes());
   Local JavaObject &props = CreateJavaObject("java.util.Properties");
   Local JavaObject &configurator =
         CreateJavaObject("org.apache.log4j.PropertyConfigurator");

   REM ** Use reflection to avoid "More than one overload matches";
   Local JavaObject &configureMethod =
         &configurator.getClass().getMethod("configure",
         CreateJavaObject("java.lang.Class[]", &props.getClass()));

   &props.load(&in);
   &configureMethod.invoke(&configurator,
         CreateJavaObject("java.lang.Object[]", &props));
```

```
    %This.getThisLogger().info("Log4j subsystem initialized from " |
          "Message Catalog Entry");
end-method;
```

The `initialize` method begins by initializing the internal logger:

```
&thisLogger_ = GetJavaClass(
      "org.apache.log4j.Logger").getLogger(&THIS_LOGGER_NAME);
Local JavaObject &appender =
      CreateJavaObject("org.apache.log4j.varia.NullAppender");

&thisLogger_.addAppender(&appender);
&thisLogger_.setLevel(GetJavaClass("org.apache.log4j.Level").OFF);
```

Just as a C++ header file will define a compile-time variable to ensure the header is included only once, `LogManager` defines a log4j `Logger` to ensure log4j is initialized only once. The preceding code initializes this internal `Logger`. The `LogManager` class will use this `Logger` to write its own trace statements to a log.

This PeopleCode `Logger` configuration code creates a `Logger` that uses a `NullAppender` and the level `OFF`. Based on this configuration, the `LogManager`'s internal logger will not generate any output. To override this default behavior, define a logger named `APT_LOG4J` in the log4j message catalog definition (which we will add after the full `LogManager` code listing).

The next lines of code in the class generate a Java `Properties` object from the contents of the log4j message catalog definition:

```
Local string &config = MsgGetExplainText(26000, 1, "");
Local JavaObject &configString =
      CreateJavaObject("java.lang.String", &config);
Local JavaObject &in = CreateJavaObject(
      "java.io.ByteArrayInputStream", &configString.getBytes());
Local JavaObject &props = CreateJavaObject("java.util.Properties");
Local JavaObject &configurator =
      CreateJavaObject("org.apache.log4j.PropertyConfigurator");
```

For this example, I chose message set 26000. Feel free to choose a different message set (and update your code accordingly).

NOTE
The idea for loading a log4j configuration from a message catalog definition arose from an online blog comment brainstorming session between John Wagenleitner and myself. You can read the full thread on John's blog at http://campus-codemonkeys.blogspot.com/2007/09/log4j-in-peoplecode.html.

After creating a `Properties` object, we can load the list of loggers, appenders, and layouts described in that `Properties` object:

```
Local JavaObject &configureMethod =
      &configurator.getClass().getMethod("configure",
      CreateJavaObject("java.lang.Class[]", &props.getClass()));
```

```
&props.load(&in);
&configureMethod.invoke(&configurator,
      CreateJavaObject("java.lang.Object[]", &props));

%This.getThisLogger().info("Log4j subsystem initialized from " |
      "Message Catalog Entry");
```

The log4j framework provides two primary Java classes for configuring log4j: `PropertyConfigurator` and `DOMConfigurator`. The code presented here uses the `PropertyConfigurator`. If you prefer the XML log4j configuration method over the properties file method, feel free to alter the code to use XML instead.

Our example uses Java reflection to call the `configure` method. The `PropertyConfigurator` Java class defines the `configure` method three times, each with a different parameter type. The technique of defining a method more than once is called *overloading*. The PeopleCode runtime is able to determine the difference between overloaded methods when the number of parameters differs or if the overloaded version you are trying to call uses a `String` parameter. With strings, the PeopleCode runtime knows the data sent to the method is a `String` and calls the appropriate overloaded method. In this case, however, there are multiple overloaded versions, and each requires a PeopleCode `JavaObject`.

The reflection code we use to call the `configure` method looks very similar to the JSON downcasting example from the previous chapter. Just as PeopleCode was unable to resolve methods of the JSON parser's return value (`Object`), the PeopleCode runtime is not able to determine the correct `configure` method to call.

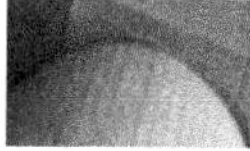

NOTE
In Chapter 11, you will see how to write Java helper classes as an alternative to Java reflection.

The Remaining Private Methods

The remaining private method implementations in the `LogManager` class are as follows:

- The `isNotInitialized` method uses the log4j `LogManager` to determine if the internal logger exists in the log4j logging hierarchy.
- The `isInitialized` method returns the opposite of the `isNotInitialized` method, and exists for convenience.
- The `getThisLogger` method ensures the private `JavaObject` instance variable is not `null`, as it would be if a think-time function were called after the `LogManager` was created, but before it was used.

The Complete LogManager Code Listing

The complete code listing for the `LogManager` application class follows.

```
/**
 * Class for ensuring log4j is initialized.
 */
import APT_LOG4J:Level;
import APT_LOG4J:Logger;
```

```
class LogManager
   method getLogger(&name As string) Returns APT_LOG4J:Logger;
   method reloadConfig();

private
   method initialize();
   method isInitialized() Returns boolean;
   method isNotInitialized() Returns boolean;
   method getThisLogger() Returns JavaObject;

   instance JavaObject &thisLogger_;
   Constant &THIS_LOGGER_NAME = "APT_LOG4J";
end-class;

method getLogger
   /+ &name as String +/
   /+ Returns APT_LOG4J:Logger +/
   If (%This.isNotInitialized()) Then
      %This.initialize();
   End-If;

   Return create APT_LOG4J:Logger(&name);
end-method;

method reloadConfig
   %This.initialize();
end-method;


/************************
 * private methods follow
 */

method initialize
   /* Create test logger used to verify system initialized.
    * Note: This is just the default config. If you want to see
    * debug statements, then create a configuration for a logger
    * named APT_LOG4J.
    */
   &thisLogger_ = GetJavaClass(
         "org.apache.log4j.Logger").getLogger(&THIS_LOGGER_NAME);
   Local JavaObject &appender =
         CreateJavaObject("org.apache.log4j.varia.NullAppender");

   &thisLogger_.addAppender(&appender);
   &thisLogger_.setLevel(GetJavaClass("org.apache.log4j.Level").OFF);

   /* Initialize loggers from a Message Catalog Entry.
    * See http://bit.ly/439d4T
    */
```

```
   Local string &config = MsgGetExplainText(26000, 1, "");
   Local JavaObject &configString =
         CreateJavaObject("java.lang.String", &config);
   Local JavaObject &in = CreateJavaObject(
         "java.io.ByteArrayInputStream", &configString.getBytes());
   Local JavaObject &props = CreateJavaObject("java.util.Properties");
   Local JavaObject &configurator =
         CreateJavaObject("org.apache.log4j.PropertyConfigurator");

   REM ** Use reflection to avoid "More than one overload matches";
   Local JavaObject &configureMethod =
         &configurator.getClass().getMethod("configure",
         CreateJavaObject("java.lang.Class[]", &props.getClass()));

   &props.load(&in);
   &configureMethod.invoke(&configurator,
         CreateJavaObject("java.lang.Object[]", &props));

   %This.getThisLogger().info("Log4j subsystem initialized from " |
         "Message Catalog Entry");
end-method;

method isInitialized
   /+ Returns Boolean +/
   Return ( Not %This.isNotInitialized());
end-method;

method isNotInitialized
   /+ Returns Boolean +/
   Local JavaObject &manager = GetJavaClass(
         "org.apache.log4j.LogManager");
   &thisLogger_ = &manager.exists(&THIS_LOGGER_NAME);

   Return (&thisLogger_ = Null);
end-method;

method getThisLogger
   /+ Returns JavaObject +/
   If (&thisLogger_ = Null) Then
      &thisLogger_ = GetJavaClass(
            "org.apache.log4j.Logger").getLogger(&THIS_LOGGER_NAME);
   End-If;

   Return &thisLogger_;
end-method;
```

NOTE
This code uses message catalog entry 26000, message number 1. If you already have a message catalog entry at that location, choose a different number and update the code listing accordingly.

log4j Metadata

The `APT_LOG4J:LogManager` class expects message catalog definition 26000, message number 1. Navigate to PeopleTools | Utilities | Administration | Message Catalog and create that message catalog definition. For entry number 1, set the message text to **log4j Configuration**, and enter the following text into the Explanation field. (If you used a different message catalog entry in the `APT_LOG4J:LogManager` application class, be sure to add the following text to the corresponding message catalog entry.)

```
# AE.test logger configuration
log4j.logger.AE.test=INFO, stdout

# App Class Framework logger
log4j.logger.APT_LOG4J=ALL, stdout

# IScript logger
log4j.logger.IScript=OFF

# IScript.test logger
log4j.logger.IScript.test=WARN, file, smtp

# IScript.test.oprid.PS logger
log4j.logger.IScript.test.oprid.PS=ALL, user_ps_file

#####
# Appender definitions

#appender configuration
log4j.appender.stdout=org.apache.log4j.ConsoleAppender
log4j.appender.stdout.layout=org.apache.log4j.PatternLayout
log4j.appender.stdout.layout.ConversionPattern=%d %-5p [%c] - %m%n

#SMTP appender configuration
log4j.appender.smtp=org.apache.log4j.net.SMTPAppender
log4j.appender.smtp.Host=localhost
log4j.appender.smtp.From=ps@hrms.example.com
log4j.appender.smtp.To=hcrusa_ku0001@hrms.example.com
log4j.appender.smtp.Subject=APT_LOG4J Notification
log4j.appender.smtp.BufferSize=1
log4j.appender.smtp.layout=org.apache.log4j.HTMLLayout

#File appender configuration
log4j.appender.file=org.apache.log4j.RollingFileAppender
log4j.appender.file.maxFileSize=100KB
log4j.appender.file.maxBackupIndex=5
log4j.appender.file.File=/tmp/log4j.log
log4j.appender.file.layout=org.apache.log4j.PatternLayout
log4j.appender.file.layout.ConversionPattern=%d %-5p [%c] - %m%n

#PSFile appender configuration
log4j.appender.user_ps_file=org.apache.log4j.RollingFileAppender
log4j.appender.user_ps_file.maxFileSize=100KB
```

```
log4j.appender.user_ps_file.maxBackupIndex=5
log4j.appender.user_ps_file.File=/tmp/ps-log4j.log
log4j.appender.user_ps_file.layout=org.apache.log4j.PatternLayout
log4j.appender.user_ps_file.layout.ConversionPattern=\
%d %-5p [%c] - %m%n
```

This log4j configuration describes five loggers and four appenders (some loggers share the same appenders, and one logger doesn't use an appender). One of those loggers is named `APT_LOG4J`. This is the logger used by our logging application class to log information about the package's methods. By defining this logger, we are overriding the default `LogManager` initialization that discards `APT_LOG4J` logging statements.

The next noteworthy logger from this configuration is the `IScript.test` logger. This logger uses the `SMTPAppender` to e-mail error and fatal logging statements. Before we move on to the appenders, look at the logger named `IScript.test.oprid.PS`. This is a user-specific logger with its level set to print every statement written to `IScript.test`, but only for the user named `PS`.

NOTE

In the appenders section, be sure to update the e-mail address and file path references. The file paths in the log4j configuration assume your application and/or Process Scheduler servers run on a Unix-style operating system. If you use a Windows operating system, change the file paths in the configuration to use Windows-style paths, such as c:\temp. Also, my use of a temporary folder for log files is for demonstration and testing purposes only. A production system should point to a permanent storage location.

Testing APT_LOG4J

To test the `APT_LOG4J` application package, create a new derived/work record named `WEBLIB_APT_L4J`. Add the field `IScript1`, and then add the following PeopleCode to the `FieldFormula` event:

```
import APT_LOG4J:Logger;
import APT_LOG4J:LogManager;

Function IScript_Reload()
   Local APT_LOG4J:LogManager &manager = create APT_LOG4J:LogManager();
   &manager.reloadConfig();
   %Response.SetContentType("text/plain");
   %Response.WriteLine("Configuration reloaded");
End-Function;

Function IScript_Test()
   Local APT_LOG4J:LogManager &manager = create APT_LOG4J:LogManager();
   Local APT_LOG4J:Logger &logger = &manager.getLogger("IScript.test");

   %Response.SetContentType("text/plain");
   &logger.debug("This is a debug statement from " | %OperatorId);
   &logger.info("This is an info statement from " | %OperatorId);
   &logger.err("This is an error statement from " | %OperatorId);
   &logger.fatal("This is a fatal statement from " | %OperatorId);
```

```
   &logger = &manager.getLogger("Not.a.defined.logger");
   &logger.warn("this is not a real logger");

   %Response.WriteLine("Logging statements written.");
End-Function;
```

Add `WEBLIB_APT_L4J` and the accompanying iScripts (`IScript_Reload` and `IScript_Test`) to your `APT_CUSTOM` permission list.

The first iScript, `IScript_Reload`, uses the `LogManager` application class to reload the log4j configuration after making changes to the message catalog entry. At the end of this function, you will see a call to the Java `LogManager` class. Since PeopleSoft delivers a log4j configuration file with preconfigured loggers, we want to ensure that the `APT_LOG4J` reload method didn't erase preconfigured loggers. If you run this code, you will see that the delivered logger still exists after using the `APT_LOG4J:LogManager` reload method. To test this iScript, navigate to a URL similar to this:

http://hrms.example.com/psc/hrms/EMPLOYEE/HRMS/s/WEBLIB_APT_L4J.ISCRIPT1
.FieldFormula.IScript_Reload

The `IScript_Test` function creates two loggers: `IScript.test` and `Not.a.defined.logger`. The first logger is our primary output test logger. The other logger exists to demonstrate how log4j ignores loggers that are not defined.

Running this code as user `PS` will produce output in the /tmp/log4j.log and /tmp/ps-log4j.log files, as well as an e-mail for each error and fatal log message. To run this test code, navigate to this URL:

http://hrms.example.com/psc/hrms/EMPLOYEE/HRMS/s/WEBLIB_APT_L4J.ISCRIPT1
.FieldFormula.IScript_Test

After running this code as user `PS`, log in as a different user and run it again. Notice that the /tmp/ps-log4j.log file does not change in size when you're logged in as a user other than `PS`.

After testing a different user, change the log4j message catalog definition and run your tests. The log4j framework will remain unaware of your changes until you reload the configuration (to reload, run the `IScript_Reload` iScript).

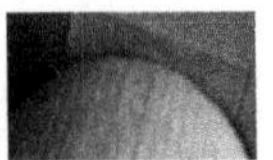

NOTE
In Chapter 15, we will discuss a testing framework that can be used to test code without creating iScripts.

Best Practice: Avoid Debuggers

Do not depend on debuggers, regardless of the language. A well-placed print statement provides just as much insight as a debugger, but does so without forcing the programmer to step through lines of irrelevant code and control structures.

Furthermore, debug print statements are permanent. They become a part of the application's code. Debugging sessions are extremely transient. Once a variable goes out of scope, its value is lost. And once you close the debugger, the information from that session is lost. Conversely, output from a print statement exists until you decide to delete the output file.

Conclusion

The log4j logging framework is one more tool for your investigative kit. Think of log4j as a wiretap or a GPS tracking device. With it, you can watch your adversary's every move, analyzing each print statement for patterns that will lead to the apprehension of the criminal (problem).

The log4j logging framework does not replace PeopleSoft's trace facilities. Rather, it complements them by providing a configurable, targeted, repeatable logging session.

A typical PeopleSoft production deployment includes multiple load-balanced application servers, each with its own JVM and file system. In this chapter, we utilized a message catalog definition to provide a single configuration method for multiple servers, rather than depending on a file system-specific log4j configuration file. In Chapter 11, we will create a custom appender that writes to a PeopleSoft table, consolidating output across load-balanced application servers.

Notes

1. Apache Software Foundation, "Logging Services" [online]; available from http://logging.apache.org/log4j/1.2/index.html; Internet; accessed 11 September 2009.
2. Apache Software Foundation, *Apache Log4j 1.2.15 API*, "Class PatternLayout" [online]; available from http://logging.apache.org/log4j/1.2/apidocs/org/apache/log4j/PatternLayout.html; Internet; accessed 11 September 2009.
3. Sun Microsystems, *Java 2 Platform SE v1.4.2*, "Class SimpleDateFormat" [online]; available from http://java.sun.com/j2se/1.4.2/docs/api/java/text/SimpleDateFormat.html; Internet; accessed 11 September 2009.

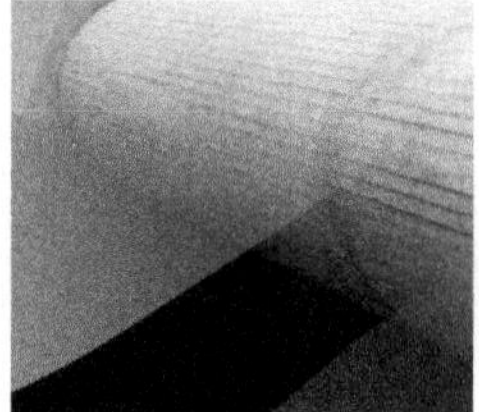

CHAPTER 11

Writing Your Own Java

The previous two chapters showed you how to call Java from PeopleCode. This chapter demonstrates the converse by showing how to call PeopleCode from Java.

As you've seen, some Java features are difficult to use in PeopleCode. For example, Java's downcasting and overloaded methods are problematic when called from PeopleCode. On the other hand, some tasks, like data access, are easier to accomplish in PeopleCode than in Java.

In this chapter, you'll learn how to create PeopleCode helper methods, as well as how to effectively use the PeopleSoft database connection from Java (eliminating the need for JDBC).

Your Java Build Environment

Java source code files are plain text files organized in directories according to their package name. A variety of vendors distribute command-line compilers for Java, allowing you to compile Java source files into Java bytecode. Rather than demonstrate the various command-line compiler features and how to manage Java source code files, we will use a Java development environment. (A variety of online tutorials demonstrate how to compile Java source code from the command line.)

Now we just need to decide which Java integrated development environment (IDE) to use. Oracle JDeveloper, NetBeans, and Eclipse are the most popular, full-featured IDEs. The examples in this chapter will use JDeveloper. If you are new to Java, check with other members of your organization to see which Java IDE they prefer. Since each editor has its own project and definition file format, it is better to use the same editor as the rest of your organization.

If you don't have a Java IDE installed, go to http://www.oracle.com/technology/products/jdev/index.html and download a copy of JDeveloper. Once it's downloaded, run the installer to install it so you can follow the examples.

Your First Java Class

In keeping with the theme of our other "first" demonstrations, let's create a Hello World Java class. We'll then deploy it to our PeopleSoft application and use it in PeopleCode.

Creating the Source Files

Launch JDeveloper (or your preferred IDE). When prompted, select the Default Role. When JDeveloper loads, create a new application by selecting File | New from the JDeveloper menu bar, and then selecting Application from the New Gallery dialog. Applications are project containers. A typical JDeveloper web application, for example, consists of a model project (data access object representations) and a view/controller project.

The Create Application wizard starts, displaying step 1 of 2. Name the application `APT_PeopleSoft` and set the application package prefix to `apt.peoplesoft`. The application package prefix indicates the starting package for your custom Java code. Generally speaking, Java developers use their company's reverse domain name as an application package prefix. For example, Oracle Corporation, which owns the domain oracle.com, would use the package prefix com.oracle. Figure 11-1 shows the completed step 1 of the wizard. JDeveloper automatically fills in the directory based on the application name you provide.

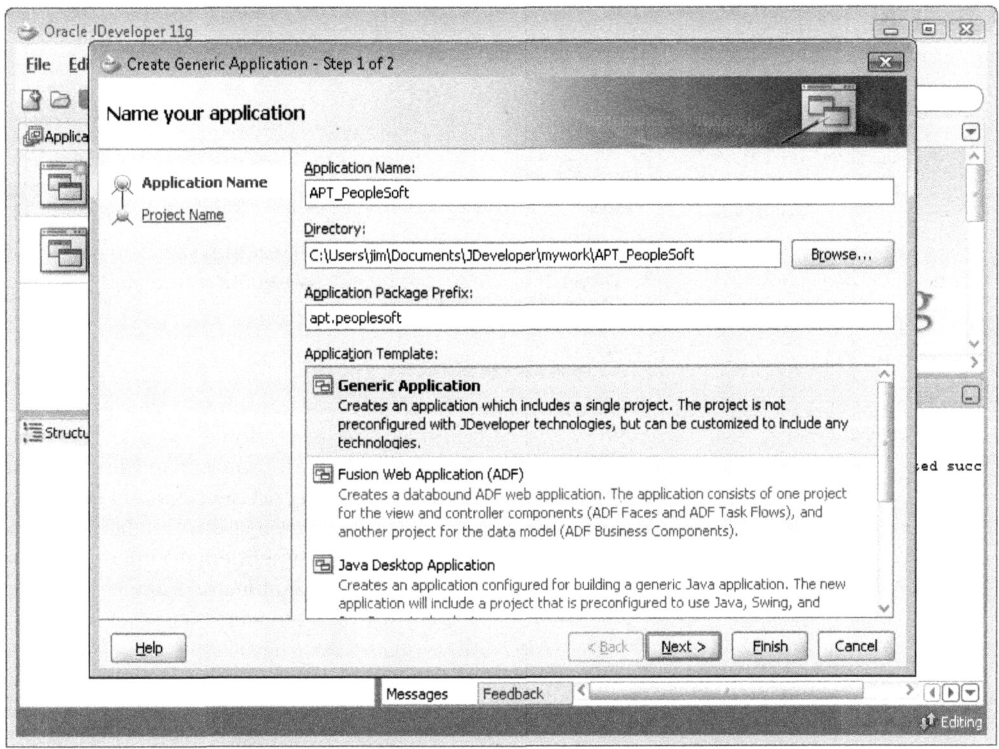

FIGURE 11-1. *JDeveloper Create Application wizard step 1*

Step 2 of the wizard allows you to specify information about the empty project that will be added to the new application. In step 2, name your project `hello`, as shown in Figure 11-2, and then click Finish.

Next, we need to add a Java class to our new project. Choose File | New from the JDeveloper menu bar. In the New Gallery dialog, choose Java from the list on the left, and then select Java Class from the list on the right. In the Create Java Class dialog, name the new class `Greeter` and enter the package name `apt.peoplesoft.examples.hello`, as shown in Figure 11-3. After you click OK, JDeveloper will open a Java text editor containing the new `Greeter` class's Java code.

In the text editor, modify the existing code by adding the `sayHello` method, as follows:

```
package apt.peoplesoft.examples.hello;

public class Greeter {
    public Greeter() {
        super();
    }
```

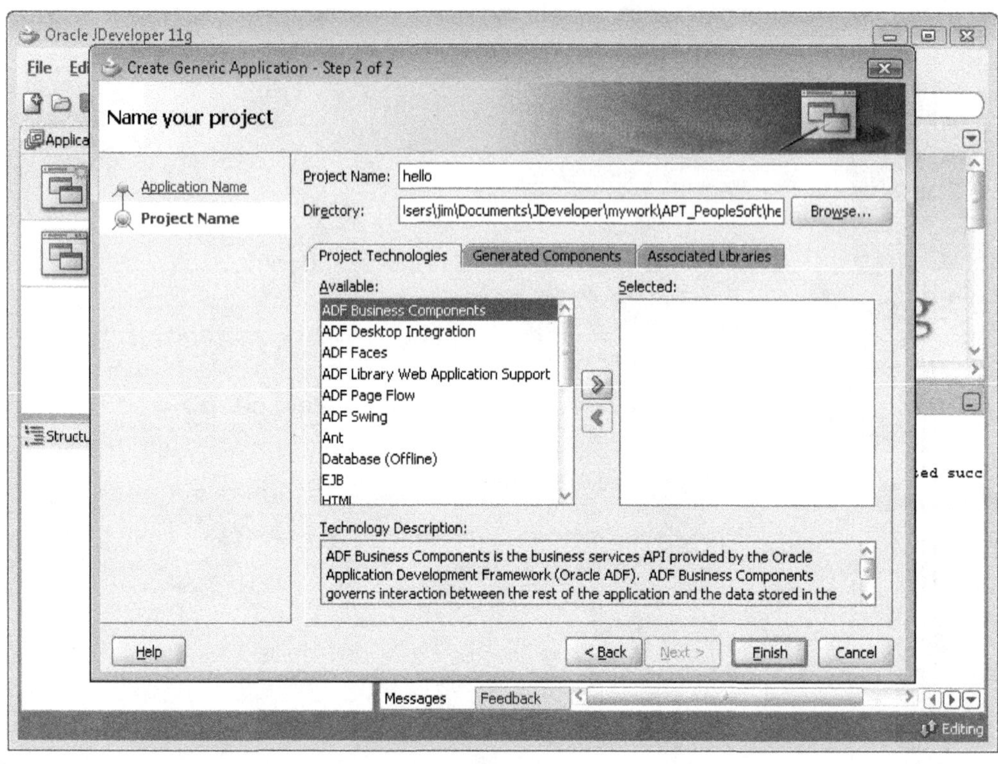

FIGURE 11-2. *JDeveloper Create Application wizard step 2*

```
    public static String sayHello() {
        return "Hello World!";
    }
}
```

Let's write another Java class to test our Java `Greeter` class. Create a new Java class and name it `TestGreeter`. For the package name, enter `test.apt.peoplesoft.examples.hello`. Since this is a test class, we will put it in a package with the same name as the class it tests (also known as the SUT, for system under test). Also, select the Main Method check box, as shown in Figure 11-4. Click the OK button to close the dialog and create the new Java class.

In the `TestGreeter` source code editor, modify the main method so that it prints the results of `Greeter.sayHello()`, as follows (additions are in bold):

```
package test.apt.peoplesoft.examples.hello;

import apt.peoplesoft.examples.hello.Greeter;
```

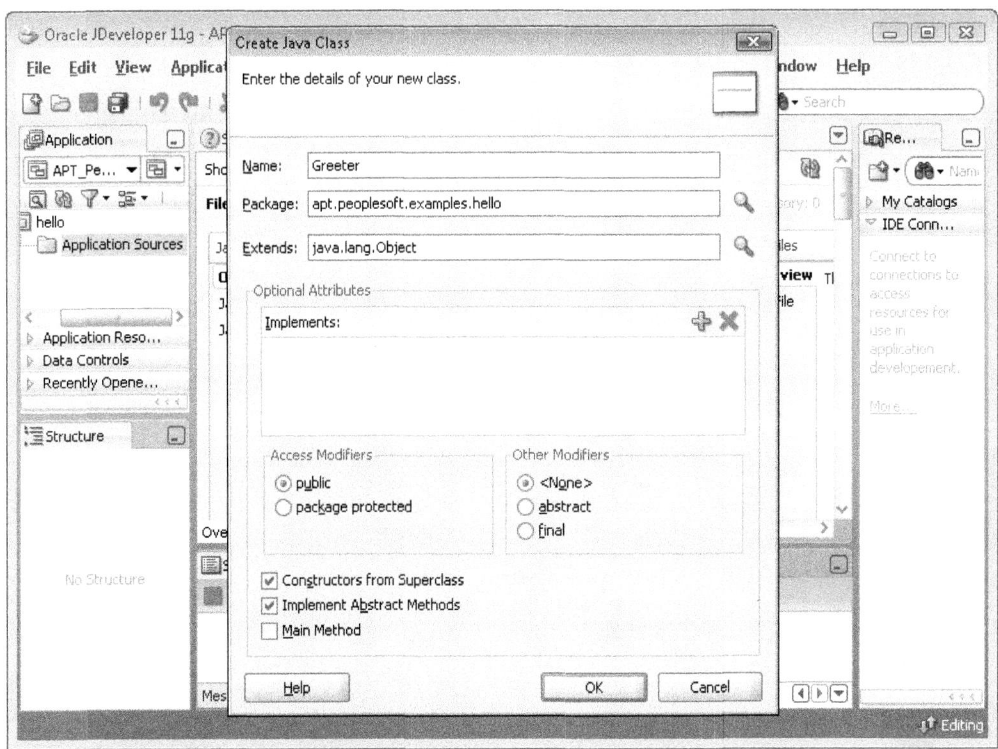

FIGURE 11-3. *Create Java Class dialog*

```
public class TestGreeter {
    public TestGreeter() {
        super();
    }

    public static void main(String[] args) {
        System.out.println(Greeter.sayHello());
    }
}
```

Since `Greeter` is in a different package than the test class, the test class must *import* the `Greeter` class. You can enter the `import` statement, as shown in the code listing, or alternatively, let JDeveloper resolve the import for you. After you type the word `Greeter`, JDeveloper will mark the word `Greeter` as an unrecognized symbol. JDeveloper will then search for the `Greeter` class definition. If JDeveloper finds the unrecognized class, it will prompt you to import the class by pressing the key combination ALT-ENTER.

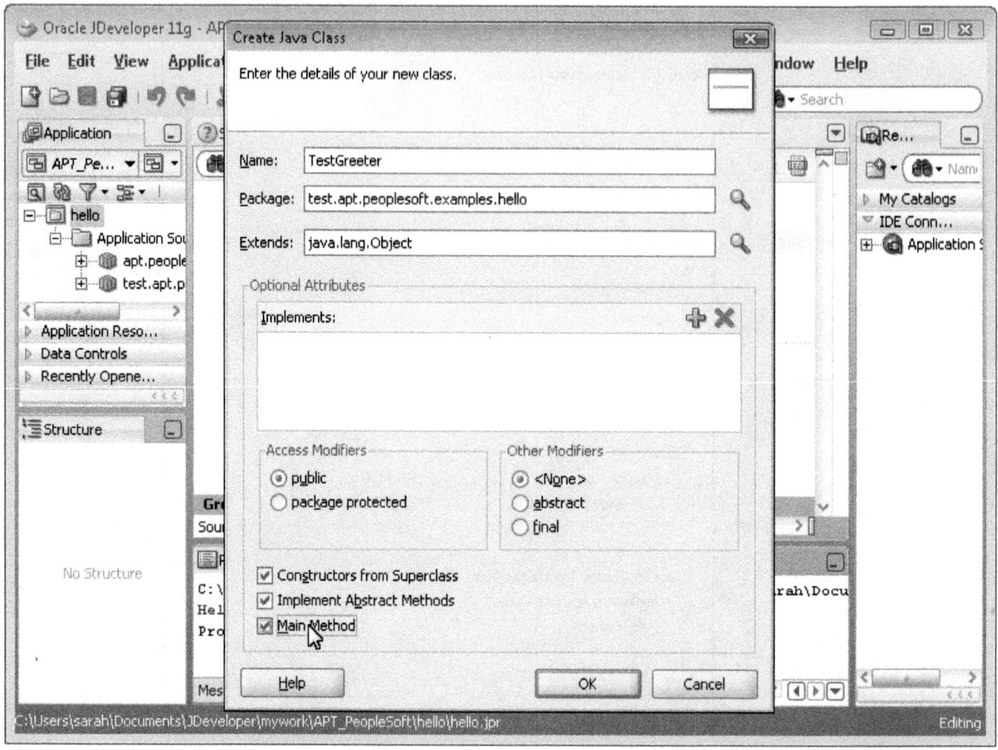

FIGURE 11-4. *Creating the TestGreeter Java class*

To run this test code, right-click in the source editor and choose Run from the context menu. If it's successful, you will see output similar to what appears in the output panel at the bottom of Figure 11-5.

Deploying Java

You can either package Java code in JAR files or deploy it directly as class files. When deploying solutions, JAR files can be easier to manage because they contain a complete, isolated file system. Since JAR files are added to the app server's class path only at startup, however, deploying JAR files requires you to restart your app server. Class files, on the other hand, can be deployed without restarting your app server. Unfortunately, if you need to redeploy, either method will require an app server restart.

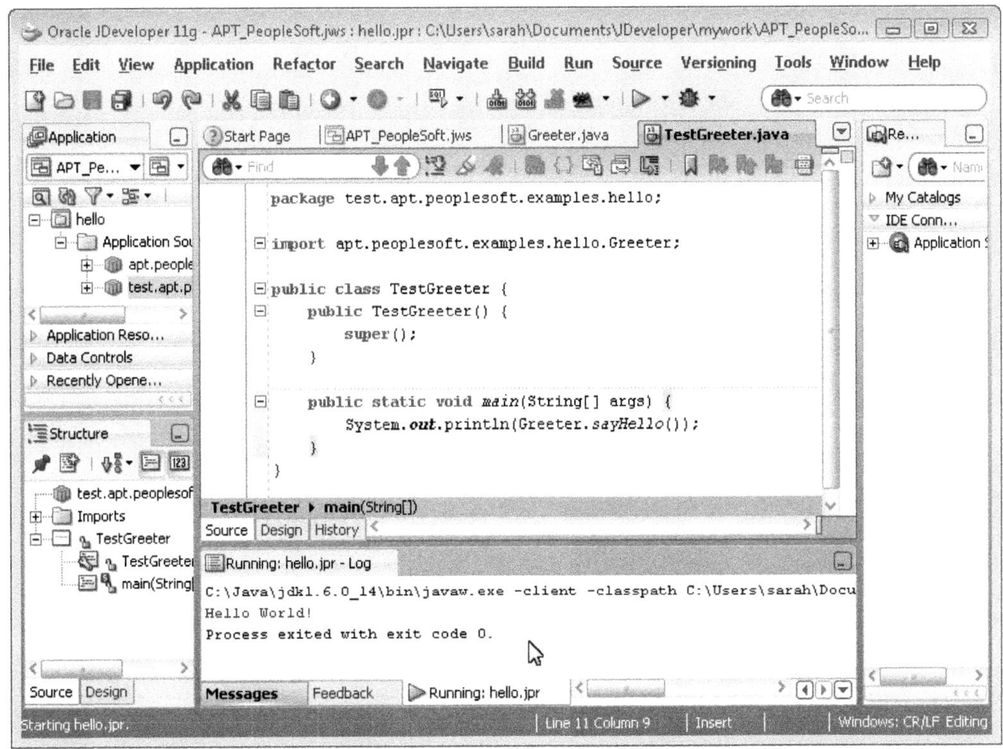

FIGURE 11-5. *Running: hello.jpr output window*

When deploying JAR files, place the JAR file in your %PS_HOME%\class or $PS_HOME/appserv/classes directory. If you deploy your Java solutions as class files, copy the class's full directory structure into your %PS_HOME%\class or $PS_HOME/appserv/classes directory.

In this chapter's examples, we will deploy Java solutions as JAR files. To create a JAR file with JDeveloper, choose File | New from the JDeveloper menu bar. In the New Gallery dialog, select General, then Deployment Profiles from the Categories list, and JAR File from the Items list, as shown in Figure 11-6.

When prompted, name the JAR deployment profile `apt_ch11_examples`. In the Edit JAR Deployment Profile Properties dialog, select File Groups, then Project Output, then Filters from the pane on the left. In the Filters section on the right, uncheck the folder named test, as shown

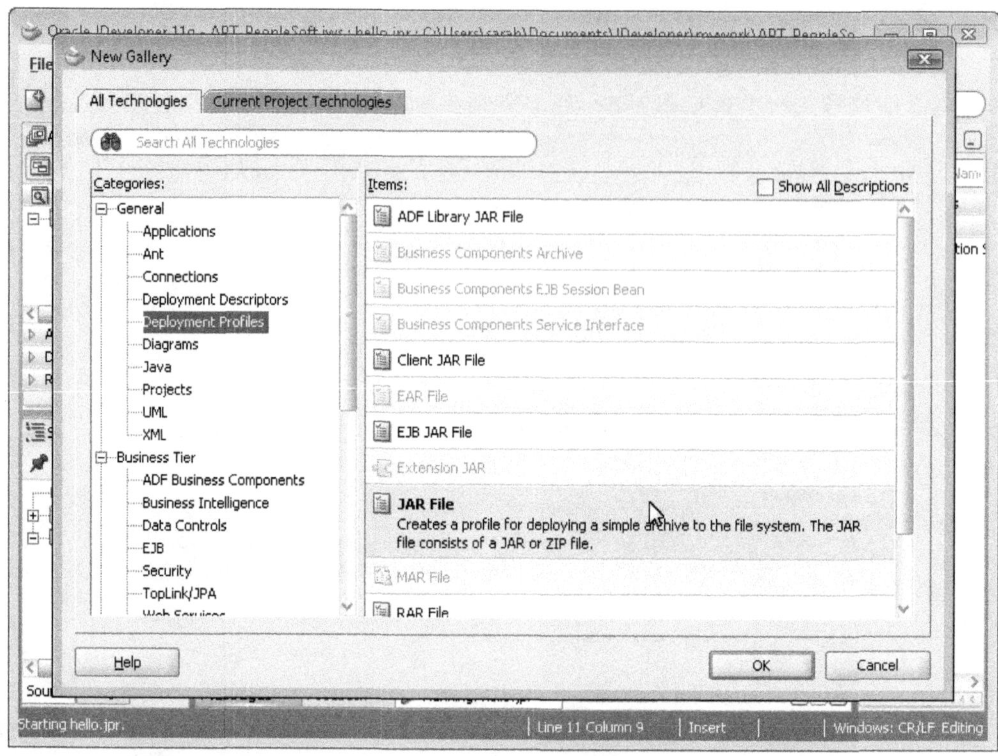

FIGURE 11-6. *Creating a new JAR file*

in Figure 11-7. The test folder (package) contains all of our test classes, so it should not exist in the deployed JAR file.

After you click OK in the Edit JAR Deployment Profile Properties dialog, the Project Properties dialog may appear (depending on your version of JDeveloper). If it doesn't appear, choose Application | Project Properties from the JDeveloper menu bar. The project's compiler compatibility setting is set to Default. Before deploying this solution to PeopleSoft, we need to change this value to the same version of Java that is used by the app server. To determine your application server's Java version, execute the following command:

```
%PS_HOME%\jre\bin\java -version
```

If you are using Linux or another supported Unix derivative, use the following command:

```
$PS_HOME/jre/bin/java -version
```

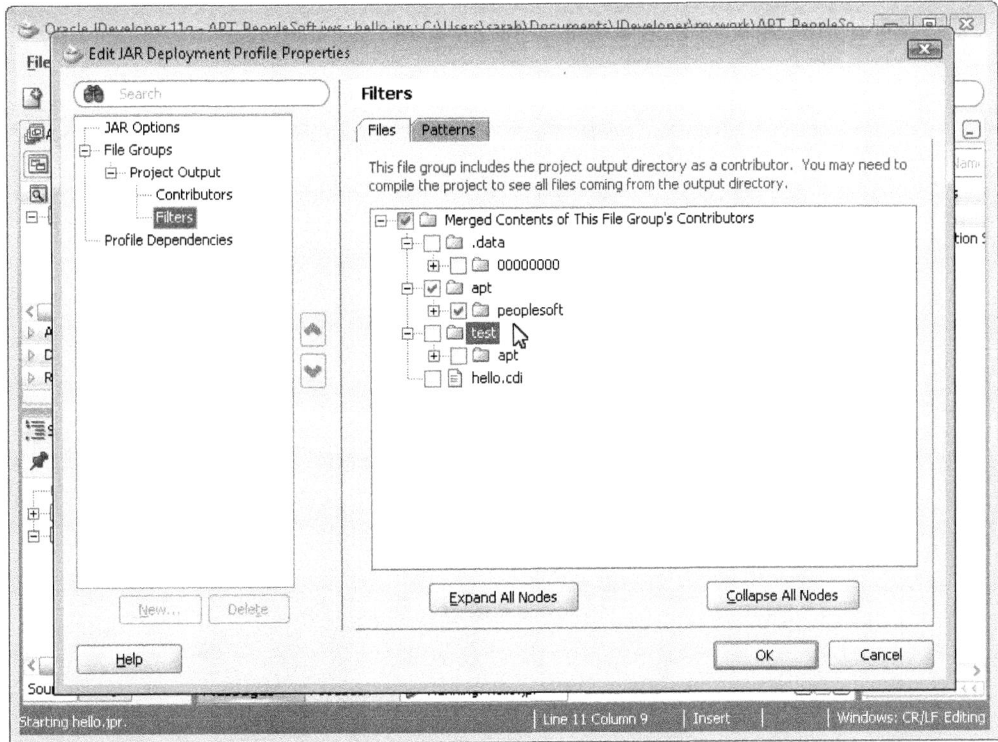

FIGURE 11-7. *Edit JAR Deployment Profile Properties dialog*

On my Windows desktop client, this produces the following output:

```
java version "1.5.0_11"
Java(TM) 2 Runtime Environment, Standard Edition (build 1.5.0_11-b03)
Java HotSpot(TM) Client VM (build 1.5.0_11-b03, mixed mode)
```

This output tells me that my PeopleSoft instance uses Java 1.5.

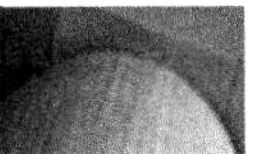

NOTE
You do not need to run the command to discover your Java versions on your application server. Your PeopleTools IDE %PS_HOME% contains the same Java Runtime Environment (JRE) information that is used by your application server.

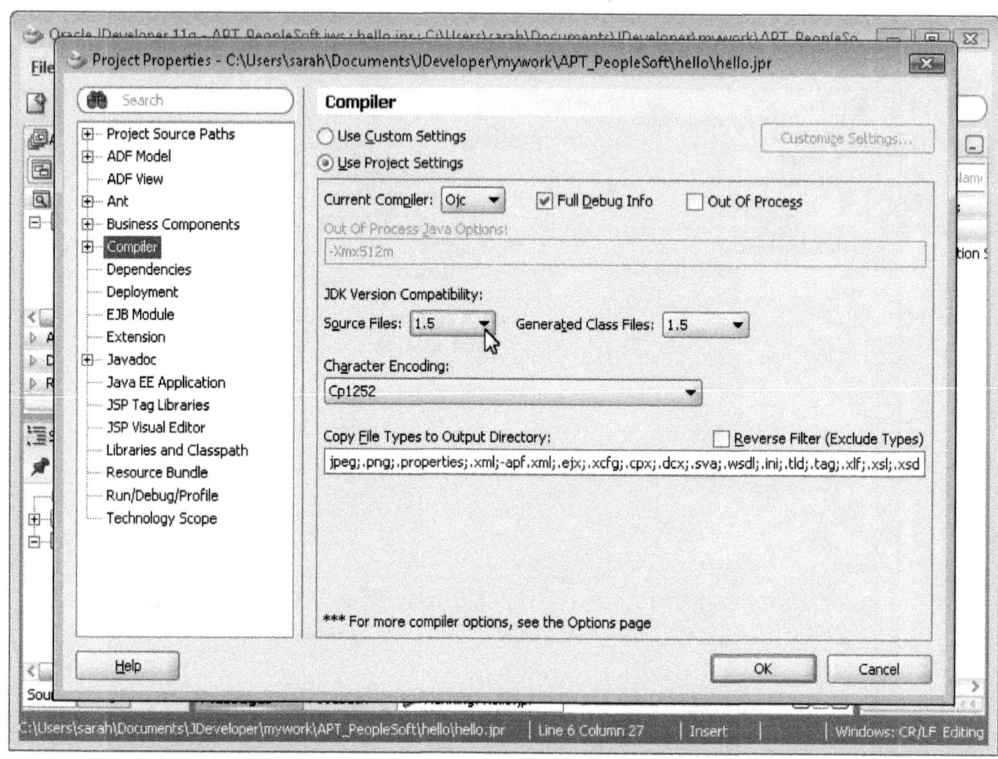

FIGURE 11-8. *Project compiler compatibility settings*

With your Java version identified, you can change the JDK compiler version compatibility setting from Default to match it, as shown in the example in Figure 11-8. When you change the source files setting here, JDeveloper will automatically update the generated class files setting. Click OK to return to JDeveloper.

Create a JAR file from this new deployment descriptor by right-clicking the project named `hello`, in the Application Navigator, and selecting Deploy | apt_ch11_examples | to JAR file, as shown in Figure 11-9.

JDeveloper will compile your project's source code and package the resultant binary files into a new JAR file located in the deploy subdirectory of your JDeveloper project's directory. You can locate the full path from the Deployment tab of the JDeveloper output window. The following listing contains the contents of my output window:

```
[11:38:26 PM] ----  Deployment started.  ----
[11:38:26 PM] Target platform is  (Weblogic 10.3).
[11:38:26 PM] Running dependency analysis...
[11:38:26 PM] Building...
```

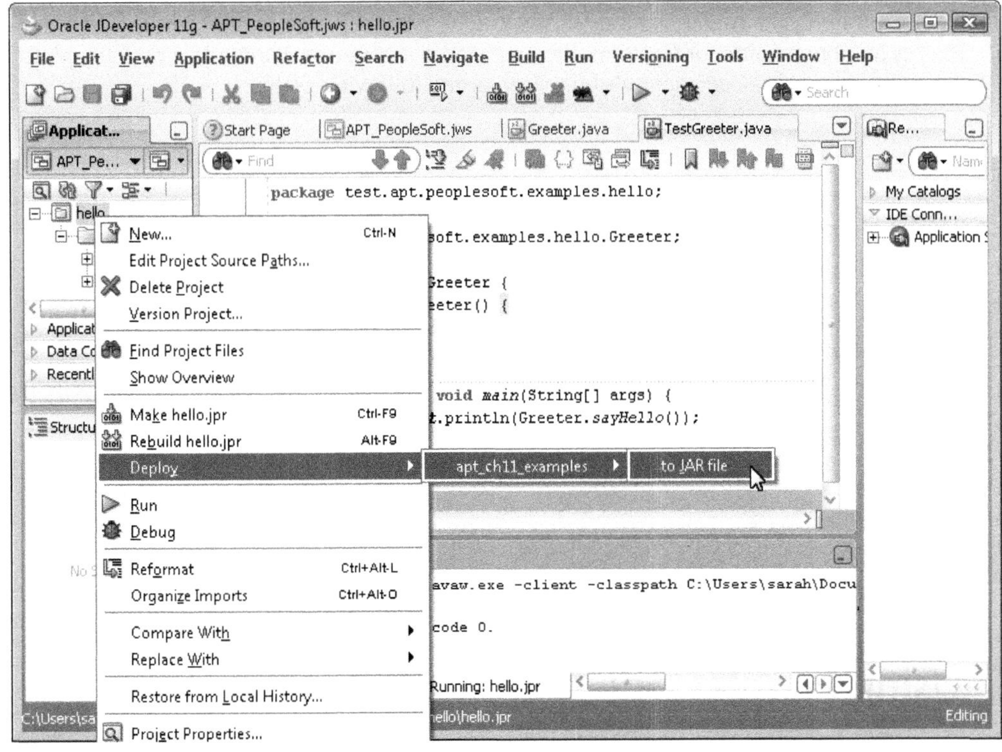

FIGURE 11-9. *Choosing to deploy to a JAR file*

```
[11:38:26 PM] Deploying profile...
[11:38:27 PM] Wrote Archive Module to
    C:\Users\jim\Documents\JDeveloper\mywork\APT_PeopleSoft\hello\
    deploy\apt_ch11_examples.jar
[11:38:27 PM] Elapsed time for deployment:  1 second
[11:38:27 PM] ----  Deployment finished.  ----
```

After JDeveloper builds the JAR file, copy it to your PeopleTools IDE %PS_HOME\class directory. Our next step is to create an App Engine program that can run this Java code.

NOTE

Since JAR files are specially structured zip files, you can view their contents with any zip file viewer (7z, WinZip, and so on).

Creating the Test Program

Open App Designer and create a new App Engine program. Name the program `APT_CST_JAVA` (`CST` is an abbreviation for Custom). Rename step 1 to `Greeter` and add a new PeopleCode action. In the PeopleCode action's editor, enter the following code:

```
Local JavaObject &greeter =
      GetJavaClass("apt.peoplesoft.examples.hello.Greeter");

MessageBox(0, "", 0, 0, &greeter.sayHello());
```

Disable the Restart property. Save and then run your new App Engine program. Running this program should produce a log file similar to the following:

```
PeopleTools 8.49 - Application Engine
Copyright (c) 1988-2009 PeopleSoft, Inc.
All Rights Reserved


Hello World! (0,0)
 Message Set Number: 0
 Message Number: 0
 Message Reason: Hello World! (0,0) (0,0)
Application Engine program APT_CST_JAVA ended normally
```

Using PeopleCode Objects in Java

PeopleSoft's pluggable encryption, data access, and the Approval Workflow Engine are a few of the many outstanding features of the PeopleTools platform that you can use with Java. Many of these features exist in Java as either part of the base Java language or as open source libraries. The difference between PeopleSoft's and Java's offerings is that PeopleSoft uses a metadata approach that supports online configuration.

PeopleSoft exposes the entire PeopleCode language to Java through the Java Native Interface (JNI)[1] programming framework. Because the PeopleCode Java library depends on JNI, PeopleCode functions and objects can be used only by Java that is running in the context of a PeopleSoft application (from an App Engine program or a PeopleSoft application server). Put another way, if you write Java that uses PeopleCode functions, you can compile it with JDeveloper (or your favorite IDE), but you can run it only from PeopleSoft.

Configuring Your Development Environment

In your PeopleTools %PS_HOME%\class directory, you will find a JAR file named peoplecode.jar. To create a JDeveloper library for this JAR file, choose Tools | Manage Libraries from the JDeveloper menu bar. In the Manage Libraries dialog, click the New button and add a new library named `PeopleCode`. The peoplecode.jar file contains both Java source files and compiled class files, so add it to both the class path and the source path, as shown in Figure 11-10. Click OK to create the new library.

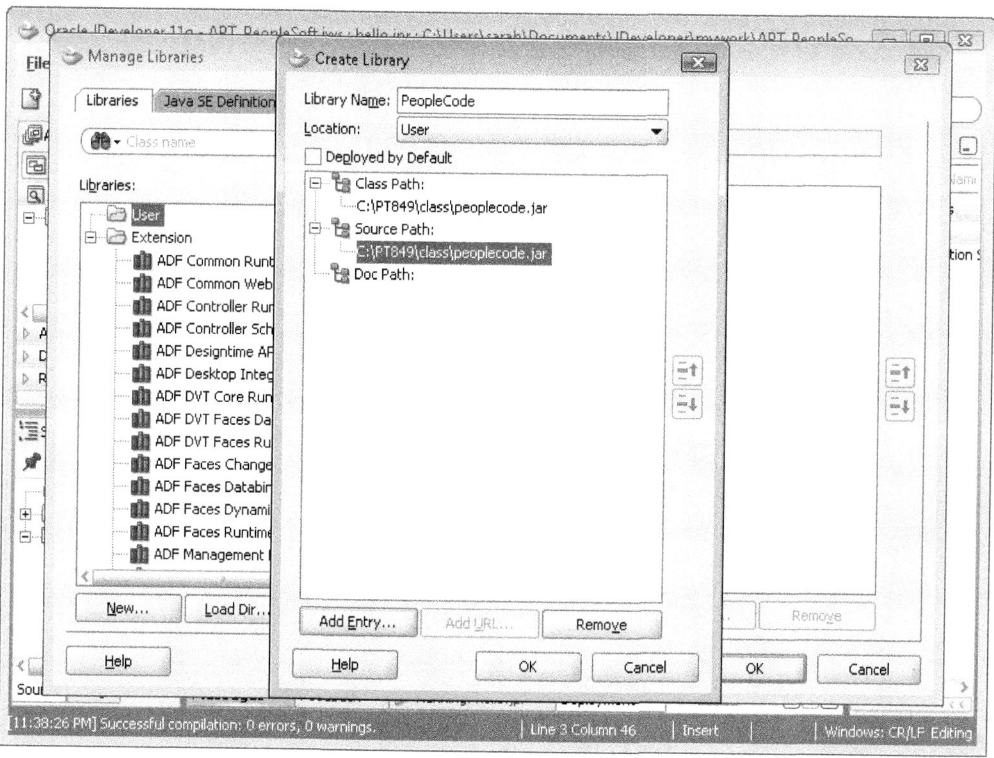

FIGURE 11-10. *Creating a JDeveloper library for peoplecode.jar*

To add the new library to your project, select Application | Project Properties, choose Libraries and Classpath from the left pane, and click the Add Library button. In the Add Library dialog, select the PeopleCode library, as shown in Figure 11-11. After adding the new library to your project, click OK to dismiss the Project Properties dialog.

Using PeopleCode System Variables

In JDeveloper, create a new class named `UserGreeter` and place it in the `apt.peoplesoft.examples.hello` package. Modify the JDeveloper-generated class file so it contains the following code (changes are in bold):

```
package apt.peoplesoft.examples.hello;

import PeopleSoft.PeopleCode.SysVar;
```

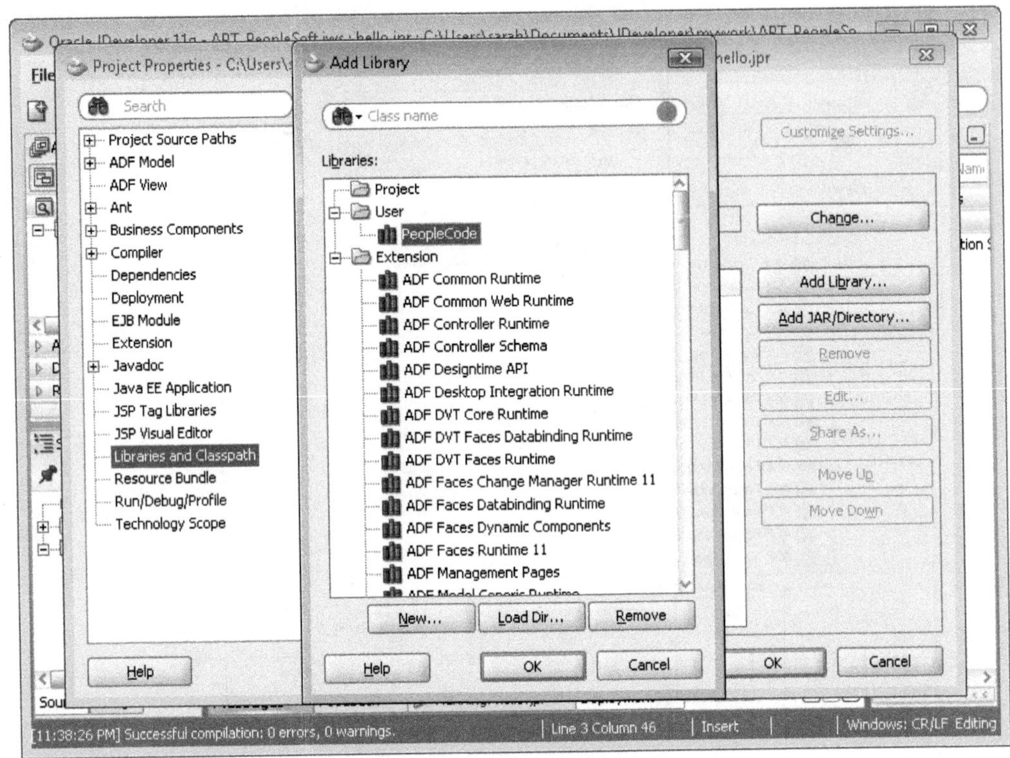

FIGURE 11-11. *Adding the PeopleCode library to your project*

```
public class UserGreeter {
    public UserGreeter() {
        super();
    }

    public static String sayHello() {
        return "Hello " + SysVar.UserId();
    }
}
```

NOTE
Are you noticing any similarities to the classes presented here and those we created in Chapter 1?

Since this new `UserGreeter` class uses the PeopleCode `SysVar` collection, we cannot test it prior to deploying it to PeopleSoft. When using PeopleCode from Java, it is imperative that you maintain access to a PeopleSoft IDE for testing your Java code.

Redeploy the `hello` project (choose Deploy | apt_ch_11_examples | to JAR file from the project's context menu), and then copy the resultant JAR file to your %PS_HOME%\class directory.

Back in App Designer, add a new step (the step's name is not important; you can keep the default name provided by App Designer) and PeopleCode action to the App Engine named `APT_CST_JAVA`. In the new step's PeopleCode editor, enter the following code:

```
Local JavaObject &greeter =
      GetJavaClass("apt.peoplesoft.examples.hello.UserGreeter");

MessageBox(0, "", 0, 0, &greeter.sayHello());
```

TIP
As you add new steps to `APT_CST_JAVA`, you may find it beneficial to disable older steps.

Running this code as user `PS` produces the following output:

```
Hello PS (0,0)
 Message Set Number: 0
 Message Number: 0
 Message Reason: Hello PS (0,0) (0,0)
```

Accessing Data

One of the most powerful features offered by the PeopleCode Java interface is data access. The Java language has database access through Java Database Connectivity (JDBC) objects. To use JDBC, however, you must have a database username and password. System and database administrators usually keep these passwords to themselves and generally frown upon providing direct database access. Using PeopleCode data objects, you can reuse PeopleSoft's database connection, eliminating the need for secondary database access.

Using the SQLExec Function

One of the most simple yet effective methods for interacting with the PeopleSoft database is by using the PeopleCode `SQLExec` function. When used in PeopleCode, the `SQLExec` function's parameters are somewhat flexible. The first parameter can be either a reference to an SQL definition or a plain SQL text string. The second parameter can be either an array or a comma-delimited list of values and variables. From Java, however, the `SQLExec` function is very rigid. When called from Java, the first parameter must be an SQL statement (as opposed to an SQL definition reference), and the second parameter must be a preallocated array containing enough elements for the SQL statement's bind variables and output columns.

We are going to write some code to demonstrate calling the `SQLExec` function from Java. To create a new project for this example, choose File | New from the JDeveloper menu bar, select General, then Projects from the New Gallery dialog's Categories list, and choose Generic Project from the Items list. Name your new project `psdao` (an abbreviation for PeopleSoft data access objects). Open your new project's properties and add the PeopleCode library as we did for the `hello` project. While still viewing the project's properties, switch to the Project Source Paths item. In the last field of the Project Source Paths properties, change the Default Package setting to `apt.peoplesoft.dao`, as shown in Figure 11-12.

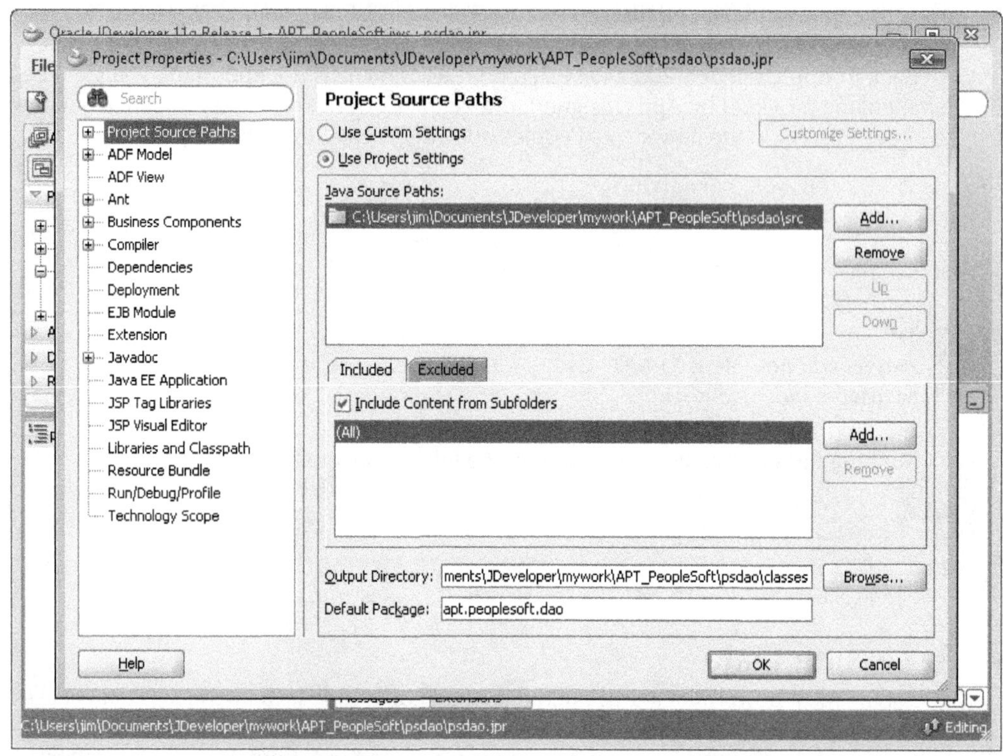

FIGURE 11-12. *Setting the psdao project source path's default package*

Next, create a new Java class named `UserInfo` and modify its code to match the following:

```
package apt.peoplesoft.dao;

import PeopleSoft.PeopleCode.Func;

public class UserInfo {
    private String oprid_;
    private String descr_;
    private String emplid_;
    private String emailid_;
    private int failedLogins_;

    /**
     * Initialize this user object at construction
     *
     * @param oprid The user's PeopleSoft login ID
     */
```

```
    public UserInfo(String oprid) {
        super();

        oprid_ = oprid;

        /* parms is an array containing input bind values when calling
         * SQLExec, and output field values when SQLExec returns.
         */
        Object[] parms = new Object[5];
        parms[0] = oprid_;

        /* Func is a PeopleSoft provided object that contains methods
         * for each PeopleCode function.
         */
        Func.SQLExec("SELECT OPRDEFNDESC, EMPLID, EMAILID, " +
                     "FAILEDLOGINS FROM PSOPRDEFN WHERE OPRID = :1",
                     parms);

        descr_ = (String)parms[1];
        emplid_ = (String)parms[2];
        emailid_ = (String)parms[3];
        failedLogins_ = ((Double)parms[4]).intValue();
    }

    public String getOperatorId() {
        return oprid_;
    }

    public String getDescription() {
        return descr_;
    }

    public String getEmployeeId() {
        return emplid_;
    }

    public String getEmailAddress() {
        return emailid_;
    }

    public int getFailedLogins() {
        return failedLogins_;
    }
}
```

NOTE

The code for this example demonstrates the Data Transfer Object (DTO) design pattern. A DTO, formerly known as a Value Object, loads its state based on constructor parameters, and then provides accessor methods for interrogating the state of the object.

The `UserInfo` class introduces the `Func` object. This object contains a method for each PeopleCode function, including think-time functions such as `MessageBox`, `WinMessage`, and `Prompt`. You can view the `Func` object's declared methods by right-clicking the word `Func` in JDeveloper's Java editor and choosing Go to Declaration from the context menu.

Add a new JAR file deployment profile to the `psdao` project and name it `apt_psdao`. Accept the default deployment profile properties and set your project's JDK version compatibility to match your PeopleTools Java version. Deploy the `apt_psdao` JAR file, and then copy it to your %PS_HOME%\class directory.

To test this code, add another step and PeopleCode action to the `APT_CST_JAVA` App Engine program. Add the following PeopleCode to the action's editor:

```
Local JavaObject &info =
      CreateJavaObject("apt.peoplesoft.dao.UserInfo",
      "HCRUSA_KU0001");

MessageBox(0, "", 0, 0, &info.getDescription());
MessageBox(0, "", 0, 0, &info.getEmailAddress());
```

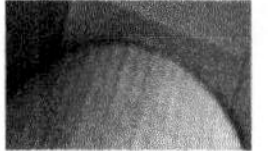

NOTE
The hard-coded operator ID in the test code here exists in the PeopleSoft HRMS demo database. You may need to substitute a different operator ID if you are using a different database instance.

Run the program. It should print the name and e-mail address associated with the hard-coded operator ID.

The Java code in this example used a hard-coded SQL string literal—something developers should strongly avoid. Even though the Java version of the `SQLExec` function requires an SQL statement, it does not need to be hard-coded. It is possible to use SQL definitions with `SQLExec`. One way to use SQL definitions with `Func.SQLExec` is to use the `%SQL` Meta-SQL, as follows:

```
Func.SQLExec("%SQL(APT_USERINFO)", parms);
```

Here is a similar method that uses an SQL definition's value property to access its SQL:

```
SQL s = Func.GetSQL(new Name("SQL", "MYSQLOBJECT), null);
Func.SQLExec(s.getValue(), parms);
```

What is the difference? You can use either method with `SQLExec`. SQL Object cursors (described next) require you to use the second method. The `GetSQL` function that is used with SQL Object cursors only fetches rows for SQL statements that start with the keyword `SELECT`, not `%SQL`.

Using SQL Objects

A common way to access the PeopleSoft database is through the PeopleCode `SQL` object. Using the `CreateSQL` and `GetSQL` PeopleCode functions, it is possible to open and iterate over a database-independent SQL cursor. To demonstrate, we'll use a PeopleCode `SQL` object to print the first ten operator definitions from `PSOPRDEFN`.

This example will use SQL stored in an App Designer SQL definition. Open App Designer, create a new SQL definition named APT_OPRDESCR, and add the following SQL:

```
SELECT OPRDEFNDESC
  FROM PSOPRDEFN
```

In JDeveloper, create a new Java class named FirstTenOperators in the package apt.peoplesoft.dao. Modify the code so that it matches the following:

```
package apt.peoplesoft.dao;

import PeopleSoft.PeopleCode.Func;
import PeopleSoft.PeopleCode.Name;
import PeopleSoft.PeopleCode.SQL;

public class FirstTenOperators {
    public FirstTenOperators() {
        super();
    }

    public static String[] getTenOperators() {
        String[] result = new String[10];
        Object[] descr = new Object[1];
        SQL sql = Func.GetSQL(new Name("SQL", "APT_OPRDESCR"), null);
        int row = 0;

        //Func.CreateSQL("SELECT...", parms);
        while (sql.Fetch(descr) && (row < 10)) {
            result[row++] = (String)descr[0];
        }

        return result;
    }
}
```

We declare the getTenOperators method using the keyword static. Static methods differ from other methods in that you can call them without creating instances of an object. In PeopleCode, this allows us to use GetJavaClass rather than CreateJavaObject. You should declare any method that does not require instance-specific variables as static.

Deploy the JAR file deployment descriptor and copy the JAR file into your PeopleTools class directory.

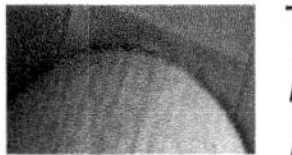

TIP
Rather than copy your modified JAR file into your PeopleTools PS_HOME directory, you can specify your %PS_HOME%\class or $PS_HOME/appserv/classes directory in your deployment descriptor's properties.

To test the `FirstTenOperators` class, create a new step and action in the `APT_CST_JAVA` App Engine program. Open the action's PeopleCode editor and add the following PeopleCode:

```
Local JavaObject &jDescrs =
      GetJavaClass(
      "apt.peoplesoft.dao.FirstTenOperators").getTenOperators();
Local array of string &descrs = CreateArrayRept("", &jDescrs.length);

CopyFromJavaArray(&jDescrs, &descrs);

MessageBox(0, "", 0, 0, &descrs.Join());
```

Running this program on my server produces the following output:

```
(Rochelle Li,Tina Palisco,[PS] PeopleSoft Mobile - User,
    [PS] Peoplesoft Superuser,[PS] Environments Mgt,,,
    Payroll User,Allowed to start web servers,) (0,0)
 Message Set Number: 0
 Message Number: 0
 Message Reason: (Rochelle Li,Tina Palisco,
    [PS] PeopleSoft Mobile - User,[PS] Peoplesoft Superuser,
    [PS] Environments Mgt,,,Payroll User,
    Allowed to start web servers,) (0,0) (0,0)
```

NOTE
I iterated over ten rows, but only seven names appear in the output. The other three names are represented by commas. It appears that three of my first ten users do not have descriptions.

Using the Record Object

For demonstration purposes, let's clone the `UserInfo` class into a new class named `UserInfoRec` and replace the `SQLExec` with a `Record` object. To clone the `UserInfo` class, open UserInfo .java in JDeveloper. Then right-click the class name in the editor, select Refactor | Duplicate from the context menu, and enter the name `apt.peoplesoft.dao.UserInfoRec`. After cloning `UserInfo` into `UserInfoRec`, modify the class's Java code as follows:

```
package apt.peoplesoft.dao;

import PeopleSoft.PeopleCode.Func;
import PeopleSoft.PeopleCode.Name;
import PeopleSoft.PeopleCode.Record;

public class UserInfoRec {
    private String oprid_;
    private Record rec_;
```

```
    /**
     * Initialize this user object at construction
     *
     * @param oprid The user's PeopleSoft login ID
     */
    public UserInfoRec(String oprid) {
        super();

        oprid_ = oprid;

        Name recName = new Name("RECORD", "PSOPRDEFN");
        rec_ = Func.CreateRecord(recName);
        rec_.GetField(new Name("FIELD", "OPRID")).setValue(oprid_);
        rec_.SelectByKey();
    }

    public String getOperatorId() {
        return oprid_;
    }

    public String getDescription() {
        return rec_.GetField(new Name("FIELD",
                                      "OPRDEFNDESC"))
            .getValue()
            .toString();
    }

    public String getEmployeeId() {
        return rec_.GetField(new Name("FIELD",
                                      "EMPLID"))
            .getValue()
            .toString();
    }

    public String getEmailAddress() {
        return rec_.GetField(new Name("FIELD",
                                      "EMAILID"))
            .getValue()
            .toString();
    }

    public int getFailedLogins() {
        return ((Double)rec_.GetField(new Name("FIELD",
                                               "FAILEDLOGINS"))
            .getValue())
            .intValue();
    }
}
```

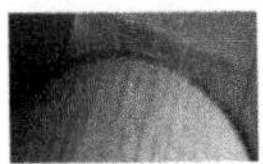

NOTE
The method declarations in `UserInfoRec` are the same as `UserInfo`, but the implementations differ.

PeopleSoft Database log4j Appender

In Chapter 10, you learned how to use the log4j logging framework. Rather than write logging statements to disparate application server-specific log files, let's create a custom appender for log4j that writes log statements to a centralized database table. This new appender will require a Java class, a record definition, and some SQL.

NOTE
The custom log4j appender example uses Oracle's autonomous transactions to commit database changes without committing the existing PeopleSoft transaction. If you are not using an Oracle database, you can obtain the same result using the log4j `JDBCAppender`. Unfortunately, the `JDBCAppender` does not share the PeopleSoft database connection and, therefore, will require database access credentials. The log4j documentation contains information about configuring the delivered `JDBCAppender`. If your PeopleSoft instance is not running on Oracle's database, I recommend skipping forward to the next example in this chapter, in the "PeopleSoft Database Velocity Template Data Source" section.

Our new record definition will require a couple of custom fields. Create the following fields:

- `APT_L4J_LEVEL`: Set its type to character, its length to 10, and its format to uppercase. Create a new field label with an ID of `APT_L4J_LEVEL`, a long name of **Log Level**, and a short name of **Level**. Figure 11-13 shows this field.
- `APT_L4J_TIMESTAMP`: Set its type to datetime and its time format to HH:MI:SS.999999. Create a new field label with an ID of `APT_L4J_TIMESTAMP`, a long name of **Log Timestamp**, and a short name of **Timestamp**. Figure 11-14 shows this field.

Create a new record definition in App Designer named `APT_L4J_LOG`. Add the fields `APT_LOGGER_ID`, `APT_L4J_LEVEL`, `APT_L4J_TIMESTAMP`, `DESCRLONG`, and `PROCESS_INSTANCE`. Figure 11-15 shows this new record definition. Save and build the record.

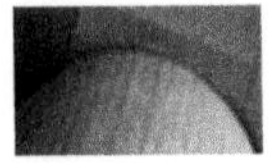

NOTE
The `APT_L4J_LOG` record does not have a primary key. To obtain optimal performance when reviewing this record definition's data, I recommend adding some indexes by selecting Tools | Data Administration | Indexes from the App Designer menu bar.

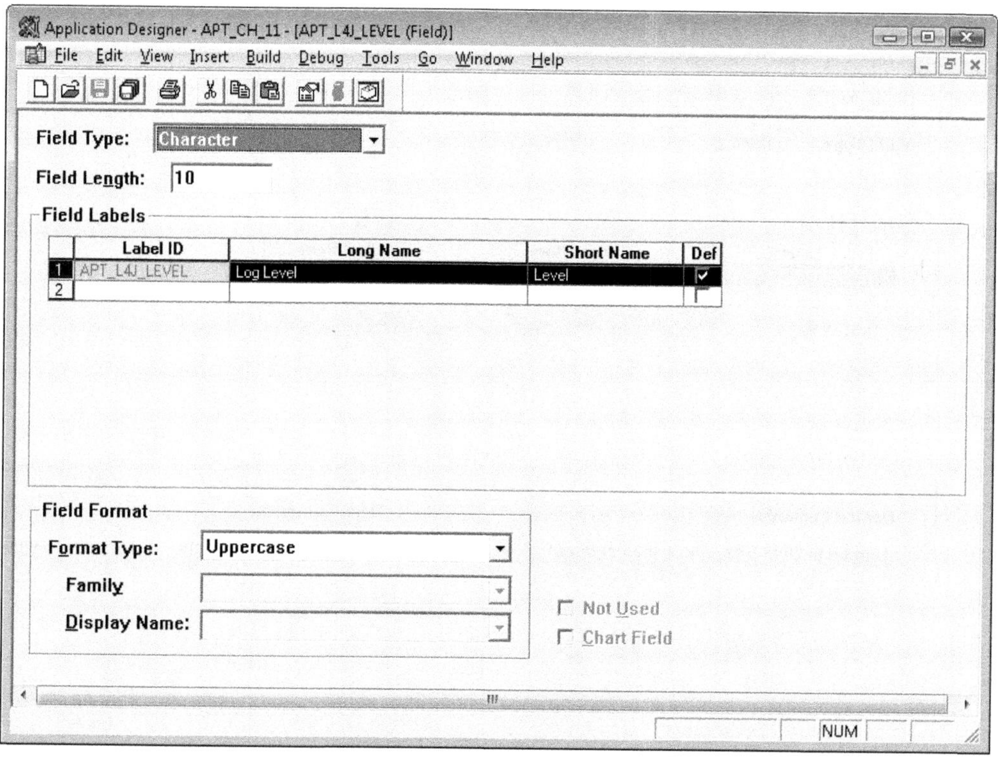

FIGURE 11-13. *The APT_L4J_LEVEL definition*

Creating the PL/SQL Autonomous Transaction

One of the objectives of logging from PeopleCode is to find and resolve errors. When an error occurs within a PeopleSoft transaction, PeopleSoft rolls back any database changes made since the transaction began. This rollback behavior poses a problem. Not only will a rollback undo transaction changes, but it will also undo any log statements your code writes to a database table. Oracle offers a solution to this scenario in the form of autonomous transactions.

With Oracle, all database operations are performed in the context of a transaction. An autonomous transaction is an independent transaction that does not share the same transaction state as a user's Oracle database session. Autonomous transactions provide a solution to our logging-within-a-transaction problem because they allow us to commit logging statements without affecting the user's main session transaction. The log statements will persist even if the user's main transaction rolls back.

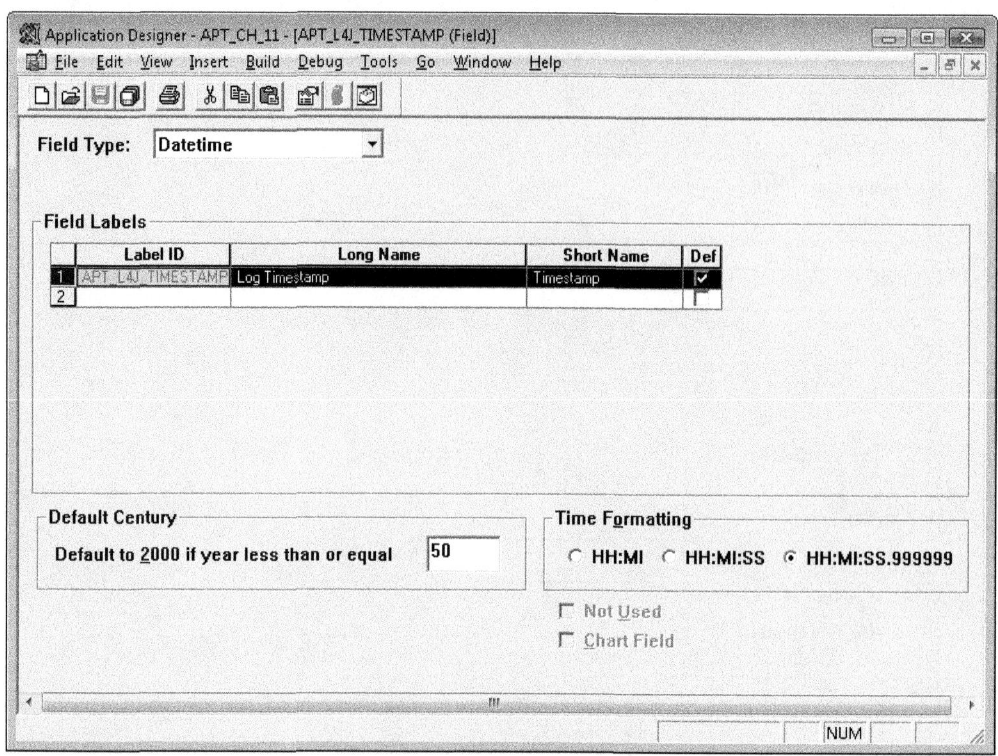

FIGURE 11-14. *The APT_L4J_TIMESTAMP definition*

Application Designer - APT_CH_11 - [APT_L4J_LOG (Record)]

File Edit View Insert Build Debug Tools Go Window Help

Record Fields | Record Type

Nu	Field Name	Type	Len	Format	Short Name	Long Name
1	APT_LOGGER_ID	Char	254	Mixed	ID	Logger ID
2	APT_L4J_LEVEL	Char	10	Upper	Level	Log Level
3	APT_L4J_TIMESTAMP	DtTm	26	MicroS	Timestamp	Log Timestamp
4	PROCESS_INSTANCE	Nbr	10		Instance	Process Instance
5	DESCRLONG	Long	0		Descr	Description

Ready NUM

FIGURE 11-15. *The APT_L4J_LOG record definition*

To use an autonomous transaction, we will need to create a PL/SQL procedure. The following code listing describes a PL/SQL package specification and package body that contains a single PL/SQL procedure named `log`. The `log` procedure uses an autonomous transaction to insert logging statements into our new `APT_L4J_LOG` record definition. Add the following PL/SQL to an empty text file and save the file in a convenient location.

NOTE
Creating PL/SQL procedures requires direct database access. You should work with your database administrator to acquire access. The SQL we will write later assumes the following PL/SQL package exists in your PeopleSoft schema. You can create the package in a different schema if you prefer.

```
SPOOL apt_l4j.log

-- Uncomment the following two lines if you are modifying the package
-- PROMPT drop package 'APT_L4J'
-- DROP PACKAGE APT_L4J;

PROMPT create package spec 'APT_L4J'
CREATE PACKAGE APT_L4J AS

    -- Note: in PT 8.48 and above, PV_MESSAGE is CLOB. Otherwise, it
    --       should be LONG
    PROCEDURE LOG( PV_LOGGER_ID IN VARCHAR2
                , PV_LEVEL IN VARCHAR2
                , PV_PROCESS_INSTANCE IN NUMBER
                , PV_MESSAGE IN CLOB
                /*, PV_MESSAGE IN LONG pre 8.48*/);
END APT_L4J;

/

PROMPT create package body 'APT_L4J'
CREATE PACKAGE BODY APT_L4J AS

    -- Note: in PT 8.48 and above, PV_MESSAGE is CLOB. Otherwise, it
    --       should be LONG
    PROCEDURE LOG( PV_LOGGER_ID IN VARCHAR2
                 , PV_LEVEL IN VARCHAR2
                 , PV_PROCESS_INSTANCE IN NUMBER
                 , PV_MESSAGE IN CLOB
                /*, PV_MESSAGE IN LONG pre 8.48*/)
    IS
    PRAGMA AUTONOMOUS_TRANSACTION;

    BEGIN
        INSERT INTO PS_APT_L4J_LOG
        VALUES ( PV_LOGGER_ID
```

```
                , PV_LEVEL
                , SYSDATE
                , PV_PROCESS_INSTANCE
                , PV_MESSAGE );

        COMMIT;

    EXCEPTION
        WHEN OTHERS THEN
            DBMS_OUTPUT.PUT_LINE('Exception in APT_L4J.LOG()');
            DBMS_OUTPUT.PUT_LINE(SQLERRM);
            ROLLBACK;

    END LOG;
END APT_L4J;
/

show errors

SPOOL OFF
```

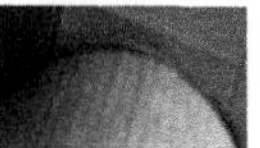

CAUTION
When using autonomous transactions, it is critical that you either commit or roll back prior to exiting the procedure that declares the autonomous transaction. Otherwise, Oracle will raise an exception.

To import and compile this PL/SQL package, open a command prompt and type the following command, replacing `SYSADM` with the name of a database user and `HRMS` with the name of your PeopleSoft database:

```
C:\> sqlplus SYSADM@HRMS
```

When you execute this command, SQLPlus will prompt you for your database user's password. After logging in, SQLPlus will present you with an SQL prompt. At the prompt, type the following, replacing `c:\projects\peopletools\chapter11\apt_l4j.sql` with the path to the text file you created in the prior step:

```
SQL> @c:\projects\peopletools\chapter11\apt_l4j.sql
```

Running this command should produce the following output:

```
create package spec 'APT_L4J'

Package created.

create package body 'APT_L4J'

Package body created.

No errors.
SQL>
```

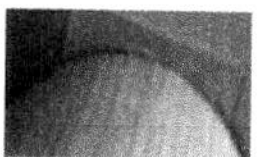

NOTE
Work with your database administrator to resolve any errors reported by Oracle while creating the package specification and package body.

Writing the Java

Appenders are Java classes that implement the `org.apache.log4j.Appender` interface. The log4j framework provides the `AppenderSkeleton` abstract class, which implements most of the `Appender` interfaces methods, leaving the `append`, `close`, and `requiresLayout` methods for final `Appender` implementations. In this section, we will create an appender that uses `Func.SQLExec` to execute the PL/SQL procedure we created in the previous section.

In JDeveloper, add a new library named `log4j` and set its class path to %PS_HOME%\class \log4j-1.2.8.jar. Next, create a new Generic project in the `APT_PeopleSoft` application and name it `l4j`. Open the project's properties and set the default package to `apt.peoplesoft.l4j`. With the project's properties still open, select Compiler from the list on the left and set the JDK version compatibility to the same value as your PeopleSoft's JRE. Switch to the Deployment item and click the New button. Create a new JAR file named `apt_l4j`, as shown in Figure 11-16. Next, move down to the Libraries and Classpath item and add the log4j and PeopleCode libraries. Then click OK to save your project.

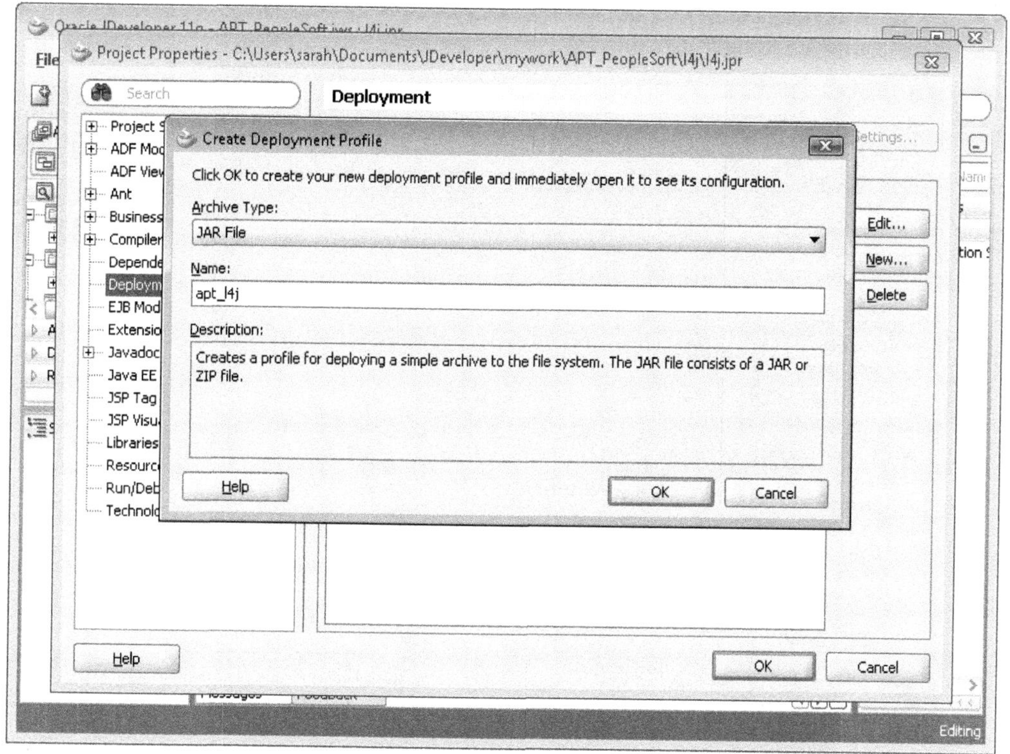

FIGURE 11-16. *The apt_l4j JAR file deployment descriptor*

Create a new Java class named `PSDBAppender`. Set the package name to `apt.peoplesoft.l4j`. In the Extends field, enter `org.apache.log4j.AppenderSkeleton`, as shown in Figure 11-17. Click the OK button to dismiss the Create Java Class dialog.

Enter the following code into the `PSDBAppender` class's Java code editor:

```
package apt.peoplesoft.l4j;


import PeopleSoft.PeopleCode.Func;

import org.apache.log4j.AppenderSkeleton;
import org.apache.log4j.spi.LoggingEvent;


/**
 * <p>Inserts data into a PeopleSoft table using the SQL statement
 * identified by {@link #setSql(String)}. See {@link #setSql(String)}
 * for details on the format of the SQL statement.</p>
 */
```

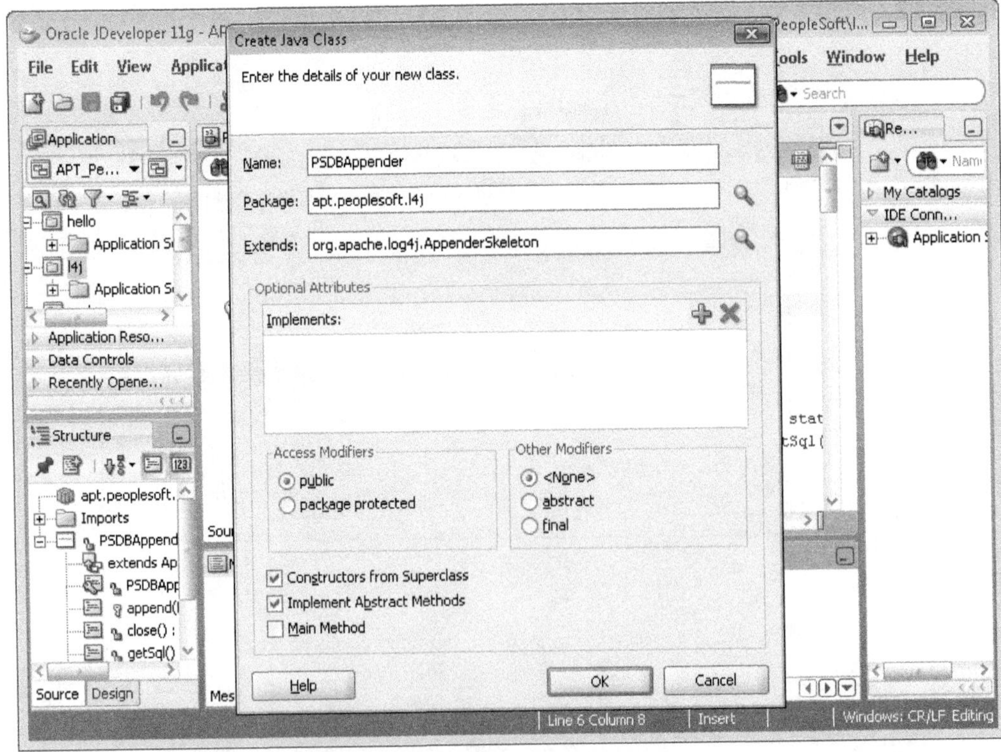

FIGURE 11-17. *Creating the PSDBAppender Java class*

```
public class PSDBAppender extends AppenderSkeleton {
    private String sqlStatement_;

    public PSDBAppender() {
        super();
    }

    /**
     * <p>Writes a logging event to a PeopleSoft database record.</p>
     *
     * @param loggingEvent
     * @see AppenderSkeleton#append(LoggingEvent)
     */
    protected void append(LoggingEvent loggingEvent) {
        Object[] parms = new Object[4];
        Object processInstance =
                loggingEvent.getMDC("PROCESS_INSTANCE");

        if (processInstance == null) {
            processInstance = new Double(0);
        }

        parms[0] = loggingEvent.getLoggerName();
        parms[1] = loggingEvent.getLevel().toString();
        parms[2] = processInstance;
        parms[3] = loggingEvent.getMessage().toString();

        Func.SQLExec(sqlStatement_, parms);
    }

    /**
     * <p>Sets the closed flag for this
     * {@link org.apache.log4j.Appender}.</p>
     *
     * @see org.apache.log4j.Appender
     * @see org.apache.log4j.AppenderSkeleton#closed
     */
    public void close() {
        closed = true;
    }

    /**
     * This Appender does not use a layout.
     *
     * @return Always returns false
     */
    public boolean requiresLayout() {
        return false;
    }
```

```
    /**
     * <p>Expects a SQL statement containing placeholders for the
     * following four bind variables:</p>
     *
     * <ol>
     *   <li>:1 Logger name (string)</li>
     *   <li>:2 Log level (string)</li>
     *   <li>:3 Message (string)</li>
     *   <li>:4 Process Instance (number)</li>
     * </ol>
     *
     * <p>To set the process instance from PeopleCode, use</p>
     * <pre>
     * Local JavaObject &mdc = GetJavaClass("org.apache.log4j.MDC");
     * &mdc.put("PROCESS_INSTANCE", STATE_REC_AET.PROCESS_INSTANCE);
     * </pre>
     *
     * <p>If you don't require a process instance, then this appender
     * will insert 0 (zero) into the log table.</p>
     *
     * @param sql SQL statement
     */
    public void setSql(String sql) {
        sqlStatement_ = sql;
    }

    /**
     * <p>Returns the SQL statement previously set by
     * {@link #setSql(String)}</p>.
     *
     * @return SQL statement
     */
    public String getSql() {
        return sqlStatement_;
    }
}
```

Let's review this code line by line. Starting at the top, you see the package declaration. Besides defining the Java class's file path, the package declaration qualifies the Java class's name to prevent naming collisions. Given the package value of `apt.peoplesoft.l4j`, this class's fully qualified name is `apt.peoplesoft.l4j.PSDBAppender`.

Next, the code listing imports three Java classes. The `import` directive allows us to use Java class names in our code without specifying the class's fully qualified name. When the compiler sees a class name in the code, it will look to the `import` directives to resolve the class name to a fully qualified class name.

The next section in our Java class file defines the `PSDBAppender` class as a subclass of `AppenderSkeleton` (or, more formally, `org.apache.log4j.AppenderSkeleton`). The class definition contains one field named `sqlStatement_`, one constructor (the method with the same name as the class), and five methods. Figure 11-18 shows the JDeveloper code editor window with the Java class Structure browser on the left. The structure browser contains text and

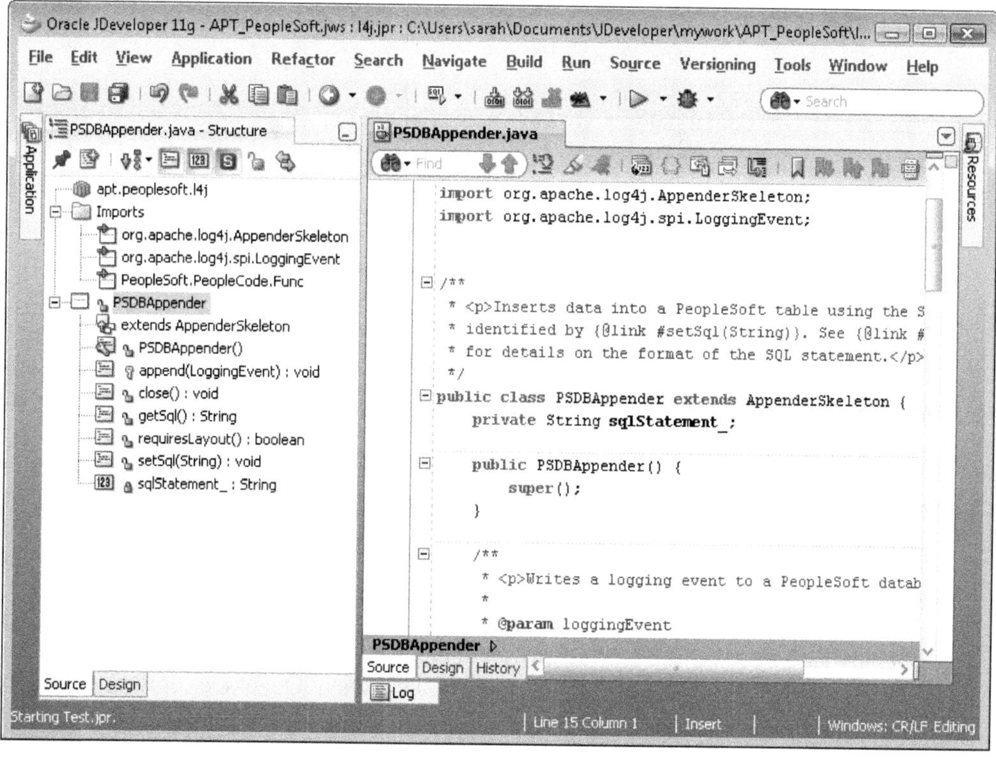

FIGURE 11-18. *JDeveloper structure browser and code editor*

icons describing each item in the list. Besides displaying an overview of the class definition, the structure browser serves as a Java class table of contents. Double-clicking any item in the structure browser will take you to the Java code for that item.

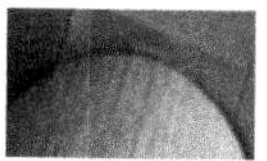

NOTE

The JDeveloper Create Java Class wizard created the default, no-argument, constructor. Since our constructor contains no additional code, we can safely delete it. In the absence of a predefined constructor that calls `super()`, the Java compiler will create an implicit constructor and make a hidden call to `super()`.

Following the constructor is the `append` method. The log4j framework calls the `append` method to send data to the appender's target. Since the `append` method is the only method in this class with any substance, let's briefly review its code:

```
protected void append(LoggingEvent loggingEvent) {
    Object[] parms = new Object[4];
    Object processInstance = loggingEvent.getMDC("PROCESS_INSTANCE");
```

```
        if (processInstance == null) {
            processInstance = new Double(0);
        }

        parms[0] = loggingEvent.getLoggerName();
        parms[1] = loggingEvent.getLevel().toString();
        parms[2] = processInstance;
        parms[3] = loggingEvent.getMessage().toString();

        Func.SQLExec(sqlStatement_, parms);
    }
```

The append method uses the PeopleCode `SQLExec` method to execute an SQL statement. As you saw in previous examples, the `SQLExec` method requires an array of bind values. The remainder of the code in this method initializes that array with values from the logging event's properties. Notice that the values in the parameter array match the `APT_L4J.LOG` PL/SQL package we created earlier.

Near the beginning of the `append` method's implementation, you see this line:

```
Object processInstance = loggingEvent.getMDC("PROCESS_INSTANCE");
```

MDC is an acronym for Mapped Diagnostic Context. The MDC is a static, thread-specific *map*, a collection of key/value pairs similar to a hashtable. In the upcoming test program, you will see how to use the MDC to pass data to an appender separate from the logged message.

Deploy the `PSDBAppender` class by right-clicking the `l4j` project name in the Application Navigator and selecting Deploy | apt_l4j | to JAR file. When JDeveloper finishes compiling the project's output into apt_l4j.jar, copy apt_l4j.jar to your local App Designer's %PS_HOME%\class directory.

TIP
When JDeveloper finishes generating apt_l4j.jar, it will print the full path to the new JAR file in the Deployment Log, an output window which is generally located at the bottom of the JDeveloper IDE.

Whether or Not to Use a Layout

Most of the log4j appenders use a layout to format logging events into messages. I considered the use of a layout with the `PSDBAppender` as well. Unlike a file or e-mail appender, which can receive/process input in a variety of shapes (XML, plain text, HTML, and so on), the `PSDBAppender` can process only one type of structured input: SQL. Nevertheless, some level of flexibility is desirable.

The log4j `JDBCAppender`[2], for example, uses the `PatternLayout` to allow for flexibility in generating SQL statements that use logging event properties. Using the `PatternLayout`, it is possible to craft a pattern that results in an SQL `INSERT` statement or stored procedure call that uses various logging event properties as input values. The problem with this approach is that the generated SQL statement will contain hard-coded, unescaped values, rather than bind variables. Consider the following sample pattern:

```
EXECUTE APT_L4J.LOG('%c', '%p', %X{PROCESS_INSTANCE}, '%m')
```

Given a logger named `my.logger`, a level of `DEBUG`, a process instance of `12345`, and the message `The employee's first name is Jim`, the `PatternLayout` would generate the following SQL statement:

```
EXECUTE APT_L4J.LOG('my.logger', 'DEBUG', 12345,
    'The employee's first name is Jim')
```

Notice that the last value passed to the `APT_L4J.LOG` procedure is actually `'The employee'` and the remainder of the text is unquoted. Given that you control log statement generation, you could escape such strings prior to logging them, but that would bind log statement generation to a particular appender, negating much of the flexibility of the configurable log4j framework. As you see with the `XMLLayout` and `HTMLLayout`, the layout is responsible for escaping logging event properties.

Besides generating unescaped values, using the `PatternLayout` for SQL statement generation suffers from two additional shortcomings: SQL injection vulnerabilities and performance. SQL injection vulnerabilities arise when we generate SQL statements by concatenating SQL with user-entered data. Since one of our reasons for logging is to review transactions for data-entry errors, we know we will be generating log statements that contain user-entered data.

The performance degradation of the `PatternLayout` approach deserves mention, but is not nearly as important as the previously mentioned flaws. As log4j demonstrates, `PatternLayout` resolution is extremely fast. The performance degradation I am referring to occurs in your database's SQL engine. When Oracle encounters an SQL statement, it generates and caches an execution plan for that statement. Thereafter, as long as the statement is in Oracle's statement cache, it will use the pregenerated execution plan. When using bind variables, the preceding statement is constant: `EXECUTE APT_L4J.LOG(:1, :2, :3, :4)`. Without bind variables, each execution generates a new statement.

To offer flexibility, I considered creating a templating engine layout. Using a template engine, such as Velocity, it is possible to offer flexibility far beyond the capabilities of the log4j `PatternLayout`. Furthermore, a Velocity SQL-generation template could use the OWASP Enterprise Security API[3] Java library's `OracleCodec` to mitigate SQL injection risk and eliminate value errors (such as misplaced quotes). I believe this solution offers the pinnacle of flexibility, but suffers greatly in performance. If the PeopleSoft SQL Access Manager were thread-safe, coupling a Velocity layout with the log4j `AsyncAppender` would present a very promising alternative.

I believe the optimal balance of flexibility and performance could be achieved by refactoring the `PSDBAppender` to accept a parameterized SQL statement and a collection designating the name of each logging event property, as well as the bind variable location within the SQL statement.

Testing the Appender

We will use an App Engine program to demonstrate the `PSDBAppender`. The Java and PL/SQL code we've written provide for a program's `PROCESS_INSTANCE`. The only way to acquire an App Engine's `PROCESS_INSTANCE` in PeopleCode is through the program's state record. Therefore, create a new state record named `APT_L4J_AET` and add the `PROCESS_INSTANCE` field, as shown in Figure 11-19. Save and build the record.

Create a new App Engine named `APT_L4J_TST`. Open the App Engine's properties by selecting File | Definition Properties from the App Designer menu bar. In the Program Properties dialog, click the State Records tab and add the `APT_L4J_AET` state record to the list of selected state records. Switch to the Advanced tab and select the Disable Restart check box. Click the OK button to dismiss the App Engine Program Properties dialog.

In the `APT_L4J_TST` App Engine program editor, add two new steps with actions to section `MAIN`. Name the first step `commit` and the second step `fail`. Open the PeopleCode editor for the `commit` step and add the following code:

```
Local JavaObject &logger =
      GetJavaClass("org.apache.log4j.Logger").getLogger(
      "AE.APT_L4J_TST.MAIN.commit");
Local JavaObject &appender =
      CreateJavaObject("apt.peoplesoft.l4j.PSDBAppender");

Local JavaObject &mdc = GetJavaClass("org.apache.log4j.MDC");
&mdc.put("PROCESS_INSTANCE", APT_L4J_AET.PROCESS_INSTANCE);

&appender.setSql("exec APT_L4J.LOG(:1, :2, :3, %TextIn(:4))");

&logger.addAppender(&appender);
&logger.setLevel(GetJavaClass("org.apache.log4j.Level").DEBUG);
&logger.debug("This data was written from the 'commit' step and "
      | Char(13) | Char(10) | "contains ' characters that would cause "
      | Char(13) | Char(10) | "a PatternLayout SQL statement to fail");
```

The code in this listing is similar to the examples presented in Chapter 10. The code retrieves a `Logger` from the log4j logger repository, configures an appender, sets the logger's level, and then prints statements to the logger instance. The differences from the Chapter 10 examples are as follows:

- It uses our new `PSDBAppender` Java class.
- It doesn't use a layout.
- It uses a Java object named `MDC` to store the App Engine's process instance.

The log4j `MDC` class allows us to place transient data into a buffer, and then access that data from layouts and appenders. The difference between MDC data and information embedded in a log message is that the layout (or appender) can determine how to format MDC key/value pairs. In our example, we used the `MDC` object to transfer a program's process instance from PeopleCode to the `PSDBAppender`, and then on to a database table. Since the process instance is separate from the logged message, we can readily query for all messages generated by a specific program.

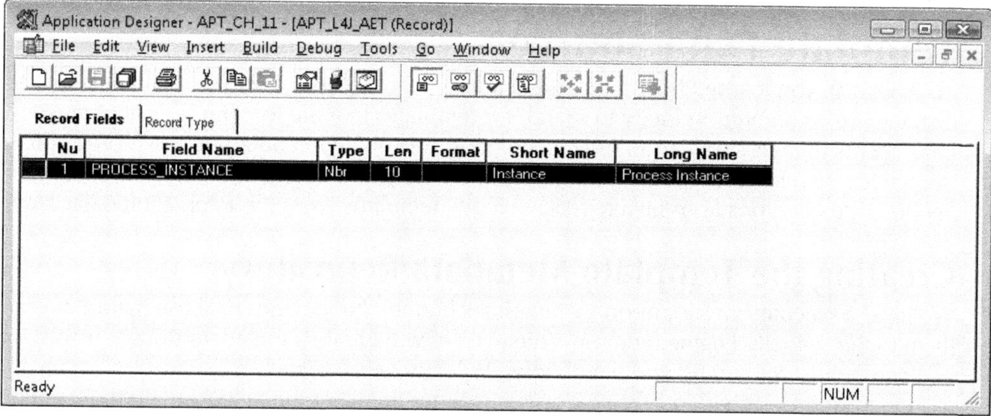

FIGURE 11-19. *APT_L4J_AET state record definition*

In Chapter 10, we used PeopleCode to configure the `RollingFileAppender`, an appender with several properties that needed to be set prior to use. Similar to the `RollingFileAppender`, the `PSDBAppender` example uses the following PeopleCode to set the appender's property:

```
&appender.setSql("exec APT_L4J.LOG(:1, :2, :3, %TextIn(:4))");
```

This SQL statement looks a little different from our prior examples. Unlike the usual `SELECT`, `INSERT`, `UPDATE`, or `DELETE` SQL statement, this SQL statement begins with the word `exec`. The `exec` keyword tells PeopleSoft to execute a stored procedure. Another abnormality is the use of `%TextIn`. The `%TextIn` Meta-SQL construct identifies bind variable `:4` as a long character field.

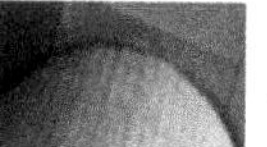

NOTE
As always, I highly recommend SQL definitions over SQL string literals. I used a string literal in this example for demonstration purposes only.

The actual log statement, the last line in the example, contains newline characters and single quotes to demonstrate that the bind variable approach accepts this type of input. This is in contrast to the `PatternLayout` strategy used by the log4j-delivered `JDBCAppender`, which fails when presented with unsafe characters.

Static Configuration

In Chapter 10, you learned how to use a message catalog entry to configure the log4j logging framework. The following code listing shows how to use the `log4j.properties` format to configure the `PSDBAppender` and a logger that uses this appender:

```
#PSDB appender configuration
log4j.appender.psdb=apt.peoplesoft.l4j.PSDBAppender
log4j.appender.psdb.sql=exec APT_L4J.LOG(:1, :2, :3, %TextIn(:4))

# IScript.test.PSDBAppender logger
log4j.logger.IScript.test.PSDBAppender=INFO, psdb
```

PeopleSoft Database Velocity Template Data Source

In Chapter 9, you learned how to integrate the Apache Velocity Engine with PeopleSoft. In that chapter, we configured Velocity to search for templates in a file folder. Given that few developers have access to their application servers, perhaps the PeopleSoft database is a more appropriate storage location for Velocity templates. The example in this section demonstrates how to call PeopleCode functions from Java to read Velocity templates from the PeopleSoft database.

Creating the Template Metadata Repository

We need a mechanism for importing templates into the PeopleSoft database before we can serve them to the Velocity Engine. For convenience, we will create a metadata storage record, page, and component for storing and maintaining Velocity templates.

Open App Designer and create a new character field. Set the field's length to 30 and the field format to mixed case. Add the label `APT_TEMPLATE_ID`, and give it a long name of **Template ID** and a short name of **ID**. Name the new field `APT_TEMPLATE_ID`. Figure 11-20 shows this new field definition.

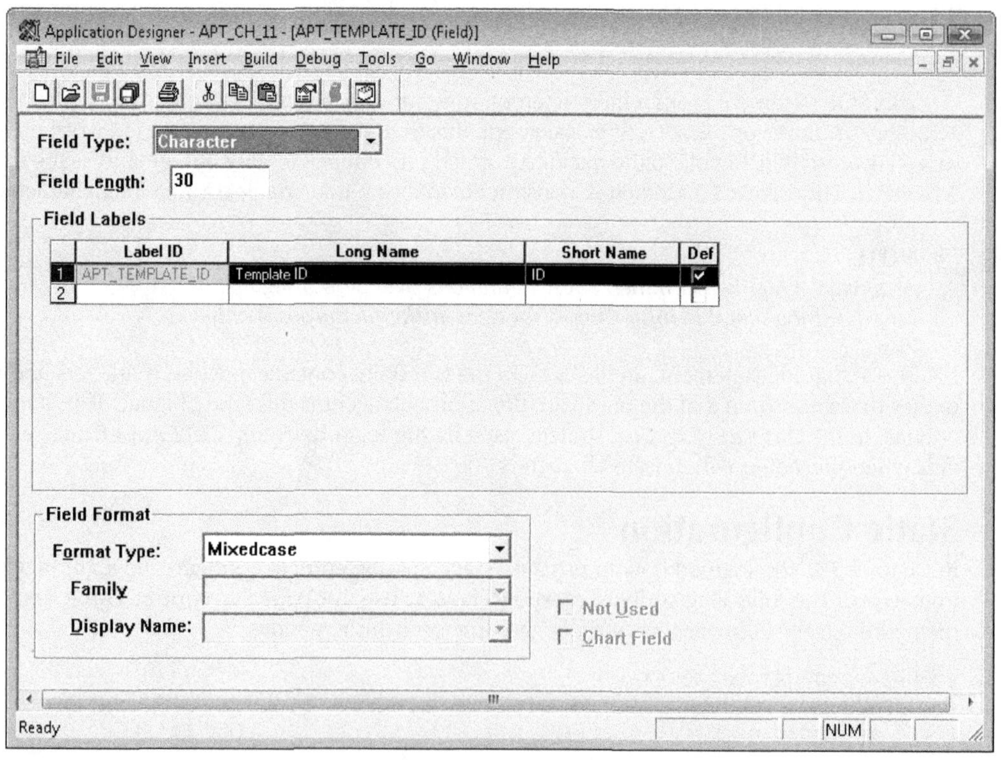

FIGURE 11-20. *APT_TEMPLATE_ID field definition*

Create a new record definition named APT_TMPLT_DEFN. We will use this record to store Velocity templates within the PeopleSoft database. Add the fields APT_TEMPLATE_ID, DESCR, HTMLAREA, and LASTUPDDTTM. Make APT_TEMPLATE_ID a key and a search key. Make DESCR an alternate search key and a list box item. Figure 11-21 shows this record definition. Save and build the record.

Did you notice that the LASTUPDDTTM field in Figure 11-21 is bold? This is App Designer's visual cue that the LASTUPDDTTM field has PeopleCode in one of its events. Later, we will write some Java to read and compare timestamps. So that your record definition matches mine, add the following PeopleCode to the SavePreChange event to update the LASTUPDDTTM field whenever a row changes.

```
/* APT_CH_11, Jim Marion, 21-OCT-2009, dttm for Velocity Resource */
APT_TMPLT_DEFN.LASTUPDDTTM = %Datetime;
```

Create a new page named APT_TMPLT_DEFN and add all of the fields from record APT_TMPLT_DEFN. Make APT_TEMPLATE_ID and LASTUPDDTTM read-only, and change the label of the field HTMLAREA to **Template Text**. Resize the HTMLAREA field as shown in Figure 11-22.

Create a new component named APT_TMPLT_DEFN. Add the APT_TMPLT_DEFN page to the new component and set the page's label to **Template Definition**. Set the component's search record to APT_TMPLT_DEFN and save the component. Register the component using the following values:

- Menu: APT_CUSTOM
- Bar: CUSTOM
- Portal: EMPLOYEE
- Folder: PT_ADMINISTRATION

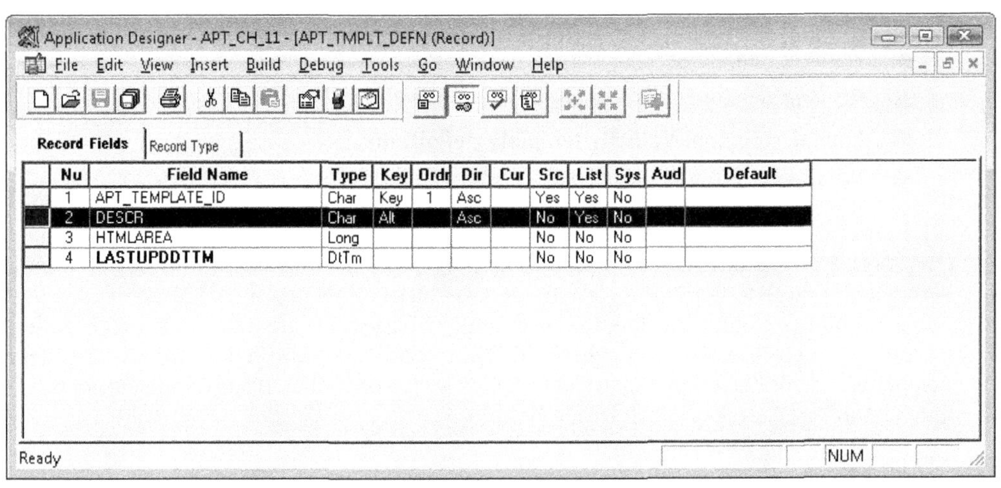

Nu	Field Name	Type	Key	Ordr	Dir	Cur	Src	List	Sys	Aud	Default
1	APT_TEMPLATE_ID	Char	Key	1	Asc		Yes	Yes	No		
2	DESCR	Char	Alt		Asc		No	Yes	No		
3	HTMLAREA	Long					No	No	No		
4	**LASTUPDDTTM**	DtTm					No	No	No		

FIGURE 11-21. *APT_TMPLT_DEFN record definition*

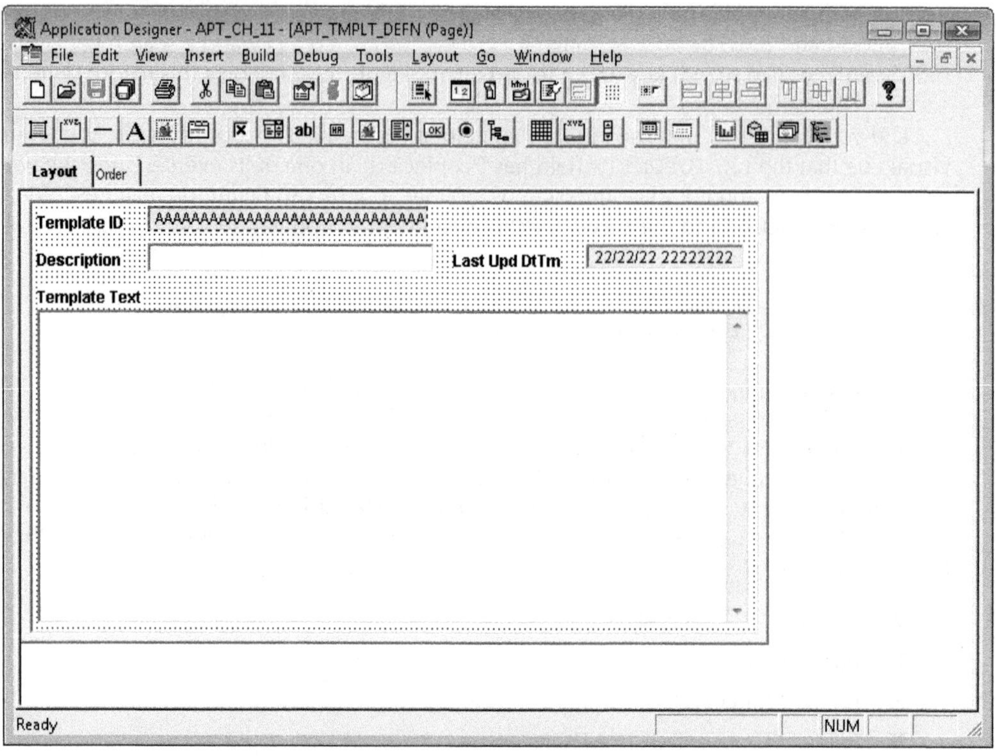

FIGURE 11-22. *APT_TMPLT_DEFN page definition in App Designer*

- Content reference: `APT_TMPLT_DEFN_GBL`
- Content reference label: **Velocity Templates**
- Long description: **Velocity template definitions**
- Permission list: `APT_CUSTOM`

To test this page, log in to your PeopleSoft application as a user with access to the `APT_CUSTOM` permission list and navigate to PeopleTools | Utilities | Administration | Velocity Templates. Switch to the Add a New Value tab and enter the value `icalendar.vm`. We are going to create a slightly modified version of the Chapter 9 iCalender Velocity template. After PeopleSoft opens the new template definition transaction, set the description to **iCalendar Template** and add the following to the template text. Notice that this text differs from the Chapter 9 template in `PRODID` only (as shown in bold).

```
BEGIN:VCALENDAR
VERSION:2.0
PRODID:-//PT Tips and Techniques//PSDB Velocity vCal 1.0//EN
```

```
#foreach ($event in $events)
BEGIN:VEVENT
DTSTART:$event.start
DTEND:$event.end
SUMMARY:$event.summary
DESCRIPTION:$event.descr
LOCATION:$event.location
CATEGORIES:$event.categories
END:VEVENT
#end
END:VCALENDAR
```

Creating the Velocity Repository Java Class

Launch JDeveloper and open the `APT_PeopleSoft` application you created at the beginning of this chapter. Create a new Generic project named `PSVelocity`, and accept the rest of the default values provided by the Create Generic Project wizard.

Velocity allows developers to create custom template loaders for loading templates from nonstandard repositories. To create a custom loader, a developer must extend the `org.apache.velocity.runtime.resource.loader.ResourceLoader` class by providing implementations for each of the class's abstract methods.

Before creating our custom loader, we need to tell JDeveloper where to find the Velocity Java library. To add Velocity as a new library, select Tools | Manage Libraries from the JDeveloper menu bar. In the Manage Libraries dialog, click the New button, and name the new library `velocity`. Add the velocity-*.jar file to the class path. You should find the Velocity JAR file in your local PeopleTools class directory (we added it in Chapter 9).

Velocity requires Apache Commons Logging, Lang, and Collections. In Chapter 9, we added these JAR files to the PeopleTools class directory, so you should find these files in the class directory as well. Create new libraries for each of these three files: commons-collections*.jar, commons-lang*.jar, commons-logging*.jar. You can add them to the Velocity library, but I recommend keeping them separate for flexibility.

After adding the four libraries to JDeveloper, we need to add them to the project's class path. Right-click the `PSVelocity` project in JDeveloper's Application Navigator and select Project Properties from the context menu. In the Project Properties dialog, select Compiler, and then change the JDK version compatibility setting to a version compatible with your PeopleSoft application. Next, select Libraries and Classpath and add the `velocity`, `commons-collections`, `commons-lang`, `commons-logging`, and `PeopleCode` libraries. We will use the `PeopleCode` library to access the PeopleSoft database.

With the project fully configured, we can create a Java class to load Velocity templates from the PeopleSoft database. Select File | New from the JDeveloper menu bar and choose to create a Java class. Name the class `PSDBResourceLoader`, set the package to `apt.peoplesoft.velocity`, and set the Extends field to `org.apache.velocity.runtime.resource.loader.ResourceLoader`, as shown in Figure 11-23. Click OK to create the new class.

JDeveloper will open the `PSDBResourceLoader` Java class in a JDeveloper code editor. Since we chose to extend an abstract class, JDeveloper created method stubs for each of the `ResourceLoader` base class abstract methods. We'll look at the implementation details for each of these abstract methods. The complete `PSDBResourceLoader` code listing appears at the end of this section.

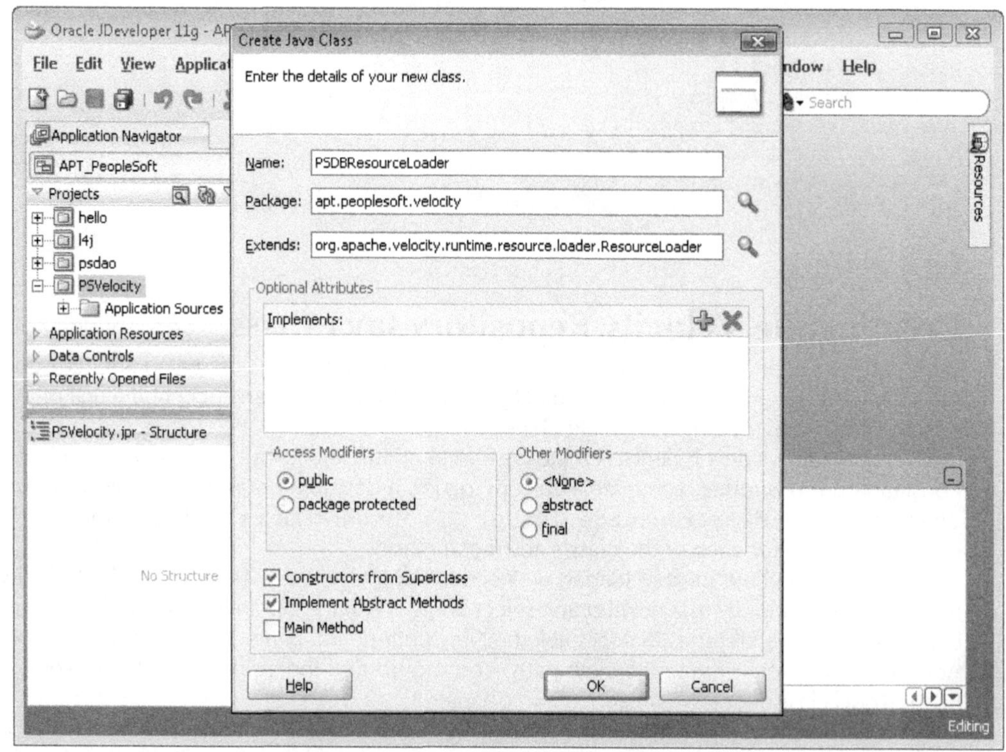

FIGURE 11-23. *Creating the PSDBResourceLoader class*

The init Method

The Velocity Engine calls the `init` method to initialize a repository from an `ExtendedProperties` object. In Chapter 9, we created an instance of the `ExtendedProperties` class to initialize the `FileResourceLoader` from values contained in our Chapter 9 velocity.properties file. Our Chapter 11 `PSDBResourceLoader` does not have initialization properties, so we will ignore this method. Even though our repository loader does not require initialization settings, we must implement this method because the base class, `ResourceLoader`, declares the `init` method as abstract.

The `init` method declaration is as follows:

```
public void init(ExtendedProperties extendedProperties) {
    // Do nothing, no properties to configure
}
```

The getResourceStream Method

The next method we need to implement is the `getResourceStream` method. This method is responsible for acquiring and returning a template's contents as an instance of an `InputStream`. Our resource loader will use the template name parameter to query the PeopleSoft database for a template's contents. The query will return a `String`, but we need an `InputStream`. We will use the `String` object's `getBytes()` method to convert the query's result to a byte array, and then wrap those bytes in a `ByteArrayInputStream`.

Here is the `getResourceStream` method:

```
public InputStream getResourceStream(String name)
    throws ResourceNotFoundException {

    if (StringUtils.isEmpty(name)) {
        throw new ResourceNotFoundException(
            "PSDBResourceLoader : No template name provided");
    }

    /* The first parameter for our SQL statement is the template
     * name bind variable. The second element in the array is the
     * SQLExec output field. Unlike PeopleCode arrays, Java arrays
     * have a fixed size. The following code initializes an Object
     * array big enough to hold the input bind variables and output
     * field values.
     */
    Object[] parms = new Object[] { name, null };
    Func.SQLExec("SELECT HTMLAREA FROM PS_APT_TMPLT_DEFN WHERE " +
                 "APT_TEMPLATE_ID = :1", parms);

    String template = (String)parms[1];

    /* Just like PeopleCode, we can use the None function
     * to determine if SQLExec returned a value. The PeopleCode
     * version of None allows for an unlimited list of variables.
     * The Java version uses an array to replicate this same
     * behavior. The following code creates a temporary, anonymous
     * Object array containing the template contents.
     */
    if (Func.None(new Object[] { template })) {
        throw new ResourceNotFoundException(
            "PSDBResourceLoader : Resource '" +
            name + "' not found.");
    }

    /* If we made it this far, then the template exists in the
     * database. The following code converts the template text to
     * a byte array and then wraps it in a ByteArrayInputStream.
     * We can return a ByteArrayInputStream from this method
     * because ByteArrayInputStream is a subclass of InputStream.
     */
    return new ByteArrayInputStream(
        parms[1].toString().getBytes());
}
```

NOTE

The Create Java Class wizard created the method `getResourceStream(String string)`. I changed the name of the `String` parameter from `string` to `name` for clarity. You will notice in the code listing here that the method signature appears as `getResourceStream(String name)`.

The isSourceModified and getLastModified Methods

For consistency, I present the last two methods, `isSourceModified()` and `getLastModifed()`, in the same order as JDeveloper. Logically speaking, however, I believe this is the wrong order, because our `isSourceModified()` method will use `getLastModified()` to determine if a template has changed. The code for `isSourceModified()` compares the last modified date from the PeopleSoft database against the last modified date within the template. If the database date is greater, then the template was modified.

The `isSourceModified()` code follows:

```
public boolean isSourceModified(Resource resource) {
    return (resource.getLastModified() <
        getLastModified(resource));
}
```

Our `getLastModified()` implementation is similar to our `getResourceStream()` method in that it queries the PeopleSoft database for a template by name. The challenge in `getResourceStream()` was to convert a `String` to an `InputStream`. The challenge presented by `getLastModified()` is to convert a PeopleCode date/time string into its Java numeric equivalent.

The following code uses Java's `SimpleDateFormat` class to parse a PeopleCode date string into a Java `Date` object. Unfortunately, Velocity doesn't want a date; it wants a number. Java internally represents dates as the number of elapsed milliseconds since January 1, 1970, 12:00 AM GMT. The following code generates a date for the purpose of calculating the number of milliseconds that have elapsed since January 1, 1970, and then returns those milliseconds.

```
public long getLastModified(Resource resource) {
    String name = resource.getName();

    if (StringUtils.isEmpty(name)) {
        throw new ResourceNotFoundException(
            "PSDBResourceLoader : No template name provided");
    }

    Object[] parms = new Object[] { name, null };
    Func.SQLExec("SELECT %DateTimeOut(LASTUPDDTTM) FROM " +
        "PS_APT_TMPLT_DEFN WHERE APT_TEMPLATE_ID = :1", parms);

    String dateString = (String)parms[1];

    if (Func.None(new Object[] { dateString })) {
        throw new ResourceNotFoundException(
```

```
                "PSDBResourceLoader : Resource '" +
                name + "' not found.");
        }

        SimpleDateFormat parser =
            new SimpleDateFormat(
                "yyyy'-'MM'-'dd'-'HH'.'mm'.'ss'.000000'");
        Date lastModified;

        try {
            lastModified = parser.parse(dateString);
        } catch (ParseException e) {
            throw new VelocityException("Error parsing date "
                  + dateString, e);
        }

        return lastModified.getTime();
    }
```

NOTE
Both the `getResourceStream()` and `getLastModified()` methods use SQL statements as embedded strings rather than App Designer-managed SQL definitions. For maintenance purposes, I recommend modifying this code to use SQL definitions instead of embedded SQL statements. If you prefer some flexibility in your resource loaders, you can make these SQL statements parameters of the `init` method's `ExtendedProperties`.

The Complete PSDBResourceLoader Code Listing

The complete `PSDBResourceLoader` class definition follows.

```
package apt.peoplesoft.velocity;

import PeopleSoft.PeopleCode.Func;

import java.io.ByteArrayInputStream;
import java.io.InputStream;

import java.text.ParseException;
import java.text.SimpleDateFormat;

import java.util.Date;

import org.apache.commons.collections.ExtendedProperties;
import org.apache.commons.lang.StringUtils;
import org.apache.velocity.exception.ResourceNotFoundException;
import org.apache.velocity.exception.VelocityException;
import org.apache.velocity.runtime.resource.Resource;
import org.apache.velocity.runtime.resource.loader.ResourceLoader;
```

```
public class PSDBResourceLoader extends ResourceLoader {
    public PSDBResourceLoader() {
        super();
    }

    public void init(ExtendedProperties extendedProperties) {
        // Do nothing, no properties to configure
    }

    public InputStream getResourceStream(String name)
        throws ResourceNotFoundException {

        if (StringUtils.isEmpty(name)) {
            throw new ResourceNotFoundException(
                "PSDBResourceLoader : No template name provided");
        }

        /* The first parameter for our SQL statement is the template
         * name bind variable. The second element in the array is the
         * SQLExec output field. Unlike PeopleCode arrays, Java arrays
         * have a fixed size. The following code initializes an Object
         * array big enough to hold the input bind variables and output
         * field values.
         */
        Object[] parms = new Object[] { name, null };
        Func.SQLExec("SELECT HTMLAREA FROM PS_APT_TMPLT_DEFN WHERE " +
                "APT_TEMPLATE_ID = :1", parms);

        String template = (String)parms[1];

        /* Just like PeopleCode, we can use the None function
         * to determine if SQLExec returned a value. The PeopleCode
         * version of None allows for an unlimited list of variables.
         * The Java version uses an array to replicate this same
         * behavior. The following code creates a temporary, anonymous
         * Object array containing the template contents.
         */
        if (Func.None(new Object[] { template })) {
            throw new ResourceNotFoundException(
                "PSDBResourceLoader : Resource '" +
                name + "' not found.");
        }

        /* If we made it this far, then the template exists in the
         * database. The following code converts the template text to
         * a byte array and then wraps it in a ByteArrayInputStream.
         * We can return a ByteArrayInputStream from this method
         * because ByteArrayInputStream is a subclass of InputStream.
         */
```

```
        return new ByteArrayInputStream(
            parms[1].toString().getBytes());
    }

    public boolean isSourceModified(Resource resource) {
        return (resource.getLastModified() <
            getLastModified(resource));
    }

    public long getLastModified(Resource resource) {
        String name = resource.getName();

        if (StringUtils.isEmpty(name)) {
            throw new ResourceNotFoundException(
                "PSDBResourceLoader : No template name provided");
        }

        Object[] parms = new Object[] { name, null };
        Func.SQLExec("SELECT %DateTimeOut(LASTUPDDTTM) FROM " +
            "PS_APT_TMPLT_DEFN WHERE APT_TEMPLATE_ID = :1", parms);

        String dateString = (String)parms[1];

        if (Func.None(new Object[] { dateString })) {
            throw new ResourceNotFoundException(
                  "PSDBResourceLoader : Resource '" +
                  name + "' not found.");
        }

        SimpleDateFormat parser =
            new SimpleDateFormat(
                "yyyy'-'MM'-'dd'-'HH'.'mm'.'ss'.000000'");
        Date lastModified;

        try {
            lastModified = parser.parse(dateString);
        } catch (ParseException e) {
            throw new VelocityException("Error parsing date "
                  + dateString, e);
        }

        return lastModified.getTime();
    }
}
```

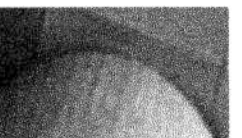

NOTE

Did you notice the redundancies between `getResourceStream()` and `getLastModified()`? Both verify the name of the template, execute an SQL statement, and then verify the `SQLExec` result. I recommend decluttering this code by extracting this common code into a separate method.

Our PSDBResourceLoader is composed of one Java class. Deploying a single class to PeopleSoft consists of creating the class's package directory structure in your %PS_HOME%\class or $PS_HOME/appserv/classes directory, and then copying the class file into that package directory. Rather than create and maintain the directory structure, cluttering up the delivered PS_HOME, I find it easier to create a JDeveloper JAR file deployment profile.

To compile and deploy your new PSDBResourceLoader, create a new JAR file deployment profile named apt_velocity. After creating the deployment profile, right-click the project's name in the Application Navigator and select Project Properties. In the Project Properties dialog, select Deployment and edit the new apt_velocity profile by changing the JAR file path to point to your App Designer's %PS_HOME%\class directory. On my workstation, the path is C:\PT849\class\apt_velocity.jar. Next, right-click the PSVelocity project in the Application Navigator and choose Deploy | apt_velocity | to JAR file from the context menu. This command will save your Java source code files, compile them into binary class files, zip them into a JAR file, and then copy the resultant JAR file to your App Designer's class path.

Testing the PSDBResourceLoader

The best way to test how your custom Java code interacts with PeopleSoft is with an App Engine run locally through App Designer. Once the JVM loads a Java class definition into memory, it stays in memory until the JVM is unloaded. If you find errors with your PSDBResourceLoader, you will need to reload your JVM. In the context of an application server, reloading the JVM requires you to restart your app server. It is much easier to restart a local App Engine program than it is to restart an application server.

In Chapter 9, we created an App Engine program named APT_VEL_TST. We can use that same program to test our new repository loader Java class. All we need to do is configure Velocity to use our new resource loader class by modifying the velocity.properties file we created in Chapter 9. You will find this file in your %PS_HOME%\class directory. Modify this file so that it matches the following listing. Notice that I removed the FileResourceLoader configuration in favor of the simpler PSDBResourceLoader configuration.

```
resource.loader=psdb
psdb.resource.loader.class=apt.peoplesoft.velocity.PSDBResourceLoader

runtime.log.logsystem.log4j.logger=velocity
```

After modifying velocity.properties, rerun the APT_VEL_TST App Engine test program. In addition to the logging and other output, you should see the following output:

```
BEGIN:VCALENDAR
VERSION:2.0
PRODID:-//PT Tips and Techniques//PSDB Velocity vCal 1.0//EN
BEGIN:VEVENT
DTSTART:20090813T160000Z
DTEND:20090813T180000Z
SUMMARY:Event One
DESCRIPTION:This is event number one
LOCATION:Conference room 1
CATEGORIES:Business,Conferences
END:VEVENT
BEGIN:VEVENT
```

```
DTSTART:20090814T160000Z
DTEND:20090814T180000Z
SUMMARY:Event Two
DESCRIPTION:This is event number two
LOCATION:Conference room 2
CATEGORIES:Business,Conferences
END:VEVENT
END:VCALENDAR
```

Notice that the PRODID at the beginning of the generated output contains the PSDB value we entered into the online template.

Multithreading

App Engine is very efficient with SQL and database interaction. Unfortunately, the only way to parallel-process data with an App Engine is to partition your data on a set of fields and values, and then run the same App Engine multiple times. Using this approach, each App Engine receives its own database connection and, therefore, its own transaction.

Several years ago, I attempted to create a Java batch processing replacement for App Engine. I wanted to see if I could improve batch processing performance by leveraging Java's multithreading features for parallel processing while sharing the same transaction. Rather than use Java's JDBC, I wanted to reuse SQL definitions, Meta-SQL, and the PeopleSoft database connection. What I discovered is that the PeopleSoft SQL Access Manager (SAM) is not thread-safe. I tried synchronizing across threads so that only one thread wrote to the SAM at a time, but that didn't help. It appears that the SAM allows only the single PeopleSoft thread to execute SQL.

Nevertheless, there are ways to use Java's multithreading model for parallel processing PeopleSoft data in a single transaction. The easiest way is to synchronize on a JDBC connection and spawn threads to process data row by row. For small amounts of data, this approach is very efficient. For larger data sets, I recommend using a JDBC connection pool and a distributed transaction. A distributed transaction (Java Transaction API) manages a single transaction across multiple connections. This allows you to commit on a per-connection basis, but still roll back all connections and prior commits if any thread fails.

I recommend the distributed transaction approach only for large data sets, because there is a small amount of overhead associated with creating connections. This overhead may counteract the benefits of parallel processing when dealing with smaller data sets. Unfortunately, these Java-only approaches do not support Meta-SQL and cannot share PeopleSoft's application security (database connection).

Conclusion

The Java language contains many features, and this chapter covered a limited subset of those features. The feature set available to you is determined by your PeopleTools Java version. For example, Java 1.4 was the first version to provide regular expressions. Java 1.5 added autoboxing, generics, and annotations. Java 1.6 (PeopleTools 8.50) added support for the scripting engines, specifically including the Rhino JavaScript engine as part of the core platform.

If your development environment uses the latest version of Java but your PeopleSoft application uses an older version of Java, be careful to limit your feature set to those features available to your PeopleSoft Java version. For example, when using Func.SQLExec with Java 1.4, specify numbers as `Double(1234)` rather than `1234`. In Java 1.5 and later, the compiler will convert `1234` from the primitive `int` type to an `Integer` object with the value `1234` through a process named *autoboxing*. Further exacerbating this issue, Java IDEs, such as JDeveloper, encourage new feature usage by displaying warnings when you fail to use the latest features such as generics and autoboxing.

Notes

1. Wikipedia, "Java Native Interface" [online]; available from http://en.wikipedia.org/wiki/Java_Native_Interface; Internet; accessed 25 September 2009.
2. Apache Software Foundation, *Apache Log4j 1.2.15 API*, "Class JDBCAppender" [online]; available from http://logging.apache.org/log4j/1.2/apidocs/org/apache/log4j/jdbc/JDBCAppender.html#sqlStatement; Internet; accessed 29 September 2009.
3. OWASP, "Enterprise Security API" [online]; available from http://www.owasp.org/index.php/ESAPI; Internet; accessed 1 October 2009.

CHAPTER 12

Creating Real-Time Integrations

he typical enterprise architecture consists of a diverse ecosystem of interconnected applications. The challenge for many information technology professionals is promoting a healthy version of this system via integration. To assist in developing a healthy integrated ecosystem, PeopleSoft applications offer a variety of integration opportunities.

Integration Technologies

The most obvious integration technology is web services. PeopleSoft's Integration Broker offers queuing, routing, and transformations much like any enterprise service bus (ESB). The features offered by an ESB and the common protocols used by web services make web services a compelling integration technology.

By far, the most common integration technology employed by PeopleSoft developers is SQR integration. A derivative of SQR integration is App Engine. App Engine trumps SQR by offering reusable business logic in the form of PeopleCode and component interfaces. App Engine programs can also leverage file layouts for creating flat file integrations. File layouts represent a metadata approach to stringing rows together in SQR.

Both SQR and App Engine are batch-processing technologies that usually use custom, complex logic to search your PeopleSoft database for data to send to an external system. The complexity of a typical integration batch program stems from the fact that PeopleSoft does not stamp database changes with the date and time. Finding changed rows usually involves complex reconciliations that use SQL to search for differences.

Integration Broker contrasts batch processing by providing a mechanism for communicating data changes as they occur. At save time, built-in PeopleCode logic publishes changes to the PeopleSoft Integration Broker. The only thing standing between you and real-time integration is configuration and a connector.

If your target system has an HTTP listener that accepts XML input, as most modern systems do, then you can readily integrate your systems. HTTP is the protocol used by web services, and therefore receives the most attention. Out of the box, Integration Broker speaks several other protocols as well. If your target system can read flat files, pick up e-mail, or listen on a Java Message Service (JMS) queue, then integration for you is a matter of configuration.

While the delivered target connectors cover a vast portion of integration protocols, there are a few unsatisfied integration scenarios. In fact, the two most common scenarios satisfied by batch-style integration are flat file and database integration. Integration Broker covers flat file integration, but stops short of database integration. In this chapter, you will learn how to use Integration Broker's SDK to develop custom target connectors for communicating with external systems that are not supported by the delivered Integration Broker connectors.

Setting Up for Database Integration

One of the most prevalent integration scenarios is database to database. In this integration scenario, a batch program such as an SQR uses database links to read data from one system, known as the *source*, and copy that data into another system, known as the *target*. In this chapter's example, you will write a custom target connector that uses JDBC to connect to a target database and execute SQL statements. To do this, you will need some files on your local file system, a database and custom table to use for testing, and a database-specific JDBC library.

Your PeopleSoft web server contains a web application named `PSIGW`. Inside that web application, you will find a subdirectory named SDK. The SDK directory contains sample connector code and documentation describing each of the Java classes that comprise the `PSIGW` web application. You can browse the SDK documentation online by navigating to http://your.peoplesoftserver.com/PSIGW/SDK/docs/SDK/index.html.

To build custom target connectors, you will need to copy the following files and folders to a directory on your local file system:

- PSIGW\WEB-INF\classes
- PSIGW\WEB-INF\lib\mail.jar
- PSIGW\WEB-INF\lib\xalan.jar

Where you place these files on your local file system is not important. I store all of my Java libraries in a folder named c:\java\lib, but you can store them wherever you prefer. For reference purposes, I recommend copying the PSIGW\SDK directory to a local folder.

After copying these files to a local directory, launch JDeveloper (or your preferred Java IDE). From the JDeveloper menu bar, select Tools | Manage Libraries. Add a new library named `PSIGW`, and then add the classes directory, mail.jar file, and xalan.jar file to the new library's class path. (See Chapter 11 for details on how to add libraries to JDeveloper.) We will use this `PSIGW` library for each target connector we create.

To test our custom target connector, you will need a target database. If your PeopleSoft web server can connect to your local desktop, you can download and install a free database, such as Oracle's XE database. Alternatively, ask your database administrators if they have a test or development database you can use.

NOTE
If your database administrator provides you with SQL access to your PeopleSoft development database, you can use PeopleTools to create a destination table.

This example will use the delivered `USER_PROFILE` integration point to insert `OPRID`, `OPRDEFNDESCR`, `EMPLID`, and `EMAILID` into a custom table. In your target database, create a table named `users` with the following fields:

- `OPRID`, as varchar2(30)
- `OPRDEFNDESC`, as varchar2(30)
- `EMPLID`, as varchar2(11)
- `EMAILID`, as varchar2(70)

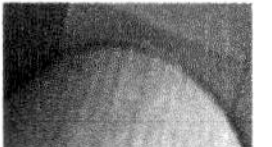

NOTE
Do not make any of the `users` table's fields into key fields. As you modify data within PeopleSoft, you will insert multiple rows with the same key structure. If your interface tables must have keys, create a separate key field and populate it accordingly.

I used the following SQL to create a `users` table in the `jim` schema of my local Oracle database:

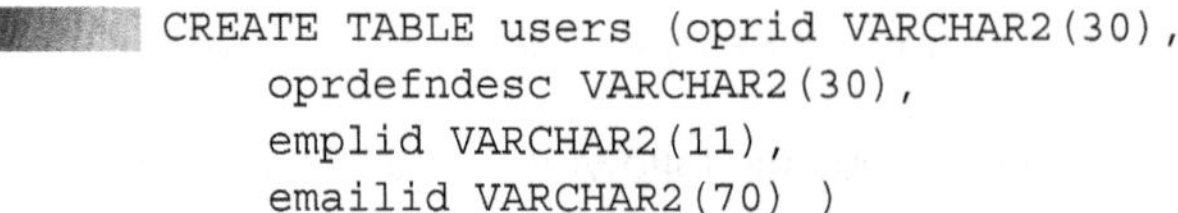

```
CREATE TABLE users (oprid VARCHAR2(30),
    oprdefndesc VARCHAR2(30),
    emplid VARCHAR2(11),
    emailid VARCHAR2(70) )
```

In addition to the `PSIGW` Java library you created a few paragraphs earlier, the JDBC target connector requires a database-specific JDBC library. If you chose a target database other than Oracle, then add the target database's JDBC driver to JDeveloper's list of managed libraries. You can download JDBC drivers for most of the popular databases. Refer to your database's documentation to determine which JAR file to use.

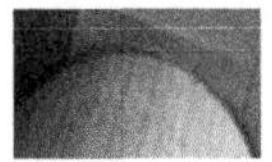

NOTE

We will use the JDBC driver for testing purposes only. Our custom target connector will be flexible enough to use with any JDBC driver. When deploying the JDBC target connector to your PeopleSoft web server, you will deploy the appropriate JDBC JAR file for your target database.

Creating a Custom JDBC Target Connector

In JDeveloper, create a new generic application named `PSIBConnectors`. Set the application's package prefix to `com.peoplesoft.pt.integrationgateway.targetconnector`. PeopleSoft requires target connectors to exist in this package. When prompted to create a new project, name it `JDBCTarget`.

After creating the new application and `JDBCTarget` project, open the project's properties. Switch to the Compiler item and change the JDK version compatibility setting to the version used by your PeopleTools installation. Switch to the Libraries and Classpath item and add the `PSIGW` library and your database's JDBC library. Since I am using an external Oracle database, I chose the JDeveloper-delivered Oracle JDBC library.

Creating the JDBCTargetConnector Class

Create a new class named `JDBCTargetConnector` and set the class's package to `com.peoplesoft.pt.integrationgateway.targetconnector`. Click the plus symbol in the Implements box to add the interface `com.peoplesoft.pt.integrationgateway.targetconnector.TargetConnector`. After you click OK, JDeveloper will present you with a class containing three empty methods:

- The `send()` method is responsible for sending data to the target system.
- The `ping()` method allows you to test connectivity between your PeopleSoft system and the target system.
- The `introspectConnector()` method specifies configuration data for a target connector.

Our connector will require the JDBC driver class name, database connection URL, username, and password. We use the `introspectConnector()` method to notify the Integration Broker of our need for this information. We'll begin with that method. The complete `JDBCTargetConnector` listing appears at the end of this section.

The introspectConnector Method

The following code listing contains the implementation of the `introspectConnector()` method.

```
public ConnectorDataCollection introspectConnector() {
    ConnectorDataCollection coll = new ConnectorDataCollection();
    ConnectorData data = new ConnectorData("JDBCTARGET");

    data.addConnectorField("JDBC-URL", true, "jdbc:", "");
    data.addConnectorField("JDBC-Driver", true,
                           "[java package.class.name]", "");
    data.addConnectorField("Username", true, "[db user name]", "");
    data.addConnectorField("Password", true, "[user db password]",
        "");

    data.addConnectorField("HEADER", "sendUncompressed", true, "Y",
        "Y|N");

    coll.addConnectorData(data);

    return coll;
}
```

All `introspectConnector()` methods perform the same task: They add configuration properties to a `ConnectorDataCollection` object. Besides the `JDBCTargetConnector` properties, the preceding code listing contains a reference to a `HEADER` property named `sendUncompressed`. This property tells Integration Broker to send messages to this target connector without compressing the message first.

The connector we are about to write receives an Integration Broker message, and then executes a series of SQL statements against a target database. The Integration Broker message will provide the data and SQL statements. The connector, however, will also need to know the target database driver and connection information.

The getConnection Method

Our `ping()` and `send()` methods will require a database connection. Let's collect the common connection logic for these methods into a couple of private methods. Add the following `getConnection()` method to the end of the `JDBCTargetConnector` Java class.

```
private Connection getConnection(IBRequest request)
        throws ExternalSystemContactException {
    ConnectorInfo info = request.getConnectorInfo();
    Connection conn = null;
    String jdbcUrl = info.getFieldValue("JDBC-URL");
    String driver = info.getFieldValue("JDBC-Driver");
```

```
        String username = info.getFieldValue("Username");
        String password = info.getFieldValue("Password");

        try {
            Class.forName(driver);
        } catch (ClassNotFoundException e) {
            String msg = "JDBCTargetConnector: " +
                "ClassNotFoundException: Unable to locate the JDBC " +
                "driver '" + driver + "'. This error usually means " +
                "that the JDBC driver class is not in the PSIGW web " +
                "application classpath.";

            String[] parms = { driver };
            throw new ExternalSystemContactException(msg,
                new MessageCatalogEntry(1, parms, 27000, null, msg),
                e);
        }

        try {
            if (username == null) {
                conn = DriverManager.getConnection(jdbcUrl);
            } else {
                conn = DriverManager.getConnection(jdbcUrl, username,
                    password);
            }
        } catch (SQLException e) {
            String msg = "JDBCTargetConnector: " +
                "SQLException: Error connecting to " +
                jdbcUrl + " using driver " + driver + ": " +
                e.toString();
            String[] parms = { jdbcUrl, driver, e.toString() };
            throw new ExternalSystemContactException(msg,
                new MessageCatalogEntry(2, parms, 27000, null, msg),
                e);
        }

        try {
            conn.setAutoCommit(false);
        } catch (SQLException e) {
            String msg = "JDBCTargetConnector: " +
                "SQLException: Unable to set auto commit to false: " +
                e.toString();
            String[] parms = { e.toString() };

            throw new ExternalSystemContactException(msg,
                new MessageCatalogEntry(3, parms, 27000, null, msg),
                e);
        }

        return conn;
    }
```

As the name implies, the `getConnection()` method is responsible for opening a database connection. The `getConnection()` method uses the following code to retrieve the database connection information from the `JDBCTargetConnector` configuration data. As you will see later, connector information is specified on a per-node basis.

```
ConnectorInfo info = request.getConnectorInfo();
Connection conn = null;
String jdbcUrl = info.getFieldValue("JDBC-URL");
String driver = info.getFieldValue("JDBC-Driver");
String username = info.getFieldValue("Username");
String password = info.getFieldValue("Password");
```

The remainder of the code in the `getConnection()` method is standard JDBC code. It uses `Class.forName` to load the JDBC driver Java class, and then obtains a JDBC database connection from the JDBC `DriverManager`.

The only other item worth mentioning in the `getConnection()` method is the method's exception handling. As you will see throughout this example, the custom connector SDK includes several Integration Broker exceptions. The constructors for many of these exception classes expect a message catalog entry. As shown in the following partial code listing, I used the message catalog entry set 27000.

```
...
    } catch (SQLException e) {
        String msg = "JDBCTargetConnector: " +
            "SQLException: Unable to set auto commit to false: " +
            e.toString();
        String[] parms = { e.toString() };

        throw new ExternalSystemContactException(msg,
            new MessageCatalogEntry(3, parms, 27000, null, msg),
            e);
    }
```

If an error occurs, the Integration Broker will display the exception's message catalog entry in the Service Operation Monitor. Here are the six message catalog entries that you will need to create:

- Message 1: `JDBCTargetConnector ClassNotFoundException: Unable to locate the JDBC driver '%1'.` (This error usually means that the JDBC driver class is not in the `PSIGW` web application class path.)
- Message 2: `JDBCTargetConnector: SQLException: Error connecting to %1 using driver %2: %3.`
- Message 3: `JDBCTargetConnector: SQLException: Unable to set auto commit to false: %1.`
- Message 4: `JDBCTargetConnector: Connection Error: Unable to contact external system. See the server's log files for more details.`
- Message 5: `JDBCTargetConnector: XmlException: %1.`
- Message 6: `JDBCTargetConnector: SQLException: SQLException: %1.`

NOTE

Be sure to create these message catalog entries in the same message set that is referenced by your code. The sample code uses message set 27000. If you choose a different message set, be sure to update all references to message set 27000.

The closeQuietly Method

Once the `ping()` and `send()` methods finish using a connection, they will need to close it to free the resources consumed by the connection. Unfortunately, JDBC may throw an exception when closing a database connection. Since our connector is not concerned with errors thrown when closing a connection, let's add a method to encapsulate the logic required to ignore connection close errors. Add the following code to the end of the `JDBCTargetConnector` class.

```
private static void closeQuietly(Connection conn) {
    try {
        // rollback anything that isn't committed
        conn.rollback();
    } catch (SQLException e) {
        Logger.logMessage("Failed while rolling back" +
                          "uncommitted transactions",
                          e, Logger.WARNING);
        // ignore
    }
    try {
        conn.close();
    } catch (SQLException e) {
        Logger.logMessage("Failed while closing JDBC connection",
                          e, Logger.WARNING);
        // ignore
    }
}
```

Even though we aren't interested in reported errors, we did add code to log connection close errors should they occur. If you configure your integration gateway log level to warnings or higher and a connection close error occurs, Integration Broker will log the error in the msgLog.html file. We will review the msgLog.html and errorLog.html files later when we discuss connector troubleshooting tips.

The ping Method

Let's implement the `ping()` method next. Replace the `ping()` method with the following code.

```
public IBResponse ping(IBRequest request)
        throws ExternalSystemContactException,
               MessageUnmarshallingException {

    Connection conn = getConnection(request);
```

```
        if (conn == null) {
            String msg = "JDBCTargetConnector: " +
                "Unable to contact external system. See the " +
                "server's log files for more details.";
            ExternalSystemContactException e =
                new ExternalSystemContactException(msg,
                    new MessageCatalogEntry(4, null, 27000, null, msg),
                    null);
            Logger.logError(e.toString(), msg, request, null,
                            Logger.STANDARD_GATEWAY_EXCEPTION, e);
            throw e;
        } else {
            closeQuietly(conn);
        }

        IBResponse response = new IBResponse();
        response.setStatusCode(IBResponse.SUCCESS);

        return response;
    }
```

The `ping()` method attempts to open a connection to the target database. If the connector is successful, it returns `IBResponse.SUCCESS`. Otherwise, the connector throws a suitable exception describing why it was not able to connect.

Before implementing the `send()` method, let's discuss its purpose and any security concerns we should address.

Connector Metadata

Since our connector will execute SQL, we want to avoid potential SQL injection flaws, as well as improve performance by leveraging SQL bind variables. The only way to accomplish this is to use hard-coded SQL statements and bind variables. To keep this connector flexible, we don't want to hard-code the SQL statements directly in the connector. As an alternative, we can hard-code them as metadata in the XML message sent to the connector. Using Integration Broker's transformation capability, we can transform a PeopleSoft structured message into an unstructured collection of SQL statements and transaction bind values. Since the connector's code depends on the structure of the XML message, let's design the XML first. The following code listing contains an XML sample that this connector expects.

Using JDeveloper, create a new XML document named sql.xml and place it in the test subdirectory of the `JDBCTarget` project src folder (the test directory may not exist yet). Replace the contents of the JDeveloper-generated XML file with the following. Later, we will use this XML file to test our connector.

```
<?xml version="1.0" encoding="UTF-8" ?>
<message>
    <statements>
        <sql id="oraSQL1">insert into table_one values (?, ?)</sql>
        <sql id="oraSQL2">
            insert into table_two values (?, ?, SYSTIMESTAMP)
        </sql>
    </statements>
```

```
    <data>
        <bindings sql-ref="oraSQL1">
            <bind>12345</bind>
            <bind>3rd St.</bind>
        </bindings>
        <bindings sql-ref="oraSQL1">
            <bind>12346</bind>
            <bind>3rd St.</bind>
        </bindings>
        <bindings sql-ref="oraSQL2">
            <bind>12347</bind>
            <bind>3rd St.</bind>
        </bindings>
    </data>
</message>
```

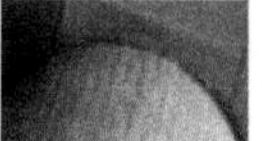

NOTE
The `id` attribute of the `sql` elements in this example contain the prefix `ora`, an abbreviation for Oracle. While the SQL may be standard SQL suitable for all PeopleSoft databases, I chose this prefix to clearly identify the use of Oracle specific functions such as `SYSTIMESTAMP`.

Notice that the XML starts with a collection of SQL statements and ends with a collection of bind values. Each bind value collection contains an `sql-ref` attribute that points to a named SQL statement from the `statements` collection. Our custom target connector will use the `sql` element `id` attribute to map between bind variable collections and SQL statements.

Our `send()` method may execute the same SQL statement multiple times. Using a JDBC `PreparedStatement`, we can send a parameterized statement to the target database for compilation and then reuse that same statement, avoiding SQL compilation and optimization overhead on each successive call.

Considering our design, the `send()` method will have to manipulate a collection of SQL statements and a collection of bind variables. To keep things simple, let's implement the SQL statement collection as a cache in a separate Java Class.

The StatementCache Class

In JDeveloper, create a new class named `StatementCache` and specify `apt.peoplesoft` as the package. Add the following code to this new class.

```
package apt.peoplesoft;

import com.peoplesoft.pt.common.XmlException;
import com.peoplesoft.pt.common.XmlNode;

import com.peoplesoft.pt.integrationgateway.common.Logger;

import java.sql.Connection;
import java.sql.PreparedStatement;
import java.sql.SQLException;
```

```
import java.util.Hashtable;


public class StatementCache {
    XmlNode statementsNode_;
    Hashtable cache_;
    Connection conn_;

    public StatementCache(Connection conn, XmlNode statementsNode) {
        conn_ = conn;
        statementsNode_ = statementsNode;
        cache_ = new Hashtable();
    }

    public PreparedStatement get(String id)
            throws XmlException, SQLException {
        PreparedStatement stmt = (PreparedStatement)cache_.get(id);

        if (stmt == null) {
            stmt = addStatementToCache(id);
        } else {
            // Only clear parameters from old SQL statements.
            // New statements won't have parameters set yet.
            stmt.clearParameters();
        }

        return stmt;
    }

    private PreparedStatement addStatementToCache(String id)
            throws XmlException,
            SQLException {
        XmlNode sqlNode = statementsNode_.FindNode(
                "sql[@id='" + id + "']");
        PreparedStatement stmt = null;
        String sql = null;

        if (sqlNode != null) {
            sql = sqlNode.GetNodeValue();
            Logger.logMessage("Caching statement \"" + sql +
                              "\" using id \"" + id + "\"", null,
                              Logger.LOW_IMPORTANCE_INFORMATION);
            stmt = conn_.prepareStatement(sql);
            cache_.put(id, stmt);
        }
        return stmt;
    }
}
```

The `StatementCache` constructor requires a JDBC `Connection` and the `statements` node from the XML document described in the previous section. We could use the constructor to iterate over the SQL statements in the `statements` node to create our collection of `PreparedStatements`. Instead, we will wait until the `JDBCTargetConnector` requests an SQL statement. It is possible that an SQL statement is declared in the `statements` node but never used by the `data` node. This lazy initialization technique will save us the expense of preparing a statement that is never used.

The `get` method appears next in the `StatementCache` definition. This method returns the JDBC `PreparedStatement` referenced by the method's `id` parameter. If the statement doesn't exist, `get` calls the private `addStatementToCache` method. The `addStatementToCache` method uses XPath to find the correct SQL statement in the `statements` node.

If you look closely at the `import` statements, you will notice that the constructor's `XmlNode` parameter is not a standard World Wide Web Consortium (W3C) DOM node.[1] Integration Broker connectors can use the same PeopleSoft `XmlDoc` used in PeopleCode. The PeopleCode `XmlNode` supports XPath, a feature that is not supported by the standard `org.w3c.dom.Node`. Also, the `XmlNode.GetNodeValue()` method returns the node's normalized text string, in contrast to W3C DOM node values, which are really a collection of text nodes disguised as a single node.

The send() Method

A target connector's `send()` method is responsible for the following:

- Extracting the message content from an `IBRequest`
- Extracting connector information from an `IBRequest`
- Reporting errors
- Logging
- Generating an `IBResponse`

Our `send()` method receives an XML string containing a collection of SQL statements and bind variables. After converting the XML string to the Java equivalent of the PeopleCode `XmlDocument` object, this method will do the following:

- Delegate statement parsing to the `StatementCache` class.
- Iterate over the `bindings` nodes from the XML document's `data` section.
- Execute each SQL statement referenced by the `bindings` node.

The code for the `send()` method follows.

```
public IBResponse send(IBRequest request)
        throws InvalidMessageException,
        MessageMarshallingException,
        ExternalSystemContactException,
        MessageUnmarshallingException {
    XmlDocument xmlDoc = new XmlDocument();
    XmlNode rootNode = null;
    Connection conn = getConnection(request);

    try {
        xmlDoc.ParseXmlFromString(request.getContentSectionAt(0));
        rootNode = xmlDoc.GetDocumentElement();
```

```
XmlNode statementsNode =
    rootNode.FindNode("/message/statements");
XmlNode dataNode =
    rootNode.FindNode("/message/data");

if ((statementsNode == null) || (dataNode == null)) {
    String msg =
        "JDBCTargetConnector: " +
        "The message did not contain SQL or data nodes";
    InvalidMessageException e =
        new InvalidMessageException(msg);
    Logger.logError(msg, request, null,
                    Logger.STANDARD_GATEWAY_EXCEPTION, e);
    throw e;
}

StatementCache cache =
    new StatementCache(conn, statementsNode);

XmlNodeList bindingsList = dataNode.FindNodes("bindings");

if (bindingsList == null) {
    String msg =
        "JDBCTargetConnector: " +
        "The message did not contain any bindings";
    InvalidMessageException e =
        new InvalidMessageException(msg);
    Logger.logError(msg, request, null,
                    Logger.STANDARD_GATEWAY_EXCEPTION, e);
    throw e;
}

int bindingsCount = bindingsList.size();

for (int bindingsIdx = 0; bindingsIdx < bindingsCount;
     bindingsIdx++) {
    XmlNode bindingsNode = bindingsList.Get(bindingsIdx);

    PreparedStatement sql =
        cache.get(
            bindingsNode.GetAttributeValue("sql-ref"));
    XmlNodeList bindList = bindingsNode.FindNodes("bind");

    if (bindList != null) {
        int bindCount = bindList.size();
        StringBuffer bindMessage = new StringBuffer();

        for (int bindIdx = 0; bindIdx < bindCount;
                bindIdx++) {
            String bindValue =
```

```
                    bindList.Get(bindIdx).GetNodeValue();
                sql.setObject(bindIdx + 1, bindValue);
                if (bindIdx > 0) {
                    bindMessage.append(", ");
                }
                bindMessage.append("'" + bindValue + "'");
            }
            Logger.logMessage("Bind values: " + bindMessage,
                null, Logger.LOW_IMPORTANCE_INFORMATION);
        }

        sql.execute();
    }

    conn.commit();
} catch (XmlException e) {
    String msg = "JDBCTargetConnector: XmlException: " +
        e.toString();
    String[] parms = { e.toString() };
    Logger.logError(e.toString(), msg, request, null,
                Logger.STANDARD_GATEWAY_EXCEPTION, e);
    throw new InvalidMessageException(msg,
        new MessageCatalogEntry(5, parms, 27000, null, msg),
        e);
} catch (SQLException e) {
    String msg = "JDBCTargetConnector: SQLException: " +
        e.toString();
    String[] parms = { e.toString() };
    Logger.logError(e.toString(), msg, request, null,
                Logger.STANDARD_GATEWAY_EXCEPTION, e);
    throw new InvalidMessageException(msg,
        new MessageCatalogEntry(6, parms, 27000, null, msg),
        e);
} finally {
    closeQuietly(conn);
}

IBResponse response = new IBResponse();
InternetHeaders internetHeaders = new InternetHeaders();
internetHeaders.addHeader("Content-Type", "text/xml");

String responseXmlString =
    "<?xml version=\"1.0\"?>\n" +
    "<JDBCResponse>" +
    "  <Status>" +
    "    <Code>0</Code>" +
    "  </Status>" +
    "  <ResponseBody>" +
    "    <Message>Update successful.</Message>" +
    "  </ResponseBody>" +
    "</JDBCResponse>";
```

```
        response.addContentSection(internetHeaders, responseXmlString);
        response.setStatusCode(IBResponse.SUCCESS);
        return response;
    }
```

An IBRequest object may contain multiple content sections. IBRequest content sections are similar to MIME[2] content sections. Later, you will see the relationship between the MIME standard and Integration Broker requests when we review the contents of the msgLog.html file that resides in your PSIGW web application. The send() method uses the following code to convert an IBRequest content section into a parsed XML document:

```
xmlDoc.ParseXmlFromString(request.getContentSectionAt(0));
```

The remainder of the send() method uses standard Java and JDBC to iterate over the list of bind variables, setting bind values for each statement prior to execution.

Complete JDBCTargetConnector Listing

The complete code listing for the JDBCTargetConnector follows.

```
package com.peoplesoft.pt.integrationgateway.targetconnector;


import apt.peoplesoft.StatementCache;

import com.peoplesoft.pt.common.XmlDocument;
import com.peoplesoft.pt.common.XmlException;
import com.peoplesoft.pt.common.XmlNode;
import com.peoplesoft.pt.common.XmlNodeList;
import com.peoplesoft.pt.integrationgateway.common.ConnectorData;
import com.peoplesoft.pt.integrationgateway.common.
    ConnectorDataCollection;
import com.peoplesoft.pt.integrationgateway.common.
    ExternalSystemContactException;
import com.peoplesoft.pt.integrationgateway.common.
    InvalidMessageException;
import com.peoplesoft.pt.integrationgateway.common.Logger;
import com.peoplesoft.pt.integrationgateway.common.MessageCatalogEntry;
import com.peoplesoft.pt.integrationgateway.common.
    MessageMarshallingException;
import com.peoplesoft.pt.integrationgateway.common.
    MessageUnmarshallingException;
import com.peoplesoft.pt.integrationgateway.framework.ConnectorInfo;
import com.peoplesoft.pt.integrationgateway.framework.IBRequest;
import com.peoplesoft.pt.integrationgateway.framework.IBResponse;

import java.sql.Connection;
import java.sql.DriverManager;
import java.sql.PreparedStatement;
import java.sql.SQLException;

import javax.mail.internet.InternetHeaders;
```

```
public class JDBCTargetConnector implements TargetConnector {
    public JDBCTargetConnector() {
        super();
    }

    public IBResponse send(IBRequest request)
            throws InvalidMessageException,
            MessageMarshallingException,
            ExternalSystemContactException,
            MessageUnmarshallingException {
        XmlDocument xmlDoc = new XmlDocument();
        XmlNode rootNode = null;
        Connection conn = getConnection(request);

        try {
            xmlDoc.ParseXmlFromString(request.getContentSectionAt(0));
            rootNode = xmlDoc.GetDocumentElement();

            XmlNode statementsNode = rootNode.FindNode(
                "/message/statements");
            XmlNode dataNode = rootNode.FindNode("/message/data");

            if ((statementsNode == null) || (dataNode == null)) {
                String msg = "JDBCTargetConnector: " +
                    "The message did not contain SQL or data nodes";
                InvalidMessageException e =
                    new InvalidMessageException(msg);
                Logger.logError(msg, request, null,
                                Logger.STANDARD_GATEWAY_EXCEPTION, e);
                throw e;
            }

            StatementCache cache =
                new StatementCache(conn, statementsNode);

            XmlNodeList bindingsList = dataNode.FindNodes("bindings");

            if (bindingsList == null) {
                String msg = "JDBCTargetConnector: " +
                    "The message did not contain any bindings";
                InvalidMessageException e =
                    new InvalidMessageException(msg);
                Logger.logError(msg, request, null,
                                Logger.STANDARD_GATEWAY_EXCEPTION, e);
                throw e;
            }

            int bindingsCount = bindingsList.size();

            for (int bindingsIdx = 0; bindingsIdx < bindingsCount;
```

```
             bindingsIdx++) {
            XmlNode bindingsNode = bindingsList.Get(bindingsIdx);

            PreparedStatement sql = cache.get(
                bindingsNode.GetAttributeValue("sql-ref"));
            XmlNodeList bindList = bindingsNode.FindNodes("bind");

            if (bindList != null) {
                int bindCount = bindList.size();
                StringBuffer bindMessage = new StringBuffer();

                for (int bindIdx = 0; bindIdx < bindCount;
                        bindIdx++) {
                    String bindValue =
                        bindList.Get(bindIdx).GetNodeValue();
                    sql.setObject(bindIdx + 1, bindValue);
                    if (bindIdx > 0) {
                        bindMessage.append(", ");
                    }
                    bindMessage.append("'" + bindValue + "'");
                }
                Logger.logMessage("Bind values: " + bindMessage,
                    null,
                    Logger.LOW_IMPORTANCE_INFORMATION);
            }

            sql.execute();
        }

        conn.commit();
    } catch (XmlException e) {
        String msg = "JDBCTargetConnector: XmlException: " +
            e.toString();
        String[] parms = { e.toString() };
        Logger.logError(e.toString(), msg, request, null,
                        Logger.STANDARD_GATEWAY_EXCEPTION, e);
        throw new InvalidMessageException(msg,
            new MessageCatalogEntry(5, parms, 27000, null, msg),
            e);
    } catch (SQLException e) {
        String msg = "JDBCTargetConnector: SQLException: " +
                e.toString();
        String[] parms = { e.toString() };
        Logger.logError(e.toString(), msg, request, null,
                        Logger.STANDARD_GATEWAY_EXCEPTION, e);
        throw new InvalidMessageException(msg,
            new MessageCatalogEntry(6, parms, 27000, null, msg),
            e);
    } finally {
        closeQuietly(conn);
    }
```

```
        IBResponse response = new IBResponse();
        InternetHeaders internetHeaders = new InternetHeaders();
        internetHeaders.addHeader("Content-Type", "text/xml");

        String responseXmlString =
            "<?xml version=\"1.0\"?>\n" +
            "<JDBCResponse>" +
            "  <Status>" +
            "    <Code>0</Code>" +
            "  </Status>" +
            "  <ResponseBody>" +
            "    <Message>Update successful.</Message>" +
            "  </ResponseBody>" +
            "</JDBCResponse>";
        response.addContentSection(internetHeaders, responseXmlString);
        response.setStatusCode(IBResponse.SUCCESS);
        return response;
    }

    public IBResponse ping(IBRequest request)
            throws ExternalSystemContactException,
            MessageUnmarshallingException {

        Connection conn = getConnection(request);

        if (conn == null) {
            String msg = "JDBCTargetConnector: " +
                "Unable to contact external system. See the " +
                "server's log files for more details.";
            ExternalSystemContactException e =
                new ExternalSystemContactException(msg,
                    new MessageCatalogEntry(4, null, 27000, null, msg),
                    null);
            Logger.logError(e.toString(), msg, request, null,
                            Logger.STANDARD_GATEWAY_EXCEPTION, e);
            throw e;
        } else {
            closeQuietly(conn);
        }

        IBResponse response = new IBResponse();
        response.setStatusCode(IBResponse.SUCCESS);

        return response;
    }

    public ConnectorDataCollection introspectConnector() {
        ConnectorDataCollection coll = new ConnectorDataCollection();
        ConnectorData data = new ConnectorData("JDBCTARGET");
```

```
    data.addConnectorField("JDBC-URL", true, "jdbc:", "");
    data.addConnectorField("JDBC-Driver", true,
                            "[java package.class.name]", "");
    data.addConnectorField("Username", true, "[db user name]", "");
    data.addConnectorField("Password", true,
            "[user db password]", "");

    data.addConnectorField("HEADER", "sendUncompressed",
            true, "Y", "Y|N");

    coll.addConnectorData(data);

    return coll;
}

private Connection getConnection(IBRequest request)
        throws ExternalSystemContactException {
    ConnectorInfo info = request.getConnectorInfo();
    Connection conn = null;
    String jdbcUrl = info.getFieldValue("JDBC-URL");
    String driver = info.getFieldValue("JDBC-Driver");
    String username = info.getFieldValue("Username");
    String password = info.getFieldValue("Password");

    try {
        Class.forName(driver);
    } catch (ClassNotFoundException e) {
        String msg = "JDBCTargetConnector: " +
            "ClassNotFoundException: Unable to locate the JDBC " +
            "driver '" + driver + "'. This error usually means " +
            "that the JDBC driver class is not in the PSIGW web " +
            "application classpath.";

        String[] parms = { driver };
        throw new ExternalSystemContactException(msg,
            new MessageCatalogEntry(1, parms, 27000, null, msg),
            e);
    }

    try {
        if (username == null) {
            conn = DriverManager.getConnection(jdbcUrl);
        } else {
            conn = DriverManager.getConnection(
                jdbcUrl, username, password);
        }
    } catch (SQLException e) {
        String msg =
            "JDBCTargetConnector: " +
            "SQLException: Error connecting to " +
```

```
                jdbcUrl + " using driver " + driver + ": " +
                e.toString();
            String[] parms = { jdbcUrl, driver, e.toString() };
            throw new ExternalSystemContactException(msg,
                new MessageCatalogEntry(2, parms, 27000, null, msg),
                e);
        }

        try {
            conn.setAutoCommit(false);
        } catch (SQLException e) {
            String msg =
                "JDBCTargetConnector: " +
                "SQLException: Unable to set auto commit to false: " +
                e.toString();
            String[] parms = { e.toString() };

            throw new ExternalSystemContactException(msg,
                new MessageCatalogEntry(3, parms, 27000, null, msg),
                e);
        }

        return conn;
    }

    private static void closeQuietly(Connection conn) {
        try {
            // rollback anything that isn't committed
            conn.rollback();
        } catch (SQLException e) {
            Logger.logMessage("Failed while rolling back " +
                "uncommitted transactions", e, Logger.WARNING);
            // ignore
        }
        try {
            conn.close();
        } catch (SQLException e) {
            Logger.logMessage("Failed while closing JDBC connection",
                e, Logger.WARNING);
            // ignore
        }
    }
}
```

Predeployment Testing

Unlike the Java we wrote in the last chapter, which depended on the application server, our custom target connector can run directly from JDeveloper. This means we can test this target connector before deploying it to the PeopleSoft web server.

As noted earlier, you will need access to a development database to test the connector described in this chapter. If you don't have access to one of your company's development databases, you can download and install one of the many free databases (such as Oracle XE, MySQL, Apache Derby, or HSQLDB). Whatever database you choose, create two tables described as follows:

- `table_one`: `field1` as varchar(30), `field2` as varchar(30)
- `table_two`: `field1` as varchar(30), `field2` as varchar(30), and `field3` as date/time

I used the following SQL to create these tables in my local Oracle database instance:

```
CREATE TABLE table_one (field1 VARCHAR2(30),
    field2 VARCHAR2(30))
/
CREATE TABLE table_two (field1 VARCHAR2(30),
    field2 VARCHAR2(30),
    field3 TIMESTAMP)
/
```

Next, in JDeveloper, create a new Java class named `TestJDBCTargetConnector`. Set the package to `test.com.peoplesoft.pt.integrationgateway.targetconnector` and select the Main Method check box. This new class will contain code to test the various methods of the `JDBCTargetConnector` class. To identify this class as the test case for the `JDBCTargetConnector` class, this new class is in a package with the same name as the `JDBCTargetConnector` class, but prefixed with `test`. The class itself has the same name as the `JDBCTargetConnector` class, but also with the prefix `Test`.

As usual, we will go over each of the methods in the class, and then present the full code listing at the end of the section.

The assertTrue Method

Add the following method to the new `TestJDBCTargetConnector` class.

```
    private static void assertTrue(boolean test, String message) {
        if (!test) {
            throw new RuntimeException(message);
        }
    }
```

We will use the `assertTrue` method in each of our test methods to ensure that the `JDBCTargetConnector` methods behave as expected.

The testIntrospectConnector Method

Our first test method verifies that the `introspectConnector` method returns the correct information. Add the following method to `TestJDBCTargetConnector`.

```
    private static void testIntrospectConnector() {
        ConnectorDataCollection coll =
            (new JDBCTargetConnector()).introspectConnector();
        String[] names = coll.getConnectorDataNames();
```

```
assertTrue((names.length == 10), "Connector data count != 10");
assertTrue((names[0].equals("JDBCTARGET")),
           "Name does not equal JDBCTARGET");

String receivedXml = coll.getConnectorData(
    names[0]).toString();
String expectedXml =
    "<Connector>" +
        "<ConnectorName>JDBCTARGET</ConnectorName>" +
        "<Fields>" +
            "<Field>" +
                "<PropID>JDBCTARGET</PropID>" +
                "<Name>JDBC-URL</Name>" +
                "<Required>Y</Required>" +
                "<DefaultValue>jdbc:</DefaultValue>" +
            "</Field>" +
            "<Field>" +
                "<PropID>JDBCTARGET</PropID>" +
                "<Name>JDBC-Driver</Name>" +
                "<Required>Y</Required>" +
                "<DefaultValue>" +
                    "[java package.class.name]" +
                "</DefaultValue>" +
            "</Field>" +
            "<Field>" +
                "<PropID>JDBCTARGET</PropID>" +
                "<Name>Username</Name>" +
                "<Required>Y</Required>" +
                "<DefaultValue>[db user name]</DefaultValue>" +
            "</Field>" +
            "<Field>" +
                "<PropID>JDBCTARGET</PropID>" +
                "<Name>Password</Name>" +
                "<Required>Y</Required>" +
                "<DefaultValue>" +
                    "[user db password]" +
                "</DefaultValue>" +
            "</Field>" +
            "<Field>" +
                "<PropID>HEADER</PropID>" +
                "<Name>sendUncompressed</Name>" +
                "<Required>Y</Required>" +
                "<DefaultValue>Y</DefaultValue>" +
                "<PossibleValues>" +
                    "<Value>Y</Value>" +
                    "<Value>N</Value>" +
                "</PossibleValues>" +
            "</Field>" +
```

```
            "</Fields>" +
        "</Connector>";

    assertTrue((expectedXml.equals(receivedXml)),
               "Connector XML strings are not equal.\nExpected: " +
               expectedXml + "\nReceived: " + receivedXml);
}
```

This test method verifies that the connector has only one connector data item, that the name of that item is `JDBCTARGET`, and that the connector data's XML matches an expected XML string. If any one of these tests fails, then the method throws a runtime exception and exits. So that we can run this test and see some results, rewrite the `main` method to match the following code listing.

```
public static void main(String[] args) {
    testIntrospectConnector();
}
```

Run this test class by right-clicking inside the JDeveloper code editor and choosing Run from the context menu. Running this test should produce the following output (which is formatted to fit on the printed page).

```
Exception in thread "main" java.lang.RuntimeException: Connector data
  count != 10
      at test.com.peoplesoft.pt.integrationgateway.targetconnector
          .TestJDBCTargetConnector.assertTrue(
              TestJDBCTargetConnector.java:17)
      at test.com.peoplesoft.pt.integrationgateway.targetconnector
          .TestJDBCTargetConnector.testIntrospectConnector(
              TestJDBCTargetConnector.java:26)
      at test.com.peoplesoft.pt.integrationgateway.targetconnector
          .TestJDBCTargetConnector.main(
              TestJDBCTargetConnector.java:12)
Process exited with exit code 1.
```

The method threw the exception `Connector data count != 10`. It actually equals 1. I intentionally coded this test to fail to make sure the test performed correctly. If we wrote the test to pass, ran it, and it passed, how would we know our test logic was correct? Correct the error by changing `10` to `1` in this line:

```
assertTrue((names.length == 10), "Connector data count != 10");
```

The updated line should read as follows:

```
assertTrue((names.length == 1), "Connector data count != 1");
```

Rerunning this test case again will produce the output:

```
Process exited with exit code 0.
```

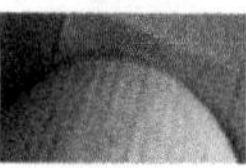

NOTE
The test case presented here validates an XML document by comparing two XML strings for equality. Even though the test passes, this is not an appropriate way to validate an XML document. Two XML documents may differ character by character, but still represent the same XML DOM tree, and therefore represent the same XML document. A better way to unit-test XML documents is with XmlUnit, an open source testing package for XML documents available from http://xmlunit.sourceforge.net/.

The generateRequest Method

The `ping` and `send` methods require an `IBRequest` parameter. The following method centralizes the creation of an `IBRequest` object. Add this method to the end of the `TestJDBCTargetConnector` class.

```
private static IBRequest generateRequest()
        throws IOException,
        MessageUnmarshallingException {
    ConnectorInfo info = new ConnectorInfo();

    info.setField("JDBC-URL",
        "jdbc:oracle:thin:jim/jim@//hrms.example.com:1521/HRMS");
    info.setField("JDBC-Driver",
        "oracle.jdbc.driver.OracleDriver");

    IBRequest request = new IBRequest();
    request.setConnectorInfo(info);

    StringBuffer msg = new StringBuffer();
    InputStream data = TestJDBCTargetConnector
        .class
        .getClassLoader()
        .getResourceAsStream("test/sql.xml");

    BufferedReader in =
        new BufferedReader(new InputStreamReader(data));

    String line = null;

    while ((line = in.readLine()) != null) {
        msg.append(line);
    }

    // add msg to request
    InternetHeaders internetHeaders = new InternetHeaders();

    internetHeaders.addHeader("Content-Type", "text/xml");
    request.addContentSection(internetHeaders, msg.toString());

    return request;
}
```

NOTE
Be sure to change the JDBC-URL value specified in this generateRequest method to match your test database's connection information. If you are using an Oracle database, change the value so that it matches this pattern: jdbc:oracle:thin:<user>/<password>@//<host>:<port>/<SID>. For Microsoft's SQL Server, change the JDBC-URL value to match the pattern: jdbc:sqlserver://<host>:<port>;databaseName=<db name>;user=<user>;password=<password> and the JDBC-Driver value to com.microsoft.sqlserver.jdbc.SQLServerDriver. For other database platforms, consult your database documentation.

This code populates the IBRequest message content with data contained in the sql.xml file we created earlier in this chapter.

The testPing() Method

Add the following method to test the ping() method.

```
private static void testPing() {
    IBResponse response;

    try {
        response =
            (new JDBCTargetConnector()).ping(generateRequest());
    } catch (Exception e) {
        throw new RuntimeException(e);
    }
    assertTrue((response.getStatusCode() == IBResponse.SUCCESS),
               "Ping did not return success");
}
```

NOTE
The testPing() code catches exceptions and then rethrows them as instances of RuntimeException. This is acceptable in test cases, but should be avoided in production code. Instances of RuntimeException are unchecked, undeclared exceptions. They represent errors that cannot be anticipated at design time.

Next, add a call for the testPing() method to the main method. Your main method should now read as follows:

```
public static void main(String[] args) {
    testIntrospectConnector();
    testPing();
}
```

Rerun the TestJDBCTargetConnector and watch for errors. If there are no errors, you should see the same Process exited with exit code 0 line that you saw in the previous test.

The testSend() Method

Let's add a final test to verify that the `send()` method works correctly. Add the following code to the end of `TestJDBCTargetConnector`.

```
private static void testSend() {
    try {
        IBResponse response =
            (new JDBCTargetConnector()).send(generateRequest());

        assertTrue(
            (IBResponse.SUCCESS == response.getStatusCode()),
            "Status code != success");

    } catch (Exception e) {
        throw new RuntimeException(e);
    }
}
```

Add the `testSend()` method to the `main()` method and rerun the test class. This time, the Java runtime will tell you it can't find the integrationGateway.properties file. Ignore this output. If you don't see any exceptions in the output, the test succeeded.

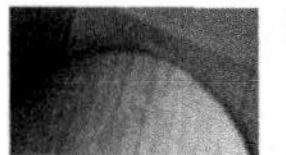

NOTE
The `testSend()` method confirms only the response code. A true automated test would include JDBC code to verify the contents of the two tables modified by sql.xml.

To confirm that the `testSend()` method succeeded, log in to your database query tool and execute the following SQL statements:

```
SELECT * FROM TABLE_ONE;
SELECT * FROM TABLE_TWO;
```

When I run these on my workstation, I see the following output:

```
SQL> SELECT * FROM TABLE_ONE;

FIELD1                         FIELD2
------------------------------ ------------------------------
12345                          3rd St.
12346                          3rd St.

SQL> SELECT * FROM TABLE_TWO;

FIELD1                         FIELD2
------------------------------ ------------------------------
FIELD3
---------------------------------------------------------------------------
12347                          3rd St.
30-OCT-09 01.18.31.367482 AM
```

Complete TestJDBCTarget Connector Code Listing

The complete `TestJDBCTargetConnector` Java class code follows.

```
package test.com.peoplesoft.pt.integrationgateway.targetconnector;


import com.peoplesoft.pt.integrationgateway.common
    .ConnectorDataCollection;
import com.peoplesoft.pt.integrationgateway.common
    .MessageUnmarshallingException;
import com.peoplesoft.pt.integrationgateway.framework.ConnectorInfo;
import com.peoplesoft.pt.integrationgateway.framework.IBRequest;
import com.peoplesoft.pt.integrationgateway.framework.IBResponse;
import com.peoplesoft.pt.integrationgateway.targetconnector
    .JDBCTargetConnector;

import java.io.BufferedReader;
import java.io.IOException;
import java.io.InputStream;
import java.io.InputStreamReader;

import javax.mail.internet.InternetHeaders;


public class TestJDBCTargetConnector {
    public TestJDBCTargetConnector() {
        super();
    }

    public static void main(String[] args) {
        testIntrospectConnector();
        testPing();
        testSend();
    }

    private static void assertTrue(boolean test, String message) {
        if (!test) {
            throw new RuntimeException(message);
        }
    }

    private static void testIntrospectConnector() {
        ConnectorDataCollection coll =
            (new JDBCTargetConnector()).introspectConnector();
        String[] names = coll.getConnectorDataNames();

        assertTrue((names.length == 1), "Connector data count != 1");
        assertTrue((names[0].equals("JDBCTARGET")),
                    "Name does not equal JDBCTARGET");
```

```
        String receivedXml =
            coll.getConnectorData(names[0]).toString();
        String expectedXml =
            "<Connector>" +
                "<ConnectorName>JDBCTARGET</ConnectorName>" +
                "<Fields>" +
                    "<Field>" +
                        "<PropID>JDBCTARGET</PropID>" +
                        "<Name>JDBC-URL</Name>" +
                        "<Required>Y</Required>" +
                        "<DefaultValue>jdbc:</DefaultValue>" +
                    "</Field>" +
                    "<Field>" +
                        "<PropID>JDBCTARGET</PropID>" +
                        "<Name>JDBC-Driver</Name>" +
                        "<Required>Y</Required>" +
                        "<DefaultValue>" +
                            "[java package.class.name]" +
                        "</DefaultValue>" +
                    "</Field>" +
                    "<Field>" +
                        "<PropID>JDBCTARGET</PropID>" +
                        "<Name>Username</Name>" +
                        "<Required>Y</Required>" +
                        "<DefaultValue>[db user name]</DefaultValue>" +
                    "</Field>" +
                    "<Field>" +
                        "<PropID>JDBCTARGET</PropID>" +
                        "<Name>Password</Name>" +
                        "<Required>Y</Required>" +
                        "<DefaultValue>" +
                            "[user db password]" +
                        "</DefaultValue>" +
                    "</Field>" +
                    "<Field>" +
                        "<PropID>HEADER</PropID>" +
                        "<Name>sendUncompressed</Name>" +
                        "<Required>Y</Required>" +
                        "<DefaultValue>Y</DefaultValue>" +
                        "<PossibleValues>" +
                            "<Value>Y</Value>" +
                            "<Value>N</Value>" +
                        "</PossibleValues>" +
                    "</Field>" +
                "</Fields>" +
            "</Connector>";

        assertTrue((expectedXml.equals(receivedXml)),
                "Connector XML strings are not equal.\nExpected: " +
                expectedXml + "\nReceived: " + receivedXml);
    }
```

```
private static IBRequest generateRequest()
        throws IOException,
        MessageUnmarshallingException {
    ConnectorInfo info = new ConnectorInfo();

    info.setField("JDBC-URL",
        "jdbc:oracle:thin:jim/jim@//hrms.example.com:1521/HRMS");
    info.setField("JDBC-Driver",
        "oracle.jdbc.driver.OracleDriver");

    IBRequest request = new IBRequest();
    request.setConnectorInfo(info);

    StringBuffer msg = new StringBuffer();
    InputStream data = TestJDBCTargetConnector
        .class
        .getClassLoader()
        .getResourceAsStream("test/sql.xml");

    BufferedReader in =
        new BufferedReader(new InputStreamReader(data));

    String line = null;

    while ((line = in.readLine()) != null) {
        msg.append(line);
    }

    // add msg to request
    InternetHeaders internetHeaders = new InternetHeaders();

    internetHeaders.addHeader("Content-Type", "text/xml");
    request.addContentSection(internetHeaders, msg.toString());

    return request;
}

private static void testPing() {
    IBResponse response;

    try {
        response =
            (new JDBCTargetConnector()).ping(generateRequest());
    } catch (Exception e) {
        throw new RuntimeException(e);
    }
    assertTrue((response.getStatusCode() == IBResponse.SUCCESS),
              "Ping did not return success");
}
```

```
    private static void testSend() {
        try {
            IBResponse response =
                (new JDBCTargetConnector()).send(generateRequest());

            assertTrue(
                (IBResponse.SUCCESS == response.getStatusCode()),
                "Status code != success");

        } catch (Exception e) {
            throw new RuntimeException(e);
        }
    }
}
```

Deploying the Connector

I find it easiest to deploy solutions as JAR files. Unfortunately, the Integration Broker requires that custom target connectors be deployed as class files to the web server's PSIGW/WEB-INF/classes/com/peoplesoft/pt/integrationgateway/targetconnector folder. Therefore, to deploy the target connector, find your project's output directory and copy the JDBCTargetConnector file into the targetconnector folder on your web server.

NOTE
To find your project's output directory, open your project's properties and switch to the Project Source Paths item. Your output directory is listed at the bottom of the Project Source Paths dialog.

To keep the `JDBCTargetConnector` project's dependencies separate from the rest of the `PSIGW` web application's classes, create a new JAR file deployment profile named `APT_JDBCTargetConnector`. For the deployment profile's Project Output Filters setting, select the apt folder and child items, and unselect everything else. We deployed the contents of the com folder as a class file, and we do not want to deploy the test classes from the test folder.

After creating the deployment profile, right-click your project's name in the Application Navigator and select Deploy | APT_JDBCTargetConnector | to JAR file from the context menu. When the deploy task completes, upload this file and the target database's JDBC driver JAR file to your PeopleSoft web server's PSIGW/WEB-INF/lib directory, and then restart your web server.

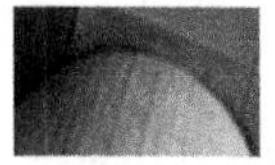

NOTE
You must upload your target database's JDBC driver to the `PSIGW` web application lib directory.

Configuring Integrations

Our next task is to configure PeopleSoft to use our new target connector. This involves configuring the integration gateway, creating a node definition, and then configuring a service operation routing.

Configuring the Gateway

Log in to your PeopleSoft web-based application and navigate to PeopleTools | Integration Broker | Configuration | Gateways. (PeopleTools 8.4*x* releases earlier than 8.48 used the navigation PeopleTools | Integration Broker | Gateways.) PeopleSoft applications are delivered with a predefined gateway named LOCAL. Open the LOCAL gateway and verify the URL. The URL should point to the same server as your `JDBCTargetConnector`. Click the Load Gateway Connectors button.

NOTE

If the LOCAL gateway URL points to a server named "You must change this URL.com," then your gateway is not configured. If it points to one of your web servers, but not the one that has your new `JDBCTargetConnector`*, then redeploy the* `JDBCTargetConnector` *to the web server described in the gateway URL.*

PeopleSoft will search your web server for connectors and load any that exist in the file system, but are not listed on the gateway configuration page. If the load process succeeded, you will see a message stating that one new connector and six new properties were loaded. Figure 12-1 shows the Gateways page after loading the `JDBCTargetConnector`.

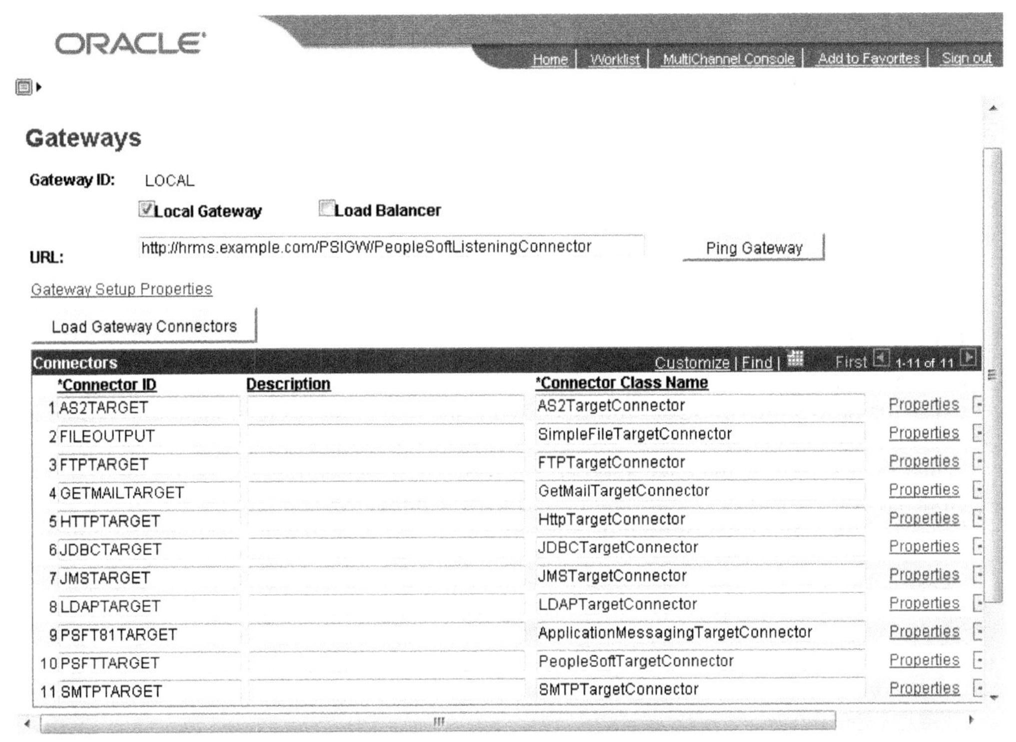

FIGURE 12-1. *Integration Broker gateway configuration*

ORACLE

Home | Worklist | MultiChannel Console | Add to Favorites | Sign out

New Window | Customize Page |

Gateways

Connector Properties

Gateway ID LOCAL

Connector JDBCTARGET

Properties — Customize | Find | First 1-6 of 6 Last

Properties | Data Type / Description

	*Property ID	*Property Name	Required	Value	Default
1	HEADER	sendUncompressed	☑	Y	☑
2	HEADER	sendUncompressed	☑	N	☐
3	JDBCTARGET	JDBC-Driver	☑	[java package.class.name]	☑
4	JDBCTARGET	JDBC-URL	☑	jdbc:	☑
5	JDBCTARGET	Password	☑	[user db password]	☑
6	JDBCTARGET	Username	☑	[db user name]	☑

OK | Cancel

FIGURE 12-2. *JDBCTARGET Connector Properties page*

Your list of connectors should now contain a connector named `JDBCTARGET`, which is the name we provided in our `introspectConnector` method. Click the Properties link to the right of the connector. The list of properties on the Connector Properties page matches the properties we described in the `introspectConnector` method, as shown in Figure 12-2.

Creating a Node

Our next step is to create a node to identify our external database system and configure the node to use the new `JDBCTargetConnector`. Navigate to PeopleTools | Integration Broker | Integration Setup | Nodes and add a new node named `JDBC_TEST`. (PeopleTools 8.4*x* releases earlier than 8.48 used the navigation PeopleTools | Integration Broker | Node Definitions.) On the Node Definitions tab, set the description to **JDBC Connector Test**, the default user ID to `PS`, and leave the rest of the fields at their default values. Figure 12-3 shows the Node Definitions tab.

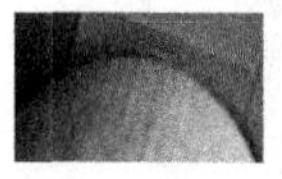

NOTE

For security purposes, create a new user with minimal permission list access. PeopleTools releases earlier than 8.48 used the default user ID to control access to component interfaces and other items.

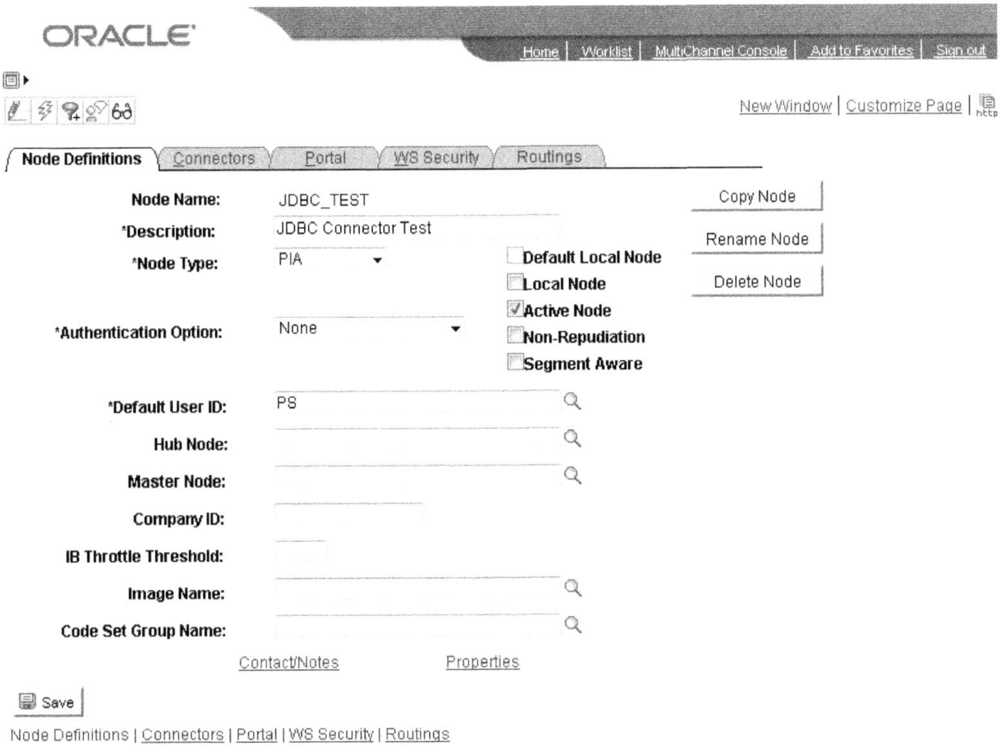

FIGURE 12-3. *JDBC_TEST Node Definitions tab*

Switch to the Connectors tab and set the connector ID to `JDBCTARGET`. PeopleSoft will display a grid containing all of the `JDBCTargetConnector` properties. Fill in the connector properties using the same values you used when you created the `generateRequest()` method for the `JDBCTargetConnector` test case, as shown in Figure 12-4.

Transforming Messages

Integration Broker transmits data in a structure called a *message*. PeopleSoft's standard messages represent rowset hierarchies (a component buffer, for example) as XML. Our target connector expects XML formatted as a series of SQL statements and bind variable collections. Here is an abbreviated example of the `USER_PROFILE XML` message generated by PeopleSoft:

```
<?xml version="1.0"?>
<USER_PROFILE>
  <FieldTypes>
    <PSOPRDEFN class="R">
      <OPRID type="CHAR"/>
```

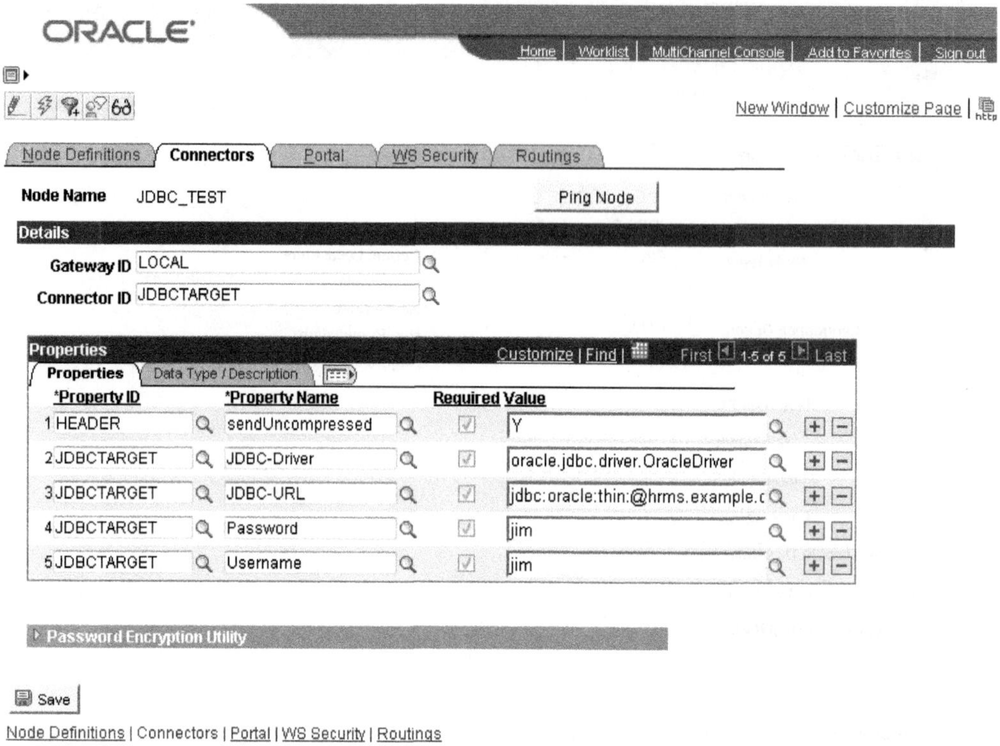

ORACLE

Home | Worklist | MultiChannel Console | Add to Favorites | Sign out

New Window | Customize Page | http

Node Definitions | Connectors | Portal | WS Security | Routings

Node Name JDBC_TEST Ping Node

Details

Gateway ID LOCAL

Connector ID JDBCTARGET

Properties Customize | Find | First 1-5 of 5 Last

Properties | Data Type / Description

	*Property ID	*Property Name	Required	Value
1	HEADER	sendUncompressed	☑	Y
2	JDBCTARGET	JDBC-Driver	☑	oracle.jdbc.driver.OracleDriver
3	JDBCTARGET	JDBC-URL	☑	jdbc:oracle:thin:@hrms.example.c
4	JDBCTARGET	Password	☑	jim
5	JDBCTARGET	Username	☑	jim

Password Encryption Utility

Save

Node Definitions | Connectors | Portal | WS Security | Routings

FIGURE 12-4. *JDBCTARGET connector properties*

```
    <VERSION type="NUMBER"/>
    <OPRDEFNDESC type="CHAR"/>
    <EMPLID type="CHAR"/>
    <EMAILID type="CHAR"/>
    <OPRCLASS type="CHAR"/>
    <ROWSECCLASS type="CHAR"/>
    ...
  </PSOPRDEFN>
  <PSROLEXLATOPRVW class="R">
    <OPRID type="CHAR"/>
    <ROLEUSER type="CHAR"/>
    ...
  </PSROLEXLATOPRVW>
  ...
  <PSCAMA class="R">
    <LANGUAGE_CD type="CHAR"/>
    <AUDIT_ACTN type="CHAR"/>
```

```
      <BASE_LANGUAGE_CD type="CHAR"/>
      <MSG_SEQ_FLG type="CHAR"/>
      <PROCESS_INSTANCE type="NUMBER"/>
      <PUBLISH_RULE_ID type="CHAR"/>
      <MSGNODENAME type="CHAR"/>
    </PSCAMA>
  </FieldTypes>
  <MsgData>
    <Transaction>
      <PSOPRDEFN class="R">
        <OPRID IsChanged="Y">HCRUSA_KU0007</OPRID>
        <VERSION IsChanged="Y">1</VERSION>
        <OPRDEFNDESC IsChanged="Y">[PS] Betty ...</OPRDEFNDESC>
        <EMPLID IsChanged="Y">KU0007</EMPLID>
        <EMAILID IsChanged="Y">hcrusa_ku0007@hrms...</EMAILID>
        ...
        <PSROLEUSER_VW class="R">
          <OPRID IsChanged="Y">HCRUSA_KU0007</OPRID>
          <ROLENAME IsChanged="Y">APT_CUSTOM</ROLENAME>
          <DYNAMIC_SW IsChanged="Y">N</DYNAMIC_SW>
        </PSROLEUSER_VW>
        <PSCAMA class="R">
          <AUDIT_ACTN>A</AUDIT_ACTN>
        </PSCAMA>
      </PSOPRDEFN>
      ...
    </Transaction>
  </MsgData>
</USER_PROFILE>
```

PeopleSoft's Integration Broker allows us to define XSL and PeopleCode App Engine transform programs to convert messages into alternative structures and formats. Let's create an App Engine transform program to convert the `USER_PROFILE` message into the format required by the `JDBCTargetConnector`. In App Designer, create a new App Engine program named `APT_USER2SQL`. Open the program's properties and select the Advanced tab. Change the program type to Transform Only, and then specify the rest of the program's advanced properties as follows (see Figure 12-5):

- Input Message Name: `USER_PROFILE`
- Input Message Version: `VERSION_84`
- Output Message Name: `IB_GENERIC`
- Output Message Version: `VERSION_1`
- Output Root Element: `message`

Rename step 1 to `Transfrm` and add a new XSLT action to the `Transfrm` step. As of PeopleTools 8.48, App Engine XSLT actions can use Oracle's XSLT Mapper. Since I am

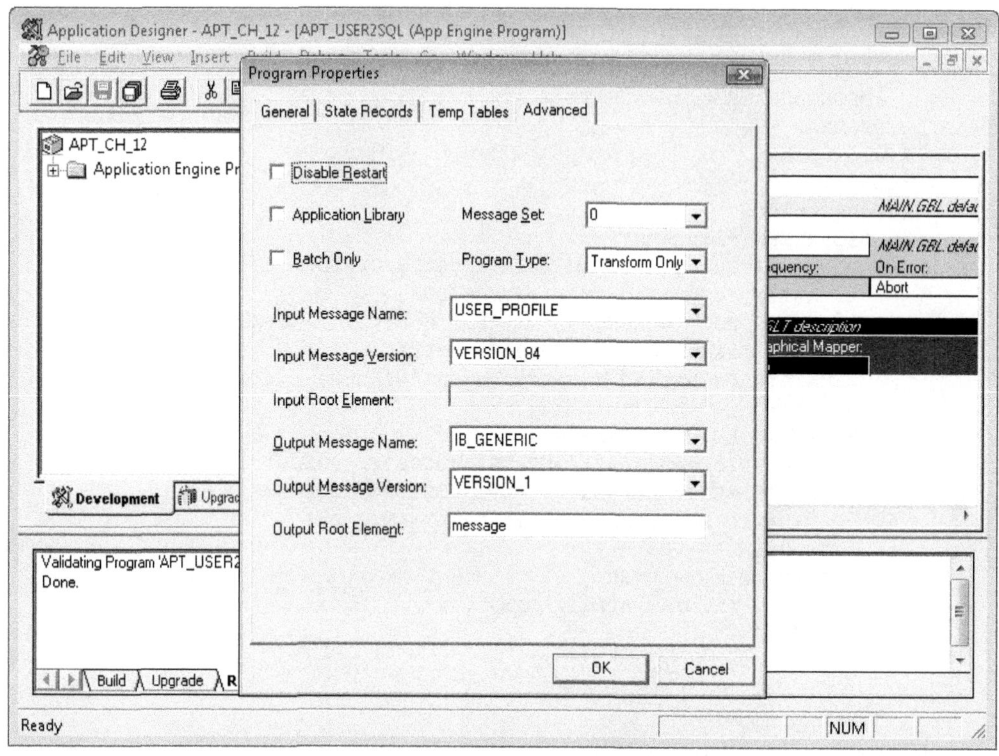

FIGURE 12-5. *APT_USER2SQL program advanced properties*

providing you with the XSL for this transformation, I recommend disabling the Graphical Mapper on this XSLT action by changing the Graphical Mapper value from Yes to No. Open the XSLT action and add the following XSL:

```
<?xml version="1.0"?>
<xsl:stylesheet version="1.0"
    xmlns:xsl="http://www.w3.org/1999/XSL/Transform">
  <xsl:template match="/">
    <message>
      <statements>
        <sql id="user-insert">
          insert into users values (?, ?, ?, ?)
        </sql>
      </statements>
      <data>
        <xsl:apply-templates
            select="USER_PROFILE/MsgData/Transaction/PSOPRDEFN"/>
      </data>
```

```
    </message>
  </xsl:template>

  <xsl:template match="USER_PROFILE/MsgData/Transaction/PSOPRDEFN">
    <bindings sql-ref="user-insert">
      <bind><xsl:value-of select="OPRID"/></bind>
      <bind><xsl:value-of select="OPRDEFNDESC"/></bind>
      <bind><xsl:value-of select="EMPLID"/></bind>
      <bind><xsl:value-of select="EMAILID"/></bind>
    </bindings>
  </xsl:template>
</xsl:stylesheet>
```

NOTE
Integration Broker XSL transformations use the Apache Xalan XSLT processor. You can download a copy of the same transformer from http://xml.apache.org/xalan-c/ to test transform programs on your local workstation. When designing transform programs, I create a test message in PeopleSoft, copy the generated XML to a local file, mock up the XSL transformation program in an XSL file, and then run the transform locally using Xalan-C. This allows me to review the results of the transform prior to running the transform online.

After entering the preceding XSL, save the transform program.

Creating a Routing

Our node and gateway are ready to send transactions to an external database using JDBC. We just need to create routings to identify which transactions to send. Since one of our objectives is to reuse delivered integration points, we will configure a routing for the delivered `USER_PROFILE` service operation.

NOTE
The following directions and screenshots pertain to PeopleTools 8.48 and higher. Earlier 8.4x versions of PeopleTools offered the same features through node transactions and relationships. Consult PeopleBooks if you require configuration instructions for earlier versions of PeopleTools.

Navigate to PeopleTools | Integration Broker | Integration Setup | Service Operations and open the `USER_PROFILE` service operation. On the General tab, verify that the Active check box is selected. If not, be sure to activate it.

Switch to the Routings tab and add a new routing named `USR_PRFL__PSFT_HR__JDBC_TEST`.

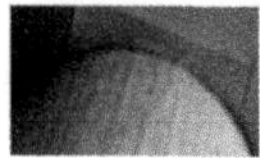

NOTE

I generally name my routings using the convention `SERVICEOPERATION__SENDER__RECEIVER`. *I use double underscores (__) to separate elements within the routing name because each element (service operation and node name) may contain underscore characters. In this example, my sender node is* `PSFT_HR`. `PSFT_HR`, *which is the delivered name of the PeopleSoft HRMS node. When implementing PeopleSoft, you should rename your default local node. Your development, test, production, and other systems should each have unique node names. Failure to rename your nodes can compromise security.*

Adding a new routing will transfer you to the Routings component. On the Routing Definitions page, set the sender node to `PSFT_HR` (or the name of your default local node) and the receiver node to `JDBC_TST`, as shown in Figure 12-6.

Switch to the Parameter tab and set the Transform Program 1 value to `APT_USER2SQL`, as shown in Figure 12-7. The component will automatically fill in the Message.Ver out of Transforms field from the transform program's metadata. Save the routing and click the Return button.

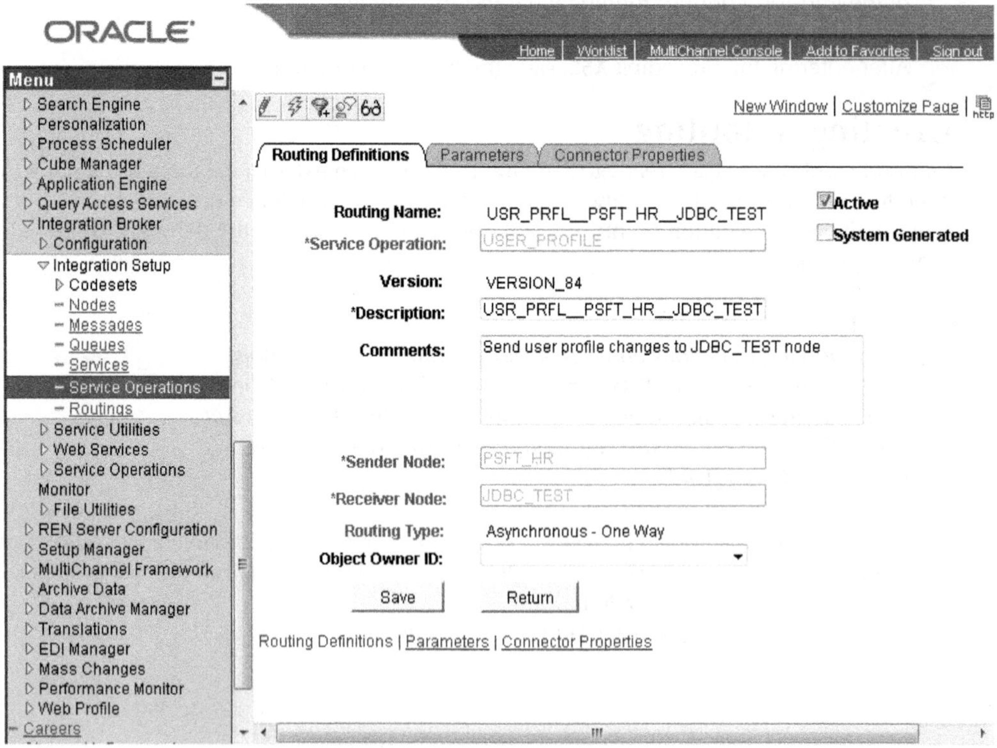

FIGURE 12-6. *Routing Definitions tab*

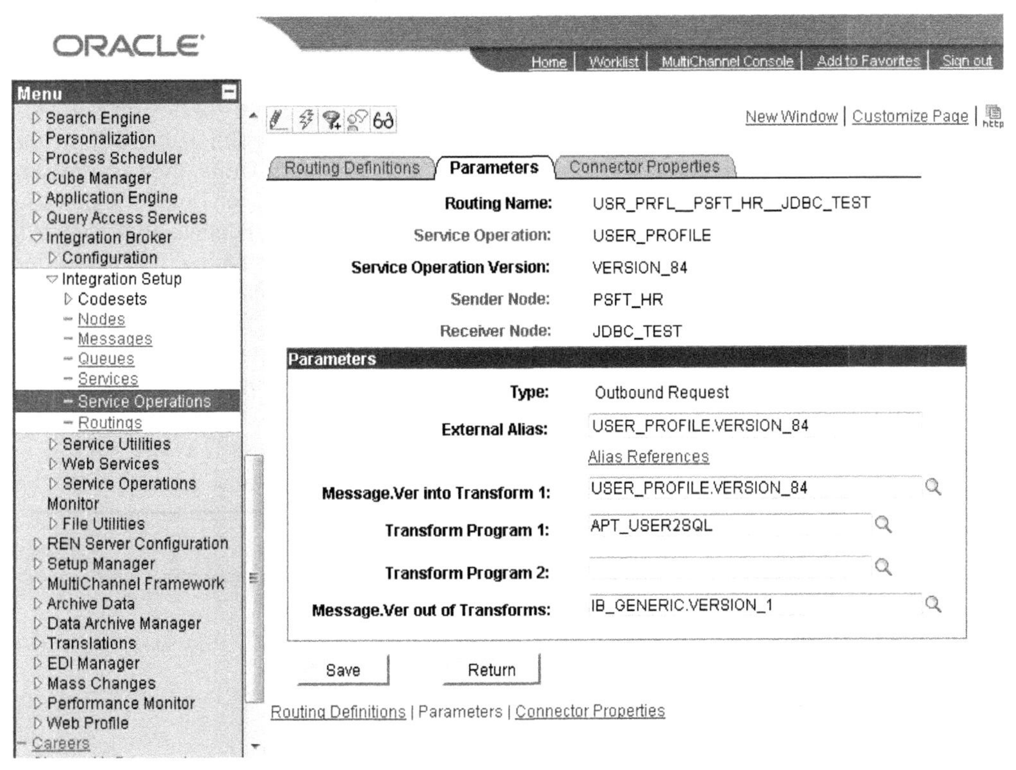

FIGURE 12-7. *Routing Parameters tab*

Testing the Integrated Connector

The code is written and deployed. Our configurations are complete. It is time to test sending a `USER_PROFILE` transaction to a database. Navigate to PeopleTools | Security | User Profiles | User Profiles and open a user profile for editing. In my HRMS demo database, I chose user `HCRUSA_KU0007`, Betty Locherty. Change a property of the user profile and click Save. I chose to set Betty's e-mail address to betty@hrms.example.com.

After saving the transaction, use your target database's query tool to select rows from the `users` table. After changing Betty's e-mail address, I see the following output in SQLPlus:

```
SQL> select * from users;

OPRID          OPRDEFNDESC                  EMPLID   EMAILID
-------------  ---------------------------  -------- ---------------------
HCRUSA_KU0007  [PS] Betty Locherty - MGR    KU0007   betty@hrms.example.com
```

If you don't see a new row in your table after a couple of seconds, continue to the next section for some tips on how to track down the problem.

Troubleshooting Custom Connectors

If your connector isn't working, navigate to PeopleTools | Integration Broker | Service Operations Monitor | Monitoring | Asynchronous Services. On the Monitor Overview tab, you will see a Queue Level field. Start with Oper Inst. If the `USER_PROFILE` service operation is in Done status, then change the Queue Level field to Pub Con and click the Refresh button. If the `USER_PROFILE` service operation is in any status other than Started, Working, or Done, then you may have a problem. If the `USER_PROFILE` service operation is in Error, Retry, or Timeout status, then click the hyperlinked number to transfer to the Queue Level details page (Publication Contracts tab).

The details page contains a grid of all messages matching the search criteria provided on the Monitor Overview tab. Scroll all the way to the right and click the Details link for the row containing the suspect message. This will open the Asynchronous Details page so you can view error messages, review the transformed XML, and so on. Figure 12-8 shows an Asynchronous Details page with one successful publication and one in Retry status, and Figure 12-9 shows the transformed XML as viewed from the Asynchronous Details page.

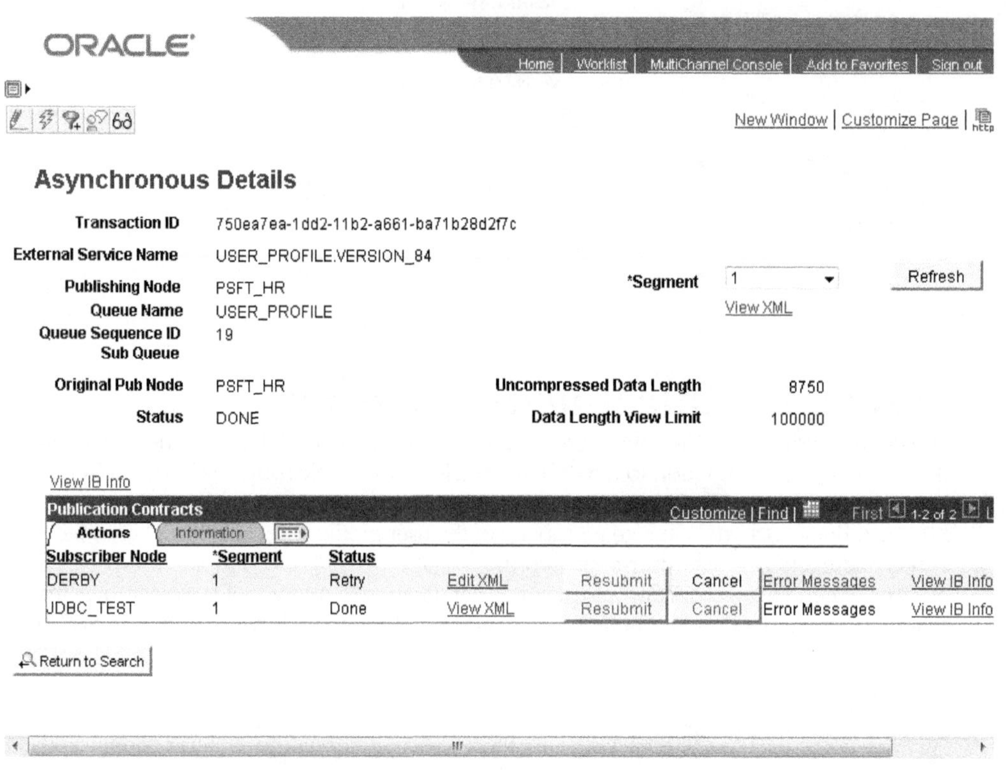

FIGURE 12-8. *Asynchronous Details page*

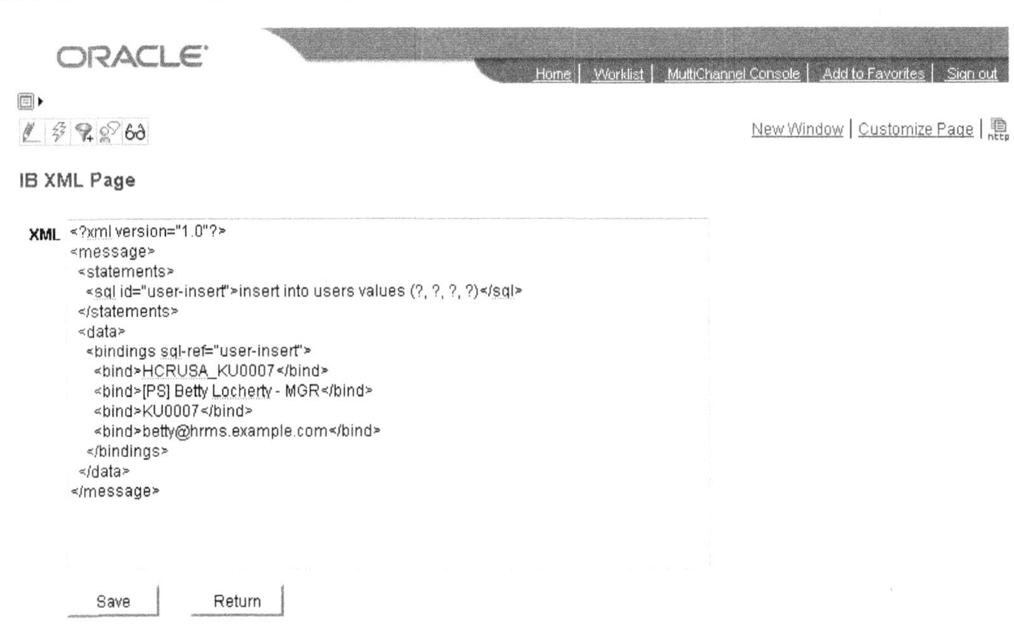

FIGURE 12-9. *USER_PROFILE XML after transformation*

If you are able to determine the issue from the information presented on the Asynchronous Details page, then resolve the problem and resubmit the transaction by clicking the Resubmit button.

If the Asynchronous Details page does not provide enough information, navigate to http://hrms.example.com/PSIGW/errorLog.html (replace hrms.example.com with your server's name and port). Scroll to the end of this file and find the error corresponding to your transaction (use the log file's timestamp for reference). The error log contains the complete Java exception stack trace.

If the error log doesn't provide enough information, navigate to PeopleTools | Integration Broker | Configuration | Gateways. Open your LOCAL gateway and select the Gateway Setup Properties link. When prompted, log in to modify the gateway properties. When the PeopleSoft Node Configuration page appears, click the Advanced Properties Page link. This will open the integrationGateway.properties file in your browser. Find the key `ig.log.level` and increase it to 5. This will write the entire integration conversation to a file named msgLog.html, which is accessible through the URL http://hrms.example.com/PSIGW/msgLog.html.

If you still can't find the error, instrument your Java code with `Logger.logMessage` statements as demonstrated in the `JDBCTargetConnector` and `StatementCache` Java classes. The `Logger.logMessage` method prints additional information to the msgLog.html file.

For tips on resolving other integration issues, such as "Messages stuck in New Status," search Oracle Support for the Integration Broker troubleshooting guide.

Conclusion

In this chapter, you learned how to create a custom target connector. I designed this connector for the purpose of converting batch SQR programs into configurable, real-time integrations. Unlike batch integrations, custom target connectors reuse delivered publishing logic and do not require complex identification logic.

Here are a couple more connector ideas to help you as you consider the possibilities afforded by the Integration Broker Connector SDK:

- Scripted connector for executing Ruby, JavaScript, Groovy, and so on using the Apache Bean Scripting Framework (BSF), available from http://jakarta.apache.org/bsf/
- Third-party API connector for integrating with systems that expose an integration API object model

I hope this chapter has provided you with some new inspiration for integrations.

Notes

1. W3C, "Document Object Model (DOM)" [online]; available from http://www.w3.org/DOM/; Internet; accessed 29 October 2009.
2. Wikipedia, "MIME" [online]; available from http://en.wikipedia.org/wiki/MIME; Internet; accessed 29 October 2009.

CHAPTER 13

Java on the Web Server

A majority of the code in this book focuses on customizing PeopleSoft applications through the app server tier. This is understandable, considering we spend most of our development time in App Designer, a tool for designing programs that run on the app server. In Part II of this book, we added client-side browser development to our list of development options. In this chapter, we look at the opportunities afforded by the web server tier.

The PeopleSoft web server is the same Java 2 Platform, Enterprise Edition (J2EE) web server used by developers around the world to build enterprise-class applications. Among other things, PeopleSoft applications use a J2EE web server to execute servlets that communicate with the PeopleSoft application server. Using standard J2EE development techniques, you can extend the PeopleSoft web server through JavaServer Pages (JSP), servlets, and servlet filters. Unlike app server development, code deployed in the web server tier does not have access to the PeopleSoft database (unless you use JDBC).

Extending the PeopleSoft Web Server with JSP

In Chapter 5, you learned how to use iScripts to generate pages and files that couldn't be represented as PeopleSoft components. If you require a nontraditional user interface that doesn't access the PeopleSoft database, then you may want to consider using JSP as an alternative to iScripts. As an example, let's create a JSP file that enumerates PeopleSoft web server session variables.

In JDeveloper, create a new generic application named `APT_ch13` and move to the next step. When prompted, name the application's project `JSPTest` and click Next. In the Project Technologies section, move JSP and Servlets from the Available list to the Selected list. When you move these Java technologies into the list of selected technologies, JDeveloper will add another step to the Create Application wizard and enable the Next button. Select the Next button to continue. On the final step of the wizard (step 3), set the default package to `apt.peoplesoft.servlets` and click Finish.

After JDeveloper creates the application and project, create a new JSP page by selecting File | New from the JDeveloper menu bar. When the New Gallery dialog appears, select Web Tier | JSP from the Categories list on the left, and then JSP from the Items list on the right. When prompted for a filename, name the new JSP file enum-session.jsp.

JDeveloper will open a new JSP page in design mode. Use the tabs at the bottom of the editor to switch to Source view. Replace the code in the JSP source code editor with the following:

```
<!DOCTYPE HTML PUBLIC "-//W3C//DTD HTML 4.01 Transitional//EN"
"http://www.w3.org/TR/html4/loose.dtd">
<%@ page contentType="text/html;charset=windows-1252"
    import="java.util.Enumeration"%>
<html>
  <head>
    <meta http-equiv="Content-Type"
        content="text/html; charset=windows-1252"/>
    <title>enum-session</title>
  </head>
```

```
  <body>
    <h1>Session Variables</h1>
    <table border="1">
    <%
        Enumeration names = session.getAttributeNames();
        while (names.hasMoreElements()) {
            String attribute = names.nextElement().toString();
            String value = session.getAttribute(attribute).toString();
            out.println("<tr><td>" + attribute + "</td> " +
                "<td>" + value + "</td></tr>");
        }
    %>
    </table>
  </body>
</html>
```

To test this file in JDeveloper, right-click the source code editor and select Run from the context menu. JDeveloper will compile the JSP file's source code, start a local instance of WebLogic server, and then load this JSP file in your web browser. Since we didn't create any session variables, the enum-session page should display only the Session Variables title. Our primary reason for testing in JDeveloper is to catch any compilation errors or obvious runtime errors prior to deploying this JSP to the PeopleSoft web server.

After testing this page, upload it to your %PS_HOME%\webserv\peoplesoft\applications\peoplesoft\PORTAL directory. (PeopleTools 8.50 uses the PORTAL.war folder instead of the PORTAL folder.) Depending on your WebLogic deployment mode, you will be able to see results by first logging into PeopleSoft online, and then navigating to http://hrms.example.com/enum-session.jsp. J2EE web servers compile JSP files into class files and then execute them like any other servlet or Java class. If you do not see results or if you need to make changes to the JSP file after running it, you will need to restart your web server.

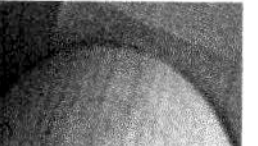

NOTE
The method employed to move a file from your desktop to your web server varies by operating system and deployment. Typically uploading a file to a web server involves FTP or some other remote copy method (SCP, FTPS, SFTP, and so on). Consult your system administrator for details.

Using Servlet Filters

In previous chapters, you saw how to use object-oriented concepts to subclass and extend existing objects. Since PeopleSoft's web tier is composed of servlets, we could manipulate the request/response cycle by subclassing the delivered PeopleSoft servlets. J2EE offers a better solution to subclassing servlets: servlet filters.

A servlet filter is a configurable Java class that preprocesses a request prior to calling a specific servlet, or postprocesses a response generated by that same servlet. The J2EE web server actually passes the incoming request to the servlet filter and lets the filter determine whether to pass the request on to the requested servlet.

Investigating iScript Caching Behavior

In Part II of this book, I showed you how to use iScripts to serve static files such as images, SWF files, JavaScript, and CSS files. In those chapters, I explained that browsers will not cache iScript responses because of HTTP headers set by the PeopleSoft web server. Let's create an iScript to investigate this behavior. After we understand how PeopleSoft is avoiding the browser cache, we can create a strategy to override PeopleSoft's delivered behavior.

In App Designer, create a new derived/work record named `WEBLIB_APT_HDR` and insert the field `ISCRIPT1`. Open the field's `FieldFormula` event and add the following PeopleCode:

```
Function IScript_CheckHeaders()
   %Response.Write("The current time is " | %Datetime);
End-Function;
```

Next, log in to your PeopleSoft application online and add the `IScript_CheckHeaders` function of `WEBLIB_APT_HDR` to the `APT_CUSTOM` permission list.

Navigate to this URL (replace the server name with your server's name):

http://hrms.example.com/psc/hrms/EMPLOYEE/HRMS/s/WEBLIB_APT_HDR.ISCRIPT1
.FieldFormula.IScript_CheckHeaders

You will see the server's current time. Since our iScript writes the server's current time to the response on each request, each page load will display a different time value.

NOTE

When I refer to loading a page, *I mean opening a particular URL in your web browser. This differs from using your browser's refresh/reload feature. The refresh/reload feature is supposed to download a fresh copy of a URL from your web server. Loading a page, on the other hand, may result in a server request or may be satisfied from the web browser's local cache.*

Browsers use HTTP headers to determine what content to cache. Using Fiddler, we can see the HTTP response headers PeopleSoft generates for iScripts, as shown in Figure 13-1. From this view, you can see that PeopleSoft controls browser caching through the `Cache-Control` HTTP response header.

As you've seen in previous chapters, it is possible to override default HTTP header values by calling the `SetHeader` method of the `%Response` object. PeopleSoft treats the `Cache-Control` header differently. Regardless of the value you specify for `Cache-Control`, PeopleSoft will always return `no-cache`. To see this in action, add a `SetHeader` line to the beginning of the iScript as follows:

```
Function IScript_CheckHeaders()
   rem one year, in seconds;
   %Response.SetHeader("Cache-Control", "max-age=" |
         60 * 60 * 24 * 365);

   %Response.Write("The current time is " | %Datetime);
End-Function;
```

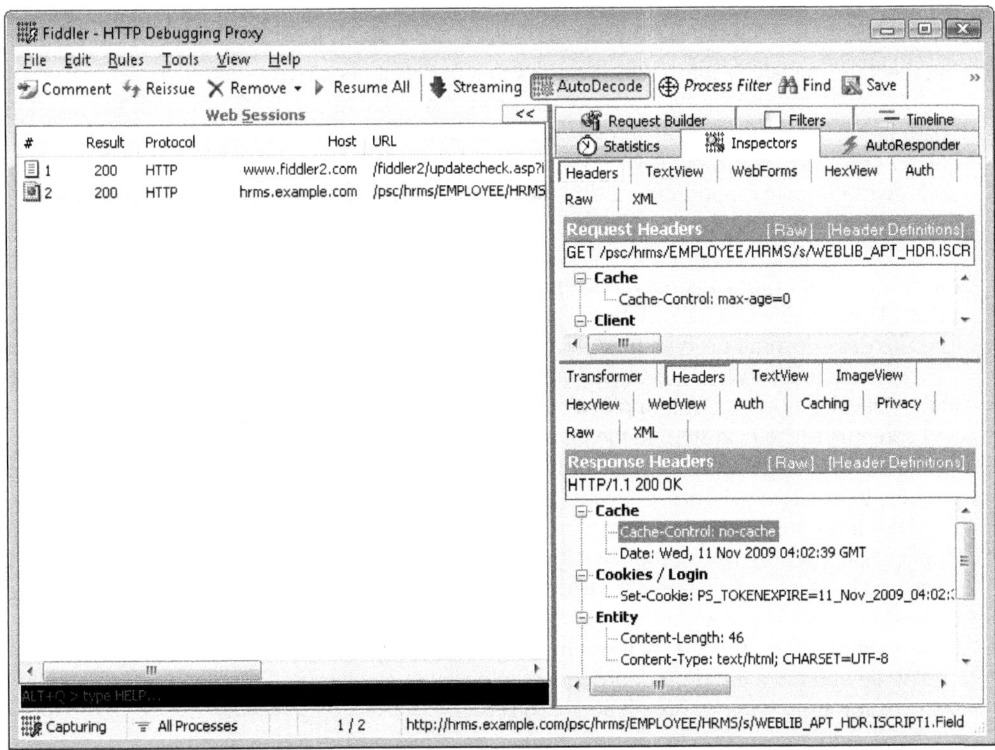

FIGURE 13-1. *iScript cache response headers displayed in Fiddler*

Reload this iScript in your browser, and then review the response headers in Fiddler. You will notice that the `Cache-Control` header is still set to `no-cache`, just as displayed in Figure 13-1. It appears that the PeopleCode language offers no solution for caching iScripts. Let's see if we can override PeopleSoft's iScript cache behavior at the web server level.

Creating an HTTP Header Servlet Filter

Servlet filters offer an opportunity to interact with (or even interrupt) the HTTP request/response cycle. A J2EE web server will not fulfill an HTTP request until that request passes through each configured servlet filter. A servlet filter can interact with a request in one of three ways:

- Modify the request by changing parameters and HTTP headers
- Fulfill the request through redirection and/or error return codes
- Ignore the request and allow it to pass through to the requested resource (or the next servlet filter)

The jCIFS NTLM HTTP filter,[1] IOPLEX Jespa Active Directory filter,[2] and OWASP Enterprise Security API filter[3] are examples of servlet filters that authenticate users by standing between the incoming request and the final destination resource. Other filters, such as the UrlRewriteFilter,[4] intercept and satisfy requests for resources that may not even exist.

J2EE web servers pass HTTP requests through a chain of servlet filters, with the last item in the chain being the requested resource handler (such as the servlet). Each servlet filter is expected to call `FilterChain.doFilter` to pass control onto the next servlet filter. The authentication and rewrite filters I mentioned modify the request object by changing headers, parameters, and other request properties prior to calling `FilterChain.doFilter`.

This same filter-chaining mechanism allows a servlet filter to modify an HTTP response after the resource handler satisfies a request. By placing code after the call to `FilterChain.doFilter`, a servlet filter can modify the `ServletResponse` returned by the resource handler. The SiteMesh decorator servlet filter[5] is an example of a filter that modifies an outgoing response.

Let's create a servlet filter to change the outgoing response's `Cache-Control` HTTP header. In the JDeveloper `APT_ch13` application, create a new generic project, name it `ServletFilters`, and continue to the next step. In the Project Technologies section, move JSP and Servlets from the Available list to the Selected list, and then click Next. On the final step of the wizard, set the default package to `apt.peoplesoft.servlets` and click Finish.

After JDeveloper creates the project, open the project's properties window and select Java EE Application from the list on the left. Change the value of the Java EE Web Context Root field from `APT_ch13-HeaderServletFilter-context-root` to `filtertest`. The Java EE web context root will become part of the URL; it is much easier to type `filtertest` than the long-winded text generated by JDeveloper.

While you have the project properties window open, set the JDK version compatibility to the Java version used by your PeopleSoft web server.

Next, add a Java class to the new project by selecting File | New from the JDeveloper menu bar. In the Categories list on the left, scroll down to Web Tier and select Servlets. In the Items list on the right, select Servlet Filter, and then click the OK button. JDeveloper will launch the Create Servlet Filter wizard. Click next on the Welcome page. To begin, select the servlet version that matches your web server's J2EE compliance level. Table 13-1 lists J2EE versions for each of the PeopleTools-supported WebLogic versions.

After selecting the appropriate servlet version, in step 1 of the wizard, name the filter `CacheHeaderFilter`, name the filer class `BasicHTTPHeaderFilter`, and specify the package `apt.peoplesoft.servlets`, as shown in Figure 13-2.

WebLogic Version	JDK Version	J2EE Version
8.1	1.4	1.3
9.2	1.5	1.4
10.3	1.6	1.5

TABLE 13-1. *WebLogic J2EE Support by Version*

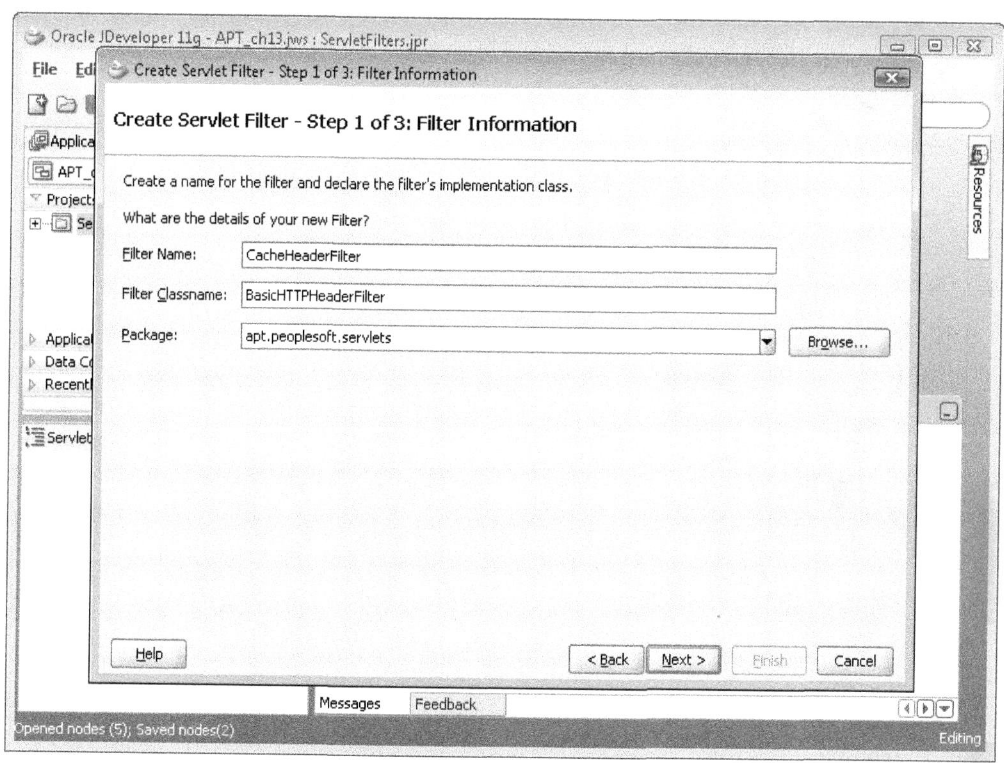

FIGURE 13-2. *Create Servlet Filter wizard step 1*

Step 2 asks for a URL or servlet mapping. Enter a slash (/) as the value. The / mapping is far too inclusive for production use, but works well for JDeveloper testing purposes.

Step 3 of the wizard asks for initialization parameters. Since we may find other headers to override, let's make this servlet filter generic enough to use with several HTTP headers by adding a parameter for the header name and another parameter for the header value. Create two initialization parameters. Name the first one `HeaderName` and give it the value `Cache-Control`. Name the second parameter `HeaderValue` with the value `31556926` (31556926 is one year in seconds). Figure 13-3 shows the filter's initialization parameters. Click Finish to create the servlet filter.

JDeveloper will use the information collected in the Create Servlet Filter wizard to generate a new Java class as well as the necessary servlet filter web.xml declaration. Replace the code inside the wizard-generated `BasicHTTPHeaderFilter` Java class with the following:

```
package apt.peoplesoft.servlets;

import java.io.IOException;

import javax.servlet.Filter;
import javax.servlet.FilterChain;
```

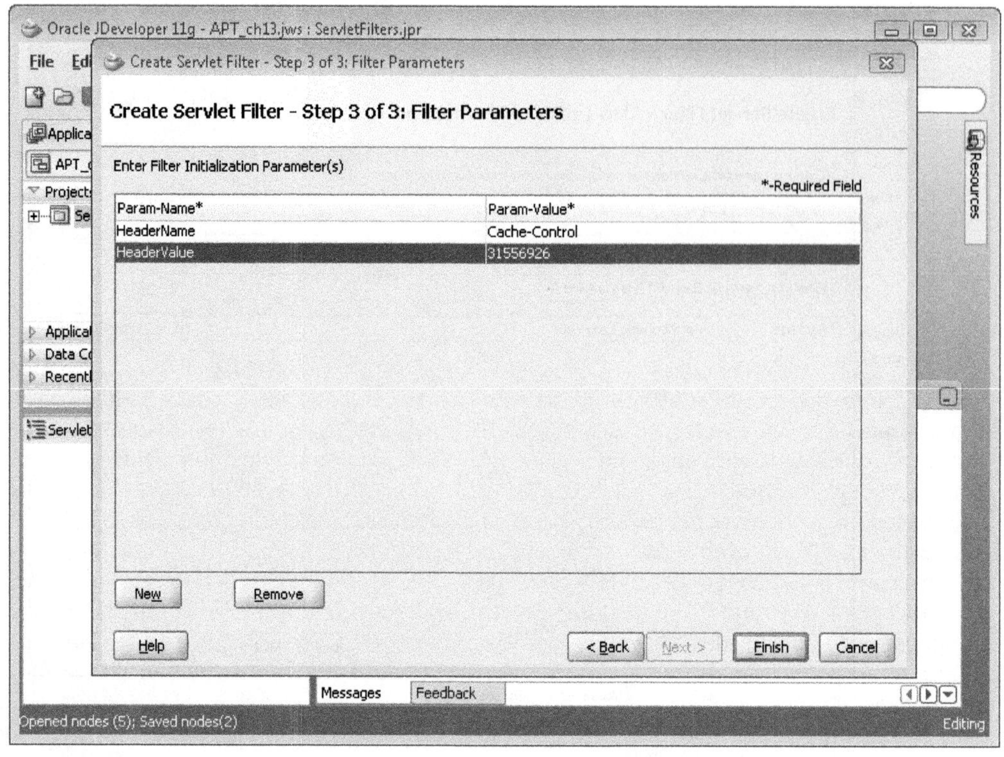

FIGURE 13-3. *Create Servlet Filter wizard step 3*

```
import javax.servlet.FilterConfig;
import javax.servlet.ServletException;
import javax.servlet.ServletRequest;
import javax.servlet.ServletResponse;
import javax.servlet.http.HttpServletResponse;


public class BasicHTTPHeaderFilter implements Filter {
    private FilterConfig _filterConfig = null;
    private String _headerName;
    private String _headerValue;

    public void init(FilterConfig filterConfig) throws ServletException {
        _filterConfig = filterConfig;

        _headerName = _filterConfig.getInitParameter("HeaderName");
        _headerValue = _filterConfig.getInitParameter("HeaderValue");
    }
```

```
    public void destroy() {
        _filterConfig = null;
    }

    public void doFilter(ServletRequest request, ServletResponse response,
                         FilterChain chain) throws IOException,
                                                   ServletException {
        chain.doFilter(request, response);

        HttpServletResponse httpResponse = (HttpServletResponse)response;

        httpResponse.setHeader(_headerName, _headerValue);
    }
}
```

When loaded, your PeopleSoft J2EE web server will call the filter's `init` method with the values specified in the web.xml declaration. The `init` method in this listing stores the header name, `Cache-Control`, and header value, `31556926`, in private member fields for later use in the `doFilter` method.

When the web server receives a request for a URL matching the filter pattern we specified in the web.xml file, the web server will execute the `doFilter` method. Our implementation of `doFilter` immediately passes the request on to the next filter in the chain by calling `chain.doFilter`. On return, the `response` variable will contain the PeopleSoft-generated HTTP response, including headers and data. Our `doFilter` method casts the `response` variable to an `HttpServletResponse`, and then sets the header as specified by the web.xml filter initialization properties—`Cache-Control: 31556926` in this case.

Testing the Servlet Filter

To test this servlet filter, create a new JSP page by choosing File | New from the JDeveloper menu bar. When the New Gallery dialog appears, select the JSP subcategory from the Web Tier category. In the list on the right, select the JSP item, and then click the OK button. When prompted, enter TestHeaders.jsp for the filename and click the OK button. JDeveloper will respond by opening a new JSP page in Design view. Use the tabs at the bottom of the JSP page designer to switch to Source view. Add the following `import` to the page directive:

```
import="java.util.Date"
```

Add the following code inside the <body> tags:

```
This file was last updated at
<%= (new Date()).toString() %>
```

The complete JSP code listing is as follows:

```
<!DOCTYPE HTML PUBLIC "-//W3C//DTD HTML 4.01 Transitional//EN"
    "http://www.w3.org/TR/html4/loose.dtd">
<%@ page contentType="text/html;charset=windows-1252"
    import="java.util.Date"%>
<html>
  <head>
    <meta http-equiv="Content-Type"
        content="text/html; charset=windows-1252"/>
```

```
    <title>TestHeaders</title>
  </head>
  <body>
    This file was last updated on
    <%= (new Date()).toString() %>
  </body>
</html>
```

To run this JSP file, right-click the code editor window and choose Run from the context menu. JDeveloper will compile your source code and then launch an embedded WebLogic instance. After starting WebLogic and deploying this project's web application, JDeveloper will launch your web browser and navigate to TestHeaders.jsp. In your browser, you should see text similar to the following:

```
This file was last updated on Thu Nov 12 00:17:57 PST 2009
```

Loading this URL multiple times should not change the displayed date and time. If you refresh the page, however, the time will change to match your current time. Figure 13-4 shows the `Cache-Control` header as specified by the `BasicHTTPHeaderFilter` servlet filter.

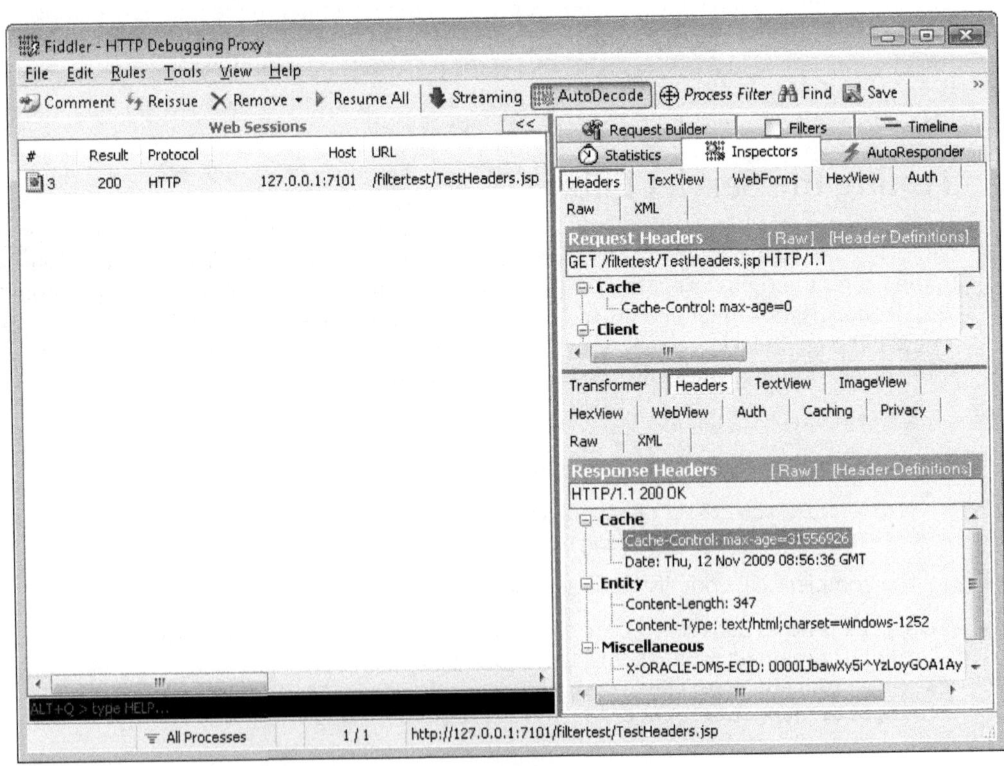

FIGURE 13-4. *Cache-Control header as seen from Fiddler*

Deploying the Servlet Filter

Even though this filter contains only one class file, I find it easier to deploy and maintain solutions as JAR files rather than creating new directory structures within the PeopleSoft web application classes directory. To create a new deployment profile, in the JDeveloper `ServletFilters` project, select File | New from the JDeveloper menu bar, select General, then Deployment Profiles from the Categories list, select JAR File from the Items list, and then click OK. Name the new JAR file deployment profile `apt_filters`. After creating the new deployment profile, right-click the project in the JDeveloper Application Navigator and select Deploy | apt_filters | to JAR file from the context menu.

After creating apt_filters.jar, copy it to your web server's WEB-INF/lib directory. On a Linux-based WebLogic instance, the directory is located at $PS_HOME/webserv/peoplesoft/applications/peoplesoft/PORTAL/WEB-INF/lib.

Next, we need to register our new servlet filter with WebLogic. Open your `PORTAL` web application's web.xml file. On a Windows based WebLogic instance, the path will be similar to %PS_HOME%\webserv\peoplesoft\applications\peoplesoft\PORTAL\WEB-INF\web.xml. Near the beginning of web.xml, you should see a filter declaration for a filter named `psfilter`. Immediately following the closing `</filter>` tag, add the following declaration:

```
<filter>
  <filter-name>CacheHeaderFilter</filter-name>
  <filter-class>
      apt.peoplesoft.servlets.BasicHTTPHeaderFilter
  </filter-class>
  <init-param>
    <param-name>HeaderName</param-name>
    <param-value>Cache-Control</param-value>
  </init-param>
  <init-param>
    <param-name>HeaderValue</param-name>
    <!-- 365.242199 days * 24 hours * 60 minutes * 60 seconds; one
      year in seconds.
      -->
    <param-value>max-age=31556926</param-value>
  </init-param>
</filter>
```

The next segment in the web.xml file is the `filter-mapping` section. This section allows you to specify servlet names or URL patterns to pass through the new filter. Add the following code immediately following the `psfilter` filter mapping:

```
<filter-mapping>
  <filter-name>CacheHeaderFilter</filter-name>
  <url-pattern>
      /psc/hrms/EMPLOYEE/HRMS/s/WEBLIB_APT_HDR.ISCRIPT1.FieldFormula
     .IScript_CheckHeaders</url-pattern>
</filter-mapping>
```

Notice that the `url-pattern` specifies a path to a specific iScript, rather than using wildcard characters. I recommend using full paths for your patterns so that you don't accidentally cache other, potentially volatile iScripts. If you have multiple iScripts that require caching, create multiple `filter-mapping` elements, each using the same `filter-name` value.

The web.xml specification also allows you to define multiple instances of the `BasicHTTPHeaderFilter`, wherein each instance has a unique name. This allows you to specify different header names and values for each filter pattern. Or you could even apply multiple filters to the same pattern for the purpose of simultaneously setting more than one header value.

Save your web.xml file and then restart WebLogic. Log in to your PeopleSoft application and revisit the test iScript. On my test system, the URL is as follows:

http://hrms.example.com/psc/hrms/EMPLOYEE/HRMS/s/WEBLIB_APT_HDR.ISCRIPT1
.FieldFormula.IScript_CheckHeaders

Repeatedly loading this page should not change the contents of the page. Reloading the page using your browser's refresh/reload function, however, will cause your browser to request a new instance of the page, resulting in an updated date/time value. In Fiddler, you can see the `Cache-Control` header now matches the result shown earlier in Figure 13-4, with a value of `max-age=31556926`.

NOTE

If your web server doesn't start correctly, verify your web.xml entry, that the JAR file was deployed, and that you compiled the project using the correct Java version. Also check your PIA_stderr.log file. If you find a `ClassNotFoundException`, this indicates that the file was incorrectly deployed, the class name in web.xml is incorrect, or the class was compiled with the wrong Java version.

Conclusion

The web server offers a unique opportunity for modifying PeopleSoft application behavior. What makes the web server unique is that we can modify the response generated by PeopleSoft without actually modifying delivered definitions.

With your new `BasicHTTPHeaderFilter` installed, I recommend adding `filter-mapping` elements for several of the iScripts in `WEBLIB_APT_JSL`, including `IScript_jQuery` and `IScript_JSON2`.

It is important to note that the `BasicHTTPHeaderFilter` described in this chapter places files in the web browser cache for the amount of time specified by the filter initialization parameter regardless of changes made to those objects. For example, if you configure an iScript URL to use the `BasicHTTPHeaderFilter` and then make changes to that iScript, your browser will continue to use the older, cached version until you delete your browser cache (temporary Internet files) or use your browser's refresh/reload feature.

Notes

1. JCIFS Project, "JCIFS NTLM HTTP Authentication" [online]; available from http://jcifs .samba.org/src/docs/ntlmhttpauth.html; Internet; accessed 10 November 2009.

2. IOPLEX Software, "Jespa - Java Active Directory Integration" [online]; available from http://www.ioplex.com/jespa.html; Internet; accessed 11 November 2009.

3. OWASP, "OWASP Enterprise Security API" [online]; available from http://www.owasp.org/ index.php/Category:OWASP_Enterprise_Security_API#tab=Java_EE; Internet; accessed 11 November 2009.

4. Paul Tuckey, "Url Rewrite Filter" [online]; available from http://tuckey.org/urlrewrite/; Internet; accessed 11 November 2009.

5. Wikipedia, "SiteMesh" [online]; available from http://en.wikipedia.org/wiki/SiteMesh; Internet; accessed 11 November 2009.

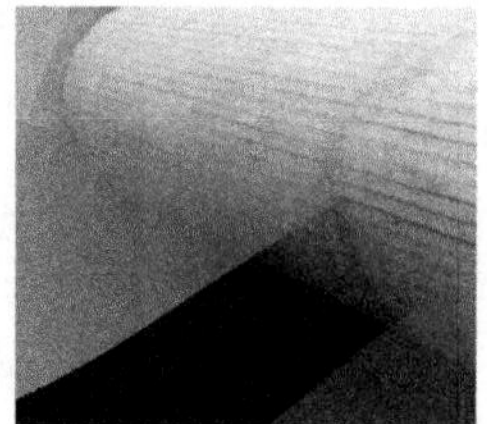

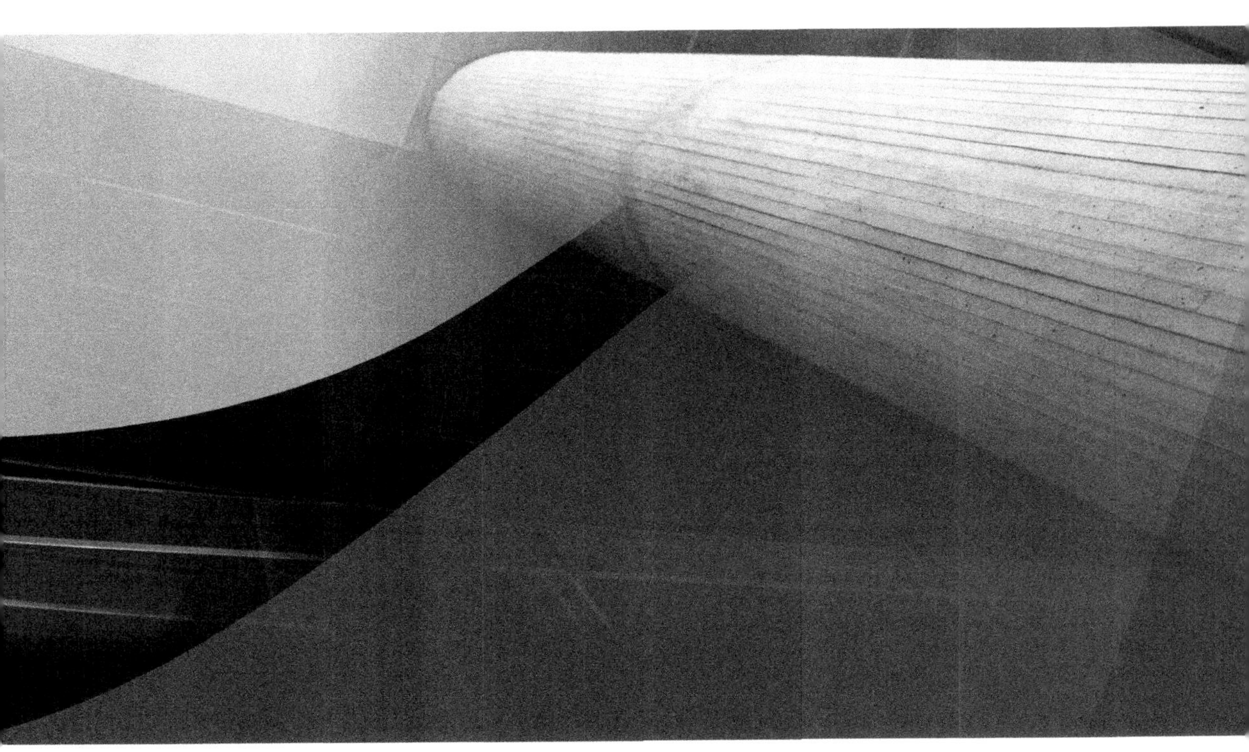

CHAPTER 14

Creating Mobile Applications for PeopleSoft

Year after year, our workforce becomes increasingly mobile. Assisted by online conferencing, chat, e-mail, and many other related technologies, the "office" has left the building. Through Wi-Fi hotspots and wireless Internet cards, employees armed with laptops can work from just about anywhere on planet Earth. But a laptop with an anytime/anywhere Internet connection is just a teaser. It offers as much freedom as a sailboat with the anchor down and no wind. The boat rocks with the waves, but it isn't going anywhere.

One of the benefits of a mobile workforce is the ability to collect transaction information at the point of transaction. For example, with a mobile laptop and an Internet connection, a field sales agent can place an order in real time. But there are other transaction points where a laptop is not convenient. Can you imagine booting up your laptop while dining at a restaurant so you could enter your travel expenses?

In this chapter, we will use Oracle Application Development Framework (ADF) and PeopleSoft's web services to create a mobile application. This chapter differs from other chapters in that we aren't going to write any code. JDeveloper's combination of wizards and drag-and-drop development makes building web applications a trivial point-and-click exercise.

Our objective in this chapter is to create the search page for a mobile, read-only personnel address book based on the `CI_PERSONAL_DATA` component interface (CI) delivered with PeopleSoft's HRMS application. We will create a single page that contains data-entry fields for search criteria and a table for displaying search results. The page itself will look very similar to a PeopleSoft component search page.

Providing Web Services

Before launching JDeveloper to build our search page, we need to expose a PeopleSoft transaction as a web service. PeopleSoft delivers a service based on the `CI_PERSONAL_DATA` CI, which means we won't need to create the web service.

Enabling a Component Interface as a Web Service

Follow these steps to enable the `CI_PERSONAL_DATA` HRMS CI as a web service.

1. If you haven't already done so, configure your Integration Broker service target location by navigating to PeopleTools | Integration Broker | Configuration | Service Configuration and filling in the Target Location field. Figure 14-1 shows the Integration Broker Service Configuration page.

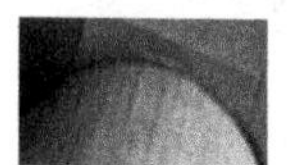

NOTE
Figure 14-1 shows a service configuration with Production status. Typically, you develop new services in a system configured with Development status.

2. Navigate to Integration Broker | Web Services | CI-Based Services. On the transaction search page, select `CI_PERSONAL_DATA`, and then click Search. Figure 14-2 shows the CI-Based Services page after the search.

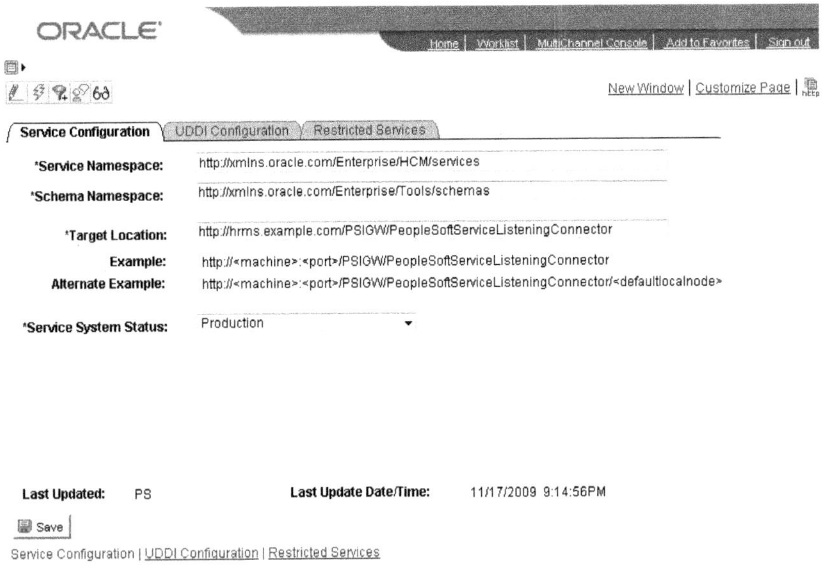

ORACLE

Home | Worklist | MultiChannel Console | Add to Favorites | Sign out

New Window | Customize Page | http

Service Configuration | UDDI Configuration | Restricted Services

*Service Namespace: http://xmlns.oracle.com/Enterprise/HCM/services

*Schema Namespace: http://xmlns.oracle.com/Enterprise/Tools/schemas

*Target Location: http://hrms.example.com/PSIGW/PeopleSoftServiceListeningConnector

Example: http://<machine>:<port>/PSIGW/PeopleSoftServiceListeningConnector

Alternate Example: http://<machine>:<port>/PSIGW/PeopleSoftServiceListeningConnector/<defaultlocalnode>

*Service System Status: Production

Last Updated: PS Last Update Date/Time: 11/17/2009 9:14:56PM

Save

Service Configuration | UDDI Configuration | Restricted Services

FIGURE 14-1. *Integration Broker Service Configuration page*

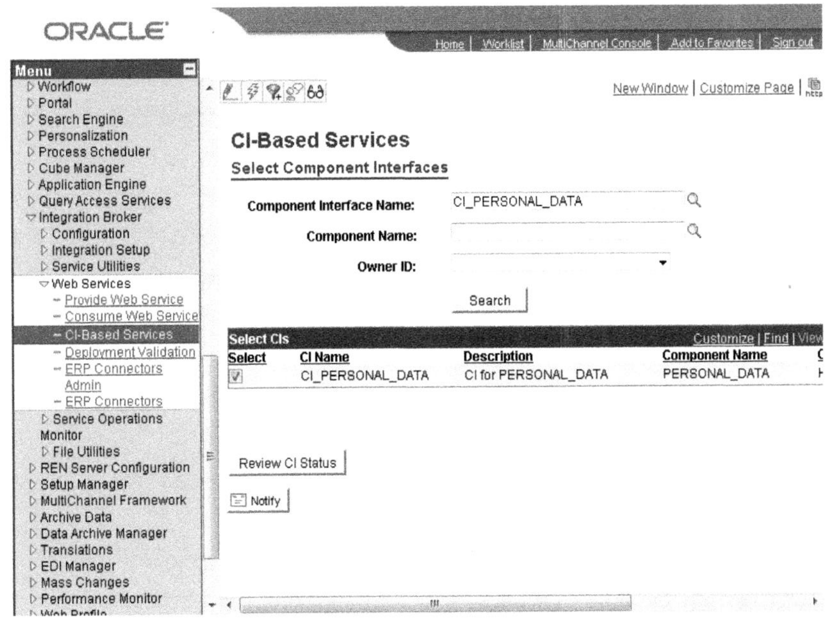

FIGURE 14-2. *CI-Based Services Select Component Interfaces page*

3. With the CI_PERSONAL_DATA CI selected, click the Review CI Status button. As shown in Figure 14-3, from this status page, you see that the web service name is CI_CI_PERSONAL_DATA, which is the name of the CI prefixed with CI_. This page shows the relationship between each service operation name and the CI method it represents. For this example, we will enable the Get, CI_CI_PERSONAL_DATA_G, and Find, CI_CI_PERSONAL_DATA_F, methods. JDeveloper shows only the service operation name and not the CI method name, so it is important to note this relationship in advance.
4. Click the View Service Definition link. From this page, you can verify the active status of each service operation. Figure 14-4 shows that each CI_CI_PERSONAL_DATA service operation is inactive.
5. Select the Provide Web Service link (located in the middle of the page). PeopleSoft will transfer you to step 2 of the Provide Web Service Wizard.
6. Select CI_CI_PERSONAL_DATA_F and CI_CI_PERSONAL_DATA_G, the Find and Get operations, as shown in Figure 14-5.

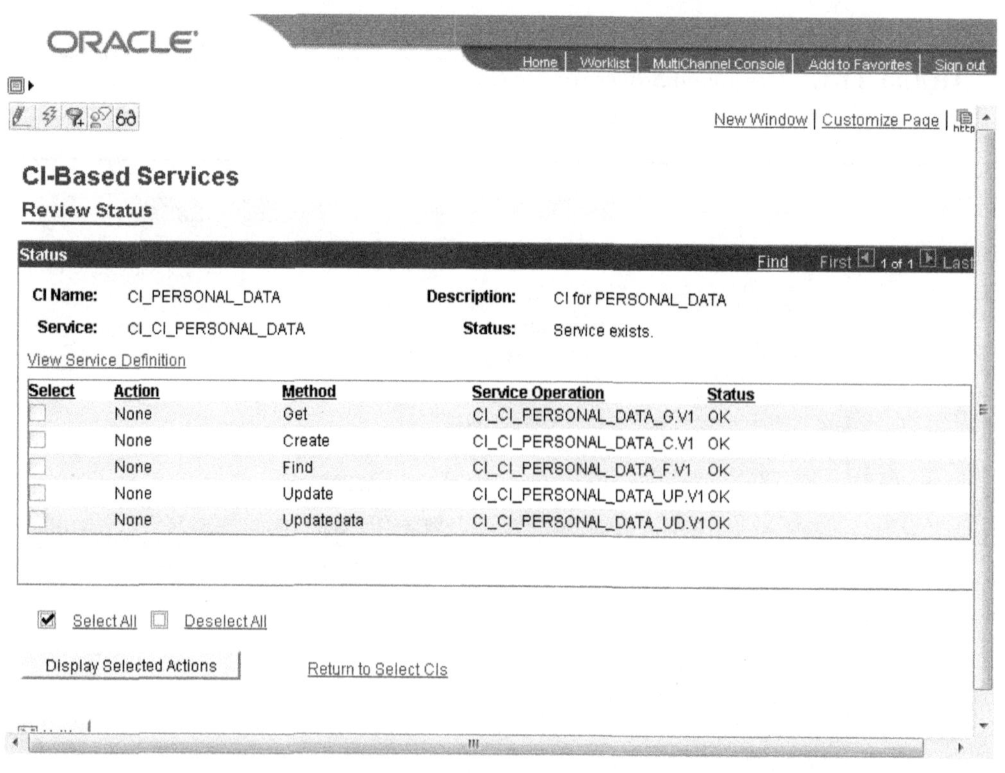

FIGURE 14-3. *CI-Based Services Review Status page*

ORACLE

Home | Worklist | MultiChannel Console | Add to Favorites | Sign out

Service: CI_CI_PERSONAL_DATA

***Description:** CI_CI_PERSONAL_DATA

Comments:

Service Alias:

Object Owner ID:

***Namespace:** http://xmlns.oracle.com/Enterprise/HCM/services

View WSDL   Provide Web Service

Service Operations

Service Operation:

Operation Type: ADD

Existing Operations   Customize | Find | View All | First 1-5 of 5 Last

Operation | Message Links

Operation.Default Version	Description	Active	Operation Type
CI_CI_PERSONAL_DATA_C.V1	CI_CI_PERSONAL_DATA_C		Synch
CI_CI_PERSONAL_DATA_F.V1	CI_CI_PERSONAL_DATA_F		Synch
CI_CI_PERSONAL_DATA_G.V1	CI_CI_PERSONAL_DATA_G		Synch
CI_CI_PERSONAL_DATA_UD.V1	CI_CI_PERSONAL_DATA_UD		Synch
CI_CI_PERSONAL_DATA_UP.V1	CI_CI_PERSONAL_DATA_UP		Synch

FIGURE 14-4. *CI_CI_PERSONAL_DATA service definition*

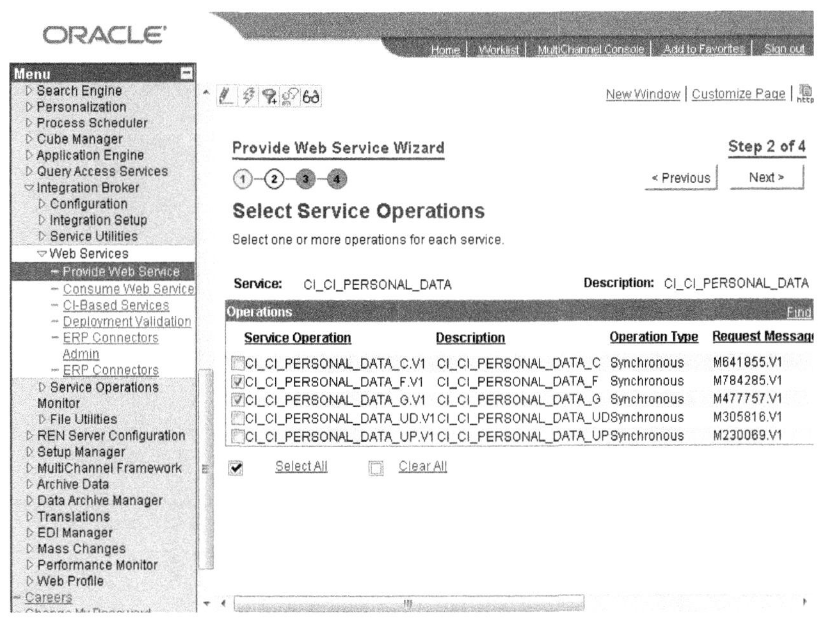

FIGURE 14-5. *Step 2 of the Provide Web Service Wizard*

7. Click the Next button to move to step 3 and then again to get to step 4.
8. Click the Finish button on step 4 to see the wizard's confirmation page, which includes the web service's Web Service Definition Language (WSDL) URL, as shown in Figure 14-6. On my system, the WSDL URL is http://hrms.example.com/PSIGW/PeopleSoftServiceListeningConnector/CI_CI_PERSONAL_DATA.1.wsdl.
9. Copy this URL and save it for later use in JDeveloper. (Notepad is a great place to store text like this until you need it.)
10. The `CI_CI_PERSONAL_DATA` CI-based web service operations are inactive by default. To enable the Find service operation, navigate to PeopleTools | Integration Broker | Integration Setup | Service Operations and select the `CI_CI_PERSONAL_DATA_F` service operation, as shown in Figure 14-7.
11. Verify that the `CI_CI_PERSONAL_DATA_F` service is active, as shown in Figure 14-8.

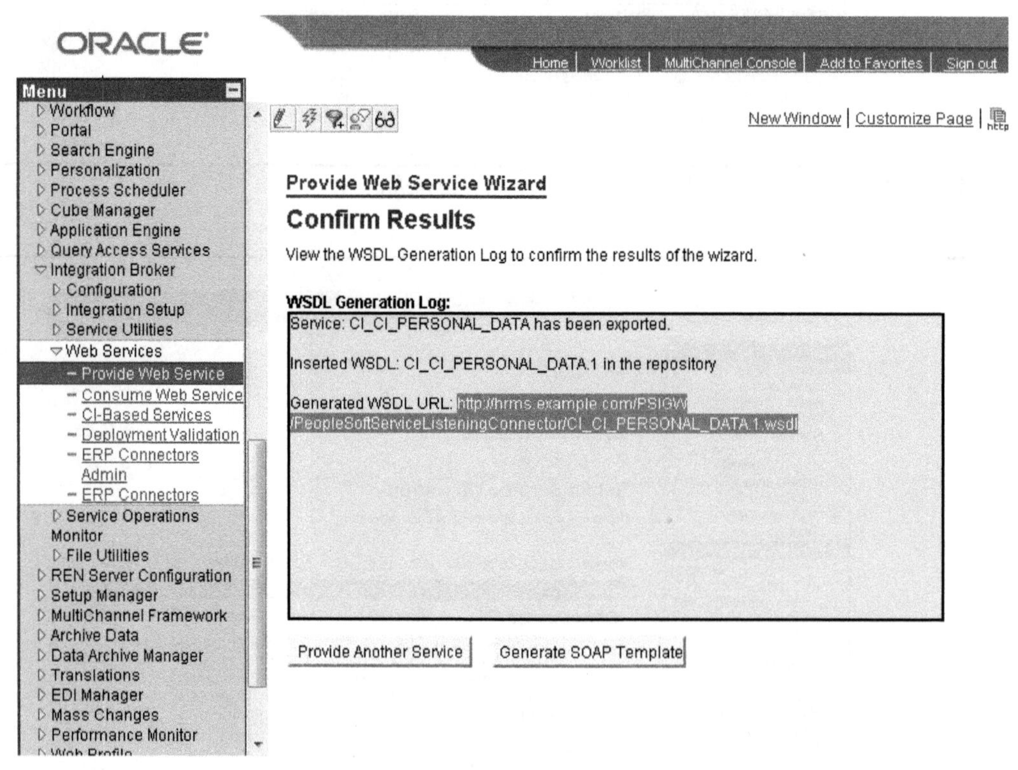

FIGURE 14-6. *Provide Web Service Wizard confirmation page*

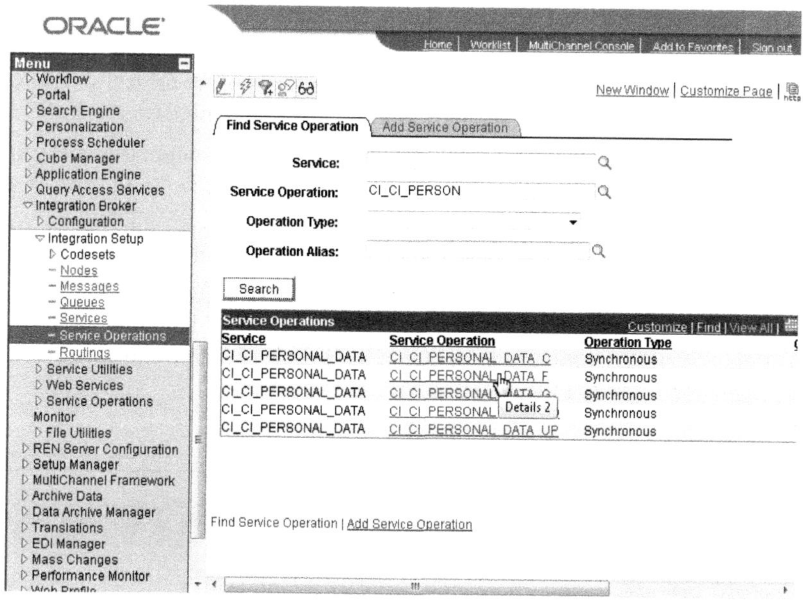

FIGURE 14-7. *Service Operations search page for the CI_CI_PERSONAL_DATA service*

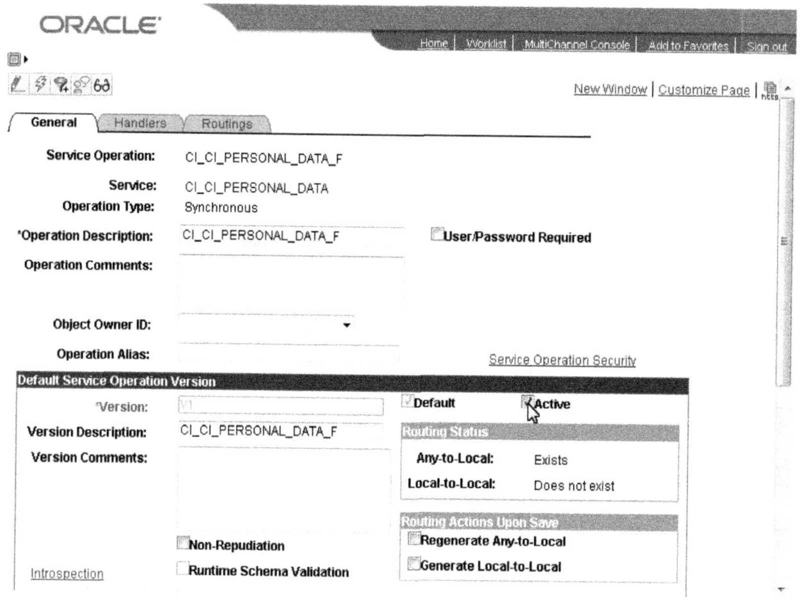

ORACLE

Home | Worklist | MultiChannel Console | Add to Favorites | Sign out

New Window | Customize Page

General | Handlers | Routings

Service Operation: CI_CI_PERSONAL_DATA_F

Service: CI_CI_PERSONAL_DATA

Operation Type: Synchronous

*Operation Description: CI_CI_PERSONAL_DATA_F

User/Password Required

Operation Comments:

Object Owner ID:

Operation Alias:

Service Operation Security

Default Service Operation Version

*Version: V1

Default

Active

Version Description: CI_CI_PERSONAL_DATA_F

Routing Status

Version Comments:

Any-to-Local: Exists

Local-to-Local: Does not exist

Routing Actions Upon Save

Non-Repudiation

Regenerate Any-to-Local

Introspection

Runtime Schema Validation

Generate Local-to-Local

FIGURE 14-8. *CI_CI_PERSONAL_DATA_F service operation*

12. Select the Service Operation Security link (just above the Active check box). This opens the Web Service Access page, where you can specify which permission lists can execute this service operation.
13. Add the `APT_CUSTOM` permission list so that members of this list can execute the `CI_PERSONAL_DATA` Find service operation, as shown in Figure 14-9.
14. From the `CI_CI_PERSONAL_DATA_F` service page, switch to the Handlers tab. The CI `OnRequest` PeopleCode event handler is inactive by default. Activate this handler, as shown in Figure 14-10.
15. The last inactive service operation definition is the routing. Switch to the Routings tab. To enable the autogenerated any-to-local routing, click the Selected check box, and then click the Activate Selected Routings button, as shown in Figure 14-11.
16. Repeat steps 10 through 15 (depicted in Figures 14-7 through 14-11) for the service operation `CI_CI_PERSONAL_DATA_G`.

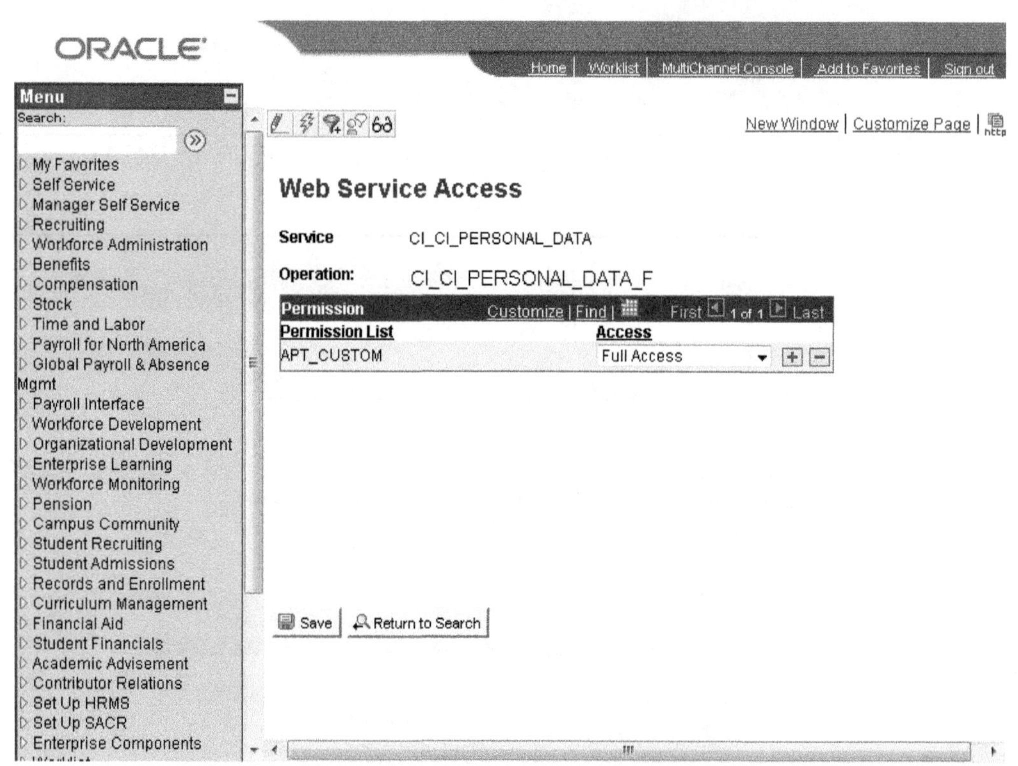

FIGURE 14-9. *CI_CI_PERSONAL_DATA Web Service Access page*

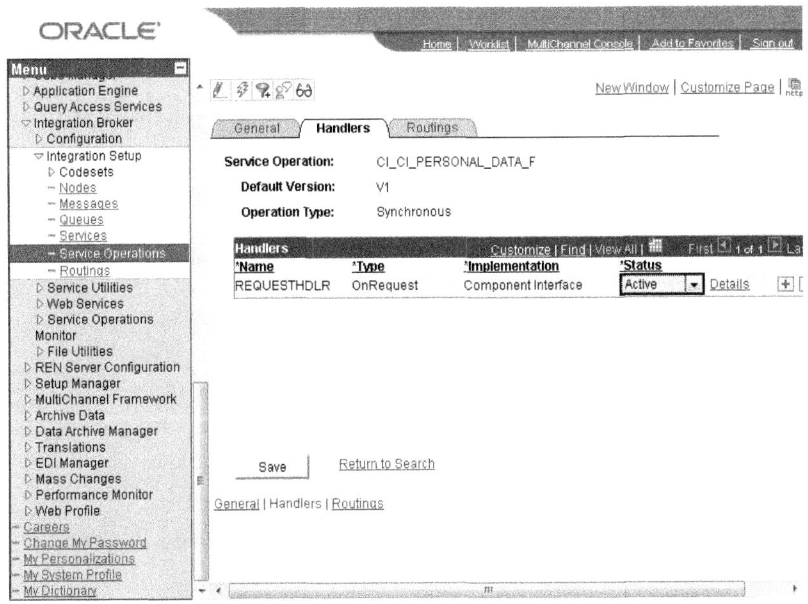

FIGURE 14-10. *CI_CI_PERSONAL_DATA Web Service PeopleCode event handler*

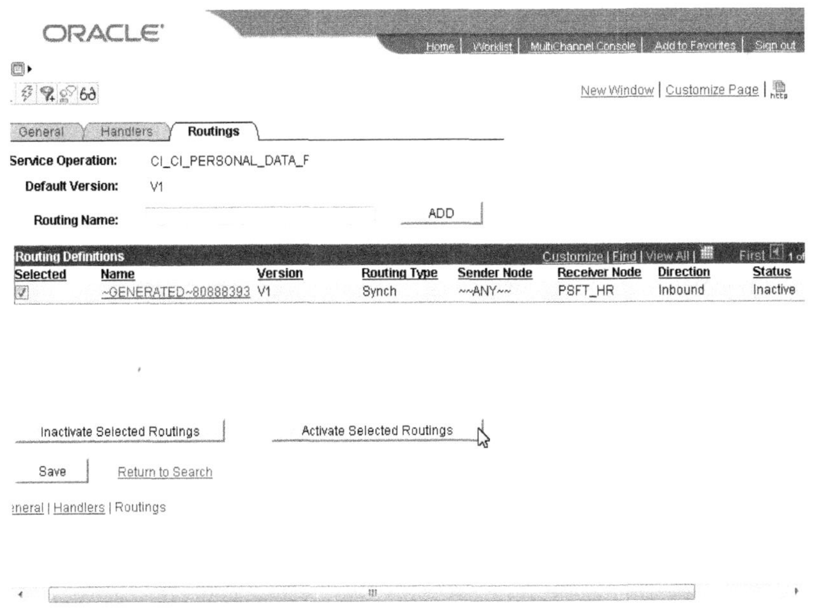

FIGURE 14-11. *CI_CI_PERSONAL_DATA service Routings tab*

Testing the WSDL URL

Before moving onto JDeveloper, I suggest testing the WSDL URL in your web browser. Navigate to the WSDL URL you copied from the Provide Web Service Wizard and verify that PeopleSoft returns an XML WSDL document. The first time I tested the WSDL URL, PeopleSoft presented me with the following error document (the important information is in bold).

```
<?xml version="1.0" ?>
<SOAP-ENV:Envelope
    xmlns:SOAP-ENV="http://schemas.xmlsoap.org/soap/envelope/">
  <SOAP-ENV:Body>
    <SOAP-ENV:Fault>
      <faultcode>SOAP-ENV:Server</faultcode>
      <faultstring>null</faultstring>
      <detail>
        <IBResponse type="error">
          <DefaultTitle>Integration Broker Response</DefaultTitle>
          <StatusCode>20</StatusCode>
          <MessageID>55</MessageID>
          <DefaultMessage>
            <![CDATA[UserName not defined in database. (158,55)]]>
          </DefaultMessage>
          <MessageParameters>
            <Parameter><![CDATA[ANONYMOUS]]></Parameter>
          </MessageParameters>
        </IBResponse>
      </detail>
    </SOAP-ENV:Fault>
  </SOAP-ENV:Body>
</SOAP-ENV:Envelope>
```

Notice the error message "UserName not defined in database." This means the user defined for the ANONYMOUS Integration Broker node does not exist. Correct this by changing the ANONYMOUS node's user ID to a valid user ID. In my demo system, I chose user PS.

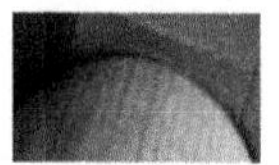

NOTE
If you receive the error "Unable to find a routing request corresponding to the incoming request message," verify that the service operations of the IB_UTILITY *service are active.*

Going Mobile with JDeveloper

The following example uses Oracle's JDeveloper 11.1.1.2.0 Studio Edition. The Studio Edition includes the Oracle ADF and JavaServer Faces (JSF) page designer. The ADF web service data control offers rapid development through JDeveloper's drag-and-drop data binding support. The remainder of this chapter describes how to create a web service data control and then bind that data control to user interface elements.

Creating a Fusion Web Application

JDeveloper uses an MVC design pattern for developing web-based applications. The Fusion Web Application template creates two projects: a Model project and a ViewController project. The ViewController project contains technologies for developing desktop web applications. We will use the Model project for our web service data control, and ignore the ViewController project.

Follow these steps to create the Fusion web app:

1. Launch JDeveloper and select New Application from the Application Navigator drop-down list, as shown in Figure 14-12.
2. In step 1 of the New Application wizard, name the application `MobileDC` (an abbreviation for Mobile Data Control) and select the Fusion Web Application template, as shown in Figure 14-13. Click Next to continue.

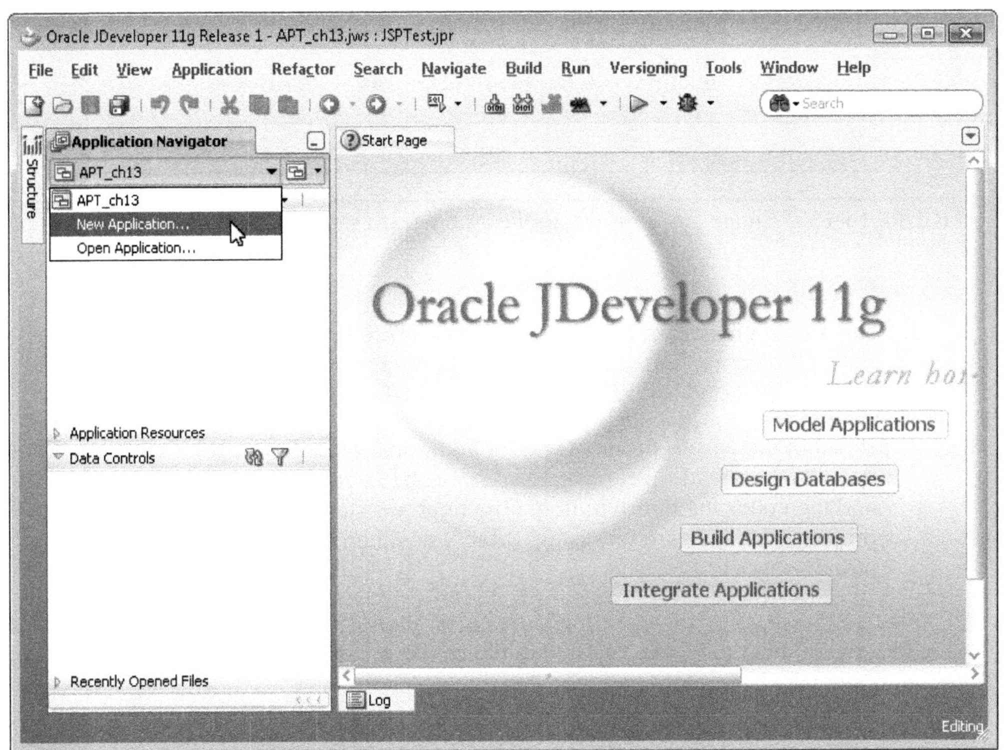

FIGURE 14-12. *Choosing to create a new application*

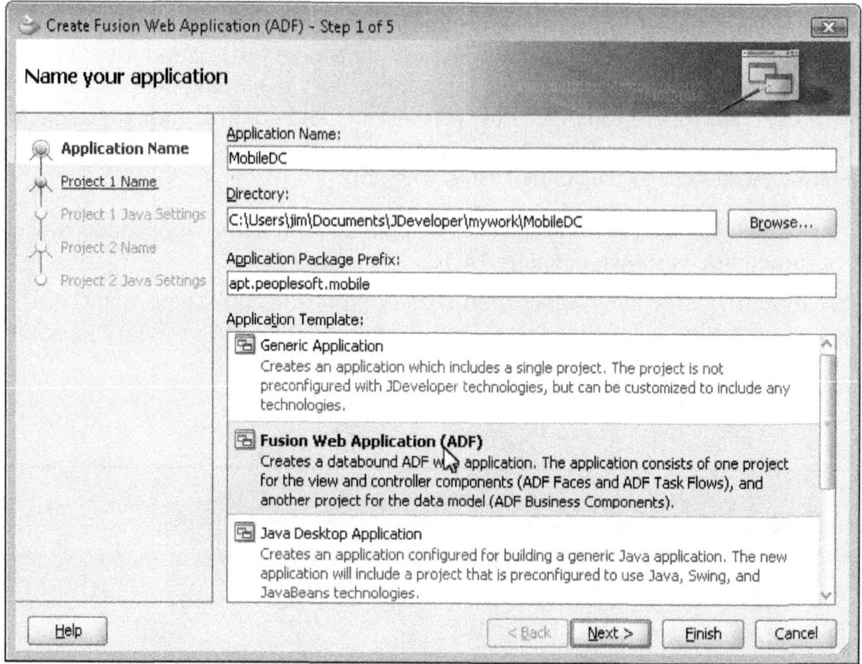

FIGURE 14-13. *Create Fusion Web Application wizard step 1*

3. Our Model project requires the Web Services project technology. In step 2 of the wizard, on the Project Technologies tab, move the Web Services technology from the Available list to the Selected list, as shown in Figure 14-14. Click Next to continue.

4. Step 3 of the wizard prompts you for additional Model project Java settings. Set the default package to `apt.peoplesoft.mobile.model`, as shown in Figure 14-15, and then click the Finish button. (The final two steps configure the ViewController project, which we are not using. Later, we will add a new project for developing mobile pages.)

After completing the Create Fusion Web Application wizard, your JDeveloper environment should appear similar to Figure 14-16. (I minimized some of the JDeveloper docked windows to reveal more of the JDeveloper designer area.)

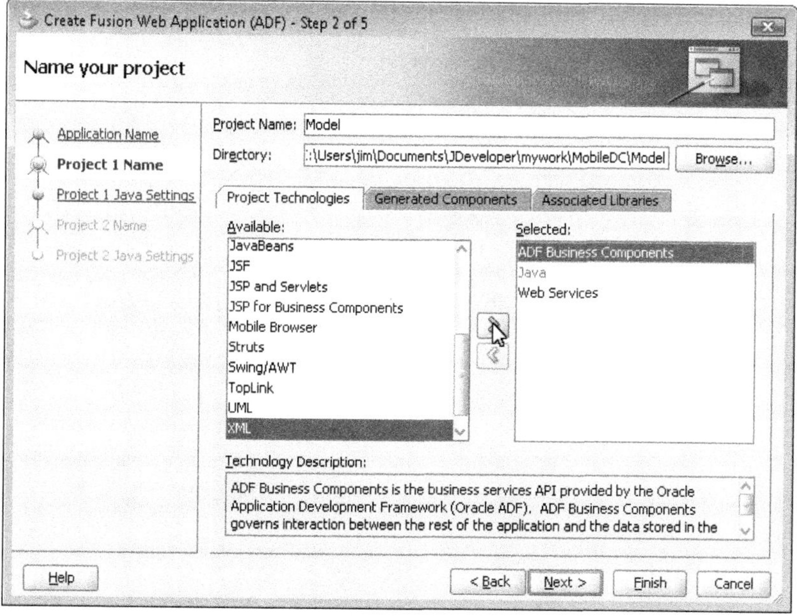

FIGURE 14-14. *Create Fusion Web Application wizard step 2*

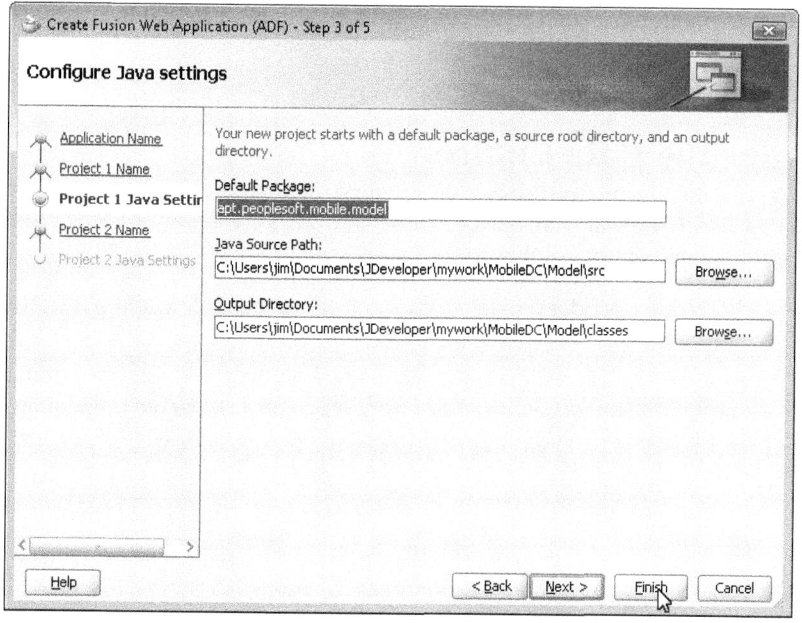

FIGURE 14-15. *Create Fusion Web Application wizard step 3*

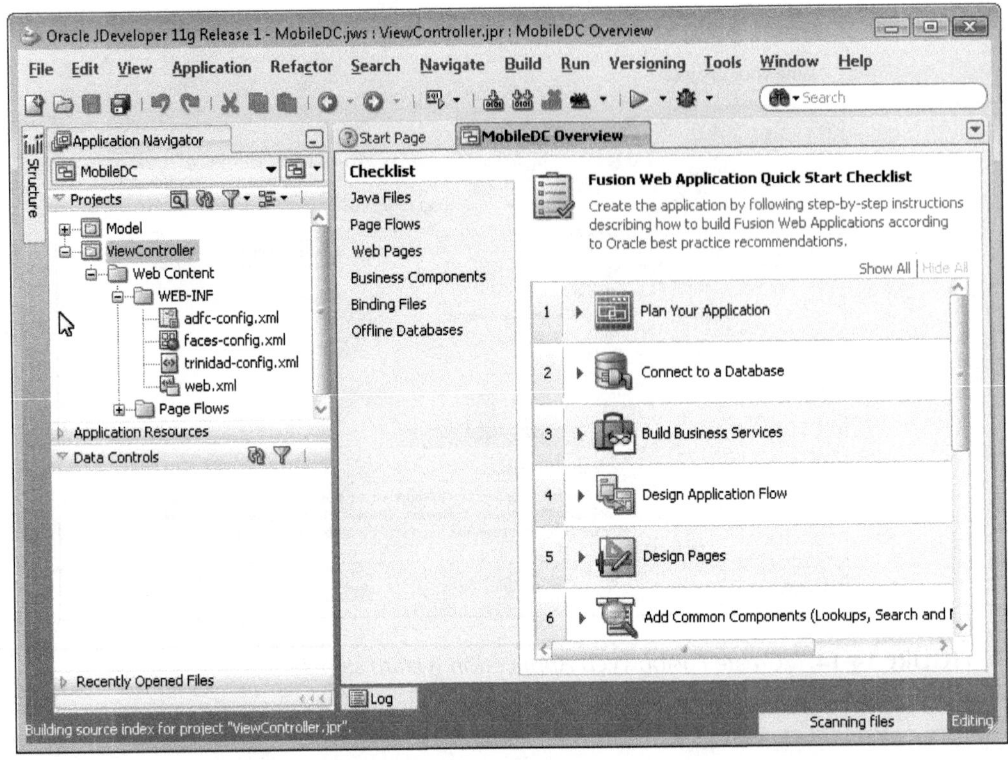

FIGURE 14-16. *JDeveloper environment after creating a new Fusion web application*

Creating the Data Control

A web service data control provides a design-time mechanism for collecting web service parameters, executing that web service, and then displaying the results of the web service. Create a web service data control as follows:

1. Right-click the Model project in the Application Navigator and select New from the context menu, as shown in Figure 14-17.
2. In the New Gallery dialog, select Business Tier, then Web Services from the Categories list and Web Service Data Control from the Items list, as shown in Figure 14-18. Then click OK.

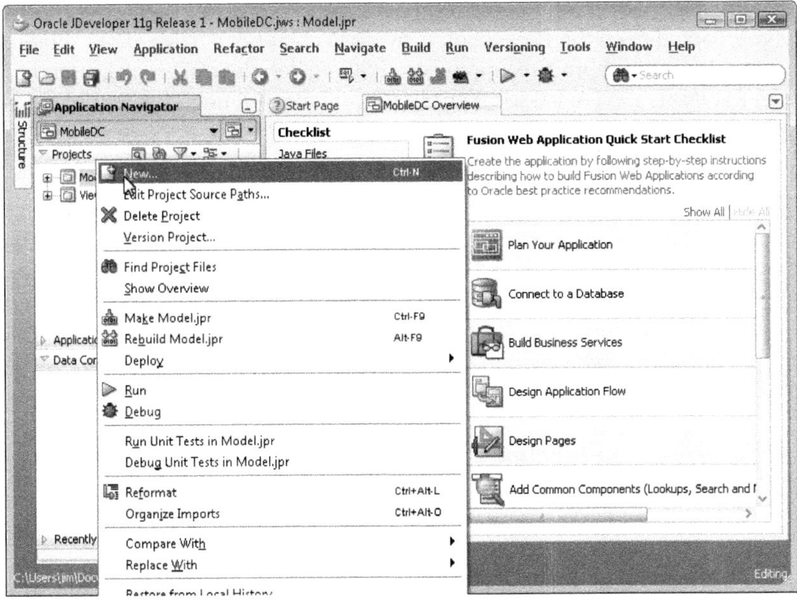

FIGURE 14-17. *Selecting to create a new project*

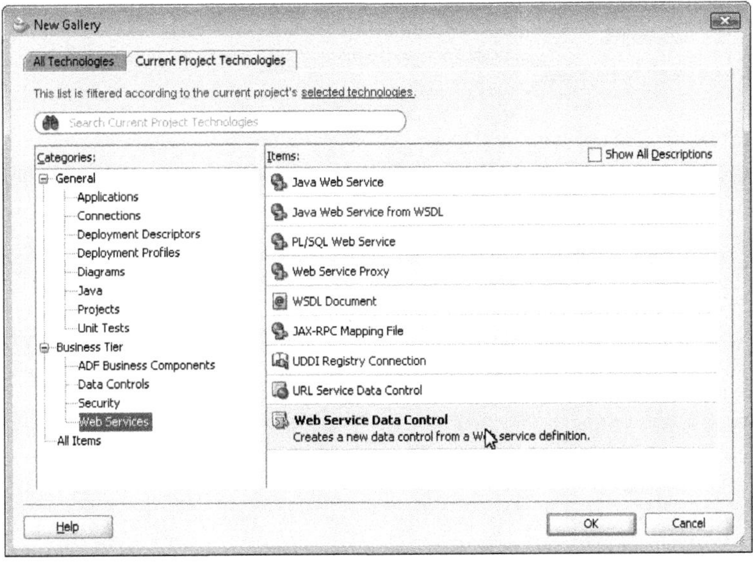

FIGURE 14-18. *Choosing to create a new web service data control*

3. In step 1 of the Create Web Service Data Control wizard, enter `PersonalData` in the Name field. For the URL, enter the `CI_CI_PERSONAL_DATA` web service WSDL URL you copied from the PeopleSoft Provide Web Service Wizard. As shown in Figure 14-19, my URL is http://hrms.example.com/PSIGW/PeopleSoftServiceListeningConnector/CI_CI_PERSONAL_DATA.1.wsdl. Your URL will have a different server name and may contain the name of your default local node.
4. Tabbing out of the URL field will cause JDeveloper to load and parse the WSDL. Click the Next button to move to step 2.
5. Step 2 of the Create Web Service Data Control wizard asks you which service operations you want to enable. Figure 14-20 shows the two service operations we enabled in PeopleSoft. The Find (_F) operation is similar to a transaction search page, in that it allows you to find transactions based on transaction key values. This differs from the Get (_G) operation, which returns an actual transaction. Click Next to continue.
6. Accept the defaults in step 3. PeopleSoft includes all the XSD information necessary for JDeveloper to parse the service operation response. Click Next to move to step 4.
7. In step 4, specify the username and password the data control will use to connect to PeopleSoft, as shown in Figure 14-21.

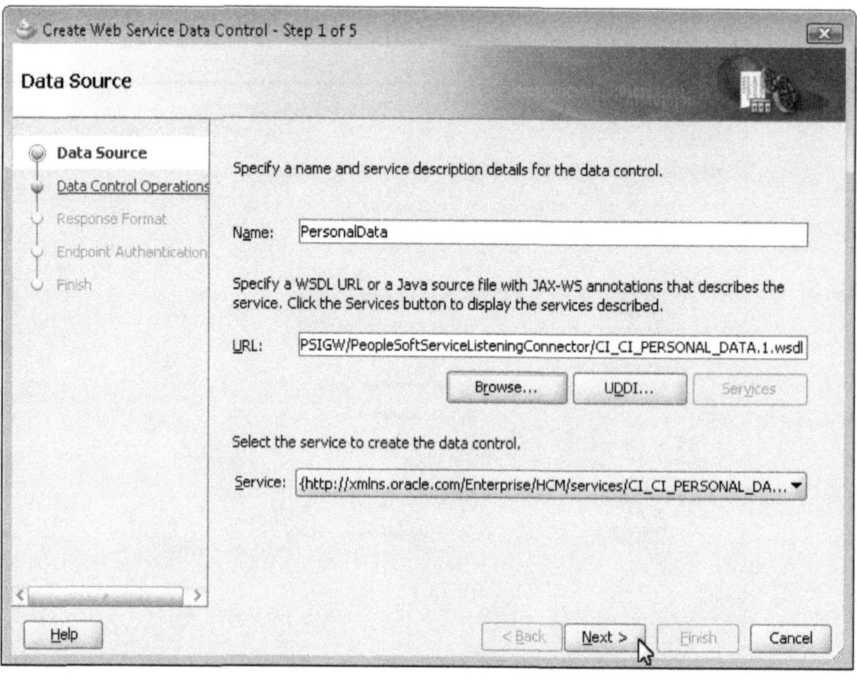

FIGURE 14-19. *Create Web Service Data Control wizard step 1*

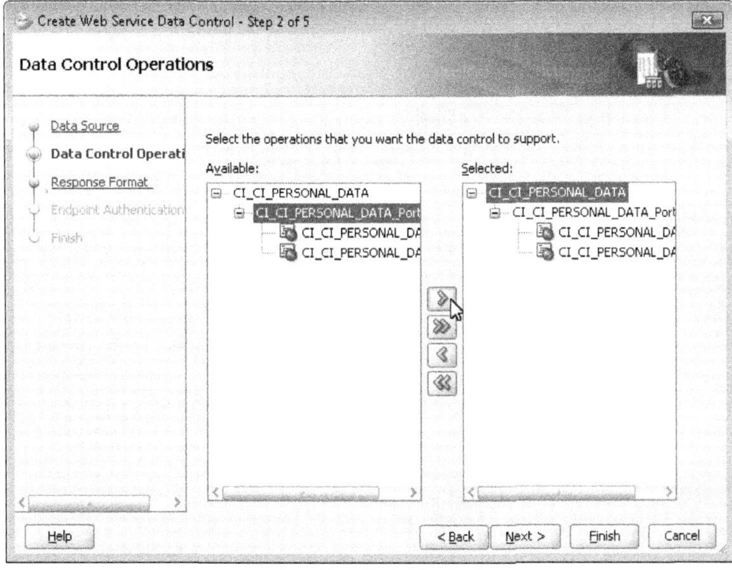

FIGURE 14-20. *Create Web Service Data Control wizard step 2*

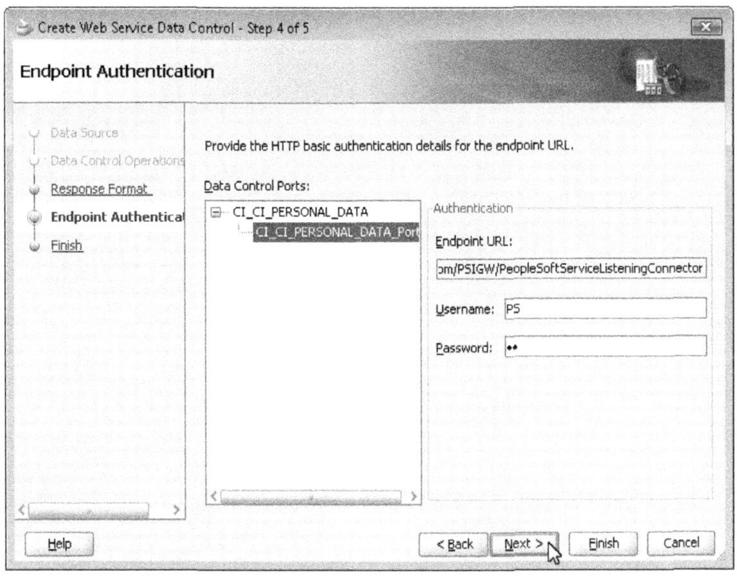

FIGURE 14-21. *The Create Web Service Data Control wizard step 4*

8. Step 5 of the wizard displays a summary of the options you selected in the previous four steps, as shown in Figure 14-22. Click Finish to create the web service data control. JDeveloper will create several source code files in the Model project.

Figure 14-23 shows JDeveloper after creating the new `PersonalData` web service data control. (I minimized several JDeveloper docked windows to display the control as well as some of the new source files.)

Creating the View

The ViewController project created by the Fusion Web Application template uses the ADF Faces JSF implementation. Unfortunately, ADF Faces components do not support mobile devices. For mobile applications, JDeveloper delivers the Trinidad[1] JSF alternative. Trinidad is a JSF component set originally developed by Oracle, and then donated to the Apache Software Foundation. Since we are creating a mobile project, we will ignore the ViewController project created by the Fusion Web Application template and build a new project that contains the appropriate scope for mobile development.

Creating the MobileView Project

Follow these steps to add a new project for our view:

1. Create a new Generic project named `MobileView`.
2. In step 1 of the wizard, select the Mobile Browser technology from the Available list and move it to the Selected list, as shown in Figure 14-24.

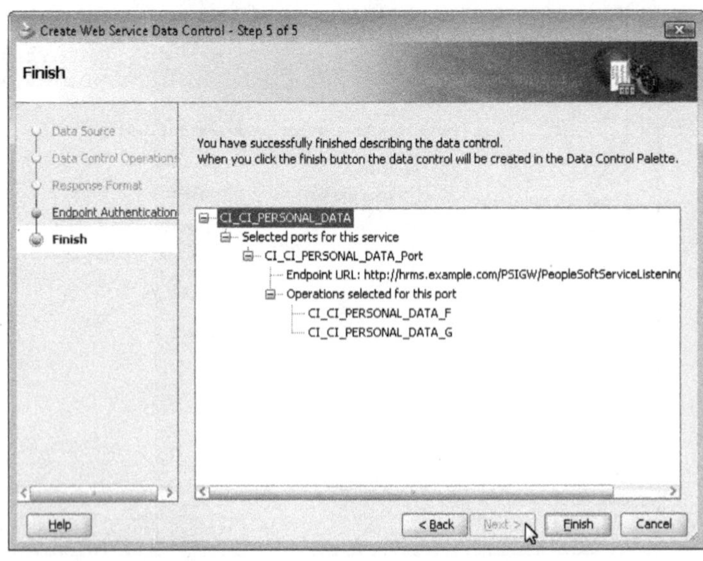

FIGURE 14-22. *Create Web Service Data Control wizard step 5*

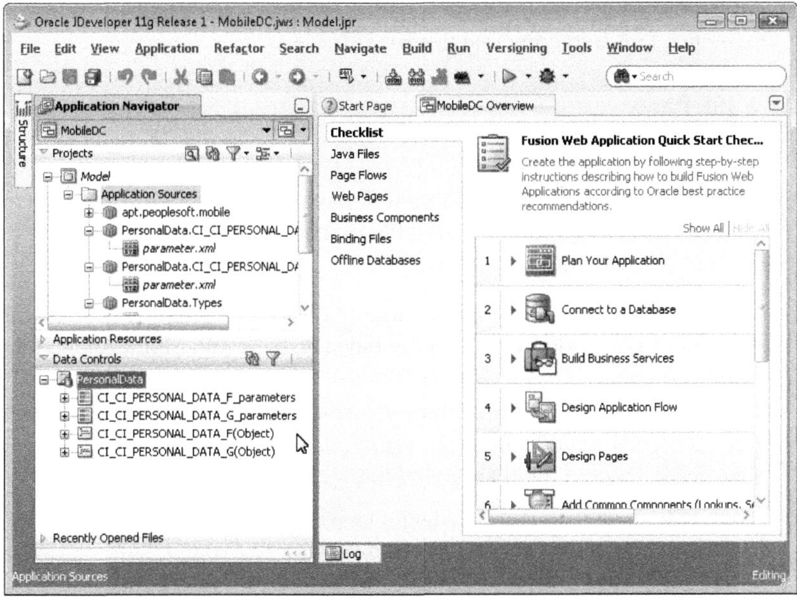

FIGURE 14-23. *JDeveloper after creating the PersonalData web service data control*

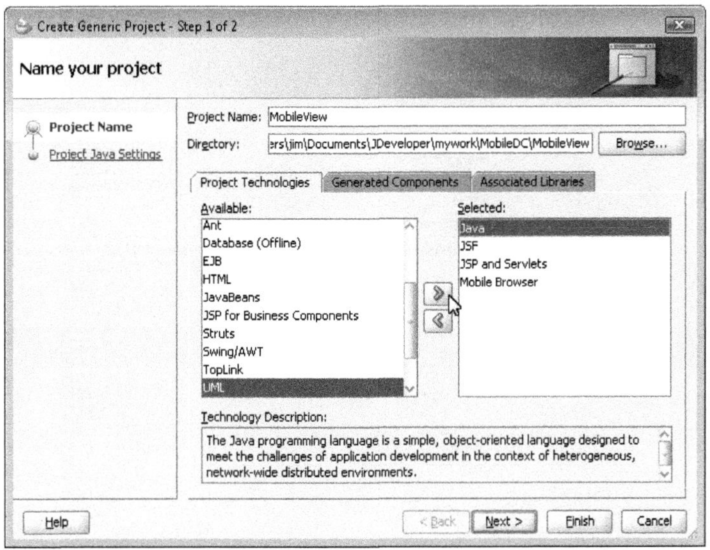

FIGURE 14-24. *Create Generic Project wizard step 1*

3. JDeveloper enables a second step for configuring the project's Java settings. Set the default package to `apt.peoplesoft.mobile.view`, as shown in Figure 14-25, and then click Finish to complete the wizard.

Adding a JSF Page

The JSF controller manages application state in a manner similar to the PeopleSoft component buffer. Rather than registering components (pages) into a portal registry, JSF uses a page flow map. JDeveloper represents this map as a diagram of pages showing the navigation cases between each page. JSF stores these navigation rules in a file named faces-config.xml.

Follow these steps to add a JSF page:

1. Open the faces-config.xml file by double-clicking the file in the Application Navigator. If the file is not readily visible in the navigator, expand MobileView, then Web Content, then WEB-INF.
2. The JDeveloper faces-config editor displays a page flow diagram editor for editing JSF controller page navigation cases. Using the Component Palette on the right, add a JSF Page component to the diagram editor.
3. When you add a new page, JDeveloper will provide a default name of untiled1.jsp. Change the name of this file to **search.jspx**, as shown in Figure 14-26. (The JSPX file format is similar to JSP, but it conforms to the XML specification.)

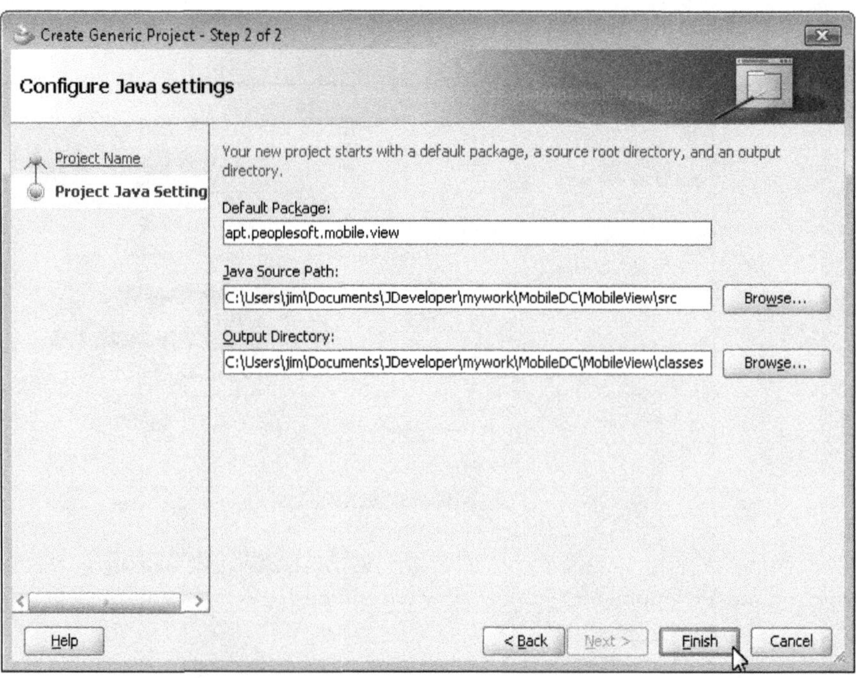

FIGURE 14-25. *Create Generic Project wizard step 2*

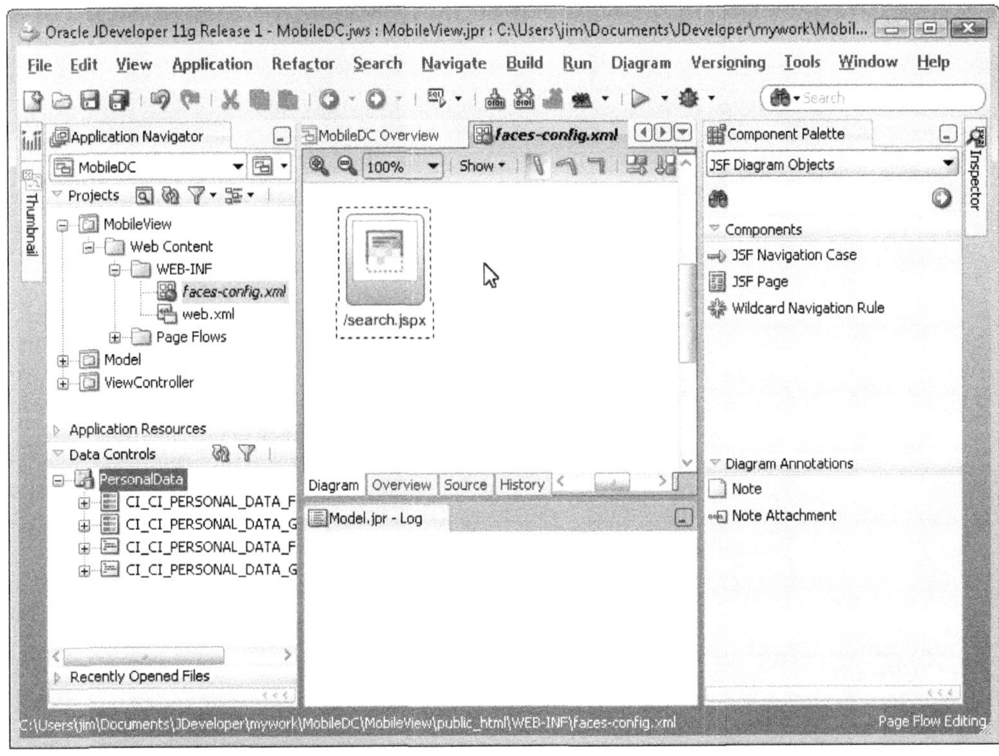

FIGURE 14-26. *The project's faces-config.xml file*

4. Adding a new page to the faces-config.xml file generates the appropriate JSF metadata for rendering and managing a page, but it doesn't actually create the page. From the page flow diagram you can tell whether a page exists by the type of icon used to represent the page. JDeveloper 11.1.1.2.0 represents missing pages as square icons showing a partial document. (Looking at the icon in Figure 14-26, you might think that half the document had been erased or dissolved.) Double-click the search.jspx page icon to create the actual search.jspx file.
5. In the Create JSF Page dialog, make sure the Create as XML Document check box and Render in Mobile Device check box are selected, as shown in Figure 14-27. Click the OK button to create the page.

When you finish with the Create JSF Page dialog, JDeveloper will create the search.jspx file and open the JSP graphical designer. Now we will design our search page.

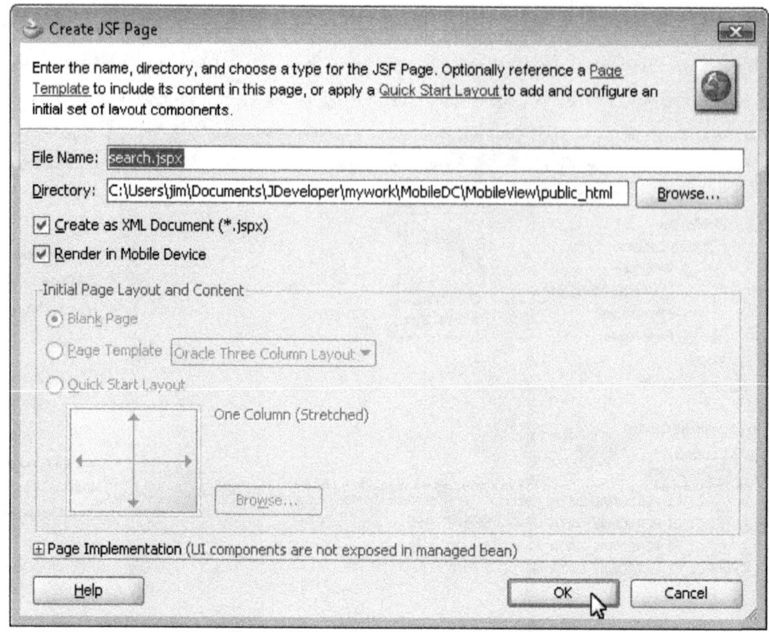

FIGURE 14-27. *Create JSF Page dialog*

Designing the Search Page

The JSP graphical designer represents the empty canvas onto which we will design our search page. First, we'll add the form.

Adding the Form Component

Follow these steps to add the parameter form:

1. With the search.jspx page open in the designer, and the Data Controls palette visible, expand the PersonalData node, then CI_CI_PERSONAL_DATA_F_parameters node. Drag the parameter child node onto the search.jspx page and release your mouse.
2. When you drag a data control onto a page, JDeveloper will try to convert the data control into a user interface component. JDeveloper will evaluate the context of the data control and display a context menu showing you a list of appropriate user interface components. Since the parameter node represents our search page criteria, select Form | Trinidad Form from the context menu, as shown in Figure 14-28.
3. In the Edit Form Fields dialog, enter a display label for each field, using Figure 14-29 as a guide. Then click OK.

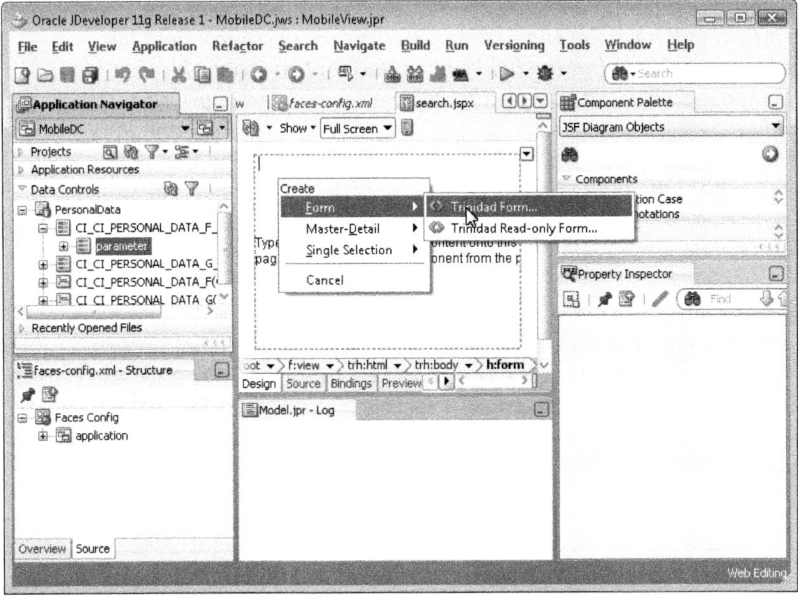

FIGURE 14-28. *JDeveloper parameter form*

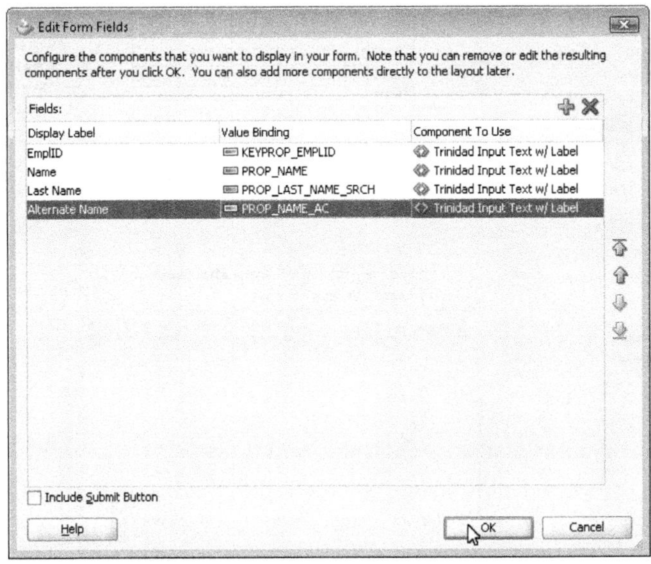

FIGURE 14-29. *The search criteria form's Edit Form Fields dialog*

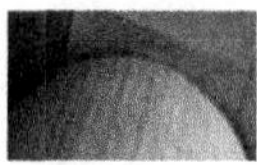

NOTE

When the Edit Form Fields dialog appears, the display label for each field will have the value <default>. Each data control field has metadata that describes the field's label, tooltip text, control type, and validation rules. If you plan to use the same data control on multiple pages, you can save time, standardize labels, and centralize administration by defining your user interface metadata within the data control rather than on a page-by-page basis. The value <default> tells JDeveloper to use the data control's metadata instead of hard-coded values.

Figure 14-30 shows the search.jspx page designer after adding the PersonalData parameter form. Take a moment to investigate the page, form, and input field properties before continuing. Notice that the EmplID field value is set to `#{bindings.KEYPROP_EMPLID.inputValue}`. The `#{}` notation tells the JSF controller that the EmplID text field value is bound to the data control's `KEYPROP_EMPLID` parameter field. You can use the `#{}` and `${}` expression language[2] constructs to set values for most JSF element properties.

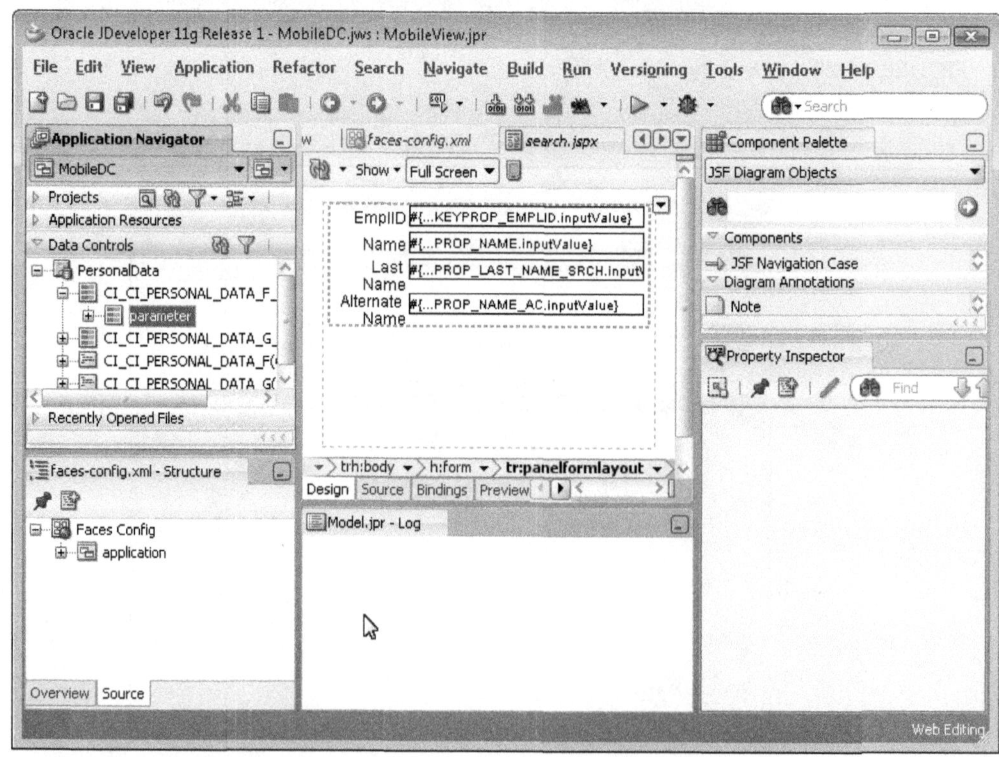

FIGURE 14-30. *The search.jspx page with the PersonalData parameter form*

When we chose the Trinidad Form component, JDeveloper added a form layout to align labels and text fields. Layouts use various HTML strategies to display user interface controls in the most natural order for the layout's designated purpose and device. You do not need to use layouts, but they are highly recommended.

Displaying the Footer Facet

We need to add a Search button underneath the search page parameters. After entering search criteria, a user will click the Search button to execute the web service and display search results. To create the Search button, we will drag the data control's find method onto the search.jspx page. We could drag the method onto the page directly below the parameter form, but there is a more appropriate place for form buttons.

Many JSF layouts contain facets. *Facets* are sections of layouts that designate a particular location within a layout. The Trinidad panelFormLayout element has a footer facet specifically designed for form action buttons.

With the search.jspx page open in JDeveloper, display the Structure window and navigate to jsp:root | f:view | trh:html | trh:body | h:form | tr:panelFormLayout. Right-click the tr:panelFormLayout element and select Facets - Panel Form Layout | Footer from the context menu, as shown in Figure 14-31. You will see the layout's facet in the page designer.

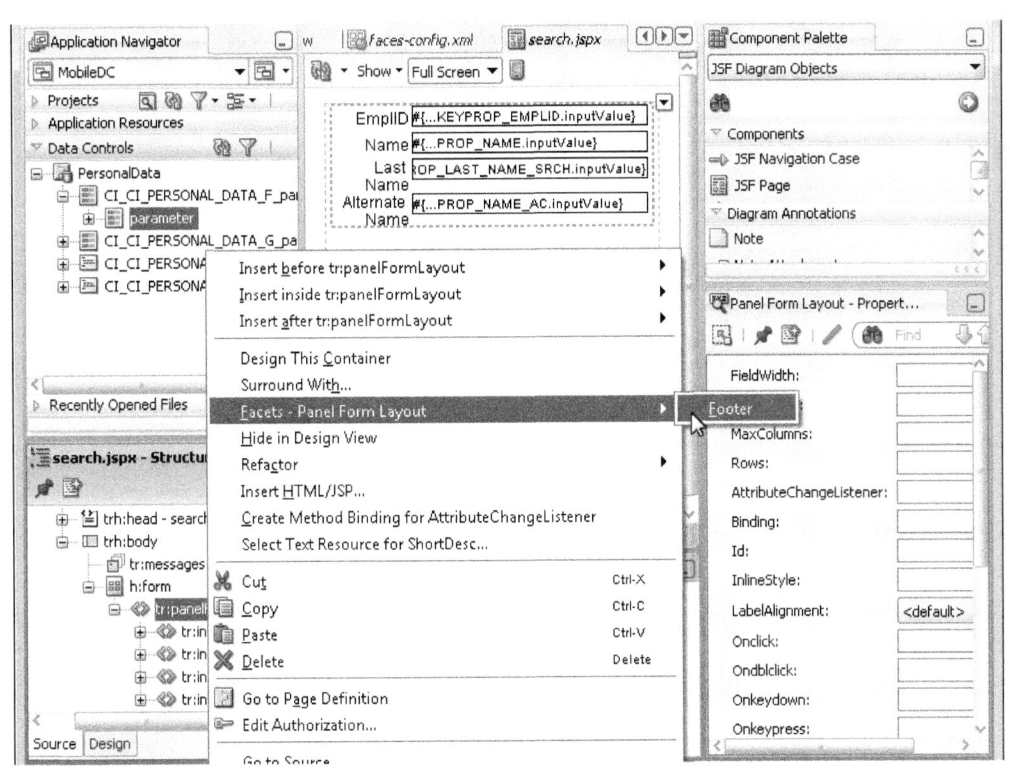

FIGURE 14-31. *Choosing the Footer layout facet*

Take a moment to review the three Insert items available on the panel form layout context menu (Figure 14-31). You will see that choosing each of these menu items shows a list of elements that you can place before, inside, or after the current element, using the Structure browser.

When adding user interface components to a page, I sometimes find it easier to use the Structure browser, rather than drag and drop. Using the Structure browser offers the same wizard-based declarative experience as drag and drop, but ensures that the inserted element lands in the exact location you desire. Sometimes it is difficult to drop a user interface component inside a particular container. If you go directly to the JSPX source code, you have absolute control over the placement of user interface controls, but lose the wizard-based experience offered by the JDeveloper design-time interface.

Creating the Search Button and Results Table

Now let's add the Search button and the search results table, with a separator after the button to delimit the criteria from the search results.

1. Drag the `CI_CI_PERSONAL_DATA_F (Object)` element from the PersonalData data control onto the panel form layout footer facet.
2. JDeveloper displays a context menu containing user interface control options. Select the Method | Trinidad Button menu item, as shown in Figure 14-32.
3. JDeveloper displays the Edit Action Binding dialog, as shown in Figure 14-33. Accept the default values displayed in this wizard and click the OK button.

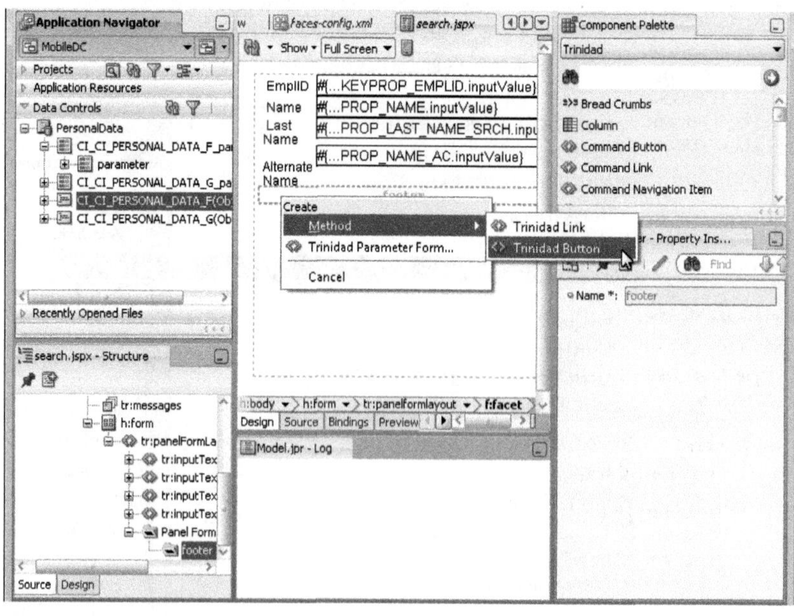

FIGURE 14-32. *Creating a button to execute a web service method*

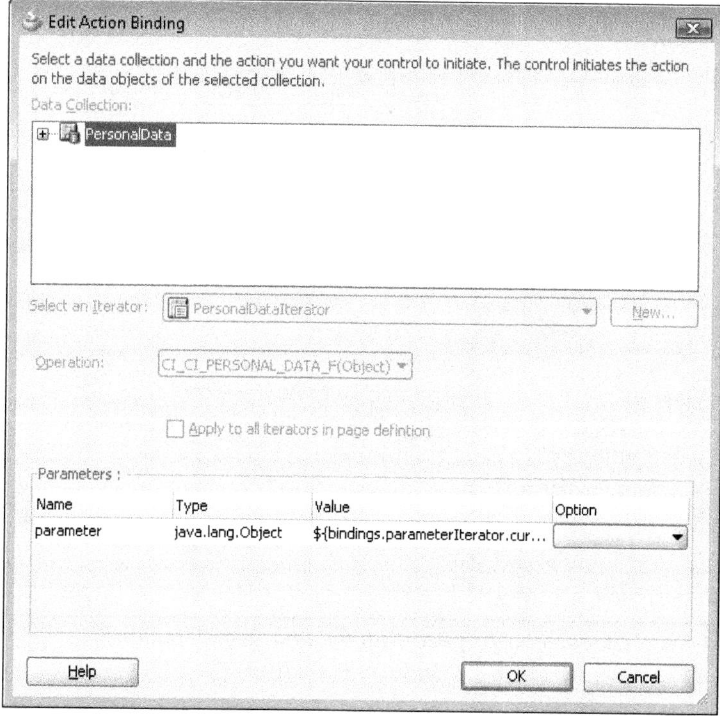

FIGURE 14-33. *Edit Action Binding dialog*

4. Our search page now has a button named `CI_CI_PERSONAL_DATA_F`. When a user clicks this button, the ADF data binding runtime will convert the parameter form into a web service request, and then call the `CI_CI_PERSONAL_DATA_F` web service operation. Highlight the button and then use the Property Inspector on the right side of the window to change the Text property to Search, as shown in Figure 14-34.
5. In the Component Palette on the top right, change the component list to Trinidad. Scroll down to the Separator component and drag it beneath the panel form layout footer (the Search button is inside the footer), as shown in Figure 14-35.
6. In the Data Controls palette, navigate to the PersonalData | CI_PERSONAL_DATA_F(Object) | Return | CI_PERSONAL_DATA node. This node contains the PeopleSoft `PERSONAL_DATA` component's search record list box fields. Drag the CI_PERSONAL_DATA node onto the search.jspx page below the separator.

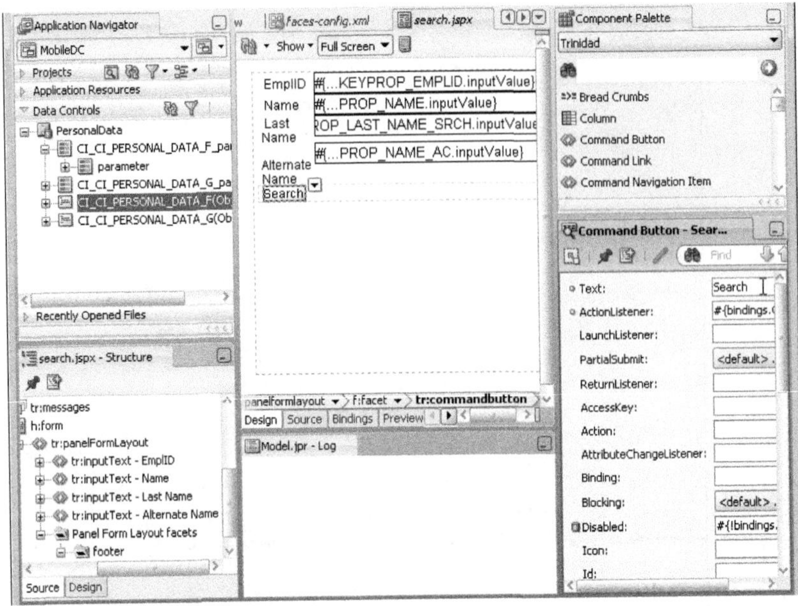

FIGURE 14-34. *The search.jspx page with the new Search button*

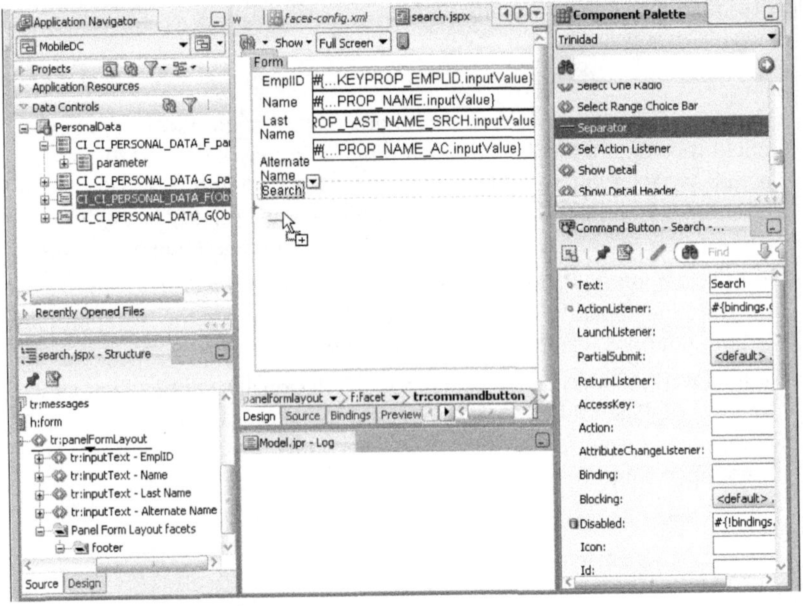

FIGURE 14-35. *The Trinidad separator control placed on the search.jspx page*

7. JDeveloper displays a context menu containing user interface elements appropriate for the data control's return value. Select Table | Trinidad Read-only Table from this context menu, as shown in Figure 14-36.
8. JDeveloper opens the Edit Table Columns dialog. Just as you did with the Edit Form Fields dialog, enter a label for each field, as shown in Figure 14-37.

Figure 14-38 shows the search.jspx page after adding the search results table.

Setting the Data Control's Refresh Properties

We have now built enough of the personal data search application to test it in a web browser. If you test this page, it will initially display as expected, with no data. After entering search criteria and clicking Search, the ADF runtime will attempt to execute the web service, but it will do so prior to updating the data control's search parameters.

The default behavior of the web service data control is to update the data control's result set on the first post after the initial display (also known as a *postback*). ADF will execute the web service again after updating the data control's parameters with the values entered in the page's

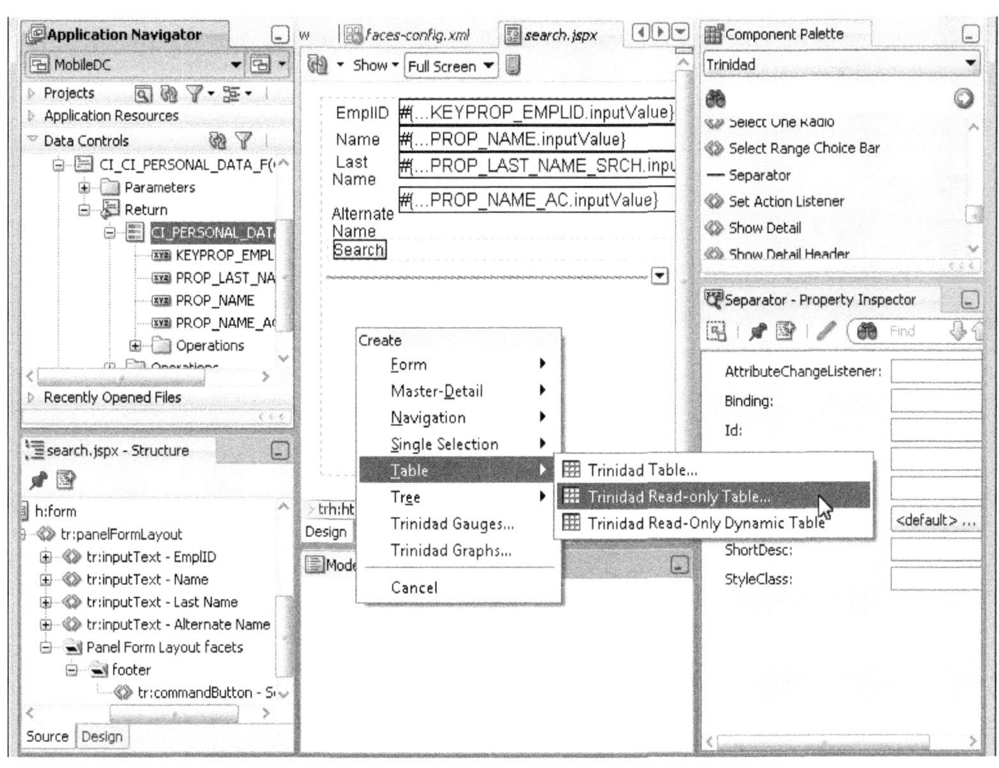

FIGURE 14-36. *Web service data control search results table*

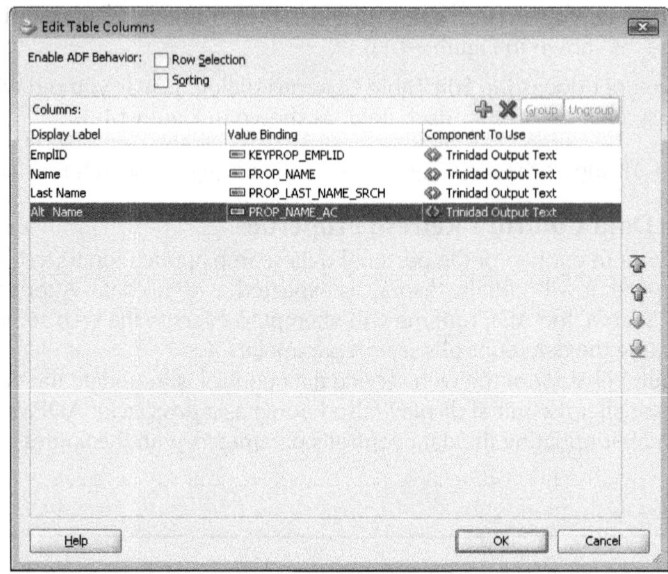

FIGURE 14-37. *The search results' Edit Table Columns dialog*

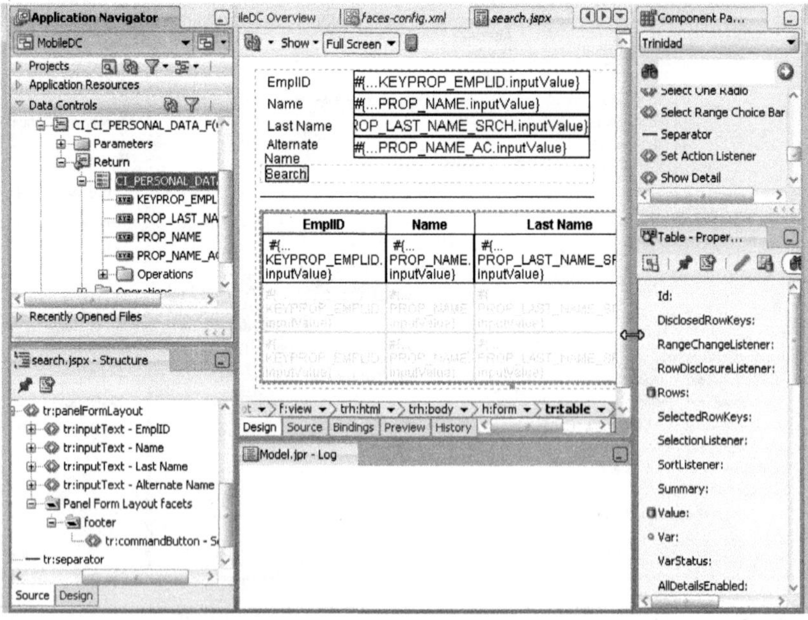

FIGURE 14-38. *The search.jspx page with the search results table*

form fields. Using network-sniffing software like Wireshark, you will see that ADF executes the web service twice. We can alter this default behavior by changing the table binding's Refresh property.

We also need to ensure that ADF doesn't refresh the data control's results if the data control has no parameters. We use the RefreshCondition property to tell ADF when it is acceptable to refresh the data control's result set. We will set the RefreshCondition property to `#{ !empty bindings.KEYPROP_EMPLID.inputValue}`. This expression tests for a value in the EmplID field.

Follow these steps to change the Refresh and RefreshCondition properties:

1. With the search.jspx page open in JDeveloper, switch to the Bindings tab by clicking the Bindings button at the bottom of the page designer.
2. On the Bindings and Executables tab, find the Executables section and highlight the CI_PERSONAL_DATAIterator.
3. In the Property Inspector, find the Refresh property. It should have a value of <default> (deferred). Change the value of the Refresh property to renderModel, as shown in Figure 14-39. This will ensure that the data control isn't refreshed until after ADF updates its in-memory representation of the data control's search parameters.
4. In the Property Inspector, click the down arrow to the right of the RefreshCondition property and select Edit from the context menu, as shown in Figure 14-40.
5. In the Expression Builder, navigate to ADF Bindings | bindings | KEYPROP_EMPLID, as shown in Figure 14-41.

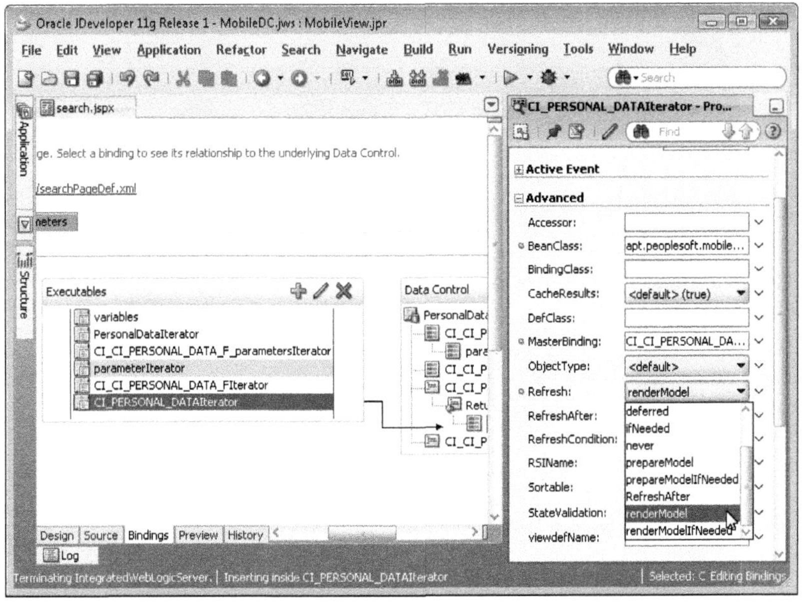

FIGURE 14-39. *The search.jspx CI_PERSONAL_DATAIterator Refresh property*

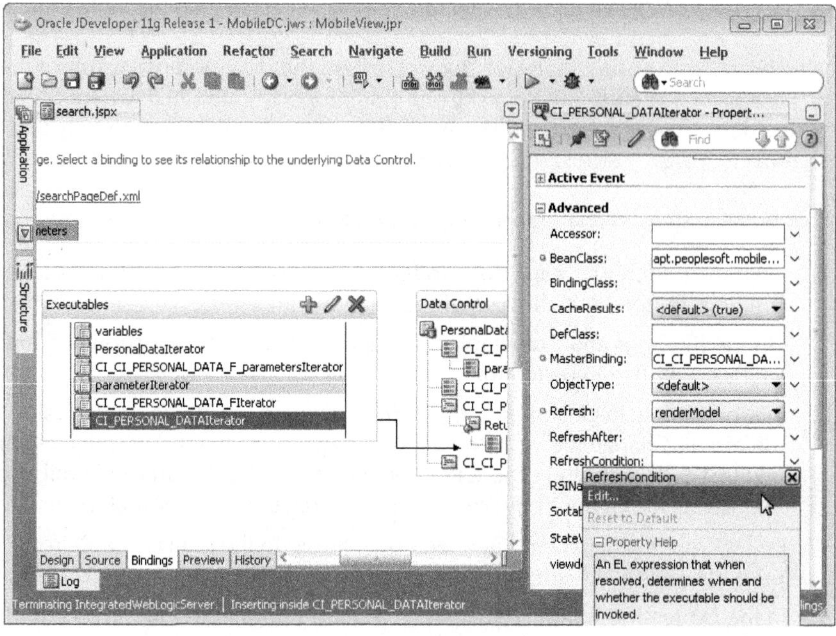

FIGURE 14-40. *RefreshCondition context menu*

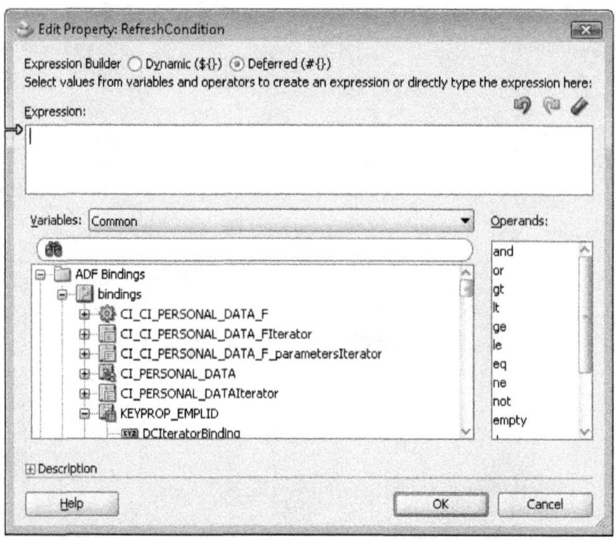

FIGURE 14-41. *RefreshCondition expression builder showing the KEYPROP_EMPLID node*

6. Expand the KEYPROP_EMPLID node, scroll down to the inputValue property, and select the inputValue. JDeveloper will create an expression similar to the one shown in Figure 14-42.
7. The expression shown in Figure 14-42 returns the actual value of the EmplID field. We want to determine only if the field has a value. The JSF expression language contains the `!empty` operator, which translates to "not empty." We can determine if the `EmplID` search parameter has a value by adding the `!empty` operator to the beginning of the field, as shown in Figure 14-43. The full RefreshCondition expression is as follows:

```
#{ !empty bindings.KEYPROP_EMPLID.inputValue}
```

Marking a Field as Required

With the data control refresh properties set as described in the previous section, it seems appropriate to mark the EmplID field as a required field.

1. Switch back to the search.jspx page's Design tab.
2. Highlight the EmplID Input Text element, and then find the Required property at the bottom of the Property Inspector.
3. Initially, the Required property will be set to an expression so that it derives its value from the data control's properties. Rather than update the data control, clear the value out of the EmplID Required field and then tab out of the Required property. JDeveloper will reset the property to its default value.
4. Revisit the Required property and select the value true, as shown in Figure 14-44.

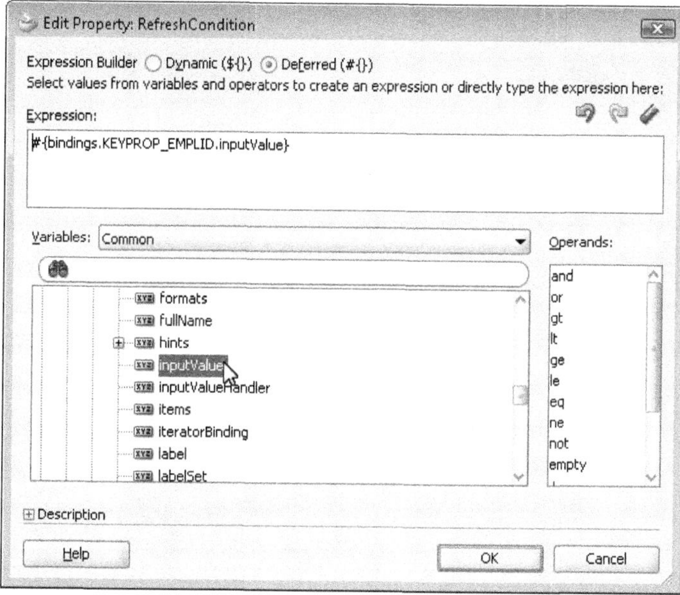

FIGURE 14-42. *KEYPROP_EMPLID.inputValue expression*

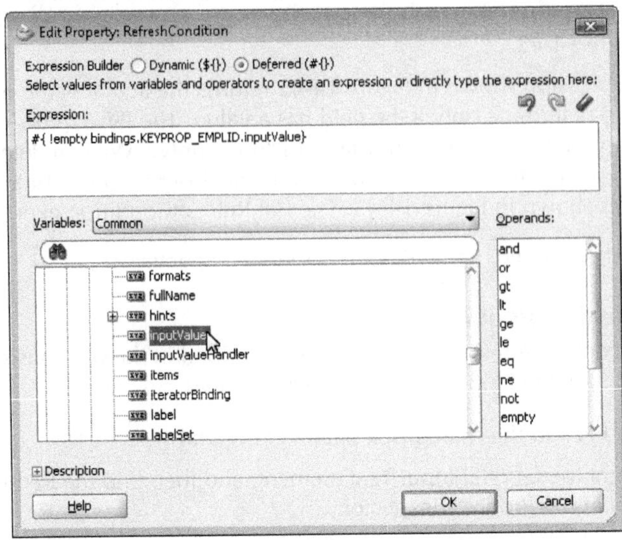

FIGURE 14-43. *Final RefreshCondition expression*

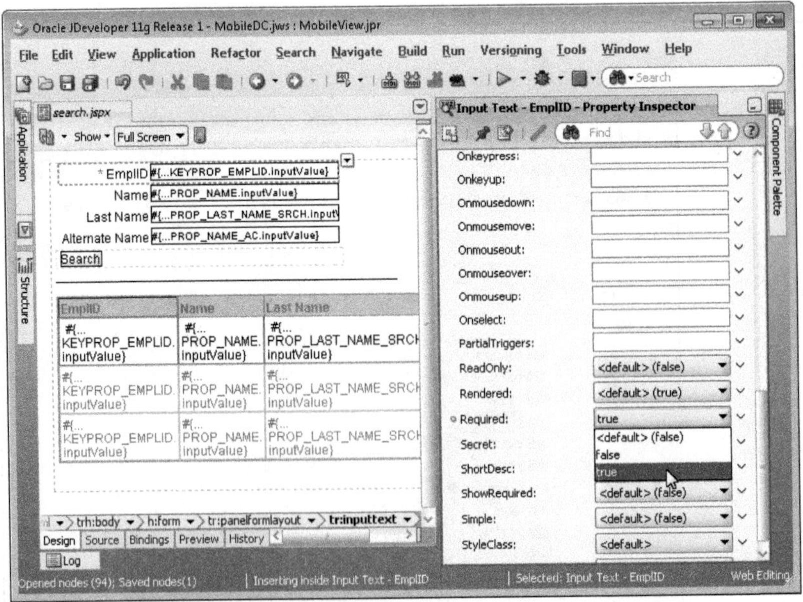

FIGURE 14-44. *EmplID Required property*

NOTE

When you switch from the page's bindings view to its design view, you may notice that the search results table background colors differ from the initial white background (see Figure 14-38). The yellow and gray background you see now are the actual background colors that your mobile device will display.

Testing the Search Page

It is finally time to test this page. Right-click in the page designer and select Run from the context menu, as shown in Figure 14-45.

JDeveloper will start the embedded WebLogic server, deploy the `MobileDC` web application, and then launch this page in your web browser, as shown in Figure 14-46.

To test the web service data control, enter **KU** in the EmplID field and **John** in the Name field, and then click the Search button. ADF will execute the web service, update the JSF component model, and display the updated results table in your web browser, as shown in the example in Figure 14-47.

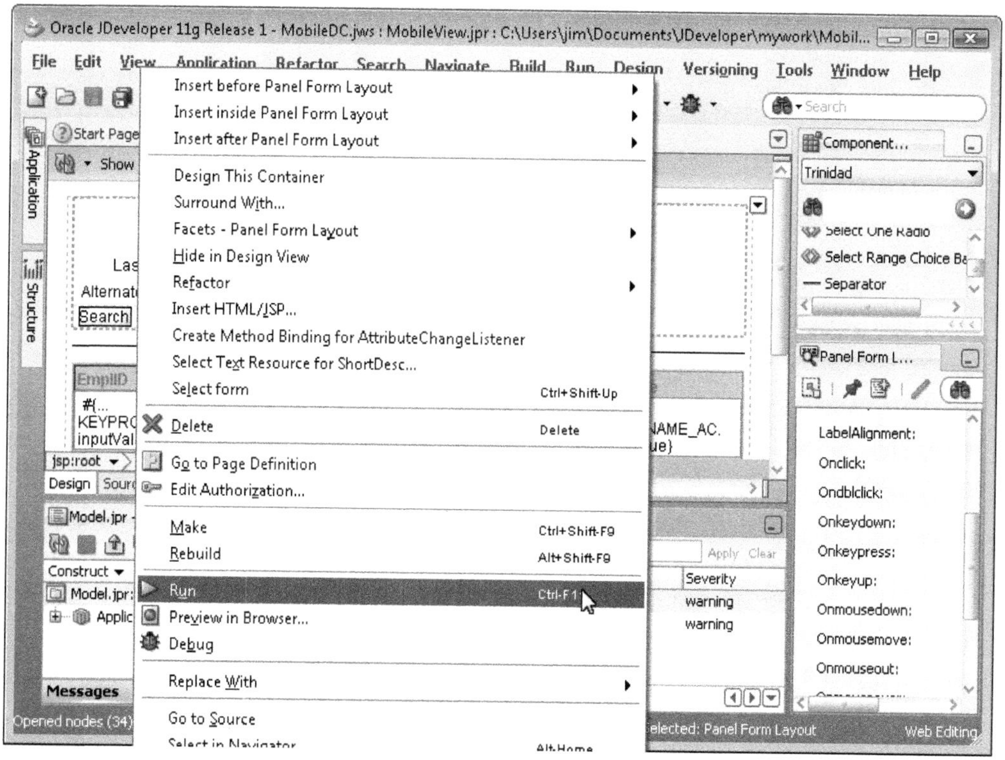

FIGURE 14-45. *Page designer Run menu item*

EmplID	Name	Last Name	Alt Name
No data to display.			

FIGURE 14-46. *The search.jspx page online*

EmplID	Name	Last Name	Alt Name
KULA09	John Baker	BAKER	
KUTZ496	John Baker	BAKER	
KULA05	John Baldini	BALDINI	
KULA11	John Baron	BARON	
KUL512	John Barry	BARRY	
KUTZ487	John Carson	CARSON	
KULA12	John Chestney	CHESTNEY	
KUTR02	John Gardner	GARDNER	
KULA13	John Grace	GRACE	
KULA06	John Harmon	HARMON	
KUI010	John Hubball	HUBBALL	
KULA14	John Huser	HUSER	
KULA01	John Kelly	KELLY	
KUL571	John Kennedy	KENNEDY	
KULA08	John Kerper	KERPER	
KULA10	John Kim	KIM	
KULA02	John Laren	LAREN	
KULA15	John Molleur	MOLLEUR	
KU0026	John Pak	PAK	
KULA03	John Schaffer	SCHAFFER	

FIGURE 14-47. *Web service data control results*

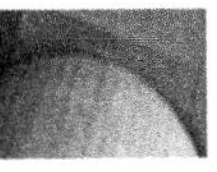

NOTE
If you are using an HR database other than the delivered demo database, enter search criteria that match your organization's employee information.

Try entering different search criteria. Enter **K** for the employee ID and **John** for the name. The Trinidad read-only table will display the first 25 results with buttons to navigate through the rest of the results. While you are testing this page, try entering criteria that will return more than 300 rows. In the HCM demo database, for example, entering just an employee ID of **K** with no other search criteria will find more than 300 entries, and PeopleSoft will return an error message saying there were too many rows for the CI. In this case, Trinidad will display an error at the top of the page, but the error will just say "Component Interface Error." To see the full error message, you need to use a network sniffer such as Wireshark.

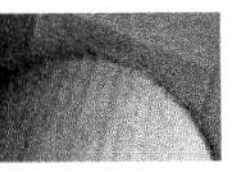

TIP
If you are having any problems with your web service data control, fire up Wireshark and watch the web service data control's HTTP posts to your PeopleSoft server. I spent a lot of time in Wireshark while learning how to use the web service data control. It's available from http://www.wireshark.org/.

While testing the search page, note the URL, which should look something like this:

http://127.0.0.1:7101/MobileDC-MobileView-context-root/faces/search.jspx

Shortening the Application's URL

Since users will access this application from a mobile browser, it would be nice to have a shorter URL, perhaps something like this:

http://127.0.0.1:7101/MobileDC/faces/search.jspx

To change the URL, open your project's properties and find the Java EE Application settings. In those settings, change your Java EE Web Context Root value to something short, like **MobileDC**, as shown in Figure 14-48. Click OK to dismiss the project's properties, and then save your project.

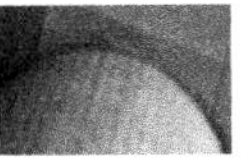

TIP
Once I have a page that functions properly in a web browser, I like to test my pages in a mobile device simulator. If your preferred mobile device has a device simulator, I recommend downloading and configuring that simulator. I use the BlackBerry device and MDS simulators to test pages that are running from my local JDeveloper instance.

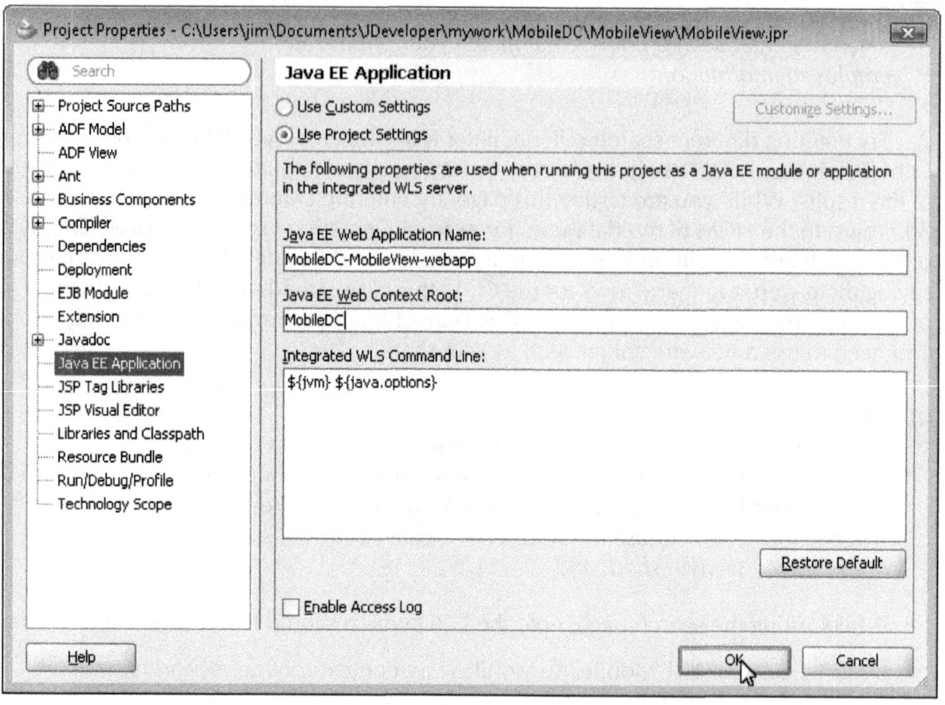

FIGURE 14-48. *The MobileView project's Java EE Application settings*

Requiring Authentication

PeopleSoft CI-based web services support authentication, a feature this example ignored. The source code for this chapter includes a sample application named `MobileDCLogin` that demonstrates how to pass credentials to the web service data control.

The `MobileDCLogin`'s model project is very similar to the example presented here. The only difference is that I added the `wss_username_token_client_policy` to the `PersonalData` control's security policy. To make this change, follow these steps:

1. Expand your model project and the project's Application Sources node. Continue to traverse these nodes until you find the DataControls.dcx file located in the `apt.peoplesoft.mobile.model` package.
2. Select this DataControls.dcx file, and then use the Structure browser to navigate to DataControlConfigs | PersonalData.
3. Right-click the PersonalData node within the Structure browser and select Define Web Service Security from the context menu.
4. In the Edit Data Control Policies dialog, use the green plus symbol (+) to add the `wss_username_token_client_policy` item to the Security list. Click OK to dismiss the dialog.

The `MobileView` project is where you will find most of the differences. The `MobileDCLogin` version includes three Java source code files:

- **UserBean.java** `UserBean` is a session-scoped bean that contains the current user's credentials and passes those credentials along to the data control upon web service execution.
- **DataControlOperation.java** The `DataControlOperation` class is a generic Java class capable of executing a web service method against a web service data control. It is responsible for setting the data control's `SecurityModel` and then executing the web service.
- **SearchMethod.java** The `SearchMethod` class replaces the Search button's execute command by executing the `DataControlOperation` instead.

The project now includes a login.jspx page for collecting a user's credentials. The login page doesn't actually verify the user's credentials; it just stores them for later use when calling the web service.

The only other user interface change is the search.jspx page's Search button. I changed the `ActionListener` to `search.execute`. The `search` bean is a request-scoped bean that is backed by the `SearchMethod` class.

Conclusion

This chapter demonstrated how to combine Oracle ADF with PeopleSoft's web services to create a web-based mobile application. JDeveloper's drag-and-drop development made it possible to implement this solution without writing any code.

The Web is just one way to deliver mobile solutions. I prefer web-based solutions because a single web application can run on multiple, incompatible devices. However, web-based solutions are available only when your users are online. For disconnected solutions, try developing applications using your mobile phone's development kit.

The example given here approached mobile development from the JDeveloper/Java angle. It is possible to create a very similar solution using any web-based application development environment. For example, you could create this same solution using Ruby.

If you plan to use the drag-and-drop approach presented here, you must license the Oracle ADF runtime. If licensing Oracle ADF is not an option for you, try one of the free alternatives. Apache's Axis2 project[3] contains code-generation utilities for converting WSDL into Java classes. Also, the Trinidad components used in this chapter are available from Apache under the standard Apache software license.

If you want to build JSF solutions but don't have a license for ADF, give Eclipse[4] a try. The Eclipse JSF design-time tools bear a marked resemblance to the JDeveloper JSF tools. I believe this is because Oracle plays a crucial role in the development of Eclipse's JSF tools project.[5]

Notes

1. Apache Software Foundation, "Apache MyFaces Trinidad" [online]; available from http://myfaces.apache.org/trinidad/index.html; Internet; accessed 24 November 2009.
2. Krishna Srinivasan, "Unified Expression Language for JSP and JSF" [online]; available from http://today.java.net/pub/a/today/2006/03/07/unified-jsp-jsf-expression-language.html; Internet; accessed 28 November 2009.
3. Apache Software Foundation, "Apache Axis2/Java - Next Generation Web Services" [online]; available from http://ws.apache.org/axis2/; Internet; accessed 28 November 2009.
4. The Eclipse Foundation, "Eclipse.org home" [online]; available from http://www.eclipse.org/; Internet; accessed 28 November 2009.
5. Oracle, "Eclipse Projects" [online]; available from http://oss.oracle.com/oracle-eclipse-projects.html; Internet; accessed 26 November 2009.

PART IV

Best Practices

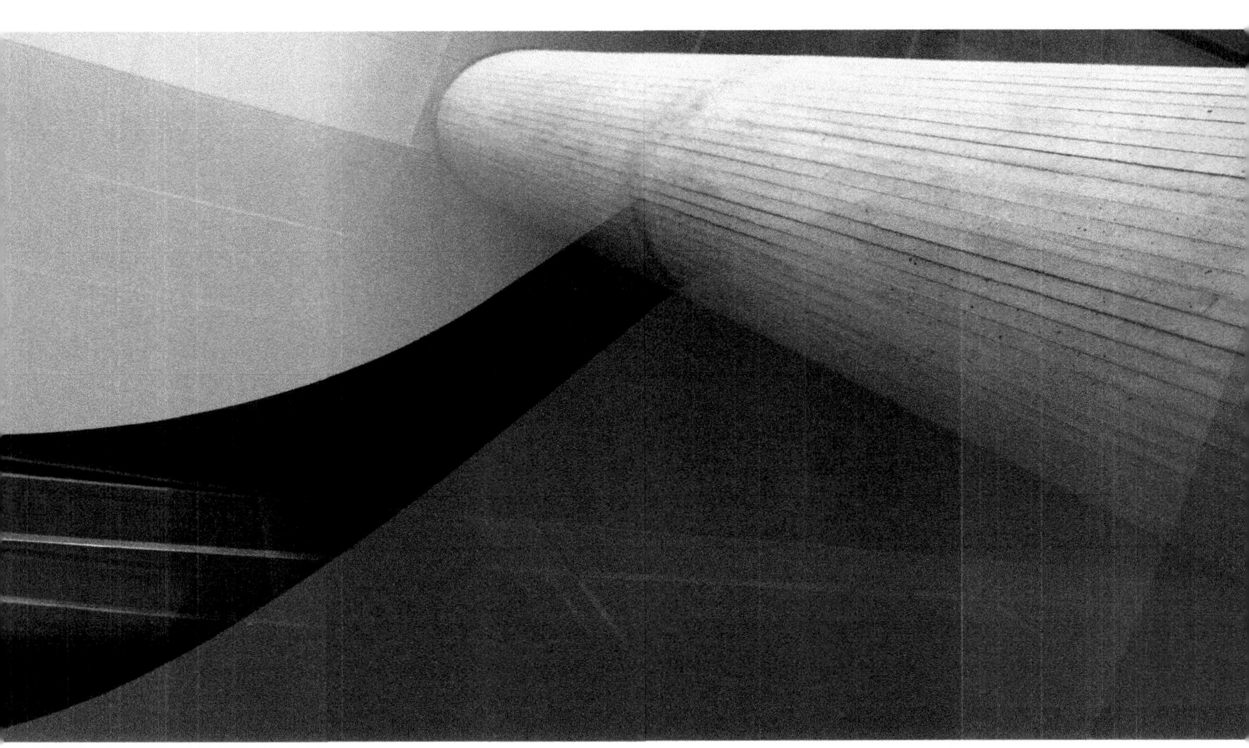

CHAPTER 15

Test-Driven Development

ow many times have you programmed and implemented a solution, and then heard from your users that your solution didn't *exactly* solve their problems? This is actually very common. So common, in fact, that we almost expect to create multiple solutions for each business problem.

Using the traditional software engineering/architecture approach, we gather requirements, design a solution, and then code that solution. Often, the final product bears little resemblance to the design. Even if the solution produced by this process satisfies the gathered requirements, we find that we misunderstood the requirements. This type of software development reminds me of the famous tree swing diagram, illustrating the disparity between the product desired and the product delivered.[1]

Test-driven development (TDD) is a discovery process where you start with what you know—the business requirements—and discover the solution. TDD differs from the engineering/architecture approach, in that TDD does not require you to know the implementation details. It is very much like solving a mystery or a mathematical equation.

In this chapter, we'll begin with an introduction to TDD, and then demonstrate how to apply it to PeopleSoft. The example in this chapter will apply TDD techniques to reimplement the meta-HTML processor introduced in Chapter 9.

Introduction to Test-Driven Development

TDD is an iterative process. It starts with a set of business requirements translated into software tests. Those tests describe the external interfaces of a system. After creating a test, you begin to work inward, creating the first layer of objects, functions, and so on. Through coding this first layer, you will discover the next layer.

You can demonstrate the system at any point in time, because you started with the external interface and mocked up the internals. When you start from the outside and work toward a solution, your functional users can provide you with usability feedback early and often. This stands in contrast to the engineering approach, where you may code the internals first and mock up the external interface only if required. Demonstrating a solution early avoids costly rework by identifying erroneous assumptions and requirements at the beginning of the development cycle.

A key point of TDD is starting with what you know. You know the system or solution requirements because someone gave them to you. From these requirements, you write a test to prove your solution satisfies the requirements. To write tests, you need to write code. That code identifies the high-level objects for your solution. The next step is to write implementations for those objects. Often, the implementations will require additional objects. As you discover the need for more objects, methods, and functions, you write tests for those items. Again, the tests expose the external interface for those items.

The TDD Approach

The steps of TDD are as follows:

1. Write a requirements-based test.
2. Run the test and watch it fail.
3. Write the shortest, simplest solution that will cause the test to pass.

4. Run the test and watch it pass.
5. Refactor the code (transform, rewrite, or restructure code for performance, readability, and reusability, without modifying the code's behavior).
6. Repeat the cycle.

After writing a test (step 1), you run the test (step 2). Notice that the cycle isn't write the test, code the solution, and then run the test. In step 2, you actually run the test before coding the solution. The point of running the test first is to *test* the test case. If your test case reports success before you implement a solution, then your test case may be incorrect. Step 2 tests your test logic.

The objective of steps 3 and 4 are similar to step 2. In step 3, you implement a solution, but it isn't the final solution. The point in step 3 is to write a solution that will prove your test case. If you hard-code the *answer* into the implementation and the test fails, then you know your test logic is incorrect.

In step 5, you begin perfecting the internal implementation by replacing the hard-coded implementation with a working solution. By running your tests after each change, you can easily identify which change caused a test to pass or fail. This allows you to catch regressions and fix them immediately. The end result is fewer bugs and better code.

Some TDD Lingo

Here are some common phrases developers use to describe TDD:

- Test early and test often.
- We don't fix bugs; we fix tests.
- Deliver early; deliver often.

Many programming languages have unit testing frameworks for designing and automating unit tests. The JUnit testing framework includes a stoplight user interface that reports success as green and failure as red. Based on the stoplight metaphor, the TDD mantra is "red, green, refactor," which means this:

1. Run a test and watch it fail (red).
2. Make the test pass (green).
3. Refactor to remove redundancies, hard-coded answers, and so on.

TDD promotes best practices such as KISS (keep it simple stupid), YAGNI (you ain't gonna need it), and DRY (don't repeat yourself). TDD often leads to solutions that use other best practices and patterns.

NOTE
If you are interested in learning more about TDD, I highly recommend Kent Beck's Book Test Driven Development: By Example *(Addison-Wesley, 2002).*

A TDD Framework

Several programming languages have TDD frameworks that assist with the TDD process, but you don't need to use such a framework. A basic PeopleCode function run from an App Engine or iScript will suffice. However, a testing framework provides design-time support in the form of assertions as well as a runtime feedback mechanism. This chapter uses a free PeopleCode unit testing framework named PSUnit.

PSUnit is composed of PeopleCode, records, pages, and components. You can find installation instructions as well as the PSUnit source project at http://wiki.oracle.com/page/Introducing+PSUnit. Download and install PSUnit before continuing with the example in this chapter.

Test Driving the Meta-HTML Processor

In Chapter 9, we wrote a custom meta-HTML processor that used Java regular expressions to convert character sequences into data. While writing each of the processor methods—`processJavaScript`, `processGenerateQueryContentUrl`, and so on—I noticed a significant amount of redundant code. Let's set that code aside and use TDD to discover a new implementation.

Writing a Test

The objective of our meta-HTML processor is to transform meta-HTML character sequences into the actual data those sequences represent. Let's follow the TDD steps by writing a test that represents our understanding of the requirement.

TDD promotes starting with what you know. Here's what we know about the meta-HTML processor:

- We will have an input string.
- The meta-HTML processor will produce string output.
- The meta-HTML processor logic must be packaged in a reusable manner, which means the code will need to exist in a FUNCLIB or an application class.

In PeopleCode, these requirements look something like this:

```
Local APT_META:HTML:Processor &p = create APT_META:HTML:Processor();

Local string &result = &p.process("%Image(MY_IMAGE_NAME)");
```

This code describes the meta-HTML processor's interface: an object named `APT_META:HTML:Processor` that has a method named `process`. From the example, we see that the method requires a `string` parameter and returns a `string` result.

If this is to be a test case, we can't stop here. The preceding code runs the meta-HTML processor, but it is not a test case because it does not perform a test. We might write something like the following, which is a basic equality test that validates the processor's results:

```
Local string &expectedResult =
      "http://hrms.example.com/cs/hrms/cache/MY_IMAGE_1.gif";
```

```
If(&result <> &expectedResult) Then
   MessageBox(0,"",0,0,"Strings do not match");
End-If;
```

We could wrap the preceding code in an iScript and print a result to the iScript response, but instead, we will use the PeopleCode PSUnit framework to aid in our TDD efforts, as stated in the previous section.

After installing PSUnit, open App Designer and create a new application package named `APT_META_TESTS`. Add a new class to this package named `ProcessorTest`.

We will write a PSUnit-based test case similar to the preceding test, but for a different meta-HTML sequence. Because the filename created by the PeopleSoft caching servlet may change, it is difficult to write a consistent test case for `%Image`. Instead, we will test drive the development of a new meta-HTML sequence: `%NodePortalURL`. The `%NodePortalURL` meta-HTML sequence expects a node name and replaces the meta-HTML sequence with the node's portal URL.

Before continuing, be sure to configure the node's portal URL. If you use Enterprise Portal, you should have already configured this. If you are using a single PeopleSoft application, such as HRMS or FSCM, you probably haven't done this configuration. To do so, navigate to PeopleTools | Portal | Node Definitions, open a node, and switch to the Portal tab. The psc URL is the content URL used to display a node's content within the PeopleSoft frameset (for example, http://hrms.example.com/**psc**/hrms/). The portal URI is used to display the node's content in its own frameset (for example, http://hrms.example.com/**psp**/hrms/). For testing purposes, I recommend using your local content node. For the Financials application, the local content node is ERP; in Human Resources, the local content node is HRMS.

Next, add the following code to the `APT_META_TESTS:ProcessorTest` application class.

```
import TTS_UNITTEST:TestBase;
import APT_META:HTML:Processor;

class ProcessorTest extends TTS_UNITTEST:TestBase
   method ProcessorTest();
   method Run();
end-class;

method ProcessorTest
   %Super = create TTS_UNITTEST:TestBase("ProcessorTest");
end-method;

method Run
   /+ Extends/implements TTS_UNITTEST:TestBase.Run +/
   Local APT_META:HTML:Processor &p = create APT_META:HTML:Processor();
   Local string &input = "%NodePortalURL(HRMS)";
   Local string &expectedResult = "http://hrms.example.com/psp/hrms/";

   Local string &result = &p.process(&input);

   %This.AssertStringsEqual(&result, &expectedResult,
         "Processor output does not match the expected results");
end-method;
```

The body of the application class is very similar to the %Image test case we created earlier. The code creates an instance of the meta-HTML processor, asks the processor to process an input string, and then compares the processor's output to an expected result. This example, however, has a few more lines of code than the former.

Starting with the class declaration, we see that the ProcessorTest class extends a class named TTS_UNITTEST:TestBase. The TTS_UNITTEST:TestBase class is the base class for all unit tests and contains convenience methods, such as the AssertStringsEqual method, as well as framework-specific methods, such as Setup and Teardown.

Since the ProcessorTest class extends a class that has a constructor with parameters, our class must also have a constructor. Test case constructors, however, cannot have parameters. The PSUnit runtime PeopleCode uses PSUnit metadata to create an instance of your test case. That PeopleCode assumes your constructor does not have parameters. Your test case constructor must create an instance of the base class by specifying the name of the test.

The Run method contains your test case-specific code. Whether a test passes or fails is controlled by assertions, or more specifically, by *exceptions*. If your test case throws an exception, then the framework marks the test as failed (failed assertions throw exceptions). The PSUnit testing framework will call the Run method to run the test.

As I mentioned, this test case exposed the need for an APT_META:HTML:Processor class. Before we can save our test case, we need to stub out the APT_META:HTML:Processor class. To do so, create a new application package named APT_META and add a subpackage to this package named HTML. To the HTML package, add a class named Processor.

Since we are still on step 1, we won't code the solution, but we do need to add enough code to the Processor class to save the ProcessorTest class. Open the APT_META:HTML:Processor class and add the following PeopleCode.

```
class Processor
   method process(&input As string) Returns string;
end-class;

method process
   /+ &input as String +/
   /+ Returns String +/
   Return "";
end-method;
```

A *stub*[2] is an object, method, or function that exists as a placeholder. A stub contains just enough code to compile without errors, but doesn't contain an implementation. The code for the Processor class is considered a stub because it contains only enough code to place the Processor class in a valid state.

As you write test cases, you will uncover the need for new objects and functions. This is a critical part of TDD. Unfortunately, you can't save test cases that make use of nonexistent objects. Once you discover the need for a new object, stop coding your test case to create a minimalistic instance of the new object. Then write the least amount of code possible to place the object in a valid state.

Running the Test

PSUnit has a facility for running tests. If you log into PeopleSoft as a user who has the TTS_UNIT_TEST role, you will see the PSUnit menu item at the bottom of the Enterprise menu. Select this item and add the new value APT_META_HTML_PROCESSOR. Figure 15-1 shows the new test suite without any tests.

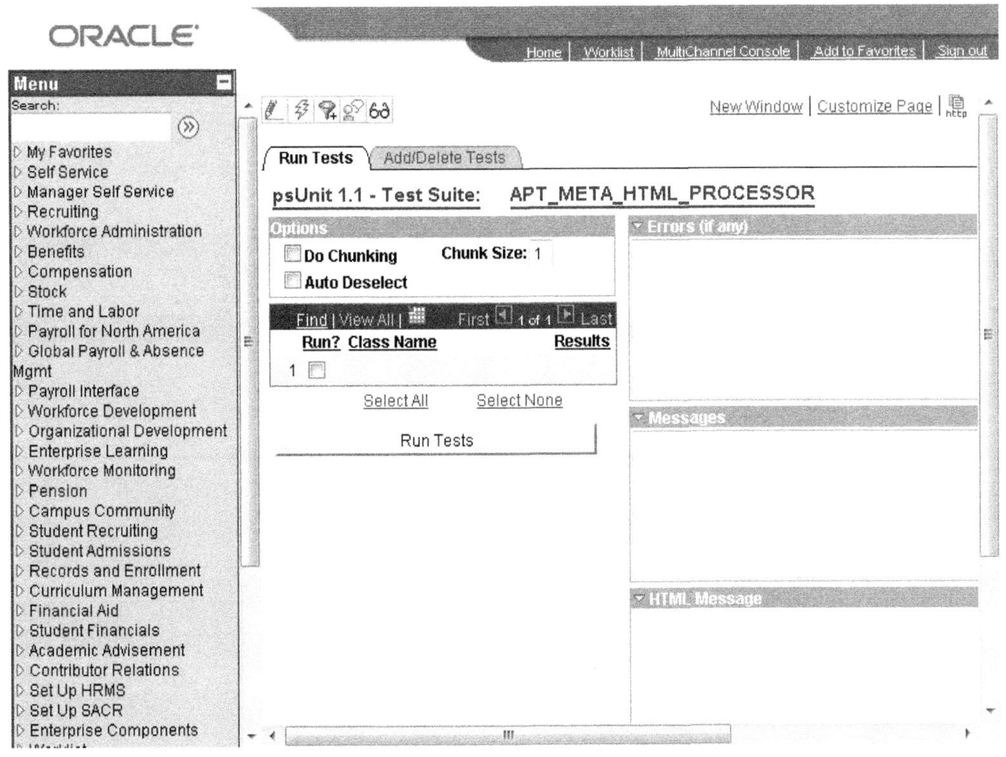

FIGURE 15-1. *A PSUnit online test suite*

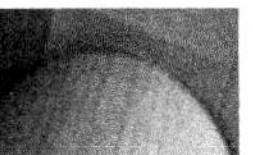

NOTE

The `TTS_UNIT_TEST` role and PSUnit menu items are part of the PSUnit project available from http://wiki.oracle.com/page/Introducing+PSUnit. If you imported the PSUnit project, but do not have the `TTS_UNIT_TEST` role, you can create a new role and add the `TTS_UNIT_TEST` permission list to your new role.

Switch to the Add/Delete Tests tab and add a new test. Our first test has the package root `APT_META_TESTS`, a class path of : (a colon), and the class name `ProcessorTest`, as shown in Figure 15-2.

Switch back to the Run Tests tab, and you will see the `ProcessorTest` class listed in the page's grid. Click the Select All link to activate all of the tests in this test suite (currently only one test), and then click the Run Tests button.

PSUnit will display "FAILED" in the test's Results column and the test's error message in the Errors group box, as shown in Figure 15-3. Since we haven't implemented the meta-HTML processor's logic, we expect it to fail. If it passed, then we would have to question our test case.

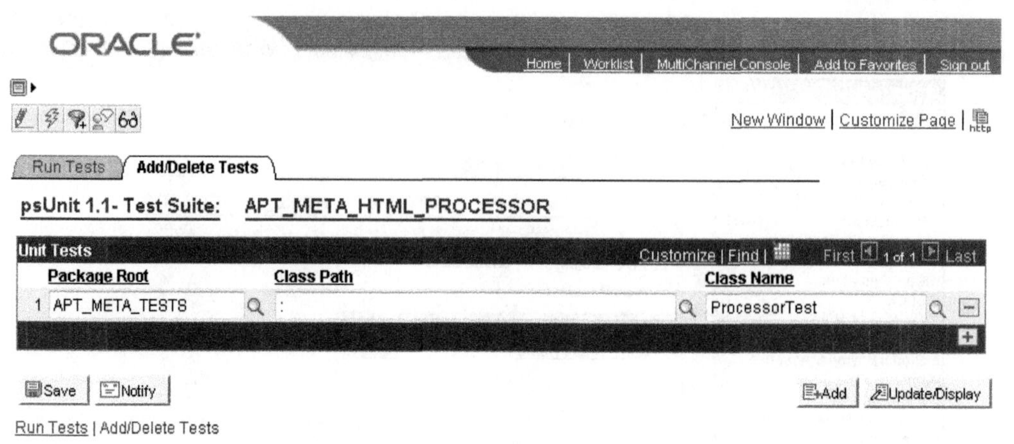

FIGURE 15-2. *The test suite's Add/Delete Tests tab*

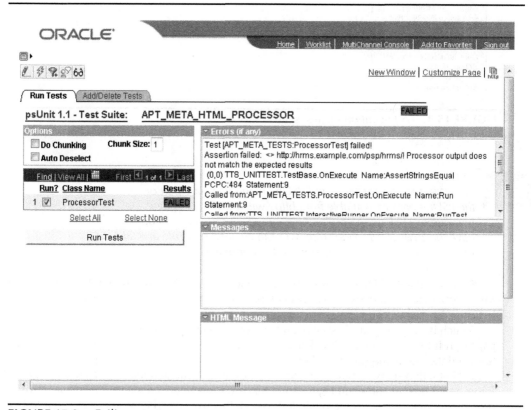

FIGURE 15-3. *Failing a test*

The red indicator next to the test is what gives this initial test the name "red" in the TDD "red, green, refactor" mantra mentioned earlier in the chapter.

Although we call this test a "failure," it actually was a success. Since our object is to write an implementation that fails, and the test actually failed, we were successful.

Making the Test Pass

Our next step is to make the test pass. Like step 2, step 3 is concerned with testing the test case, not the actual implementation.

Considering our objective for step 3, let's write the smallest implementation possible that will pass the test. Change the `process` method of the `APT_META:HTML:Processor` application class to match the following code.

```
method process
   /+ &input as String +/
   /+ Returns String +/
   Return "http://hrms.example.com/psp/hrms/";
end-method;
```

You probably think I cheated by hard-coding the answer, don't you? You are right. If the implementation isn't obvious, then fake it. We will refactor this implementation later. At this stage we are still interested in testing the test case, not the implementation. Hard-coding the answer may seem highly unusual, and it is—from a traditional application development perspective. In step 5, we will write a real implementation for the `process` method. For now, I can't think of a better way to test the test case than to hard-code the result.

Looking at this hard-coded implementation, you might notice another test we should write. If the input is `%NodePortalURL(HRMS)`, and the expected result is `http://hrms.example.com/psp/hrms/`, then perhaps we should write another test for our Financials (ERP) node. This second test will act as a cross-check against fake answers such as the one in the preceding code. Now is not the time to implement new tests. Write that idea in a list so you don't forget it. We will come back to it after working through the TDD cycle.

Lists are very important in TDD. As you work through the TDD cycle, writing tests and refactoring code, you will identify new test cases and refactoring opportunities outside the current step. When you identify these necessary distractions, write them down and save them for later. It is very important that you avoid interrupting the TDD cycle. And if you write down your ideas, you will have a better chance of remembering them.

TDD is an iterative cycle of small, incremental steps. You will run through the cycle often. Don't shortcut the process by trying to combine steps. For example, if you are at step 2 and already know the implementation, avoid the temptation to code the solution and use step 4 as a confirmation of your success. Most of the time, skipping steps in this manner will work. But the time that it doesn't work will cost you hours or days, as you try to track down an incorrectly written test that passed even though the implementation was incorrectly coded.

Running the Test Again

Run the test again and watch the red failed indicator change to "Passed" with a white background, as shown in Figure 15-4. (Yes, the white is anticlimactic; green would be much better.)

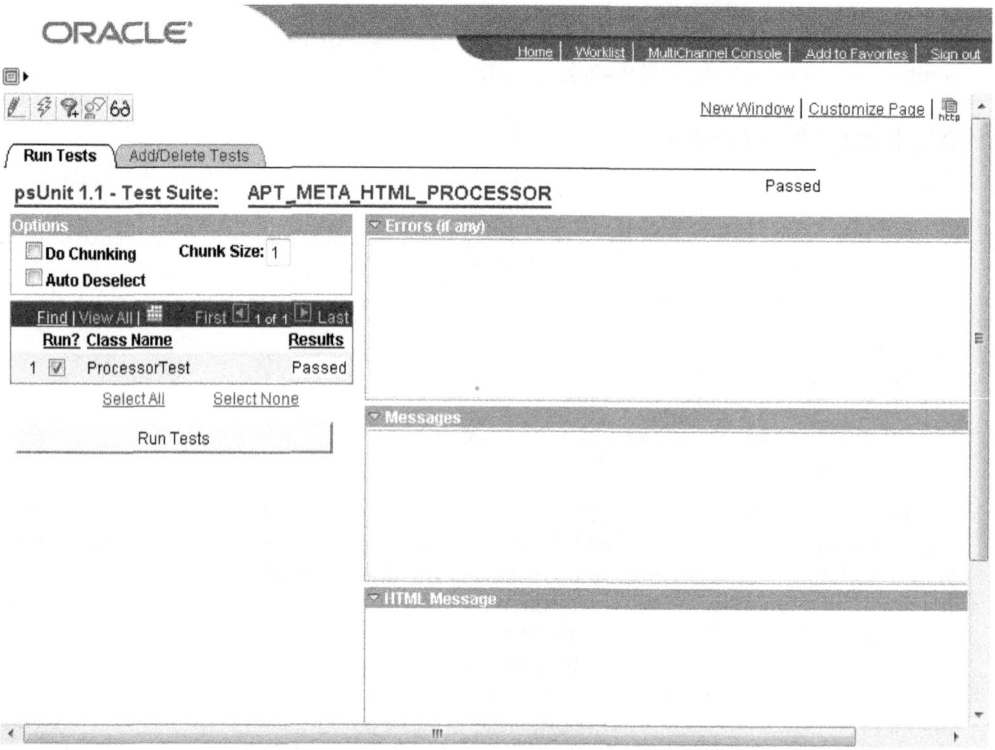

FIGURE 15-4. *Passing a test*

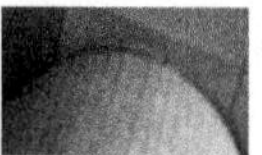

TIP

If you are interested in changing the background color, search for the text `TTS_RUN_STATUS` in the `TTS_UNITTEST:Controller` application class. The PeopleCode uses delivered style sheet class definitions to set the Results field's background color. Copy the `PSNORMAL` style class into a new style class and change the background color of this new style class.

Refactoring

Here is where the rubber meets the road. It is now time to write a real implementation. We won't write the entire implementation at once though. This is an iterative process. With each change, we will run back through the test cycle to verify that the code still functions properly.

Refactoring the Test Case

In step 3, we hard-coded a solution (also known as *faking it*) and decided we should add another test as a cross-check for such fake answers. Let's refactor the `ProcessorTest` to confirm our results.

NOTE

If your PeopleSoft installation uses only one node (one application) and you haven't configured any external nodes, open the ERP node and set the URL to a fictitious location. For this example, you need to have two configured nodes. The code we write won't test to make sure the location actually exists. Our code will just compare the node's configured value with an expected value.

Since we are going to execute the same test twice, but with different strings, let's first inline all of our variables so the code will contain only one declaration and two executable lines.

```
method Run
   /+ Extends/implements TTS_UNITTEST:TestBase.Run +/
   Local APT_META:HTML:Processor &p = create APT_META:HTML:Processor();

   %This.AssertStringsEqual(&p.process("%NodePortalURL(HRMS)"),
         "http://hrms.example.com/psp/hrms/",
         "Processor output does not match the expected results");
end-method;
```

Update your `APT_META_TESTS:ProcessorTest` class's `Run` method with the preceding code, and then rerun your test. The test should pass.

Update the `Run` method again, this time adding a test for another node. The following code contains an additional test for the ERP node.

```
method Run
   /+ Extends/implements TTS_UNITTEST:TestBase.Run +/
   Local APT_META:HTML:Processor &p = create APT_META:HTML:Processor();

   %This.AssertStringsEqual(&p.process("%NodePortalURL(HRMS)"),
         "http://hrms.example.com/psp/hrms/",
         "The resultant HRMS node URL is incorrect.");

   %This.AssertStringsEqual(&p.process("%NodePortalURL(ERP)"),
         "http://fscm.example.com/psp/fscm/",
         "The resultant ERP node URL is incorrect.");
end-method;
```

One way to identify a test is by the error message it throws. The original error message was quite generic. We modified it here so that it identifies which line failed.

Run the test again, and you should see the results indicator switch to "FAILED." Success! As you remember from our fake `Processor` implementation, the `process` method always returns the HRMS node's URL. The Errors group box confirms that the ERP line failed, not the HRMS line:

```
Test [APT_META_TESTS:ProcessorTest] failed!
Assertion failed: http://hrms.example.com/psp/hrms/ <>
http://fscm.example.com/psp/fscm/!
The resultant ERP node URL is incorrect.
```

Refactoring the Implementation

Now we have a reasonable, failing test case proving the `process` method doesn't work. Let's refactor the `process` method so that the test will pass.

We need a mechanism for finding meta-HTML sequences within a text string. Our original meta-HTML processor from Chapter 9 used regular expressions to find and parse meta-HTML sequences. That approach seems reasonable, so let's continue using regular expressions. The regular expression `(?i)%NodePortalURL\((\w+)\)` will find the expected meta-HTML and its parameter. Here is our first "real" implementation of the `Processor` class (additions are in bold):

```
class Processor
   method process(&input As string) Returns string;

private
   method processNodePortalUrl(&input As string) Returns string;
end-class;

method process
   /+ &input as String +/
   /+ Returns String +/
   Local string &result = &input;
   &result = %This.processNodePortalUrl(&result);

   Return &result;
end-method;

method processNodePortalUrl
   /+ &input as String +/
   /+ Returns String +/
   Local JavaObject &pattern;
   Local JavaObject &matcher;
   Local string &node_url;
   Local string &html = &input;

   REM ** Resolve %NodePortalURL(NODENAME) tags;
   &pattern = GetJavaClass("java.util.regex.Pattern").compile(
         "(?i)%NodePortalURL\((\w+)\)");

   &matcher = &pattern.matcher(
         CreateJavaObject("java.lang.String", &html));

   While &matcher.find()
      SQLExec("SELECT URI_TEXT FROM PSNODEURITEXT " |
            "WHERE MSGNODENAME = :1 AND URI_TYPE = 'PL'",
            &matcher.group(1), &node_url);
      &html = Substitute(&html, &matcher.group(), &node_url);
   End-While;

   Return &html;
end-method;
```

Update your `APT_META:HTML:Processor` class to match the preceding code and run the test suite again. This time the test should pass.

Repeating the Cycle

The `%NodePortalURL` test case works, but what about other meta-HTML sequences? Let's expand the test case to include another meta-HTML sequence: `%Message(MESSAGE_SET, MESSAGE_NBR)`. Here is the refactored test case (additions are in bold):

```
import TTS_UNITTEST:TestBase;
import APT_META:HTML:Processor;

class ProcessorTest extends TTS_UNITTEST:TestBase
   method ProcessorTest();
   method Run();
end-class;

method ProcessorTest
   %Super = create TTS_UNITTEST:TestBase("ProcessorTest");
end-method;

method Run
   /+ Extends/implements TTS_UNITTEST:TestBase.Run +/
   Local APT_META:HTML:Processor &p = create APT_META:HTML:Processor();

   %This.AssertStringsEqual(&p.process("%NodePortalURL(HRMS)"),
         "http://hrms.example.com/psp/hrms/",
         "The resultant HRMS node URL is incorrect.");
   %This.AssertStringsEqual(&p.process("%NodePortalURL(ERP)"),
         "http://fscm.example.com/psp/fscm/",
         "The resultant ERP node URL is incorrect.");
   %This.AssertStringsEqual(&p.process("%Message(3, 51)"),
         "Working...", "The resultant message does not match.");
end-method;
```

Run this test immediately to prove that it fails.

Now let's write some code to resolve the `%Message` meta-HTML sequence. Add the following method declaration to the private section of the `APT_META:HTML:Processor` class declaration:

```
   method processMessage(&input As string) Returns string;
```

Add the following code to the end of the `APT_META:HTML:Processor` class:

```
method processMessage
   /+ &input as String +/
   /+ Returns String +/
   Local JavaObject &pattern;
   Local JavaObject &matcher;
   Local string &msg;
   Local string &html = &input;

   REM ** Resolve %Message(MESSAGE_SET, MESSAGE_NBR) tags;
   &pattern = GetJavaClass("java.util.regex.Pattern").compile(
         "(?i)%Message\((\w+), ?(\w+)\)");

   &matcher = &pattern.matcher(
         CreateJavaObject("java.lang.String", &html));
```

```
   While &matcher.find()

      &msg = MsgGetText(&matcher.group(1), &matcher.group(2), "");
      &html = Substitute(&html, &matcher.group(), &msg);
   End-While;

   Return &html;
end-method;
```

Update the process method to match the following.

```
method process
   /+ &input as String +/
   /+ Returns String +/
   Local string &result = &input;
   &result = %This.processNodePortalUrl(&result);
   &result = %This.processMessage(&result);

   Return &result;
end-method;
```

Run the test again, and it should pass.

Removing duplicate code is part of refactoring. Looking at the implementations of `processNodePortalUrl` and `processMessage`, you can see a lot of redundant code. Both create regular expression matchers, and both use loops to perform replacements. It seems as though we could eliminate this redundancy by changing the regular expression to match any meta-HTML sequence and then executing a method that has the same name as the meta-HTML tag. Here is the refactored `APT_META:HTML:Processor` class:

```
class Processor
   method process(&input As string) Returns string;

   method processNodePortalUrl(&nodeName As string) Returns string;
   method processMessage(&messageSet As string,
         &messageNumber As string) Returns string;
end-class;

method process
   /+ &input as String +/
   /+ Returns String +/
   Local JavaObject &pattern;
   Local JavaObject &matcher;
   Local string &tag;
   Local string &parmList;
   Local array of string &parms;
   Local string &replacement;

   Local string &html = &input;

   REM ** Regular expression that matches %SomeTag(with, parameters);
   &pattern = GetJavaClass("java.util.regex.Pattern").compile(
         "(?i)%(\w+)\(([\w, ]*)\)");
```

```
   &matcher = &pattern.matcher(
         CreateJavaObject("java.lang.String", &html));

   While &matcher.find()
      &tag = &matcher.group(1);

      /* If the Meta-HTML tag had parameters, then split them into an
       * array
       */
      If (&matcher.groupCount() > 1) Then
         &parmList = &matcher.group(2);
         &parmList = Substitute(&parmList, " ", "");
         &parms = Split(&parmList, ",");
      Else
         &parms = Null;
      End-If;

      /* Use a PeopleCode function to dynamically execute a method with
       * the same name as the tag, but prefixed with process. For
       * example, if the Meta-HTML tag is %Message, then call the
       * method named processMessage.
       */
      &replacement = ObjectDoMethodArray(%This, "process" | &tag,
            CreateArrayAny(&parms));
      &html = Substitute(&html, &matcher.group(), &replacement);
   End-While;

   Return &html;
end-method;

method processNodePortalUrl
   /+ &nodeName as String +/
   /+ Returns String +/
   Local string &node_url;
   SQLExec("SELECT URI_TEXT FROM PSNODEURITEXT " |
         "WHERE MSGNODENAME = :1 AND URI_TYPE = 'PL'",
         &nodeName, &node_url);

   Return &node_url;
end-method;

method processMessage
   /+ &messageSet as String, +/
   /+ &messageNumber as String +/
   /+ Returns String +/

   Return MsgGetText(Value(&messageSet), Value(&messageNumber), "");
end-method;
```

Run this test again, and PSUnit should show that the test passed.

Our test case verifies positive outcomes. It proves that known meta-HTML sequences return the correct results. But what about unknown meta-HTML sequences? What will happen if the input string contains a meta-HTML sequence that doesn't have a corresponding method? Let's refactor the test case to find out.

First, we need to decide what we want the `Processor` to return if the method does not exist. For this test, let's ask the `Processor` to ignore unknown meta-HTML sequences and just return the input as the output. Here is what that test would look like:

```
%This.AssertStringsEqual(&p.process("%Unknown(Tag)"), "%Unknown(Tag)",
      "The Processor does not handle unknown Meta-HTML sequences.");
```

Add this line to the Run method of `APT_META_TESTS:ProcessorTest` and run the test. You should see the test failed, with this error message:

```
Test [APT_META_TESTS:ProcessorTest] failed!
Invalid parameter No class/method info for function ObjectDoMethod.
```

PSUnit is telling us that the method `processUnknown` does not exist. One way to ignore unknown meta-HTML sequences is to wrap the call to `ObjectDoMethodArray` in a `try/catch` construct. This, however, would have the unfortunate side effect of ignoring all exceptions raised by legitimate `process`*`XXX`* methods. Another alternative is to maintain a list of known meta-HTML sequences and verify the existence of a sequence in that list prior to executing the corresponding method. The following code listing contains this modification (changes are in bold). This is our final iteration of the `APT_META:HTML:Processor`.

```
class Processor
   method process(&input As string) Returns string;

   method processNodePortalUrl(&nodeName As string) Returns string;
   method processMessage(&messageSet As string,
         &messageNumber As string) Returns string;

private
   Constant &SEQUENCES = "NodePortalUrl Message";
end-class;

method process
   /+ &input as String +/
   /+ Returns String +/
   Local JavaObject &pattern;
   Local JavaObject &matcher;
   Local string &tag;
   Local string &parmList;
   Local array of string &parms;
   Local string &replacement;

   Local string &html = &input;

   REM ** Regular expression that matches %SomeTag(with, parameters);
```

```
   &pattern = GetJavaClass("java.util.regex.Pattern").compile(
         "(?i)%(\w+)\(([\w, ]*)\)");

   &matcher = &pattern.matcher(
         CreateJavaObject("java.lang.String", &html));

   While &matcher.find()
      &tag = &matcher.group(1);

      REM ** Only replace if Meta-HTML tag is in a list of known tags;
      If (DBPatternMatch(&SEQUENCES, "%" | &tag | "%", False)) Then

         /* If the Meta-HTML tag had parameters, then split them into
          * an array
          */
         If (&matcher.groupCount() > 1) Then
            &parmList = &matcher.group(2);
            &parmList = Substitute(&parmList, " ", "");
            &parms = Split(&parmList, ",");
         Else
            &parms = Null;
         End-If;

         /* Use a PeopleCode function to dynamically execute a method
          * with the same name as the tag, but prefixed with process.
          * For example, if the Meta-HTML tag is %Message, then call
          * the method named processMessage.
          */
         &replacement = ObjectDoMethodArray(%This, "process" | &tag,
               CreateArrayAny(&parms));
         &html = Substitute(&html, &matcher.group(), &replacement);
      End-If;
   End-While;

   Return &html;
end-method;

method processNodePortalUrl
   /+ &nodeName as String +/
   /+ Returns String +/
   Local string &node_url;
   SQLExec("SELECT URI_TEXT FROM PSNODEURITEXT " |
         "WHERE MSGNODENAME = :1 AND URI_TYPE = 'PL'",
         &nodeName, &node_url);

   Return &node_url;
end-method;

method processMessage
   /+ &messageSet as String, +/
```

```
    /+ &messageNumber as String +/
    /+ Returns String +/

    Return MsgGetText(Value(&messageSet), Value(&messageNumber), "");
end-method;
```

Is the `APT_META:HTML:Processor` class case-sensitive? In other words, is `%Message` treated the same as `%MESSAGE`? Let's add another test to find out:

```
%This.AssertStringsEqual(&p.process("%MESSAGE(3, 51)"), "Working...",
      "The resultant message does not match.");
```

This test passes, proving that the `APT_META:HTML:Processor` is not case-sensitive.

Conclusion

TDD has many benefits from a software design and productivity perspective. I prefer TDD because it keeps me focused on requirements and tasks. The solutions I create with TDD often have a simplicity and elegance that I can't seem to achieve when using the traditional design-and-build technique.

TDD works well with AWE and Integration Broker handler classes. It also works well for developing specialized utility classes and functions. The key to successful TDD usage is designing loosely coupled code modules. The usage of context-aware functions and system variables, such as `%Component` and `GetRow()`, effectively break TDD.

TDD does more than just help you write better software. With TDD, each project becomes a mystery to solve. Many people are better at solving problems and fixing programs than creating new solutions. Instead of trying to create designs, TDD allows us to create tests, which are really problems to solve. Tests become the creative engine driving programmers toward a solution.

Notes

1. Businessballs, "Tree Swing Pictures" [online]; available from http://www.businessballs.com/treeswing.htm; Internet; accessed 5 December 2009.
2. Webopedia, "stub" [online]; available from http://www.webopedia.com/TERM/s/stub.html; Internet; accessed 5 December 2009.

CHAPTER 16

PeopleCode Language Arts

Programmers apply various coding standards, practices, and patterns to mainstream programming languages. This chapter describes how we can use some of these standards, practices, and patterns with PeopleCode.

Composition over Inheritance

In Chapter 1, we used application classes to create a PeopleCode logging framework. Our logging framework consisted of a `Logger` interface, a `LoggerBase` abstract class, and two concrete `Logger` implementations named `FileLogger` and `MessageBoxLogger`. This inheritance-based design decision served us well for Chapter 1, but let's consider some more complex examples.

What if we want to add encryption to logging targets? How and where would we implement encryption? If we implement encryption at the lower-level `LoggerBase`, how would we account for targets that don't support encryption? If we implement encryption at a higher level, such as within the `FileLogger`, we may need to repeat the same encryption code in other `Logger` implementations.

An alternative to inheritance is composition. Consider the encryption scenario in relation to the `FileLogger` and `MessageBoxLogger`. It is possible to write encrypted data to a file and later decrypt that data, but displaying encrypted data in a `MessageBox` is useless. Instead of creating an inheritance hierarchy, we could make `Logger` a top-level class that expects a `Target` object as a constructor parameter. This would allow us to chain targets together. We could create a target that encrypts content, and then delegates the actual logging task to another target. Another useful target might be a message-formatting target. Using this approach, a `Logger` could chain a message through a formatter, then to an encrypter, and finally write it to a log file. Here is some code that demonstrates how we might use a logging API written in this manner:

```
Local APT_LOG4PC:Target &file =
      create APT_LOG4PC:Targets:FileTarget("c:\path\to\file.log");

Local APT_LOG4PC:Target &encrypter =
      create APT_LOG4PC:Targets:Encrypter("TRIPLE_DES_ENC_B64", &file);

Local APT_LOG4PC:Target &formatter =
      create APT_LOG4PC:Targets:PatternFormatter("%d %s", &encrypter);

Local APT_LOG4PC:Logger &logger =
      create APT_LOG4PC:Logger(&formatter);

&logger.debug("This statement was formatted, encrypted, and then " |
      "written to a log file");
```

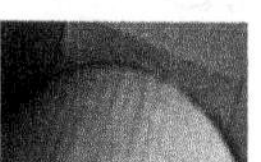

NOTE
The `TRIPLE_DES_ENC_B64` parameter mentioned in the preceding code is the name of a delivered pluggable encryption profile. For more information about PeopleTools pluggable encryption, see PeopleBook: Security Administration, *"Securing Data with PeopleSoft Encryption Technology."*

Notice how the targets are chained together: `&formatter > &encrypter > &file`. Composition lends itself to reuse. The `Encrypter` class has no knowledge of the `Formatter` class in front of it or the `FileTarget` class behind it. Each target contains the code necessary to perform its specific duty.

Façades

The prototype in the previous example references a `Formatter`, an `Encrypter`, a `FileTarget`, and a `Logger`. Let's prototype those objects, starting from the outside and working inward in a manner similar to the TDD approach described in Chapter 15.

Here's the `Logger` class:

```
REM ** Declare the facade logger class;
class Logger
   method Logger(&target as APT_LOG4PC:Target);
   method info(&message as string);
   REM ** other helper methods go here;

private
   method writeToLog(&level As APT_LOG4PC:Level, &message as string);
   instance Target &target_;
   REM ** other instance members go here;
end-class;

method info
   If (%This.isFatalEnabled()) Then
      %This.writeToLog(
         (create APT_LOG4PC:Level()).enableForFatal(), &message);
   End-If;
end-method;

method writeToLog
   &target.write(&level, &message);
end-method;
```

Notice that the `Logger` class constructor requires a `Target`. The following code describes the `Target` interface:

```
REM ** Declare the interface responsible for writing messages;
interface Target
   method write(&level As APT_LOG4PC:Level, &message as string);
end-interface;
```

An implementation of the `Target` interface could look similar to this:

```
class Encrypter implements APT_LOG4PC:Target
   method Encrypter(&target as APT_LOG4PC:Target);
   method write(&level As APT_LOG4PC:Level, &message as string);
```

```
private
  instance APT_LOG4PC:Target &target_;
end-class;

method Encrypter
   &target_ = &target;
end-method;

method write
   Local string &encryptedString;

   REM ** code to encrypt string goes here;

   &target_.write(&level, &encryptedString);
end-method;
```

Considering the `Formatter`, `Encrypter`, and `FileTarget` described here, we don't actually need the `Logger` class. We could generate the same results using the following code:

```
Local APT_LOG4PC:Target &file =
      create APT_LOG4PC:Targets:FileTarget("c:\path\to\file.log");

Local APT_LOG4PC:Target &encrypter =
      create APT_LOG4PC:Targets:Encrypter("TRIPLE_DES_ENC_B64", &file);

Local APT_LOG4PC:Target &formatter =
      create APT_LOG4PC:Targets:PatternFormatter("%d %s", &encrypter);

&formatter.write((create APT_LOG4PC:Level()).enableForFatal(),
      "This is a fatal message");
```

However, the `Logger` class is useful because it hides the complexities of the internal logger API. The `Logger` class is a *façade*—it provides an external interface to an internal API.[1]

Factories

The preceding façade example wires together `Logger` and `Target` instances prior to use. We could centralize `Logger` creation in a class method or FUNCLIB function. With a FUNCLIB function, using a `Logger` would be as simple as this:

```
Declare Function get_logger PeopleCode
      APT_LOGGER_FUNC.FUNCLIB FieldFormula;

Local APT_LOG4PC:Logger &logger = get_logger();

&logger.debug("This is a debug statement");
```

The `get_logger` function would contain most of the code from our first example:

```
Function get_logger() returns Local APT_LOG4PC:Logger
   Local APT_LOG4PC:Target &file =
      create APT_LOG4PC:Targets:FileTarget("c:\path\to\file.log");
```

```
   Local APT_LOG4PC:Target &encrypter =
      create APT_LOG4PC:Targets:Encrypter("TRIPLE_DES_ENC_B64", &file);

   Local APT_LOG4PC:Target &formatter =
      create APT_LOG4PC:Targets:PatternFormatter("%d %s", &encrypter);

   Return create APT_LOG4PC:Logger(&formatter);
End-Function;
```

In this example, the Factory pattern offers centralized configuration.

Inversion of Control

A factory centralizes construction and configuration, with the configuration hard-coded at design time. The configuration, therefore, is controlled by the programmer. Inversion of control (IoC)[2] is a design pattern that moves configuration from the control of the programmer to the control of an administrator (or even a user). Our `DBLoggerFactory` in Chapter 1 is an implementation of IoC. An administrator, not a programmer, specifies which `Logger` implementation class to use by modifying configuration data.

IoC facilitates reuse and loose coupling by forcing developers to code using interfaces rather than concrete implementations. It improves flexibility by allowing administrators to change application behavior without recompiling application source code. IoC promotes extensibility by allowing administrators and other developers to modify the behavior of delivered objects through interjection.

Well-known IoC containers, such as Java's Spring[3] and .NET's Castle Windsor[4] provide a mechanism for acquiring an instance of an interface from a configuration. PicoContainer,[5] for example, uses the factory-like method `getComponent`. We experience IoC on a small scale through the configuration of a PeopleSoft service operation or an AWE configuration.

PeopleSoft does not deliver an IoC container, so let's build one ourselves. Our IoC container will offer only customizable configuration. The container will expose a single `get_instance` function that returns a preconfigured instance of the requested interface.

NOTE
The common mainstream language IoC containers offer many features beyond IoC.

Let's use TDD to build this IoC container. As you learned in the previous chapter, TDD starts with a test case. To begin, create a new application class named `APT_IOC_TESTS` and add a new class named `ContainerTest`. Open the `ContainerTest` PeopleCode editor and add the following PeopleCode.

```
import APT_META:HTML:Processor;
import TTS_UNITTEST:TestBase;

class ContainerTest extends TTS_UNITTEST:TestBase
   method ContainerTest();
   method Run();
end-class;
```

```
Declare Function get_instance PeopleCode
      APT_IOC_FUNCLIB.FUNCLIB FieldFormula;

method ContainerTest
   %Super = create TTS_UNITTEST:TestBase("ContainerTest");
end-method;

method Run
   /+ Extends/implements TTS_UNITTEST:TestBase.Run +/
   Local APT_META:HTML:Processor &p =
         get_instance("APT_META:HTML:Processor");

   %This.AssertStringsEqual(&p.process("%NodePortalURL(HRMS)"),
         "http://hrms.example.com/psp/hrms/",
         "The resultant HRMS node URL is incorrect.");
end-method;
```

Our test case asks the `get_instance` function to return an instance of the meta-HTML processor we created in Chapter 15. Even though our stated intent is to map interfaces to implementation classes, this example requests an instance of a concrete class. For now, we just need to create an instance of an object and then test one of the object's methods. This example leverages the test case we built in the previous chapter. Later, we will create another test for interfaces.

Following the TDD six-step process, we started with a test case, not an implementation. This means the test code will not work until we stub out the system under test, or more precisely, the `get_instance` function. Create a new derived/work record named `APT_IOC_FUNCLIB` and add the delivered field named `FUNCLIB`. Open the `FieldFormula` event of the `FUNCLIB` field and add the following PeopleCode.

```
Function get_instance(&interfaceName As string) Returns object
   Return Null;
End-Function;
```

Next, log into your PeopleSoft application online and create a new PSUnit test suite named `APT_IOC`. Add the `APT_IOC_TESTS:ContainerTest` test case to the suite and then run the test. As shown in Figure 16-1, the test fails (TDD step 2) because the `get_instance` method returns `Null` instead of the expected `APT_META:HTML:Processor` class.

Now we can move on to step 3 by writing the simplest implementation possible that satisfies the test case. Open the `get_instance` function and replace its contents with the following PeopleCode.

```
import APT_META:HTML:Processor;

Function get_instance(&interfaceName As string) Returns object
   Return create APT_META:HTML:Processor();
End-Function;
```

We are ready for step 4. Rerun the test suite and watch it pass.

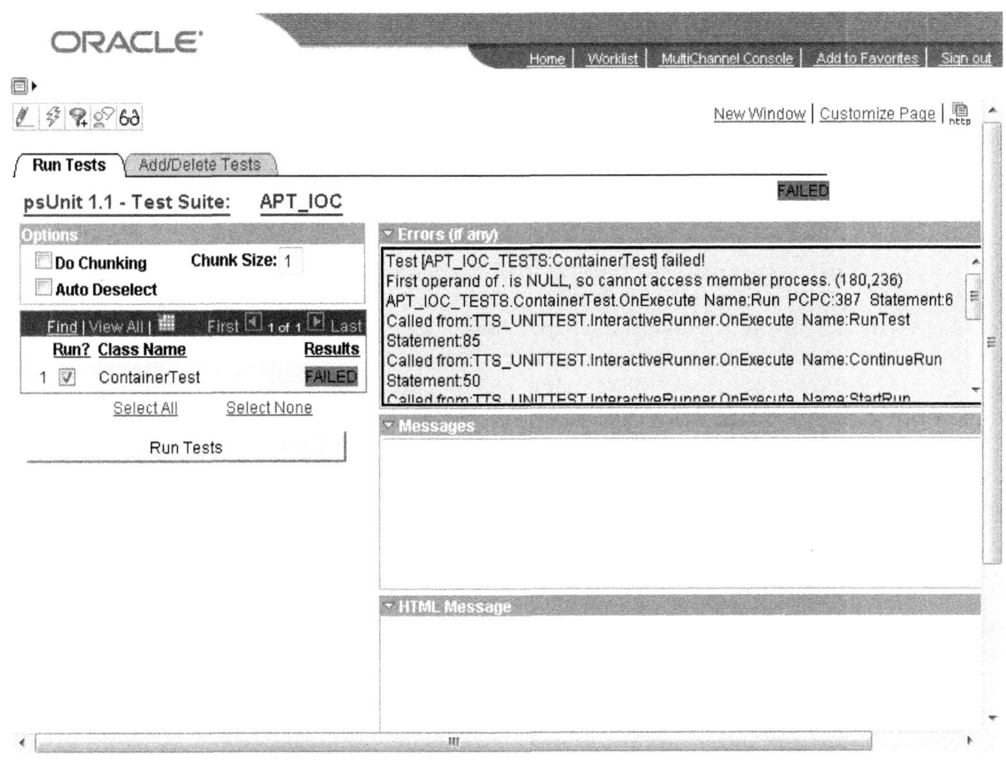

FIGURE 16-1. *First run of the APT_IOC test suite*

In step 5, we refactor our code. It was easy to create a bogus implementation for our test case because we knew exactly what the test case required. Let's refactor the test case by adding another test. It is more difficult to falsify answers for two tests. In this iteration, our test case will additionally ask the `get_instance` method to return an `APT_LOG4PC:Loggers:Logger`. Modify the PeopleCode in the application class `APT_IOC_TESTS:ContainerTest` so that it matches the following code listing (additions are in bold).

```
import APT_LOG4PC:Loggers:Logger;
import APT_META:HTML:Processor;
import TTS_UNITTEST:TestBase;

class ContainerTest extends TTS_UNITTEST:TestBase
   method ContainerTest();
   method Run();
end-class;
```

```
Declare Function get_instance PeopleCode
      APT_IOC_FUNCLIB.FUNCLIB FieldFormula;

method ContainerTest
   %Super = create TTS_UNITTEST:TestBase("ContainerTest");
end-method;

method Run
   /+ Extends/implements TTS_UNITTEST:TestBase.Run +/
   Local APT_META:HTML:Processor &p =
         get_instance("APT_META:HTML:Processor");

   %This.AssertStringsEqual(&p.process("%NodePortalURL(HRMS)"),
         "http://hrms.example.com/psp/hrms/",
         "The resultant HRMS node URL is incorrect.");

   Local APT_LOG4PC:Loggers:Logger &l =
         get_instance("APT_LOG4PC:Loggers:Logger");
   %This.Assert(&l.isDebugEnabled(),
         "Logger is NOT enabled for debug");
end-method;
```

When this test runs, considering the current implementation of `get_instance`, we expect the PeopleCode runtime to throw an exception as it tries to store the result of `get_instance` in a variable of type `APT_LOG4PC:Loggers:Logger`. Rerun the `APT_IOC` test suite to confirm this expectation. After modifying the test case and running the test, the test suite reports the following exception:

```
Test [APT_IOC_TESTS:ContainerTest] failed!

Cannot convert type APT_META:HTML:Processor to object type
      APT_LOG4PC:Loggers:Logger. (180,604)
      APT_IOC_TESTS.ContainerTest.OnExecute
      Name:Run  PCPC:639  Statement:7
```

The code failed on the second call to `get_instance`. The `get_instance` function actually returned a value, but the PeopleCode runtime was not able to coerce the result into a `Logger` variable. This is because `get_instance` is hard-coded to always return an `APT_META:HTML:Processor`.

We need to refactor the `get_instance` function so that it maps interfaces to object instances, but we don't want the `get_instance` function to perform the mapping directly. We want the `get_instance` function to derive its mapping from some form of configuration metadata.

The point of IoC is to *configure* rather than *code* logic. When considering configuration we must ask, "What form should we use for configuration files?" Spring uses XML files. A format that may be more appropriate for a PeopleSoft application is database tables, similar to the logging metadata tables we created for Chapter 1. Using database tables would allow us to present administrators with online configuration forms tailored to each configurable component. JSON is another form that merits consideration. JSON offers the flexibility of XML, but uses a syntax that is more familiar to programmers.

After determining the form of our configuration files, we must determine where to store those configurations. File systems and databases are common locations for storing PeopleSoft configuration information, but they aren't the only choices. We could, for example, use a load-balanced web service and an HTTP connector to access configuration information.

Even in the implementation of an IoC container, we recognize use cases for an IoC container. For example, we could code our IoC business logic around a `Configuration` interface and then create multiple storage engines (HTTP, file, database, and so on), leaving the actual storage implementation decision to an administrator.

Google Guice[6] is a Java IoC container that takes a different approach to configuration. Rather than placing configuration in the hands of an administrator, Guice uses configuration *modules*, which are compiled Java classes that map interfaces to implementations. While a coded solution reduces flexibility, it allows developers to express the configuration using syntax and semantics that are compatible with the system. This type of IoC delegates configuration to the business logic writer rather than the individual component developer. Considering that the component developer and the business logic writer are often the same person, the real benefit of a module-based IoC is its emphasis on small, focused components and code reuse.

To keep the text succinct, our example uses Guice's module-style configuration to map interfaces to fully configured implementation objects. Guice users benefit from Java's ability to represent class definitions as objects of type `Class`, a feature that allows for strong compile-time type checking. PeopleCode has no complement to this Java feature. Instead, our modules will use strings to refer to interfaces and classes by name.

Strongly or Loosely Typed?

PeopleCode allows us to declare variables and parameters as specific data types: number, string, record, and so on. These typed variables stand in contrast to undeclared variables. We don't distinguish typed variables from untyped variables, because all variables actually have a type. The PeopleCode compiler implicitly assigns the type `Any` to untyped variables. Instead, we classify variables as *strongly typed* or *loosely typed*.

When you declare a variable to be a `number`, you strongly type that variable. The compiler will not allow you to store a `string` in that `number` variable. A variable of type `Any`, however, can store strings, numbers, or anything.

The PeopleCode configuration module example uses strings, which are considered strongly typed variables, to represent object types. Because those object types masquerade as strings, the compiler will not perform compile-time validation. As a general rule, any time one type masquerades as another, the object it represents is loosely typed. Consider an array. An array that contains a collection of strings, fields, and so on is a strongly typed array. Once you expect an array to contain specific instances of objects, numbers, or strings, that array ceases to be a collection and begins to behave similar to a *value* object. The following PeopleCode fragment demonstrates the proper use of a PeopleCode array as a collection of strings (strongly typed).

```
class Processor
   method process (&strings as array of string);
end-class;

method process
   Local number &index;
```

```
   For &index = 1 to &strings.Len
      Local string &item = &strings[&index];
      REM ** process this string;
   End-For;
end-method;


REM ** Processor use case
Local MY_PKG:Processor &p = create MY_PKG:Processor();
Local array of string &stringsToProcess = CreateArray(
      "string1", "string2", "string3");

&p.process(&stringsToProcess);
```

The following example differs from the previous example in that the `Processor` class expects each element of the array to contain a specific type of value.

```
class Processor
   method process (&properties as array of string);
end-class;

method process
   Local string &emplid &properties[1];
   Local string &jobCode = &properties[2];
   Local string &supervisorId = &properties[3];

   REM ** Place code to process this employee here;
end-method;
```

There is nothing wrong with representing an object as an array, as long as you understand the risks associated with your decision. Sometimes the flexibility offered by an array is preferable to strongly typed application classes. The problem arises when you code a method or a function and then expect other developers to call that function or method.

The next example calls the `process` method from the prior example, but has the array elements out of order. The `process` method expects an employee ID as the first element, but the following code places the supervisor ID in the first element. The employee ID and job code are out of place as well. This code will compile and save, but may generate a runtime error.

```
Local MY_PKG:Processor &p = create MY_PKG:Processor();
Local array of string &properties = CreateArray(
      "supervisor123", "employee123", "job123");

&p.process(&properties);
```

An alternative to the previous "array as an object" example is an application class value object, as shown in the following listing.

```
class JobTransferData
   method setEmplid(&emplid as string);
```

```
    method setSupervisorId(&supervisorId as string);
    method setJobCode(&jobCode as string);
end-class;

REM ** class method implementations go here;


REM ** How to use the value object;
Local MY_PKG:Processor &p = create MY_PKG:Processor();
Local MY_OTHER_PKG:JobTransferData &data =
      create MY_OTHER_PKG:JobTransferData();
&data.setEmplid("employee123");
&data.setSupervisorId("supervisorId");
&data.setJobCode("job123");
```

A more subtle example of strongly versus loosely typed variables is the common record scenario. We often pass record objects as function and method parameters. The compiler will confirm that the input parameter is a record object, but the PeopleCode language will not ensure that the record object represents a particular named record. For example, you may write a function that expects a `JOB` record, but a developer calls the function with the `PERSONAL_DATA` record.

While a value object offers better design-time confirmation, it may also require more code. For example, we rarely convert a record to a value object because of the effort required.

To allow for some level of configuration within module implementations, we will create a one-row, one-field configuration table that stores the fully qualified name of an application class IoC configuration module. Using App Designer, create a new field and record. Set the field's type to character with a length of 254. Set the field's label to `APT_IOC_MODULE`, the label's long name to **Module Name**, and the label's short name to **Module**. Save the new field as `APT_IOC_MODULE`. Add this new field to a new record, and then name the record `APT_IOC_CONFIG`. Save and build the record definition. In the record, insert a single row with the value `APT_IOC:Modules:Module1`. Here is the Oracle SQL I used to insert a row into the `APT_IOC_CONFIG` record:

```
INSERT INTO PS_APT_IOC_CONFIG VALUES('APT_IOC:Modules:Module1')
/
COMMIT
/
```

We will create the `APT_IOC:Modules:Module1` application class after we deal with the `get_instance` function.

It is time to refactor the `get_instance` function. We know that the function will delegate object creation to an unknown module class. We also know that the name of the module class is stored in a database table. Let's start with what we know and discover the rest.

```
Function get_instance(&interfaceName As string) Returns object
   Local object &module;
   Local string &moduleName;
```

```
   SQLExec("SELECT APT_IOC_MODULE FROM PS_APT_IOC_CONFIG",
         &moduleName);

   &module = CreateObject(&moduleName);

   Return &module.getInstance(&interfaceName);
End-Function;
```

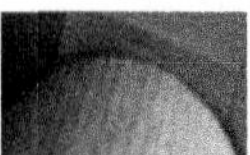

NOTE
TDD recommends small, incremental changes. In this iteration, we completely rewrote the `get_instance` *function. Technically, we should break this refactoring into multiple iterations and run the test suite after each change. I eliminated these extra iterations to keep you awake.*

In the preceding code listing, the bold text emphasizes the `&module` variable's object type and the `&module` method our code will execute. Since we don't know the actual module application class name, we can use the less restrictive `object` variable type.

Even though we don't know the module object type, we do know that the object must implement a `getInstance` method. By calling the `getInstance` method of `&module`, our code implicitly enforces a contract. It is a best practice to refactor such implicit contracts into explicit contracts by creating and implementing application class interfaces.

To create an interface for the IoC container, create a new application package named `APT_IOC`, add a new class to this package named `Module`, and save the application class. Open the `Module` class's PeopleCode editor and add the following PeopleCode.

```
interface Module
   method getInstance(&interfaceName as string) returns Object;
end-interface;
```

We can now write our first module. Add the subpackage `Modules` to the `APT_IOC` application package. To the `Modules` package, add a new application class named `Module1`. Our module will create object instances from the interfaces listed in our test case. We can accomplish this by returning an `APT_LOG4PC:Loggers:FileLogger` when asked for a `Logger` and then using the PeopleCode `CreateObject` function for all other requests. Add the following PeopleCode to `Module1`.

```
import APT_IOC:Module;
import APT_LOG4PC:Loggers:FileLogger;

class Module1 implements APT_IOC:Module;
   method getInstance(&interfaceName As string) Returns object;
end-class;

method getInstance
   /+ &interfaceName as String +/
   /+ Returns Object +/
   /+ Extends/implements APT_IOC:Module.getInstance +/
   Local object &result;
```

```
   Evaluate &interfaceName
   When "APT_LOG4PC:Loggers:Logger"
      &result = create APT_LOG4PC:Loggers:FileLogger(
            "c:\temp\ioc_test.log");
      &result.setDebugEnabled();
      Break;
   When-Other
      REM ** No mapping so try to create an instance;
      &result = CreateObject(&interfaceName);
   End-Evaluate;

   Return &result;
end-method;
```

NOTE
The preceding code listing uses an `Evaluate` *statement to determine what type of object to create. It then configures that object within the* `When` *block.*

Refactor the `get_instance` function again by changing the `&module` variable from an `object` to an `APT_IOC:Module`. The complete `get_instance` implementation follows (this is the final iteration of the `get_instance` function contained in the record field `APT_IOC_FUNCLIB.FUNCLIB FieldFormula` event).

```
import APT_IOC:Module;

Function get_instance(&interfaceName As string) Returns object
   Local APT_IOC:Module &module;
   Local string &moduleName;

   SQLExec("SELECT APT_IOC_MODULE FROM PS_APT_IOC_CONFIG",
         &moduleName);

   &module = CreateObject(&moduleName);

   Return &module.getInstance(&interfaceName);
End-Function;
```

The PeopleCode runtime will now enforce this contract at object-creation time. The previous implementation deferred enforcement until the runtime executed the `&module.getInstance` method.

Run the `APT_IOC` test suite again. This time, your test should pass. You now have an extremely lightweight IoC container for use with your next PeopleCode development project.

Enumerated Types

In this chapter, I've demonstrated that it is possible to use primitive data types to implement loose, or implicit, method and function parameter contracts. It is a best practice, however, to avoid implicit contracts. Explicit contracts use great detail to describe the interaction between objects.

Implicit contracts use vague language to allude to a contract, leaving room for misinterpretations. Bit flags, numbers, and predefined strings are examples of implicit contracts. The best way to describe this type of implicit contract is with an example.

The delivered `ProcessRequest` PeopleCode object contains a property named `RunStatus`. The property is described as a number, so it should accept any number. However, this property accepts only numbers in the range of 1 to 16. The list of valid values for the `RunStatus` property forms an unenforceable contract. Other programming languages describe and enforce this type of contract through *enumerated types*, which are a list of constants. Even though the PeopleCode language doesn't support enumerated types, we can emulate the same behavior through application classes.

The following PeopleCode listing describes a `RunStatus` application class that could be used for the `RunStatus` property of a fictitious `ProcessRequest` object. The difference between this `ProcessRequest` class and the delivered `ProcessRequest` class is that this example's `RunStatus` property is defined as having the type `RunStatus` as opposed to the delivered type of `number`.

```
class RunStatus
   method cancel() Returns APT_PRCSRQST:RunStatus;
   method delete() Returns APT_PRCSRQST:RunStatus;
   method hold() Returns APT_PRCSRQST:RunStatus;
   REM ** the other 13 method declarations would go here;

   method isCancel() Returns boolean;
   method isDelete() Returns boolean;
   method isHold() Returns boolean;
   REM ** the other 13 "is" method declarations would go here;

   method equals(&otherRunStatus As APT_PRCSRQST:RunStatus)
         Returns boolean;

private
   method getRunStatus() Returns number;
   instance number &runStatus;

end-class;

method cancel
   /+ Returns APT_PRCSRQST:RunStatus +/
   &runStatus = 1;
   Return %This;
end-method;

method delete
   /+ Returns APT_PRCSRQST:RunStatus +/
   &runStatus = 2;
   Return %This;
end-method;

method hold
   /+ Returns APT_PRCSRQST:RunStatus +/
   &runStatus = 4;
```

```
   Return %This;
end-method;

method isCancel
   /+ Returns Boolean +/
   Return (&runStatus = 1);
end-method;

method isDelete
   /+ Returns Boolean +/
   Return (&runStatus = 2);
end-method;

method isHold
   /+ Returns Boolean +/
   Return (&runStatus = 4);
end-method;

method equals
   /+ &otherRunStatus as APT_PRCSRQST:RunStatus +/
   /+ Returns Boolean +/
   Return (&runStatus = &otherRunStatus.getRunStatus());
end-method;

REM ** private methods;
method getRunStatus
   /+ Returns Number +/
   Return &runStatus;
end-method;
```

If the `ProcessRequest` object defined the `RunStatus` property as an `APT_PRCSRQST:RunStatus` object, then you would use the `RunStatus` class as follows:

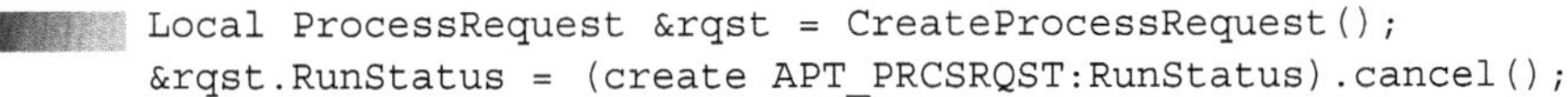

```
Local ProcessRequest &rqst = CreateProcessRequest();
&rqst.RunStatus = (create APT_PRCSRQST:RunStatus).cancel();
```

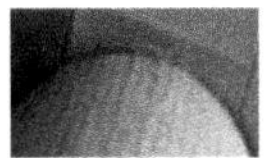

NOTE
The `RunStatus` class described here is a fully functional class. Given the implementation of `ProcessRequest`, however, it can't be used with the delivered `ProcessRequest` class. The last example that sets the `RunStatus` property to a `RunStatus` object is fictitious and is for demonstration purposes only.

Language Diversity

In an effort to control costs, IT departments often try to limit the number of redundant technologies. I believe this is a worthwhile endeavor. For example, PeopleSoft's applications support multiple server operating systems. Whenever possible, it makes sense for an organization to learn one server operating system well and eliminate the others. If the same applications run on both operating systems, then these operating systems are clearly redundant technologies.

Unfortunately, I often see organizations categorize various technologies as redundant when, in fact, they are very different. In an effort to eliminate redundant technologies, I see organizations try to limit the number of available programming languages by considering all languages to be redundant, when, in fact, most languages are very different.

Consider the array of languages we used in this book: PeopleCode, Java, JavaScript, HTML, and SQL (as well as some XML and other configuration file-specific syntaxes). As PeopleSoft developers, we can't afford to limit ourselves to a single language. Languages are the tools of a programmer. Just like any skilled craftsman, we need multiple tools, and we need to know how to use them well. You would no more use PeopleCode to write a web browser user interface than a carpenter would use a hammer to drive a screw.

This book presented code samples and patterns from several different programming languages. I encourage you to take the advice of Andrew Hunt and David Thomas in their book *The Pragmatic Programmer* (Addison-Wesley, 1999) and learn a new language. By "learn a new language," I don't mean just the syntax, functions, and routines. I mean learn how to communicate effectively in that language.

In my tenure as a PeopleSoft developer, I've surveyed code written by programmers from a wide variety of backgrounds. I can usually discern programmers' language experience by reviewing their code. For example, Java programmers tend to write PeopleCode using a Java style, and COBOL programmers write PeopleCode using a very different style.

When you learn a new language, learn that language's style. Doing so will make you a better programmer and a more effective communicator.

Notes

1. Wikipedia, "Facade pattern" [online]; available from http://en.wikipedia.org/wiki/Facade_pattern; Internet; accessed 16 December 2009.
2. Martin Fowler, "Inversion of Control Containers and the Dependency Injection Pattern" [online]; available from http://www.martinfowler.com/articles/injection.html; Internet; accessed 16 December 2009.
3. SpringSource, "Spring Source Community" [online]; available from http://www.springsource.org/; Internet; accessed 30 December 2009.
4. Castle Project. "MicroKernel" and "Windsor Container" [online]; available from http://www.castleproject.org/container/index.html; Internet; accessed 30 December 2009.
5. PicoContainer Committers, "What is PicoContainer" [online]; available from http://www.picocontainer.org/; Internet; accessed 30 December 2009.
6. Google, "google-guice" [online]; available from http://code.google.com/p/google-guice/; Internet; accessed 30 December 2009.

Index

* (asterisk), 234
= (equal sign), 21
" (quotation marks), 284
' (quote marks), 373, 374–375
// characters, 234
( ) parenthesis, 21, 24
3D Cover Flow effect, 220

A

abstract classes, 25, 27
abstract methods, 27
access control, 19–21
accessor/mutator design pattern, 20–21
Add button, 56, 57, 58, 60–64
AddAttachment function, 62–64, 68–77
add_attachment function, 62–64, 72, 73
address book application. *See* CI_PERSONAL_DATA HRMS CI
addStatementToCache method, 474
ADF (Application Development Framework), 520, 528, 545–549, 557
ADF Faces, 536
AdhocAccess class, 135
Adobe Flex, 211–220
  considerations, 209, 211
  Hello World example, 211–220
  modifying Flex source code, 269–270
  requirements, 211
AJAX, 263–302. *See also* HTML; XML
  adding animation via, 266–267
  "Ajaxifying" Direct Reports display shelf, 268–275
  "Ajaxifying" pages, 264–266
  configurable user interfaces, 275–293
  creating HTML AJAX service, 271–273
  custom scripts. *See* Custom Scripts component
  described, 264
  Fiddler HTTP proxy, 298–301
  Hello World example, 264–268
  modifying container page, 273–275
  postback issue and, 142
  security issues, 268
AJAX request handler, 264, 272
AJAX requests, 264, 272, 298–301
allowDelete method, 135
allowInsert method, 135
animation
  adding via AJAX, 266–267
  loadingAnimation graphic, 255, 350–353
anonymous function, 238–239, 244–245, 287

ANONYMOUS node, 528
antipatterns, 156
Apache Ant, 213
Apache Axis2 project, 557
Apache Commons, 365–372
Apache Velocity, 368–372
    creating repository Java classes, 453–460
    data source, 450–461
    JAR files, 368–369, 453
    templates, 370–372, 447, 450–461
Apache Xalan XSLT processor, 499
App Designer, 4–12
    adding code, 15
    comments, 12
    creating new application package, 4–5, 95
    creating records, 111
    saving/naming application package, 4–5, 12, 95
    vs. iScripts, 188
App Designer definitions, 190, 217–220, 225–227
App Engine
    disabling Restart property, 8, 9
    multithreading and, 461
    testing code, 6–10, 31–32, 36–38
    vs. SQR integration, 464
append method, 445–446
appenders, 441–446
application classes, 3–40
    access control, 19–21
    coding, 5–6
    comments, 12
    considerations, 39
    construction phase, 17
    constructors, 17, 24, 27–33
    creating, 4–5
    dynamic execution, 17
    example of, 4–12
    expanding, 11–12
    features, 17–21
    inheritance, 13–16
    logging framework example, 21–38
    misuses of, 38–39
    states, 17–19
    testing code, 6–10, 15–16
    user list, 100–101
    workflow functions, 117–120
Application Designer. *See* App Designer
Application Development Framework. *See* ADF
application packages
    adding classes to, 13, 95, 100, 399, 400
    creating, 4–5, 95
    data types and, 149
    inheritance, 13–16
    saving/naming, 4–5, 12, 95
    testing, 411–412
application pages. *See* pages
application servers
    environment variables, 86
    file storage locations on, 86
    file system, 33
    iScripts and, 225
    JAR files and, 365
    Java and, 365, 423
    loggers and, 391, 404
    pub/sub handlers, 149
    restarting, 460
    state blocks, 225
applications
    adding attachments to, 77–85
    address book. *See* CI_PERSONAL_DATA HRMS CI
    background colors, 553
    creating with JDeveloper, 416–418
    deploying Java classes to, 416–426
    Fusion, 529–532
    Java EE Application, 510, 555, 556
    mobile. *See* mobile applications
    requiring authentication, 556–557
    shortening URLs, 555–556
    web. *See* web applications
approval buttons, 110–113
approval event handlers, 94–97
approval flag, 95, 108, 270

approval process
- e-mail messages, 97–100
- tracing approvals, 125–126

approval status field, 108–109
Approval Status Monitor, 113–114, 129–132
Approval Workflow Engine. *See* AWE
ApprovalManager class, 117–120, 122, 124
approvals. *See also* AWE
- ad hoc access, 132–135
- e-mail templates for, 97–100
- overview, 92
- web service-enabling, 138–140

arrays
- Java, 341, 347–348
- JavaScript, 238
- PeopleCode, 238, 349, 373

assertTrue method, 483
asterisk (*), 234
ATTACHADD field, 57, 58, 60, 61, 66, 76
ATTACHDELETE event, 64, 84
attachment buttons
- Add button, 56, 57, 58, 60–64
- adding to application page, 80–81
- adding to transaction page, 53–64
- button states, 66–68, 112
- Delete button, 64
- enabling/disabling, 64, 65, 66
- initializing, 65
- properties, 56, 57, 58
- testing, 65
- View button, 64–65
- writing PeopleCode for, 59–65

attachment fields
- adding to application page, 78–81
- adding to transaction page, 53–59

attachment storage record, 49–53
attachments. *See also* File Attachment API
- accessing, 86
- adding to applications, 77–85
- adding to transactions, 42–77, 85
- file data, 53
- names, 53–54
- processing, 85–87
- serving via iScripts, 209–210
- storage of, 49–53, 56–57, 87
- UCM, 85
- URLs for, 56–58
- validating, 87–89

authentication, 556–557
autoboxing, 461, 462
autonomous transactions, 437–441
AWE (Approval Workflow Engine), 91–140. *See also* approvals
- ad hoc access, 132–135
- configuring metadata, 102–108
- configuring transactions, 104–105
- event handler iterator, 136–138
- event handlers, 94–97
- modifying transactions, 108–126
- overview, 92
- process definitions, 105–108
- registering transactions, 102–103
- supporting definitions, 93–102
- testing approvals, 126–129
- thread IDs, 94
- tracing approvals, 125–126
- transaction tables, 94
- user lists, 100–102
- web service-enabling approvals, 138–140
- workflow-enabling transactions, 92–129

Axis2 project, 557

B

backups, 51
batch processing, 464
best practices, 559–594
binary data, 50, 89
binary files, 42, 50, 65–89
bind variables
- advantages of, 14
- e-mail templates, 97–99
- employee ID, 272
- HTML definitions, 200, 244

bind variables (*cont.*)
managing, 472, 474
performance and, 14, 471
setting, 477
BlackBerry devices, 555
bookmarklets
adding to browser toolbar, 196–197
calling iScripts via, 192–197
considerations, 314
creating, 194–197
general information, 192, 197
trace, 194, 195, 237–239
URLs in, 194–197
bookmarks, 192, 194
bootstrap code
described, 247
JavaScript and, 247–251
modifying, 285–291, 316–324
parsing JSON, 285–287
separating from common code, 316–317
bootstrapping, 247
browsers. *See* web browsers
buttons. *See also* toolbar buttons
approval, 110–113
attachment. *See* attachment buttons
deny, 109, 110, 112
hiding, 112
images, 304, 310
metadata repository, 304–312
permission lists, 305, 315–316, 329–331
states, 66–68, 112
styles, 266
submit, 110–112, 122, 127, 128
trace, 314–316
workflow, 122–126

C

cache, parameter, 200–203
caching
browser, 292, 360
iScripts and, 302, 350, 508–509, 516
performance issues, 261
web server, 241
calendar content, 198–200
callHandlers method, 138
Cascading Style Sheets. *See* CSS
case sensitivity, 12, 343
Chrome browser, 275, 285, 292
chunked data, 53
CI_PERSONAL_DATA HRMS CI
creating data control, 532–536
creating Fusion web app, 529–532
creating view, 536–540
designing search page, 540–553
providing web services, 520–528
requiring authentication, 556–557
shortening application's URL, 555–556
testing search page, 553–555
class definitions, 6
class directory, 365, 453
class files, 420–421, 424, 460
classes. *See also specific classes*
abstract, 25, 27
adding methods to, 11–12
adding to application packages, 13, 95, 100, 399, 400
application. *See* application classes
instances, 17, 27, 31
Java, 364–372, 416–426
Logger, 25–30, 390, 392, 400–402
naming, 12
repository, 453–460
thread, 131–132
UserGreeter, 13–17
Clone method, 159
cloned databases, 51, 57
closeQuietly() method, 470
code. *See also* coding; PeopleCode
bootstrap. *See* bootstrap code
comments, 12, 63, 72, 234, 266
common, 318–324
highlighting, 251–254
iScript. *See* iScripts
procedural, 4, 17

strong vs. loosely typed, 587–591
testing, 6–10, 15–16
UI loader, 294
code refactoring, 12
coding. *See also* code
application class, 5–6
custom data types, 149–168
for exceptions, 156
iScript, 189–190
spartan, 8
color, background, 240, 249, 553
comments, 12, 63, 72, 234, 266
Commons library, 365–368
components. *See also specific components*
adding PeopleCode to, 81–85
buffer utilities, 114–116
configuring as web services, 520–527
launching, 324–328
pagelets, 148–183
registering, 44–48
composition, 29
compression, 241
connector metadata, 471–472
ConnectorDataCollection object, 467
connectors, integrated. *See* integration technologies
construction phase, 17
constructors, 17, 24, 27–33, 566
content references (CREF), 48, 324–328
context-sensitive variables, 38
control flow statements, 161
Create Application wizard, 416–418
create function, 36
Create Java Class wizard, 445, 456
create keyword, 7, 17
CreateObject function, 7, 17, 36
CreateObjectArray function, 7, 17, 36
credentials, 557
CREF (content references), 48, 324–328
cross-reference record, 93, 95
cross-scripting, 268
CSS (Cascading Style Sheets), 230, 249
CSS files, 359, 360
css method, 245
CSS selectors, 244, 245
CSS specification, 240
Custom Scripts component
changing search operators, 293–298
downloading scripts, 287–289
highlighting active fields, 291–293
importing scripts, 289–291
limitations, 297
testing, 291
custom tools, 303–334. *See also* toolbars
buttons. *See* buttons; toolbar buttons
CREF information, 324–328
launching components, 324–328
modifying bootstrap code, 316–324
obtaining permission lists, 328–329
repositories. *See* metadata repository
URL-generation functions, 317–318
viewing query results, 328–333

D

data. *See also* metadata
binary, 50, 89
chunked, 53
recovery, 51
source, 148
test, 33, 279–283, 291
data control fields, 542
data controls, 532–536
data source parameters, 146
data sources, 143–146, 177, 210–227
Data Transfer Object (DTO), 431
data types
application packages, 149
coding, 149–168
custom, 148–168
described, 148
pagelets, 143, 180–183
provided by PeopleTools, 148–177
registering, 168, 169
database integration. *See* integration technologies
database tables, 86

databases
    attachments stored in, 49–53
    backups, 51
    cloned, 51, 57
    connections, 467–470, 471
    development, 465, 483
    free, 483
    Java Database Connectivity. *See* JDBC
    join options, 98
    target, 465
DataControlOperation class, 557
dataFilter function, 286–287
dataRetrieved function, 270
DataSource abstract class, 150, 168
DataSource properties/methods, 168
debug messages, 22, 31–32, 38
debug method, 28, 32
debuggers, 412
definition criteria, 106
definitions
    App Designer, 190, 217–220, 225–227
    AWE, 93–102, 105–108
    common, 245–246
    HTML. *See* HTML definitions
    JavaScript, 246
    process, 105–108
    record, 78–79, 193
    SQL, 14, 97–101, 271–272, 457
    supporting, 93–102, 255–256
    WEBLIB, 190
Delete button, 64
delivered record definitions, 78–79
deny buttons, 109, 110, 112
Deployment Log, 446
DEPT_SALARIES__NVISION_ query, 146
derived/work record, 234
desktop integration, 197–209
development databases, 465, 483
Direct Reports display shelf. *See* DisplayShelf component
Direct Reports service, 270–271
directories
    class, 365, 453
    output, 492
    package, 460
    SDK, 465
    working, 86
display formats, 148
DisplayShelf component
    "Ajaxifying," 268–275
    creating, 220–227
    modifying, 269–271
document management systems, 85
Document Object Model. *See* DOM
Document Type Definition (DTD), 89, 168
document.ready() method call, 244, 294–296
DOM (Document Object Model)
    HTML, 239, 240, 244
    JavaScript and, 243–245, 347
    script loading and, 291
DOM injection, 268
DOM methods, 245
downcasting, 338
download prompts, 207–208
drag-and-drop approach, 254, 520, 528, 557
drivers, JDBC, 466, 467, 469, 492
Driver's License Data component, 77–89
DTD (Document Type Definition), 89, 168
DTO (Data Transfer Object), 431
dynamic execution, 17
dynamic logger configuration, 32–36

E

EBNF (Extended Backus–Naur Form), 20
Eclipse JSF design-time tools, 557
Edit CREF toolbar button, 326–328
elements, styling, 239–240
e-mail notifications, 138
e-mail pagelets, 169–176
e-mail servers, 148, 173

e-mail templates, 97–100
EMailDataSource listing, 162–168
embedded strings, 11, 457
employee photo iScript, 220–225
!empty operator, 551
encryption, 580
enterprise service bus (ESB), 464
enumerated types, 591–593
environment variables, 86
equal sign (=), 21
error notifications, 64
errorLog.html file, 470, 503
errors. *See also* messages
    authorization, 194, 253
    autonomous transactions, 437–441
    Integration Broker, 467, 469–470
    log4j, 372
    logging, 390, 392, 397, 402
    PSUnit, 567
    scroll, 78, 79
    test, 567, 571, 576
    unable to find routing request, 528
    undefined user name, 528
ESB (enterprise service bus), 464
EscapeHTML function, 268
EscapeJavaScriptString function, 284
Evans, Eric, 24–25
event handler iterator, 136–138
event handlers
    activating, 526
    approval, 94–97
    HTTPService element, 270
    onclick, 270
    user lists, 100
event properties, 446–447
events, PeopleCode, 59, 60, 62
exceptions, 156, 470, 485, 566
exec keyword, 449
execute method, 159–161
explicit contracts, 590, 591
Extended Backus–Naur Form (EBNF), 20
Extensible Markup Language. *See* XML
Extensible Stylesheet Language. *See* XSL

F

facades, 581–582
facets, 543, 544
factories, 582–583
factory design pattern, 33–38
factory objects, 33
factory test program, 36–38
fatal messages, 22, 33–34, 38
fatal method, 28, 32
Fiddler, 298–301, 508–509
FieldChange event, 122–123, 210–211, 234
FieldFormula event, 67, 121, 188, 189–190
fields
    approval, 108–110
    attachment. *See* attachment fields
    building, 33
    disabling at runtime, 114–116
    hidden, 54
    highlighting active, 291–293
    labels, 542
    names, 67
    required, 551–553
File Attachment API, 41–89
    accessing attachments, 86
    adding attachments to applications, 77–85
    adding attachments to transactions, 42–77, 85
    customizing file attachment behavior, 65–77
    described, 42
    processing attachments, 85–87
    storage methods, 49–53, 56–57, 87
    validating attachments, 87–89
file attachments. *See* attachments; File Attachment API
file contents validation, 89
file extensions, 87–89
file paths, 86
file systems, 33, 241, 586

FILE_ATTACH_SBR subrecord, 53
FileLogger class, 25–26, 29–30
filename validation, 87–89
files. *See also specific files*
  accessibility of, 52
  attaching. *See* File Attachment API
  backups, 51
  binary, 42, 50, 65–89
  class, 420–421, 424, 460
  CSS, 359, 360
  iCalendar, 198–203
  JAR. *See* JAR files
  JavaScript, 241, 248, 300
  JSP, 506–507, 514
  log. *See* log files
  names, 63, 64
  recovery of, 51
  size, 63
  SWF, 209, 214–215, 223
  trace, 21, 388, 389
  XML, 161, 392, 471–472, 486
  XSL, 499
Firebug browser plug-in, 236–238, 293–295, 298
Firefox browser, 199, 236, 275, 285, 299
fireShelfChange function, 270
Flex. *See* Adobe Flex
fluent interface design, 24–25, 294
footer facets, 543, 544
form component, 540–543
Fowler, Martin, 24–25
FTP-based storage, 49–52, 56–57
FUNCLIB functions, 66–67, 188, 247
FUNCLIB records, 66–67
function library, 65–77
functions. *See also specific functions*
  anonymous, 238–239, 244–245, 287
  JavaScript, 238
  self-invoking, 238
  undocumented, 334
  URL-generation, 317–318
Fusion web applications, 529–532

G

gateway properties, 503
%GenerateQueryContentURL meta-HTML resolver, 356–361
generateRequest method, 486–487
get methods, 378–382, 474
get modifier, 19
GetAttachment function, 86
getConnection() method, 467–470
GetHTMLText() function, 75, 270
get_instance function, 583–586
GetJavaScriptURL method, 241
getLastModified() method, 456–457, 459
GetParameter method, 193
getResourceStream method, 454–456, 459
GetUsers method, 100–101
global namespace, 238
global scope, 117
Globally Unique Identifier (GUID), 201–202, 206–207
globals, PeopleCode, 331–333
Google AJAX libraries, 217
Google Guice, 587
GUID (Globally Unique Identifier), 201–202, 206–207

H

&handle_error parameter, 73
hashtables, 349, 373
Heller, Chris, 192
Hello World example
  Adobe Flex, 211–220
  AJAX, 264–268
  iScripts, 189–192
  Java, 339–345, 416–426
hidden fields, 54
highlighting active fields, 291–293
highlighting code, 251–254
HTML (HyperText Markup Language)
  dynamic, 234
  injecting via AJAX. *See* AJAX
  malicious, 268
  meta-HTML processor, 350–364

HTML AJAX service, 271–273
HTML Area controls, 218–219, 231, 233–234
HTML definitions
    bind variables, 200, 244
    common, 246, 253
    considerations, 241
    creating, 217–218, 235–236
    File Attachment API, 74, 75
    iScripts imported into, 253, 255
    JavaScript, 241, 246
    jQuery and, 243–244
    size of, 241
    static, 368
    vs. templates, 161
HTML DOM, 239, 240, 244
HTML hyperlinks, 257–258
HTMLAREA field, 234–235
&html_header parameter, 73
HTTP (Hypertext Transfer Protocol), 49, 464
HTTP header servlet filters, 509–513
HTTP headers, 508
HTTP listener, 464
HTTP proxy, 298–301
HTTP redirects, 190, 299
HTTP requests, 211, 264, 298–301, 509–510
HTTPService script, 216–217, 223–225
hyperlinks, 196, 203–209, 257–258. *See also* URLs
HyperText Markup Language. *See* HTML
Hypertext Transfer Protocol. *See* HTTP

I

IBRequest object, 477, 486–487
IBRequest parameter, 486
iCalendar files, 198–203
IDE (integrated development environment), 416
IE Developer Toolbar, 236
IETF (Internet Engineering Task Force), 198
%Image meta-HTML resolver, 350–353
image URLs, 223–225
ImageCoverFlow.mxml file, 222, 269–270
ImageCoverFlow.swf file, 223, 270
images
    button, 304, 310
    included with PeopleSoft, 304
    placeholder, 224
    toolbar, 353
IMAP (Internet Message Access Protocol), 148
implicit contracts, 590, 591–592
import directive, 444
importScript function, 291
inclusion sequence, 275
inheritance, 13–16, 29, 580–581
init method, 454
initializeSettings method, 150–154
instances, 17, 27, 31, 33
instantiation, 17
integrated connectors. *See* integration technologies
integrated development environment (IDE), 416
Integration Broker
    described, 464
    exceptions, 469
    gateway configuration, 493–494
    messages/errors, 467, 469–470
    service configuration, 520–521, 524
    transforming messages, 495–499
    troubleshooting connectors, 502–503
integration technologies, 463–504
    configuring integrations, 492–501
    connector deployment, 492
    creating routings, 499–501
    gateway configuration, 493–494
    integration setup, 464–466
    JDBC target connector, 466–492
    node creation, 494–495
    overview, 464
    predeployment testing, 482–492
    testing integrated connectors, 501
    transforming messages, 495–499
    troubleshooting connectors, 502–503

Internet Engineering Task Force (IETF), 198
Internet Explorer, 236, 240, 275, 285
Internet Message Access Protocol (IMAP), 148
introspectConnector() method, 466, 467
inversion of control (IoC), 583–591
IoC (inversion of control), 583–591
iScript URLs, 248–255
iScripts, 187–227
  Adobe Flex, 211–220
  caching behavior, 302, 508–509, 516
  calling via bookmarklets, 192–197
  coding, 189–190
  as data sources, 210–227
  described, 188–189
  desktop integration, 197–209
  DisplayShelf component, 220–227
  employee photo, 220–225
  Hello World example, 189–192
  HTTP headers, 508–509
  imported into HTML definitions, 253
  JavaScript and, 246
  JSON results in, 284
  JSP as alternative to, 506–507
  loading as JavaScript files, 248
  modifying code, 191–192
  modifying transactions, 203–209
  naming conventions, 188
  obtaining CREF information, 324–325
  parameter cache, 200–203
  permission list, 190
  securing, 253
  serving calendar content, 198–200
  serving file attachments, 209–210
  serving SQL results to browser, 281–285
  testing, 190–191, 284, 289
  vs. App Designer, 188
  vs. FUNCLIB functions, 188
  WEBLIB_APT_JSL code, 260–261
isSourceModified() method, 456–457
IsUserInRole function, 135

J

J2EE web servers, 506, 507, 509–510, 513. *See also* web servers
JAR files
  application servers and, 365
  considerations, 365, 375, 515
  creating with JDeveloper, 421–422, 424
  deploying connectors, 492
  deploying Java, 420–425
  Velocity, 368–369, 453
  viewing contents, 425
Java arrays, 341, 347–348
Java build environment, 416
Java classes, 364–372, 416–426
Java collections, 349
Java Database Connectivity. *See* JDBC
Java EE Application, 510, 555, 556
Java language
  advantages of, 338–339
  autoboxing, 461, 462
  configuring development environment, 426–427
  considerations, 461–462
  creating source files, 416–420
  creating test program, 426
  data access, 429–436
  deploying, 420–425
  examples, 339–349
  Hello World example, 339–345, 416–426
  log files, 340–341
  logging framework, 389–413
  meta-HTML processor, 350–364
  multithreading, 461
  objects vs. classes, 338
  overloading, 378
  overview, 338–349
  regular expressions, 341–345
  string formatting, 345–347
  using PeopleCode objects, 426–436
  using PeopleCode system variables, 427–429
  versions, 384

vs. JavaScript, 338
on web server, 505–517
writing, 441–447
Java libraries, 338–339, 364–372, 384, 465
Java Message Service (JMS) queue, 464
Java Native Interface (JNI), 426
Java objects, 338, 340–341, 426–436
Java Runtime Environment (JRE), 423
Java Server Faces. *See* JSF
Java Server Pages. *See* JSP
Java strings, 339–347
Java Virtual Machine (JVM), 377, 460
JavaScript, 229–262
bookmarklets. *See* bookmarklets
bootstrap code, 247–251
considerations, 240, 293, 297
dynamic script, 233–236
Firebug browser plug-in, 236–238
iScripts and, 246
PeopleCode globals, 331–333
performance issues, 242, 261
static script, 230–233
styling elements, 239–240
testing, 231, 237
vs. Java, 338
web browsers and, 231–233, 240, 243–244
JavaScript arrays, 238
JavaScript definitions, 246
JavaScript files, 241, 248, 300
JavaScript functions, 238
JavaScript libraries, 217, 240–245, 264
%JavaScript meta-HTML resolver, 353–356
JavaScript Object Notation. *See* JSON
JDBC (Java Database Connectivity), 488, 499
JDBC connections, 461, 464, 466–474
JDBC drivers, 466, 467, 469, 492
JDBC library, 466
JDBC objects, 429
JDBC target connector, 466–492
JDBCAppender, 436, 446, 449
JDBCTargetConnector class, 466–482, 483
JDBCTargetConnector listing, 477–482
JDeveloper
creating applications, 416–418
creating data controls, 532–536
creating Fusion web app, 529–532
creating Hello World class, 416–426
creating JAR files, 421–422, 424
creating mobile applications, 528–556
creating search page, 540–555
creating views, 536–540
JSP and, 506–507
managing libraries, 465
servlet filters and, 510–515
shortening application URLs, 555–556
versions, 528
JDeveloper libraries, 426–427, 428
JDK compiler, 424
JDK versions, 466
JMS (Java Message Service) queue, 464
JNI (Java Native Interface), 426
join options, 98
jQuery calls, 294
jQuery library, 240, 242, 243–245, 285
jQuery load method, 266
jQuery plug-ins, 254–260
JRE (Java Runtime Environment), 423
JSF (Java Server Faces), 528, 536, 538–540, 551, 557
JSF controller, 538, 542
JSF metadata, 539
JSF pages, 538–540
JSON (JavaScript Object Notation), 373–384
consuming, 376–384
described, 281, 373
producing, 373–376
JSON parsing, 284, 285–287, 376
JSON2 JavaScript library, 291
JSP (Java Server Pages), 505–507
JSP files, 506–507, 514
JVM (Java Virtual Machine), 377, 460

L

labels, 542
LaunchManager class, 117–120, 124, 128
layouts, 446–447
"lazy initialization," 119
leave portal button, 333–334
Level class, 22–24, 28
Level object, 24–25, 32
libraries
  Apache Commons, 365–372
  function, 65–77
  Google AJAX, 217
  Java, 338–339, 364–372, 384, 465
  JavaScript, 217, 240–245, 264
  JDBC, 466
  JDeveloper, 426–427, 428
  jQuery, 240, 242, 243–245, 285
  managing, 465
  PeopleCode, 426–427, 428
  SQLObject JavaScript, 217
  third-party, 364–372
license agreement, 214
Lightbox plug-in, 254
loadingAnimation graphic, 255, 350–353
log files
  Deployment Log, 446
  errorLog.html file, 470, 503
  Java, 340–341
  msgLog.html file, 470, 477, 503
log4j appender, 436–449
log4j configuration, 369–370
log4j error, 372
log4j logging framework, 389–412
log4j metadata, 410–411
Logger classes, 25–30, 390, 392, 400–402
logger factory, 32–36
Logger interface, 25–29
LoggerBase class, 26–28, 29
loggers, 390–391, 404
logging event properties, 446–447
logging frameworks
  custom appender for, 436–449
  examples, 21–38, 369–370
  integrated, 398–411
  log4j, 389–412
  testing, 31–34, 411–412
  Velocity. *See* Apache Velocity
logging levels, 22–25
logging strings, 32
logging tools, 388–389
login.jspx page, 557
LogManager class, 403–409

M

Mapped Diagnostic Context (MDC), 446
maps, 446, 538
MCF (MultiChannel Framework), 148–149
MDC (Mapped Diagnostic Context), 446
MDS simulators, 555
members
  described, 20
  instance, 346
  protected, 24, 27
  public, 24
  static, 346
message boxes, 21, 25–29, 31, 234, 291
Message not found error, 11
message sets, 11
MessageBox function, 21, 25–29, 31
MessageBox statement, 389
MessageBoxLogger class, 25–26, 28–29
messages. *See also* errors
  debug, 22, 31–32, 38
  fatal, 22, 33–34, 38
  Integration Broker, 467, 469–470
  Java Message Service, 464
  not found, 11
  transforming, 495–499
metadata. *See also* data
  AWE, 102–108
  connector, 471–472
  JSF, 539
  log4j, 410–411
metadata repository
  creating, 275–276
  maintaining, 276–279
  serving scripts, 279–285

template, 450–453
toolbar buttons, 304–312
working with, 33–36
meta-HTML processor
creating, 350–364
testing, 564–578
meta-HTML transformer, 178–180
Meta-SQL, 240
method chaining, 24–25, 28
methods. *See also specific methods*
abstract, 27
access control, 19–20
adding to classes, 11–12
creating, 6
fluent, 24–25, 294
naming, 12
private, 20
protected, 19, 20
public, 19, 20
static, 433
vs. properties, 21
mobile applications, 519–558. *See also* web applications
address book app. *See* CI_PERSONAL_DATA HRMS CI
background colors, 553
creating data controls, 532–536
creating Fusion web app, 528–532
creating views, 536–540
overview, 520
providing web services, 520–528
requiring authentication, 556–557
search pages, 540–555
shortening URLs, 555–556
using JDeveloper for, 528–556
web browsers, 528, 536, 555
WSDL URL, 524, 528, 534, 557
mobile browsers, 536, 537, 555–556
mobile workforce, 520
MobileDCLogin project, 556–557
MobileView project, 536–538, 556, 557
MsgGet function, 11
MsgGetExplainText function, 11
MsgGetText function, 11
msgLog.html file, 470, 477, 503
MultiChannel Framework (MCF), 148–149
multithreading, 461
mxmlc Flex compiler, 214

N

namespaces, 238, 247–248, 289, 319, 340
naming conventions, 12, 500
navigation rules, 538
notifications, 64, 92, 135, 138

O

object state, 17–19
object-oriented programming (OOP), 4, 29
objects. *See also specific objects*
changing types, 380
Data Transfer Objects, 431
DOM. *See DOM entries*
downcasting, 338
factory, 33
in-memory, 7, 17
instances, 27, 33
Java, 338, 340–341, 426–436
JDBC, 429
Record, 434–436
SQL, 432–434
stateful, 17–19
upcasting, 338
OnFinalApproval event, 136
OOP (object-oriented programming), 4
OOP inheritance, 29
Open Web Application Security Project (OWASP), 268
operator IDs, 100, 101, 119, 432
options object, 318
Oracle Application Development Framework (ADF), 520, 528, 545–549, 557
overloading, 378
OWASP (Open Web Application Security Project), 268

P

page flow map, 538
pagelet transformers, 148, 177–180
Pagelet Wizard, 141–183. *See also* pagelets
  considerations, 17, 183
  data types, 148–177
  display formats, 180–183
  extending, 183
  templates, 161
  XML/XSL considerations, 180–181
pagelets
  adding to home page tabs, 176–177
  advantages of, 142
  components of, 148–183
  creating, 143–147
  data types, 143, 180–183
  described, 142
  display formats, 180–183
  e-mail, 169–176
  headings, 168, 170
  test, 168–177
  title, 143, 144
  XML/XSL considerations, 180–181
pages
  adding fields/buttons to, 78–81
  adding hyperlinks to, 203–209
  adding Thickbox to, 256–260
  "Ajaxifying," 264–266
  attaching toolbars to, 312–316
  buttons on. *See* buttons
  creating, 230
  download prompts, 207–208
  fields on. *See* fields
  JSF, 538–540
  loading, 508
  permission lists, 45–48, 190, 328–329
  search. *See* search page
  for toolbar maintenance, 308–310
parameter cache, 200–203
parameter form, 540–543
parenthesis ( ), 21, 24
PASSTHRU transformer, 177, 178, 180
path criteria, 107
PatternLayout, 447
PeopleCode, 579–594. *See also* code; coding
  adding to components, 81–85
  best practices, 559–594
  binary files and, 50, 89
  composition vs. inheritance, 580–581
  copying for source records, 193
  enumerated types, 591–593
  facades, 581–582
  factories, 582–583
  inversion of control, 583–591
  language diversity, 593–594
  PostBuild, 117–120
  SQL in, 14, 98, 472
  strongly vs. loosely typed, 587–591
  writing for attachment buttons, 59–65
PeopleCode arrays, 238, 349, 373
PeopleCode editor, 5–6, 62, 120, 235
PeopleCode events, 59, 60, 62
PeopleCode globals, 331–333
PeopleCode libraries, 426–427, 428
PeopleCode system variables, 427–429
PeopleTools, 6, 13, 499
performance
  bind variables and, 14, 471
  CSS, 261
  JavaScript and, 242, 261
  logging, 397
  PatternLayout and, 447
permission lists
  for buttons, 305, 315–316, 329–331
  considerations, 316
  custom tools, 328–329
  iScripts, 190
  obtaining via queries, 328–329
  for pages, 45–48, 190, 328–329
Permission Lists grid, 308–310
personal information management (PIM) systems, 197–198
PIA (Pure Internet Architecture), 188
PIM (personal information management) systems, 197–198
ping() method, 466, 467, 470–471, 487
PL/SQL autonomous transactions, 437–441

point-in-time recovery, 51
POP (Post Office Protocol), 148
Post Office Protocol (POP), 148
postback issue, 142
postback technique, 142, 547
PostBuild event, 117–120
PreparedStatement, 472–474
&preserve_case parameter, 73
primary key, 436
printing levels, 22
private access control, 20
problems, investigating, 388
procedural code, 4, 17
process definitions, 105–108
process queries, 100
processSettingsChange method, 154–158
programming. *See* coding
Project Source Paths item, 492
projects. *See also specific projects*
  Axis2, 557
  migration, 48
  MobileDCLogin, 556–557
  MobileView, 536–538, 556, 557
  output directory, 492
  OWASP, 268
  ViewController, 529, 530, 536
properties
  access control, 19–20
  attachment buttons, 56, 57, 58
  changing values, 18–19
  defining, 19
  in-memory, 19
  protected, 19, 20
  public, 19, 20
  read-only, 18
  refresh, 547–551
  vs. methods, 21
protected access control, 19
Provide Web Service Wizard, 522–524, 528, 534
PSDBAppender, 442–449
PSDBResourceLoader, 453–461
PSIGW application, 465, 477
PSIGW library, 465
PSUnit, 564–567, 576
public access control, 19
pub/sub handlers, 149
Pure Internet Architecture (PIA), 188
PutAttachment function, 87

Q

queries. *See also jQuery entries*
  bind variables and, 101
  obtaining permission lists via, 328–329
  as user lists, 100
  viewing query results, 328–333
  XQuery, 338
query toolbar button, 329–333
quotation marks ("), 284
quote marks ('), 373, 374–375

R

ready method, 244
real-time integrations. *See* integration technologies
&RECNAME parameter, 72
record definitions, 193
Record objects, 434–436
record URL protocol, 56–58
record-based storage, 49–53, 56–57
records
  building, 33
  cloning, 193
  copying source record's PeopleCode, 193
  creating, 43, 52, 111
  cross-reference, 93, 95
  delivered record definitions, 78–79
  FUNCLIB, 66–67
  names, 43, 53, 57, 67
recovery, data, 51
recursion, 116
redirects, 190, 299
refactoring, 12, 570–572
reflection, 376

refresh properties, 547–551
registering data types, 168, 169
registering transactions, 102–103
Registration Wizard, 44–48
regular expressions, 341–345, 574
repository Java classes, 453–460
repository tables, 304–308
Request for Comment (RFC), 198
%Request system variable, 193
requests
    AJAX, 264, 272, 298–301
    approved, 98–99
    denied, 99
    HTTP, 211, 264, 298–301, 509–510
    servlet filters and, 507, 509–513
Response object, 190
Restart property, 8, 9
results table, 544–547
&RETCODE parameter, 73
return values, 25
RFC (Request for Comment), 198
RGB macro, 240
rich Internet technologies, 42, 210–211
roles, 46, 49
routings, creating, 499–501
RowInit event, 234, 244
row-level security, 272
Run method, 566
Run Program button, 8, 10
Run Request dialog, 8–10
RunStatus application class, 592–593
RuntimeException, 487

S

Safari browser, 240
SAM (SQL Access Manager), 461
SavePostChange event, 118, 119, 123–124, 125
scripts. *See also* iScripts
    custom. *See* Custom Scripts component
    inclusion sequence, 275
    serving, 279–285
scroll errors, 78, 79
SDK directory, 465
search bean, 557
search button, 544–547
search operators, 253, 293–298
search page
    adding form component, 540–543
    changing search operators, 253, 293–298
    designing, 540–553
    footer facets, 543, 544
    refresh properties, 547–551
    required fields, 551–553
    results table, 544–547
    search button, 544–547
    testing, 553–555
search page application. *See* CI_PERSONAL_DATA HRMS CI
SearchMethod class, 557
security
    access control, 19–21
    AJAX and, 268
    authentication, 556–557
    encryption, 580
    iScripts, 253
    malicious HTML, 268
    PatternLayout and, 447
    permission list, 45–48
    row-level, 272
    SQL injection, 14, 447, 471
select element, 294
send() method, 466, 467, 472, 474–477
SendMail function, 135
servers. *See also* web servers
    application. *See* application servers
    e-mail, 148, 173
    J2EE, 506, 507, 509–510, 513
    WebLogic, 507, 553
servlet filters, 507–516
set modifier, 19
SetTraceSQL function, 192, 193–194
source data, 148
spartan programming, 8

SQL
  embedded strings, 457
  in HTML AJAX service, 271–272, 279–285
  join options, 98
  Meta-SQL, 240
  in PeopleCode, 14, 98, 472
  Resolve Meta SQL option, 281
  serving results to browser, 281–285
  string literals, 449
SQL Access Manager (SAM), 461
SQL definitions, 14, 97–101, 271–272, 457
SQL injection vulnerabilities, 14, 447, 471
SQL INSERT statements, 33–34
SQL objects, 432–434
SQLExec function, 429–432
SQLExec method, 446
SQLObject JavaScript library, 217
sql.xml file, 471, 487, 488
SQR integration, 464
stateful objects, 17–19
StatementCache class, 472–474
states, button, 66–68, 112
static keyword, 433
static methods, 433
static strings, 32
step criteria, 107
string literals, 11, 14, 449
string utilities, 366
string-escaping utilities, 366–368
strings
  embedded, 11, 32
  escaping, 366–368
  Java, 339–347
  logging, 32
  static, 32
stub, 566
style object, 245
style property, 245
styling elements, 239–240
SUT (system under test), 418
SWF files
  considerations, 209
  uploading, 214–215, 223
&sys_dir parameter, 72
&sys_filename parameter, 73
system under test (SUT), 418

T

tables
  database, 86
  destination, 465
  results, 544–547
  transaction, 93, 94
  users, 465–466
target connectors, 464, 465, 466–492
target database, 465
target transactions, 42–49
TDD (test-driven development), 561–578
  considerations, 578
  introduction to, 562–563
  IoC containers, 583–584
  making test passes, 569
  procedure for, 562–563
  running tests, 566–570
TDD frameworks, 564
template engines, 368–369
template metadata repository, 450–453
templates
  Apache Velocity, 370–372, 447, 450–461
  e-mail, 97–100
  Fusion Web Application, 529–532
  Pagelet Wizard, 161
  vs. HTML definitions, 161
  XSL, 180
test data, 33, 279–283, 291
test errors, 567, 571, 576
test pagelets, 168–177
test-driven development. *See* TDD
testing
  application code, 6–10, 15–16
  application packages, 411–412
  approval process, 126–129
  attachment buttons, 65
  Custom Scripts component, 291
  factory test program, 36–38

testing (*cont.*)
  integrated connectors, 501
  iScripts, 190–191, 284, 289
  JavaScript, 231, 237
  log4j appender, 448–449
  logging framework, 31–34, 411–412
  meta-HTML processor, 564–578
  PSDBResourceLoader, 460–461
  search page, 553–555
  servlet filters, 513–514
  target connectors, 482–492
  WSDL URL, 528
testIntrospectConnector method, 483–486
TestJDBCTargetConnector listing, 489–492
testPing() method, 487
testSend() method, 488
text editors, 211
Thickbox plug-in, 254–260, 327, 328
thread classes, 131–132
thread IDs, 94
time zones, 202
toolbar buttons. *See also* buttons
  edit CREF button, 326–328
  leave portal button, 333–334
  metadata repository for, 304–312
  query button, 329–333
  trace button, 314–316
toolbars
  attaching to pages, 312–316
  button metadata repository for, 304–312
  creating maintenance page for, 308–310
  defining custom script for, 312–314
  defining HTML for, 311–312
tools, custom. *See* custom tools
trace bookmarklet, 194, 195, 237–239
trace files, 21, 388, 389
trace toolbar button, 314–316
tracing
  log4j, 392–393
  in PeopleSoft, 388–389
  turning off, 194–196
transaction page, 53–64
transaction tables, 93, 94
transactions
  adding approval fields to, 108–110
  adding attachments to, 42–77, 85
  autonomous, 437–441
  canceled, 52
  configuring, 104–105
  considerations, 93
  modifying, 108–126, 203–209
  multiple attachments, 85
  PL/SQL, 437–441
  registering, 102–103
  requirements for, 42–49
  storage location, 63–64
  target, 42–49
  workflow-enabling, 92–129
transformers
  described, 148
  meta-HTML, 178–180
  pagelet, 148, 177–180
  PASSTHRU, 177, 178, 180
  XSL, 177, 178, 180
Trinidad component, 536, 540, 543–547, 555, 557
troubleshooting. *See also* errors
  connectors, 502–503
  problem investigation, 388

U

UCM (Universal Content Management System), 85
UCM attachments, 85
UI (user interface)
  configurable, 275–293
  global changes to, 245–254
  inspecting with Firebug, 236–238, 293–295
  metadata repository, 275–285
  updating code for, 121–122
UI (user interface) code, 121–122
UI loader code, 294
Universal Content Management System (UCM), 85

upcasting, 338
update_ui function, 121–122
URL-generation functions, 317–318
URLs. *See also* hyperlinks
  base, 248–249
  in bookmarklets, 194–197
  case sensitivity, 194
  component/query functions, 316–324
  HTML hyperlinks, 257–258
  image, 223–225
  iScript, 248–255
  opening, 508
  redirects, 190, 299
  shortening, 555–556
  specifying storage location with, 56–58
  WSDL, 524, 528, 534, 557
user IDs, 494
user interface. *See* UI
user lists, 100–102
user profiles, 465, 495, 497, 499–503
user queries, 100
UserBean.java file, 557
UserGreeter class, 13–17, 233, 264
users
  anonymous, 528
  authentication, 556–557
  credentials, 557
  undefined, 528
users table, 465–466

V

validation, 63, 87–89, 268, 587
validation rules, 542
validator, 126
Value Object. *See* Data Transfer Object
variables
  bind. *See* bind variables
  context-sensitive, 38
  copying, 126
  environment, 86
  PeopleCode system variables, 427–429
  private, 20
  strongly vs. loosely typed, 587–591
  temporary, 25
Velocity. *See* Apache Velocity
View button, 64–65
ViewAttachment function, 65, 84
view_attachment function, 65, 84
ViewController project, 529, 530, 536
Virtual Approver, 92

W

W3C (World Wide Web Consortium), 474
web applications. *See also* mobile applications
  address book app. *See* CI_PERSONAL_DATA HRMS CI
  considerations, 416, 465
  Fusion, 529–532
  Java EE Application, 510, 555, 556
  URLs for, 58, 555–556
web assets
  approvals for. *See* approvals
  binary files as, 42
  event handlers, 94–97
  serving, 209–210
  workflow-enabling, 92–129
Web Assets component
  adding file attachments, 42–77
  uploading SWF files, 214–215, 223
web browsers
  bookmarklets. *See* bookmarklets
  bookmarks, 192, 194
  caching and, 292, 360
  Chrome, 275, 285, 292
  Firefox. *See Firefox entries*
  highlighting active fields, 291–293
  Internet Explorer, 236, 240, 275, 285
  iScript and, 191–192
  JavaScript and, 231–233, 240, 243–244
  JSON parsing and, 285
  mobile, 528, 536, 555
  mobile browsers, 536, 537, 555–556

web browsers (*cont.*)
Safari, 240
serving SQL results to, 281–285
testing WSDL URL in, 528
web servers. *See also* servers
extending with JSP, 505–507
J2EE, 506, 507, 509–510, 513
Java on, 505–517
PSIGW application, 465
Web Service Definition Language (WSDL) URL, 524, 528, 534, 557
web service-enabling approvals, 138–140
web services
creating with JDeveloper, 528–556
data controls, 532–536
enabling component interface as, 520–527
integration technologies, 464
providing, 520–528
requiring authentication, 556–557
Web Services for Remote Portlets (WSRP), 142
WEBLIB definitions, 188, 190, 193
WEBLIB naming conventions, 188, 190
WEBLIB records, 189, 193
WEBLIB_APT_JSL code, 260–261
WebLogic, 507, 510, 514–516
WebLogic server, 507, 553
Wireshark, 192, 549, 555
workflow buttons, 122–126
workflow notifications, 135
workflow-enabling transactions, 92–129
working directories, 86
World Wide Web Consortium (W3C), 474
WSDL (Web Service Definition Language) URL, 524, 528, 534, 557
WSRP (Web Services for Remote Portlets), 142

X

Xalan-C, 499
XML (Extensible Markup Language). *See also* AJAX
Adobe Flex and, 211
escaping, 367–368
Pagelet Wizard, 159
pagelets and, 159, 180–181
XML files, 161, 392, 471–472, 486
XML strings, 474, 485, 486
XmlDocument object, 474
XmlNode parameter, 474
XmlUnit package, 486
XPath, 474
XSL (Extensible Stylesheet Language), 159, 180–181, 497–499
XSL files, 499
XSL templates, 180
XSL transformations, 499
XSL transformers, 177, 178, 180
XSLT processor, 499
XSS attacks, 268

GET YOUR FREE SUBSCRIPTION TO *ORACLE MAGAZINE*

Oracle Magazine **is essential gear for today's information technology professionals. Stay informed and increase your productivity with every issue of *Oracle Magazine*. Inside each free bimonthly issue you'll get:**

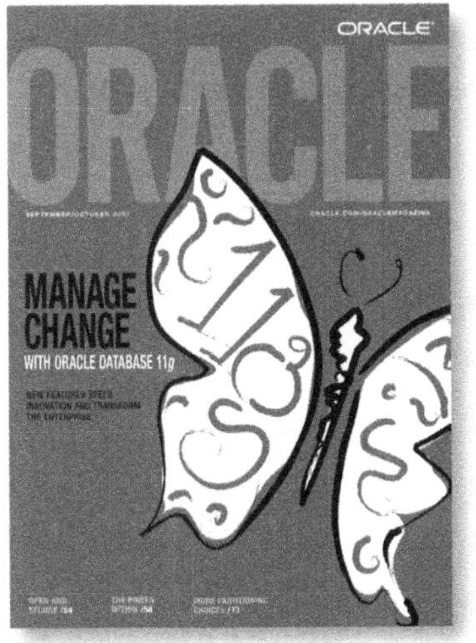

- Up-to-date information on Oracle Database, Oracle Application Server, Web development, enterprise grid computing, database technology, and business trends
- Third-party news and announcements
- Technical articles on Oracle and partner products, technologies, and operating environments
- Development and administration tips
- Real-world customer stories

If there are other Oracle users at your location who would like to receive their own subscription to *Oracle Magazine*, please photocopy this form and pass it along.

Three easy ways to subscribe:

① **Web**
Visit our Web site at **oracle.com/oraclemagazine**
You'll find a subscription form there, plus much more

② **Fax**
Complete the questionnaire on the back of this card and fax the questionnaire side only to **+1.847.763.9638**

③ **Mail**
Complete the questionnaire on the back of this card and mail it to **P.O. Box 1263, Skokie, IL 60076-8263**

Want your own FREE subscription?

To receive a free subscription to *Oracle Magazine*, you must fill out the entire card, sign it, and date it (incomplete cards cannot be processed or acknowledged). You can also fax your application to +1.847.763.9638. **Or subscribe at our Web site at oracle.com/oraclemagazine**

○ **Yes, please send me a FREE subscription *Oracle Magazine*.** ○ No.

○ From time to time, Oracle Publishing allows our partners exclusive access to our e-mail addresses for special promotions and announcements. To be included in this program, please check this circle. If you do not wish to be included, you will only receive notices about your subscription via e-mail.

○ Oracle Publishing allows sharing of our postal mailing list with selected third parties. If you prefer your mailing address not to be included in this program, please check this circle.

If at any time you would like to be removed from either mailing list, please contact Customer Service at +1.847.763.9635 or send an e-mail to oracle@halldata.com. If you opt in to the sharing of information, Oracle may also provide you with e-mail related to Oracle products, services, and events. If you want to completely unsubscribe from any e-mail communication from Oracle, please send an e-mail to: unsubscribe@oracle-mail.com with the following in the subject line: REMOVE [your e-mail address]. For complete information on Oracle Publishing's privacy practices, please visit oracle.com/html/privacy/html

X

signature (required) date

name title

company e-mail address

street/p.o. box

city/state/zip or postal code telephone

country fax

Would you like to receive your free subscription in digital format instead of print if it becomes available? ○ Yes ○ No

YOU MUST ANSWER ALL 10 QUESTIONS BELOW.

① WHAT IS THE PRIMARY BUSINESS ACTIVITY OF YOUR FIRM AT THIS LOCATION? (check one only)

- □ 01 Aerospace and Defense Manufacturing
- □ 02 Application Service Provider
- □ 03 Automotive Manufacturing
- □ 04 Chemicals
- □ 05 Media and Entertainment
- □ 06 Construction/Engineering
- □ 07 Consumer Sector/Consumer Packaged Goods
- □ 08 Education
- □ 09 Financial Services/Insurance
- □ 10 Health Care
- □ 11 High Technology Manufacturing, OEM
- □ 12 Industrial Manufacturing
- □ 13 Independent Software Vendor
- □ 14 Life Sciences (biotech, pharmaceuticals)
- □ 15 Natural Resources
- □ 16 Oil and Gas
- □ 17 Professional Services
- □ 18 Public Sector (government)
- □ 19 Research
- □ 20 Retail/Wholesale/Distribution
- □ 21 Systems Integrator, VAR/VAD
- □ 22 Telecommunications
- □ 23 Travel and Transportation
- □ 24 Utilities (electric, gas, sanitation, water)
- □ 98 Other Business and Services ________

② WHICH OF THE FOLLOWING BEST DESCRIBES YOUR PRIMARY JOB FUNCTION? (check one only)

CORPORATE MANAGEMENT/STAFF

- □ 01 Executive Management (President, Chair, CEO, CFO, Owner, Partner, Principal)
- □ 02 Finance/Administrative Management (VP/Director/ Manager/Controller, Purchasing, Administration)
- □ 03 Sales/Marketing Management (VP/Director/Manager)
- □ 04 Computer Systems/Operations Management (CIO/VP/Director/Manager MIS/IS/IT, Ops)

IS/IT STAFF

- □ 05 Application Development/Programming Management
- □ 06 Application Development/Programming Staff
- □ 07 Consulting
- □ 08 DBA/Systems Administrator
- □ 09 Education/Training
- □ 10 Technical Support Director/Manager
- □ 11 Other Technical Management/Staff
- □ 98 Other

③ WHAT IS YOUR CURRENT PRIMARY OPERATING PLATFORM (check all that apply)

- □ 01 Digital Equipment Corp UNIX/VAX/VMS
- □ 02 HP UNIX
- □ 03 IBM AIX
- □ 04 IBM UNIX
- □ 05 Linux (Red Hat)
- □ 06 Linux (SUSE)
- □ 07 Linux (Oracle Enterprise)
- □ 08 Linux (other)
- □ 09 Macintosh
- □ 10 MVS
- □ 11 Netware
- □ 12 Network Computing
- □ 13 SCO UNIX
- □ 14 Sun Solaris/SunOS
- □ 15 Windows
- □ 16 Other UNIX
- □ 98 Other
- 99 □ None of the Above

④ DO YOU EVALUATE, SPECIFY, RECOMMEND, OR AUTHORIZE THE PURCHASE OF ANY OF THE FOLLOWING? (check all that apply)

- □ 01 Hardware
- □ 02 Business Applications (ERP, CRM, etc.)
- □ 03 Application Development Tools
- □ 04 Database Products
- □ 05 Internet or Intranet Products
- □ 06 Other Software
- □ 07 Middleware Products
- 99 □ None of the Above

⑤ IN YOUR JOB, DO YOU USE OR PLAN TO PURCHASE ANY OF THE FOLLOWING PRODUCTS? (check all that apply)

SOFTWARE

- □ 01 CAD/CAE/CAM
- □ 02 Collaboration Software
- □ 03 Communications
- □ 04 Database Management
- □ 05 File Management
- □ 06 Finance
- □ 07 Java
- □ 08 Multimedia Authoring
- □ 09 Networking
- □ 10 Programming
- □ 11 Project Management
- □ 12 Scientific and Engineering
- □ 13 Systems Management
- □ 14 Workflow

HARDWARE

- □ 15 Macintosh
- □ 16 Mainframe
- □ 17 Massively Parallel Processing
- □ 18 Minicomputer
- □ 19 Intel x86(32)
- □ 20 Intel x86(64)
- □ 21 Network Computer
- □ 22 Symmetric Multiprocessing
- □ 23 Workstation Services

SERVICES

- □ 24 Consulting
- □ 25 Education/Training
- □ 26 Maintenance
- □ 27 Online Database
- □ 28 Support
- □ 29 Technology-Based Training
- □ 30 Other
- 99 □ None of the Above

⑥ WHAT IS YOUR COMPANY'S SIZE? (check one only)

- □ 01 More than 25,000 Employees
- □ 02 10,001 to 25,000 Employees
- □ 03 5,001 to 10,000 Employees
- □ 04 1,001 to 5,000 Employees
- □ 05 101 to 1,000 Employees
- □ 06 Fewer than 100 Employees

⑦ DURING THE NEXT 12 MONTHS, HOW MUCH DO YOU ANTICIPATE YOUR ORGANIZATION WILL SPEND ON COMPUTER HARDWARE, SOFTWARE, PERIPHERALS, AND SERVICES FOR YOUR LOCATION? (check one only)

- □ 01 Less than $10,000
- □ 02 $10,000 to $49,999
- □ 03 $50,000 to $99,999
- □ 04 $100,000 to $499,999
- □ 05 $500,000 to $999,999
- □ 06 $1,000,000 and Over

⑧ WHAT IS YOUR COMPANY'S YEARLY SALES REVENUE? (check one only)

- □ 01 $500, 000, 000 and above
- □ 02 $100, 000, 000 to $500, 000, 000
- □ 03 $50, 000, 000 to $100, 000, 000
- □ 04 $5, 000, 000 to $50, 000, 000
- □ 05 $1, 000, 000 to $5, 000, 000

⑨ WHAT LANGUAGES AND FRAMEWORKS DO YOU USE? (check all that apply)

- □ 01 Ajax
- □ 02 C
- □ 03 C++
- □ 04 C#
- □ 05 Hibernate
- □ 06 J++/J#
- □ 07 Java
- □ 08 JSP
- □ 09 .NET
- □ 10 Perl
- □ 11 PHP
- □ 12 PL/SQL
- □ 13 Python
- □ 14 Ruby/Rails
- □ 15 Spring
- □ 16 Struts
- □ 17 SQL
- □ 18 Visual B
- □ 98 Other

⑩ WHAT ORACLE PRODUCTS ARE IN USE SITE? (check all that apply)

ORACLE DATABASE

- □ 01 Oracle Database 11*g*
- □ 02 Oracle Database 10*g*
- □ 03 Oracle9*i* Database
- □ 04 Oracle Embedded Database (Oracle Lite, Times Ten, Berkel
- □ 05 Other Oracle Database Release

ORACLE FUSION MIDDLEWARE

- □ 06 Oracle Application Server
- □ 07 Oracle Portal
- □ 08 Oracle Enterprise Manager
- □ 09 Oracle BPEL Process Manager
- □ 10 Oracle Identity Management
- □ 11 Oracle SOA Suite
- □ 12 Oracle Data Hubs

ORACLE DEVELOPMENT TOOLS

- □ 13 Oracle JDeveloper
- □ 14 Oracle Forms
- □ 15 Oracle Reports
- □ 16 Oracle Designer
- □ 17 Oracle Discoverer
- □ 18 Oracle BI Beans
- □ 19 Oracle Warehouse Builder
- □ 20 Oracle WebCenter
- □ 21 Oracle Application Express

ORACLE APPLICATIONS

- □ 22 Oracle E-Business Suite
- □ 23 PeopleSoft Enterprise
- □ 24 JD Edwards EnterpriseOne
- □ 25 JD Edwards World
- □ 26 Oracle Fusion
- □ 27 Hyperion
- □ 28 Siebel CRM

ORACLE SERVICES

- □ 28 Oracle E-Business Suite On Den
- □ 29 Oracle Technology On Demand
- □ 30 Siebel CRM On Demand
- □ 31 Oracle Consulting
- □ 32 Oracle Education
- □ 33 Oracle Support
- □ 98 Other
- 99 □ None of the Above

08014004